1850 CENSUS, EASTERN KENTUCKY

Counties of Breathitt, Carter, Floyd, Greenup, Johnson, Lawrence, Letcher, Morgan, Perry and Pike

VOLUME 5

By

BYRON SISTLER, BARBARA SISTLER,
and SAMUEL SISTLER

JANAWAY PUBLISHING, INC.
Santa Maria, California
2012

Notice

In many older books, foxing (or discoloration) occurs and, in some instances, print lightens with wear and age. Reprinted books, such as this, often duplicate these flaws, notwithstanding efforts to reduce or eliminate them. The pages of this reprint have been digitally enhanced and, where possible, the flaws eliminated in order to provide clarity of content and a pleasant reading experience.

Copyright © 1994, Byron Sistler & Associates, Inc.

Originally published:
Nashville, Tennessee 1994

Reprinted by:

Janaway Publishing, Inc.
732 Kelsey Ct.
Santa Maria, California 93454
(805) 925-1038
www.janawaygenealogy.com
2012

ISBN: 978-1-59641-170-8

Made in the United States of America

INTRODUCTION

The entries appear in the same order as on the original schedules. In general an entry comprises all members of a given household, except that any individuals whose surname differed from that of the household head are shown as a separate unit.

An asterisk (*) identifies each entry which does not consist of an entire household.

The symbol (B) identified black or mulatto individuals or families. If the (B) follows the first name in the entry it means the entire household is black. Where the household is mixed, each black person is separately identified with the (B).

The symbol (I) was supposed to identify Indians, but actually was used by the enumerators to represent various racial mixtures.

The number after each name is the person's age. The "Schedule Page" number is the stamped number in the upper right hand corner of every other page of the original schedules. The page following the numbered one assumes the same number.

Transcription for the six counties is followed by a full name index listing the first name of each entry—usually the household head. Page numbers referred to in the index are the Schedule page numbers, not the page numbers of this book.

County of residence is identified in the index by appropriate county symbols. They are as follows:

Breathitt	BE	Lawrence	LW
Carter	CT	Letcher	LE
Floyd	FO	Morgan	MG
Greenup	GN	Perry	PE
Johnson	JO	Pike	PI

As of this writing it is our intention to publish the entire 1850 Kentucky in a series of regional volumes, after the completion of which a single every name index for the entire state is projected. This index would show all names, not just household heads.

As always, we urge the researcher to refer back to the original schedules where possible, as there is important information on those schedules not contained in this book. Data such as occupation, real estate value and state of birth are all very meaningful, and a full genealogical search is not obtainable without this additional information.

The Sistlers

TABLE OF CONTENTS

Breathitt County 1

Carter County 23

Floyd County 61

Greenup County 93

Johnson County 155

Lawrence County 177

Letcher County 215

Morgan County 231

Perry County 275

Pike County 293

INDEX 327

1850 Census Breathitt County Kentucky

Schedule Page 1

PENSE, Andrew 51, Rebecca 44, Henry 23, Angy 21, Jo. A. 18, Jackson 16, Fanny 14, Charity 13, Lucinda 7, Sytha 5, Rebecca 2
PENSE, John S. 24*, Sally 23, Greenville 3, David 2
FRILEY, Henry 24*
GILLS, Washington*
TAULBEE, Isaac 19, Margaret 15
HOLLAND, George 61*, Elizabeth 54
MULLIS, Ambrose 75*
PUCKETT, Meredith 25*
BRUER, Dennis 27, Ailsey 25, Littleton 7, George 5, Mary 2
VANCLEAVE, Ebenezer 73, Elizabeth 55, Tolbert 15
CRAWFORD, Gideon 62, Nancy 51
HOLLAND, John 29, Polly 30, Patsy 13, Washington 10, Nathan 8, Charity 6, Philip 4, Charley 3, John 2, Lucinda 7/12
BRUER, Thomas 25, Elizabeth 24, Bracken 6, Wm. R. 4, Mahala 1
KING, Lewis 23, Louisa 25, Armina 11, Jeremiah 9, Caloway 7, Oliver C. 5, Wm. D. 3, J. W. 2 (m)
BANKS, Danl. 27, Nancy 28, William 4, Happy 1 (f)
KING, Fleming 30, Josephine 21, Rosilla 5, Franklin 3, Lewis L. 3/12
HOLLAND, Ambrose 38*, Happpy 42
BRYANT, Martha 13*
COCRELL, William 60, Rhody 30
MALONEY, McKinley 32, Malinda 31, AnnEliza 12, Wm. 10, Eleanor 8, Susannah 5, Elizabeth 4, Sally 2
BANKS, John 26, Katharine 23, Henry 5, Sandford 1
HOLLAND, Hiram 32, Mary 25, Arena 9, Sephus 7, Fanny 5

Schedule Page 2

BRUER, Isham 20*, Sally 20, Willis 2
PELFRY, Alexander 22*, Eliza J. 18, Moses G. 2, Alsey J. 1
CRAWFORD, F. B. 18 (m)*
SIMPKINS, William 19*
DUNN, Jesse 35, Sally 29, Comfort 8, John 6, Algium 4, Granville 2, Angeline 5/12
DAVIS, William 40, Elizabeth 30, Evilene 14, Katharine 13, Juliann 11
CHILDERS, James M. 31, Nancy 28, Gillian 5, James M. 4, Sarah J. 2, Jeremi 1
LOVELACE, Jeremi 65, Pheobe 51, James 25, Ann Eliza 14, Columbus 11, John H. 9
SMITH, Hardin 37, Elizabeth 30, Ellen 10, Eliza J. 9, Wm. N. 8, James A. 7, Greer 6, Polly 5, John M? 4, Lewis H. 2
VANCLEAVE, Andrew S. 25, Messmia 22, Anderson 6, Tolbert 3, Wm. 9/12
WOOD, Luke 35*, Susan 29, Andrew J. 6, Sarah E. 5, Martha J. 2, James F. 7/12
CRAWFORD, Katharine 55*
KIDD, John 25, Perliann 28, Jincy Ann 6, Saml. 4, David 2, Elijah 2/12
SIMPKINS, Polly 38, Nancy 21, Sally 15, Lucinda 13, John 11, Louisa 7, Rosannah 5, Jane 1
ROSE, Bowen 56, Cumfort 30, Powell J. 11, Sylvania 9, Polly J. 7, Nancy 3
HOLLAND, Simon 19, Nancy 21, Sandford 11/12
TAULBEE, Saml. 22, Nancy 17
KING, Jeremi 39, Elizabeth 28, Lewis 10, William 8, Lydia 6, Caroline 5, Elmira 3, Adison 7/12

1850 Census Breathitt County Kentucky

Schedule Page 3

KING, Moses 57, Polly 56
BRYANT, Evin 35, Elizth. 27, Sarah 10, Hiram 7, Jasper 5, Hurum 2
KING, George 35, Polly 30, Margaret 17, Ambrose 11, Moses 10, Serilda 8, Eliza 5, John 2, Elijah 1, Delila 10/12
BAILEY, Martin 29, Almeda 22, Malinda 3, Katharine 53
FRILEY, Sally 55, Sidney 25, Margaret 17
MALONEY, John 39, Elizabeth 26, Justin 4, Eliza Ann 2, Susan 79
PUCKETT, Morgan R. 49, Susan 50, Elizabeth 22, Gardner 18, Clarinda 16, Minerva 11, John 10, Green 8, Polly 5
HOLLAND, James 31, Elizabeth 36, Sarah 19, Betsy 11, Jackson 8, Paulina 6, Wm. 3, Rebecca 1, Polly 1
ROSE, Anderson N. 32, Eleanor 28, Nancy 4, Lydia Ann 3, Wm. R. 2, Logan S. 7/12
COLDIRON, George 22, Priscilla 19
STAMPER, James W. 40*, Margaret 39, John W. 15, Eliza J. 13, Joel 12, Henry 7, Emiline 4, Stamper 3/12 (m)
TOLSTON, Wm. 22*
STAMPER, Richard 72*, Martha 72
DUNN, Julian 19*, Rachel 1
TRENT, Henry 43*, Charity 43, James 21, William 18, John W. 16, Nancy E. 14, Eliza 12, George 10, Henry 7, Stokeley 2

Schedule Page 4

SMITH, Elcana D. 23*
TURNER, James 50, Mary 27, Jemima 12, Anna 9, Thomas 17, Johnston 21, Sally 12, Wm. 11, Nancy 7, Fannie 6, Rebecca 3, John 2, Emiline 1
SHEPHERD, John M. 51, Eve 25, Sally F. 4, George W. 3, Celia D. 1
HURST, Hardin 26, Dulcina 28, Saml. H. 7, Wm. L. 5, Andrew T. 4, Zachry T. 2, Richd. E. 7/12
DAMRELL, Saml. 37, Sally 29, John 12, Wm. 10, Joel 7, Margaret 4, Franklin 11/12
TRENT, Alexr. 25, Nancy 22, Mahala 3, Lucinda 1
TRENT, Wm. 24, Mahala 22, Elizh. 5
SPENCER, Andrew 20, Pheobe 16
SPENCER, Elijah 47, Mary 37, John C. 14, Mary A. 11, Elizth. 9, Patience 5, Saml. 3, Elijah 1
GIBBS, John 63, Elizabeth 51, Wm. 21
GIBBS, Green B. 21, Jemima 18, Polly 1
PELFRY, Alexander 21, Ellen J. 18, Moses G. 2, Ailsey J. 1
TYRA, John 35, Sally 28, James H. 13, Polly 11, Daniel 9, John 7, Wm. 6, Ebenezer 5, Eli J. 4, Asbury 1
HOLLAND, William 42, Cardus 40 (f), Nancy 17, Preston 15, Orlena 11, Wilson 10, Nelson 8, Mahala 6, Kilson 4 (f), Lusinda 2, Charlotte 8/12
HOLLAND, John 72, Charity 72

1850 Census Breathitt County Kentucky

Schedule Page 5

BANKS, Wm. W. 39, Fiba 30, Charley 15, Sally 10, Charlotte 12, Elizabeth 8, Danl. 7, William 5, Polly 4, James 3, George 1
WADKINS, Jackson 26, Keziah 26, Sally 7, W. O. W. 3 (m), Andrew 2
HATTON, John 18, Angy 14, Wm. J. 5/12
BANKS, John 41*, Polly 41, Nelly H. 12, Barbara 6
WADKINS, Andy 21*
BANKS, William Sr. 73, Sally 73
BAKER, Alexander 30, Mary 32, Elizth. 13, Sally 9, Eliza 7, Mahala 3, Polly 1
HATTON, William 60, Betsy 43, Benjn. 12, Wm. 9, Isham S. 1
STUFFLEBEAN, Hiram 46*, Mourning 40
BRYANT, Sally 9*, Josiah 7
BANKS, David 47, Sally 40, William 20, Levina 18, Adam 17, Hannah 14, David 12, Polly 10, Eviline 8, Louraney 6, Caroline 5, John 3, Richard 1
SHACKELFORD, Sandford 31, Sarah 3, Marion M. 10, Caroline 9, Amanda 7, Nancy 6, Louisa 2
SHUFFIELD, Wm. P. 26, Eviline 21, Nancy 2
SHACKELFORD, Alfred 25, Mary 23, John W. 1
MILLER, George 46, Sidney 46, Vancey 18, Susan 15, Arminta 14, Armina 12, John 10, Christena 8
CARPENTER, Sarah 36*, Andrew 18, Malinda 7, Stephen 16, John 14, Nancy 12, Saml. 10

Schedule Page 6

MILLER, George 6*, Letcher 4, Abner 2
MILLER, Owens 23, Matilda 20
SHUFFIELD, James 60, Elizabeth 50, Susan J. 17, Elizth. 6
NEWTON, William 46, Alsey 35, Ansil 17, Ransom 14, Elizth. 12, John 9, Demerias 7, Dillard 5, America 11/12
LYKINS, E. Isaac S. 22*, Lucinda 21, Louisa 2, Louraney 1?/12
WRIGHT, Betsy 57*
BACK, Lewis Sr. 52, Elizabeth 45
FIELDS, Acey 63, Rachel 54, Ace 14, Polly 13
FIELDS, Abram 25, Polly 17
FIELDS, Turner 35, Rebecca 25, Thomas J. 6, George W. 4, DAnl. B. 2
FIELDS, Stephen B. 23, Katharine 19
HOUNSHEL, Franklin 50, Sally 35, Polly Ann 14, Nancy J. 8, Thomas J. 7, Floyd 6, Eliza 5, Susan 4, Rachel 2, George 9/12
SEWELL, Margaret 38, Joseph 16, Harriett 13, Mary 11, George 8, John H. 5
MCQUINN, Charles B. 60, Lucy 57, Haney 21 (f), Alexander 18, Louisa 17, Shadrack 12
MCDONALD, Elizabeth 60, Ursula 50
SMITH, Edmund 54 (B), Lucinda 31, Mary 11, William 8, Matilda 5, Edmund 3, Sally 1
JONES, Daniel 28, Nancy 24, James H. 4, Henry 2, Granville 4/12
CLEMONS, John C. 28, Betsy 24, Lafayette 2, Benjamin 8/12
WILLIAMS, Coleman 60, Elizabeth 21, James 23
WHITAKER, William J. 29, Betsy 30, Nancy 4, Hurum 3, Anderson 1

1850 Census Breathitt County Kentucky

Schedule Page 7

CLEMONS, Benjamin 53, Polly 39, Isaac 18, Moses 17, Benjamin 15, Frances 14, Elizabeth 12, Sally 11, William 7, Jackson 5, Rebecca 8, Johnston 4, Nancy 9/12
FUGATE, Jesse 28*, Farinda 23, Peggy 3, Henley 25
HELTON, Francis J. 22*
SMITH, Benjamin 72, Nancy 50, Rhoda 21, Levina 12
FUGATE, William 18*, Rachel 16
NOBLE, Sally 22*
DEATON, Lucinda 22*
DAVIS, Elizabeth 65, Robert 26, Rebecca 33, Elizabeth 24
CLEMONS, Francis 28, Fanney 26, Manford 11, Rhody 8, Polly 7, Nancy 5, Martha 4, Samuel Miller 2
HOWARD, Preston 40, Sally 38, Russell 15, Wily 12, S. 10 (m), Elizabeth 9, Eliza 7, Esther 5, John 2
WILLIAMS, Wyatt 33, Nancy 22, Chandler 11/12
WILLIAMS, Henry 36*, Nancy 32, Hiram 12, Sally 10, Lucinda 8, Gilbert 6, Peggy 3, Daniel 6/12
FUGATE, Jonathan 96*
NOBLE, John 18, Katharine 22, Rebecca 1
FUGATE, John 20, Ritty 68 (f), Andrew 17
COLLINS, William 40, Polly 37, Levisa 18, Mary J. 15, William P. 13, Polly 12, Nancy 9, John 7, Eliza 5, James 2, Sally 4/12
MCDANIEL, John 60*, Celia 24, Polly 18, Vasa 16, Thomas 14, Wiley 13, Shadrach 11, Mary 9, Matilda 7, Lucy 4
FUGATE, Hannah 49*, Alfred 7

Schedule Page 8

CARPENTER, Benjamin 21, Sally 36, Andrew 18, Stephen 16, John 14, Nancy 12, Samuel 10, Malinda 7, George 5
GREEN, Elijah 36*, Ally 27 (f), Mary J. 6, Sally 4, Ceatta 3, Columbia 1 (m)
HOWARD, Celia 60*
CARPENTER, Felix 75, Delphia 73, Elisha 26
DAVIS, William 31*, Sally 22, Robert 4, Calvin 1
SHEPHERD, Benjamin 28*
CARPENTER, Wilson 20*, Nancy 22
FITCH, Henderson 2*
BRADLEY, James 38, Elizabeth 32, Polly 12, American 10 (m), George 8, Celia 6, William 4, Elizabeth 2, Arty 2/12 (f)
SHEPHERD, David H. 57, Rebecca 42, Margaret 14, William R. 8, George 5, Elias 3, Susan 5/12
SHEPHERD, Henderson 26, Mary 24, William E. 6, George 5
HOWARD, James 90*, Elizabeth 70, Green 33, Peggy 32, Morgan 14 (m), William 12, Martin 10, Franky 8 (f), James 6, Daniel 5, John 4, Green 2, Elizabeth 5/12, Amanda 3/12
ALLEN, Nancy 19*
WADKINS, William 30, Peggy 40, Henry 20, John 12, Polly 15, Susan 11, James 10, Barbara 8
MILLER, Samuel 46*, Franky 30 (f), James W. 11, William 8, Samuel 6
BRADLEY, George 22*, Ann 21
MULLENS, Allen 22, Phoebe 21, Eveline 3

1850 Census Breathitt County Kentucky

Schedule Page 9

MULLENS, Ambrose 47, Matty 46 (f), Levina 20, Booker 18?, Sally 14, Agness 10, Rebecca 8, Sumantha 5, Ambrose 1
GEARHEART, William 55, Rachel 53, Hetty 19, Manford 17, Polly 15, William 13, Harrison 10, Henderson 5
GILBERT, Joseph 40, Suckey 35 (f), Eliza 16, John 14, Ben 12, Susan 10, Thomas 8, William 6
JONES, John 60*
GIBSON, Duvenberry 30*, John 6
GOODMAN, Enoch 35, Susan 30, Miriam 15 (f), Eleanor 13, Jackson 11, Obediah 9, Sarah 7, _____ 4/12 (m)
PATTON, Granville 45, Polly 30, Adam 15, John 17, Linsey 12 (m), Jane 10, Andrew 6, Littleton 4, Ruben 4/12
CORLEY, David 27, Lourinda 27, Polly 6, Peggy 4, Jackson 2, Albert 1
PATTON, Sarah 35, Fanny 15, Granville 12, Eliza 18, James 10, Nancy 8, Cynthian 6 (f), Daniel 4, John 2, Sarah 4/12, William 2
JOHNSTON, John 32, Peggy 32, William 15, Adam 12, Sarah 9, Lemuel 7 (f), Peter 2, Ann 4, Benjamin 6/12
CARPENTER, Samuel 23, Katharine 20, Rosannah 3, George 1
MULLENS, Isaac 34, Polly 30, Jemima 10, Ambrose 8, Malinda 7, John 11/12
ALLEN, George 42, Malinda 36, Rhoda 18, Elizabeth 16, William 13, Simon 10, Woodson 9, Sarah 5, Louisa 1

Schedule Page 10

CONLEY, John 25*, Luester 25 (f), John 3
LAWHORN, Elijah 27*, John 2
HUNTER, Robert 30, Elizabeth 25, John 7, Winney 4, Elizabeth 2
BRADLEY, George 68, Susan 47, Cynthia 18, John 16, Jacob 12, Willis 7, Briton 7, Anne 5
ALLEN, William 67, Katharine 58, Ira 29, Dulaney 19, Nancy 18, Fanny 16
ALLEN, James 22, Elizabeth 20, Farlena 1, Lourancy 3/12 (f)
COLLINS, Shepherd 38, Polly 38, John 16, Hiram 14, Sally 11, Fereby 10, Susannah 7, Dicey 5
LOVELEY, Ruben 20, Levisa 17, Alperson 1
LOVELY, William 45, Nancy 36, Thomas 19, Elijah 17, Allen 15, Drisana 11, Daniel 9, William 7, Tiritha 5, Louisa 3, Samuel 2, Elizabeth 1
MORGAN, Enoch 47, Jerusid 41 (f), Henry 18, Rufus 15
MANN, William 41, Rhoda 37, George 17, Sally 15, Samuel 11, Eliza 10, Nancy 7, John 5, William 3, Polly 3, Jackson 1
HOWARD, Samuel 25, Ann 27, Sally 7, John 5, Calvin 3, _____ 1 (m)
HOWARD, William 67, Polly 50, John 24, Riley 20, Andrew 18

Schedule Page 11

CARPENTER, Fielding 26, Jane 25, Alexander 7, William 5, Babe 1 (f)
HOWARD, Ben 34, Nancy 30, Rhoda 15, Nathan 12, Martin 10, Lucinda 8, Eliza 6, Larkin 3
MANN, John 27, Lucinda 27, Adam 3, Eve 1

1850 Census Breathitt County Kentucky

HOWARD, George 20, Betsy 20, Wilson 2, Polly 10/12
MCDONALD, Arthur 30, Polly 20, Elijah 5, John 3/12, Sarah 50
HAGINS, Thomas 50, Rebecca 47, John 25, Mahala 17, Luraney 17, Eliza J. 10, Nancy 8, Delila 5
MCCOY, Curtus F. 37, Elizabeth 31, Louisa 12, William 10, Mary 8, Cynthia 6, George W. 3, Louraney 5/12 (f)
CROFT, William 27, Rhody 25, Arzela 5, Sarah J. 1
MANN, Thomas 28, Eliza 26, Minerva 9, Susan 7, Mary 5, Rebecca 1
CROFT, Susan 47, Daniel 19, John 16, Preston 14, Elijah 12, Allen 10
ROBBINS, Joshua 40, John W. 10, Wiley 10
ALLEN, William 32, Elizabeth 25, Eli 9, John 4, Mahala 7/12, Katharine 35
PATTON, George 23*, Polly 28, Thomas 5, Samuel 1
ROBBINS, Kiza 18 (f)*
TRUSTY, John 29, Peggy 25, Olbert 5, Sally 4, Samuel 1, William 27
TRUSTY, David 27, Sally 34, Abram 6, Ann 5, Polly 3, Lucinda 1

Schedule Page 12

PUCKETT, Caleb 26, Polly 24, Elizabeth 5, John 3, Susan 1
MARSHAL, William 45, Nancy 35, Jefferson 13
COCKRELL, Jereme 62
SMITH, William 25, Elizabeth 22, Rebecca 4, Malissa 2, Babe 1 (m)
ALLEN, Joseph 27, Fanny 24, Rebecca 6, Katharine 4, Levisa 2, Ervine 7/12 (f)
CLEMMONS, Richard 40, Rebecca 31, John 9, William 7, Mahala 1
SMITH, Thomas 52*, Sarah 44, Benjamin 23, Martha 22, Mary 20, Richard 17, Matilda 14, Elias 11, Lewis 9, Aggy 5 (f)
ALLEN, George 18*
CALHOUN, Evins 23, Deary 20 (f)
RIMES?, Isaac 25*, Polly 23, Martha 1, Louisa 10/12
MILLER, Mary 63*
HOLBROOK, John 53, Susan 45, Susan 20, Mary Ann 19, Hargis 15, William 5, Isaac 4
MATTOCKS, Emery 38, Mary 36, Rebecca 13, Willoby 8, Jesse 6, Carline 5 (f), Elijah 1
FLETCHER, James 38, Betsy 27, Louisa 7, Nancy 5, Susan 3
HALBROOK, John jr. 30, Levisa 30, Elizabeth 8, Hiram 6, James 4, Jacob 2, Calvin 1
CLEMONS, William 37, Katharine 36, William 18, Elizabeth 16, Polly Ann 14
CALHOUN, James 47, Polly 43, Lucinda 21, Dulcina 19, James 16, Polly 16, Jepthy 14 (m), Robert 11, Nancy 8, Sally 5, Milan 3 (m)

Schedule Page 13

CALHOUN, Thomas 65, Nancy 60, Delila 14
MOREFIELD, David 23
HOWARD, Micajah 26, Dred 49, Julian 49, Sam 13, Mary 8, Hiram 6, Hurum 3, Clay 1 (f)
CHURCH, Joseph 22, Martha 24, Sampson 2, Lewis 5/12
BACK, John 40, Elizabeth 37, Minerva 13, Polly 11, William 9, Henry 7, Alfred 5, Eliza 3
BACK, Solomon 38*, Jane 34, Katharine 14, Isaac 12, John 10, Lewis 8, Joseph 4, Solomon 2, Susan 10/12
DAVIS, John 98*

1850 Census Breathitt County Kentucky

BACK, Alfred 46, Isabel 42, Mary 21, Elizabeth 19, Henry 17, John 15, Joseph 12, Alfred 9, Benjamin 7
WILLIAMS, Stephen 27, Sally 25, Levina 8, Emiline 6, Gilbert 4, Greenville 2
BIRCHFIELD, William 39, Fanny 33, Angeline 11, Elizabeth 8, Adam 6, James 9/12
COPE, James D. 51, Elizabeth 47, Louraney 23, James 18, Lucinda 14, Eviline 12, Caroline 10, Geenville 8, Elizabeth 5
WILLIAMS, Caleb 20*, Nancy 15, James V. 38, Jane 38, Belinda 16, Jeptha W. 14, Wiley O. P. 12, Clarinda 10, Joseph D. 9, William S. 4
BUFFINGTON, Ailsey 13*
JONES, John 60*, Darcus 60
VIERS, Anna 35*
TAULBEE, William 48, Polly 45, John W. 18, James P. 16, William W. 14, Martha Ann 10, Nancy C. 8, Green 12, Elsbury 5, Silas 1

Schedule Page 14

TOLBY, Jefferson 25, Temperance 26, William L. 5, James P. 4, Paulina 2
TOLSTON, Thomas 25, Rebecca 21
TOLSTON, Peter 57*, Polly 52, James 16, tamer 13 (f), Warren 13, Jo. E. 9 (m), Peggy 28, Polly 6, Sally 4, Peter 1
TRUSTY, Daniel 28*
GARNER, William 54*, Lockey 30 (f)
DEATON, John 41, Malinda 50, Thomas 18, Edward 13, Jemima 11, Elizabeth 9, Alexander 7, John 5, Joseph 5, Lewis 1
MILLER, Benjamin 51, Nancy 42, Miriam 9 (f)
MILLER, Elijah 24, Nancy 16
RUSSELL, John 33, Sally 33, Absalom 14, James 12, David 10, William 6, John 4, Nancy 2
MILLER, John 27, Tabitha 19, Ruben 3, James 9/12
HAYS, John B. 17, Sarah 17
COMBS, Alfred 36*, Peggy 36, Polly 17, Nancy 16, Henderson 13, Shadrach 12, Jerry 10, Rachel 8, Paulina 6, Delila 4, Delaney 3 (m), Isaac 11/12
NOBLE, William 16*
FIELDS, Ephraim 32, Lydia 32, Nancy 7, Mary 5, Nathan 2, Stephen 9/12
SOUTHERS, Isaac 42, Polly 36, Frankey 13 (f), Nancy 10, Levina 8, Sampson 6, Nelson 7/12
HICKS, Robert 25, Polly 21, Isaac 5, Samuel 3, Elizabeth 2, Nancy 8/12

Schedule Page 15

SOUTHERS, Abram 42, Rosy 33, Sally 13, Linda 8, Peggy 5, Rebecca 2
COMBS, Henry 31, Temperance 34, Dulcena A. 11, Stephen 9, Larkin 8, Elizabeth 7, Alfred 5, Asbury 3, William 1
MCINTOSH, Nimrod 27, Nancy 25, Vardeman 10, Eviline 7, Andrew 4, Ambrose 2
MILLER, John 50, Patsy 35, George 15, Peggy 13, Sally 11, Haney 9 (f), Alfred 7, Nancy Ann 5
MCINTOSH, Zechariah 30, Martin 16, Frankey 14 (f), Mary 10, William 8, Andrew 6, Chaney 4 (f)
HARVEY, William 40*, Elizabeth 41, John 22, Robert 12, Easter 7, Elizabeth 2
COMBS, James 12*
HARVEY, William 23, Ellis 17 (f)
FUGATE, Samuel 25, Frankey 26 (f), Mahala 10, Nancy 9, Solomon 2

1850 Census Breathitt County Kentucky

FUGATE, John 24, Margarett 22, Nancy 9, Delila 7, Benjamin 5, James 3, Henly 1 (m)
RICE, George 50, Sally 54, Sam 16, Ben 14, Wesley 21
NOBLE, Jackson 37*, Elizabeth 27, Clabourn 12, William 4, Matilda Ann 2
COMBS, Simon 16*
MILLER, William 42, Sally 39, Polly 17, Nathan 15, Jackson 12, Juda 11, Nancy Ann 9, Lawson 8, Levina 7, William 6, Stephen 3, Clabourn 2
NOBLES, John 26, Jane 18, Sally 8/12

Schedule Page 16

FRANCIS, Hiram 50, Sarah 44, William 19, Lucinda 17, Hiram 14, Daniel 11
MILLER, John 36, Sarah 30, Speed 12, Daniel 8, James 6, Kaleb 5 (m), Stephen 2, Nancy 3/12
NOBLE, James 24, Polly 23, Sarah 1
BARNETT, Wilson 42, Polly 37, George 22
WOODS, Woodson 30, Jane 30, Polly 12, Lucinda 10, Martha 5, _____ 1 (m)
MILLER, Elias 50, Nancy 50
MILLER, Samuel 38, Nancy 25, Tabitha 12, Polly 9, Andrew 7, Patsy 5, Isaac 3, Richard 5/12
NOBLE, Ira 35, Rachel 30, William 12, Samuel 10, Mary 8, Losson 7 (m), Nancy 6, Katharine 5, Louisa 4
DAVIS, Henry 30, Eliza 25, Gabriel 4, Nancy 1
CAMPBELL, Jackson 58,, Patsy 50, John 18, Susannah 15, Katharine 12, Lewis 10, Judah 8, Rolly 5 (f)
CAMPBELL, Alexander 30*
FRANCIS, Temperance 19*, William 7, Washington 4, Lucinda 11/12
CAMPBELL, Caleb 32, Delila 30, John 6, Alfred 3, Susan 4/12
FRANCIS, William 50, Polly 38, Adam 16, Minerva 12, Mary Ann 12, Washington 12, Daniel 10, Preston 8, Elizabeth 6, Rachel 4
DAVIS, Jeremi 25 (m), Miriam 25 (f), John 6/12
NAPIER, Patrick 28, Rhody 25, Lewis 6, Leaner 4 (f), Matilda 3, Micajah 6/12

Schedule Page 17

FUGATE, John 25, Rebecca 21
FUGATE, Mary 70, Martin 22, Mary 18
FUGATE, Isaac 22, Sarah 22, Delphia 5, Sena 1 (f)
FUGATE, Andrew 20, Elizabeth 20, Nancy 1
FUGATE, Martin 20, Susan 18, Sarah 40
JOHNSTON, John 22, Peggy 18
FUGATE, Andrew 42, Martin 14, William 12, Mary 10, John 7, Isaac 6, Andrew 2
MCINTOSH, James 55, Katharine 55, Nancy 26, John M. 21, Rhody 18, Fugate 15, Hannah 100, Pheobe 21, Guildean 2/12 (f), Nancy 7
HENSLEY, John 22, Betsy Ann 16
HENSLEY, Lewis 19, Fanny 20

Schedule Page 18

HARGIS, John 48, Eliza 29, Samuel 20, Kenay F. 17 (m), James H. 14, Thomas J. F. 8, Sabina 19, Eliza 12, Emiline S. 9, Ann 3, Attila 1 (f)

1850 Census Breathitt County Kentucky

BRADFORD, Saunders C. 27, Sarah Ann 19, Louiza 4/12
DUNN, John 37, Margaret 40, Jessee 16, John 15, Sally 14, Polly Ann 12, Fanny 9, Elizabeth 4
CREECH, Hiram 23, Alexander 7
DARTER, Alexander M. 23, Martha Ann 22, Susan E. 4, E. Jane 2, Babe 4/12 (m)
COMBS, Isaac B. 27
NOE, Jackson 26, Jane 16
COPE, A. C. 22 (m)
CHAPMAN, Edmund 53, Nancy 41, Virginia 12, John 16, Marion 11 (m), Lafayette 2, George 82
COMBS, William M. 22
CARDWELL, John 60, Ariminta 50, Mary M. 17, Isaac N. 23, Thomas 21, A. Edward 15
MYERS, Michael 58, Margaret 53, Strother 21, David 19, Eliza 9
DINKINS, James 22, Charlotte 20, George 3, Babe 1/12 (m)
BACK, Lewis jr. 43, Margaret 39, Susan 9, Sally 3, John 19, Barnabas 16, Solomon 22
PATRICK, A. B. 31 (m), Prudence 31, Mary M. 6, Armina C. 3, Samuel H. 2, Babe 2/12 (m)
ROARK, John 58, Polly 51, Susannah 20, Arminta 6, Jesse 15, Isaac 10
WISEMAN, Thomas B. 49, Levina 27, Nancy Ann 11, David 9, James 17, Henry 7, Abner 4, Thomas 9/12

Schedule Page 19

OVERBEE, Alexander H. 33, Lucinda 33, R. W. 6 (m), William S. 4, James C. 1?
PETERS, John H. 53, Ann 33, James 29, Samuel 3, Emily 1
GABBARD, Michael 56*, Polly 54, Michael 19, Henry 15, Margaret 13, William 11
JOHNSTON, Emily 4*
JETT, Stephen jr. 22*, Polly 15
SALLINS, Susan 19*
COMBS, Edin 21, Sylvania 18, Eliza 2, William 1
HERRALD, Alexander 65, Lizzy 55, Alexander jr. 22, Richard J. 16
HERRALD, Harris 23, Mary 25
ANGEL, Mathena 50, Ruben 16, Levi 15, Vanburen 6
JETT, Newton 41, Elizabeth 38, Morton 15, Hercanus 13, Granville 10, Sytha 11 (f), Martha 9, Julian 4, Timeandra 3 (f), Rachel 3
JETT, Stephen sr. 75
JOHNSTON, Isaac 33, Nancy 23, Granville 4, Caloway 2 (f), Thomas 7/12
TERRY, Elisha 30, E. Jane 26, Jackson 9, Nancy 7, Geo. W. 6, Isaac 4, Malve? 1 (f)
WILLIAMS, John 30*, Nancy 26
ADAMS, Green 8*, Polly Ann 6, Susan 4, Wm. 4, James 5
ROBERTS, Moses 45, Patsey 43, Rebecca 19, Rosilla 8/12
BROCK, Joshua 50, Polly 35, James 15, John W. 12, Nancy J. 10, Allen 7, David 5, Elijah 2
BOWMAN, Henry 34, Rachel 27, Permilia 10, E. Green 8, Amanda G. 7, Greenbury 5, Malvina 4, Jenara 3 (m), Lucinda 9/12, Gamble 1 (f)

Schedule Page 20

CRAWFORD, Archibald 78*, Anderson 17, Abner 19, Margaret 19
SPICER, Eviline 7*, Nancy 5
EVINS, John 58, Nancy 54, Vardeman 17, Perry 12, Nancy 20

1850 Census Breathitt County Kentucky

EVINS, Lewis 23
BROADDUS, Wm. 30, Eleanor 27, Mary F. 6/12, John E. 4, M. Beverly 2 (m)
EVINS, Henry 47, Lucinda 37, Sally 15, Margaret 12, Ann 12, Lydia Jane 10, Nancy 5, Henry 4, John 2, unnamed 5/12 (m)
CRAWFORD, Owens 33
WARNER, James 23, Nancy 19
PLUMMER, Elizth. 42, Sally 15, Nancy 12, Elizth 7, Jeremi 18, Isaac 16, John 21
PLUMMER, Samuel 25*, Rachel 21, America 5/12
BASH, Nancy 21*, Mary 2
CHAMBERS, Elijah 46, Rachel 45, John R. 19, Joseph 15, Polly 14, Lydia Ann 12, Sarah J. 10
GIBSON, Alexander C. 34, Mary 35, G. Washington 19, Ewing 17, Emily 15, Henderson 15, T. J. 9 (m), Orson 7, Anderson 5
TINCHER, William 45, Matilda 40
TINCHER, James 23, Elias 21, Joseph 16, Thomas 11, Martha 8
BOWMAN, Nicholas 53, Wesley 19, Fletcher 8, Isabel 51, Miriam 17, Martha 15, Deborah 12, Rachel 10
BOMWARS, Henry C. 23
CRAWFORD, Valentine 39*, Isabel 30, Liberty 12, Simeon 9, Elizabeth 7
THOMAS, Peter 25*, Allen 21
ANGEL, Joseph 21*, Katharine 23, Margaret 3/12
JOHNSTON, E. J. 6 (f)*, Elizabeth 12

Schedule Page 21

BRYANT, Elijah 56, Mary 45, Dison 11 (m), Roes 9, Martisia 12, Siras 22 (m)
GILBERT, Jackson 30*, Lydia 31, William 15, Martha 11, Elizabeth 9, Lucinda 8, Robert 7, James G. 5, Malvina 1
FOX, Martha 16*
BRYANT, Sarah 48, Margaret 14
BRYANT, Hurum 23, Polly 21, Serilda 3/12, Ansil 21 (m)
HENSLEY, William 26, Sebrina 20, Margaret 4, Eliza E. 2
GIBSON, Burwell 30, Synthian 28 (f), Levina 11, Fanny 10, Allen 4, Tyra 3 (f)
BRYANT, Hiram 27*, Sarah 26, Margaret 7, Joshua 3, Hiram 2, William 9/12, Eliam 17 (f)
HARGIS, Mary 50*
CRAWFORD, Oliver 35, Elvia 27, Wickliffe 9 (m), Susan 7, Archibald 5, Luraney 4, Babe 2 (m)
CRAWFORD, Harrison 31, Ibby 33 (f), Delina C. 7, Paulina 5, Babe 3 (m), Babe 1 (m)
BOWMAN, Elisha W. 35, Eviline 33, Liberty B. 13, Wilbourn 11, Mahala 9, Caloway 7, Sally 5, Rachel 3, Elijah 2
SLIDHAM, Preston 35, Rebecca 30, Henry 6, Wesley 3
BOWMAN, Joseph 42, Sytha 40, Adison 18, Angeline 17, Armina 15, Meranda 12, George W. 10, Andrew J. 8, Margaret 5, Zechry T. 3, Madison 9/12
HADDIX, William 22, Elizabeth 22, John H. 4, Mary J. 3
WALTERS, B. 41 (f)

Schedule Page 22

CRAWFORD, Clabourn 45, Susan 37, America 18, Luraney 16, Caloway 14, Elvira 12, William H. 10, Green 8, Kenaz? 5 (m), Elizabeth 3, James 3

1850 Census Breathitt County Kentucky

VIER, Moses 37, Nicey 33, James 15, John 13, Elizabeth 11, Nancy 9, Randal 7, Sarah J. 5, Almeda 3, Babe 2 (m), Babe 1 (f)
LITTLE, Paulina 19, Elizabeth K. 2
MAINARD, Pleasant 37, Mary 34, Susan 18, John M. 16, William 14, Wesley 12, Margaret 10, Lucinda 8, Mahala 3, Alexander 4/12
KING, S. Darrell? 20(m), Rosannah 17, G. W. 1 (m)
SPICER, Roger S. 30*, Julian 25 (f), Elizabeth 6, Nancy 3, William 2
COVEY, Nixon 59*, Susannah 40, William L. L. 17, Josephine 9, Jeremi W.L.M.O. 5, Daniel B. F. 1
WELLS, Margaret 18*
HILL, William P. 29*, Nancy M. 23, Mary 2, Robert C. 9/12
HARDIN, Henry 17*
SOUTH, Richard L. 38*, Sarah 30, John 12, Kit 9 9f), Richard 7, Letitia 5, William 3, Jerry 1
FARLEN, William 34*
BARNETT, Harmon 24, Eleanor 20, Nixon 3, Alexander C. 1
NOE, John D. 38, Polly 27, Hiram 8, David 7, Margaret 5, Michael 2, Daniel 9/12
MCMARR, Godfrey 56* (B)
BUSH, Harmon 21*
ALLEN, James 28
DOLTON, Peter 41, Sally 38, Peggy 18, Riley 16, Samuel 13, Susan 12

Schedule Page 23

HOURSHEL, Andrew 35, Lavina 36, Minerva 14, William P. 12, Susannah 10, Jackson 8, Harvey 6, Sally 4, Lydia 3, Rosan 2 (f), Armina 1
STURGEON, William 36, Sarah 32, William 14, Jonathan 12, Robert 10, Elizabeth 8, John 6, William 4, Jackson 5/12
MCDANIEL, Daniel 18
RANEY, William 35, Louisa 35, Ruben L. 5, Albert F. 1
SEWELL, Thomas 47, Joannah 41, B. F. 18 (m)
SEWELL, William 22*
POTELE?, Ben F. 31*
LITTLE, Edmund 31, Ede L. 26 (f), Ann 8, William 5, Emeline 3, Polly 1
SPARKS, Colburn 27
SPICER, James 23*
CUNDIFF, Stephen 22*
COMBS, Henry 23
COMBS, Stephen 45, Patsy 43, Stephen 22, Ephraim 18, William 17, Jackson 14, James 10, Lucinda 8, Nancy 6, Wilson 4, Hugh 1
SPENCER, Jesse 51, Elizabeth 42, William 20
SIZEMORE, Felix 22, Salina 21
BAKER, William 23, Nancy 21, Eliza J. 1
BOHANNON, Robert 70 (B)
HOLMES, Samuel 38, Elizabeth 33, John D. 14, Huldah Ann 12, Emiline 10, Zerilda 8, Franklin 6, Arminta 4
MARKHAM, James 22*
MCQUINN, Charles B. 30*, Esther 24, Jerry 6, Ruben 2, Emily 4/12
THOMAS, Susan 21*

1850 Census Breathitt County Kentucky

BARRETT, David 33*, Nancy 32, Thomas 11, William 9, Polly 7, John 5, Abram 3, Babe 6/12
WHITAKER, W. J. 21 (m)*

Schedule Page 24

FRAZIER, John 45, Hannah 41, Sarah 21, Nancy 20, George 18, Samuel 16, Jackson 14, Solomon 12, Polly Ann 10, James 8, Martha 6, Elizabeth J. 5, William 1
JONES, George 39*, Elizabeth 34, Louisa 15, Nancy Ann 13, Sarah 11, Sylva 8, Emiline 3, Lewis 1
THOMPSON, Eli 21*
COUCH, Andrew 42, Ann 41, William 11, Jefferson 9, Polly Ann 7
FEE, Henderson 30*, Peggy 25, Jane 3, David 2, J. C. Masor 1 (m)
MCQUINN, Zechariah 22*
MCDANIEL, John 22*
BRUER, Forrest 25*
SIZEMORE, William 53, Ann 47, Hardin 18, Edmund 15, Dillon 12, Lewis 9
BARRETT, Joshua 35, Jane 30, James 11, Sarah 9, Nancy 7, Mary 5
CARDWELL, John O. 25
OAKS, James 41*, Polly 42, Fanny 18, James 13, Micajah 6, Caldwell 9, Samuel 2
MILLER, Jeremi 22*, Mary M. 18, Fanny 1
DAMRON, Joseph jr. 38
DAMRON, Nancy 20
BAKER, John 38, Margaret 40, Nancy 16, Clarinda 13, Rebecca 10, Sarah 8, Jackson 5, John 1, Elijah 65
COCKRELL, John 40, Deborah 29, D. Dillon 5, Emilia 4, Asa 3, Martha 7/12, Mary 7/12
COCKRELL, Emilia 68
ANGEL, Adrain 42 (m), Eliza 35, Thomas 17, Berry 16, Zerilda 9, Frank 11, Lurinda 6, Emily 5

Schedule Page 25

SMITH, James 51, Louisa 28, Frances 11, Isham 9, Charles 7, Ann Eliza 5, Polly 3, Annetta 2, Bud 8/12
ROBERTS, Sampson 47, Hiley 39 (f), Preston 21, James 19, Lewis 14, Turner 12, Caleb 7
COCKRELL, Simon 78, Mary 56, B. F. 15 (f), Simon 13, Henry B. 9, John M. 9
CUNDIFF, Joseph 26, Hannah 22, Sarah J. 9/12
COCKRELL, James 33*, Ann 33, Eliza 10, E. Logan 8, Zerilda 6, Mary 4, Melissa 2
MCMARR, Letty 84* (B)
DUFF, Alexander 29, Katharine 24, Martha ann 7, Orlena 5, Marcus 3, Logan 2
COCKRELL, Harrison 22, Fanny 20
WILLIAMS, John J. 26*, Paulina 18, David 1
MARTIN, James 24*
ANGEL, Nicholas 36, Mary 35, Sarah 16, Luraney 14, Guilda Ann 12, America 10, Jane 8, Louisa 6, Arberry 4 (m), Cass 1 (m)
MONSEY, Benjamin 27, Sally 26, John 6, McKinley 4, Caloway 2, Squire 2
ANGEL, Philip 28, Nancy 26, Peter 10, Andrew 8, Polly ann 6, Sally ann 4, Betsy ann 1
DAVIS, Pleasant 26
MAYABB, John 25*, Eliza 21, Daniel 2, William T. 11/12
BEVERLY, Jacob 30*
HOGG, James 45, Barbara 37, Nancy 13, Sally 10, Stephen 7, Pollyann 5, Missourie 1

- 12 -

1850 Census Breathitt County Kentucky

Schedule Page 26

CRAFT, William 28*, Rhoda 24, Sarah J. 1
ROARK, John B. 25*, Lucinda 20, Rachel 2
COPE, Wiley 31, Susannah 28, Luraney 9, Paulina 7, Louisa 4, Delila 1
HAGINS, David 38, Susannah 30, Sally 16, Betsy 11, Clinton 7, Eliza 4, Elisha 2, Babe 6/12 (m)
SPICER, William 35, Esther 28, Saml. 12, Haney 10 (f), Jesse 8, Granville 6, Nancy 4
KETCHUM, George 33, Susan 24, Marcus W. 4, Jerry 3, Ellen 10/12
ANGEL, William 34
ANGEL, Delila 26*, Mary J. 9, Amanda 7, Selina 5, Babe 1 (f)
COMBS, Matthew 60*, Francis __
HADDIX, George C. 17*
JONES, Elizabeth 67*
BACK, Isaac 33, Rachel 25, Polly 7, Katharine 5, Louisa 2, Henry 1, Alexr. 8
FIELDS, Elizabeth 26, Deborah 11, Jane 9, Luraney 5, Wm. T. 2, Rachel M. 2/12
ROBINSON, John 38, Polly 46, John 15, Emiline 13, Malissa 12, Minerva 8, Danl. 6
TRENT, Isaiah 22, Lucinda 17
SPURLOCK, Wm. 39, Levicy 39
SPURLOCK, Jesse 72*, Jane 70
WILLIAMS, John 18*
PHIPPS, Preston M. 23, Nancy 29
WILLIAMS, Nancy 33, John H. 3
BACK, Joseph 48*, Permelia 47, Hiram 18, James 16, Nancy 10, Stephen 23
HOGG, Stephen sr. 79*
BACK, John sr. 75, Katharine 70
SPURLOCK, Saml. 33, Polly 34, Eviline 10, Miles F. 8, Chistean 6, Nancy 4, Clementine 1

Schedule Page 27

KASH, William 41, Sally 41, Levi 19, James 17, Priscilla 14, Alfred 11, Caleb 8, Pheobe 5, Polly ann 1
COPE, James P. 64, Polly 64, Alfred 24, Eliza J. 21, James Dial 18, Louisa 16
COOPER, Rebecca 37*
JONES, Polly ann 17*, Caloway 1 (m), Green C. 5
MCQUINN?, Francis 20*
COPE, William 27, Delila 25, Louiza 6, Semantha 3, JohnFrenando 2/12
HADDIX, Zechariah 41, Katharine 40, Jesse 15, Jinsey 13, Pheobe 11, Edi 8, Matilda 3
MCQUINN, Wm. 58, Elizth. 53, Haney 21 (f), Nancy 8, Eleanor 22, William 10, James 16
SHACKELFORD, Abner T. 53, Rebecca 56, Caroline 19, Polly 17, Servilla 13, James 11, Julia ann 9, Sally Jane 7, Berry 21
GAMBLE, Wm. 51, Elizth. 48, Fanny 18, Sally 12, Alfred 6, Squire 4
RALEIGH, James 25, Margaret 25, Sarah 4, Wm. 2
FRILEY, Andrew 27, Sarah Ann 25, Mary Jane 10, Rebecca 4, Susan 3, Babe 11/12 (m)
KETCHUM, Joseph 55, Susan 18, Eliza 16, John 27
CHANEY, John 35, Sally 27, George 11, Elizth. 9, William 7, James 4, Thomas 3, Babe 3/12 (m)
COLE, Isaac 24, Polly 18

1850 Census Breathitt County Kentucky

Schedule Page 28

MILLER, Martin 45, Nancy 39, Rebecca 15, Sally 13, James 12, George 10, Prudence 8, Hiram 5, Louisa 4, Fanny 4
LITTLE, Jason 25, Minerva 19, Samantha 2, George 1
BOHANNON, Henry C. 33, Paulina 28, Mary F. 7, Logan 5
HADDIX, Saml. B. 41, Suffy 35, Andrew D. 16, Lewis 14, Sally Ann 12, Katharine 10, James 8, M. Vendable 5
WILLIAMS, Gilbert 36, Polly 26, Jasper 14, Dicey 11 (m), Emiline 7, Polly 1
MULLENS, Joseph G. 28, Joannah 24, Jas. K. P. 5, Joseph 2, Nelly 1/12
NOBLE, Enoch 53, Leah 50, Edward 21, Wm. 18, Polly 16, Stephen 14, Washington 12
RALEIGH, Jacob 22, Elizth. 18
DAVIS, Henry 23, Eliza 23, Gabriel 3, Nancy 1
MARSHALL, Ruben 34, Katharine 24, Elizth. 3, John 1, Susannah 1
HAYS, Wm. 25*, Polly 18
TOLBY, Ira 20*
NIECE, Jacob B. 36, Polly 25, Peggy 8, John 6, Pater 4, Martha 2
ALLEN, Thomas 25, Etha 25, Polly 3, Babe 1 (m)
NIECE, Austin 23, Katharine 18
WYATT, Nathaniel 20*, Elsey 20, E. Jane 2/12, Wm. L. 15
SPENCER, Franklin 23*, Louisa 17
MCQUINN, Wiley 35, Sally 40, Josephine 14, Minerva 9, Palmyra 7, Julian 5, Nancy 3, Armina 1

Schedule Page 29

ANGEL, Arch. 27*, Franky 26 (f), Nancy J. 9, Polly Ann 7, Matilda 4, Philip 2
DOAN, Sally 46*
BARNETT, Mary 63
STRONG, Edward C. 26, Nancy 20, Greenville 1, Sarah 10/12
HENSLEY, Lewis 20, Fanny 21, John 7/12
HENSLEY, John 23*, Elizth. 18
HARRIS, William 34*
WILSON, Auskin 22*
COCKRAM, James 19*
RALEIGH, Elizth. 16*
MCINTOSH, Edward 29, Katharine 16, Daniel 14, America 12, Henry 10, Haney 8 (f), Marshall N. 4
CAMPBELL, Zechariah 26, Paulina 18, Mahuldah 1
HADDIX, William sr. 66*, Sarah 65, Wm. G. 27
THOMAS, Wm. 21*
THOMAS, Isaac 51*, Elizth. 40, Merchant 20, Richd. 18, Katharine 16, Rachel 12, Jemima 10, Mary 4, Pleasant 2, Marchant 79, Jemima 76
BEVERLY, Jacob 30*
WELLS, John 30, Sarah 21, Mary E. 2
FUGATE, Charles D. 63*, William 25
NIX, Leonard 42*, Fanny 28, Patsy 14, Nancy 12, Nancy J. 9, Sarah 6, Levi 3, Emily 1
WATERS, Jane 30, Letty 8, Nancy 5, Katharine 2
MCINTOSH, Absalom 39, Rachel 36, Nimrod 12, Wm. 10, Rebecca 7, Nancy 5, Stephen 3

1850 Census Breathitt County Kentucky

JOHNSTON, James 26, Dolly 21, Alfred 6, Elizth. 4, Nancy J. 2
JOHNSTON, John 35, Elizth. 30, Colbird 14, John H. 12, Sylvania 10, Jane 9, Levi 5, Granville 3, Haney 3 (f)

Schedule Page 30

WATTERS, Bradford 41, Margaret 28, Thomas C. 13, James P. 9, Josephine 7, Nancy 5, Polly Ann 2
ISHAM, Gideon 70*
DELANEY, Margaret 30*, Rosanna 9
HADDIX, Henly 70, Lydia 47, Wm. D. 19, Elizth. 18, Henly 15
BOWMAN, John 40, Prudence 45, Eliza 16, Lucinda 14, Rachel 12, Betsy 10, Wm. 8
NOBLE, Nathan 66, Jane 58
NOBLE, Henry 23, Ibby 25, Sarah J. 8, Nancy Ann 7, Washington 5, Polly Ann 3, Granville 2
CAMPBELL, John 23, Nancy 20, Matilda 1
NOBLE, Lawson 39, Peggy 32, Wm. 14, Elizth. 13, Katharine 10, Nathan 8, Jane 5, Lucy Ann 3, James 1
NOBLED, James 43, Polly 22
JOHNSTON, Ephraim 29*, Syntha 25, Sally 7, James E. 5, Madison C. 4, Drury F. 2
PARKER, Drury 21*, Nancy Ann 19
NIECE, Jacob 63, Polly 52, Polly 18, Nancy 13, Henry 15, Delila 10
FUGATE, Henly 49, Matilda 33, Pricey 15, Fanny 14, Lewis 12, Alfred 10, Danl. 8, Jeremi 8, Polly 6, Benj. 3, Susan 5/12
FUGATE, William 25, Rachel 22, Zechriah 7, Abitha 4 (f), Joshua 3, Ellis 1
FUGATE, Henly Jr. 23*
FUGATE, Zeckariah 22, Polly 21, Henly 1, James 1/12, Hourshel 1/12

Schedule Page 31

NIECE, Austin 65, Malinda 55, Joshua 23, Ann 18
NIECE, Saml. Jr. 26*, Nancy F. 29, Malinda 7, Austin 5, Micajah 4, Mary Ann 2, Polly 1/12
BUSH, James 43*
FUGATE, Wm. 19*, Nathan 18, Polly 16
ALLEN, Polly 31*, Pheobe 13, Franklin 5
NOBLE, William 41, Letty 39, Polly 23, James 18, Lavina 16, Alexander 13, Sally 10, Simpson 7, Washington 5, Frankey 4, Levicey 1
MILLER, Wiley 31, Elizth. 31, Nancy Jane 8, Peggy 4, Letty 3, Nathan 1
GWYNN, Drury F. 24*, Jane 19, Wm. 1, James 3/12
GWYNN, Wm. 55*, Polly 45
NIECE, Jacob Jr. 28*, Mariah 20, Polly 7/12
FUGATE, John B. 35*, Sally 28, Jane 10, Turner 8, Henly 6, Ellis 3, Ursula 1
HAY, Ursula 46, Gabriel 15, Henly 11
JOHNSTON, Saml. 23, Sarah 23, Lydia 4, Ira 2, Wm. 5/12
HADDIX, Jo. E. 23*, Ellen 20, Mary L. 1
BOWMAN, Wm. 30*
LEWIS, Rebecca 20*, Wm. S. 1/20
FLINCHUM, Danl. 33, Elizabeth 35, John J. 13, Wm. P. 10, Abram J. 8, Winny 5, Danl. D. 3

1850 Census Breathitt County Kentucky

FLINCHUM, John 36*, Elizabeth 34, Nancy J. 11, Polly Ann 9, John H. 7, Margaret E. 4, Eliza E. 2
GWYNN, James 17*, Polly 15

Schedule Page 32

FRAZIER, Thomas J. 38*
HOURSHEL, Jacob 30*
GRIFFING, Wm. L. 35
HARGIS, John S. 29
NOBLE, George 26, Pheobe 21, Lewis H. 2, Missourie 10/12
DAVIDSON, Jeremi 21
FOUTZ, Wm. 40*, Rachel 45, Wm. H. 9, John S. 1, Ewell W. 3
MAPLEWHITE, Polly 46*, Priscilla F. 15, Woodard 2
CALHOUN, Lister 21*
DIKES, Wm. 26, Eliza 25, Margaret 5, James 3, Polly Ann 2
TERRY, Isaac 30, Barbara 28, Angeline 10, Thomas 7, Stephen 6, Miles 5, Isaac T. 4, Patsy 2, Babe 1/12 (f)
ANGEL, John 30*, Peggy 27, Henry 11, John 9, Danl. 7, Emiline 5, Priscilla 4, Matilda 1
MOORE, Abner 1*
MARCUM, Alfred 47, Joannah 28, America 11, Edwards 10, Thomas 8, Mahala 6, Robert 4, Elizth. 2
STRONG, Robert 26, Charlotte 23, Harrison C. 1
BACK, Alfred 43, Isabel 41, Mary 21, Elizabeth 18, Henry 17, John B. 15, Joseph B. 13, Alfred 11, Benjn. 7
HOWARD, Micajah 27, Nancy 21, Hurum 3, Chloe 1
HOWARD, Driden 49, Julian 49, Samuel 13, Poly 8, Hiram 6
CAMPBELL, Lewis 50, Matilda 48, Caleb 17, Colbird 16, Polly 14
SWATNAM, Wm. P. 27, Nancy E. 20
BIRCHFIELD, Adam 57, Nancy 66
MOORE, Wm. 25, Anadatha 27, John 5, Abner 1

Schedule Page 33

SOUTH, Jeremi W. 41, Mary M. 39, Eliza 19, Ellen 18, Saml. 17, John 15, M. Vanburen 12, Celia 11, Wm. T. B. 7, Jas. K. P. 5, Patsy 4, L. Cass 2, Moore 5/12
STACY, Benjn. 30, Hannah 25
MEDLOCK, James 20*
RILEY, Richd. 20*
CARDWELL, Danl. 24*
BOOTHE, Wm. 25*, John 23, Mathias 19
WELLS, Anderson 19*
SPARKS, Ephraim 27*
CHAPMAN, George 25, Jemima 21, Nancy 3, Fulton 1
LANDRUM, R. W. 39 (m)*, Margaret 31, Ruben 13, Wm. S. 12, Martha Ann 9, Francis A. 7, Albert B. 5, Robt. S. 3, Babe 1
BELEW, John L. 27*
HADDIX, John S. 39, Emilia 34, Hiram 14, Wm. A. 13, John M. 12, Wm. A. 13, John M. 12, Henrietta 10, Sally P. 8, Danl. 6, Alexr. 5

1850 Census Breathitt County Kentucky

VIER, Randal 27, Celia 25, John M. 5, LuEllender 4, Elisha 3, Babe 6/12 (m)
VIER, David 30, Sally 25, Elizth. 5, Polly 2
MCINTOSH, Ben. 31, Katharine 27, Fanny 13, Henly 12, Mary Ann 10, Delila 8, Wm. 5, Ibby 1
SHORT, Wm. 54, Nancy 52, Wm. 12, Anderson 10, George H. 6
JOHNSTON, Elisha 27, Julia 24, James 7, Nancy 4, Luraney 2
JOHNSTON, Jesse Jr. 22, Clara 15
JOHNSTON, Thomas Sr. 79, Mary 72
JOHNSTON, Jesse Sr. 56, Polly 55, Madison 18, Nancy 16, Henderson 12, Jefferson 8

Schedule Page 34

COMBS, Saml. 51*, Nancy 47, Wiley 23, Nicholas 21, Nancy 18, Garrett 13, Lucy 10, Andrew 6, Malinda 4
EDWARDS, Jackson 26*
JETT, Curtus 31, Nancy 25, Malvre 10 (f), Eleanor 3, Jett 2
COMBS, Benjn. 57, Patsy 48, Elvira 9, Maranda 9
MULLENS, Joshua 55, Polly 45, Patsy 19, James 15, John 12, David 10
BARRETT, James 38*, Matilda 40, Andrew 16, John 12, Wm. 9, Harrison 8, Martha 6, James 4, Nancy 1, Fanny 2, Nancy 2, Pealy B. 3/12 (m)
JOHNSTON, Elizth. 22*, Hurum 1
STAMPER, Joel 72*
JOHNSTON, Thomas 23, Rebecca 29
BURNS, Wm. B. 30, Sarah 30, Margaret J. 10, Nancy J. 10, Nancy E. 8, Christian 6, Mariah M. 4, Sarah E. 2, Polly 4/12
BARRETT, Isham Jr. 22*, Eliza 17
JOHNSTON, Madison 16*
BARNS, Elizth. 15*
FOX, Nancy 16*
STURGEON, Fanny 30*
ANGEL, James 87*
BARRETT, Isham 60*, Elizabeth 52
CHADWICK, James 16*
HOURSHEL, Geo. W. 22*
VIER, Fleming 32, Polly 23, Richd. 10, Isaac 8, Margaret 6, Sally 4, Rebecca 2, Polly 1
CAUDLE, John 54*, Nancy 45, Moses 19, Pleasant 17, Tabitha 16, Preston 14, Nancy 12, John 10, Sytha Ann 8, Christian 6
OLIVER, Betsy 24*, Margaret J. 5, Martha Ann 2

Schedule Page 35

CAUDLE, Henry 27, Lucinda 27, Levisa 6, Armina 4, Alfred 2, Lewis 1
COMBS, Joseph 24, Delila 24, Calvin 5, Wiley 4
COMBS, Sira 26*, Polly 26, Tarlton 7, Jackson 5 (f), Jenira 3, Ferinda 1, Jos. 3/12
CAUDLE, Polly 21*, Sira 1
SPICER, Benjn. 55*, Nancy 45, Jemima 17, Irvine 15, Benjn. P. 13, John 8, Bryant 6
SPICER, Saml. 22*
SPICER, Jackson 24*

1850 Census Breathitt County Kentucky

COMBS, Buonapart 40, Susan 36, Eliza J. 16, Minerva 15, Artemesia 13, Synthian 11, Caroline 7, Mary Ann 4
MCINTOSH, Wm. 60*, Ibby 50, Thomas 11, Elizth. 9, Charity 6
MAYS, Lydia 29*
TURNER, Wm. 25, Nancy 25, Sally 6, Ellis 5, John 3, Nancy 1
GRIFFITH, Thomas 80, Eleanor 65, James C. 15, Ursula 18
MURRELL, Larkin 24, Nancy 22, Elijah 4, Susannah 3, William 1
LEWIS, Zera 30, Chaney 30, Dulaney 8, John 6, Zera 3, Elisha 1
MCINTOSH, Henly 30, Rachel 30, Hannah 8, Abram 6, Wm. 3, John 1/21
MAYS, John 27, Patsy 27
MCINTOSH, Wm. 30, Margaret 27, Vicey 3, Sally 1
MCINTOSH, Peter 35, Jane 30, Wm. 9, Henry 5, Tabitha 3, Fanny 1
GROSS, Henry 26*
ROBERTS, Vicey 30*, Jerry 16, Moses 14, E. Jane 12, Malvre? 3 (f), Simon 9/12

Schedule Page 36

MCINTOSH, John 35, Katharine 32, Wm. 15, Henly 13, Nimrod 11, Peter 9, Benjn. 7, Jane 5, Polly 2
MULLENS, Jesse 27, Elizabeth 24, Luraney 4, Arzanney 2, Harrison? 6/12
COMBS, Hardin jr. 35, Dicey 31, Mariah 14, Emilia Ann 12, Lessley 10 (m), Granville 7, Woodson 5, Babe 2 (f)
SIZEMORE, Russell 25, Susan 18, Nancy 5/12
GROSS, Simon 52, Darcey 46, Giles 14, Wm. 11, Polly 9, John 7, Edward 5
GROSS, Thomas 25*, Sally 25, Levi 6, Saml. 4, Wm. 6/12
STAMPER, Martha 72*
HOWARD, Patrick 25, Jane 23, Elijah 2, Chloe 1/12
COMBS, Preston 46*, Nancy 45, Clabourn 19, Buonapoparte 15, Andrew 12, Mason 10, Chistena 7, Preston 4
STORY, Elizth 11*, Ben 87
COMBS, Tarlton 24, Jemima 23, Jane 1
TURNER?, John 41, Jane 41, Nancy 19, Henry 17, Adaline 14, Sally 12, Edward 9, Jane 7, Darius 5, Wm. 4, Mary Ann 2
MAYS, William 26, Patsy 36
MAYS, Grace 48*, Gran 20, Marilda 15, Henly 13
BECKNEL, Jane 75*
MAYS, Thomas 43*, Nancy 38, Abram 18, Rachel 16, Sally 14, Wm. 12, Higy 10, Samuel 8, Darcus 2

Schedule Page 37

HALL, John 20*
LADD, Thomas 24*
SPICER, Edward 37
TURNER?, Thomas 38, Polly 35, Jesse 15, Timothy 13, Elliott 11, Edward 9, John 7, William 5, Mary 4, Paschal 3, Shadrach 1
BECKNEL, Wm. 32, Sarah 25, Saml. 7, Mary J. 5, Sarah Ann 4, Elizth. 4/12
FALLIERS, Nelson 21, Susan 17, Carr 6/12
SIBASTIAN, John 66, Sally 54, Caloway 22, Lewis 16, Benjn. 13

1850 Census Breathitt County Kentucky

STAMPER, Joel 45, Polly 44, Sally 19, Patsy 18, Delita 16, Edward 14, Nancy 12, Richd. 10, John 9, Polly 7, Joel 5, Susan 3, Margaret 2
SEBASTIAN, David 26, Elizabeth 20, Susan 1, John 6/12
SEBASTIAN, Henderson 29, Lizzy 20
TURNER, Thomas 40, Jane 38, Sylvania 12, John 10, Saml. 8, Charlotte 7, Wm. 4, Polly 2
TURNER, Thomas sr. 60, Delita 26, John W. 8, Nancy 24
TURNER, Edward sr. 69, Sally 63, Betsy 19, Boyd 15
TURNER, Edward jr. 34, Rachel 31, Elliott 10, Edward 8, Thomas 6, Meredith 4, Rachel 3, Sally 2/12
MAYS, Moses 33*, Mary 32, Abram 14, Sally 12, Charity 10, Hannah 9, Ibby 8, Eli 6, Grace 4
TURNER, Shadrach 12*, Sarah 18

Schedule Page 38

TURNER, David 53, Sarah 50, Hampton 18, Nancy 16, Alfred 14, Roger 12, Sally 10, Matilda 8
TURNER, Saml. 35, Sarah 34, Betsy 15, Jane 13, Polly 11, Agness 9, Bud 7, Lucinda 5, Babe 1/12 (m)
TURNER, Roger jr. 24, Nancy 16
SHIFLY?, James Turner 46, Jane 38, Polly 17, Sally 15, Betsy 14, David 12, Jessee 10, Katharine 8, Nancy 4
TURNER, Larkin 30, Polly 25, Lizzy 7, Sylvania 5, Jane 2
HERRALD, Thomas 37, Elizth. 37, Felix 19, Roger 17, Jesse 15, Alexr. 13, Sarah 10, Thos. 7, Elizabeth 4, Nancy 2, America 3/12
TURNER, Wiley 24, Susan 20, Sally 6/12
BOLING, Dulaney 26, Sarah 26, Wm. 4, R. P. Letcher 2, Sidney 1
BOLING, Elijah 52, Mary Ann 32, Elisha 18, Elihu 15, Martha J. 5, America 3, Kenay? F. 1
BOLING, George 40, Pheobe 35, Marinda 18, Elizth. 16, John 11, Lucinda 9, Malinda 7, Nancy 5, Elly 1
KEEN, John 32, Martha 31, May Ann 4, James 3, Ellen 9/12
BOLING, Jesse 27
CAMPBELL, Charly 47*, Polly 46, Elijah 19, Sarah 12, Elihu 15, Henry 3
MAYS, David 7/12*
COMBS, Nicholas 21*, Polly 15
COX, Henderson 22*

Schedule Page 39

BOLING, William jr. 25*, Elijah jr. 21
NEAL, Wm. 59
RILEY, Zachriah 30, Sarah 28, Betsy 8, James 6, Emilea 4, Zechr. 3, John 2
RILEY, John 50, Betsy 50, Wm. 18, Peggy 20, John 15, Lucinda 12
RILEY, John 45, Jane 42, Nancy 18, Ludema 16, Squire 14, Granville 12, Riley 10
RILEY, Saml. 22, Mary B. 18
MOSLEY, James 28, Sarah 25, Wm. 7, James 5
LUCEY, Harvey 28
SMITH, Joshua 32, Elizth. 26, Wm. 9, Jarvis 7, Margaret 6
SMITH, Whitley 34, Elizth. 30, James 13, Josh. 12, Caroline 10, Wm. 8, Simon 6, John 3, Esther 4, Henry 1
JOHNSTON, Elliott 32, Esther 29, Robert 9, Malinda 7, Marinda 5, Mahala 3, Palestine 2 (m), Matilda 6/12

1850 Census Breathitt County Kentucky

FOX, John 28, Sally 22, Sally 1
HACKER, Dudley 24, Elizth. 19, Melvin 6/12 (f)
SANDLIN, John 24, Mary 21, Levina 1
BROCK, Wm. 46, Mourning 30, Rebecca 13, Ballinger 11, Elizth. 9, Minerva 7, Wm. Owsley 5
JOHNSTON, James 46, Mary 44, Elliott 24, John S. 14, Rachel 8
JOHNSTON, Robert sr. 72, Rachel 66
JOHNSTON, Paschal 26, Rhoda 24, Robert 9/12
MCGEORGE, P. W. 35 (m), Elizth. 30, Mariah 15, Alfred 13, John 11, James 3, Danl. 8/12

Schedule Page 40

BAKER, Isaac 32, Jane 30, Savina 12, Esther 11, Emiline 9, Clarissa 4, Wm. 2, Wm. 2, America 5/12
HERRALD, William 33, Polly 24, Lewis 9, Lizzy 7, Mahala 4, John 2
HERRALD, John 30, Mahala 20, Sally 2
SPICER, Samuel 66, Jane 66
TURNER, Roger 55, Esther 25, Wessley 20, Henry 18, Henderson 2
GRIFFITH, Danl. 20, Isabel 22, Emilia 1/12
STAMPER, Enoch 40*, Mary Isabel 42, Susan 17, Albert 15, Peter 13, Polly 11, Peggy 9, Jonathan 7, Katharine 5, Sally 3, James 6/12
BAKER, Ira 21*
STAMPER, Jonathan 68
STAMPER, Lewis 30, Emilia 25, Ellis 8 (f)
STAMPER, Jonathan Jr. 30, Nancy 29, Wessley 9, Enoch 7, Eviline 5, Wm. 3, Polly 1
TURNER, Edward 50, Susannah 44, Edward 18, Jesse 16, Lewis 12, Levis 11, Preston 8, Sally 6, Betsy 3, John 1
STAMPER, Lewis 22, Jane 20, Richard 2
COUCH, Elijah 40, Serana 44, Katharine 19, Patsy 17, Rosannah 15, Anna 11, Sally 7, Levisa 5, Serana 2
WOMBLES, Cornelius 40*, Anna 44
DAVIS, Betsy 20*, Barbara D. 13, Eliza 9, Poly 7, Nancy 5, John 2
SPURLOCK, Wm. 62*

Schedule Page 41

LITTLE, Joseph 35*, Nancy 35, John 11, Joannah 10, Thos. F. 8, Eliza 6, Minerva 5, Jere. W. 2, Jos. 5/1, James 14
SPARKS, John 16*
BROWN, George A. 45, Mary 36, Araba J. 22, George A. 17, Jacob C? 14, Napoleon D. 12, McKee 10, Margaret 7, Arthusela 4
DUNAWAY, Caleb 34, Sally 28, James 10, Isaac 8, Mary 5, Geo. Ann 3, Amanda 9/12
KILLBURN, George 35*
KING, Hiram 34*, Isham 25
HAGINS, Danl. 42*, Elizth. 35, Emilea 16, Polly 15, William 12, Patsy 9, Hiram 7, Nancy 5, Mary J. 3, John L. 1
WHITAKER, Edmund 20*
BROWN, Geo. A.F.Co. –*
GIBSON, T. J. 9 (m)*, Orson 7, Anderson 5

1850 Census Breathitt County Kentucky

BOWMAN, Wesley 19*
MOORE, Allen 50, Margaret 46, Polly 15, Rebecca 13, John 11, Drucilla 8, James 5
WILSON, John 28, Polly 22, Jackson 3
CRAWFORD, M. N. 30 (m), Rebecca 26, Sally 6, Volentine 4, Arminta 2, Jephtha 1
WHITE, Alsor 23, Sally 20, Saml. 18
CLAY, Elijah 35, Elizth 32, John 13, Levina 11, Eliza 9, Sally 7
COCKRAM, Danl. 24*
MILLER, Hiram 32*, Elizth. 24, Granville 4, Meranda C. 2
DEATON, John 21*
JONES, Wm. 66, Peggy 62
RILEY, Wm. 46, Susan 42, Betsy 15, Sally 13, Nancy 11, John 9, Susan 7

Schedule Page 42

STRONG, William 52, Jemima 43, Thomas 20, John 17, Jane 14, Isabel 12, Malissa 7, Wiley 6/12
DAY, Willoughby 41, Levina 35, Ambrose 20, Serilda 16, Mahuldah 14, Whitier 11, Rosannah 8, Fanny 6, Barbara 2
BARNETT, James 40, Ellis 36, Anna 19, Betsy 15, Vina 13, Joshua 11, Patsy 9, Siba 7, Nancy 5, Sally 3, Munda? 1
STRONG, Edward (Col.) 59, Elizth. 58, William 24, John 20, Elizabeth 18, Alexander 14
LITTLE, John 37, Jane 35, Mahala 16, Haney 14, Sylvania 11, Alfred 11, Edward 8, Joseph 6, WM. 4, Robert 3, Katharine 1
DEATON, Isaac 25, Sarah 25, Malinda 8, William 6, Nancy 4
DEATON, William 22, Rachel 21, Lewis 3, James 1
SPENCER, Alfred 24, Ibby 20
WHITE, Rachel 50, Mahala 16, James 14, Jane 12
DAVIDSON, Robt. 47, Nancy 43, Jerry 20, Susan 16, Darcus 14, Edward 12, Polly 12, Mary 5, Nancy 3
AIKMAN, John 71, Sally 50, Peter 24, Alexander 15, Daniel 19, James 13, Elizth. 11
DAVIDSON, John 25, Miriam 23, Robt. 2
AIKMAN, Abner 21*, Effa 20, Allen 5/12

Schedule Page 43

MULLENS, Franklin 18*
TRUEMAN, Hiram 27*
BACK, John Jr. 21, Mary B. 23, Greenville 2
BUSH, Hugh 35, Katharine 35, Polly 19, Rebecca 12, Peggy 10, Sarah 8, Rachel 6, Nickelbury 2
BUSH, John 45, Rachel 35, Drury 17, John 15, William 11, Elizth. 13, Hugh 9, Thomas 7, George 3, Eliza 5, Sally 6/12
MORRIS, Elias 44, Rebecca 44, Julia 16, Margaret 14, Rebecca 11, Lydia 9, Elias 7, Wiley 5, John 2, Jeremiah 5/12
MORRIS, Wesley 19, Sytha 18
AIKMAN, John Jr. 27, Jane 26, Henry 10, John 8, James 6, Mary 3
GWYNN, John 28, Sarah 28, Nancy 9, Allen 7, Margaret 5, Elizabeth 3, James 2
GAMBLE, John 24, Elizth. 20, Granville 6, Delila 3, Joseph 2
LITTLE, James 25, Polly 21, Jaason 2
WATTS, Washington 30, Polly 30, Ambrose 7, Susan 5, Emilia 3, Babe 1

1850 Census Breathitt County Kentucky

WATTS, George 75, Emilia 75
FUGATE, Eli 55, Elizth. 50, David 5, Jeptha 7
COMBS, Mason 55, Matilda 43, Patsy 17, Margaret 16, John 14, Enoch 11, Malinda 8, Granville 6, Levina 3, George 1
WATTS, Polly 30, Enoch 10, Ambrose 7, Joannah 5, John 1

Schedule Page 44

DEATON, Bryant 25*, Lucinda 24, Mahala 5, John 8
MARTIN, Fitney 24 (f)*
WATTS, Emilia 22*
LITTLE, William 41, Patsy 35, Polly 16, John 13, James 11, William 9, Jane 5, Armina 1
STIDHAM, James 38, Polly 35, William 13, Saml. 11, Ebenezer 9, Nelly 7, Andrew 5, Prudence 3, James 1
FORTNER, Joseph 34*, Mary 34, Timothy 12, Martha 10
WATTS, Ambrose 27*
SEWELL, Joseph 50, Nancy 44, Lucinda 21, Benjn. F. 18, James A. 13, John L. 10, Thomas J. 7, Elizabeth 5, McKinley 4, Stephen 2
DAMRON, Joseph Sr. 64, Elizth. 79
HOWARD, Mongomery 27*, SArah 22, William 4, Louisa 10/12
WHITAKER, Edmund 20*
BREWER, Frank 18

1850 Census Carter County Kentucky

Schedule Page 214

NETHERCUTT, George 58, Rebecca 55, Sarah 22, William 22, George 17, Stephen 14, Rebecca 12
GOBLE, Stephen M. 38, Emily 32, Eliza 14, Hannah 12, William 9, Elizabeth 7, Ephraim 1
MONTGOMERY, John Y. 40, Mary 35, Matilda 14, James 12, Martha 11, Elizabeth 7, Henry 4, Joseph 1
DAWSON, Olive 49*, Harriet 18, Mary 16, James 13, Larkin 10, Elizabeth 9
MARTIN, John 18*
MCCARTY, Milla 38*, Dewet 11, Sarah 9, Eliza 6
DAVIS, William 21*, John 18, Enoch 15, James 13, Charlotte 3
DAVIS, Hezekiah 41, Martha 41, Jonas 16, Sarah 12, Jerimiah 9, Terissa 6, Nancy 4, Robert 1
GEE, Champness M. 45*, Nancy 37, Henry 20, Mary 14, Isabinda 12, John 10, Robert 8, Margaret 4, Martha 2
WALTON, Jame 23*
RUTHERFORD, William 38*, Rachael 33, Lelira 7, Olena 6, Sarah 4, Louis 2, George 7/12
SMITH, ---- 25 (f)*, Sarah 6
HERN, Perry 29, Louisa 25
HUNT, William H. 30, Martha 24, Susan 17, Mary 7/12
ANGLIN, Gabriel 37, Mary 28?, Adron 28, James 9, Tarlton 7, Virginia 4, Nancy 4/12
MIRANDY, William 51, Leaner 37, Mary 8, Henrietta 6
BAKER, Robert 52, Ann 55, Hiram 19

Schedule Page 215

LOW, Alfred 23, Sarinda 21, Emily 4, Clarinda 1
HANNAH, Alexander 48, Lucinda 37, Peter 25, Nancy 15, Lucinda 12, Alexander Jr. 10, John 8, Charles 6, Comadore 4, James 2
SMITH, Edward G. 23, Matilda 22, James 4/12
ANGLIN, Abram 32, Orenas 22, Malicah 14, Nancy 10, Mary 7, Lucy 2, William 10/12
ANGLIN, John Sr. 65, Mary 63, John Jr. 30, William 24, Eliza 18
BALL, John C. 43*, Jelina 40, Susan 15, John 14, Rebecca 12, Elizabeth 10, Henry 8, Sarah 6, Thomas 4, Robert 2, James 4/12
COLEGROVE, Edwin 30*
BALL, William D. 38, Cynthia 30, Ralph 8, Walter 6, William 4
CLARK, James 39, Mary 36, Mary 10, Heloise 7, Lucy 4, Ann 1
BOLEY, William B. 38, Nancy 29, Elias 9, Marietta 7, Nancy 5, William 2, John 1/12
HORD, John N. 44, Ann 37, Louis 20, Mary 18, Bainton 15, Arthur 12, John 5, William 1
MORRIS, Luana 35, Amy 17, Martha 15, Madison 13, Susan 10, Elizabeth 8, James 5
MORRIS, Benjamin 7i5, Elizabeth 50, William 30, Henry 24, Elizabeth 16
RICE, Elijah 43*, Elizabeth 39, Sarah 17, Mary 15, Granville 13, John 10, Elijah 7, Willian 4, Michael 2

Schedule Page 216

WOOLFORD, Michael 41*
JACOBS, Carter H . Jr. 25, Mary 26, Landon 5, Martha 1
SPERRY, Alfred 40, Elizabeth 36, Lydia 14, Calphurnia 10, John 8, Samuel 6, JKames 4

1850 Census Carter County Kentucky

JACOBS, Carter H. 56*, Mary 51, Joseph 23, Isabel 23, John 20, William 19, Frances 16, Daniel 15, Madison 13, James 10, Katharine 8, Permelia 6
HOOVER, Emanuel 90*
SYRUS, Benjamin 95* (B)
BURCHETT, Burrell 45, Sarah 43, John 24, Elizabeth 19, Benjamin 17, Nancy 15, Thomas 13, Silas 10, Drewra 8, Burrell 6, Ann 3, Susana 10/12
BURCHETT, James 33*, Elendor 30, Susana 73, Cynthian 8, Francis 4, Lydia 3, John 1/12
HANEY, Mary 24*
BLANKENSHIP, Obediah 69*, Elizabeth 55
THOMAS, William 34*, Tarsha -0?, Henry 16
GALION, Thomas 56, Ruth 51, James 29, Louis 19, Mary 14, Alfred 9
GALION, Johnathan 27*, Elizabeth 20, William 5, America 1
LUNFORD, John 13*
BURCHETT, Benjamin 36, Elizabeth 35, Susana 14, James 15, Eliza 13, John 11, William 9, Burrell 7, David 5, Benjamin Jr. 3
ALEXANDER, William 28*, Sarah 20, Rebecca 1
WADE, William 12*
WILSON, James 30, Hetta 20, Robert 6/12

Schedule Page 217

JONES, William 57*, Nancy 23, Andrew 4
WADDLE, Mary A. 57*
THOMAS, Jonathan 31, Delena 28, Mary 5, Elizabeth 3, William 1
GULLET, John 55, Elsa 58, Rhoda 33, Jane 30, William 9, Reese 6, Susana 2
BRADLEY, Jesse 63, Elizabeth 50, Phebe 19, Ira 16, James 14, Mary 12, William 10, Rhoda 8
CLARK, Mitchel 30, Sarah 27, James 7, William 6, Mary 4, John 1
FANNIN, Bryan 48*, Mary 43, Lindsey 18, Almira 13, William 7
MCCARTY, Sarah 38*
LAMBERT, James C. 15*
SEXTON, James 52, Milla 52, James 17, Aaron 13, Enoch 9
FLOWHER, James 29*, Margaret 27, James 4, Chrisley 10/12, Elizabeth 3
WELCH, Napoleon 21*
RUGGLES, James 17*
CRAWFORD, George W. 40*, Eliza 40, Mary 2, John 6/12
ALLEN, James S. 25*
BARNS, James 13*, Thomas 11
SMITH, Maria L. 6*
HARPER, David M. 46*, Cynthia 45, Nancy 20, Susan 17, Elizabeth 15, James 12, George 8, Mary 6, Louis 4
PARSONS, Gabriel 25*, Sarah 23, Nancy 10/12
PRATER, Harvey 16*
HORD, Philip B. 47, Katharine 42, Hebe 14, Mary 7
VIRGIN, Lamack 41*, Amanda 30, Katharine 6, Nancy 2, James 18
CURRY, Lena 34*
PUGH, Martin 36*
GOBLE, Amos 16*
COOK, Hiram 35*, Henry 7, Thomas 2

1850 Census Carter County Kentucky

Schedule Page 218

VIERS, Henry 21*
COOK, Johnson 62, Mary 58, Edwin 23
WAMACK, William 41, Jacintha 38, Nancy 19, Moses 17, Martha 13, Archy 11, Ebgert 9, James 6, Sally 3, Ephraim 1
BRYSON, Isaac 75, Nancy? 60
BRYSON, James 40, Nancy 35, Rebecca 14, Mary 12, John 10, Rutha 8, Sarah 6, Martha 4, Nancy 2
BRADFORD, John 44*, Cassander 44, Eliza 16, Susan 14, Mary 13, Lydia 11, Cyntha 9, William 5, Henry 1
BRADSHAW, Sarah J. 21*
SCOTT, Henry 42*, Jane 37, Elizabeth 20, William 16, Sarah 13, Thomas 11, Jackson 6, Katharine 1
BRADFORD, Sarah 55*
SCOTT, Thomas 69, Elizabeth 66
SCOTT, Andrew J. 33, Rhoda 23, Delila 4, Nancy 2
HORD, Thomas T. 54*, Clarinda 44, Mildred 20, Moses 18, Sarah 8
DUNCAN, Alamander 73*
JONES, Griffith 44, Elizabeth 42, Martha 17, James 15
STEWART, James 47, Eda 42, Emily 16, Joicy 15, Harriet 14, Elmina 12, James 10, Joseph 9, Phebe 7, Charles 5, Mary 3, William 3/12
LAWHORN, George W. 57, Amra 42, Mary 22, William 20, Melcena 16, Malaciah 13, John 12, George 10, James 8, Finetta 6, Alonzo 3, Cerrilda 8/12

Schedule Page 219

EVERMAN, Moses Sr. 53*, Elender 55, Rebecca 22, Delila 20, Tignel 18, Caroline 13
JORDAN, James 17*
KIBBEY, Jacob 46*, Malinda 43, William 19, Harriet 17, John 15, George 12, Samuel 10, Francis 8, James 6, Mildred 3
SHEPHERD, John T. 26*
RATCLIFF, William 19*
DUNCAN, Leroy 71*, Hagga 72, Losson 36
JAMES, Phebe 14*
RICHARDS, Pheola A. 4*
DUNCAN, Eli 43, Jalia 43, James 18, Isaac 17, Rebecca 16, Louis 15, Robert 14, Parthena 6, William 3
WRIGHT, Charles 64, Dorothea 65
WRIGHT, William 36, Polly 34, Cerena 16, Charles 14, John 12, Dorothea 10, Harrison 6, Robin 10/12
ZORNS, Andrew 56*, Elizabeth 36, George 18, Rosana 15, Martha 14, Elizabeth 12, Louisa 11, John 9, Garret 7, Ricaroa 5, James 4
GLASSFORD, Sarah 45*
GUY, David 54, Elizabeth 40, Enoch 18, William 17, Rachael 15, Andrew 12, Katharine 5, Tennessee 10/12
MCGINNIS, Reuben 28*, Caroline 27, William 5, Rachael 1, John 73, Rebecca 65
MEAD, Larkin 14*, Elizabeth 12
HOSLEY, Hiram 41, Mary 41, Amanda 19, Emily 17, Louisa 15, Cynthiana 13, Stephen 11, Silas 9, Fielding 7, Frederick 5, Preston 8/12

- 25 -

1850 Census Carter County Kentucky

Schedule Page 220

HARVEY, Calvin L. 66*, Katharine 43, John 26, Calvin 24, Sarah 21, James 19, William 16, Martha 13, Elizabeth 7
DUZAN, Eli C. 10*
SHAW, John Aa. 45, Martha 40, William 22, Francis 20, Mary 15, Elizabeth 13, Harvey 11, Lorenzo 7, Flavius 3, Samuel 2, Katharine 8
DUNCAN, Edward R. 27*, Mary 21, Lafayette 3, Rosilla 1
WILBURN, Patterson 30*
RISTER, John 64*, Sarah 55, Francis 18, Katharine 15
SMITH, Sarah 14*, Richard 21
LAMBERT, Burrel 49, Elizabeth 46, John 26, Sarah 22, Elizabeth 14, Susana 12, Burrel 19, Finetta 5, Benjamin 1
GILBERT, John 22, Darcus 21
ROE, Joshua 49*, Nancy 42, Robert 20, Nancy 17, Joshua 15, Ariel 13, Martha 11, William 9, Matilda 6, Eliza 4
HUNTSMAN, John 25*
KEATLEY, William 50*, Mary 39, Eveline 16, Elender 14
GILBERT, Jane 20*, Samuel 17, Mary 15, Alexander 12, America 10, Elizabeth 7, Helen 4, George 6?/ 12
WOOTON, Randal 42, Lydia 41, Charles 20, Perlitha 16, Clarinda 13, Eveline 12, Fanny 8, Perlania 4, Martha 1
FURGASON, Elijah 40, Elsa 28, Almira 10, Napoleon 8, Louisa 6, Lucy 4, Phelonesse 1
RIGGS, George W. 42, Delila 41, Saraj 16, Zerelda 10, Clarinda 6, William 4, Theodore 3/12

Schedule Page 221

CARVER, George 32, Cynthia 28, Harriet 13, Mary 11, Phebe 9, Nancy 7, Robert 4, John 2
JACOBS, William 42, Rhoda 46, William 22, Ira 21, Carter 20, Hiram 18, John 17, Celetha 15, Jackson 9, Rhoda 7, Geroge 5, Francis 2, Nancy 25
GILBER, Samuel 25, Nancy 25
KIBBEY, Oliver 28, Nancy 27, Delila 7, Moses 5, Willis 4, Eugene 1
LAMBERT, Philip 51, Margaret 49, John 26, Levi 22, Hannah 16, Milton 13, Simpson 11, Henderson 9, Anthony 7, Mahala 3
GLOVER, Thomas J. 45, Margaret 27, Thomas 18, John 16, Rebecca 8, William 7, Benjamin 5
LAMBERT, Ezekiel 48, Margaret 47, Elizabeth 23, McKinney 21, Malinda 19, Hannah 16, Polly 15, Matilda 13, Lafayette 9?, John 7?, Cassandre 4?, Castoria 2?, Louisa 10
FURGASON, Jeremiah 27, Melissa 23
FURGASON, Vincent 26*, Olivia 19, Elizabeth 3
LAMBERT, Polly 57*
RICE, Nancy 39, Delila 15, Olivia 12, Richard 10, Matthias 8
HOOD, William P. 45, Matilda 44, James 17, Charles 15, Martha 13, Sarah 11, Mary 9, Nancy 6, William 2

1850 Census Carter County Kentucky

Schedule Page 222

BANFIELD, John 51, Katharine 46, Chrisley 20, Thomas 18, Martha 18, John 15, Eliza 14, Sydney 12, William 5
HOGAN, Isom 43*, Lenna 42, Alvira 20, John 14, Melvina 13, Andrew 10, Edward 7, Lenna 5
MURPHY, David 21*
HENSLEY, Madison M. 37, Elizabeth 31, Joseph 13, Hannah 9, Mordic 7, Mary 4, James 1
MCBRAYER, Solomon S. 24, Mary 23, Cecilia 2, Eliza 6/12
DUNAFIELD, John 63*, Leanna 55, David 21, Sarah 17, Virginia 17, John 15, George 13
EARTHEM, Adaline 2*, Rosana 1
HOGAN, David 91*, Betsey 75, William 41, Andrew 32, John 8, Elizabeth 6, harrison 7, Mary 4
SIMS, William 33*
FRAD, Charles 27*
CHAFIN, Sally 25*
DIXON, Sophrona 24*
WHITE, Samuel 48, Elizabeth 41, William 23, Alfred 19, Mary 16, Sarah 14, James 12, Bathany 10, Susan 7, Elizabeth 4, Henry 2
COLLINSWORTH, Anderson 44*, Margret 24, Thomas 17, nancy 2, Mary 6/12
ROMAN, Mary 15*
LOVEJOY, David 24, Jane 21, Mary 2, Nancy 3/12
ARTHUR, Eli 29*, Margaret 30, Octavo 9, Alifair 7, Levi 4, Alvin 1
CHOCKEY, John 75*, Elizabeth 68
RUSSEL, Mahala 38*
BLANKENSHIP, Thomas 53*, Permelia 53, Asa 20, Henson 18, Mary 17, Adaline 16, William 12

Schedule Page 223

HOOD, Elizabeth 23*, Charles 8, John 5, Nancy 2
KEESER, Martin 40*, Katharine 38, John 13, Emeline 12, Elizabeth 7, Frances 4, Martin Jr. 1
TURNER, Stephen 36* (B)
KEESER, Thomas 22, Sarah 21, Elizabeth 5, Jane 4, Albert 3, Mary 2, Adalaide 1/12, Jane 46
WOOTON, John 77, Elizabeth 41
BATTEN, James P. 56*, Delila 54, Robert 17, Cerilda 13
VAUGHN, Benjamin 9*, Sarah 7
BURTCHETT, William 33*, Martha 28, Benjamin 8, Mary 6, William 3, John 3/12
GALAWAY, Mary 16*
BIAS, Berry 24, Sarah 16
NORTH, Loyd 28, Alice 17, Cammomile 8/12
RUNYAN, Harvey 39, Mary 42, Cynda 15, Henry 13, Nancy 10, Sophia 8, Martha 6, Matilda 3, John 1
WHITE, James 67, Nancy 49, Mary 22, Alfred 10
CALDWELL, William 24, Jane 23, Andrew 2
KIRK, Susan 60*, Thomas 21, Susan 18, Elizabeth 16, Elsa 13
WHITE, Mary 39*, Eli 15, Henry 12, Robert 3
KIRK, Solomon 29*, Rachael 22, Susan 2, Adaline 8/12
WALKER, Mary 43*, Rutha 17
HOWE, Mary E. 4/12*

1850 Census Carter County Kentucky

BOWLING, Hannah 41, William 24, Elizabeth 22, John 20, Jasper 15, Mary 8
SWEARENGEN, John 27, Mary 29, Louis 11, Mary 9, Sarah 8, Vanburen 7, George 5, Roxa 2, Amanda 1/12

Schedule Page 224

DAVIS, David 57, Katharine 56, Solomon 14
EASTHAM, John C. 22, Elizabeth 18
KIRK, George 27, Hannah 25, Susan 7, Solomon 5, Joseph 3, Mary 1
MCGINNIS, James 38, Eliza 33, Elizabeth 12, Jasper 9, Celia 6, John 4, George 1
MCGINNIS, Thomas 35, Sarah 33
DAVIS, William 29, Elizabeth 31, Margaret 6, Sarah 4, Edward 3, Volney 1
DAVIS, Aaron 34, Miram 35, Christiana 9, Frances 8, Marietta 6, Louisiana 4, Henson 2
MCBROYER, James 46, Anne 43, James 18, Mary 16, William 12, Susan 8, Henry 1
KOUNS, George W. 46*, Elizabeth 46, Charles 23, Mary 20, John 18, Stephenia 16, Miram 14, Sarah 12, Caroline 10, George 8, Leanora 5, Olive 11/12
MCCONAHA, J. L. 28 (m)*
EASTHAM, John H. 34*, Elizabeth 25, Virginia 3, Miram 3/12
MCBROYER, Louis P. 23*
DAVIS, Edmund Sr. 46, Weneford 43, nancy 16, Amos 13, Lucinda 12, Mary 10, Ibba 9, Sarah 3, Edmund Jr. 1
MCBROYER, William G. 35*, Elizabeth 39, John 16, James 14, Mary 12, susan 10, Esther 8, Araminda 4, America 2, Hartwell 6
FISHER, Joseph 20*

Schedule Page 225

NORTON, Pleasant 48, Anne 49, Hetta 20, William 11, Martha 9
STEPHENS, James 52, Mary 40, James 19, Eliza 15, Mary 14, Sarah 12, John 10, William 7, George 4
SAVAGE, Peter 34, Sarah 28, William 4, Chrisley 2, Archibald 4/12
CLARK, Joseph 29, Polly 32, Stephen 9, Sarah 6, Owen 5, Ama 2
SLOANE, James 43*, Cena 47
HALL, Wesley 16*, Rutha 14, Andrew 12, Sarah 10, Holeman 8, Ephraim 4
JONES, William 26, Mary 22, Comadore 3, Nancy 1
LUSK, James 34, Elizabeth 25, Perlina 7, Emily 5, Nancy 3, America 1
ADKINS, Isaac 47, Polly 42, Eliza 23, Sarah 20, Daniel 15, Henry 13, Weiser 11, harrison 7, Andrew 5, Martha 9?, Anthony 1, William 2
HALL, James 27, Susan 23, William 6, Elizabeth 4, Emily 2, Sarah 6/12
SMITH, Claiborn 48, 4Cloa 31, James 15, Delila 14, Russell 12, Lucindad 10, John 8, Martha 7, Nancy 5, George 4, Ann 2, Roxa 6/12
LUSK, Sarah 72, Russell 35, William 24, Samuel 22, Emily 19
WILLIAMS, Mary 70*, Samuel 33
HALL, Fielding 21*, John 20
PARSONS, Robert 21*
RIGGS, Charles B. 67*, Greenville 47, Samuel 45, Charles 41, Anthony 39, Adaline 33, Sarah 26, Frances 24, Malinda 22

1850 Census Carter County Kentucky

Schedule Page 226

PLUM, John 23*
LAMPTON, James 59*, Susan 58, Robert 30
WAMACK, Ann 34*, James 14, Polly 12, Susan 6, Nancy 2
SMILEY, Polly 54*
RILEY, James W. 22*
MONTGOMERY, George 28, Julia 23, William 5, George 3
SMITH, William 29, Lydia 23, John 10/12
LOCKE, Lindsey 38, Martha 34, Eliza 18, William 16, Nancy 14, Sarah 12, John 10, Mary 10, Martha 9, Lindsey 7, George 1
HALL, William 32?, Cyntha 27?, James 6?, Pleasant --, Margaret --
GAY, William 27*, Mary 22
BETTYS, Mary 8*
GARD, William 33, Margaret 31, Jane 10, Ann 8, Otho 6, John 4, Margaret 10/12
HANEY, Ancil T. 37, Rachael 30, Irvin 10, Christopher 5, Henry 10/12
WOOD, James F. 26*, Eliza 23, Nancy 5, John 4, James 2
WOOD, Andrew J. 21*
BROWN, Irvin 32, Jane 20, Mary 1
WILSON, Isaac D. 24*, Elziabeth 18, John 10/12
HARDIS, Andrew J. 8*
GAY, Samuel 67, Maria 54
LANE, Harvey 26, Martha 19, Mary 2, James 2/10
WILSON, John 24*, Nancy 30
HORNER, Joshua 15*, Peter 13, James 7, Cordelia 5
BAYS, Samuel E. 22, Elizabeth 18, Mary 2, John 1

Schedule Page 227

LOCKE, Rachael 59*, Hiram 24, Nathan 22, Martha 18
WARD, William 30*
RIDGEWAY, Benjamin 30, Jane 25, Newton 3, John 1
VIRES, William 25, Sarah 25, James 4, Martha 2, Nancy 1
SHORT, Stephen Sr. 39*, Lydia 39, William 11, Stephen Jr. 9, Daniel 6, John 4, Lucy 2, Andrew 1
MONTGOMERY, Nathan 26*
CRAIG, Stewart 25*
IRVIN, Isaac 23, Temperance 17, Joshua 2/12
WILSON, Henry 29, Mary 22, William 3, Margaret 2
ROBISON, George 34, Martha 28, Greenville 12, Nancy 9, Phebe 5, Perlina 4, Roxa 1
BRANNUM, Edward 77, Polly 69, Wiley 24, Riley 20, Edward 10
GEARHART, Allen 36*, Eliza 31, Alexander 11
THORNSBURY, Edward 38*, William 13
JUSTICE, Harrison 18*
MONTGOMERY, James 49, Elizabeth 33, Taylor 16, Ann 8, Henry 7, Rebecca 5, Eunice 2, Maria 1, James 10/12
COX, Joshua 30*, Rosan 30, Sarah 11, Nancy 8, John 6, Mary 4, James 2

1850 Census Carter County Kentucky

SENATE, Thomas 40*
THOMAS, John 35*
DAVIS, John 40*
JONES, Evan 38*
EDWARDS, Edward 35*
OSETER, Casper 31*
MURPHY, John 30*
BOYLE, Martin 27*, James 25, Morgan 20
JONES, David 26*
RYOST, Michael 27*
LEE, James 25*
HELONY, Thomas 22*
JONES, Isaac 26*
RICHARDS, Daniel 34*
THOMAS, Evan 23*

Schedule Page 228

GORE, Gracy 70*
PRINCE, Jane 20*
BOYD, Milton 20*
EDWARDS, Volatine 18*
WORTHINGTON, John 49*, James 21, David 19, William 17
WADE, Jackson 21*
BELL, Samuel 20*
JACOBS, Roley 32, Susan 30, Andrew 5
HAMMON, Robert 28, Rebecca 28, Charles 1
HAMMON, Richard 22, Nancy 24, Thomas 2, Margaret 1
BRADFORD, William 31, Icybinda 28, Margaret 2
DEVORE, Alfred 39*, Katharine 28, Mortimore 14, Warren 10
SCOTT, Henry 34*
REEVES, John 45*, Cynthian 43, Orena 17, Greenville 13, Belinda 10, Eventine 8, Aramenta 5, Alfred 2
BAYS, William 20*
REEVES, Brackston P. 24, Margaret 23, John 3, Cynthian 7/12
BELLOW, Asa 42*, Martha 32, Elizabeth 12, Mary 9, Lycurgus 7, Martha 5, Emiline 3, William 2
HAGERTY, Hugh 23*, John 31
MCGOWEN, William 25, Polly 25, Andrew 4, Albert 3, Martha 2
HILL, William 54, Nancy 54, Francis 21, Margaret 19
STONE, Cudbert 35, Polly 32, Delila 10, Albert 8, William 5, Nancy 2, Margaret 4/12
STONE, Enoch 24, Polly 25, George 4, Elizabeth 6/12
STONE, Iraby 30, Jane 29, Mary 12, Manervia 9, Sarah 7, Delila 5, John 4, Thomas 1
RISTER, John J. 47, Mary 39, William 19, Susana 15, Nancy 13, Samuel 18, Eastham 12, David 3

Schedule Page 229

SCOTT, Judy 58, Thomas 28, Louis 15, James 8
MADDEN, Matthew 24, Sophia 21, David 10/12

1850 Census Carter County Kentucky

MOORE, John 39, Katharine 42, Christopher 12, SArah 10, William 9, Nancy 6, Julia 3, Amanda 9/12
HORSLEY, Gabriel 30, Maria 22, Artemesa 4, Jacob 2
BLOOMFIELD, Reuben 33, Elizabeth 29, Jasper 14, Newton 9, Phebe 8, Eda 6, Reuben 4, George 2/12
BLOOMFIELD, George 28, Pracilla 21, Melissa 3, Thomas 1
MCCLEESE, Marshall 27*, Mary 25, Charles 3, Hiram 2, Thomas 4/12
CARVER, Percival 8*
SIMMONS, Rolen 40, Mary 47, Oliver 18, Nathan 16, Susan 14, Ephraim 12, Henry 10, Louisa 7, Rutha 4
SMITH, Caswell 35, Cela 19, Allen 13, Thomas 12, Eveline 10, Darcus 8, Hannah 4, Elzira 3
KEYTON, Lovina 32, Polly 14, Nelson 13, Hulda 10, Julia 8, Jefferson 6, William 2
SMITH, Thomas Sr. 59, Corta 55, Thomas Jr. 23, Nancy 21, Corta 19, Creed 13, Manervia 8
SMITH, William 50*, Betsey 49, Richard 34, Edward 24, Wesley 20, Jane 18, Darcus 15, Sarah 13, Nancy 6, Dellila 9, William 6
SMITH, Sally 100*
MCCLEESE, Thomas 51*, Pelana 46, Thomas 23, Malinda 19, Ruhama 10, Martin 9, Polly 4, Daniel 2

Schedule Page 230

BAILEY, Nancy 73*
COOLEY, John 38*, Milla 26, Robert 10, John 5, Katharine 3, Charles 2/12
COOLEY, Richard 21*
CASTEEL, John J. 64*, Christena 44, Elizabeth 15, Mary 12
ROTEN, Betsey 47*
COOPER, Wyatt 45, Nancy 37, Elizabeth 18, Cynthian 16, Wyatt 12, Polly 10, Thomas 8, Ammun 6, James 2
STAFFORD, James 72*, Polly 46, Sylvester 17, Rebecca 14
COOPER, Malinda 21*
RAMACH?, Elizabeth 12*
CARVER, Jackson 5*
MCGLOME, James 42, Elizabeth 42, Eda 14, Owen 13, Ezekiel 12, Sanford 10, Thomas P. 8, James 4, Polly 2
YATES, Wiliam 56, Sally 46, Eda 23, Betsey 20, Nancy 17, Sally 12, Allen 22, Benjamin 15, William 14, Jackson 9, Joshua 6
YATES, Levi 27, Sally 23, George 4, William 2, Ambrus 3/12
MCGLONE, Ambros 30, Nancy 30, Mary 6, William 3, Alfred 4/12
SARTIN, Elijah 30*, Letta 38, SArah 8, Margaret 6, Joseph 2
CARVER, Jackson 12*
MCGLONE, Joseph 36, Margarett 31, David 4, Silas 1, Joseph 1
MCGLONE, Alfred 35, Mary 35, Joseph 11, Robert 8, Henry 6
MCGLONE, Owen 70, Mary 65, Prudence 11

Schedule Page 231

OSBURN, John G. 37, Lucinda 41, James 14, Owen 13, Mary 11, Sarah 10, John 8, Margaret 7, Prudence 6, Cyntha 5, Robert 3, Manoah 16
MCGLONE, Squire 39, Mary 33, Cordelia 15, James 13, William 12, Mary 8, Eliza 5, Patrick 7/12
MCGLONE, Robert 44, Margaret 39, Amanda 14, Mary 13, Daniel 12, SArah 9, Martha 6, Rebecca 4

1850 Census Carter County Kentucky

WOOTEN, Thomas 24*, Fanny 59
JONES, Barella 10*, Mary 5
BURRISS, Ridgway 50, Nancy 40, Samuel 23, William 21, Louisa 12, Lucinda 10, Clarinda 8, Joseph 6
ZORNS, Jeremiah 23, Nancy 24, Betsey 3, Clarinda 9/12
ZORNS, Philip 65*, Sarah 56, Martha 13
ZORNS, Eli 23*
EVERMAN, Elza 33, Eveline 27, Martha 10, Jemima 8, James 6, Moses 4, John 1
MOORES, Silas 42*, Paulina 42, Elizabeth 17, Wayne 9, Louisa 5
GILKERSON, Francis M. 13*
TRUMBO, George 28, Olivia 19, Paulina 2, Nancy 9/12
HONAKER, Charles W. 42, Sarah 39, Cornelius 18, Jesse 16, Peter 13, Mary 10, Martha 6, Lucy 2
FRIEND, Jonas 30*, Sarah 27, Andrew 2, Silas 1
FRIEND, Percival 35*
PLUMMER, John 55, Jane 49, William 23, Sarah 19, James 16, Susan 14, John 12, Louisa 12, Mahala 7

Schedule Page 232

BURTCHETT, Robert 42, Polly 34, Nelson 15, Charles 14, Elizabeth 9, Elenor 6, John 4, Susan 2, Sarah 5/12
HUFF, Caleb 28, Jane 29, Mary 5, John 2, Charles 4/12
MCALISTER, Alexander 36, Elizabeth 36, James 12, Sarah 8, John 5, Elexander 2
BAGBY, James 32, Elizabeth 34, William 10, Isaac 6, Sarah 3, Adolphus 6/12
BUSH, John 67, Margaret 55, Thomas 19, Rebecca 17, Charles 14, David 11
BUSH, Sanford 36, Martha 23, Mary 4, James 1
ZORNS, Martin 28, Lucinda 28, Martha 9, Thomas 7, Mary 5, Elizabeth 1
BURRISS, Sanders 24, Elizabeth 25, Rachael 5/12
ZORNS, Andrew Jr. 32, Martha 28, Sander 10, Samuel 7, Emily 6, Allen 5, Edward 2
PATTEN, James 45, Kissiah 43, Margart 19, Charlotte 18, Jane 16, SArah 14, William 9, John 6, Thomas 2
MCGLONE, William Sr. 47*, Jemima 38, Alfred 20, Elizabeth 16, Nancy 14, George 12, John 7, Martha 5, Jemima 3, William Jr. 7/12
HELMORE, Daniel O. 4*
JORDON, Julia 38, John 20, Joseph 18, Rachael 16, James 14, Manervia 13, William 8, George 6, Albert 5, Levi 1

Schedule Page 233

MULLENS, Isom 47, Leary 41?, John 24, Sarah 21, Mary 19, Perlina 10, Booker 7, Marinda 3, Julia 1
SMITH, Ambrose 24, Nancy 24, Thomas 6, Cynthian 4, Joseph 3, Elizabeth 1
FULTZ, Joseph 31, Elizabeth 24, Mary 10, James 4, Ambrose 3, Hezekiah 19
BUCKNER, Mack 60, Elizabeth 59, Henry 25, Julia 23, Martha 2, Nancy 3/12, Lucinda 8, Jane 28
BUCKNER, Overton M. 38, Elizabeth 39, James 17, Martha 14, William 12, John 10, Mary 9, Sarah 8, Emanuel 5, Harrison 4, Cornelius 1
FULTZ, Wesley 34*, Silvia 27, James 8, John 7, Obediah 5, Martha 3, George 2, Martha 75
STAMPER, Jackson 23*
KITCHEN, Alexander 36, Delphia 26, James 16, John 13, George 11, Eliza 9, Alexander Jr. 5, Martin 3, Polly 1

1850 Census Carter County Kentucky

JORDON, George 34, Abbey 29, Martha 7, Rachael 4, Lear 2, Betey 1
FANNIE, David 50, Julia 47, Burrell 27, Joseph 22, Matilda 19, Susana 15, John 12, Lear 10, David 8, James 4
JORDAN, Joseph 39*, Abarilla 40, Abarilla 6
MEAD, Nancy 35*, Martha 9
JORDAN, George W. 28, Nancy 23, John 1

Schedule Page 234

JORDAN, Lindsey 34, Abigal 27, Elizabeth 10, Delila 7, James 1
JORDAN, James 75, Martha 70
KITCHEN, Nehemiah 24, Martha 21, John 1
FANNIN, John 25, Sarah 19, Joseph 6/12
JORDAN, James 34, Sarah 33, Lindsey 13, Julia 10, Nancy 7, Nehemiah 4, Sarah 2
RAMY, Charles 41, Charity 38, William 20, Elizabeth 15, Thomas 15, James 12, Nancy 10, Eliza 7, Elzira 2, Mary 1/12
HALL, William 51, Polly 45, Amy 21, Susan 19, Sally 16, Polly 12, Elizabeth 9, Hezekiah 8, James 5
BOCOCK, William W. 65, Sarah 55, Eliza 21, Nancy 17, Jackson 16, George 12
LARGE, Thomas 43, Nancy 33, Louisa 11, James 7, Marinda 6, William 3, Mary 2, John 2/12
HARRIS, David K. 32, Margaret 30, Nancy 9, William 7, Lucinda 6, James 4, Sarah 1
GILLUM, Richard 50, Nancy 40, Daniel 17, Susan 16, Martin 14, John 9, Hiram 2
STAMPER, John 50, Sarah 50, Milla 22, Jefferson 18, Nancy 16, Washington 13, William 11, Joanna 6
ISOM, Charles 48, Lucinda 46, Nancy 20, Elizabeth 17, Esla 15, Joshua 12, Anne 10, Lucinda 6, George 3

Schedule Page 235

ISOM, Martin 23, Leanner 21, Charles 1
WILLIAMS, Lucas P. 35, Elizabeth 26, Thomas 8, Aramenta 5, Sanford 3, Noah 1
PERREY, Robert H. 40, Amanda 36, Mary 13, Thomas 11, James 7, William 5, Nancy 10/12
WILLIAMS, Jefferson B. 37, Mary 25, Robert 10, Nancy 9, John 7, Norman 7, Martha 4, Hughy 1, James 12, Jefferson 11
FULTZ, Robert 43, Elizabeth 39, Thomas 20, Zachariah 18, Abraham 16, David 13, Perry 11, William 10, Mansford 9, John 6, Robert 1
WILLIAMS, Lameck 38, Martha 34, Matilda 13, Emily 12, Harrison 9, Eliza 8, Elizabeth 5, Ralph 2, Lucinda 1
ERWIN, John L. 59, Elizabeth 47, Eliza 18, Oscar 17, Martha 10
ERWIN, John B. 25, Susana 19
JONES, John 26, Eveline 26, Mary 6, Sophia 5, Margaret 3
SEEGRAVE, Stephen 40, Susan 36, Polly 17, Joseph 16, Martha 14, Lviller 12, Aly 10, Theresa 9, Gordon 7, Carlo 5, Sina 2, Jacob 4/12, Sarah 4/12
SMITH, William P. 38, Elizabeth 31, John 9, Eda 4, Louis 1
MCMAHAN, Alexander 48, Eve 43, Mary 14, William 8, George 4
SMITH, Thomas J. 27, Sarah 23, William 7, Thomas J. Jr. 5, Sarah 3, Clarinda 1

1850 Census Carter County Kentucky

Schedule Page 236

INGRAM, Sylvanus 24, Nancy 19
INGRAM, Silas 35, Letha 33, Michael 8, John 5, Thomas 1
INGRAM, Thomas 29, Sally 20, Tobitha 4, James 1
JARVIS, Solomon 48*, Susan 22, James 17
GULLY, Branson 8*
RICHARDS, James 68, Elizabeth 49, Robert 39, John 16
MCCARTY, William 33, Lucinda 34, Margaret 12, Harvey 10, James 7, Andrew 6, Abner 4, Robert 2
ROSS, Samuel 58*, Mary 57
PADGET, Nicholas 33*, Cordelia 28, Adison 6, William 4, George 1
STANLEY, James 28*, Sarah 20, Hannah 2/12
WATSON, Hannah 56*
COOK, Fielding B. 31, Elsa 32, Martha 5, John 1
HOOBLER, Samuel 40, Sarah 36, Susana 11, William 9, Mary 5, Thomas 2
GORMAN, David 45*, Nancy 41, David 18, Samuel 17
JONES, Eveline 8*
BRINIGER, Morgan 37, Elizabeth 30, John 13, Elizabeth 8, Solomon 6, Marinda 4
FULTZ, Daniel 30*, Rebecca 29, Andrew 5, Nancy 3
PRESLEY, Rachael 17*
ROSS, Reuben 26*, Rebecca 19, Abraham 1
JAMES, Mary 17*
ROSS, John N. 31, Nancy 31, John 10, George 9, Reuben 7, Mary 5, Austin 2
JONES, James M. 34, Mary 33, Martha 13, Mary 9, Margaret 6, Sarah 2, Albert 12

Schedule Page 237

FLANEGAN, Joshua 63*, Betsey 56, Linda 15, Bewford 12
ROSS, Susana 25*
JONES, Elijah 72, Margaret 67, Martin 20, William 9, Emily 4
GULLY, John 36, Matilda 31, Mary 14, Eveline 12, John 11, Nancy 9, George 5, Mertilla 3, Simon 8/12
WILLIAMS, George W. Sr. 50, Rebecca 35, Americus 20, Sarah 18, Visa 15, Kathairne 15, William 14, Hetta 13, Jesse 12?, Elendor 11, Emily 7, Henry 3, Rebecca 2, George Jr. 1
ALEXANDER, Louis 45, Elizabeth 41, Margaret 20, Allen 19, James 16, Malinda 15, Easter 14, Ann 12, Katharine 9, Andrew 7, Louisa 6, William 4, Robert 2, Louis 8/12
HALE, Thomas 63, Frances 49, James 18, John 18, Robert 15, Thomas 10, Lucinda 14, Mary 12, Mildred 8
MILLER, John 49, Mary 30, Oliver 11, Mary 8, Mareamra 7, Delila 30
STAPLETON, Charles 45, Mary 45, Richard 24, Joshua 16, Nancy 15, Alexander 12, Thomas 9, Katharine 6, Martha 3
BOND, Bazel Sr. 36, Nancy 41, Mary 14, James 12, George 10, Bazel Jr. 7, Elizabeth 4, Barbary 1
TABOR, Laurderdale 23
MAUK, Peter C. 32, Mary 31, Mary 10, Amanda 9, John 6, Peter 3, Robert 1

1850 Census Carter County Kentucky

Schedule Page 238

SAWYER, James 26, Polly 16, William 5, Polly 3
TABOR, Bazel M. 51, Nancy 53, Adolphus 20, Lilburn 25, Ira 16
TABOR, Addison 27, Matilda 29, Napolean 8, Bazel 4, Lafayette 1/12
MANNIN, Tarlton 39, Hester 30, Susana 12, Amos 8, James 7, John 5, Louisa 2
HENDERSON, Robert J. 34, Ama 26, James 10, SArah 8, Mary 6, Robert 4, George 2, Oliver 2/12
RAY, Samuel 52, EAster 36, John 25, William 22, Andrew 17, Milla 11, Lucy 7, James 3, Sarah 22
HENDERSON, James 33, Rebecca 30, James Jr. 12, John 10, William 8, Sarah 6, Samuel 4, Jane 1
SUTTER, Uriah T. 30, Mary 28, James 5, Julia 3, Elizabeth 1
SUTTER, John 34*, Harriet 41, Elizabeth 5, Uriah 3, Harriet 6
ZORNS, Martin 29*, Perlitha 28, Sarah 4, James 1
PATRICK, Nancy 50, Delila 25, James 22
HOLLAND, Oliver 31, Mary 42, Mary 9, Jane 7, James 5, Martha 3
GILLUM, Archablad 29, Lucinda 26, Elizabeth 3, William 1
BROWN, James 31*, Nancy 34, Thompson 6, Elizabeth 4, Mary 1
GILLUM, James A. 23*
BROWN, George 54, Sarah 48, Elizabeth 20, Frances 13, Delila 10

Schedule Page 239

PHELPS, William 35, Mary 30, William 9, Zachariah 6, Lovina 4
KINDER, William G. 26, Lucind 25, Barnabas 4, William 3, James 1
PENLAND, George 53, Susana 38, Elizabeth 20, James 16, Mary 15, Alexander 12, John 10, Sibian 9, Lovina 3, Nancy 2
KINDER, Barnabus 51*, Elendor 41, James 9
COMBS, Hugh 17*
RABOURN, Henry 59, Priscilla 58, Enoch 22, Samuel 20, Elizabeth 16, Henry 15, Jane 12
LOGAN, Tobias 30*, Eliza 29, Elizabeth 6, Lucy 4, Delila 2
GRAY, Sarah F. 18*
GRAY, Preston 26, Jane 22, Ann 3, Sarah 1/12
HAM, Peter A. 25, Rebecca 23, John 1/12
ENOCH, Amariah 32, Matilda 31, Lucinda 9, Eliza 7, John 6, James 4, Nancy 7/12
HAM, Joseph 58, Nancy 57, Mahala 18, Perry 16, Susan 13, Cheton 9
WOOD, Robert 71*, Elizabeth 52, Durret 22
HAM, Thomas W. 20*
HISEY, Willis 29, Sarah 31, Harriet 4, Leander 3, Mary 1
HAM, Harvey 34, Mary 31, Joseph 10, James 7, Rebecca 5, Phebe 4, William 3
SHIELDS, James L. 24, Harriet 20
HAM, Jeremiah 29, Sarah 25, Wesley 7, Fantly 4, Nancy 3, Isaac 2

Schedule Page 240

COGSWELL, William 55, Ellen 21, Elizabeth 20, Polly 18, David 15, Martha 14, Zahariah 13, Sarah 12, Amanda 1, Drusilla 9, Johnson 7, Acenith 5
SHIELDS, Alexander 26*, Elizabeth 24, William 4, Robert 2, James 8/12

1850 Census Carter County Kentucky

GRAY, Maria 47*
KNAP, Joshua 76*, Mary 67, Ann 33, Malinda 30, Mary 19, James 20
BRAMMER, William 23*, Robert 11, Malinda 9
JOHNSON, John W. R. 23, Nancy 22, James 1
PARRISH, Oliver P. 65, Elizabeth 40, Robert 14, Sarah 13, George 11, Melissa 9, Maranda 9, Malaciah 8, Rosana 4, Barney 1
MARKWELL, Sandy 28, Diana 25, Elizabeth 9, James 7, William 3
HARGET, Benjamin 26, Elizabeth 23, James 3, Israel 1
JOHNSON, James 37, Emily 30, John 13, Elizabeth 12, Ann 10, Mary 8, Benjamin 6, William 4, James 3, Isaac 3/12
EVANS, Isaac 48, Miram 48, Edward 22, Delila 21, Sarah 19, Benjamin 15, Samuel 13, Nancy 11, Robert 9, John 6
LOCKERS?, Andrew 56, Sarah 48, Alexander 21, Nelson 18, Louis 15, Elizabet 12, Eliza 9, Andrew 6
PARK, William O. 24, Mary 20
REEDER, Joseph 39, Manervia 35, James 17, Malinda 16, Mary 14, George 12, Joseph 10, Elizabeth 7, John 5, Eliza 2, Cornelius 1/12

Schedule Page 241

THOMPSON, John 50*, Mary 30, Amos 14, Mason 10, Elizabeth 9, Lucretia 4, Henry 7, Amanda 2
RICE, Martha A. 25*
GARVIN, Joshnson 63, Elizabeth 64
RUNNER, Isaac 55, Ann 49, Ann 16, George 14
SCOTT, Gabriel 60, Martha 55
WILBURN, Cynthian 16*
TYREE, Zachariah 44, Eliza 36, Elzira 17, Sarah 15, Chrisley 12, William 10, James 8, John 6, Jerome 4, Perry 2, Lafayette 6/12
GOBLE, Ephraim S. 30*, Elizabeth 25, William 5, Jane 3, Burtis 2
BRAMMER, Joshua 20*
DEBELL, Alfred 48, Susan 33, Emily 8/12
HENDERSON, James 67, Jane 66
HENDERSON, Alexnader M. 31*, Lucinda 26, James 7, Mary 5, Alexander 3, Nancy 1
YULETT, William 52*, Mary 61, James 13
DENNIS, John L. --, Martha 22?, Samuel 1
TYREE, Jerome 29, Margaret 22, Sarah 2, Mary 3/12
OSENTON, Samuel 67*
HANKS, William 17* (B), Martha 15
MOORE, Hiram 30*, Mary 34, Louisa 7, jackson 5, Olivia 4, Gelena 1
RICE, Elijah 19*
ENOCH, Alfred 39, Mary 30, George 10, Elizabeth 7, William 4, Lafayette 3/12
MILLER, William 58, Easter 58, Jala 24, Mahala 23, Thomas 21, Jane 19, Robert 17, Martha 15, William 13

Schedule Page 242

SCOTT, James W. 37, Jane 35, Calvin 12, Martha 11, Mary 9, Louisa 7, Johnson 4, Sarah 1
JAMES, George 53*, Sarah 34, Phelona 15, Emily 12, Elizabeth 10, Henry 8, Ephraim 3, Margaret 1

1850 Census Carter County Kentucky

FLANEGAN, Volantine 20*
JAMES, Andrew J. 26, Julia 25, George 6, Louisa 4, Gabriel 3, James 6/12
MOODY, George 31*, Rebecca 18, Logan 1, Nancy 2/12
MCMAHON, Isaac W. 25*
JORDAN, John 39, Louisa 28, William 10, Elizabeth 7, Joseph 4, Martha 1, Mary 64
SKEIN, Elcanah 52*, Maria 40, James 5
YORK, Nancy E. 14* (B)
STROTHER, Joseph H. 32, Sarah 26, Emogene 4, Sarah 2
STROTHER, Philip 71*, Sarah 55
BROWN, Deborah 35*, Sarah 13, Mary 8, Melvin 6, Frances 5, Joseph 3, James 1
DAVIS, Sarah K. 13*
WILBURN, Reuben 22, Celia 22, Sarah 2, James 3/12
MCGUIRE, John 32*, Eliza 28, Emily 10, James 8, Stephen 6, William 4, Thomas 1
RICE, Jelina 16*, Harvey 12
CARVER, Morgan 66*, Letta 46, Pierce 11, Emily 10, Thomas 6, Cyntha 4
WELLMAN, John H. 12*
JAMES, Bazel 43*, Narcissa 47, Martha 20, Lovina 19, John 16, Emily 13, Sarah 12, Amanda 9, William 7, Thompson 4

Schedule Page 243

WILLIAMS, Malan 22*
GEE, David P. 38, Sarah 38, Martha 16, Champness 14, Mary 12, Robert 11, Rintha 8, Macager 6, David 3, Mertilla 1
EVERMAN, John Jr. 20, Martha 21, Mary 6/12
JAMES, William R. 30, Mertilla 33, Polly 9, Patty 7, John 5, Jeremiah 2
EVERMAN, John Sr. 72, Sarah 63, John 19
CRAWFORD, Sanders 37*, Lovina 31, Mary 13, James 11, Elizabeth 9, Jane 4, America 1
CRAWFORD, Robert 31*, Elizabeth 18
EVERMAN, William 41*, Elizabeth 37, Samuel 18, George 16, William Jr. 14, Henry 12, James 8, Charles 4, Francis 2/12
TOLER, Stephen 77*, Margaret 76
BIGGS, Jeremiah 48, Louisa 48, Henry 27, Harrison 25, Nancy 24, Polly 23, Benjamin 20, Eliza 18, Jarrus 16, Sydney 14, Hannah 7, Martha 5
VIRGIN, Rezin 46*, Louisy 56
JONES, Mary 54*, Martha 20
SMITH, Mathew S. D. 12*
PLUMMER, Reuben 52*, Louis 38 (f), Thomas 6, Theresa 4
WARD, Theresa A. 46*
PRUETT, Henry 56*, Fanny 44, Mary 22, Hiram 17, Neoma 15, Isaac 11, Louisa 8, Fannya 6, Nancy 2
RODEN, Rebecca 19*, Fanny 1
BECKWITH, Arthur C. 35, Louisa 29, William 7, Clarisa 6, Mary 5, Sophia M. 1

Schedule Page 244

BOTTS, James R. 29*, Mary 25, James 2, Joseph 8/12
EVERMAN, Moses Jr. 31*

1850 Census Carter County Kentucky

SHEPHERD, Benjamin F. 39, Elizabeth 29, William 12, Mary 11, Sarah 8, Jesse 4, Alsa 2, Zachariah 1
COOK, Weley 28, Delinda 18, John 1
WARD, Charles L. 25, Nancy 24, Benjamin 6, Joseph 4, Charles 2/12
OSENTON, Henry K. 29*, Lewtha 22, Lucy 4, Temperance 2
DOOLY, Nicholas 45*
PRICE, Richard W. 55, Sarah 42, Stephen 27, Anderson 22, John 21, William 16, Robert 12, Martha 10, Sarah 8, James 5, Lee 2
DUNCAN, Allen 29*, Nancy 22, William 2, Mary 1
ROBISON, Elizabeth 11*
EVERMAN, Jacob 24, Elizabeth 21
KIBBEY, James H. 23*, Martha 20
KIBBEY, Sarah 67*
MCGUIRE, James 22, Nancy 19, Ephraim 6/12
DAVIS, Job 62*, Susan 63, Ellen 3
CANNON, Susan 14*
WILLIAMS, William 4*
NORRIS, Edward 55* (B)
BECKWITH, Matilda 58
MARTIN, George 34, Polly 35, Martha 10, Margaret 8, Thomas 6, Elizabeth 4, George 2, Robert 7/12
DAWSON, James 56, Hannah 45, Benjamin 22, Martha 19, Stephen 15, Emily 12, Lucy 10, Hannah 5, Jessie 2
LONG, George W. 29, Martha 24, Mary 6, America 4, Charles 2
GEE, Robert 83, Elizabeth 69, Elizabeth 19, William 29

Schedule Page 245

VIERS, Daniel 49, Harriet 40, Jacob 19, Brice 18, Mary 14, Frances 12, Elizabeth 8, Harriet 7, Lucy 5, Rebecca 2
ACRES, Edward 50, Lovina 48, James 17, Betsey 15, Nancy 13, Solomon 11, Christena 9, Emily 7
PRINCE, David 35, Fanny 34, William 13, James 11, Elizabeth 8, Mary 7, Margaret 3, Ann 1
HACKETT, James L. 38, Martha 27, Margaret 9, Temperance 7, Emiline 4, John 2
DAVIS, Isaac 28*, Leander 26, Marinda 6, Easter 5, Sarah 2, Susan 4/12
DEFOE, James 8*
GILKISON, Malinda 62*
BURTON, Isaac 42, Lucretia 43, Caleb 21, James 20, Juda 18, Hulda 16, Nancy 14, Mary 11, Eliza 8, David 6, Caroline 5, John 3, Helen? 2
DRAKE, Hulda 23, Josiah 3, James 2, Susana 9/12
GREEN, Helma? 62, Elizabeth 29, Nathan 25, Robert 21, Margaret 11
SELVAGE, James 56, Jemima 50, Sinclair 17, Nancy 15, Betsey 12
ADAMS, Thomas 24, Martha 23, Martin 4/12
COLE, Jeremiah 22, Polly 22, Isaac 6, Julia 3, James 1
STEWART, William 26, Luana 25, Thomas 7, James 5, John 1
ENGLAND, Stephen J. 30*, Clarinda 29, Elender 10, Cornelius 8, Mary 6, Jesse 4, Sarah 2

1850 Census Carter County Kentucky

Schedule Page 246

BARTEE, Thomas 17*
OSENTON, James 38*
STOPHER, Charles 45* (B)
EVERMAN, Samuel 45*, Phebe 41, Brunetta 19, William 18, Joseph 12
COOK, James 7*
BLACK, Robert 50* (B), Malinda 42, James 13, Alfred 16, Eliza 20, Finetta 19
BITTERWATER, Joseph 112* (B)
HAMPTON, Preston 31*, Emiline 28
CHRISTIAN, Jackson 21*
THROOP, Benjamin B. 36, Ann 32, Elizabeth 9, Mary 6, Thomas 5, Hannah 2, Arabella 8/12
KENNEDY, Wayne 38, Esther 33, Mary 12, Asbury 10, William 8, Andrew 2/12
TRIMBLE, Elizabeth A. 33*, Elizabeth 7, John 5
WINN, Mary 75*
MONTGOMERY, William 36*, Elizabeth 23, Miliner 1
PARSCALL, John 63*
HILLIS, James 15*
RATCLIFF, John T. 28, Sarah 25, Martha 5, Charles 3, Lafayette 2, Moes 1
WHITE, Edward 25, Katharine 26, John 10
ROBERTS, George W. 36*, Elizabeth 41, Lucy 18, Hiram 16, Sabina 12, Phineas 10, Emma 7, Martha 3?, Anan 5/12
HORD, Polly 32?*
OXIER, Rebecca 70*
ADAMS, Robert 53, Anne 72
DUNCAN, Marshall 55, Martha 31, Urial 7, Amanda 6, Naomi 4, Anne 2, James 1
ENGLAND, Hannah 66, William 27
COLLINS, John W. 30, Mary 21, Alonzo 1

Schedule Page 248

COX, Mrk 36, Sarah 31, Jackson 12, Ross 10, Annes 8, Lucinda 7, Julia 5, Zerelda 2, Ballard 8/12
TABER, William 24, Nancy 28, Luemmy 5, Henderson 3, Rhoda 2, Stephen H. 11/12
BROWN, Low 55*, Mary 38, Julia A. 15, Mary E. 14, Cintha M. 11, Nancy L. 9, Sarah M. 7, James A. 4, Samuel H. 2
BROWN, William A. 22*
NICKELL, Joseph 40, Lexey 34, Marinda 17, Andy 15, Susanna 10, John M. 7, Sarah Ann 5, Trumbo 4, James M. 2, Thomas J. 2
NICKELL, John 67*, Feraby 55
SLOAN, John 22*, Airey 28, Nancy 20, Serintha 9, William 7, Mary 5
PROCTOR, Jeremiah 43*, Mary 41, Sarah 19, Elbert 17, Francis 16, Elizabeth 14, Jeremiah 12, Susanna 10, Joseph W. 8, John A. 6, Charles 4
PURVES, Elizabeth J. 16*
HAMILTON, David K. 45, Drusilla 45, Wesley 24, Benjamin 23, Edward 20, Elizabeth 18, John 9, Nancy 7, David K. 5, George W. 1, John M. 4, Timpa Jane 2
HAMILTON, Nancy 24
DAY, Daniel 23, Anna 16

1850 Census Carter County Kentucky

DAY, Eli 28, Elizabeth 22, Mary Emely 5, Riley 4, John 3, Alexander 1
MANNEN, Meradith 48, Rachel 47, Tubal 20, Reuben 17, Cathrine S. 15, John 13, Mahala 12, Sarah 10, Zachary 8, Tarlton 6

Schedule Page 249

MANNEN, Thomas 24
MANNEN, Isaac 25, Louisa 25
JONES, Ryal M. 42, Mary 38, Thomas 16, Hester Ann 15, William 12, Levi 11, Ellen 9, Goodan 8, Mary F. 5, James 4, Eady 1, Nancy 17
BUNYARD, James 40*, Martha 39, Susanna 18, Sarah 15, Barbara 13, Elizabeth 9, John J. C. 5, Anna 2
JONES, John M. 5*
SPARKS, Isaac 21*, Nancy 23
JONES, Susanna 8*, Martha E. 4
DAY, John W. 39, Mary 35, John M. 17, Daniel 15, William 13, Sarah Ann 11, Elizabeth 9, Sidney 7, Philip 7, Martha 2, Mary J. 2/12
KISSICK, Robert 47*, Milly 43, William 20, Henry 17, John 14, Milly 12, Benjamin F. 10, Fleming 6
MCROBERTS, John 10*, Jane 11
PRICE, David 27, Nancy Ann 22, Eliza Ann 11/12
MANNEN, John 50, Sarah 46, Tubal 19, Francis 18, Carlyle 17, Jeptha 15, Anos B. 14, Enoch 13, Jasper N. 12, John C. 11, Lucinda LLLF 7, Samuel 21
TACKETT, Moses 44, Rodicy 32?, James W. 16, Sherwood 15, Zerelda 12, Louicy 10, Sarah A. 7, Elizabeth A. 6, John Kufus 7
MCGLOTHLAN, Jacob 39, Margaret J. 23, Walker K. 3, William P. 2, SArah E. 1/30
MANNEN, John B. 35, Sarah A. 31, Tarlton 9, Susanna 8, Charles W. 6, William W. 3, SArah 11/12, John 16?

Schedule Page 250

DAY, John 53*, Sarah 53, John L. 24, Isaac 21, Peter 20, David 18, Thomas 14
JONES, John C. 2*
GOODAN, Philip W. 41*, Sidney 32, John 12, Mary 10, Daniel 8, Sarah 6
KAY, Thomas 36*
PELFREY, James 36, Jamima 36, William J. 18, Alexander H. 16, Barbara 14, Louisa 12, Isaac 9, Clarinda 6, John 5, Mary K. 2, Martha E. 2/12
PARKER, John 38, Cathrine 41, James 13, Mary 11, Sary J. 9, Cathrine 7, Daniel A. 5, John M. 3, Nancy E. 1
THACKER, Daniel 30*, America 28, Marth 5, Lewis 3, Isaac 1
YOUNG, Eddy 33*, Phebe 40
MOCKBEE, Hamilton 10*
MOCKBEE, David 39, Anna M. 38, Elizabeth H. 12, Nancy M. 11, Granville A. 9, Lucretia B. 8, Caroline J. 7, John C. 5, Govel 3, Winfield S. 1
UNDERWOOD, Stephen 34*, -ady 31 (f), Wm. A. 9, Malvina 8, Philip S. 7, John W. 5, Emaline 3, Amanda 5/12
WAREN, Harrison 31*
GOODAN, Levi W. 43, Cathrine 30, George Ann 7, Samuel 6, Philip 3, William F. 2, Martha J. 1
GOODAN, Daniel 69*, Mary 68

1850 Census Carter County Kentucky

SHUMATE, George W. 15*
ROSS, Joseph? 25, Lucy 22, Elijah 3, Job 2
OFFICE?, John 56*, Eleanor 50, Johnson 22, Elizabeth J. 20, Allen 18, Margaret 15

Schedule Page 251

MCLONG, John 4*
BRAMMER, Samuel 50*, Jailey 38, Martha 21, George W. 19, Harrison 15, Margaret 13, Susan 11, Elizabeth 10, Robert B. 8, Dawson 5, Richard 2, John 4/12
SHUTTS, Phebe 32*
HAM, Bazzel 52*, Ambrose 20, James M. 17, Edward M. 14, George W. 11, Ignsius J. 9, Wm. A. 7
UNDERWOOD, Dolly A. 20*
PARK, Thomas J. 38*, John J. 1, Thos. O? 2/12
HAM, Malinda 39*
HAM, Ignasius G. 44, Margaret 40, James H. 14, Mary 7, John W. 6, Isaac A. 4, Dicy A. 2
RICHARDS, George W. 47, Eleanor 45, Eliza 24, Charles W. 22, John W. 20, Van S. 18, William W. 14, Amanda 12, Davis H. 9, Julia 7, Samuel N. 2
JONES, Zachary 63, Sidney 38, Stephen 21, Mary A. 21, Sarah 19, Jemima 19, Elijah 18, Elizabeth J. 15, Frances 14, Eliza 12, --- 10 (m), Zerelda 9, Amanda 6, Martha T. 6/12
LANSDOWN, James W. 33*, Sarah A. 28, Margret E. 5, William M. 4, Stephen R. S. 2, John C. M. 4/12
CLARK, Lucinda J. 27*, George W. 6
HILL, Thomas 33*
LANSDOWN, David S. 26, Nancy A. 27, Charity 7, James W. 5, Sarah S. 2
WILLIAMS, Thomas 45, Martha 24, Elizabeth S. 19, John P. 16, Sarah A. 13, Margaret 11, Thomas J. 8, Mary J. 2, Eliza E. 4/12
GILBERT, James 32*, Lotty 22, Sarah E. 2

Schedule Page 252

SWINN, Sanford 21*
GARVIN, John 40*, Elizabeth 25, St Clair 12, Johnson 8
UNDERWOOD, Nelson 22*
DEHART, Sarah 40*, Martha 24, Mary 15, Amanda 13, Stephen 12, Frances 9, Gabriel 7, James 5, Henry H. 2/12
DICKERSON, Absailom 32*
SWIM, Michael 48, Sarah 51, Trumbo 17, Michael E. 12
POWERS, William B. 30*, Elizabeth 28, Benjamin F. 4, Henry S. 2, Louisa R. 8/12
BRAMMER, John 16*
BOCOOK, John 40*, Eliza J. 28, Rhoda 11, Elizabeth 13, David 8, Sarah 1
HENDERSON, Hervey H. 30*
HOWARD, David J. 22, Jamima 21, Thomas J. 3
HENDERSON, Robert 68*, Sarah 57, Narcissa 32, Henry E. G. 20, Mary E. 20, George W. 16
HOWARD, Nancy 60*
SHUMATE, William 50, Nancy 22, Elizabeth 8, Daniel H. 6, Francis M. 4, Eliza F. 2
SAVAGE, James N. 22*, Sarah 32, James M. 4/12
BELAMY, Townley H. 19*, Julia A. 17, Andrew J. L. 9, Richard F. 4

1850 Census Carter County Kentucky

CLARK, William 48, Mary 37, Nancy C. 20, Mary M. 17, Ann 16, Louisa 13, James H. 10, Lucinda J. 6, William 4, Elizabeth 1
PERRY, Amanda 29, Nancy 7, John 8, Andrew J. 4
CLARK, Joseph N. 32, Emritta 30, Mary F. 9, Sarah Ann 4
GILBERT, John 31*, Rachel 24, Andrew J. 5, James M. 5, Sarah E. 3, Martha E. 4/12
KEETON, Mary 15*
MCLONG, James 50, Elizabeth 44, Mary A. 22, Alexander 20, Delila 18, Maranda 13, Joseph 6, Lucinda 3

Schedule Page 253

HAM, Alexander 42, Mary Ann 34, Martin P. M. 14, Elizabeth J. 13, Mary 9, George W. 6, Angeline 3/12
THOMSON, James J. 25, Elizabeth 20, James M. 9, John W. 2
MYERS, Jameson 30, Margaret 28, Eli 10, Elizabeth 9, Carlisle 6, John 3, Jeremiah P. 2/12
GARDNER, James 81*, Malinda 46
PARK, John J. 24*
BROWN, Delila 10*
TRUMBO, John L. 58, Sarah 38, Margaret A. 15, Penina 14, Elkana 10, Mary J. 8, Benjamin F. 7, Lucinda 3, Thomas J. 18
TRUMBO, Oliver H. 29, Nancy A. 30, Elizabeth 5, John J. 4, Leander 1
PEARCE, Daniel T. 53, Elizabeth 45, James W. 22, Sarah A. 19, Charlotte 12, Eliza J. 10, Harriet E. 8, Mahala 6, Allice Anna E. 5, Jesse O. 8/12
BRINEGAR, Jacob 54, Elizabeth 67
JARVIS, Mathias 27, Mary 29, William E. 10, Cathrine 7, James S. 5, Flora A. 3, John L. 7/12
CLINE, Levi 40*, Sarah 40, Samuel 20, Henry 17, John 15, Mary 12, Barney 10, James 8, Martha 5
CLINE, William 21*, Malinda 18, Sarah E. 1, Martha J. 2/12
BRAMMER, William 28, Mary A. 26, Sarah E. 4, George A. 2
WATTERS, Mathias 54, Martha 48
OFFICE, Elzaphan 45*, Martha 39, Sarah J. 18, Mary E. 15, Elizabeth 13, Martha 12, Mahala 8, Louisa 5, John E. 2

Schedule Page 254

CLINE, Samuel 22*
BURD, Thomas 36, Lavina 23, John J. 3, Joshua 11/12
CLINE, Levi W. 24*, Lydia 35
COLLINS, Caroline 17*, Nancy A. 10, Paulina 6, Josiah W. 3
CHAIN, John 28, Telitha 23, Ambozeor 8, Sarah J. 6, Mary E. 3, Minerva A. 2
GARVIN, James 33, Sophia 31, Wm. H. H. 10, Sarah J. 8, Amanda M. 6, Martha 4, Julia 2
THOMSON, John L. 30*, Susan 34, Malinda 9, Sarah 7, John E. 4, Mary H. 2, Amanda J. 2/12
THOMSON, Charles 28*
SHULTS, Phebe 7i2*
UNDERWOOD, James 43, Permelia 44, William 17, Silas 16, Clarinda 13, Rebecca J. 12, Olive 10, Eleanor 8, Margaret A. 6, James M. 4
UNDERWOOD, George W. 36, Rebecca J. 17, Elveston 16, George L. 14, Alfred A. 11, David C. 10, Jessee M. 8, William C. 6

1850 Census Carter County Kentucky

OFFICE?, Alem 46, Louisa 43, Daniel O. 24, Elzaphan 22, Aaron S. 20, John M. 19, America E. 17, William 15, Israel H. 14, Francis M. 12, James A. 8, Mathias W. 7, Louisa A. 4, Richard 3/12
SHUMATE, Alfred 27, Eliza J. 22, James W. 1, Reuben 19
GARVIN, William H. 38*, Eleanor D. 40, Elizabeth 8, William W. 6, James F. 3, Eliza F. 1
RICHARDS, Elijah 28*, Eliza J. 21
UNDERWOOD, Gideon 42, Mary C. 47, Hervey 15, Cordelia 9, Malinda 8

Schedule Page 255

OFFICE, James 31, Mary A. 24, Martha 8, John F. 6, Marion 3, Matthias 1
DUNWAY, Joseph 54, Cintha 41, William 15, Cintha A. 13, Mary A. 11, Levi H. 9, Eleanor 7, Jeremiah 4, John F. 3, Sytha C. 3/12
GILBERT, William 34, Jane 39, Sarah J. 12, John 10, James M. 8, William H. 5, George W. 4, Daniel M. 3, Lucinda 1, Robert 4/12
DINSMORE, Wm. F. 21, Nancy A. 21, Sarah Ann 10/12
ROE, Isom 31, Eleanor H. 28, John 8, Sarah 6, Martha E. 5, Rachel 3
GILBERT, Sarah 52, Samuel 16
STAGGS, John M. 37, Minerva 32, Sarah A. 13, Alexander 11, William N. 9, Albert 7, Elizabeth J. 5, John M. 4, Malinda 2
BROWN, Elihu 24, Malinda 21, Allen C. 3/12
FABER, James 35, Sarah 29, Mary E. 12, George H. 10, Erastus G. 8, James M. 6, Teresha A. 4, Elihu A. 1
SPARKS, Nelson 31*, Margaret 30, Peter 6, Paulina 4, John 3, Sarah 1
MAUK, Daniel 21*
NETHERCUTT, Moses 25, Cathrine 25, Mary S. 10/12, George 16
MAUK, Peter 69, Eleanor 58, Fredrick 23, Henry 18, Peter 16, Martha 14, Mary J. 11
PRINCE, Thomas 40, Hanah 35, Miles 16, Jane 14, Thomas 12, John 10, Paulina 7, Arthur 4, Malinda 1

Schedule Page 256

ARMSTRONG, William 27*, Susan 27, Sarah K. 4, Amelia 3, Elziabeth Z. 1
NETHERCUTT, Stephen 14*
HARPER, Allen 38, Elizabeth 33, Thomas 15, Samuel 13, John 9, Elihu 8, Elizabeth 4, James 2, Mary 1, Jane 80
BARKER, Solomon 50, Mary 50, Henry W. 24, Mary 20, Cathrine 17, Solomon 15, Joseph 13, Henderson 11, Minna J. 7
WHITT, Richard 54*, Rebecca 44, Hanah 28, James B. 22, Lavisa 15, James G. 13
MCFARLAND, Virginia L. 7*
REYNOLDS, John B. 36
BEAR, Avery 34, Susannah 26, Mary A. 11, Henry W. 9, Lawson 6, Amanda S. 4, Solomon L. 1
WHITT, Emund 24, Mary J. 15, Sabery 2/12
SPARKS, James 27, Susan 25
BROOKS, John 45, Julia A. 29, Elizabeth 11, Eliza J. 9, Francis M. 7, Hampton P. 5, Richard P. 3, Price W. 3, John E. M. 11/12
REYNOLDS, Pleasant 27, Nancy M. 22, John H. 11/12
COX, William 21, Belcenia 18
HOLBROOK, Simeon 32, Sarah 28

1850 Census Carter County Kentucky

WHISMAN, David 33*, Nancy 33, Louisa 10, Susan 9, Harrison 8, Henderson 5, John 3, Richard 10/12
HALLIOME, Samuel 20*
BARKER, William 28, Minnia 28, William O. 5, Elizabeth 2
COX, Rebecca 62, Rebecca 8
COX, Odom 30, Sidney 22, Elijah 6, Missouri 3, Helena 1

Schedule Page 257

DARNELL, William 31, Tabitha 31, Mary 10, William J. 5, Wm. R. 22
HORTON, Elijah 39, Nancy 37, Henry 11, Travis 9, Rees 7, William 5, Phebe 1
WARD, J. B. 33 (m)*, Louisa 26, Robert 9, Mary 7, Elizabeth J. 5, James 5, Susan 3
WARD, Mary 70*
DAVIS, E. P. 40 (m)*, Mertilla 36, Elizabeth 13, Mary 7, Richard 5
WOOD, Joshua 35*
FLOYD, Thomas 40*
VIERS, William 23*
BURROUGHS, Thomas 25*
TOLER, Henry 40*
DAWSON, Larkin 55*
MOBLEY, Telitha 45, Samuel 24, Thomas J. 20, Elizabeth 16, William 15
WIESS, Daniel K. 34, Hannah 32, Faris R. 8, Allice 7, Josephine 5
LEWIS, Charles 36*, Louisa A. 33, Jesse 13, Sarah A. 9, Lucy 8, Charles N. 5, Hervey 2
LEWIS, Milton 42*
WARD, James 54*
HARLOW, William 26, Amanda S. 5, Grasilla 63
HUNTSMAN, James E. 27, Eleanor 21
JAMES, John W. 41, Eliza G. 38, John E. H. 18, Marinda J. 16, Phebe A. 14, Elizabeth 11, William J. 6, Martha E. 4, Samuel B. 2
JAMES, T. S. 39 (m), Emely C. 38, John W. 16, Mary S. 13, Amanda E. 11, John B. 10, Landoff H. 8, Bermetha 6, Wat A. 4
WILLIAMS, James 63, Sarah 49, Silas 21, Nancy J. 18, James 14, Malvina 11, Meldon 7
JAMES, William 31, Elizabeth 31, John A. J. 10, Margaret A. 5, Reuben T. 3, Lucinda O. 2

Schedule Page 258

JAMES, George 22, Eliza J. 20, Hannah 1
RATLIFF, James 40, Frances E. 34, Marion B. 13, Sarah C. 11, Mariah E. 10, Philip S. 9, William A. 8
RICE, Elijah 63, Sarah 54, Paris 23, Abbert G. H. 18, Elizabeth 15, Anthony L. 13, Kenos F. 10, John D. 8
OFFELL, James 52*, Mary L. 35, James P. 17, John P. 17, John H. A. 15, Gabriel M. 11, Martha J. 9, Louisa 6, Therissa E. 4, Amanda H. 1
SWIM, Barbary 15*
WAUGH, William 33*, Eliza 32, Lafayette 8, Syntha A. 6, John 5, Rebecca 3, Sarah J. 2, Mary 5/12
CARRELL?, Patsey 23*
RICE, William P. 27*, Oliva 31, Valinta V. 3
MCCANE, Mariah 13*
JOURDON, Edward 33, Mary A. 25, Martha J. 1

1850 Census Carter County Kentucky

RICE, Danel 29, Flora A. 22, William J. 3, Mary E. 1
MCGLOTHLIN, James 38, Cinthia A. 38, Josephas 14, Andrew L. 11, Martha 10, Samuel 7, Nancy A. 6/12
BROMEGAR, William 22, Agler 24, Nancy B. 1
JARVIS, John 22, Elizabeth 20, John H. 2, Sarah E. 7/12
WILBOURN, Robert 34, Mariah 24, Francis 10, William 5, Reuben A. 3, Mary L. 1
JARVIS, Joshua 19, Mary 20
SAVAGE, James 43*, Martha 41, William 17, Eleanor 16, Mary A. 14, John E. 11, Hiram B. 9, James S. 7, Nicholas 3
HALE, John 21*
SHOAT, Richard 68, Elizabeth 37, Tilla 17, Terissa 14, Mary 11, Zachariah 10, Emaly 8, Namon 6, Malvina A. 5, Eliza E. 3, Abraham 1

Schedule Page 259

RICE, Ezekiel 30*, Margaret 31, Almira E. 12, Jeremiah 11, James J. 6, Travis M. 8, Mary E. 4, Jury F. 1
SPENCER, Henry 21*
RICE, Wm. M. 24
PENINGTON, Jonathan 32, J— 32, Elizabeth 11, John 9, Mary A. 8, William J. 7, Jourdan 5, Abel 3, David 1
BOGS, Hugh 36, Louisa 32, James M. 11, John 8, William 6, David 5, Whitt 3, Abijah 2, Benjamin F. 6/12
ROE, Eleanor 54, James H. 21, Malinda R. 15
COX, Henry 29, Eleanor 28, Odom 9, Malinda A. 6, James 4, David 1
DICKERSON, Levi 34, Lucinda 38, Benjamin 14, Mary 12, Rebecca 11, John 10, Frances 8, Elizabeth 7, Washington 6, Jackson 6, Lousia 5, Lucy 5, James 1, Griffitt 4/12
ROE, John 26, Elizabeth 26, Phebe 8, Mary A. 6, Henry 4, Louisa 11/12
NETHERCUTT, Jourdan 59, Rebecca 51, David 24, Solomon 19, Jourdan 17, Sarah 14, Rebecca 7
PENINGTON, Isaac 27, Abigail 23, Rebecca 4, Jourdan 3, Jamima 7/12
NETHERCUTT, George 20, Sarah 20
JOHNSTON, Philip 53, Thirsey 39, Pleasant L. 20, Elijah 18, Margaret 15, George W. 12, Evaline 10, Mary J. 9, Robert H. 4, Harmon 3, Zachariah 2, Richard J. 6/12

Schedule Page 260

TACKETT, James 28, Nancy 25, Lydia M. 10, William 5, James M. 3, Wiley 1
TABER, Robert 72
OAKLEY, Anderson 45, Mariah 41, James 15, George Ann 13, Benjamin 9, Samuel 7, Jane 5, Susan 3, Minerva 1
ELLIOTT, Samuel R. 37, Minerva 36, Jane E. 12, Amanda 10, John M. 9, James H. 7, Mary A. 5, Benjamin F. 1
BARKER, John 61, Macey 38, Levi 21, Mary J. 13, John 10, Nancy 8, Sarah 6, Cathrine 2
HOLBROOK, William 61*, Sarah 54, Leurena 17, Israel 15, William 13
HOLBROOK, Albert 36*, Elizabeth 30, Finley P. 8/12
KERNOOT, William 39, Mary 37, John 21, Tursey 17, Nancy 15, James 13, Elizabeth 12, William 9, Mary J. 7, Elisha 5, Thompson B. 3, Martin F. 7/12

- 45 -

1850 Census Carter County Kentucky

MAUK, Joseph 34, Sarah 28, Samuel 8, Peter 4, William 3, Mary F. 1
HOLBROOK, William B. 50, Delila 47, John 26, Allen H. 24, Paulina B. 17
TACKETT, Robert 35, Amy 25, James W. 13, Elisha T. 11, Elijah T. 11, Celia 7, Matilda 6, Nancy 4, America 1
HOLBROOK, Jesse 24, Mary 20, Granville 1/12

Schedule Page 261

THARP, Robert 43, Mary 43, Elias 16, Nathan 14, Calvin 13, Sarah 12, Jesse 10, William 8, Isaac 6, Siney 5, Bazzel 4, Robert 1
LYON, Jesse 37, Mary 35, Jarret C. 12, Jeremiah 8, Elizabeth 10, John 7, Fleming 5, James 3, William 3/12
BOGS, James 39, Aretta 39, John 18, Tyra T. 16, Elijah 14, Hugh 11, James 8, Elizabeth 6
DEBOARD, Jeptha 50*, Maney 45, John 20, JosAnna 18, Luraney 16, Ira 14, Isaac 13, Frances 11, Solomon 8, Amos 5
MIDDLETON, Luraney 56*
BINION, James 23, Nancy M. 20, Annis 3/12
BARKER, Hardin 50, Annis 46, Elizabeth 18, Cathrine 16, Annis 15, Hervey 12, Sarah 10, William 9, Rebecca 6
KNIPP, Alexander 29, Adaline 23, Sarah 10, Henry J. 8, Hannah 4, George 7/12
SMITH, Martha A. 30*, McSilas 4, William 2, Elizabeth 50, William S. 15
MCFARLANE, Hiram 26*
WILSON, William 34, Rachel 32, Solomon 14, William 13, Mary 10, Rebecca 7, Nancy 6, Sarah 6, Henry 3, Levi 1
BLEVINS, Sarah 65, Mary 24, Sarah 8
WINER, Jophnn 24, Elizabeth 25, Margaret 5, Christopher 4
BLEVENS, Ryal 33, Sarah 30, ― 14 (f), Elisha 12, Mary 10, Elizabeth 8, HEnry 5, Annis 1

Schedule Page 262

BLEVINS, William 35, ― ― (f), Nancy 5, Ryal 2
BLEVINS, James 38, Cathrine 37, Nancy 20, Rebecca 16, William 15, Luraney 13, Mary A. 11, James 9, Rachel 7, Robert 5, Phebe 4, Solomon 1, Henry B. 1/12
BARKER, William 55, Phebe 44, William 20, Matilda 17, Nancy 15, Hardin 13, Jesse 8, Jourdan 5, Hervey 2
STEPHENS, William 23*, Elizabeth 22, John 1, Phebe 6/12
BARKER, Annis 9*
RENTFROE, William 28, Mary 26, Sarah E. 6, John W. 4, Mary E. 2, Matilda J. 6/12
MARLOW, Joel 27, Mary 22, William 3, James 1
GILBERT, William 32, Osiller 32, Spud 10, Daniel 8, nancy A. 7, Susanna 5, Matilda 1
LOWE, William 51, Mariah 46, Franlin 21, Cathrine J. 13, Amanda 10, Melvina 10, America 7, George W. 6
LOWE, Miles 34, Mary 21, Mitchell 10, William 5
SPARKS, john 26, Almeda 24, Minerva 3, Cynthia 1
MADDOX, Nathaniel 52*, Susannah 40
HOLLAND, Drusilla 70*
THOMAS, Susannah 13*

1850 Census Carter County Kentucky

CARRELL, Daniel 54, Maryann 28, Thomas 17, Solomon 11, Samuel 8, David 5, Phebe 2, Luke 7/12
CARRELL, Daniel 26, Sirena 28, Martha J. 4, Rebecca 1, Elizabeth 18

Schedule Page 263

CARRELL, Nelson 26, Angelina 24, Elizabeth 4, Susanah 2, George W. 1
LYON, Nathaniel 32, Jane 25, Daniel 7, William 6, Rebecca 2
LYON, Susannah 55, George W. 20, David 16, Elizabeth 18
STEPHENS, John 44, Phebe 39, Malinda 17, John P. 16, Isaac H. 14, Andrew 12, Daniel K. 10, George W. 8, Mary A. O. 5, Susannah 3, Elkaney 1
STEPHENS, James M. 21, Susannah 18, Mary A. 4/12
MADDOX, Abraham 52, Mary 53
MADDOX, Syrus G. 22, Elizabeth 20, Frances 10/12
ROBERTSON, Isaac 39, Clarissa 19, Francis M. 8, Milton 4, James? 10
BISHOP, Hannah 52*, Elizabeth 30, Sampson 22, Mary A. 14
HALE, Mary A. C. 6*
COUNTS, Christopher 33, Mary A. 31, Martha J. 10, Margaret E. 8, Mary J. 4, Philip A. 1
MCCOY, Ryland D. 35, Nancy 26, William 13, Palmera A. 9, Rebecca A. 8, Mary J. 5, Granville A. 4, Winfield S. 3, Zachara T. 1, George W. 4/12
WILLIAMS, Laban 39*, Mary A. 36, Borceal 17, Laban J. 13, Nancy J. 5, Telitha A. 2
COUNTS, John S. 23*
HUX, Ishmael H. 33*, Sarah A. 28, William R. 9, Daniel 8, Jesse 4, Martha J. 2
WINEGAR, John 25*
HUX, Nathan 65, Ruth 40
NOLAND, Jesse 24, Nancy 25, Syrena 4, Frances E. 3, Nathan H. 2/12
NEWELL, Aaron 48, Margaret 41, Elizabeth 19, John 16, Phebe 12, William F. 10, Porter 7, Eliza B. 5, George A. 1 (f)

Schedule Page 264

WAUGH, John 59, Augusteen 56, Jacob P. 22, George W. 21, Zeir 18, Sarah A. 16
WAUGH, John 28, Margaret 26, Columbus 2, Augusteen 4/12
MCLOVY?, William 28, Lucinda 23, Alexander 6, James 4, Permelia A. 2, Leander 5/12
JAMES, John M. 28*, Eliza J. 29, Martha A. 6, William 5, Zerelda 2, George 1
MOWRY, John 22*
ROSS, Susannah 23, Mary A. 20, Alonzo 1
HICKS, Henry 28, Sarah 28, Christeena 10, Nancy 9, Cinthia 7, Reuben 5, Wm. S. 2, Louisa 4/12
CHAPMAN, Nancy 39*, Miinerva 15, Susan 13, James R. 9
BIRCH, Oliver 22*, Martha 17
TOLER, Christopher 45*, Nancy 50, Thomas Burns 3
CHAPMAN, Wm. 19*
MOOR, Frances A. 16*
TERRY, Thomas 53, Mary 40, Samuel W. 21, Leonard 14, Isaac 12, Elijah 8
WILBOURN, Lewis 42, Elizabeth 42, Elizabeth 15, Mary A. 13, Susanna 9, Hervey 6, Nelson 3, Elizzabeth 23, Martha J. 5, Christopher 3
RUGGLES, James 52, Elizabeth 41, Elizabeth 93, Harriet A. 13, Michael 11, Alfred 8, Clement 6, James 3, Martha E. 1

- 47 -

1850 Census Carter County Kentucky

STEWART, Lewis 31, Jane 15
KITCHEN, William 33*, Nancy 30, Allen 5, Caroline 2

Schedule Page 265

BAYS, Seana G. 17*, Samuel L. 15
HORR, Elizabeth 33*
MCCREAN, Mariah E. 14*, William L. 11
HORR, Emly V. 7/12*
MCKINNEY, Daniel 59*, Elziabeth 34
COOK, Joel 59*, Cowden 12
POPE, Evaline 23*
COUNTS, George W. 26, Sarah 21
SALSBERRY, Milton 46*, Levicy 36, William 13, Nancy 11
JOHNSTON, Eada 87*
LITTLETON, John 60, Talitha 43, Jesse 17, John 17, Amanda J. 12, Andrew V. 10, William L. 8, James M. 4
LITTLETON, George C. 19, Mary A. 20
POPE, Lewis 43, Mary 44, William 14, John 13, Hiram 10, Deborah 8, Louisa 6, Mary E. 3, James F. 5/12
ALEXANDER, Fleming 18, Rebecca 17, Elizabeth 1/12
COUNTS, William 29, Mary E. 23
DEBORD, James 50*, Eliza 36, Harriet A. 19, Alfred 17, Mary E. 17, Caroline C. 13, Lucy 9, Arabell 7, James H. 4
NOLCINA, Charles 21*
MILLARD, Malvina 21*
ROGERS, Nancy 20*
BLACK, Washington 45* (B)
WELBOURN, Jackson 35, Jane 32, Robert 6, John H. 3, Mary A. 2/12
SKIDMORE, Joicy 73*
THROOP, Joseph 30, Mary 30, Phares 67
FRIZZELL, Alfred H. 42, Eliza A. 34, Mary E. W. 10, Martha E. 8, Thomas A. 7, Allice G. 5, Henry J. J. C. 4, Margaret A. 2
LANSDOWN, A. J. 33 (m)*, Mary 25, Lucy 7, Mary 6, George 1
JONES, William D. 19*
KIBBY, William 31, Casander 31
PARKER, Andrew J. 27, Elizabeth 19, Julia W. 2
CRAWFORD, B. F. 43 (m)*, Elizabeth A. 26, Dorathy S. 6, Mary 3, Laury 1

Schedule Page 266

ROGERS, Susan 43*
WARD, George W. 26*, Susan 15
CARTER, R. G. 50 (m)*, Sophia 40, Robert 10, Hebe 7, Susan 5
HOOD, Thomas J. 30*
STROTHER, John R. 44*, Ruth 35, Martha J. 14, Robert S. 10, Nancy A. 8, George W. 5, Elizabeth B. 3
TANNER, John 22*

1850 Census Carter County Kentucky

WHITE, Manlius 19*
MADDIX, William 32, Eliza 30, John W. 8, Elizabeth C. 6, William L. 3, Abraham 1
MILLER, Marcus 30, Amanda 28, Stephen P. 8, Robert H. 6, James F. 4, Arthur P. 2, George W. 2/12
THOMPSON, James W. 33*, Sarah 33, George A. 7, Elizabeth 5, Julia A. 1
SAVAGE, Tabitha 15*, Sarah 15
SOUTHERLAND, Cornelius 25*
ROBERTSON, James 26, Ezekiel 75, William H. 18
HICKS, William J. 35, Mary 25, Elizabeth S. 11, John 9, Nancy 7, Hardin 4, Peter 3
MONTGOMERY, Edington 31, Sylvester K. 29, Lavina 23
HOOD, John 40*, Eliza 35, Samantha J. 12, Amanda M. 9, Arastus 8, Synthia A. 4, Louisa E. 2, Emely L. J. 8/12
HERVEY, Calvin 23*
OSTER, Andrew 27, Amanda 19
WALKER, Jeremiah 37, Teresy 34, George W. 17, William R. 15, Sarah 12, Silas 8, James 2
WALKER, Rachel 66, Rachel 17, Robert B. 4
LAMMONS, William 30, Cathrine 30, Benj. F. 10, William T. 7, Mary E. 6, James L. 3, George W. 2

Schedule Page 267

SCAGGS, Hervey M. 26*, Mary A. 20, Nancy J. 3, Silva 4/12
HYTTON, Rodrick 74*, Nancy 50
CHAFIN, Julia A. 15*
SCAGGS, Jeremiah 53, Eleanor 50, Martha 20, Moses 19, Matilda 17, Linny 15, Joseph 12, John L. 8
PARSONS, John 25, Juda 49, Elizabeth 16, Armilda 11, John T. 2
SCAGGS, Solomon 53, Telitha 30, Mary 19, Ananias 17, Susanna 15, Luraney 10, Peter 8, James 7, Silva B. 5, Laney C. 1
PARSONS, Thomas 30, Clarinda 39, James P. 5, Squire 3, Robert T. 2
GRIZZEL, John 38, Cinthia 36, Sally 18, Elizabeth 16, Leucretia 15, George 13, Thomas 9, Linnea 7, Nancy 4, Rebecca 3, Lafayette 1
ROSE, Robert 38*, Sarah 39, Henderson 18, John P. 12, Julia A. 10, Jesse 8, Robert 6, William 4, Lucinda 2
BAKER, James 30*
BIRCHFIELD, John 38*
WHITT, Richard P. 43, Sally 43, Hannah A. 19, Elias H. D. 22, John S. 16, Clarinda 14, David C. 12, Henry C. T. 10
WHITT, Abijah 37, Nancy 37, Rebecca A. 13, Louisa 12, John 9, Elizabeth 7, Emely 5, Richard D. 3, Linny 3/12
WHITT, Hannah 77
MCFARLANE, William 66, Rachel 50, Miles 36, Luraney 25, Nancy 17, Rachel 15, Jincy 10
MCFARLANE, John 33, Christina 22, Faris 7, Mahaley 4, Fady 3, Hiram 1

Schedule Page 268

COX, John F. 27, Linnia 36, Squire 14, Lavisa 12
KING, Elkana 34, Mary 34, James M. 9, Lucinda 8, Hiram 6, William 5, Samantha 3, Laban 1
KNIPP, William 34, Violet 30, William H. 10, George 6, John L. 10/12
LANE, Lewis P. 25, Mary J. 27

1850 Census Carter County Kentucky

KNIPP, George 60, Sally 56, Talitha Q. M. 22, Malinda J. 19, George W. 17, Elizabeth 11
SEXTON, William 27, Frances 28, Sarah A. 5, George R. 4, James L. 1
MOBLEY, Harris 22, Malinda 18
LANE, Corbin 47, Mary 45, William 18, Martin 16, Nathan B. 14, Margaret E. 11, Sarah D. 9, Martha J. 7, James E. 6, Helen A. 4, Caroline Va 2
LANE, Samuel 23*, Nancy B. 19
BENTON, William T. 24*
MILLER, William H. 30, Melvina 36, Mary 11, William R. 7, Robert H. 3, John B. T. 1
BALEY, _____ 26 (m), Lucinda 16
WALLACE, George 55, Nancy 36, William 24, Henry 17, Odom 15, Phebe 11, Martha 9, James 6, Elizabeth 4, Mary 2, Elijah 1, Rebecca 21
FISHER, Joseph 49, Prissilla 48, Alfred M. C. 22, Mourning M. 26, Sintha 19, Elizabeth 17, Nancy 14, Edmund H. 8
MADDEX, John 31*, Eliza 22, Mary 3
LOWE, Baley 25*, Martha 19, Mary 1

Schedule Page 269

GILBERT, Thomas 27, Rachel 24, Susan 4, James 2
GILBERT, Stephen 23, Mahala 17, Elizabeth 7/12
CROAN, Thomas 52, Elizabeth 48, Rachel 19, Sidney 17 (f), George T. 15, Nancy 13, Frances 11, Hannah 9, John A. 7, Joseph M. D. 5
DERBY, Mary 23
CROAN, William 30, Ann 20, Susan 3, Francis M. 1
SAMMONS, Fleming 41, Nancy 37, James R. 15, Thomas 13, Elizabeth 11, Martha 9, George W. 6, Mary A. 3, Comodore P. 10/12
ALEXANDER, Mary 52*, Robert 21, Sidney 17 (f)
NUNLEY, Mary 3*
ALEXANDER, Greenup 44, Dosha 34, Sintha 17, Wm. N. 14, James 11, Elizabeth 9, Washington 7, Greenup 5, Cathrine 4/12
ALEXANDER, Thompson 24, Phebe 19, Greenberry 1, Mary A. 1/12
POPE, Jacob 85*, Rebecca 76, Hetty 18
RUGGLES, Michael 65*
DAMRON, Hiram 43*, Margaret 43, Richard 21, John 21, Elizabeth H. 8
CARROLL, John 22*, Nancy 19, Hiram 9/12
MCGUIRE, Temperance 52*, Nehemiah 20, Francis M. 13, Comodore P. 10
BUFFINGTON, William 23*
LONG, Benjamin 21, Margaret 17
MCGUIRE, Robert 28, Margaret 25, Sidney A. 5 (f), Elizabeth A. 4, Lavina 2
SAVAGE, C. P. 26 (m), Rebecca C. 25
FARNEY, David 36, Malinda G. 36, Minerva 16, Amanda 14, Mary E. 11, John D. 10, Francis M. 8, George W. 4, Ruth A. 3
BANFIELD, Thomas K. 27*, Ailsey A. 22, James T. 3, Prudence 84

1850 Census Carter County Kentucky

Schedule Page 270

CAMPBELL, David 19*
KENEDA, John 22*
CARSON, Elijah 28*
GREEN, Caney 25*
ADAMS, Pleasant 47*, Eleanor 24, Richard 21, Elizabeth 18, Sylvester 16, Daniel 14, Amanda S. 13, Jesse 9, Manerva 2, Elijah 6/12
JONES, Elijah 6*
TRIPLETT, Elijah 18*
BURTON, Eleanor 54*, Martin 14
ADAMS, James 22, Freelove 24 (f)
ADAMS, William 23, Elizabeth 19, John 1
MESSER, William 37*, Letty 30, Charley 18, Samuel 16, William B. 13, Nancy A. 11, Ellen 9, Archibald 7, Benjamin 5, James 3, Henry 1
CARVER, Frances 20*, Harriet A. 3
STEWART, James R. 32*, Nancy A. 29, George W. 9, James N. 4, Elmira 1
WILBOURN, Elizabeth 29*, Martha 1
SLATER, John 46*
JAMES, William 24*
ADAMS, William C. 22*
MORRIS, John 33, Rebecca 27, Elizabeth 11, Lucy 5, Wesley 3, Lafayette 1
OWENS, Hugh 28*, Vance 24 (f), Angeline 6, Elias 3, Leaner 2
CRAME, William 16*
OWENS, Elizabeth 45*, John 19, Archibald 16, Joseph 14, Hervey 12, George 10
ROBERTSON, Frances 20*
SAVAGE, Edward 52, Nancy 50, Jackson 19, Elizabeth 17, Ellen 17, Francis M. 14, Edward 8, John 40
MULLENS, Elias 24, Eleanor R. S. 27, Susan A. 3, Mary M. L. 3/12, Burrell 14
MULLENS, James 23, Aranetta 18, Martha A. 2

Schedule Page 271

BELL, Sarah 55
ELSWICK, William 26*, Louis 26, James 7, Carroll 3
LEWIS, William 23*, Lucy 23
BUSH, Telitha 35 (B), Nancy J. 8, William M. 5, Ann E. 3, Sarah 3/12
WILBORN, William 29, Nancy 23, James 10, William H. 7, Mary A. 5, Robert 3, Ephraim 8/12
GOAD, Elizabeth 20*
ARMS, Mary 70*
RICE, Jane 23*, William N. 2
WHITLOCK, Lewis 34, Elizabeth A. 25
WILBORN, Burrell 32, Cathrine 26, Edward R. W. 11, Phebe R. 8, Nancy A. 6, Reller 3, Elizabeth 9/12
TAYLOR, Stephen 24, Mary 55, Nancy E. 14
GEE, Robert A. 32, Teresse 32, Thompson 10, Elizabeth 8, Lewis 5, Roxey A. 3, Henry 1
HUMPHREYS, John 37, Margaret 36, Eleanor 13, Virginia 7, Ann E. 5, John 1
WALFORD, Michael 35, Sarah A. 18

1850 Census Carter County Kentucky

DEVORE, David 41*, Sarah 38, Jane 21, Robert 19, Jasper 16, Elizabeth 14, John 10, Margaret 7, Lafayette 5, Cathrine 2
WHITAKER, William 22*
KOUNS, Nelson 22*
WILSON, John 21*
MOUTHEN, James 24*
WOOD, Andrew 19*
OSTER, John 30*
CARR, Miles 30*
REED, Samuel 20*, Thomas 16
MCALISTER, Hervey 25*
CARSIN, Elijah 25*
FUGATT, Moses H. 35, Mary 35, Sarah 12, Phebe 10, Benjamin 8, George W. 4, Marion J. 4/12, Lydia 75
FAIN, Arthur C. 32, Jane 20, Richard 2, Reuben 1
GRAY, James 40, Susannah 24

Schedule Page 272

JENKINS, Levi 27, Mary J. 18, Mary E. 1
SELLERS, ___ y 41 (f)*, Mary J. 8, Ensy E. 6
PRUETT, Henry 26*, John 18, Luanny 23
ADAMS, William 23*
NICKELL, George 25, Elizabeth 23, Henry 1/12
GEE, Micajah 33, Martha 19, William 3, Mary A. 2
CHRISMAN, Ira G. 34, Rebecca 32, Morton B. 15, James M. 11, Isaac 8, America V. 6, Elijah 5, Josephine 3/12, Logan L. 19
BUTTENSHAW, Bernard 25, Mary 20, Eliza 2
DAVIS, John 40, Elizabeth 36, David 14, Emanuel 12, Frances 11
TACKETT, William 24*, Jane 26, Lewis 5, Nancy 2, Joel 1
LEWIS, Isaac 20*, Nancy 21
YARNALL, David 30, Ann 35, Mary 5, Andrew 3
COOK, George 40*, Jane 35, Cathrine 15, George 11, Sarah 6, Jeremiah 1, Lewis 30
ROOK?, George 25*
DUNCAN, Lewis 24, Elizabeth 21, John 1
RUCKER, Absailom 40, Nancy 36, James D. 19, Mary 16, Eleanor 14, Nancy J. 12, Henry W. 10, Susan 7, Robert 5, Allice 11/12
BURTONSHAW, James 23*
BIGGS, Andrew 22*, William 20
VOLDINER, L. C. 26 (m)*
JACKSON, Isaac 25* (B)
TURPIN, Andrew 19* (B)
BONDURANT, Isaac 22* (B)
JAMES, William 22, Mary 19
JAMES, Ephraim 49*, Hannah 42, Dudley 22, Mary 20, Henry 15, Rolley 13, Hannah 11, Ephraim 9, Milton 8, George 5, Charles 10/12

1850 Census Carter County Kentucky

Schedule Page 273

BIGGS, James P. 20*, Sarah A. 17, Campbell 15, Reuben A. 14, Landron 10, Jackson 8
STRAIN, Barney 25*
HARKINS, Barney 22*
JAMES, John 75, Margaret 35
TROUT, Daniel 43, Rhoda 43, Philip 20, Elizabeth 18, Noah 15
GLANCY, Thomas 38*, Ameter 27 (f), David M. 7, Frances J. 4, Charles 3, John 7/12
RICE, Delina 16*
HARRIS, Willis 26*
ISOM?, Lewis 38*
HAMILTON, Isaac 18*
COUNTS, Samuel 20*
HALL, John 26*, Casander 24
DAVIDSON, Isom 35, Elizabeth 27, Landsen C. 16?, Sarah A. 9, Elisa 8, Elizabeth 7, Joseph 5, Nancy 4, Olevi 1
BOGUS, Reuben 37*, Frances L. 34, Nancy A. 15, Cathrine jr. 9, John M. 7, Wm. L. 5
GAMBREL, Nancy 54*
BOW, Argus 33, Sarah 30, Jackson 10, James 8, William T. 6, John 4, Nancy E. 5/12
LUNSFORD, James 27, Frances 19
ACRES, Burrell 26, Malinda 23, George M. D. 4, Lavina J. 1, Mary J. 9
BUSH, James 39, Margaret 38, William 20, James 18, Elizabeth 15, Lafayette 11, Eliza 9, Cathrine 5, Ellen 1
WILLIAMS, Alfred 39, Dicey 33, Dilila 7, Amanda 6, Jehu 4, Mary 2
BLANKENSHIP, Sarah 69
STEWART, Hiram 27*, Arametha? 24, Albert 7/12
BLANKENSHIP, Vincent 8*
EVANS, A. J. 17 (m)*
KUCKER, Thos. J. 26*, Martha 22, Elizabeth N. 1

Schedule Page 274

BOGS, Cathrine 16*, John 20
KISEE, Jeremiah 27, Elizabeth 26, Paulina E. 9, Emaly J. 8, John H. 5, Oliver F. 2, William A. 1/12
JAMES, Edward 50, Paulina J. 25, Rachel 9, Albert W. 8, Rebecca 6, Paulina 4, James 8/12
HOWELL, James 62*, Jainima F. 32, Samuel P. 10, Martha A. 5
CRANE, James 14*, Joseph 12
HANEY, John 63*, Elizabeth 27, Elizabeth 18, Sarah J. 1
COOK, Angeline 8*, Martha A. 5
MARTIN, John P. 51, Sarah 34, William F. 14, Ellen W. 12, John 10, Mary J. 8, Elizabeth A. 6, Benj. F. 3, Caroline 1
RICE, Sherod 46, Margaret 37, William S. 20, Perry W. 18, Henry M. 16, Benj. J. 12, Cintha E. 9, Sarah H. 7, James K. P. 5, George M. D. 3, Elias C. M. 8/12
RICE, Wm. 94, Margaret 89, William 51
SEXTON, Mark 37*, Cathrine 41, Henry P. 15, Bartlett 75, Cathrin 71
BLAIR, Leann 7*
GALION, Hiram 23, Elizabeth 20, Larkin 1

1850 Census Carter County Kentucky

ARTRIP, John 38, Elizabeth 37, Sarah 13, Henry 9, Francis M. 6, Eliza A. 4, Wm. J. 1
RICE, Archibald 55*, Cindarilla 49, Ezekiel M. 25, John E. 17, Sarah J. 16, Wm. M. 7, Lucinda 14
BURTON, Margaret 18*
CAMPBELL, Riley 20*
JAMES, Andrew T. 31*, Eliza A. 30, Joseph A. 10, John F. 6, James M. 2, Sarah J. 2/12
PEREBOYS?, Jacob 24*

Schedule Page 275

BLANKENSHIP, Wm. R. 28, Amanda 22, Avery 1 (f), William A. 2/12, Casander 9
RICE, Ezekiel T. 37, Tabitha 30, Lewis P. 12, Malinda 10, America 8, Montraville 5, Elisha G. 3, Charles W. H. 1
OWENS, William 27, America 18
STEWART, Charles 40, Jane 34, Albert 17, Landon 15, Braxen 11, Benj. F. 7, Martha 5, Daniel 1
STEWART, Andrew 53, Rachel 27, Missouri 16, Henry 13, Alfred 10, James 8, Greenville 7
COOK, Joel 83*, Eada? 54, John 22, Eli 20, Franklin 13
MCGUIRE, Eada 21*, Frances 6/12
EVANS, Mary 34*, Andrew J. 16, Wm. W. 15, Hiram 12, Nancy A. 9, Mary A. 9, George W. 6, Emly 2
MULLENS, James 21*, Arametha 18, Martha A. 2
ARMS, John 68*
TOLIVER, William 21*
TOLIVER, Hamton 35*, Malinda 28, Hiram 9, James 7, Andrew T. 5, John 2, Jane 20, James R. 7/12
STEWART, Jonston 25*
SAVAGE, Isaac 27, Cintha A. 25, Andrew J. 4, James H. 2, Missouri 1/12
NIPP, Elizabeth 29, Bazzle R. 11, Archibald 9, Sarah J. 7, James W. 8/12
SHEARER, Walter 36*, Nancy B. 28, Sarah J. 9, Charles W. 7, Nancy E. 4, Ann R. 1
REEVES, Miram 16*
RICE, Margaret A. 28, Sarah E. 10, Eliza F. 8, Charles N. 6, Amanda H. 3
RICE, Fleming B. 46, Eliza 43, Hiram A. 19, Jefferson 15, Campbell 13, Berryman S. 18, Caroline 5, Thomas F. 2

Schedule Page 276

REEVES, Bartlett 59, Matilda 45, Rachel 18, Miram A. 16, Samuel C. L. 14, Sarah B. 12, Elizabeth 10, John W. 7, Matilda E. 5
SHORT, Aaroon 35, Susanna 27, Sarah A. 3, Elizabeth 3, Hugh 2/12
JOURDAN, James 23, Sarah 26, Winfield S. 3/12
MCGUIRE, John 48, James 18, Joel 16, William 14, Nancy 10, Emily J. 8, Rebecca 3
JOURDAN, Ann 48, George W. 19, William 18, Absailom 16, Nancy 12, Burrell 8, David 7, Pleasant 5
BURCHETT, David 39*, Julia A. 32
REEVES, Jasper N. 20*, Jane 16, Emely 14, Benjamin 11, Rhoda 10, James 8, Eliza 5, Mary 3, John 6/12
MCDOLE, Peter 20, Sarah 16
JOHNSON, Hiram 48*, Susanna 45, Jonas 15, Robert 11, Hiram 9, Henry P. 3, Lavina 3, John M. 2
JONES, Luraney 14*, Elizabeth 12, Anna 9
KISSEE, Jessee 46, Elizabeth 46, Andrew J. 16, Allen W. 13, Sarah E. 9, John L. 4
KITCHEN, Fleming 29, Rachel 24

- 54 -

1850 Census Carter County Kentucky

WILSON, William 54, Mary 49, James 25, John 23, Andrew 18, Sarah 16, William 13, Lewis 10
STANLEY, Andrew J. 21, Barbary 21, Elizabeth 11/12, George W. 21
KITCHEN, Andrew 58*, Mary 58

Schedule Page 277

HARRIS, John M. 10*
SEXTON, Alva 24 (m)*
KITCHEN, Lewis H. 23, Jane 23, Louisa 1
JONES, Jane 46, Lelia 16, Andrew 13, Sarah 8
BARNETT, James 28, Barbary 21, Ananias 8, Margaret 4, Cathrine 3
LACEY?, Philomen 49, George R. 14, Kenaz F. 12 (m), Joel R. 9, Frances 7
TACKETT, Hardin G. 25, Sarah A. 22, George W. 7, James F. 5, Mary J. 3, Elizabeth 1
RICE, Elizabeth 71*, Wm. W. 41, Charles 30, Nelson T. 39, America F. 30, James H. 13, Alfred H. 11, Elzaphan C. 8, Taylor 3, Wm. N. 24
MILLER, Wm. 22*
NOLAND, Leonard 23*, Angeline 18
BALEY, Samuel R. 27*, Elizabeth 21
HALL, James 24, Matilda 24, Henry 6, Amanda S. 5, William 3, Julia A. 2
RUCKER, Syria 34 (m), Susan 21, Columbia 4, Columbus 2?, James 8/12
RUCKER, Elizabeth 50
BAYS, William 52, Leonard 17, William 9
ARMS, John 23?, Mary 18
GOOD, William 47, Amanda 22, John 16, Sarah 13, Nancy A. 7
GOLAHUE, John 39, Sarah S. 20, Cindarella 13, James W. 11, Barbary Ellen 8, John W. 7, Phebe P. 2, Henry 8/12
GOLAHUE, Ruth 37, Elihu 9, Elizabeth 6, Levi 3
WELBOURN, Robert 63*, Prissilla 54, James 14, Gilly 22
GOLAHU, Mary J. 4*
RICE, Ezekiel 72, Deanna 65
RICE, Jacob 44*, Amanda 37

Schedule Page 278

BELCHER, Isaac 21*
ROGERS, David 40, Jane 40, Hiram 10, William 9, Henry G. 5, Missouri 1
GRANT, Sarah R. 31, John 8, Rhoda 6, Eliza 2, George W. 6/12
ROGERS, Jonathan 44, Mary A. 34, Arta 15, Maryatt 13, Elizabeth 11
ROBINS, Joshua 21, Mary 23, Emery 2 (f)
RUCKER, Elzaphan 70*, Mary 62, Elizabeth 29
WADE, Mary 25*, Henry T. 1
ROBINS, Daniel 42, Anna 50, Mary 18, Elizabeth 17, James 14, Lucinda 13, John 11, William 10, Merrell 8
WARD, Joseph R. 52, Adelaid 47, Sidney A. 13 (f), Susan H. 9, John B. 5, Milton L. 2/12
WOMACK, Richard 37, Harriet 32, James A. 14, Adalaid 12, Tignal 9 (m), Lavinia 7, Nancy E. 5, George 4, William 10/12
BANFIELD, Zedakiah 55*, Lavina 47, Alfred 17, James R. 15, William A. 9

- 55 -

1850 Census Carter County Kentucky

ROACH, Hiram 24*, Elizabeth 21
BALL, Mansford 37, Rachel 36, Rebecca J. 16, Nancy A. S. 16, Margaret 12, Joseph 8, William 6, Henry J. 5, Amanda 1
RUCKER, Bazzel 40, America 40, Elizabeth 15, Mary 12, John 10, Thursa A. 8, Margaret 7, Jane 6, Amanda R. 4, Emely 2
RUCKER, Elzaphan 32?, Elizabeth 22, Thomas J. 3, James M. 1, Jacob R. 2/12
ISOM, Hetty 46, Archibald 23?, Isaac 22, Ira 21, Hamilton 18, William 11, Mary 18, Elizabeth 14, Lucinda 9

Schedule Page 279

FIELDS, William J. 30*, Rebecca 23, Matilda F. 5, Christopher C. 3, James A. 1
BIGGS, James 19*
BOGGS, Mary A. 27*, Ebby F. 3, Ephraim 1/12
BOGGS, Frances 58, Elihu 21, Temperance 18, John 18
TRIPLETT, John 22, Mary 19
ISOM, Isom 21, Hannah 17
WILHITE, James A. 33, Matilda 29, Ephraim 16, Frances 5, Nancy J. 2, Eleanor 1
BALEY, James F. 56*, Phebe 40, Rebecca 21, Margaret 19, James 18, Jamima 14, John 12, Henry 10, William 8, Mary 5, Samson 1
SERGEANT, William 16*
KENEDA, Milton 30, Eleanor 24, James J. 7, Elihu S. 15, Salina E. 4, Hannah A. 3, Margaret 1
STURGIL, Solomon 45*, Rebecca 41, Elizabeth 16, Nancy 14, John F. 11, Matilda 9, Jamima 7, Rebecca 5, Solomon 3
SERGEANT, Robert 28*
HALL, Isaac 30, Lucy 31, Elizabeth M. 9, Elisha P. 8, Martin McC. 7, Hiram K. 5, Emely J. 3, Rebecca 1
MAHAY?, John B. 19, Eliza J. 15
CRAWFORD, Benjamin 27*, Rebecca 33, Eli 11, James 10, Benjamin 7, George 5, Mary 4, Henry 2
WILLIAMS, Eli 69*
STURGIL, Hervey 30, Mary 32, Elizabeth 5, Hamilton 3, Elijah 1, Ruth 9
STURGIL, Benjamin 23, Nancy 23, George W. 1, Isaac 15

Schedule Page 280

KITCHEN, Andrew __*, Winny 24, Eleanor 6, Charles 5, James 2, William -/12
MOORE, George 35*
MULLINS, Jonston 23, Aivey 20, Mary 2, Sarah 3/12
LEDINGHAM, Jacob 34, Frances 29, Mary 9, Peter 7, William 5, Sararah 3, James 10/12
LEDINGHAM, Peter 65, Sarah 65, Hetty 30, William 24, Thomas 22, Sarah 18, Nancy 16
ROBERTSON, Sarah 40, Rhoda 12, Margaret 6, Mary A. 2
PENINGTON, James 22*, Sarah 19, Nancy Va 1
WALKER, Mordecai 15*
ROBERTSON, Charity 29*
ADKINS, George W. 11*, Eliza J. 5
CHAFEN, John 39, Harriet 46, Eliza 17, Mordecai 14, Rebecca 7, Harriett 4
RIGHT, Calvin 24*, Rebecca 24, Delila A. 1
YATES, John 16*

1850 Census Carter County Kentucky

ELDRIGE, Mary 29, Nancy 8, William 4
RIGHT, Henry 25, Matilda 23, Enoch 4
MCDAVID, John 33, Permelia 30, Samuel 5, Amanda 4, Sarah J. 2
MCDAVID, George 58, Mary 49, Samuel 26, Daniel 21, Martha 19
WELLS, Franklin 29*, Nancy 24, Mary E. 6, William 4, James W. 1
ROBERTSON, Siba 73*
BURTON, William 24, Rebecca J. 23, Amelia 1, Samuel 4/12
BURTON, Samuel 66*, Amelia 61
RIGHT, Malinda 15*
ROBERTSON, Jacob 38, Malinda 28, Alfred H. 10, Elihu 7, Sarah A. 6, Mary T. 4, John M. 1

Schedule Page 281

PORTER, Bartlett 21, Tabitha 20, James 2, Elihu 3/12
SLOES, Henry 36, Mary 29, Franklin 5, Emely 3, Anny 2, Matilda 11/12
SLOES, Jesse 29, Elizabeth 29, John 9, Mary A. 4, Nancy V. 1, Martha J. 1
CLARK, Joshua 44, Elizabeth 43, Amanda M. 17, Robert 15, Nancy 13, Martha 10, William H. 8, James 4, Franklin 1
BOGGS, Bryant 33, Elizabeth 21, Mary 2
CLARK, Joseph 28, Jane 28, Mary E. 5, Sarah F. 3, America 3/12
BOGGS, Charity 32, Franklin 9, James C. 3
CLARK, James 24, Elizabeth 20, William T. 1
CLARK, John 40, Mary 70
GILLEM, Chesley 39, Sarah 27, John 13, Mary 10, Richard 6, Delila 6, Isom 3, Joseph 1
WATSON, John 43, Malinda 35, William 17, Eliza 14, James 11, Mary 8
JONSON, Mason 43, Elizabeth 40, John 18, Frances 16, William 14, Mary 13, Henry 11, Elizabeth 9, James 6, Nancy J. 5, Hulda 4, Sintha A. 2
JONSTON, Lightle 30, Cathrine 25, William 9, Jesse 8, James 5, Henry 4, John 1
WELLS, Lewis 26*, Lucinda 16
JONSON, Malinda 36*, Alfred 13
JACKSON, Sarah 49, Elizabeth 13, William 8, Lucinda 3
WADDELL, James 46, Frances 43, Meradith 25, Mary 25, James 9/12

Schedule Page 282

WADDLE, Alfred 21, Anna 19, Jesse 1
ELDRIGE, James 32, Eleanor 30, Anna 15, William 12, Tabitha 9, Susan 6, Robert 4, Nancy 3, Samuel 3/12
JOHNSTON, Jesse 50*, Mary 43, Alington 22, James 16, Jesse 14, William 12, Hugh 10, John 8, Francis M. 6, Doctor W. W. 5, Mary 2
ROBERTSON, Martha 14*
ISOM, Nancy 40*, Charles 19, William 18, Joshua 16, Reuben 14, Martin 8, Sidney 5
HAMILTON, Sarah 18*
ADAMS, Charles 26*, Sarah 20, Nancy A. 2, Richard 11/12
BOZE, Jane 14*
HUNTER, Squire 25, Mary 24, Nancy J. 3, James F. 2, William 1

- 57 -

1850 Census Carter County Kentucky

FRALEY, Britain 42, Abigail 37, Sarrah 18, Martha J. 16, Abigail 15, Louisa 12, John T. 4, George W. C. 3, Amanda S. 1?/12
LEWIS, Nathan 62, Juda 61, Andrew 19, Elisha 15
LEWIS, Jeremiah 22, Delila 21, Jonathan 5/12
WAGGONER, Jacob 23, Nancy 22, James H. 2, Jemima 1
WAGGONER, David 27, Elizabeth 24, Isom 5, Mary E. 3, Daniel 1
LEWIS, Samuel 40, Nancy 33, Nancy A. 15, Malinda 13, Sarah A. 12, Nathan? 9, Juda 6, Mary 5, Aaron 2
LEWIS, Charles 43, Elizabeth 44, Mary 22, Jerusha 21, Jesse 19, Stephen 17, John 17, Elizabeth 15, James 13, Allen 11, Hannah 9, Gideon 5, Charles 3

Schedule Page 283

BEAR, Richard 37, Martha 36, Henry 16, Avery 14, John 13, Minerva A. 11, Abigail J. 9, Rufus H. 7, Mary 4, Huston 1
OLVER, Daniel 35, Martha 20
LEWIS, Andrew 28, Hannah 23
BARE, Peter 48, Christina 47, Elias 17, Rebecca 14, Martha V. 12, Sarah 9, Derinah 8, Susan 6, Phebe 4, Mary J. 1
BEAR, George 50*, Sarah 50
LEWIS, Winney 13*
BRANHAM, Jonathan 45, Mary 42, Martha 18, Judy 17, Richard 13, Nancy 11, Mary 9, Paulina 2
BEAR, Elias 26, Rachel 23, Sarah S. 1
BEAR, Henry 65*, Dorina 65, Sarah A. K. 21, Phebe R. 18
BEAR, Reuben C. 22*
JASPER, David 1*
CASSIDA, Enoch 21
BEAR, Ambrose J. 29, Mahala 26, Francis M. 5, George W. 4, Matilda B. 7/12, Mary 15
SCAGS, David 32, Martha 24, Walter 7, Mahaly F. 2, Solomon 1
MIDDLETON, James 26, Darcas 26, John 5, Isaac 3, Luraney 11/12, Luraney 64
HOLBROOK, Robert 22, Frances 23, Wm. B. 1, John 20
KELLY, John 19, Nancy 20
GRIFFITH, Abel 35, Ailsey 38, Wm. P. 18, Zilphy 13, Elizabeth 11, John 9, Cintha 7, Abel 5, George W. 4, David 2, Rees 8/12

Schedule Page 284

HORTON, Rees D. 34, Susan 23, Martha E. 9, Elizabeth 8, James P. 6, Wm. L. 4, Flanry 11/12
KING, Elias 45*, Isabel 43, Sabery 18, Francis M. 16, Elkana 14, Houston 12, Vanburen 9, Sarah 6, Jasper 4, Calous R. 1 (f)
HORTON, Louretta 2*
HORTON, Travis 32*, Rebecca 25, Elijah 8, John 6, Letitia 4
FRALEY, Andrew 27*
HORTON, John 28, Elizabeth 23, Francis H. 7/12, Rebecca 70
SAMMONS, Lewis 49, Elizabeth 71
VINCENT, John 64, Sarah 42, John M. 22, Christopher H. 20, Delila A. 16, James A. 14, Henry W. 11, Francis M. 9, Michael A. 7, Lewis S. 5, Emly A. 3, Thomas C. 4/12

1850 Census Carter County Kentucky

WALKER, John 41, Olevi 40, Sarah J. 18, William 15, Alfred 13, Rachel 11, Jacob 9, Hamilton 7, Robert 4, Amos 3, Eli 1
ARMSTRONG, John 40, Lucinda 29, Eliza J. 12, Mary E. 10, William H. 8, Nancy V. 6, Martha A. 3, Amanda G. 1, James H. 19
WILLIAMS, Eli 25, Lucinda 19, Alvin 1, Bazzel 19
WILLIAMS, Thomas 30, Jane 25, Shadrick 6, Mary 4, Telitha 2, Nathan 1/12
MULLENS, Larkin 18, Aurena J. 18
MULLENS, Pleasant 49
MILLER, Robert 66*, Elizabeth 70, John 24, Judy 17

Schedule Page 285

EVANS, Zerelda 10*
MILLER, Adison 26, Anna 20, Arestus 4, Allen 2, Albert 1/12
BALEY, Henry 23, Angeline 21, Margaret 2, Elizabeth 1
SAVAGE, John 29, Mary 27, Nancy A. 5, Chrisley 4, John E. 4, Rebecca E. 1, William 2/12
FRALEY, William 23*, Clary E. 17, James H. 4/12
BALL, Mary A. S. 6*
THOMSON, Thos. T. 43*, Julia A. 25, Martha 9, William 7, Elizabeth 70, Harris W. 45
SAVAGE, John 44*, Nancy A. 21, Thomson 19, Samuel 11
FRALEY, Jesse 50, Barbary 51, James 20, Elziabeth 18, Mary M. 17, DAniel 13, Christina 12, Stephen 7, Sidney 5, John 2
HALL, Elkana 25, Elizabeth 18
STURGIL, David 25, Margaret 25, WAshington 6
MULLINS, John 52, Mary 52, Samson 18, Jemmima 13, Enoch 19
SMITH, Abraham 31, Sarah 25, John H. 7, James E. 3, Wiley L. 1, Frances 62
FRALEY, Wm. B. 25, Sidney J. 25, Unis E. 4, Emanuel R. 3, Augustus M. 1, Ellen B. 1/12
ONEY, Martha 23, Hannah 51, William W. 7, Richard H. 4
FRALEY, Julia A. 52, Christina E. 19, Cloe Jane 18, Wm. W. 15
SPARKS, Solomon 30, Nancy 29, Peter 11, Ananias 8, Nancy 5, Jesse 2
PRINCE, Mary 78
SPARKS, Jesse 53, Nancy 49, Rebecca 19, Eli 13, Eda 13, Sarah J. 10, Thomas 23

Schedule Page 286

SPARKS, John 24, Lucinda 26, Thomas 2, Jesse 1
ELLIOTT, John L. 55, Jane 55, Leonidas H. 32, Ephraim B. 21, Wm. R. 19, Benj. F. 16, Henry W. 16, Ephraim B. 76, Jas. W. S. 35, Rebecca J. 5, John L. 3
RICHARD, Jeremiah P. 32*, Amanda S. 26, Janie M. 7, Rebecca S. 4, John W. 2, Zerelda E. 1
COX, John 16*
TABER, Alfred 30*, Tolitha 30

- 59 -

Page 60 Blank

1850 Census Floyd County Kentucky

Schedule Page 407

STEEL, Daniel 59*, Samuel P. 22, John 19, Amanda 18, Catharine 17, Mary E. 15, Daniel W. 13
HALE, James 11* (B)
OSBORN, Jemima 40*, Charles 12, Nancy 10, William 7
FRIEND, Nancy 75*
CASEBOTT, Nancy 52, Henry 25, Mary 20, James 14
REYNOLDS, Michael 31*, Mary 22
BANKS, Nimrod 18*, male child 8/12
LEWIS, Thomas 39, Sophia 39, William 18, Katharine 16, Aremartha 14, Thomas J. 9, Benj. 7, James K. 5
GALLOWAY, John 51, Katharine 42, Sarah 17, Peggy 14, John 9, Joseph 6, Katharine 4
LEWIS, Squire 44, Katharine 25, Rachael 11, Samuel 9, William 6, Elizabeth 4, Jarrard 1
CRUM, John jr. 35, Hannah 25, Wilson 7, Henry 6, Elijah 4, Mary 6/12, Marcus 12
JOHNSON, Jacob 65, Elizabeth 55, Gordon 30, Elizabeth 24, Martha 16, Gabriel 21
JOHNSON, Jacob jr. 28, Elizabeth 23, _____ __ (f)
GARRETT, Jane 55, Caroline 25, James M. 23, Barton 21, Emily 20, Elizabeth 19
EARLS, John 30, Milly 35, Sarah 14, David __, John 5, James 3
LAYNE, Nancy 55, George 24, Zerilda 22, Lindsey 16
HUNT, William 50, Sarah 50, Elizabeth 23, Levisa 22, Levina 18, Sarah A. 16, Mary 13, Lucinda 9

Schedule Page 408

GARRETT, Sarah 83*
MCGUIRE, Elizabeth 48*, Louisa 24, Garrett 21
SALMONS, Weeks 34, Arreta 22, Daniel Webster 4, Martha A. 1
LAYNE, Elizabeth L. 41*, James 18, Richard P. 16, Mary M. 14, John H. 12, Samuel G. 10
HERRON, William 27*
LAYNE, Elizabeth M. 40, Louisa 17, Emily 15, Mary 14, James T. 13, Elizabeth J. 10
GARRETT, Rebecca 39, John W. 23, Jesse 20, Middleton 16, Selina 13, Julaan 11, Saml. P. 9, Lucy 7
SELLARDS, Susannah 55, Jarard S. 21, Arrilla 16
STRATTON, Harvey G. 26, Phoebe 19, Louisa 1, Coustina 2/12
STRATTON, Henry 76, Anna 56, Harvy 43
POWELL, John W. 34*, Thirza 32, Polly M. 15, Caroline 14, Juliann 6, James H. 4, George J. 1
WORSHAM, Thomas 24*, Elizabeth 17
BOYD, James 34, Mary 32, Henry 14, Lucinda 13, Jane 10, Susan 6, Caroline 5, Elizabeth 3, Margaret 2, Polly M. 1
EARLS, Jesse 45, Mary 40, David 17, Susan 15, Elizabeth 13, Arretty 11, John 9, William 7, Jesse jr. 5, James 3, Daniel 1
STRATTON, Solomon 52, Jane 46, John 22, Lindsey 18, Solomon jr. 14, Samuel 9, Allen M. 4
STRATTON, Tandy 52, Mahala 42, Hezekiah 23, Mary 21, Margaret J. 18, Hiram W. 16, Lucinda 14, Lorena L. 12, Araminta 9, Amanda 5

1850 Census Floyd County Kentucky

Schedule Page 409

STRATTON, James W. 31, Nancy 30, Vincent 7, Caldwell 1
STRATTON, John J. 32*, Katharine 23, Rhoda 1, Polly 53
BROWN, William 26*
LAYNE, James S. 69*, Katharine 69, Araminta 10
SMITH, William 27*
LAYNE, Lindsey 38*, Adaline 37, John L. 18, James C. 15, Moses S. 12, William H. 9, Tandy M. 6, Samuel T.? 4, Cyrus J. 1
SMITH, Pernina 20*
HOWELL, Thomas 59*, Elizabeth 58, Stephen 19, Emeline 16
SALSBERRY, Sarah 7*
BOOTH, Harris 24, Charloote 22, James K. 4, G. W. 2 (m)
YATES, Luke 24, Ida 20, John 2
HERRON, James 50*, Hannah 55
REYNOLDS, Susannah 25*
FLANNERY, John 40, Arty 37, James 14, Minta 12, Sarah 9, William 7, Rosa 5, John 4, Leo 5/12
KEATH, William 41, Ann 32, Letitia 13, Thirza A. 9, English 7, A. H.? Rany 4, Lucy J. 3, Columbus 11/12
WILLIAMS, Isaac 30, Mary 28, Fanny J. 6, Nancy A. 4, Elizabeth 1
MEAD, Moses 63*, Polly 56, Hannah 13, Rhodes 22, Emmah 20, John L. 9/12
RICE, William 25*, Elizabeth 24, Phoebe 1
MAYRES, Thomas 26, Mary 24, Napoleon 6, Seripta 5, Lorenzo 2, Daniel 1
CECIL, James 36, Mary 34, Cynthia 9, Katharine 7, Andrew? 6, William W. 2, James 2/12

Schedule Page 410

HATCHER, Anthony W. 26*, Nancy J. 18, Nancy 67
ALLY, Jonathan 26*
BRANHAM, Isom 57, Lucy 50, Luanna 30, Saml. H. 16, Lucinda 12, Isom H. 8, Milly L. 7, Geo. W. 5, Mary J. 4, Martha A. 2, Wm. A. 8/12
HADEN, Thomas 65*, Elizabeth 50, Joseph 25, Moses 18, Barbary 15, Jilla 11, Wm. 8
PRICE, Rebecca 33*
HATCHER, James G. 45*, Christiana 40, A. J. P. 18 (m), John L. 16, Elinor L. 14, James H. 12, Kenas? 9 (m), Geo. M. 7, Ferdinand C. 2
HUNTER, David M. 19*
CLARK, Lorenzo Dow 43*, Patience 30, Morgan 15, Samuel 12, Serena 10, Malinda 8, Robert 6, James 4, Kenias 1 (m)
WILLIAMS, Katharine 60*
MARSHALL, William 13*
LYNCH, William 33*, Meriba 21, Elizabeth 5, Nancy J. 8/12
GUNNELLS, Jane 74*
KIDD, George 36, Frances 23, William 12, Patience 9, James 6, Elias 5, Serena 10/12
GUNELLS, Austin 47*, Lucy 37, James M. 14, Ahirale? 12 (m), Louisa T. 10, Lucy J. 8, Geo. W. 5, Austin G. 2, Katharine E. 3/12
MARSHALL, John 16*

1850 Census Floyd County Kentucky

LEWIS, Geo. W. 42, Frances 48, Lucy A. 19, Mahala 17, Sarah 15, James M. 10, Louisa 3
WILLIAMS, John 51*, Eveline 30, Rebecca 13, Emily B. 11, Amanada 8, John K. 67, Harris 3

Schedule Page 411

YATES, Eluster 18*, Thirza 31
YATES, Susannah 50, Jackson 20, Franklin 14
WILLIAMS, Jackson W. 21, Lucy A. 19
JESSE, John 45, Mary 35, William P. 17, David 13, Isaac 10, Rebecca 8, Mary A. 6, Rhoda 1
WILLIAMS, Abraham 28, Mary 25, Margaret 2, Isaac 3/12
WILLIAMS, James 22*, Margaret 23, Alexander 5, Saml. P. 2
MEAD, Ann 30*
JOHNSON, Ruth 47, Sarah 19, Campbell 16, Jackson 14, Letta 12, Abigail 10, Parallee 8, William 21, Mahala 11
MEAD, William 30, Elizabeth 26, Rosana 6, Sittrany? 3 (f)
MEAD, Abraham 22, Jane 24
OWENS, Berry 30, Susan 27, Elizabeth 10, Clarinda 8, Vina 5, Elias 2
HALL, Nimrod 23, Elizabeth 20, Squire 2, Rosanna 7/12
AKERS, Daniel 28, Arta 23, Andrew 6, Margaret 5, Sarah 4, Kin S. 2, James H. 6/12
HALL, Squire 50*, Eleanor 46, Mehulda 18, Wilson 16, Lilburn 15, Jarvy 10, Florinda 7, James M. 6, Preston 3, Messiah J. 7/12
STURGEON, Patsy 40*
BLEVINS, Alexander 5*
FRAZIER, Robert 36, Frances 33, John 16, Cyrus 15, Caroline 13, Ansa 12, Nancy 10, Elizabeth 8, William 6, Rotiman? 5 (m), Margarett 3, Malinda 10/12

Schedule Page 412

HAMILTON, Jesse 49, Penina 38, Thomas 20, Lurana 17, Russell 15, Craig 13, Freeman 11, Dulany 9, Hogan 7, Seltana 5, McDonald 3, Lydia 1, Mary 9/12?
HAMILTON, William 38*, Elizabeth 29, John 13, Sarah A. 10, Araminta 8, Martha 5, Frances 3
FRAZIER, Nancy 60*
MCKINNY, Peter 47, Nancy 37, Mary 17, Robert 16, James 14, Jane 12, Milton 10, Emily 8, Elijah 2
AKERS, David 49, Elizabeth 43, Joseph 19, Andrew 17, Caleb 15, Loenna? 13, Sarah 11, John B. 8, Elijah 6, Nelson 2
BALDWIN, Solomon 40*, Sarah 39, Alexander 15, John W. 14, Rebecca 11, Elijah 8, Jarvy 6, Matilda 4, Martha 2, Sarah E. 1
AKERS, Valentine 23*, Hannah 26, Mahala 3
HALL, Elijah 42, Margaret 38, Arminda 14, Elizabeth 12, Greenberry 9, Sylvester 9, Darcus 7, Mary 4, Robert J. 1
AKERS, Levi 25, Nancy 17, Mary J. 8/12
HALL, Jarvy 46*, Elizabeth 38, Owen 17, John 16, Una 13, Olly 11 (f), Wilson 8, William 5, Wilburn 2
HICKMAN, Pleasant 12*
HAMILTON, Preston 23, Matilda 18, Kinas F. 3, Wilburn 2, Martha E. 10/12
HAMILTON, Thomas 50, Jemima 28, Mary 11, Leonard 9, Katharine 7, Nancy 5, Preston 4, Letta 2

1850 Census Floyd County Kentucky

Schedule Page 413

BLANKENSHIP, Wm. 60, Spica 36, Anna 19, Candaca 17, Prica 16, Milly 13, Mitchell 17, Wm. 9, Vina 6, Lucinda 5, Elizabeth 3, Spencer 1/12
JONES, John 40, Phoebe 24, Nathaniel 20, James 19, Claiborne 18, Ambrose 14, Lemuel 12, Wm. 11, Tandy 10, Alina 8, Francis 3, Martha 2, Nathaniel sr. 79, Nancy 75
CARTER, Joseph 40, Sarah 36, Nancy 18, Matilda 14, John 12, Charly W. 9, William 6
ELLIOTT, Robert 23, Elizabeth 43, Phena 18
ELLIOTT, John 30, Sarah 29, Emily 13, Susanna 11, Elizabeth 9, William 7, Isaac 6, Mary 4, Harvy 1
AKERS, Stephen 24, Sarah 18, Arminda 1
HAMILTON, Samuel 50, Jane 35, William 21, Hannah 19, Jesse 17, Margaret 15, John 13, Sarah A. 11, Saml. 9, Allen 6, Harvy 4, Stephen 2
HALL, Robert 24, Nancy 21, Louisa 3, Martha J. 2, Andrew J. 7/12
NEWSOM, Henry 26, Unica 29, Rebecca 20, Harman 7, Lucinda 6, Letta 5, John T. 3, James H. 1

Schedule Page 414

HALL, Jesse 55, Nancy 46, Morgan 20, Amanda 16, Margaret 13, Charlotte 10, Christena 8, Colbert 7, Mahala 5, Sittana 2
HALL, James 25, Mary 24, Hiram 3, William 2, Rachael 10/12
ALLY, Elisha 23, Mary 24, Martha 3
HALL, Henderson 22, Amy 20
STURGEON, Eli 46, Delinda 23, John 22, Leroy 19, Miles 17, Elizabeth 15, Emanuel J. 12, Joseph C. 3, Martha J. 2
STURGEON, Blackburn 24*, Lucinda 20, Priscilla 4, John R. 2
CLAY, Jane 45*, Victoria 5
SLOAN, Harvy 25, Catharine 24, Luanna 7, Elizabeth 2
SOUTHARD, Sarah 50, Hiram 18
AKERS, Tolbert 50, Mary 39, Hiram 22, Jacob 16, Nancy 14, Nimrod 13, Eleanor 11, Susannah 9, Elijah 6, Mary 4, Tolbert 2
HALL, David 22, Nancy 20, Jasper 2
HALL, Rodden 66, Mary 64, Preston 19, Miles 16, John 12, Lemuel 9, Jackson 5, William 2, Anna 26
TACKETT, Taply 23, Elizabeth 20, Kedene 3 (f), Stinson 2, Greenberry 1
DEEL, Thomas 90, Elizabeth 37, Campbell 17, Granville 15, Tolbert 4
MCKINNEY, Elijah 36, Agga 31, Wm. H. 11, Jackson 8, Nancy 5, Luana 3, Peter 1

Schedule Page 415

HOWELL, Henderson 32*, Elizabeth 28
JOHNSON, Zachariah 60*
WATSON, Abraham 32, Agga 34, Elizabeth 15, Jonathan 12, Sarah 10, Rosemin 9, John 7, Arissa 3, Mary 2/12
HOWELL, David 37*, Mary 37, Elizabeth 13, Nimrod J. 12, Sarah M. 9, John G. 7, Millissa 4
ALLY, William 60*
ALLY, Turner 32, Rebecca 22, Eveline 9, David 4
BRANHAM, Turner 90*

1850 Census Floyd County Kentucky

ALLY, Usly 50 (f)*, Judah 15 (f)
BRANHAM, Elisha 46*, Rhoda 44, Solomon 23, Hiram 24, John 20, David 16, Jonathan 11, Abigail 13, Judah 7 (f), Mary 19
HOWELL, John 28*, Jane 27
STURGEON, Dicy 34*, America 4, Tamsa? 2 (f)
STURGEON, Lewis 33, Hulda 20, James 1
SALSBERRY, Lucky 33, Margaret 22, Thomas 6, Munrah? 1 (f)
AKERS, Jonathan 35, Sarah 32, Marion 6, Matilda 5, Elizabeth 4, Emily J. 3, Thomas W. 1, Nancy 1
HOWELL, Jesse 22, Elizabeth 22
JUSTICE, Amos 50, Sarah 45, William 18, Nancy J. 14, John 12, Joseph 10, Jonathan 8, Gracy 4
BRANHAM, Turner jr. 21, Katharine 20
MEAD, Robert 54, Susan 40, Samuel 19, Mehulda 16, Leanah 14, John R. 12, Robert A. 10, Rhody 8, James K. 6, Joseph 4, Richard 2, James 12
MARSHALL, Hugh 49, Mary 44, Thomas 20, Mary 19, John 18, Nancy 10, Huey 9, Hiram 8, Elizabeth 7, Mehulda 6

Schedule Page 416

JARRELL, Thomas 52, Sarah 37, Morgan 18, Lewis 11, Mary 9, Esther 7, Louisa 5, Sarah 3
YATES, James 40, Elizabeth 36, Esther 14, Jackson 12, Alexander 10, John 7, Charlotte 4, Barney 2
WATSON, Jonathan 45, Elizabeth 30, Alexander 21, Henry 18, Arminda 16, Mary J. 12, Lorenzo Dow 10, Wm. J. 6, Rachael 5, Geo. W. 4, Katharine 3, Carroll 1
SPEARS, William 30, Rosanna 29, Charlotte 8, Rebecca 6, Andrew 4, James M. 1
WOODS, Delila 30*, Alexander 14, Mary J. 12, Nancy A. 10, Henry M. 8, John W. 6, Susan C. 4, Wm. J. 2
BOYD, William 70*, Nancy 80
WOODS, Alexander 40, Susan 41, James 15, Mary 13, Nathan 11, Nancy 9, Lucinda 8, Sarah 6, Elizabeth 5, Emeline 4
CECIL, Thomas 60, Jane 60, Katharine 33, Margaret 30, Sarah A. 27, Susan E. 24, Elizabeth 21, Zachariah 18
BOYD, John 32*, Nancy 31, William 14, Madison 10, Harvy 7, John 5, Julia A. 4, Andrew 3, Barton 1
WOODS, Fanny 20*, Louisa 1
CECIL, William 37*, Lucy 36, Alexander 13

Schedule Page 417

JARRELL, Hiram 19*
JARRELL, Elizabeth 38, Mary J. 14, Parks 10
JARRELL, Lucy 38, Frances 18, Nancy 16, Henry C. 15, Elizabeth 12
DILLION, George 21, Dianna 18, Ruel? 6/12 (m), Rosanna 40, Mary 17, Katharine 15, Susan 13
JARRELL, Ruel 44, Nancy 50, Alexander 18, Martin 15, Sarah 80
CONN, Ira 25, Eleanor 30, Jesse 11, Wm. J. 9, John 5, Sylvester 4, Hiram 2, Andrew 9/12
CONN, William 23, Sarah 22, Mary C. 2, Rosanna 5/12
CRUM, Susan 31, Elizabeth 11, Sylvester 3, Adam 8/12
CRUM, Michael 56, Vastia 56, Mary 22, Michael 17
EARLS, James 28, Sarah 20, Meoma 3, Harrison 1
CRUM, Henry 33, Katharine 28, Mary E. 8, Minerva 4, Henry W. 3

- 65 -

1850 Census Floyd County Kentucky

WEBB, Jonathan 42, Elizabeth 42, William 22, Jonathan 20, James W. 14, Susan 13, Margaret 12, Judah 10 (f), Wallis 6, Zachariah T. 3
CECIL, Harvy 31, Mary J. 27, Julia 7, Minerva 4, Sevega 2
NESBITT, John 40*, Sophia 36, Wm. H. 4, Tandy M. 2, Sarah R. 3/12
LAYNE, Martha A. 16*, Thomas G. 15, James 13, John W. 11
MORGAN, David 45, Nelly 40, Thomas 20, Rebecca 18, Eleanor 16, David jr. 14, Wm. 12, Dorothy 8, James H. P. 6, John G. 3

Schedule Page 418

CRUM, William 24*, Amanda 20, James W. 1, Elizabeth 3/12
ROBINSON, Susan 40*, Andrew H. 18
MAYO, Lewis P. 25*, Ann 22, Jane 2, Mary E. 1/12, Jane 16, Jacob 8
WILLIAMSON, William 23*
HUBBARD, Solomon 50*, Mary A. 41, Mary A. 13
PARKER, Mary A. 19*
BARNARD, Joshua 80, Mary A. 38, Julia A. 20, Ira 15, Washington 14, Ross 12, David 9, Jonathan 8, Lydia 7, Sarah 6, Caroline S. 5, Solomon 3
BARNETT, Notty 58, Elizabeth 37, James 22, Oliver 20, Mary 17, Hicks 16, William 14, Hiram 12, Samuel 10, Sarah 7
FERGUSON, Malachi 45*, Nancy 41, Louisa 21, Telitha 18, Jane 16, Sarah A. 14, Isabella 11, Thomas 6
LEEDS, Benjamin 19*
MOORE, Andrew 24*
HALE, Franklin 26, Elizabeth 27, Rhoda 2
BURCHETT, Armstead 55, Elizabeth 50, James 27, Morgan 19, Edward 16, Drury 14, Thomas 12
MORRIS, Daniel 37, Nancy 35, Mary E. 13, Levina 11, Katharine 8, Elizabeth 4, John J. 2, Martha 4/12
HUTTON, James G. 38*, Elizabeth 33, William 13, Jane 11, Mary E. 7, James 3, Mary A. 13
SHEETS?, John 43*
HARRIS, John B. 39*, Tabitha 38, Andrew J. 14, Edwin 13, William J. 11, Thomas M. 9, James P. 6, John Q. 2, California 8/12

Schedule Page 419

BLEDSOE, Sampson W. 26*
GOBBLE, William 30, Martha 28, Nancy J. 9, Eliza A. 8, James 6, Martha 4, Geo. W. 2, William 3/12
GOBBLE, Elijah 28*, Rebecca 27, Nancy J. 7, Adam 5, Elizabeth 3, Isaac 1
HARMAN, Rachael 24*
MITCHELL, Wiley 18*
HARMAN, Adam 49, Rhoda 47, Rosanna 21, Daniel 19, Anderson 17, Margaret 15, Susanna 12, Lydia 11, Wm. F. 7
SKEAN, Wm. 30, Nancy 26, Rhoda K. 2, Adam H. 7/12
HERRELL, James 40*, Elizabeth 47, John W. 16, Elizabeth 14, Harvy 12, Wm. 10, Theadosia 6, Adam 2
WOODS, Elizabeth 86*
KINDRICK, David 29, Sophia 18, James W. 6/12
MITCHELL, Stephen 50, Anna 46, Mary A. 16, Malinda 14, Sarah 12, Wm. 10, John 8, Thomas 6

1850 Census Floyd County Kentucky

BURCHETT, Drury 60, Elizabeth 61, Drury jr. 21, Araminta 18, Alifer? 17 (f), Martha L. 14
JERVIS, James L. 28, Evelina 27, Drury 4, Elizabeth 2
BOYD, William 49, Jane 36, Malinda 18, Mel 15, Levi 13, Louisa 11, Manderville 10, Mary Ann 5, William 3, Rebecca 1
GEARHART, Adam jr. 26*, Sarah 28, Wm. L. 3, Richard 6/12
WADE, Peter 30*, Agnes 24
FITZPATRICK, Tho. S. 41, Nancy 32, Jefferson 13, John W. 11, James M. 9, Willis 7, Daniel 3, Archibald 1

Schedule Page 420

MCGUIRE, Samuel 35, Emily 25, Susan 11, David 10, Prissa 9, William 5, Mary 8/12
BANKS, Samuel 31, Nancy 25, Wm. F. 3, James A. 1
BANKS, David sr. 65, Jane 55, Elizabeth 33
DILLION, James 47, Nancy 46, Rebecca 20, Margaret 17, Arminta 15, James 11, Henry 7
LEWIS, Thomas sr. 80, Delila 38, Matilda 20, Martha 19, Mary 14, Benj. 12, Solomon 9, Columbus 6, Jane 3
HALE, Smith 32*, Elizabeth 28, John 13, Jarutha 11, Sarah 9, Nancy 7, Samuel 5, James 4, William 4/12?
TAYLOR, Isaac B. 31*
MCGUIRE, Isaac 38, Delila 25, William 13, John 11, Richard 9, Obadiah 7, Jackson 5, Meranda 3
SLUSHER, Philip 42, Mary 40, Rily 19, John 17, Gordon 15, David 12, Jarvy 9, Wm. 7, Minerva J. 3
JARRELL, Carrel 64, Mary 66, Rachael 24, Carrell 20, George 30
SALMONS, Thomas 48, Susanna 21, Elizabeth 19, John C. 16, Nancy 13, Weeks 12, James H. 10, Minerva 9, Cynthia 8, Anna 8, Thomas 6, Hezekiah 5, Solomon 3
CRISP, Joel 49, Elizabeth 43, Abel 21, Bailey 18, Peletha 16, Susanna 14, Dyer 11, Jones 8, Malinda 6, Sarah 4, Jasper 2

Schedule Page 421

SPRADLIN, Abraham 50, Sarah 45, Wm. 19, Henry 16, Anna 14, Nehemiah 10, Katharine 8, Abraham jr. 6, Benj. 4, Samuel 3
HUNT, James 26, Martha 23, William 6, Elizabeth 4, Thomas 2
HAYWOOD, Lewis 56, Elizabeth 48, Elizabeth 21, William 19, George B. 17, Samuel 15, Robert 14, Hiram 11, James 9, Anna 7, Jane 2
FORTNER, John 44, Rachael 36
SELLARDS, Thomas A. 42, Mary 35, James W. 15, Clarinda 11, John 8, Delinda 5, Samuel 3
CLAY, Matthew 34, Elizabeth 33, Fleming 15, Susanna 12, Katharine 10, Solomon 6, Elizabeth 4, Margaret 2
SCARF, Jeremiah 27, Sarah 26, Britain 5, Cynthia 3, Wm. 1
MANION, Joseph 26*, Elizabeth 32, Elijah 11/12
CLAY, Solomon 80*
JOHNS, Thomas P. 33, Elizabeth 31, John 10, Rebecca 7, Julia A. 4, Elizabeth jr. 1
ALLEN, John 42, Suda 22, Adam 16, George 14, John 13, William 11, Joseph 9, Sarah 7, David 6, Allen 4, Katharine 3
HALE, John 25, Katharine 30, Mary 10, Malinda 7, Martha 5, Claborn 3

1850 Census Floyd County Kentucky

Schedule Page 422

HALE, Sarah 61, Claiborn 24, Thomas 20
ROBINSON, William 45, Mary 37, Jefferson 18, Harrison 13, Wm. T. 9, Patrick 6, Rebecca 6/12
CRUM, John 51, Mary 42, Charlotte 22, John 21, Jacob 19, Samuel 16, Mary A. 13, Isaac 11, Rebecca 9, Riley 8, Susan 6, Amanda 4, Henford 2
CLARK, John W. 30*, Rebecca 26, James W. 7, Wilson M. 5, Mary A. 4, Minta J. 3
MAYO, John W. 18*, Jane 17
CLICK, James 50, Jane 45, Frances 22, Carter 20, James B. 18, John W. 15, Weeks 13, Susan 12, Lucinda 10, Nancy C. 7, Daniel N. 1
CLICK, Alexander 24, Martha 22, Lindsey 2, Wm. J. 6/12
SALMONS, Carter 38, Cynthia 30, William 9, Sylvester 6, Martha 4, Alexander 2, Frances 82
OSBORNE, Albert 31, Mary 30, James T. 9, Drury J. 7, Albert 6, Elizabeth 3, Arminta 1
OSBORNE, Thomas 51, Nancy 45, Arta 18, Jones 12, Wm. T. 10, Nancy 7, Martha S. 1
OWSLEY, Shadrick 50, Margaret 45, Elizabeth 22, John 20, Peter 19, Mary A. 17, Colly 16, James T. 14, Hagel? 12, Edward 2, Lurinda 2
JARRELL, Aulse? 25 (m)*, Mary 63
CRUM, Matta 30 (f)*
FRAZIER, Wm. B. 47, Susan 37, Nancy 18, Elizabeth 16, Rhoda 14, Caroline 12, Geo. M. 11, Wm. T. 7, Sarah 4, Susannah 4

Schedule Page 423

CRISP, William 25, Mary 22, Francis M. 5, Alexander 3, William J. 1
OWSLEY, Benjamin 25, Jemimah 24, Sarah 11, John 10, Nancy 6, William 3, Robert 2, Edwqard 2
CRISP, William sr. 53, Milly 40, Minerva 18, Angelina 16, Abraham S. 13, Joel 10, Sarah 8, Alvina 5, Lucinda 3
OSBORNE, Edward L. 45, Rhoda 43, Eleanor 19, Kips B. 18, David 17, Susannah 14, Sarah 11, Thomas 9, Samuel 6, Edward 5, Fanny 3?, John 6/12?
OWENS, Squire 24, Mary A. 23, John H. 4/12
EVANS, Jonathan 40, Allis 25, William 12, Jane? 8, John 6, Arta 4, Morgan 2
HOLBERT, William 28, Lucinda 20, Rebecca 3, Frances 7
HUNTER, William 48, Mariah 43, James 20, Washington 16, Elizabeth 14, John 11, Sarah A. 8, William 5, Joseph 1
MULLINS, Booker 55, Mary 54, Rutha 21, Rhoda 19, Mary A. 17, Robert 15, Matilda 13, Andy 10
KENNEDY, Elijah 40, Elizabeth 17, Meonia 12, Martha 10, Andrew J. 5, Elijah G. 1
HOLBERT, John sr. 60*, Elizabeth F. 46, John 21, Martha 19, Sarah B. 16, Rhoda V. 11, Victoria J. 9, Levinia 7, Elizabeth F. 5

Schedule Page 424

JOHNSON, Peter 31*, Susan 29, Frances 6, William J. 3, Martha J. 2
BALDRIDGE, John 28, Levisa 24, William 8, Andrew 6, Elizabeth 4, Sarah J. 1
SPURLOCK, Martha 54*, Elizabeth 23, Keziah F. 18
MORGAN, Arta 33*
PENDLETON, James 40, Fanny 33, Sarah A. 15, Patience 13, Cosby 11, James K. 7

1850 Census Floyd County Kentucky

MULLINS, William 28, Sarah 30, Mary 9, Nancy 7, John 3, Tandy 5/12
FLANNERY, Isaac 40, Caroline 29, John L. 13, Nancy 9, Arta 7, Mary 5, Tandy 1
SALSBERRY, Morgan 28, Rhoda 16, Morgan 1
SALSBERRY, William 65, Elizabeth 57, Anna 18, Sarah A. 15, Robert 22, Jane 20
SALSBERRY, Hiram 47*, Nancy 45, Greenville 14
GULLETT, Francis 13*
MARTIN, Job 40, Jenning 28, Mary A. 14, Sarah 13, Elizabeth 11, William 9, Fanny 7, David 4, Tandy 2
TURNER, Burris? 25, Nancy 60, Morgan 18, Irza? 16 (m), William 30
MARTIN, Simpson 30, Elizabeth 35, Judah 9 (f), James 8, John 7, Milly 3
MARTIN, Joel D. 32, Judah 27 (f), Allen 7, David 5, Alamander 4 (m), Frederick 2, Elizabeth 8/12
TURNER, Adam 38, Margaret 28, Wm. J. 9, Elizabeth 7, Nancy 6, John 5, Sarah 4, Samuel 3, Judah 2 (f)

Schedule Page 425

SIZEMORE, Lewis 50*, Katharine 49, Sarah 28, Rhoda 24, Elizabeth 20, Frances J. 17, William 15, John 12, Richard 10
TURNER, Alexander 23*
GEARHART, Peter 22*
SALSBERRY, Greenville 24, Buddy 4, Morgan 1
COLLINS, Simpson 33, Elizabeth 20
DYKES, Isom 50, Nancy 44, Lewis 19, Lindsey 17, Katharine 14, Milly 9, Rhoda 6, Sarah 1, James 21
BURNETT, William 88, John B. 50, Hanna 48, Adam 46, Hood 14
STRUMBO, Frederick 40, Nancy 40, William 21, John 19, Elizabeth 17, Christiana 15, Samuel D. 14, Judah 12 (f), Nancy 10, Alexander 8, Greenville 7, Sarah 6, Fanny 5, Joel M. 1
JUSTICE, Jonathan 54, Hannah 52, Katharine 18, Jackson 26, Darcus 23, Mary 5/12
JUSTICE, James 29, Keesa 26, Wm. R. 7, Thomas 5, Cambridge 3, Saml G. 1
HALL, Owen 30, Cynthia 29, Spica 10, Alexander 5, Owen 3, Nancy 1
BROWN, Lewis 40, Lydia 35, Minerva 15, Marion 8, Phena 6, Uriah 4, Jasper N. 3, John 2, Jeffry 2/12?
HALL, Cynes 75, Umsiah? 74, Cynes jr. 30, Dicy 29, Vina 3
GEARHART, Daniel 30, Adaline 26, John 9, Jane 7, Richard 6, Lindsey 4

Schedule Page 426

GEARHART, Valentine 40, Sarah 36, Mary 16, John 13, Jonathan 11, George W. 9, Allen 6
DAMEREL, Moses 30, Nancy 30, Right 13, Mary 10, James 7, William 4, Seatha 6/12
SALSBERRY, Elijah 65, Keziah 61, Susannah 19, Harriet 10, Parasade 3
JUSTICE, Izra 57, Ailsa 50, Turner 16, Ceatta 15, Christiana 13, Katherine 10, Right 5, Allen 21
MOORE, John 40 (B), Rachael 38, Sarah 26, Andy 24, George 23, Edmond 22, Eliza 20, Fanny 18, John 16, Mary 14, Rhoda 12, William 11, Calvin 9, Winfield 6/12
MOORE, Andrew 63 (B), Elizabeth 30, Orta 15, Joel 9, Isaac 7, Andrew 5, Eliza J. 1
MOORE, Archibald 27, Sarah 26, William H. 6, Florence 4, Jackson 3, Manford 2
MOORE, Edmond 50, Rhoda 49, Mary 24, Mariah 22, Arminda 20, Jeremiah 16, Rachael 13, Sarah 9
SUTTON, Lewis 23*, Edward 3, John 2
MOORE, Rycene 24 (f)*
MILUM, Edward 33, Elizabeth 40, Susannah 8

1850 Census Floyd County Kentucky

TACKETT, Joshua 33, Elizabeth 23, Margaret 8, Louisa 6, Henry 4, Matilda 3, Rhoda 3/12
JUSTICE, Aulsy 37 (m)*, Leanah 22, Solomon 14, Hannah 12, Mary 10, Jonathan 8, Valentine 6, Jocca 1

Schedule Page 427

TACKETT, Nancy 25*, Ava 55, Rebecca 15
SLONE, Hiram 53, Temperance 50, Wright 24, Hulda 20, John 16, Monroe 15, Cynthia 14, Woodroe 11, Henry T. 8, Mary 100
MEAD, Thomas 46, Mary 44, Rhody 20, Robert 18, Reuben 17, Katharine 15, Rebecca 13, Christiana 10, Riley 9, Madison 7, Albert 5, Mary 3, Rachael 1
SLONE, Marvel 28, Susan 20, Alvira 4, Amanda 4/12
REYNOLDS, Hamilton 40, Malinda 40, William R. 14, Jane 13, Phoebe 10, Lewis 9, Renias? F. 6 (m), Frances 4, James 1
SLONE, Martha 19, Serelda 16, Paris 1
COLLINS, Elizabeth 46?, Mary 33, Elizabeth 30, Susannah 26, James W. 12, William H. 7, Alexander 6
HALL, Riley 44, Jane 42, Riley 15, Lucinda 11, Mary 9, Margaret 7, Matilda 5, Henry 2
MEAD, Thomas jr. 23, Elizabeth 21, Rhodes 1
HALL, Clinton 19, Nancy 18, Jackson 2
HALL, Alfred 24, Temperance 23, Lewis 6, Emeline 4, Jane 2
HAMMOND, Stephen 33, Elizabeth 23, Rhoda 3, Mary 3/12, Rhoda 20
JUSTICE, Izra 45*, Matilda 50, Arty 13, Martin 11, Mahala 9, Sarah 7, Elizabeth 4
KEENE, Margaret 15*, Elizabeth 6

Schedule Page 428

JOHNSON, John 43, Sarah 36, Gilbert 18, Hannah 16, Nancy 13, Elizabeth 12, Mary 10, Joseph 8, Patrick 3, Anna 3/12
JOHNSON, Harvy 33, Oavala 30, Elija? 14, Basha? 12 (m), Caleb 9, Lucinda 6, Mary J. 3, Lydia 9/12
LITTLE, James 27, Mary 18, Henry 1
CAUDELL, Abner 53, Nelly 54, Abner 15
CAUDELL, Abijah 25, Drusilla 26, Ephraim 9, Elizabeth 7, Jackson 5, David 3, Tandy 2
JOHNSON, David 35, Anna 34, Harvy 14, Elisha 12, Susan 10, Sarah 6, David 2
ADAMS, Priscilla 28, Rily 7, Anna 2
CAUDELL, Abijah 33, Elizabeth 27, Preston 13, Harvy 11, Isaac 3, Jarva 1 (m)
ROBERTS, Owen 25, Dylila 24, Eleanor 7, Mary 4, Dicea 3, Nancy 2
JOHNSON, Patrick 79*, Delila 74, Peyton 33, Abisha 10, Joab 6, John 5, Mary 4, Kendrick 3, Meoma 5/12
HAMMONS, Elizabeth 27*
JOHNSON, Abisha 37, Nancy 36, Sarah 19, William 17, Mahala 14, Peyton 11, Lucinda 9, Nancy 7
LITTLE, Isaac 26, Lucinda 22, William 7, Sarah 7, Abner 5, James 3, Oda 6/12
HAMMONS, Joseph 35, Mary 32
INGLE, Thomas 26, Sarah 22, Lucinda 7, Wilson 3, James 1

1850 Census Floyd County Kentucky

Schedule Page 429

MULLINS, William 46, Sarah 49, Rebecca 25, Alexander 22, Elizabeth 20, Mary 18, Ava 17, James 15, Hiram 13, Florinda 10, Merilda 10, Sarah 7
MULLINS, Owens 27, Lydia 25, Elisha 7, Mary 4, Auzy 3 (f)
BURKS, Rolling 23, Rebecca 25, Sarah 5, Anna 3, Barner 1
MULLINS, William sr. 84*, Rutha 70
ESTEP, Joel 19*, Nancy 17
BRYANT, David 46, Vina 31, James 20, Louisa 17, Lita 15, Selina 13, Jacob 11, Nancy 7, John 5, Jane 2
ESTEP, Samuel 47, Susan 37
JOHNSON, Elisha 30, Elizabeth 28, Mary 9, Andrew 7, David 4, William 4/12
CAUDLE, Jesse 35, Nelly 34, Mathews 15, Rebecca 13, Rachael 11, William 9, Matilda 6, Wilson 4, John 2
HALL, David 46, Anna 47, William 27, Lydia 25, Mary 23, Clinton 19, Nelly 17, John 14, Marshall 8, Tarlton 10/12
HALL, William 54, Margaret 57, Susan 26, William J. 24, Ruthy 23, John W. 20, Miles 16, See? 12 (m), John H. 15
HALL, James 29, Emma 23, John W. 9, Uriah 5, Elizabeth 8, William 4, Susan 2

Schedule Page 430

VANCE, John W. 35, Patsy 31, Susan 11, Margaret 9, Authur C. 6, Mary 4, John 3, Rutha 2, Geo. W. 6/12
ISAACS, Samuel 36, Malinda 31, Clinton 11, Furman 9, Jerman 8, Martin 4, Christena 2
KING, Lewis 49*, Eada 36, Tandy 20, Wilson 17, Elizabeth 16, James 13, Margaret 8, Rebecca 5
DAVIS, Asa 22*
FLANNERY, James 75, Rebecca 77, Jerusha 35, Elizabeth 33, Susan 13
DAVIS, Thomas 49*, Fanny 36, Nancy 17, Jackson 14, Thomas 11, Margaret 7
SHORT, Elizabeth 20*, William 3, Nancy 3/12
ISAACS, William 54*, Sarah 60
HAYS, William 27*
HALL, Ausey 27 (f)*, Harrison 4, Sarah 2
TRIPLETT, Wilson 28, Eleanor 34, Merilda 4, Marinda 4, Henderson 9/12
BATES, John 36, Elizabeth 31, Eliza 13, Patsy 12, William 10, Sally 9, Margaret 8, John 6, Elizabeth 5, Robert 4, Washington 1
TRIPLETT, Bryant 27, Latha 21, John 3, Martha 2, Oma 1, William 3/12
TRIPLETT, Daniel 50, Sarah 52, Susannah 16, Nimrod 12
ROBERTS, James 35*, Eliza 12, Henry 9, Nancy 7
HALL, Lydia 40*, Sarah 2, Andrew J. 2/12
BAKER, James 28, Nancy 27, Didamy 12, Sileana 10, Noah 8, Nathaniel 4

Schedule Page 431

TRIPLETT, Lee 36, Rachael 35, Nancy 14, Sarah 10, William 8, Lee 5, Ellen? 3, Lindsey 1
TRIPLETT, Joel 28, Milly 25, Clayton 5
THORNSBERRY, Eleanor 47, Martin 19, Ata 15, Malinda 14, Allis 10, Mahala 19, Susan 4, Eleanor 1

1850 Census Floyd County Kentucky

THORNSBERRY, James 23*, Anna 22, James 3, Isaac 1, Cynthia 18
ADAMS, Allen 21*
MARTIN, Alexander 35, Malinda 38, Nancy 8, Wyatt 6, Simpson 4, Mahala 2
HALL, Samuel 35, Susanna 28, Anthony 12, Martin V. 10, Patsy A. 8, Arta 6, Susan N. 4, Laura 3, Katherine 1
MARTIN, Allen 28, Katharine 20, Mary 5, Martha 2, Christopher 9/12, George 15
JONES, Claborn 45, Milly 43, Florence 21, Florinda 20, Frances J. 17, Elizabeth 14, David 12, Joel 10, William 8, Clariza 4
THORNSBERRY, Geo. 25*, Rebecca 22, Jno. 5, Cynthia 4, Anna 11/12
GIBSON, Joel 15*
GIBSON, Leonard 35, Nancy 34, Winston 14, Miles 12, Hiram 10, Isom 7, John P. 6, Druida? 4, Arenda 2
MARTIN, Wyatt 34, Jane 23, Anna 20, Jemima 18, Tandy 14, Milly 63
KELLY, James 35, Elizabeth 24, Sarah J. 5, Milly? 3, Joseph 1

Schedule Page 432

SLOAN, Alexander 26, Matilda 35, Tandy 12, Spencer 10, Mary J. 9, Martha 8, Judah 7 (f), Amy 5
THONESBERRY, Walter 38, Hanna 37, Matilda 13, Sarah 11, Nancy 5, Geo. 2
SLOAN, Reuben 30, Sarah 29, Mary 13, Isom 12, Rosana 10, Luanah 8, Jasper 6, Newton 5, John P. 4, Henry C. 2
HOFF, William 32, Nancy 27, James A. 7, Margaret 9, Mary 5, John W. 4, William 1
TERRY, Leonard 56, Mary 54, Isom 20, Thomas 18, Nancy 14, Isaac 12, Nathaniel 7
HOFF, John 75
TERRY, William 26, Anna 22, Seatha 2, Rebecca 5/12
SLONE, Isom 56, Seatha 18, Mary 16, Pleasant 14
NOLEN, Stephen 22, Levisa 21, Leonard 3, Levina 1
SLONE, Shade 62*, Katharine 60
TIRA?, Judah 18 (f)*
HARRIS, Susannah 38*, Luana 17, William H. 15, Katharine 13, Mary J. 9, Benj. F. 6, Joseph J. 4, Lindsey 1
SLONE, James 36, Milly 35, Jacob 14, Headrick 13, George W. 10, Nathan 8, David 5, Rebecca 2
OWENS, Reese 50, Mary 49, Mahala 22, Jane 20, Vincent 14, Sarah 11, Nancy 9, Aloa? 4 (m)
HALE, James 45, Christena 35, Matilda 13, Wiley 10 (f), William 9, Martha 4, John 3, James 1

Schedule Page 433

TRIPLETT, Linville 35, Levisa 37, Usly 11 (f), Troy 9, Nancy 6, Franklin 4, French 1
TRIPLETT, Jesse 21, Rebecca 17
SLONE, William 40, Sarah 39, Susanna 21, Elizabeth 19, John 17, James 15, Hardin 13, Nancy 12, Isom 10, Mary 6, Julia 4
SLONE, Shade 22, Rachael 19, Susanna 2
TERRY, William 60, Sabre 58 (f)
SPARKMAN, William 60, Jerusha 50, Ira 23, Nancy 21, Wm. 20, Thomas 18, Samuel 15, Richard 13, Mary 10, Elizabeth 7
SPARKMAN, John 23, Phoebe 21
SLONE, Isom jr. 27, Frances 20, Andrew 3, Lurana 2

1850 Census Floyd County Kentucky

HUGHES, Daniel 82*, Sarah 47, Katharine 20, Walter 10
TYRA, Sarah 15*, Susanna 12
SLONE, Greenville 26*, Elizabeth 25, Morgan 3, Wiley 7/12
JACOBS, John 33, Mahala 37, Mary A. 14, Lois 12, William 10, George 7, Rhoda 4, Ann 11/12
JACOBS, Mary 50, John 25, Mary 24, Henry C. 22, Minerva 10, Sarah 6, Henry C. 2
MAYO, Wm. J. 29, rhoda 16, Matha J. 3, Solomon C. 12, Usal? M. 14 (m)
MARTIN, John 45, Anna 36, William 17, Susannah 15, Adam 12, Katharine 10, Sarah 8, Joseph 6, Jackson 4, Joel 1, Susannah 86

Schedule Page 434

GIBSON, Brison 65, Francis 60, Kenaly 16, Hezekiah 14, Dicy 12, Jefferson 10, Ira 25, Francis 19, Squire 23, Mary 20
MATHEWS, Samuel 25, Mary 30, Nelly 10, Fanny 8, Delila 6, Ava 4
WILLIAMS, William 40, Elizabeth 35, Henderson 5, Mack 2
WALKER, Christopher 56, Elizabeth 55, Mary 16, Ely 21
WALKER, Thomas 21, Nancy 18, Sarah J. 1
WALKER, James 24*, Clarissa 20, Rhoda C. 2
MARTIN, Susannah 18*
OWENS, Hardin 53, Delila 35, Mary 17, Sarah 9, Levina 7, Sintha 2/12
WALLEN, John 45, Mary 47, Shelby 18, Fanny 16, Jane 14, Martin 12, Susan 11, John 7, Sarah 6, Marion 1 (m)
HAYS, John 36*, Mahala 37, Malinda 12, Seatha 10, Arminta 8, Sylvester 6, Mary 4, Martha 1
CHAFIN, Samuel 20*, Nancy J. 16
WICKER, Jesse 22, Eliza 23, Robert 6, John 2, Mary 1
TERRY, Miles 36, Rachael 25, Samuel 12, Elmina 10, Armina 8, Frances J. 6, Jackson 4, Miles 2/12
HICKS, Reuben 55, Christena 56, Charles 22, Reuben R. 13
HICKS, George W. 34*, Rebecca 42
CALHOUN, David A. 15*
PRIDEMORE, Daniel 34, Rebecca 30, John 12, Sarah 10, Daniel 8, Nancy 2

Schedule Page 435

HICKS, William 24, Oma 20, Elizabeth 4, Mary 2
HUGHES, Tolaver 43, Elizabeth 40, Mary 16, Ann C. 14, Sandetta 11, Susan 8, Emmy 5, Ony 4
EASLEY, Silas 35, Arla 26, Rebecca 10, John 8, Thomas 6, Oma 4, Allen 2
DAVIS, Reece 33, Levisa 30, Malinda 10, Elizabeth 7, Mary 5, Rachael 4, Rebecca 3, Thomas 3/12
HICKS, Smith 25, Sarah 26, Elizabeth S. 5, Alexander 4, Lurana 2, Henry C. 5/12
HICKS, James H. 30, Ony 26, Mary J. 8, George W. 7, Sarah 4, Seatta 3, Andrew J. 1
SUTTON, Seatta 30, Nancy J. 17, Elizabeth 14, Ritta 12, William J. 10, Katharine 8, Preston 5, Eliza 3
MORRIS, John 68*, Ony 45, Zachariah 20, Sarah 18, Seatta 16, Amy 13, Biddy 11, Ezekiel 7
BALDRIDGE, Robert 22*
HAYS, John 76, Elizabeth 56, Nelson 24, Wesley 12
HAYS, David 22, Elizabeth 18
HAYS, Anderson 30*, Rachael 27, James 7, Elizabeth 5, George 3
GRIFFY, James 22*
MARTIN, Joel 58*, Mary 38, Richard 18

1850 Census Floyd County Kentucky

MCKEE, William 55*, Sarah 57, Jackson 13, Jane 11
SIZEMORE, William 35*, Martha 29, John 9, William 7, Susanna 5, Vincent 3

Schedule Page 436

PATTON, Charles 29, Nancy 26, Martha 6, Edward 4, John 2, William 10
PATTON, David 42, Rebecca 30, John 15, Fanny 14, Roberson 13, William 12, William 11, Henry C. 11, Christopher 9, Margaret 7, Almirah 5, Washington 19, John 17
PATTON, Sarah 40*, William 18, Frances 15, Elizabeth 13, Amy 12, Mary 10, Stephen 8, John 5, Ambrose 4
SIZEMORE, George 22*
GOODMAN, Alla 54 (f)*
MARTIN, Andrew 36, Elizabeth 38, George 12, Martha J. L. 10, Hulen A. 8 (f), Judah 6 (f), Emeline 4, Josephine 3, Emmena 2, Jeffre 20
GEARHART, Joseph 52*, Sarah 50, John B. 20, William 18, Elizabeth 16, Rhoda 14, Frances 12, Adam 10, Katharine 8, Reese 6
KENDRICK, Margaret 36*
WILLIS, George 23, Joanna 22, McCoy 2
HALE, Sarah 79*
JOHNSON, Agnes 41*, Wm. 19, Sarah 14, Mary 12
WALLEN, John 55, Prudy 40, John 15, William 14, Mary 12, Matilda 10, James 9, Pleasant 6, Mourning 4, Henry 3, Sarah 1
ALSOP, Joel 45, Elizabeth 36, William 19, Nancy 17, Gilbert 13
SALYERS, William M. 71, Dorcas 33, Ranna? 5, Rily 3, Franklin 1

Schedule Page 437

SHEPHERD, John 38, Elizabeth 35, David 15, Enoch 13, Mary 11, Daniel 8, Cresia 7, Elias 5, Nancy 4, Wesly 2
PRATER, Lorenzo D. 30, Sarah 25, Thomas 7, Susan 5, George 4, Wiley 2
CONLEY, Sampson 35, Eliza 27, Ashford 7, Margaret 5, Martin 3
CONLEY, David sr. 63, Margaret 53, William 23, Dorcas 18, Joseph 16, Thomas 11, Margaret 9
COBOURN, David 41, Sarah 37, Mary 7, William O. 16, John M. 15, Alexander 13, Joseph L. 12
ONY, William 43, Susannah 43, Bunyan? 17, David C. 15, Mary 12, Margaret 10, Samuel A. 7, John C. 5, Nancy J. 2, Sarah 19
COBOURN, Samuel jr. 40, Mary 24, Nancy 3, William 6/12
COBOURN, John P. 26?, Agnes 25, Jeremiah 5
PRATER, Jonathan 60, Margaret 60, Amanda J. 15
COBOURN, Samuel sr. 67*, Mary 72, John C. 37, Phoebe 29, Amanda 10, Mary 8, Sarah A. 6, James R. 4, William J. 2, Jeremiah 40
WALKER, Jesse 45*
PRATER, Harvy 30, Mariah 30, William 13, Rhoda 7, John W. 5, Greenville 4
SMITH, Katharine 30, Benjamin 13, Sarah 9
GEARHART, Woodson 22, Sarah 22
MARTIN, David 26, Susan C. 22, Rebecca J. 5, Wesley L. 3, Wilson T. 1

1850 Census Floyd County Kentucky

Schedule Page 438

NEAL, John 34, Mary 32
PRATER, Adam 37, Newman 15, William 6, Glatha 4
PRATER, John 25, Mary 20, John 8
PRATER, William 26, Sarah 23, Byly 12, Mary 10, John 8, Biddy 6, Nancy 4
HANSHAW, Harris 30*, Eve 31, Andrew 15, William 13, Mary 11, Alexander 9, Adam 7, Biddy 5, Martha 3, Brice 2
PRATER, Biddy 56*
PRATER, Joseph 34, Elizabeth 22, Mary 14, Elizabeth 9, Orny 6 (f), John 4, Daniel 2
PRATER, James 23, Elizabeth 19, Jackson 14
ALLEN, George J. 32, Susan 24, Amanda 6, Louisa 5, Sarah 2, Cynthia 1
THORNSBERRY, John 50, Frances 46, Mickey 17 (f), Jno. M. 15, Samuel 13, Wm. H. 11, Mary 8, Malinda 6, Joseph M. 4
ALLEN, Cynthia 65, William 40, Archibald 21, Florinda 17, Martha 7, Anna 4
ALLEN, John 20, Parthena 20, Thomas 2, George 1
JUSTICE, Abraham 21, Mary 17, George 4, Minervy J. 17, Emond? 12 (m)
HOOVER, John 25*, Nancy 29, Sarah 4, George 2
STURGEON, Lucinda 24*
ALLEN, Adam 41, Jemima 33, John 12, Joseph 8, Hezekiah 8, Katharine 6, Adam 4, James H. 2, George 5/12
WEBB, Hezekiah 26*, Martha 22, Joseph 5, Mary 3

Schedule Page 439

EDWARDS, James 30*, Louisa 28, Nancy 5, America 5, William 3, Minervy 1
GEARHART, Joseph jr. 27, Susan 24, Adam 6, Sarah E. 4, Thomas 2
KINDRICK, Adah 50, Augustus 20, Joseph 12
HARRIS, John 33, Elizabeth 29, Anna 10, William N. 7, Frances 5, Esther 2
BERRY, John 40, Florence 41, George A. 18, Isaac 15, Reuben 13, Sarah 11, Cynthia 9, John W. 6, Florence 4
GOODMAN, Pleasant 42, James 30, John 14, Hiram 12, Elizabeth 11, Parthena 9, Dolly 7, Moses 4, Susan 10/12
PATTON, Delila 32, Mary 11, John B. 6, Robert 4
SIZEMORE, Jane 42, Frances 14, Katherine 12, Elizabeth 7, John 5, Rebecca 4, Merella 3
PATTON, Henry 35, Lydia 50, Kenaz? 16 (m), Kelly 14, Anna 12, Biggs 11, Elizabeth 9, Florence 2
STONE, Jane 28, Florence 12, Nancy 8, Cynthia 6, Sarah 4, James 2
PATTON, Malinda 39, Abby 14, Mary 9, Reuben 7, Rily 6, David 4, William 2, Sarah 10/12
HAYS, Daniel 32, Mary 24, Angeline 8, Apperson 6, John 5, Alleatha 3
WHITT, John L. 32, Louisa 27, John B. 9, James P. 7, Sarah 5, George 3, Hezekiah 6/12

Schedule Page 440

WHITT, Hezekiah 25, Mary 23, Martha 3, Bunyan 2
ONY, Allen 36, Agga 23, Zachariah 4, Oney 2 (f)
JUSTICE, Neal 25, Nancy 18
WHITT, Bunyan 50, Sarah 60, Elizabeth 14, Douglass 12, Sydney B. 10

1850 Census Floyd County Kentucky

PATTON, Samuel 62, Elizabeth 55, Allen 35, Samuel A. 23, James 14, Henry C. 11
MAY, Sarah 39, George 21, William 19, Wesley 18, John 17, Jackson 16, Cynthia 15, Sarah 10, Reuben A. 9
GOODMAN, Andrew 38, Penina 33, Andrew J. 12, Wm. C. 10, Pleasant 7, James 3, Elizabeth 3
PATTON, Frazier 38, Esther 33, Elizabeth 16, Nancy 14, Allen 12, Margarett 10, Sarah 8, Malinda 6, Kelsey 3
CLICK, David 42, Nancy 41, Harvy 20, William 17, Margaret 14, Elizabeth 12, Susannah 10, Sarah 7, John P. 6, Samuel 1
ALLEN, Felix 35, Rhoda 27, Reuben 9, Joel 7, George 5, James K. 3, Miranda 1
PITTS, Thomas 30, Rachael 28, Alfred 9, Elizabeth 7, Mary 5, Washington 3
PRATER, Samuel 28, Rebecca 26, Winny 7, Biddy 4, Sarah 2
BARNETT, James 36, Sarah 31, John 14, Wesley 12, Rebecca 10, Nelson 9, Irena 7, Feraby 5, Jackson 4, Tabitha 2, Samuel 3/12

Schedule Page 441

PATTON, Henry 70, Rachael 50, John 13, Isabel 11, Samuel 8
MCKEE, Jesse 25, Sarah A. 25, Mary A. 2
LEEK, Mary 40, Florence 22
ALLEN, George 32, Rebecca 27, Cynthia 10, Samuel D. 9, Reuben M. 6, John B. 5, Louisa 3, David K. 2, William J. 9/12
STEPHENS, Samuel 49, Florence 49, James P. 25, David 23, Andrew J. 22, Thomas M. 20, Saml. A. 19, Reuben M. 18, Cynthia 15, John B. 14, Mary A. 12, Alexander L. 11, William D. 10, Morgan G. 8, Dorcas 7
LACKEY, Alexander 78, Mary 69, Greenville 42, James M. 38, Rebecca 32
ALLEN, Samuel 29*, Sarah A. 23, Andrew J. 7, Thomas G. 5, Cynthia 3, Newton 1
CRUM, Michael 9*, Henry W. 1
MAYO, Mial 55, Susannah 57, Elizabeth 31
CRUM, Jonathan 34, Margaret 32, Susan C. 14, Six? 12 (f), Meal M. 11, John W. 7, Littleton S. 6, Melissa A. 4, Elizabeth M. 3, Lewis 1
AKERS, Randle 41, Nancy 42, Margaret J. 14, Emily C. 7, Eliza E. 6, Amanda M. 5
MAYO, Jacob 50*, Rebecca 43, William 20, Susan C. 17, Tabitha 14, Julian 13 (f)
MOSELEY, Peggy 47*
DAMRON, Samuel 37, Louisa 23, Sarah 4
CRUM, Henry 47*, Priscilla 55, Matha 70
DILLION, James 24*

Schedule Page 442

SLOAS, John 36, Elizabeth 23, Frances 4, David 1
MEADOWS, Isah 50, Hannah 46, Thomas 23, John 22, Eada 20, Elisha 18, Jordan 15, Joseph 13, Manderville 11, Hannah 5, Burwell 2
MARSHALL, Johnson 41, Bersheba 43, Pelina 16, Thomas 14, Reuben 12, Jane 10, Sarah 8, George 6
MARSHALL, Washington 20, Nancy 16
ADAMS, Johnson 22, Susan 19, William 3, Beeshebe 1
BLEVINS, Eli 25, Nancy 23, Jefferson 6, Mary 4, William 2
HILL, Burton 28, Sarah 25, Thomas 8, Mary 6, Jane 4, Isabella 2, Hannah 1

- 76 -

1850 Census Floyd County Kentucky

HYTON, William 25*, Elizabeth 26, Sarah 2, John W. 6/12
ROWLAND, Isabella 66*
SPRADLIN, Margaret 46*, George 24, Agnes E. 18, John W. 16, William J. 14, Thomas 12, Lydia 10, Sarah 8, Susannah 7, Andrew S. 23
MEADOWS, John 22*
LANGLEY, Joseph 55, Delila 50, Mary 18, Mathew 16, Joseph 14
DOTSON, Mitchell 30, Elizabeth 30, Andrew 6, William 4, Arta 2
HICKS, Aulse 70, Sarah 60
FORTNER, John 45, Rachael 40
SPRADLIN, Jonathan 27, Mary A. 18, Solomon 26
CAVERN, William 35, Mary 36, Sarah 16, Amanda 14, Jonathan 12, Delpha 10, Caleb 8, James 5, Solomon 3, Levina 7/12

Schedule Page 443

BRADLY, William 33, Elizabeth 32, Mary 16, Jane 15, Susan 13, Elias 12, Rebecca 11, Margaret 9, James 7, Riley 4, Amanda 1
HANSHEW, Henry 22, Elizabeth 21, Andrew 5, Sarah 3, Martha 1
BROWN, George 67, Anna 65, Robert 30, Henry 24, Jane 19
THACKER, Reuben 70, Nancy 60, Tabitha 30, John 21, Jane 18, Nancy 15, Reuben 14
HICKS, Hiram 44, Fanny 32, Solomon 19, George 17, Pilana 14, Sarah 12, Jane 10, Henry C. 6, Hiram 4, Anna 2
WADKINS, Benedict 95, Keziah 50, Minta 8
POE, James 60, Barbary 50, Thomas 14, Katharine 12
POE, John 22, Mary 19, James 1
POTTS, James 50, Sarah 50, Sylvester 22, Isaac 16, William 13, Nancy 9
FITZPATRICK, Jacob 45, Polina 43, Jonathan 17, James 14, Samuel 11
FITZPATRICK, Geo. H. 22, Sarah 20, Jacob 8/12
HACKWORTH, Esther 60, Charlotte 30, Elizabeth 26
HACKWORTH, Benjamin 30, Mahala 19
PRATER, Elias 24, Zelpha 19, Preston 3
HAYWOOD, John 54, Arty 42, William L. 24, Hiram 22, Greenville 17, Henry 12, Robert 10, Lurana A. 8, John H. 5, Thomas 5/12
SHEPHERD, Brice 28, Nancy 25, Elizabeth 8, Sarah 6, David 4, Frances J. 2, John R. 1

Schedule Page 444

LANGLY, John 25, Sarah 24
HALE, James 45, Jane 43, Susan 18, Nelson 16, Katherine 14, Eleanor 12, John 10, William 8, Elizabeth 4
RATLIFF, William 30, Malinda 28, James 14, William 12, Lucinda 10, Elizabeth 6, John B. 3
STEPHENS, George 30, Margaret 24, Minerva 6, Mary A. 3, Florence 3/12
TUSSY, Craig 25, Mary 21, Jaratha 9/12
BARNALL, Nelson 40, Susannah 38, Wilson 15, Rebecca 13, Susannah 10, Mary 9, William 7, Charlotte 5, Martha 3
JONES, John 49, Virginia 28, John 15, Amanda 10, Louisa 8, Achsah 5, Elizabeth 3
COBURN, Jeremiah 76*, Jemima 58

1850 Census Floyd County Kentucky

DRUGIS?, Peter 21*
HANSHAW, Andrew 58, Patsy 51, Nancy 18, Rhoda 16, Elizabeth 11
BRADLY, Elias 31*, Luanah 28, Minerva J. 7, Solomon 4, Louisa 2, Jackson Morgan 13, Fanny Morgan 13
PRATER, Thomas 60, Elizabeth 71
HAMILTON, David 57, Sarah 50, Ira 22, Rhoda 16, Mary 14, William 13, Mary 12, Susanna 10, Peggy B. 8, William 7
TUSSY, Jonathan 57, Ann 55, Katharine 16, Caleb 13
TUSSY, John 34, Nancy 30, James 11, Jonathan 7, Elizabeth 5, Amanda J. 1?

Schedule Page 445

WHITAKER, Wiley 24, America 20, Johnson 1
WHITAKER, Johnson 58*, Susanna 54, William 23, Mary 20, David 18, Morgan 16, Elijah 14, Selia 13, Cynthia 12, Elmore S. 9, Wesly 2
LIFORD, Lazarus 23*
HOWARD, Samuel 31*, Delany 30, Lurana 10, Nancy 8, Peggy 6, William 4, Wiley 3
SPRADDEN, Edward 18*
COLE, Charles 24 (B), Lotta 23, Wallis 3, Shepherd 1
AUXIER, Margaret 40 (B), Elbea? 22 (f), Barbary 17, Ezekial 13, French 9, Hiram 7, Clarah 6, Doctor 3, Teira 8/12
WISEMAN, John 54*, Rebecca 45, Malinda 18, Fielding 16, Morgan 8
ROW, William 16*
WISEMAN, John 21, Florence 18, Katharine 3
WISEMAN, Jacob 27, Susan 26, Sarah 7, Nancy 6, Abraham 5, Rebecca 3, Lemma? 1 (f)
STONE, Enoch 70*, Mary 23
ROWE, Alexander 7*
WADKINS, Thomas 33, Lucinda 28, Mary 14, John 12, William 10, Lewis 7, Nancy 4, Luquena 2
WADKINS, Thomas 98*, Elizabeth 40
ROWE, Anna 35*, William 16, George 13, Andrew 5, Rebecca 9/12
HOWARD, Lewis 23, Elizabeth 22, John 4, Samuel 3, Nancy 48, Sophia 15
HALE, Brice 53*, Mary 60
SHEPHERD, Jacob 25*, William 10

Schedule Page 446

WADKINS, Sylvester 23, Hetty 21, Jonathan 1
SHEPHERD, John 30, Sarah 25, David 9, Martin 7, Elizabeth 5, Jacob 3, Clabourn 2
SHEPHERD, Brice 33, Elizabeth 28, Cresa 12, Florinda 11, Mary 10, Susan 9, Brice 5, Andrew 3, Amanda 1
SHEPHERD, Sylvester 25, Cynthia 19, Wesley 8/12
SHEPHERD, Jacob 68*, Elizabeth 50, William 21, Abel 16, Brice 9
HOWARD, Elizabeth 19*
SLONE, Nancy 55*
HALE, John 48, Vina 30, James 16, Samuel 11, Mary 9, Brice 7, Susan 6, Benjamin 4, Louisa 3, Vincent 1, Mary 80
BROWN, David 40, Isanah 35, Lorena 8, Marion 6 (m), George 4, Sarah 3

- 78 -

1850 Census Floyd County Kentucky

SALYERS, David 34, Susan 30, Calvin 11, Nelson 10, Lurany 6, Samuel 4, Delany 2 (f)
SALYERS, Isaiah 36, Phoebe 32, Cambridge 12, Nancy 10, William 8, Elizabeth 5, Stephen 3, Abby 9/12
MORGAN, Reuben 25, Susannah 22, Wiley 8/12
SALYERS, William 26, Luquena 25, Louisa 3, Esther 1
TUSSY, Jacob 36, Mary 34, Jonathan 14, William 12, David 7, Mary 5, Martha 3, Alexander 2
HOWARD, John 21, Susan 18, Amanda 3, Reuben 1

Schedule Page 447

JONES, Rebecca 37*, James 18, Jackson 10, Oscar 5
GIBSON, Cynthia 26*, Leanah 10/12
JONES, Charles 60*, Jemima 65, Wiley 26, Jonathan 13
ARNOLD, John 80*, Sarah 50
SLONE, William 47, Asia 46, Jane 24, Enoch 21, James 19, William 13
SLONE, Cudbetts? 25, Claranda 22, Jane 3, James 1
RISNER, William 35, Abigail 27, Sarah 9, John 4, Phoebe 1
BAILEY, Samuel 25, Nancy 23, William 7, Lucinda 5, Wallis 3, Henry 8/12
PRATER, Jonathan 35, Margaret 31, John 10, Susan 8, Margaret 6, Charles 4, Jackson 2
BAILEY, John 35, Katharine 25, Andrew 16, Jesse 6, Mary 2
PATRICK, Jeremiah 35, Sarah 31, John 12, Andrew 10, Nancy 8, Mary 6, Samuel 5, Isaiah 4, Abby 2
BAILEY, John sr. 62*, Susan 56, James 16, Sarah 12
PINKERTON, Susan 27*, Mary 6, Eliza 4, William 2
ARNETT, Reuben 40, Susan 28, Harris 19, Jinsa 27, Reuben 15, Jackson 14, Sarah 12, Stephen 11, Louisa 5, Anna 3, Elbert 1
SALYERS, John 48, Mary 45, John 18, Wiley 15, Arty 13, Mary 10, Morgan 8, Benjamin 6

Schedule Page 448

ARNETT, Stephen 68*, Elizabeth 67, David 38, David 21, Melinda 19, Sarah 13, Stephen 11
PRATER, Ibba 19*, John E. 2
PATRICK, John 45*, Mary J. 23, Minerva 2
JORDAN, John 9*
WHITAKER, James O. 46*, Lurana 40, William 20, Francis 19, Martin 18, Matilda 15, Thomas 11, Johnson 5, George 2
HOWARD, Benjamin 43*, Nancy 45, Stephen 23, William 21, Benjamin 19, Phoebe 17, Larkin 14, Henry C. 11
ARNETT, Juicy 20 (f)*
POE, Hugh 26, Sarah 36, Jane 5, Rebecca 4, Merida 3, Elizabeth 2, Emily 6/12
ADAMS, Joel 36, Elizabeth 28, Louisa 8, Nancy 6, Fanny 4, Rebecca 1
ADAMS, Johnson 21, Susan 18, William 3, Bashebe 1
RISNER, James 41, Margaret 40, William 18, Idris 16 (f), Martin 15, Mitchell 13, Wilson 11, Francis 9, George 6, Mary J. 4, James P. 2
RISNER, Jacob 35, Mary Ann 30, Dial 11 (m), Bethany 10, Delany 10, Miles 9, Marshall 6, James 4, Gardner 1
RISNER, Merida 20 (m), Elizabeth 17, Jaris 1 (f)

1850 Census Floyd County Kentucky

OWINGS, Robert 47*, Rutha 46, Louisa 23, James 21, Elizabeth 18, William 16
JOSEPHS, John 46*, Usley 40 (f), Abner 21, Nelson 18, Charles 17, John 16, Mary 15, Sarah 7

Schedule Page 449

CRAFT, George 6*
CONLEY, Elijah 28, Nancy 20, Mary 2
SALYERS, William 24, Anna 22, Henderson 2
SALYERS, Thomas 26, Violet 25, Cynthia 5, Caroline 4, Elizabeth 2
WADKINS, William 43, Elizabeth 43, Thomas 23, Jane 16, Keziah 13, Isaac 11, William 10, Barbara 8, Mary 7
WHITAKER, Francis 56*, Margaret 56, Mark 31, Robert 25, Thomas P. 21, Margaret 11, Nancy 9, Amanda 1, Nancy 21, Emeline 18
KILGORE, Madison 5*, Martha 3
COLE, William 59, Rebecca 28, William 8, Luanna 10, Biddy 7, Wilson 6, Cynthia 5
FLETCHER, George 53, Levisa 49, Elizabeth 18, Epperson 16, Menda 14 (m), Rebecca 10, Johnson 6, Mason 5
FLETCHER, Reuben 26, Patsy 24, Emeline 8, Levisa 6, Susan 5, Serena 4, Jasper 2, George M. 4/12
FLETCHER, Isaac 29, Susannah 25, Jesse 5, Louisa 3, Gilbert 1
FLETCHER, Simon 23, Mary 22, Alsey 2
FLETCHER, Henley 25, Nancy 24, Bethany 3 (f), Rebecca 2
BEVINS, Joseph 30, Nancy 26, Elizabeth 9, Margaret 8, Susan 4, James 1
MCCARTY, Jeremiah 34, Malinda 26, Lora 6, Harmon 2
SALYERS, Abner 52, Nancy 48, Fielding 21, Samuel 19, Andrew 14, Martin 13, Benjamin 12, Abner 10, David 7, Rufus 5, James 4, Usley 3 (f)

Schedule Page 450

PATTON, Elizabeth 39, Rhoda 21, Henry 12, Abby 7
SALYERS, John 23, Emeline 22, Sarah 2
NICHOLS, Elizabeth 55, Hassey? 25 (f), John 20, Daniel 8, Glotha 6, Anderson 4?
BAYS, Rufus 30*, Sarah 26, Elizabeth 5, Seana 2
GRIFFY, Mary 7*, William 6
SALYERS, Samuel 34, Malinda 33, Abner 18, Martha 16, Henderson 18
JORDAN, Sarah 36, James 17, Lewis 13, Anna 11, John 9, Robert 5, George 4
COLE, John 42, Katharine 34, William 17, Dial 15 (m), Sarah 13, Cynthia 11, Melissa 6
MERRIX?, John 43, Sarah 21, Dial 2 (m), Fanny 70
POE, Merida (m), Angeline 21, Nancy 3, Mary 1
MERRIX?, James 40, Fanny 33, Mary 15, Margaret 14, America 12, Charles 9, William 6, Greenville 3
PICKLESIMER, James 31*, Mary 31, Sarah 6, John 4, Mary 3, Elizabeth 1
PERSMAY?, Pelina 14*
PATRICK, John 35, Elizabeth 25, Francis 9, Violet 7
PATRICK, Brice 33*, Margaret 22, Elizabeth 12, Charles 8, Juicy 3 (f), Nancy 1
SIMER, Charlotte P. 17*

1850 Census Floyd County Kentucky

Schedule Page 451

COLE, George 22, Nancy 22, Amanda 2
MERRIX, Charles 37, Margaret 33, Rebecca 16, Emeline 15, Taza 12, Noah 9, Lewis 6, James R. 4, Jackson 1
ADAMS, William 80*, Fanny 70
MERRIX, Charles 76*
MONTGOMERY, Silas 26, Agnes 24, Elizabeth 1
MARSHALL, Reuben 69, Elizabeth 67
MARSHALL, Mason 27, Mary 26, Jackson 10, William 8, Luana 5, Thomas 3, Mary 1
MARSHALL, George 36, Elizabeth 33, Andrew 16, William 14, Jane 10, Martin 8, Elizabeth 6, John 4, Reuben 2
HUGHES, James 60, Jane 40?, Anna 15, James 12, Henderson 10, Thomas 8
CRAFT, John 54, Elizabeth 33, Henry 5, Mary 3, Fanny 2
BARNETT, William 33, Dicey 28, Nancy 14, Preston 11, Wesley 9, Sarah 8, Sarah 6, Martha 4, Daniel 10/12
COLLINSWORTH, Mason 40, Margaret 38, Isabella 13, Thomas 9, James 7, Elizabeth 4
DYKES, James 34, Arty 20, Abner 8/12
MONTGOMERY, James 29, Nancy 21, Eady 10, Nancy 8, Cynthia 7, Martha 5, John 4, Isaac 2
ARNETT, Wiley 35*, Elizabeth 37, Russell 14, William 12, Martha 9, Paris 7, John 4, Kendall 2, Jackson 3/12?, Malinda 20
SIZEMORE, Granville 15*, Vina 25, Sarah 13

Schedule Page 452

MONTGOMERY, John 57, Vina 46, John 17, Samuel 16, Jackson 15, Jane 13, John 11, Eliza 10, Martha 5, Julia 1
RISNER, Eli 35, Arta 18, Jacob 15, William 13, Anna 11, Elizabeth 10, Kelsey 6
JOSEPHS, William 28, Eliza 29, Epperson 8, Nelson 7, Susannah 5, Usley 3 (f)
HOSKINS, Moses 54*, Margaret 70, Benjamin 31, Sarah 27, Rhoda 21, Rosana 19, Merida 7 (m), Rebecca 5
WILLIAMS, Mary A. 4*
VANDERPOOL, John 27, Nancy 25, Enoch 8, Robert 6, Margaret 5, Jacob 1
HELTON, Andrew 32, Delpha 26, Emeline 8, Eada 6, Malinda 5, Melissa 2, Dial 7/12 (m)
HOSKINS, Robert 24*, Sarah 28, Moses 3, Emily 2
BAYS, Judah 15 (f)*
ALSOP, Robert 22, Jinsey 19, Margaret 3/12
PICKLE, Sarah 50, Margaret 21, Alfred 13
MCFARLAND, William 23, Caroline 20, Sandford 3, Josephine 6/12
PERKINS, Thomas 23, Nancy 36, Louisa 9, Elizabeth 5, Mary 3, William 1
PUCKETT, Isaac 40, Katharine 40, William 16, John 12, Benjamin 6, Fleming 5, Greenville 3
CONLEY, Elizabeth 33*, James 12, William 10, Lewis 8, Eveline 6, Elizabeth 2
BAYS, Lucy 7*

1850 Census Floyd County Kentucky

Schedule Page 453

BAILEY, Lemuel 58*, Nancy 45, Jinsey 14, Patsey 12, Preslie 10 (f), Pelina 8, Mary 5, George 3, William 23
DYKES, Mary 88*
STURGEON, William 45, Elizabeth 34, John 22, Matilda 19, Mary 18, William 16, Nimrod 14, Jesse 12, Sarah 8, Noah 6, David 2
REA, Sarah 70, Jesse 16
KANARD, Samuel 45, Anna 45, Louisa 25, James 23, Julia Ann 22, Thomas 16, Pelina 12
ARNETT, Stephen 18, Levisa 20
ARNETT, William 40, Jemima 20, Thomas 14, Susan 8, Martin 6, Pelina 3, Anna 7/12
ARNETT, Stephen 3rd? 44, Eliza 32, William 16, Fleming 13, Wiley 10, Frank 8, Reuben 5, Stephen 1
ARNETT, David 38*, Lydia 31, Louisa 15, Nancy 10, Susan 8, Rebecca 4, Mary 2
BINGOM, Elijah 15*
ARNETT, Ambrose 37*, Susan 19, Logan 5, Harrison 2, Mary 4/12
BAILEY, James 30*, William 20
REA, James 22, Lucy 20, Martin 2
BAILEY, John 35, Mary 32, Elijah 15, Elizabeth 13, Sarah 11, Francis 8, Patsy 6, Wiley 3, Jane 1
ARNETT, Hiram 30*, Arrena 28, Catlett 10, Elizabeth 8, Ambrose 6, Burdine 2, Letty 3/12
BAILEY, Elijah 20*

Schedule Page 454

CARTY, David 30, Letty 28
ARNETT, Reuben sr. 64, Susan 63, Reuben 28
RISNER, Michael 30, Clarinda 20, Sarah 3, Idris 1 (f)
MCNEW, William 29, Mary 28, John J. 9/12
FLINT, John 40, Fady 35 (f), Elizabeth 16, William 14, Ann Eliza 12, Hiram 10, Rebecca 8, Sillah 2, James 7/12
POWER, John 42, Nancy 37, Elizabeth 17, Sarah J. 16, Sandford 14, Mason 12, Mary 4
POWER, Lewis 64, Elizabeth 59, Celia 25, William 22, James 20, Cynthia A. 17
LITTERAL, John 32*, Mary 36, James 12, Martha 10, Pelina 8, John 6, Elizabeth 4, Rebecca 9/12
FITZPATRICK, Isaac 12*
PATRICK, Wilson 26*, Parthena 21, Emeline 3, Nancy 1
KENARD, Jane 52*
PRATER, Washington 24*, Jane 23, James 2, Susan 1
CONLEY, Caly 25*, Jane 2, Sarah 1
PRATER, Irvin 22, Mary 21, Dial 1 (m)
MAY, David 43, Nancy 40, James 15, Clarinda 14, William 10, Cynthia 9, John W. 6, Mary 5, Thomas 2, Emily 6/12
ROSE, Jesse 35, Sarah 27, Henry 6, Thomas 4, William 2
PRATER, William sr. 63*, Nancy 60, Rebecca 34, William W. 21
PATRICK, John S. 14*, Emily J. 13
PRATER, Thomas L. 24*, Mary 21, Nancy 2, William 8/12

1850 Census Floyd County Kentucky

Schedule Page 455

PERKINS, George 10*
GULLETT, Christopher 70*, Patsey 30, Nancy 20, James 18, Eveline 16, Artisa 14, William 13, Daniel 10, Wiley 8, Mary 7, Harvy 5
BAILEY, Patsy 100*
CONLY, William 40, Disa 25, Washington 19, Rachael 17, Elizabeth 15, David 13, James 11, Mary 9, Disa 7, Leroy 5, Josiah 3, Susan 1
GULLETT, Wiley 31, Jane 30, Daniel 5, Presley 3, Lydia 1
GULLETT, Martin 21, Judith 17
CRASE?, Stephen 30, Mary 20, John 3/12
PERKINS, Lewis 24, Mary 18, Eli 1, Elizabeth 60, Joshua 40, Dorothy 38, Peggy 36, George 30, James 25, Lewis 23, Jane 22
CRASE?, Henry 30, Elizabeth 28, Nancy 10, Campbell 8, Alfred 6, Mary 4, Hetty 2
MAY, Caleb 20, Pelina 19
BROWN, Peggy 40, Martha 15, James 13, Rhoda 16
CAUDILL, James 25, Angaline 20, Nancy 3
CONLEY, Henry 55, Nancy 50, David 12, James 11, Sussannah 2
PRATER, Jilson 24, Cyntha 22, Jane 6, Emeline 4, William 8/12
PATRICK, John 53*, Martha 51, Elizabeth 25, Richmond 23, Arty 18, Lucrecy 18, Seripta 16, John W. 14, William 11
KINARD, Mary 82*
CAUDILL, Abel 22, Phebe 22, Jesse 2, John 9/12

Schedule Page 456

COLLINSWORTH, Thomas 65, Hannah 56, Sarah 28, Louisa 20, Atchison 18
PATRICK, Allen 29, Elizabeth 21
PATRICK, Meethe? M. 23 (m), Susan 18, Martha 2
PRATER, Thomas 26, Rebeca 23, Martha 2, Marinda A. 1
PRATER, John 65*, Mary 67, Sarah 43, John 36, Jemimah 32, Rebecca 11, Angaline 8, Sarah 6, Isaac 4, Zackariah 2
COOK, Eliza 19*, Mary 17, Elizabeth 14, Miles 12
POWER, Holloway 38*, Clerinda 30, Sarah J. 12, John 10, Elizbeth 8, Henry C. 6, Thomas J. 4, Emily 2, James L. 9/12
PRATER, Richard M. 14*, Caroline 13
BAILEY, Walis 46*, Mary 42, Albin? C. 23, John D. 21, Melisa 17, William P. 19, Lewis P. 15, James F. 13, Narcisa P. 11, Wallis W. 9, Nancy J. 7, Alexander L. 5, Enoch M. 1
ADAMS, Wiley 23*
FOSTER, John 38, Nancy 40, Miles 16, Joseph A. 13, Elizabeth 11, Mary 9, Nancy 7, Araminta 1
BAILEY, Alfred 25, Margaret 25, Sanford R. 6, Rebecca 4, John A. 3, Jackson T. 6/12
PATRICK, William 56, Nancy 48, Grenville 26, Robert 20, Mary 11, Rebecca 7
PATRICK, Meredith 46*, Rebecca 41, Herod 26, Elijah 22, Reuben 20, Senna 17, Wiley 14, Alexander 12

1850 Census Floyd County Kentucky

Schedule Page 457

POE, Nancy 27*
NICHOLS, Joseph 28*, Orny 27 (f), Grenville 4, Martin 2, Elizabeth 4/12, William 20, John 18
COLE, Jemimah 26*, Riley 7, Lydia 4/12
PATRICK, Jeremiah 52, Nancy 43, Jackson 22, Elizabeth E. 15, Louisa A. 13, Richard 48, Ellen 43, William 20, Adaline 17, Amisinda 15, Araminta 13, John 8, Martha 5
PATRICK, Thomas C. 26, Rebecca 20, Reuben 5, John 3, Jefferson 4/12
HAMPTON, Levisse 64 (m), Sarah 46, Elisa 1
PRATER, William 28*, Mary 25, Emily 4, John 3
SCOTT, William 28*, Sarah 27, Rebecca 6, Mary 4, Thomas 1
COLLINWORTH, John 23, Susan 18, Rebecca 1
FLETCHER, Elizabeth 64*, Kelsey 25 (f)
MEDLEY, Julius 22*, Selia 27, Elizabeth 2
RICE, Samuel 38, Jane 24, Eveline 16, Daniel J. 13, Martin 12, Thomas J. 8, George W. 7, William M. 5, Nancy E. 3, Henry C. 2
CRASE?, Alfred 32, Berthy 25, Henry 2
BAYS, Isom 55, Susan 28, William 14, Nancy 8
ADAMS, Gilbert 35, Nancy 32, Sarah 21, William 18, Preston 17, John 14, Jane 12, Frances 10, Zelpha 8, Moses 6, Grenville 3
KENDRICK, William 55, Margaret 51, George 26, Rachael 24, Elisha 22, Esabel 20, Joseph 19, Clerisa 16, Caroline 14, Cynthia 12, William J. 7

Schedule Page 458

MAY, Blair 42, Sarah 35, William 16, Harvy 14, Henry H. 12, Robert W. 10, Samuel 8, Dial 6 (m), Stephen L. 4, Rebecca 4/12
SPRADLIN, Henry 25, Rosanna 18, Thomas G. 5/12
ADAMS, William 28, Margaret 24, Alfred 8, Mary 5, Rosannah 4, Sarah 2, Margaret 5/12
BARNETT, John 35, Abagale 36, Elias 16, Spicy 14 (f), William 12, Robert 10, Branson 9, Milly 8, Sarah 6, Daniel 4
REY, Daniel 38, Martha 33
REY, William 30, Nancy 28, Andrew 3
CAUDILL, Isaac 28, Elizabeth 27, William 5/12, Rachael 40
ADAMS, Daniel 50, Jane 49, Mahala 15
RICHARDSON, Daniel 48*, Mary 33, Joseph 9, Sarah 8, Biddy 6, William 4, Nancy 1
BROWN, Clerinda 16*
MAY, Mary 50*
BROWN, James 21, Nancy 18
PATRICK, Hiram 40*, Mary 35, William 16, Lewis 15, Elizabeth 12, Sarah 10, Margaret 8, Agnis 6, Mary 4, Emaline 3, Rebecca 2
HOLBROOKS, Kelsey 21*, Randall 16
COLLINSWORTH, Samuel 26, Nancy 24, Jane 3, Thomas 1
PATTON, David 43, Mary 37, John 17, William 15, Martha 11, Susan 9, Sarah 6, Phebe 3, Rebeca 1

1850 Census Floyd County Kentucky

Schedule Page 459

WADKINS, Thomas 31, Susan 27, Elisa 9, William 8, Margaret 3
HAMILTON, Stephen 36, Sarah 28, Mary J. 11, James J. 9, Martha 8, Andrew 4, Elizabeth 2
HACKWORTH, George 40, Magy 33 (f), John 16, Jeremiah 13, Andrew 11, Margaret 9, Benjamine 5, James 3, Harris H. 1
HAMILTON, James 26, Olly 23 (f), Sarah 4, Malinda 1
FITZPATRICK, William 31, Henry 23, Nancy 22, Stephen 3
HAMILTON, Cynthia 45*, Alexander 21, Thomas 19, Henry 17, Tandy 14, Solomon 12, Stephen 9
BROWN, Elizabeth 20*
SKEEN, Joseph 45, Julian 36 (f), Jonathan 15, Elisa 13, George 11, Mary 10, William 8, Thomas 6, Daniel 4, Margaret 2
HARRIS, Joseph S. 36, Sarah 30, Hiram 3, Arty 2, Richard 3/12, Nancy 38
HERRELL, William 43*, Malinda 42, Elary 17 (f), Elizabeth 14, Eliza 9, Hone 4 (f)
BROWN, Samuel 18*
ELLISON, John 6*
FITZPATRICK, Thomas sr. 60*, Jane 50, James 22
DYER, William 18*
VAUGHAN, Patrick 50*, Susan 50, Patrick 23, Elizabeth 18, Van Buren 14, Sarah 12, John 10
HATFIELD, Nuson 17*
SHEPHERD, George 38*
BROWN, James 38, Martha 25, Susan 4, George 1
MOORE, Obadiah 58 (B), Mary 47, Louisa 33, John 23, Catharine 19, Jackson 18, Jane 16, Obadiah 14, Joab 21

Schedule Page 460

HEREFORD, James H. 53*, Meriah 34, James 9, Mary 6
HOBBS, Hardin 24*
CLARK, Edward 34*, Sarah 33, Martha 10, Ahyra 8 (m), Mary 6, Joseph 4, Lucinda 2, Edward 5/12, Lucy 76
SALMON, Elizabeth 21*
FRALEY, Benjamin 43, Margaret 40, Mary 14, Daniel 13, Enoch 11, Remember 2 (m)
HARRIS, James 42, Jane 43, Cothestus? 18 (m), James 16, Elizabeth 14, Mary 12, Thomas J. 10, Easther 7, Kelsey 6, John 2
VANHOOSE, Joseph 46, Mary 41, Mary J. 18, Eady 15, Martha A. 13, Isabella 10, Julia 7, John W. 5, Sarah 3, Wallis W. 1
BROWN, Francis 64, Eady 64, Jeffry 19
HACKWORTH, Abner 40, Darcus 37, Luannah 17, Susannah 15, Cynthia 12, Christopher 11, Mary 7
PATTON, Christopher 61*, Susan 62, Phebe 39, Sarah 30, Anna 28
SPRADLIN, Cajor 20*, Mary 23, Phebe 4/12
BROWN, Thomas C. 91, Mary 50
JENKINS, Hannah 33, Nancy 15, Sarah 10, George 9, Elizabeth 7, Wilson 4
BROWN, Wilson 22*, Abagale 17, Thomas C. 11/12
MCCALASTER, Mary 45*, America 18, George 11, James 8
STURGEON, Nimrod 35, Susan 30, Josephine 8, Sarah 6, Nancy 5, Caroline 2, Armanda 7/12

- 85 -

1850 Census Floyd County Kentucky

Schedule Page 461

JENKINS, John 25, Rachael 28, Jackson 5, William 3
BAYS, Margaret 54*, Jonathan 23, Eilha? 15 (m), Asa 12, Mary 29
SPRADLIN, Richard L. 26*, Nancy 20, Elizabeth 1
BAYS, William 44, Ruth 38, Elizabeth 13, Rebecca 6, John W. 3
SPRADLIN, Thomas 30, Mary 30, Narisa 4, Sarah 3, Charles 3/12
BOYD, Joseph 51, Sarah 32, Claborne 21, Eli 16, Caroline 14, Joel 12, Sarah 10, Nancy 9, Mary 7, Susan 1
STANDERFER, William 23*, Elizabeth 19, Calvin 2, Catharine 6/12, Floyd 20
PATTON, Christopher 35*, Scheriah 34 (f), John 11, Susan 3
RAMEY, Ephraim 37, Mary 46, Samuel 11, Joseph 3
GEORGE, Wilson 29, Anna 24, Frances 4, Martha 1, Robert 23
MILAM, Elizabeth 35, Lydia 17, James 14, John 9, Samuel 7, Henry 4, Margaret 9/12
HAGIS, William 30, Charlottee 38, Darthuly 13
HANNON, Roseannah 70, Rachael 40, George 21, Adam 16
VAUGHAN, John P. 45, Catharine 42, Gabriel 19, Midleton 16, Margaret 14, Nancy 11, John P. 7, Elizabeth 5, Sarah 3
WILLIAMS, Charles 30*, Jane 28, Joseph 8, James 6, Elizabeth 3
LUCAS, Margaret 60*
WILLIAMS, Joseph 65, Patsy 60, Charlotte 22, Nancy 2

Schedule Page 462

WILLIAMS, Alfred 25*, Vina 25, Catharine 8, Jane 1
HANNON, Lorenzo D. 48*, Mary 37, John 16, William 11
TATE, Joel 23, Charlotte 21, John 1
SARTIN, Elijah 26, Aggy 22, William 4, John 2, James 1
EVANS, Samuel 38, Nancy 35, Agnes 16, Nehemiah 14, Sarah 7, Thomas 3, Delilah 9/12
BANKS, David 46, Barthina 33, Joseph 23, Nancy 22, Nimrod 18, Elizabeth 17, Mary 15, James 12, John 10, Louisa 7
BURCHETT, Thomas jr. 23, Lettitia 15
VAUGHAN, Leroy 37, Amanda 32, Barton 10, Mary 7, Melissa 5, Aremintta 3
MILLS, John 21, Mary 21, William 3, George W. 3/12
BAYS, John 37*, Margaret 29, Martin 5, William 3, Mary 1
TRAVIS, Grenville 18*
DAVIDSON, Samuel P. 50, Judith 40, Alexander A. 21, Mary M. 18, Elizabeth J. 16, Joseph 13, Martha 11, Grenville 8, Andrew J. 5, Victoria 2
PORTER, William B. 39, Jane 29, John 9, James 8, Elgin 5, Grenville 3
GEORGE, John 55, Elizabeth 44, Samuel 22, Robert 19, Margaret 17, James 16, Nancy 12, Malinda 8, Persillia 6
HARMON, William 52, Jane 24?, Lorenzo 19, James 14, Nancy 11, Roseannah 2

1850 Census Floyd County Kentucky

Schedule Page 463

LEEK, Shelton 54*, Sarah 45, John 23, William 19, Catharine 17, Andrew 15, Thompson 14, George 12, Sarah 6
WILLIAMS, Catharine 65*
WILCOX, Owen 38, Mary 27, George 8, Mary 6, Henry 4
HAGAR, Harmon 29, Lettitia 26, James 4, William 2
WILCOX, James 41, Caroline 34, Andrew 11, Jeremiah 9, George 7, Samuel 5, Lorcene 3
SPENCE, Amon 53, Mary 44, Emanuel 23, John 20, Johnson 17, Martha 13, Wallis 9, George 7
AUXIER, Daniel sr. 64, Mary 56, Sarah 21, Samuel 18, Fletcher 16, McKinsey 13, Eliza 11
AUXIER, Daniel jr. 27*, Lucinda 22, Mary 2, George 1
LYNTICUM, Jerishia 65*
BALDRIDGE, Robert 39, Eleanor 35, Charles 15, Sarah 12, Mary 9, Nancy 6, Stalla? 4 (f), Rebecca 2
HAGAR, James 50, Susannah 43, Catharine 25, Sarah 17, George 16, Lydia 14, David 13, Richard 8, Amanda 7, Daniel 4
BURCHETT, William 33, Frances 27, Richard 8, Sarah 7, Daniel 5
KELLY, Joseph 40, Nancy 35, Emeline 16, Washington 9, Araminta 6, John 2
STINSON, Zackariah 30*, Milly 25, Minerva 5, James 4, Sarah 3, Cynthia 4/12
BALDRIDGE, William 13*

Schedule Page 464

STEVENSON, William 40, Lucinda 42, Sarah 7, William 5, Jalgin? 4 (m), Martha 3, Zackariah 8/12
YOUNG, Sarah 60*
JONES, Isom 21*, Nancy 21
HATFIELD, Winney 38, Rhoda 14, James 12, Frances 7, Jasper 3
SPRADLIN, Nehemiah 45, Hester 30, Abraham 25, Isabella 23, Sarah 20, Jonathan 17, Samuel 14, Thomas 12, Margaret 10, Benjamin 3, Patrick 2, Susan 1
STRICKLAND, Britten 67, Edah 50, Elizabeth 24, Edah 16, John 7, Jonah 4, Isaac 1
ALLEN, David W. 43, Jane 34, Joel 18, George 16, Susannah 14, William 13, Felix 12, Samuel 10, Rebecca 8, Cynthia 6, Andrew 4, David 1
HANSHAW, Samuel 22, Mary 18, Jane 4, David 2
FRALEY, Daniel 60, Mary 54, Nancy 28, Daniel 26, Elizabeth 25, Harvey 22, Temperance 18, Mary 16, Washington 13
HARRIS, Lawrence 30, Cynthia 28, Remathy 7, William 5, Alefer 3 (f), Sarah 1
GEORGE, Robert M. 50*, Martha 45, Mahala 26, William 21, Lindsey 18, Jane 15, Martha 13, Sussannah 10, Naancy 6, William 5, Cynthia 4, James 26, Martha 81
PORTER, William 19*
MEADOWS, Elisha 37*, Mary 43, Nancy 12, Clerissa 10, Alexander 5

Schedule Page 465

GREY, Joseph 22*, Jane 17
WIZEMAN, Abraham 53, Aarah? 45 (f), Malinda 29, Gilbert 20, Temperance 17, Wilburn 15, Jasper 14, Julia 10, Rebecca 7, James 5

1850 Census Floyd County Kentucky

SALMONS, Joseph 26, Mary 20
SALMONS, Jonathan 55, Martha 44, Henry 30, William 23, Elizabeth 20, Mary 18, Martha 16, Robert 13, David 11
FORTUNE, Jesse 55, Martha 30, William 16, Eliza 9, Julia 7, John 6, Thomas 4, Martha 3
GOBBLE, David 25, Elizabeth 26, William 2
BALDRIDGE, William 40, Emeline 25, James 10, Jane 7, Lucinda 4
GOBBLE, William 46, Cady 45 (f), Jeremiah 18, John 15, Patsey 12, Mary 9, Eliza 6, Sarah 3
WALLER, George 24, Elizabeth 21
PORTER, John 50, Mary 41, Samuel 23, Martha 21, William 14, Cornelius 8, Minerva 4, John 2, Mary 3/12
WEBSTER, William 65, Nancy 60, Sylvester 19, Alexander 16
FLANERY, Singular 42, Delia 39, Sarah 14, Tancy 13, Albert 11, William 10, Morgan 8, Littleton 5
CLARK, Morgan 33, Elizabeth 27, Samuel 5, Mary 36, Minta 17, Lorenzo 13
CLARK, John 47*, Mary 46, Sarah 16, Mouring 14 (f), Phee 12, Alexander 11, Rosemon 9, Josephine 8, Metilda 7, Taylor 3

Schedule Page 466

MEAD, Lorenzo 11*
HYLE, Julius 42, Nancy 40, Ann 18, Robert 16, John 14, Henry 12, Andrew 10, Sussannah 7, Nicholas 5, Lucinda 3
COLLINS, William 30, Milly 24, Mary 4, William 1
DAWSON, Joseph 33, Susannah 34, Mary 12, John 10, Elizabeth 8, Archibald 6, Martha 2
MERRITT, John 30, Nancy 28, Jacob 7, William 5, John 2, Robert 1
MULLINS, Benjamine 32, Dorothy 28, Riley 9, Nancy 4, Catharine 2
COLLINS, John 45*, Emily 24, Alsey 3
BURCHETT, David F. 30*
BURCHETT, Thomas 54*, Milly 52, Jesse 21, Emily 14, Thomas J. 27, Anna 18
HALE, Henderson 21*
GEORGE, Robert 27, Mary 22, James 2
SHATTON, Tandy L. 27, Martha 22, Milly 2
JARRELL, Hiram 39, Lucinda 32, Cynthia 16, William 14, Nancy 11, John 9, Rhoda 5, Mary 3, George 6/12
DAWSON, Isaac 23, Elizabeth 21, Ephraim 9/12
HATFIELD, Andrew 26, Lydia 20, John 4, Samuel 3
CRIDER, William 31, Elizabeth 24, Jackson 8, Wesley 6, Angeline 4, Martha 1
OWENS, James 38, Roseannah 27, Phebe 15, Louisa 2
STONE, Charles 30*, Zelpha 40, Mary 14, Elizabeth 12, Stephen 2, Margaret 2/12?

Schedule Page 467

MANN, George 21*
SITZER, John 26*, Mary 22, Alfred 5, Martha 2
LAWHOM, Catharine 20*
GARRETT, George 29*
HOWARD, James 48, Mary 44, Margaret 23, Ruth 20, Elisha 18, Moses 16, Elijah 14, James 12, Lewis 9, Sarah 7, Esther 5

1850 Census Floyd County Kentucky

MOORE, Samuel 36, Thursy 29, Tamsey 11, Mary 9, Nancy 7, Seliah 5, Elizabeth 3
JAMES, Abner 46, Margert 46, Nancy 16, Susannah 14, Rachael 8
SPRADLIN, Jesse 60, Sarah 58, Thomas 12, Solomon 8
SPRADLIN, Michael 25, Elizabeth 23, Lee 3/12
PEARY?, Low B. 39, Seeney? 35 (f), Martha 12, Mary 10, James 7, Elizabeth 5, Julia 3
RATLIFF, William 36, Malinda 30, James 13, William 10, Lucinda 7, Elizabeth 5, John 3
MAY, Harvy 25*, Louisa 24, Mary 3, Theadore 1
WILLIAMS, Alexander 22*
GOBBLE, Jacob 58, Susannah 30, Christopher 19, Charles 16, Armstrong 13, Margaret 11, Hugh 9, John 7, Sarah 5, Elizabeth 3
MOSELY, Samuel 24, Elizabeth 22, Minerva 3, Margaret 4/12
CRIDER, John 54*, Sarah 45, John 19, Elizabeth 16, Eliza 13, Jane 9, Catharine 6
SETZER, Samuel 21*
WALKER, Elizabeth 44*, John 20, Emily 17, Louisa 15, James 13, Thomas 8

Schedule Page 468

HACKWORTH, Charity 17*, Nicholas 6
PARSONS, Gabriel 28, Mary 21, Colbert 6, Elizabeth 5, William 3, Russell 1
MCCOY, William 35, Sarah 33, John 13, Melinda 11, Lansey 9 (f), Pleasant 7, Andrew 4, William 4, Jane 3
PRIEST, John 26, Mehala 21, Susannah 2
ROOP, John 26, Malinda 25, James 6, Samuel 4, David 2
MULLINS, Isom 55, Rose 52, Mary 20, Ambrose 17, Sarah 15, Arty 11
MULLINS, Elijah 27, Catharine 25, Mary 7, John 6, Sarah 4, Emma 3, William 1
MULLINS, Marshall 28, Nancy 22, Isom 5, Isaac 4, Disa 2
MULLINS, Solomon 30, Darcas 30, Allin 18, Minerva 16, Melinda 12, James 8, Anna 4, Preston 3, Lettitia 3/12
STACY, Elizabeth 55, Simon 20, Patcey 16
KELLY, James P. 32, Darcus 26, Jackson 11, Nancy 9, Spencer 4, James 1
NUSOM, Elizabeth 40, Metilda 20, Henry 14, Hotwell 10, William 9
NEWSOM, James 21, Sarah 23, Isaac 2
RUSSELL, Ira 35*, Tamsey 26 (f), Sarah 5, William 3
JAMES, Pennina 56*
RATLIFF, William 39, Rachael 31, James 8, Julia 6, Susan 1
FRALEY, John 48*, Louisa 39, William 18, Henry 15, Mary 13, Elizabeth 12, George 10, Susannah 7, John 5, Louisa 3, Milly 2

Schedule Page 469

LAWHORN, Disa 76*
CLAY, Robert 30, Elizabeth 35, Jane 5, Julian 1 (f)
JAMES, William 20, Disa 16
PARSONS, George 48, Susannah 44, Sarah 21, Lydia 20, William 18
BURTON, James 28, Margaret 23, Nancy 5, Crissie 3, Susannah 1
SMITH, John 30, Nancy 26

1850 Census Floyd County Kentucky

THOMPSON, John 44, Jane 42, Burwell 16, Layfaette 14, Permelia 13, Jane 12, Ernisthia? 10, Martha 8, Mary 4, John 3, Francis 2
THOMPSON, William 70, Jane 60, Melinda 19, James 7
TURNMIRE, Jemimah 38, Martha 5, Malinda 14, Luannah 13, Ellen 10, Isaac 7, William 5
SETZER, Adam 60, Mary 53, Margaret 18, James 15
CRIDER, Resso? 25 (m), Catharine 24, Julia 4, William 3, Samuel 1
FRANKLIN, Abel 53, Elizabeth 50, Bird 19, Abel 17
FRANKLIN, William 23, Elizabeth 26, Mary 4
VAUGHAN, Iris? sr. 60 (m), Sarah 58, Susan 28, Strother 17, Sarah 8, Elizabeth 5, John 1
MUSICK, John 24, Mills 20 (f), Julia 5/12
MCGUIRE, William 48, Mary 44, John 21, Harvy 17, James 15, Rhoda 12, Jane 10, Alexander 8, Esther 6, Casimore? 2 (f), Solomon 5/12, Whitten 46

Schedule Page 470

RATLIFF, Joseph 35, Sarah 24, Mary 11, Drury 7, Milly 5, Thomas 10/12
JONES, William 27*, Mary 23, Phebe J. 2, Evan 30
CUMMINS, William 27*
DAVIS, David J. 40, Mary 30, William 12, Ann 10, Jane 6, Elizabeth 3, Ezra 6/12
MANUAL, Elisha 23, Julian 17 (f)
JONES, Thomas 43*, Lucinda 43, John 16, Wiley 13, Martin 10, Binty 7 (m), Peter 5, George 2
PLAIN, Alfred 26*
WADKINS, Reese 20*
POWELL, William 32*
BENTLY, Thomas 20*
STEPHENSON, William 30*
WILLIAMS, Watkin 32*
MOLES, Emanuel 37*, Elizabeth 37, Jane 20, Elizabeth 18, John 17, John 15, Harriett 11, Manor 7, Catharine 5, Mary 1
DAVIS, Daniel 6*
WILLIAMS, John J. 27, Pelina 20
WILLIAMS, Edward 40, Nancy 26
ROY, Isaac 40, Elizabeth 45, Elizabeth 18, William 15, Charles 11, James 8, Seatha 6, Alamander 3
HARRIS, Edward 30*, Jane 30, Mary 4, Hannah 6/12
HUBBARD, Sarah 30*
HUBBARD, William 45, Malinda 30, Marshall 20, Harvey 17, Martha 16, Theopholus 14, William 13, Jane 10, Harvey 6, Araminta 5, Rebecca 4
PORTER, William G. 23, Jane 26, John 5, David 3, Rhoda 2
VAUGHAN, Burwell 56, Susan 54, Thomas J. 24?, Charles W. 21, Susan 20

Schedule Page 471

PARKER, John 47, Joice 49, Mary 23, Jemima 15, Oldaman 14, Joice 12, William 9, Sarah 7
HUEY, Robert S. 30*, Minerva 25
DANBY, Henry 24*
SMITH, Walter 28*
MELLEN, William P. 36*, Isabella 21, William 8, Mary 6/12, William 65

1850 Census Floyd County Kentucky

MCCOY, Susan 19*
MOSELY, William 29, Susannah 21, John 10, Luannah 8, William 6, Nancy 3, James 1
WOOD, Zebede 41, Luderia 27
HORTEN, Harvey 22*, Mary 21
GIPSON, Samuel W. 23*
VAUGHAN, Ivie jr. 27, Isabell 22, Abraham 4
CRUTCHER, Robert 33*, Martha 23, Elizabeth 3, Henry 6/12
HANNON, Daniel 23*
RAMSEY, David J. 27*
VAUGHAN, William 31, Isabella 24, Patrick 3, Samuel 1
COURTNEY, Robert 26*, Elizabeth 18
ROGGERS, John 23*
HATFIELD, Samuel 57, Mary 42, John 34, Owen 31, Alta 28, Samuel 16, Martha 14, Susan 13, Shadrick 11, William H. 9
FRALEY, Samuel 24, Mary 17
FIDLER, John 24*, Melinda 23
JONES, Robert 17*
PRICE, Daniel 18*
WIN, Robert 28*
STANFORD, William 25*
BAKER, Helton 18*
THOMAS, David 25*
POWELL, Lewis 28*
WATTERS, Wallen 30*
DAVIS, Thomas 26*
STEWART, John 35*
DELANEY, Thomas 32*, Elizabeth 21, William 8/12?
ROBINSON, John 32?*
BRIEN, Daniel 31*
MELLEN, Patrick 45, Catharine 40, William 11
MAYO, George 32, Caroline 25, Benton 3, Ann C. 1, Jeremiah 10 (B)

Schedule Page 472

LOASER?, Peter 35*, Catharine 28, Samuel P. 9/12
JESSE, Joseph 21*
CAMPBELL, Richard 30, Rhoda 25, Louisa J. 6, Joice A. 2
BAYS, Charles 65, Susannah 58, Charles 20, Mary 19, Jackson 18, Gerge? 16
BURNETT, John 31, Amanda 25, Samuel 3, Martha 1
LAYNE, James 37, Mienrva 31, Newton 11, Samuel 10, James 8, Peres? 6
GEARHART, Adam 66, Esther 44, Fhoda 24, John 17, Arty 15, James 14, Jefferson 11, Myram 8, Apperson 7, Adam 5
VAUGHAN, Burwell 26, Susan 20, Jane 8/12
MAY, Samuel 67*, Catharine 57?, Wilsey 18 (m), Catharine 9, Jane 7
MORGAN, Rhoda 29* (B)
HILL, Edward P. 30, James 26, Victoria 6, James P. 4, Melisa 1
FRESE, Melton 30*, Minerva 25, Frank 1
FRIEND, John P. 21*

- 91 -

1850 Census Floyd County Kentucky

HILL, John 22*
FRIEND, John 59, Rachael 45, Susan 18, Edward 15, Bud 10, Elizabeth 8
MARTIN, John P. 39, Elizabeth 36, Mary 12, Alexander 9, Fom? 4 (f), Elbert 21
HARKINS, Hugh 41*, John 14, Elizabeth 11, Emily 9
GREEN, Francis 25*
FRIEND, Charles 65, Martha 26, Susan 16, Lavina 14, Manford 11, Jerome 6
STRATTON, Elizabeth 34*, Mandeville 9?, Adalade 6
MCREYNOLDS, Mary 10* (B)
SMITH, John W. 24, Jane 23, James 2

Schedule Page 473

DEROSSETTS, Tolbert 24*, Madusa 19
DEAN, John 16*
ELLIOTT, John M. 26, Susan 17
BELL, Archibald 24, Judah 17, Robert 6/12
BOW, Joel 49, Nancy 47, Rusha 21, Darcus 18, James 15, Julian 13 (f)
KELLY, Joseph T. 30, Mary 25, Samuel 7, Butler 5
BAKER, George 36*, Hester 32, John 13, Susannah 10, William 7, Thomas J. 2
SMITH, James 23*
FORD, James T. 35*, Lucy F. 36, Margaret 9, Henry 9, Edward 3, Charlotte 65, Martha 40
MCREYNOLDS, William 14* (B)
HILL, Thomas R. 25*
COOLEY, David 42*, Eliza 36, Joseph 13, Peter 10, James 7, Lauran 5 (f), David 2
EMERSON, Elizabeth 65*
VINCENT, Gabriel M. 28, Zerilda 20, Carnilus 5, Mildred 2
DEROSSETT, James 51, Milly 46, Mary 23, Thomas 11
HARRIS, James P. 38*, Sarah 30, Adam 4, James 2
HALL, Nancy 13* (B)
GARUTT?, Bernard 26*
FRIEND, Isaac B. 40*, Cealah 32, Aramitta 14, Henry 12, Charles 10, Samuel 8, Joice 7, Bud 6/12
VAUGHAN, Jacob 20*
DILY, Lewis C. 30*
GILES, William D. 30, Charlotte 19, Thomas 2, Mary 1
JUSTICE, Wright 47, Clearah 47, Isaac 12
GIPSON, Riley 36 (B), Mary 35 (B), Mary 8, Lewis 6, Joseph 1
SEGIMOREL?, John 35, Esther 29, Jefferson 7, Apperson 5, Farris 3 (m), Whitten 1

Schedule Page 474

AUXIER, Samuel jr. 23, Rebecca 18
TRIMBLE, Edwin 42, Dorothy 41, James 20, Edwin 13, William F. 10, Josephine 7, Thomas G. 2, Robert 3/12, Meggy 3/12

1850 Census Greenup County Kentucky

Schedule Page 157

CORUM, William 39, Edith D. 31, Hannah S. 15, Charles 13, William 11, George 9, Edith 7, Harriett 5, Edwin H. 3/12
CORUM, Jesse 40, Salma? 36 (f), Jesse 12, John 14, James 8, Lewis 6, Nancy 5
EVANS, JEfferson 45, Mary T. 39, Virginia 17, Martha O. 12, Amanda P. 9, Addell 7, Hannah C. 5, Bell J. 3 (f)
RIBBLO, Henry 41, Naomi 28, Charlotte 10, Mary 8, Eliza Ann 6, Cornelius 3 (f), Henry N. 1
WINN, John E. 31, Nancy S. 27, Elizabeth 7, Harriett 5, John 3
BURBY, Matthew 44, Margaret 41, James 18, Emily 16, Ruth 14, Eliza 12, James 10, Charles 5
BARNEY, Jacob 33, Rachel 35, John 9, Amanda 5, David 4, George W. 3, Rachel 1
NICHOLS, Rachel 65, John H. 27, Lucy Ann 14
DAY, K. B. 44 (m), Lucy 25, Clara 5, Loiz 3 (f), Jr. 1 (m)
SMITH, Benjamin 46*, Sarah 45, Hannah 15, Alexander 14, Charles 11
PATTEN, Mary 60*
DAY, John F. 38, Eliza 34, Eliza Ann 14, John B. 12, Charity B. 6
BROWN, John 55, Charity 53, Thomas 17
GUILKEY, Scott 37*, Elizabeth 34, Margaret 15
LAWHORN, Melissa 6*
DAVIS, F. W. 5 (m)*
KING, Mary 25* (B), Francis 3, Amanda 1
MEEK, Joseph 30*
RILEY, G. B. 21 (m)*
YORK, Francis 23*

Schedule Page 158

WILLS, Samuel 35*, Martha 47
OLLIVER, Martha 21*
DAVIDSON, Jeremiah 34*, Eliza 32, Alfred M. 14, Henry C. 12, Caroline A. 10, William 8, Theodore 5, Edgar 1
CALLOWAY, Mary 15* (B), John 12
RAISIN, C. L. 28 (m), Amanda 22, Charles 1, Lewis 16, Eveline 17
WILSON, C. M. 47 (m)*, Charlotte 40, David H. H. 11, Cornelia F. 5, Minor 20
MEEK, Anna 14*
SPANGLER, Hannah S. 16*, Durphin 16 (B,m)
VANBIBBER, Cyrus 51*, Mary S. 51, Charles 17, Mary Ann 15, Haney 13, Sidney 11 (m), Rachel 9, Oba 7 (m), Harriet 4
HEDGES, John 18*
DAVIS, William 14*
VANBIBBER, James 48, Naomi 34, Eliza 13
THORNTON, E. C. 33 (m), Sarah Ann 30, Adeline 8, Wesley 7, Bascom 6, Chatty 4 (f), Sarah 1
HERTEL, Joanna 43, Jacob 17, Frederick 13, Charles 10
JACKSON, James S. 26, Patsey 25, David 2
SMITH, Martin L. 28, Hellener B. 20, Mary M. 3, Areana? 1
MCMULLAN, James 57*

1850 Census Greenup County Kentucky

WILSON, Susan M. 33*, James 10, Thomas J. 8
KING, John 40*, Frances M. 30, Nancy B. 6, Mary F. 2
WESTFALL, John W. 10*
MYERS, Allen 48*, Sarah Jane 20, Mary 23, Charles 17
FOLMER, Charles 21*
CHILDERSTON, George W. 38, Malinda 24, Sophia 4, Sarah 1
WHITE, J. W. 30 (m), Julia A. 34, Eliza Ann 12, David W. 7, Nancy J. 5, John A. 2
MYERS, John 38*, Isabel 39, Hannah J. 13, Laura 8, Thomas 6, John 4

Schedule Page 159

WHITE, Nancy 50*
BARNEY, John R.? 34*, Emeline 38, Mary Jane 6
STORMS, Alfred 15*, Ary Ann 13
WURTS, George 40*, Mary A. 34, Sarah 15, Rebecca 12, Alice 10, Ann 8, Samuel 4, Mary 3
PETERS, Amanda 18*
KING, Samuel W. 16*
HOLLINGSWORTH, Edward 33, Betsy Ann 28, John 4, Mary S. 2, Lydia J. 1
SEATON, N. K. 55 (m), Nancy D. 50, Harriet E. 16
GRUBB, William 33, Mary 22, Ellinor 1
COLLINS, Joseph D. 51*, Mary 33
GREEN, F. F. 17 (f)*
KOUNS, William S. 33, Caroline 28, Amelia 7, Anna 5, Mariah 4, William 1
FORBS, Christopher 30, Mary 18
RYE, Henry 28, Mary 19, Edgar 2, Elizabeth 50, Eliza 14
MAYLONE, John 25, Malvina 20, Matilda 1
HEISLER, Edward 30, Rebecca 19, George 2, Martha 1
CORUM, Martha 57, James 17
RAMEY, Thomas jr. 21, Sarah 21, America 1
HARD, Moses 43, Mary 30, D. C. 12 (m), Cyrus S. 10, Sarah L. 8, Elona 5, Harriet E. 1
HOLLISTER, Lyman 37*, Margaret 30, Esther 7, Kindry 17 (m)
POLLOCK, Joseph 38*
WILSON, David 26, Nancy 16
CAULY, William 39*, Ann 22, Isabel 2, James 1
FAIRTRACE, William 12*
SINNETT, John H. 51, Sabellah 42, John 16, Thomas 14, Elizabeth 12, Leonidas 6

Schedule Page 160

NICHOLS, William 24*, Ann 20
KOUNS, Jacob 18*
CRETZER, Samuel 32*, Rebecca 40, George 7, John 5, Andrimeda 3
BARNEY, Benjamin 19*, Amy 16
GREEN, Adell 39, Elvira 19
WARNOCK, Nelson 35 (B)
MAYLONE, George 23, Gilliann 17
SINNETT, Jefferson 24, Mary Ann 20, Matthew 2

1850 Census Greenup County Kentucky

TANNER, John P. 49, Rhoda 41, George 18, Letha 14, Lois 12, Lydia Ann 10, John 8
BEAN, James 41*, Rachel 30
DAVIS, Mary Ann 14*, Norman 7, Isaac 3
MCMULLEN, J. S. 31 (m)*, Susan 23, Susan 1
MEARS, Susan 53*, George 21
BLACK, Sarah 27*, Henry 8, Charles 5
FOSTER, Joseph 34, Elizabeth 33, Hopkins 10, Frances 5, Mary E. 3, Joseph 1, Mary 27
SPALDING, Alfred 30, Rebecca 24, George 1
NELSON, Tom 45 (B), Amey 60
UTZ, George 22, Mary 22
KOUT?, John 38, Catharine 34, John 12, Malinda 8, George 6, Catharine 3, Eveline 1
NELSON, Emeline 44, Margaret 17, William 15, Emeline 13, Amanda 12, John 10, Benjamin 6, Francis 4
CHAPMAN, C. P. 33 (m), Eliza 23, Malinda 1
POSEY, John 32, Mariah 27, E. A. 10 (f), Virginia 5, Sarah E. 3, John W. 1
HOWE, Jacob 60*, Jane 56, Henry W. 11
LONG, Henry 68*, William H. 7
HOWE, Hosey 26 (m), Rachel 26, William 4, Charity 2, Nancy J. 1

Schedule Page 161

BURNS, Benjamin 39, Jane 32, M. J. 13 (f), M. A. 10 (f), George 7, Nancy 4
BYRNE, Peyton 41, Sarah A. 28, Victoria 11, Patrick 10, Amanda 5, Granville 2, Thomas 49, Julia 20
STAGG, George 56, Jemima 45, John 20, Thomas 17, Jane 15, George 13, Alva 7 (m), Almira 4, Joseph 1
CRUMP, Simpson 48, Elizabeth 46, Margaret 22, Malinda 18, Holley 17 (m), Olivia 14, Charles 12, Nancy 10, Eliza 5
GASTIN, Robert 44, Sophia 34, Priscilla 17, Elizabeth 15, William H. 13, J. K. 6 (m)
MYERS, Henry 59, Lydia 48, Hezekiah 19, William 17, Harrison 6, John 38
MYERS, James 35, E. A. 24 (f), Louisa 1
FERGUSON, David 38*, Darcus 39, Cathrine 9, Margaret 8, Clarinda 3, James 1
MCCRUM, Mary 15*, Naomi 12
WOMACK, Archer 52, Myram 46, George 24, Samuel 18, Elizabeth 20, Thompson 16, Charles 14, Watson 12, Myram 10, Mildred 8, Benjamin 5
COLLINS, John 42, Mariah 35, Polly A. 16, Arminda 14, Lucinda 12, Nancy 10, Matilda 8, Simpson 6, Debby 4, America 3, Helen 1
ROGERS, M. A. 44 (f), T. A. G. 16 (m), M. P. 6 (m)
WHITE, William 41*, Emeline 28, Leonora 1

Schedule Page 162

SPANGLER, Leonora 23*
FITTY, Levi 19*
COLLINS, John L. 38*, Amanda 38, Eliza 8, Lewis 5, John W. 1
PEARCE, Gilbreath 25*
BRAMMER, Joseph 56, Nancy 58, William 32, Mary 30, Sarah 28, Nancy 26, Martha 24, Corbly M. 22 (m), Brazilla 20, James A. 19, James M. 17

1850 Census Greenup County Kentucky

MCCONNELL, C. L. 24 (m)*, Caroline 17
LEATHERS, Elizabeth 30*, William 10, Sally 5, Harriett 1
MCMAHAN, Stephen 56, Nancy 47, Mary Ann 7, J. K. P. 4 (m), Letitia 2
CAUDELL, Benjamin 25, Mary 30, Sarah A. 2, Emeline 8/12
COHEN, Harrison 35*, Mary 30, Simeon 9, Leak 7 (f), Philip 6, Ann J. 4, William R. 2
NORRIS, Philip 69*, Louisa 47, George 18
GUTHERY, Mary Ann 6*
CLARKE, James 30, Elizabeth 26, William 6, John 4, George W. 3, James R. 1, Mary K. 3/12
STEWART, James 51, Nancy 50, Harvey 21, Elizabeth 23, George G. 18, Nancy 17, Mary A. 14, Martha J. 13, Cintha A. 9
BARTLEY, James 62, Cassandra 52, Martha 28, Mary 22, Amanda 17, Cassandra 15, Sophia 13, James 11, William F. 8
MEAD, Benjamin F. 32, Mary A. 28, Lott 6, Jane 4, H. A. 1 (m)
MYERS, Samuel C. 51*, Mary 51, Elizabeth 16, Louisa 12
HELM, Benjamin 20*
HOOD, Andrew 66*, Mary 62, Jesse 21, William 15, Frances 21

Schedule Page 163

CAIN, Anthony 50*
COLE, Allaniah 49 (m), Louisa 28, Ann 20, Emily 16, Rucarta? 11 (f), Lovica 9, Jacob 8, Nancy 4, Susan 2
GARTHEE, Catharine 49*, John 22, Elizabeth 21, Sichy 19 (f), Joseph 15, Amey 11, E. J. 9 (f), George 6
SHINGLETON, James 22*
HOCKASAY, E. J. 39 (m), J. E. 39 (f), Eugene 15, Martha 13, James S. 11, George 9, Margaret 6, Edwin 1, Helen 22, John 17
BARNEY, Thomas sr. 55, Barbara 55, Leonard 17, Henry 15, James 12, Mary 12, Naomi 76
ROGERS, S. M. 37 (m), Sarah 32, John W. 10, Rebecca 19
HALL, Levi 25, Rebecca 25, Sarah A. 5, R. 2 (m)
FRENCH, John 21, Julia 19, Rebecca 6/12
BIGGS, R. M. 43 (m)*, Ann 32, Virginia 13, Elizabeth 11
BALDWIN, Mary E. 20*
RICE, Jehu 56*, Amanda 20, Ann 17
FISHER, Jacob 48, Levina 35, Mariah 12, Joseph 10, Adeline 8, Eliza 6, George 4
WEST, Thomas 38*, Sarah 24, James F. 10, B. G. 6 (m), James T. 7/12
SHORT, Rebecca 20*
ENSTMIER, Amon 45, Joanna 26, Rebecca 16, Edith 13, Nancy 8, F. M. 2 (m), Amon 5
POWELL, Ellis 27*, Parthenia 24
CLANCY, Nancy 54*, George P. 18
HAYS, Henry 54*, Mary 57
POWELL, Luke 28*, Lucy 21

Schedule Page 164

PAYNE, Lucy A. 24*
WARD, Isaac 22*, Thomas 20
FOSTER, John M. 40, Elizabeth 31, Charles F. 14, Martha 12, Pamelia 10, Ann E. 7, Mary K. 4, HElen A. 1

1850 Census Greenup County Kentucky

MEAD, Elizabeth 77*
CHINN, Sophia 36*, Mary E. 14, Thomas 12, Benjamin F. 10, John 7
RIGG, Joseph 66*, Elizabeth 65, Emily 33, Eliza 30, S. H. 24 (m), William E. 23, Elizabeth B. 16, Joseph W. 14, Susan A. 12, Henry C. 10, William H. H. 7
GILBERT, Thomas 30*, David 23
DAWSON, ____ 45 (m)*
RILEY, William H. 23, Mary 20, Eliza 2
WILLIAMS, Henry 37, Jane 34, Julia Ann 15, Sarah A. 13, Mary H. 12, Elizabeth 10, John T. 7, James A. 2, Naomi 2/12
BURK, James P. 56, Elizabeth 23, James M. 16, Martha A. 1
TACKETT, Thomas 47, Louena 40, Lewis 16
TRAMER, Peter 50, Ann 50
WURTS, Samuel 39*, Matilda 28, Ann E. 9, George 7, William 4, Mary 2
SCHER, Mary A. 20*
WALKER, George 22*
MCGREW, William H. 25*
SHEPHERD, Charlton 59*, Alexander 26, Lucinda 21, Charlton 20, John 16, Hezekiah 14, Leonard 12, Sarah 10
HOSKINSON, Mary M. 19*
TACKER, Richard 37*, Nancy A. 25, John H. 9, Fanny 3, Nancy 1
BOBBIT, Absalom 24*
LAWDON, William 34*
HARRIS, Ephraim 22*
HUTCHMAN, James 55*, Mary 47, Nancy 7
WARD, John 22*
BLACK, David 19* (B)

Schedule Page 165

RHEED, John 25, Sarah A. 21, Susannah 1
STEWART, John 51*, Ellenor 46, James E. 18, William H. 15, Louisa J. 13, E. E. 9 (f), John P. 7, George W. 3
MORRISON, Prudence 66*
RUNDY, Lewis 34, Hannah 28, Henry 4, Fanny 4/12
MEE, David 55, Catharine 55, John 19, Richard 15, William 7
NICHOLS, James E. 59, Matilda 40, Helen 18, John 17, Benjamin 14, Orlando 10
FANNER, Lewis 27*, Harriet 23, Edward 1, Mahala 8/12
RICHARDSON, John 16*
HARVEY, James J. 42, Nancy 40, Mary V. 13, James M. 7, Henry 5
CHINN, Benjamin 66*, George 28
RUBY, John 34*
RUTTER, William 49, Elizabeth 42, George 20, Edward 19, Hannah 15, James 12, Martha 8, Elizabeth 4, Ellen 2
LOWRY, William 33, Mary A. 26, John 8, Leticia 6
HENRY, Samuel W. 28, Mary A. 16
CARR, Jacob 38, Priscilla 34, James 11, Samuel 9, William 7, Harvey 4, Charles 2
PAGE, Jacob 29 (B), Elizabeth 24, Lafayette 9, William 3, George 3/12
HUTCHINSON, Benjamin 47*, Alcey 37, John W. 17, Eliza J. 16, James V. 13, Charles 10/12 (f)

1850 Census Greenup County Kentucky

HIGHTON, John 28*, Nancy 17
URICK, Elizabeth 14*
PRICE, Jacob 22*
WILCOX, Gains (m)*, Martha 23, Charlton 2, Stephen 1
KAYSER, J. M. 36 (m)*
PRATT, Ben F. 13*
MURPHEY, Pearce 34, Margaret 35, Mariah 21, George 13, Mary 12, Samuel 10, Joanna 9, Sarah 8, John 4, Theodore 6/12

Schedule Page 166

CARTRIGHT, Jesse 40, Catharine 35, Joseph 18, Hannah 16, lucy 14, Cyrus 12, Margaret 10, Narcissa 8, Matilda 6, Fanny 3, Caroline 6/12
EICHER, Joseph 45*, Ellen 37, Margaret 18, William 16, Hannah 15, Ann 10, Moses 9, Cyrus 7, Matilda 4, Samuel 2, Rebecca 1
KYLE, Henry 27*
CARTRIGHT, Moses 66, Hannah 66, Cyrus 5
SHERMAN, James 26, Mary 24, James 2, Samuel 1/12
KIFFER, Hiram 26, Margaret 20, Ezekiel 1
MILLER, Joseph 31*, Lorena 23, Martha A. 4, James 2, Eliza J. 4/12
STEWART, Robert 22*
BLACK, Charlotte 41* (B), Peyton 14, David 17, Lansdown 11
LEWIS, David 27*, Julia A. 23
STOCKHAM, P. 27 (m)*
JOHNSTON, William 26*
LOWTHER, Thomas 30*, Jessee 21 (f)
POLLOCK, John 26*
CHINN, C. C. 32 (m)*, Mahal 28, Lucy A. 7, Alfred S. 3
FARMER, Henry 18*
JAMES, A. W. 23 (m)*
BRADLEY, William H. 35, Mary A. 30, William 10, Sylvester 9, Elizabeth 4, Sarah A. 2
SHOAF, John 27, Eliza 23, Jehu 2
HOOD, Jacob 43*, Phoebe 41, Hezekiah 16, Nancy A. 13, Pleasant 10, Tabitha 6, Bluford 4
BARBER, Nancy 72*
FULTS, Hiram 25*, Mary Ann 21, William H. 2, James 17

Schedule Page 167

ARMS, William 25*, Letitia 30, Eliza A. 18
KELLEY, Ephraim 17*
BAKER, James 25*
STANLEY, Jasper 30*, Polly 18, James M. 4/12
BOWEN, Lewis 24*
TURNER, Martin 44, Parthenia 31, Martha A. 3, Angelino 1 (m)
SKEEN, Joseph 25, Polly 20, Charles 5/12
CAINS, Hiram 40, Frances 27, Thomas 10, Perry 8, Marcus 5, Hiram 2, Sarah A. 2/12
FRILEY, William 45, Celia 52, Nancy 20, Tivis 18 (m), Polly 16, David C. 14, George W. 12, William R. 8, Chloe 5

1850 Census Greenup County Kentucky

ALEXANDER, John 52*, Catharine 56, Levi 19, Peyton 17, Hiram 14, John H. 11, Alexan 17, Kate 70
LONG, William 19*
YOUNG, Paschal 3*
YATES, Sarah 57*, Martha 18, Susanna 15, George 18
CARTRIGHT, Elizabeth 18*
LANE, Reubin 22*, Catharine 21, Henrietta 8/12, Margery 8/12
DEVAN, Hester A. 18*
CRAWFORD, John 33, Elizabeth 28, Samuel 14, John 13, Andrew 9, Juli Ann 10, William H. 6, George 6/12
COLBERT, Jonathan 49*, Mary 48, Elizabeth 24, Isaac 21, Lewis 19, Archer 1
SHAFER, David 23*
WEST, Thomas 23*
WALLACE, James 18*
GAVER, Charles P. 26, America 21, Mary F. 1
HARDWICK, Henry 46*, Matilda 44, Samuel W. 18, John R. 16, Henry V. 11, Sally A. 8
MCADAMS, Robert 50*
DAVIS, Eilza 45*
LITTERELL, James 30*

Schedule Page 168

GULLET, Christopher 24*
HARDWICK, William 33*, Sarah 30, Sally A. 2, Samuel W. 1
AKINS, Elizabeth 14*, John 12, Thomas 9
HARDWICK, Samuel 52*, Jane 33, Polly A. 17, John H. 19, Lucy J. 9, Jourday E. 5 (m), James S. 4, George W. 3, Christopher P. 1, William P. 14
HUGHES, Absalom 21*
HORNBUCKLE, Samuel 31*, Elizabeth 22, Alpheus 2, Margaret 1
DAVIS, Agnes 9*
GANTS, Joseph 39*, Eveline 33, Susan 11, Mary 3, Theodore 6/12
CAIN, Anthony 50*
CLARKE, Margaret 54, Cynthia A. 15
WEEKS, Cornelus 44*, Ary A. 42 (f), Charles 20, Martha 18, John 16, Emeline 14, George Ann 10, Henry 8, Hannah 7, Eliza V. 1/12
TAYLOR, William 30*
MAGILL, Ferdinand 22*
WAUGH, Thomas P. 30, Margaret E. 25, William N. 4, Matilda F. 2, Chrisley A. 5/12
HARDWICK, Nimrod 41*, F. J. 31 (f), LEvey A. 6, Eliza 4, _____ 6/12 (m)
BRADFORD, C. S. 14 (f)*
LEE, Ellis P. 24*
HUGHES, John 30*, Mary 29, Susan J. 6, Henry 4, George W. 2
HARDWICK, Jordan 45*
GHOLSON, Willis 25, Mary 22, Martha A. 1
HERN, Harvey 32, Mary 34
WILSON, Elzy A. 42 (f)*, Debby 32, Angeline 11, William 9, Clay M. 7, George W. 5, Hiram H. 3, H. Taylor 4/12
CAIN, Ann 55*
JENT, Carlos 16*

1850 Census Greenup County Kentucky

ALEXANDER, William 23*
ABRAMS, Samuel 30, Nancy 25, Minerva 6, Polly 4, Joseph 3
CRAWFORD, Milton 42*, Elizabeth 34, James 17, McDonald 9, Francis M. 7, Elizabeth 4

Schedule Page 169

ABRAMS, Elizabeth 67*
MURPHEY, Mary 40, John 19, William 18, Clarke 12, C. H. 9 (m), Lewis 6
WORTHINGTON, Alex 34*, Eliza A. 30, Hannah 11, Joseph 9, James 6, Nancy E. 4, Mary 1
HAGGERTY, Eliza 20*
HARVEY, Isaac 48, Rebecca 42, Edith 21, Alice 19, John 18, James W. 16, Lydia 13, Henry H. 10,
    Joseph M. 8, Caroline 6, Oliver P. 3, Eliza A. 2/12
GHOLSON, Malinda 54*, Emily 21, Harvey 19, James 17, Mary 16, Cynthia A. 13, Joseph C. 11
DITTY, Nathaniel 22*, Clarinda 27, Emily 2, James Harvey 1
BUSH, James 42, Eliza 35, Polly A. 14, William H. 4, Sarah Jane 3, James M. 1, Eliza A. 4/12
PATTON, William M. 46*, Rebecca 36, George B. 7, James S. 4, William A. 1
BOAL?, William K. 18*
ALLISON, Eliza 32*
HARRIS, Catharine 12*
PATTON, Ellen R. 9*
PATTON, John S. 44, Catharine 33, Elizabeth 13, Margaret 11, Caroline 9, William P. 7, Samuel 1,
    Rebecca 18, Silas 5
COLLIER, William D. 32*, Esther A. 25, Mary K. 1
DOUGHERTY, Mary J. 14*
KINNIER, Joseph 60*
FIELD, Joseph 45*
ANDERSON, Andrew 28, Elizabeth 24, Juli Ann 2/12, William 22
IRONS, Henry 38, Albina 38, George 12, Jane 10, John 8, James 5, Mary 3, Thomas 1

Schedule Page 170

CUNNINGHAM, James 36, Eliza 38, William 15, Joseph 13, Mary A. 10, John 8, Mariah 6, James 4,
    George 1, William 23
CALLAHAN, Thomas 36, Mary 36, Gabriel 12, Thomas J. 7, America 3, Mary 1, Edward 28, Jefferson
    6
SMILEY, James 39, Mary 31, John 10, Ellen 8, Nancy J. 6, James 3, Alexander 1
HASTINGS, Hiram 35, Sarah 35, Alfred 15, Elvira 11, James M. 9, America 4, Alexander 1
JOHNSON, Amos 23, Rebecca 17
CAMPBELL, Willis 42, Catharine 40, James 13, Mary K. 10, Russell 4, William 2, Willis 1
NORMAN, Stephen 55, Sarah J. 30, Elizabeth J. 3
SHAFER, Philip 42, Louisa 32, Louisa 11, Charles 10, Augustine 4, Lewis 2, George 1/12
ARMS, Moses 35, Emily 28, Malinda 9, Louisa 7, Sarah J. 4, Martha A. 3, William 1
SPRADLING, Robert 52*, Louisa 46, Nancy 17, Elizabeth 14, Polly 12, William H. 9, Harry 7, William
    4, Jackson 3, Henry 1, Samuel 21, Robert 23
CAMP, James 18*
PILES, Henry 24*, Sarah E. 21, Isaac 2
MARTIN, Ann 45*, William 24, James 21, Henry 15, John 7

1850 Census Greenup County Kentucky

COOPER, Junius 23*
GILLIS, George 30*, Lucinda 28, Martha 7, Mary A. 5, Louisa 4, William 4/12, Charles 18

Schedule Page 171

CAMPBELL, William 18*
ULEN, Benjamin 60, Elizabeth 34, Frederick 26, Sarah Ann 17, Arematha 8, Lewis 4, Margaret 7/12
CALVIN, Aquilla 40*
SUTHERLAND, Nelson 38*
KOUNS, Eleanor 8*
ELZICK, Jane 28*
BAILEY, Mary 5*
DAVIS, Jonathan 38, Sarah 34, Elizabeth 14, Matthew 10, William 6, Benjamin 4, Charles 2
HERN, Harrison 35*, Lutinea? 29, Angeline 10, Thompson 7, Henry 5, Elizabeth 3, Sarah 1
RUSSELL, Sarah 14*
SPARKS, Richard 21*
MILLER, Charles 25*, Mary 27, Lewis 4, Sophia 2
CROWDER, Coonrod 28*
BOYCE, James 28, Sarah 22, Amanda J. 2, Virginia 6/12
APPLEGATE, L. V. 28 (m)*, Margaret 33, Gertrude 16, Eliza 2, Catharine 11/12
JOHNSON, T. W. 24 (m)*
MORRIS, J. C. 25 (m), Elizabeth 22, William 2, John 3/12
MORRIS, Isaac 55*, Elizabeth 46, John 24, William 20, Sarilda 13, Betsy A. 10
BLACK, Andy 30* (B)
CARTER, Frank 23* (B)
ANTIS, Hiram 40, John W. 15, George W. 10, Nancy J. 5, Rebecca A. 2, Margaret 76
SPRADLING, Jerry 28*, Susan 22, Samuel 1, John 1/12
WILSON, Samuel 17*
ANTIS, Samuel 32, Nancy 29, Lavina 10, Calfurna 7, John W. 4, Stephen 2
YATES, Joseph 25*, Frances 22, Rozelle 3
NORRIS, George 20*
KINNEAR, Alexander 30*, Mary 20, William 1

Schedule Page 172

BRYANT, Amey 4*
BRYANT, Isaac 45*, Clarinda 34, John 16, Abraham 11, Amanda 7, William 5, Alfred 4, Alexander 1
VANDINE, Ellen 66*
JOHNSON, Eliza 30, Sarah A. 11
REED, Stephen B. 51*, Rachel 50, Amos 25, Samuel 21, Thomas 20, John 18, Rebecca 15, Isaac 13, George 11, Benjamin 9, Stephen 5, Samuel 4/12
WARD, Martha 23*
SHORT, William 25, Leana 22, William M. 4/12
TUFTS, William 26, Angeline 22, William 4, Wealthy A. 2 (f), Amasa 6/12, H. C. 21 (m)
HAWKINS, John B. 77, Polly 50
TUFFTS, Wealthy A. 50 (f)*, Aaron 31, Benjamin 17, Leven 12 (m), Mathias 10
CLUTS, Mary 32*

1850 Census Greenup County Kentucky

HARDIN, Frances 26, Eliza 2, Sarah E. 1
BRANT, Michael 47, Agnes 39, Dinah 14, Charles 8, Mary 6, Edward 10/12
BEGINBACK, John 36*, Marget 30, Marget 4, Jacob 2, Barbary 1, Michael 1/12
RUNDY, Christian 40 (m)*
HARN, George 48*, Lydia 38, Francis 12
FRY, Elizabeth 62*
WILLIAMS, James 25, Nancy J. 21, Henry 1/12
COLEGROVE, J. D. 39 (m)*, Elizabeth 37, John 16, James 12, Harriett 10, Jerry 8, Emily 7, N. C. 5 (m), Thomas H. 3
COYLE, Sarah 67*
COLEGROVE, Jeremiah 65, Olivia 59, Sanders 22
PUTHUFF?, John 65*, Kate 62
MASON, Martin 28*
DEVORE, John 52, Sophia 35, Henry 9, Lewis 5, Elizabeth 4, Coonrod 1

Schedule Page 173

BOLLING, William P. 19, Eveline 17
WORTHINGTON, James 47*, Ellenor 41, James 22, Nancy 19, Orlando 16, Isabel 14, Charles 11, Renald 9/12
MORRIS, William 21*
ARNOLD, Andy 49, Sarah 26, Robert 17, Josiah 15, Emeline 12, Phoebe A. 6, Hope J. 4, Mary E. 2, Thomas W. 1
RUTHERFORD, Scott 28, Barbara 27, Joseph H. 8, Allen 7, Elizabeth 5
SUMMERS, John 24*, Elleanor 24, Margaret A. 11/12
ANDERSON, John 24*
SPRADLING, John 26, Mary J. 25, Robert 4, Sandford 3, James 2/12
ARTIS, Daniel 33, Louisa 25, George W. 5, Mary J. 3, Cyntha A. 2, Elizabeth 4/12
FITZPATRICK, Nathan 40, Mary A. 33, Joseph 11, John 8, Charles 6, James 4, Daniel 2
ARTIS, William 28*, Eliza 26, Harvey 5, Elizabeth 3, Louisa 2
WHEELER, Elizabeth 45*
NORRIS, John 25*
WHEELER, Edward 46, Milly 40, John 20, Joseph 17, Henry 16, Sarah 15, Nancy 9, Elizabeth 7
PULLY, John 77, Mary 77
COGSHELL, Levina 38*
BELLAMY, John 22*
COOK, Levi 30, Elizabeth 28, John 8, Ann 7, Susan 4, Rohama 1
LAWRENCE, Joel 60, Sarah 55, Catharine 23, Martha A. 21, John 19, Henry 15, Rachel 13, Rebecca 11, Levina 1, Virginia 6/12

Schedule Page 174

DIALS, Eli 21, Matilda 28, Elizabeth 3, Granville 1
MCALISTER, Robert 28*, Sarah 25
BEVINS, John M. 32*, Virginia 10
SHAFER, George 32*
RAVENSTART, John 22*, James 19

1850 Census Greenup County Kentucky

SHROAT, John 19*
MCALISTER, George W. 39, Mary 27, Sarah A. 12, Nancy 10, Jane 8, Balinda 6, James 3, Emily 2, Harvey 24
POWELL, Joseph 25, Huldah 19
DAVIS, Benjamin 23*, Pamelia 24, Jane 1, John 19
MCCARTY, Eliza 5*
DARBY, George 29*, Elizabeth 29, John 7, Hugh 5, Ransom 1
BRYANT, Julian 10 (f)*
YOUNG, Poss? 29 (m)*
WOMACK, Charles 45
CULBERTSON, Samuel 48*, Mary 34, William W. 14, Kennady 10, Mary E. 7, Susan B. 5, John J. 1
CANTERBURY, Elizabeth 15*
WILLIAMS, George S. 28, Margaret C. 26, Blanch 2, Laura 1
NICKOL, Joseph 41, Arney 24, Charles 3, Joseph William 1, Charles F. 24, Aphalona 33, Josephine 7
WILSON, Seth 37, Isabel 30, Elvira 12, Elizabeth 7, Andrew J. 5, Joseph B. 3
BUCKLEY, A. J. 34 (m), Sophia 34, Emeline 11, William H. 9, Sarah A. 7, Alfred D. 5, Susan A. 3
DIXON, George 32, Satha 35 (f), Emily E. 10, Thomas 9, George 8, J. K. P. 4 (m), Robert 2, Nancy A. 1/12
CAZELL, Joseph 33*, Lorena 32, Almanza 10 (m), Isabel 8, Mary A. 4, James H. 2, ____ 1/12 (f)

Schedule Page 175

HENSLEY, Jane 21*
HALL, George 21*
WALTERS, Harrison 32, Mary 25
FITCH, Daniel 27, Sarah 23, Sarah E. 1
BURK, William 60, Sarah 50
WILSON, Andrew 23, Susan 23, Josephene 2, George W. 2/12
ARTES, Mary 37, John 19, James 17, Elizabeth 12, Rebecca 8, Henry H. 7, Nancy A. 3
COPLEY, Robert 30*, Mary A. 29, William 11, James 9, Sarah J. 7
BEASON, John 30*
JONES, John 30*
HENNIFUR, Matthew 23*
MCDONALD, Mike 35*
CULBERTSON, E. D. 45 (m)*, Sarah 35, John 11
FRICK, Christena 20*
WALK, Benjamin 50, Jane 52, Martin 23, William 18, MArgaret 21, Benjamin 17, Hezekiah 15, James 14, Elizabeth 12
FITCH, Elias 29, Mary A. 28, William N. 6, Eliza A. 4, Eliza W. 2/12, Laura L. 21, Alexander 21
BOYLS, John 46, Agatha 41
GALLION, William 24*, Martha A. 21, Rutha 4/12
LANCEFORD, William 21*
CURTEEL, William 45*, Nancy 35, Juli Ann 15, Betsy J. 13, Joseph 11, George W. 8, Harrison 5, Nancy 2
GRIFFITS, James H. 21*
GORE, James C. 22, Lucinda 20
DAVIS, Henry 33*, Elizabeth 30
JONES, Matilda 1*

1850 Census Greenup County Kentucky

GEE, William 29*
PERKINS, Lewis 26, Hesther A. 18, Margaret E. 6/12, James E. 5
PENICKS, John 31*, Elizabeth 33, Robert A. 8, Sarah A. 6, William J. 4, John D. 1
HANNAHS, Ann 60*
MCALISTER, John V. 35*, Elizabeth 31

Schedule Page 176

WILLIAMS, Don 21*
DOODY, William 27*
STEERER, John 25*
FRY, Jacob 30*
ROGAN, James 30*, Reuben 25
DAVIS, Thomas 35*
JONES, John 17*
HINKLE, John 40*
FERGUSON, Elizabeth 14*
BACK, Jacob 57*, Leann 47, John 23, Samuel 21, Jacob F. 14, William 12, James 7
MCCARRAN, Daniel 23*
CARR, Willis M. 30*
MCFADDEN, William 21*
FREELS, Frank C. 37*
DAVIS, Peggy 80*
HANNAHS, Perry 30, Jane 31, Benjamin 8, Ellis 4, Winfield 2, Sarah 1, William 34
PEARCE, Charles 29, Adelina 17
FOX, Joseph 25, Emeline 22, Asa 4
FOX, Asa 65, Elizabeth 45, Caroline 13, Daniel 21, Mary 11, Francis 7, Penina 5
NEAL, Larkin 40*, Marinda 55, Elijah 11, William J. 7, Myra 5
FRAIL, John 25*
WELCH, michael 41*, Artimica 28, Mary 2
DUNN, George 42*
SAVAGE, Ann 10*
SMITH, John 28*, Barbara 20, John 10/12
SHOBIT, Crist 23 (m)*
SHARP, William 35, Ellen 21, Elizabeth 3, Mary Ann 1
KEATON, Jefferson 36*, Rebecca 36, Catharine 18, Jesse 14, Polly 13, Lewis 11, Cytha 7, Mary 1
HATFIELD, Stephen 15*
TACKET, Lucy 60*
BUTLER, James 35
BRADLEY, David 26*, Angeline 21, Margaret E. 2
CARTER, William 30*
WADE, David 42*, Nancy 24, Sarah J. 14, William 12, James 9, Delana 7 (m)
GULLET, Moses 30*
RUGGLES, John 44*
PERKINS, Lewis 24, Lis 20 (f), James E. 4

1850 Census Greenup County Kentucky

Schedule Page 177

GULLET, Daniel 28, Nancy Jane 16
NOLEN, Jeremiah 22*, Syrene 55, Nancy 21, James 15
BOLIN, John 20*
HEGREITE, James 20*
WILDER, Deniss W. 30*
PRIDEMORE, John 23*, Nancy 16
HARVEY, Andrew 22*
TACKETT, Lewis 31, Leander 20, Richard 2, Henry 6/12
GULLET, Daniel 45, Jenny 50, Mary Jane 22, Charles 28, Clarinda 20, Telitha 18, Eliza 16, Jincy 8, Levi 6, Elizabeth 4, Esther 1
BAYS, Robert 38, Easter 20, John H. 5, Mary E. 3, Nancy J. 1/12
MCCONNELL, Matthew 31, Nancy 32, William 12, Mary J. 10, James 7, Elizabeth 6, Eliza 3, Kate 1
PENICKS, John 31*, Elizabeth 33, Robert A. 8, Sarah A. 6, William J. 4, John D. 1
HANNAH, Ann 62*
HARDING, Fielding 30, Nancy 25, Mary J. 7, Lemar W. 5, Sarah 1
COOK, Peter 45, Nancy A. 40, George W. 20, E. J. 18 (f), Margaret 14, W. H. H. 11 (m), Horace W. 8, Emily E. 4, Harriet M. 1
DARBY, James 64, Sarah 54
DARBY, John 26*, Aremetha 26, James 25
WILLIAMS, Nancy J. 17*
STEWART, Alex 22*
PREWETT, Henry 25*
BALLOO, Lincy 26 (m), Abinida? 22, John W. 3, Alice 7/12
BALLOO, Garrett 32, Mary 30, John 62
STEWART, George 33, Harriet 31, Emma 1
DEERING, William 57, Sarah 49, Henry 18, Nancy 13, John 9, Mary 6

Schedule Page 178

HOWE, Daniel 39*, Polly 34, Rebecca 14, Mary J. 12, Charles 10, William 9, Martha 7, Sarah E. 6
MONTGOMERY, Sarah 25*
FARMER, John 41, Nancy 40, Louisa 16, Mary E. 15, Christina 12, Martha 10, Lewis 8, John W. 5, Charles 5/12
SARGANT, Robert 30*, lucy A. 24, John H. 3
DEBOW, Eliza 9*
CASTEEL, John 32*, Jane 30, William F. 10, Elizabeth 9, John W. 8, Jana 6 (f), Josep 4, America 3, Mary 2
ROBINSON, Samuel 15*
HANNAH, Elizabeth 38, Isabella 7, John 5, K. S. 1 (f)
MCLAIN, Daniel 40*, Ann 23, Thomas 11/12
MCGINLEY, Roger 28*
GOLLIHER, Charles 23*
BURGESS, Robert 55*, Margery 54
DRAVENSTOT, Tobias 15*

1850 Census Greenup County Kentucky

WOOLDRIDGE, Samuel 45, Lucy 37, Nancy 19, Jane 16, Rebecca 13, John 11, William 9, Elizabeth 7, Martha 5, Sarah 1
CALLAHAN, George 24, America 20, John W. 1
MCALISTER, James 30*, Hiram 25
LOWRY, George 37*
CALLAHAN, Daniel 36, Nancy 32, Robert 12, Denabe 11 (f), James M. 9
FERGUSON, William 44, Aramatha 35, James R. 16, Elizabeth 13, Benjamin 11, Mary J. 9, John T. 6, William H. 1
WILLIS, William G. 27, Cassander 17
YOUNG, John 84, Mary 80
HARDING, Semar? 39 (m)*, America 56, Samuel 18, Huston 11

Schedule Page 179

CAIN, Charles H. 16*
NUTTER, William 28, Aramatha 23, Matthew 3, Walter 11/12
KISER, Hiram 27, Polly 21, Mary 6, John 4, _____ 1 (f), Henry 65
WILLIS, Alfred 22, Mary 23, George 4
WILLIS, John 60, Jane 17, Benjamin 14, Thomas 12, Aramatha 10, Lewis 8, Antinett 6 (f), Mary 4, James 21, John 19
WILLIS, Jacob 22, Burrilla 19, Seymour W. 8/12
HARDING, Leander 25*, George W. 5, Henry C. 4, America 2, William H. 6/12
CURRINGTON, Rosan 22*
THOMAS, Madison 32*, Nancy 31, Thomas J. 11, Eli 10, Catharine 7, Phoebe 6, George W. 5, James M. 2, Eliza J. 7/12
JOHNSON, Joseph W. 13*
LITTERELL, Perry 29, Mary A. 23, Elizabeth 6, Mary J. 4, James W. 3, Margaret 1
KOUNS, John C. 63*, Elizabeth 55, Sarah 23, Mariah 19
HOLLISTER, Hudson 32*, Mary 21
GILLY, Alfred 26, Amanda 21, William 2, Helen 10/12
MEAD, Armstead 44, Elizabeth 34, Ann 14, Eveline 12, Naomi 10, Sarah B. 7, Lucy 5, Charles 1
LANGHSIRE, Thomas J. 38, Emily 35, Cintha A. 14, Eliza 12, Sarah J. 9, Allen B. 7, Margaret 5, Mary 3
MARTIN, Phillips 34, Mary A. 29, Lucinda 11, William 9, Martha A. 5, Andy 4, John D. 5/12
FRANKLIN, Lawson 45, Polly 36, Harriet 12, Elizabeth 10, Mary 5, Reuben 4

Schedule Page 180

TOWNSEND, Jackson 55, JAne 25, Benjamin 18, Susan 15, George 13, Mariah 10, James 8, Martha 5, Richard 2
POWELL, Samuel 45, Lucy 48, Wealthy A. 19, John W. 16, James N. 14, Charles H. 12, Elizabeth 10, Thomas S. 8, Helen 6/12
MORRIS, Phil 24*, Lucinda 23, Mary 1
TAYLOR, Mary J. 10*
FISHER, Jacob 35, Sarah 24, Mary E. 4, Martha J. 3, Alexander 1
CRESSEL, Martha A. 28, William H. 13, James A. 10, Nancy J. 8
JOHNSON, Samuel 25, Sarah 25, Eliza F. 1

1850 Census Greenup County Kentucky

NOBLE, James M. 38*, Sarah 37, Levi 13, Elizabeth 16, Ann M. 7, Susan 5
NORRIS, William 20*
MORROW, John 35, Jane 33, Sarah A. 13, Elizabeth 10, Nancy 9
THOMAS, William 66, Ann 63, Nicholas 23, William 21
THOMAS, Evander 26, Juli Ann 23, William 3, Abner 10/12
WHITON, William H. 25*, Sarah 23, Elizabeth 3, Edward 1, Mary 28
BLACK, Daniel 30* (B)
CLAVIS, Coonrod 37*, Augusta 20, Charles 10/12
NAUGER?, Frederick 43*, Amanda 47, Amanda 12, Charles 10, Julia 6, Caroline 3
JOHNSTON, John 33, Isabella 27, William W. 9, Elizabeth A. 8, Mary A. 6, Lucy B. 1
JOHNSTON, Isaac 22, Rebecca 22
ZEEK, William 54, Mary 44, Thomas 16, Lieuceste? 12 (f), Nancy J. 9, John 4, Susan 1

Schedule Page 181

MAYHEW, John 24*, Mary A. 24, Eleanor 1
WHITE, George 24*
JUDSON, William 24*
SHUFF, Solomon 34, Mary A. 32, William H. 5
JONES, John D. 24*, Elizabeth 20
ABDON, Lucinda 18*
HENROTT?, E. 30 (m)*
SMITH, Henry 28, Christian 29 (f), Doler 5 (f), Rosanna 3, Catharine 1, Elizabeth 6/12
SNIDER, Daniel 26, Caroline 22
LAVENDER, Mary 53*, Henry L. 14, Harriet F. 12
BRECKENRIDGE, James 5*
SMOUT, John 32*
MAYBERS?, Charles 32, Christian 26 (f), Pauline 11/12
FEELING, John 50*, Agnes 38, John 11, Mary E. 8, Mary K. 6, Sophina 3, Mary B. 5/12
PICKEL, Frank 26*
BROWN, Clarissa 39* (B)
LACY, George 30* (B)
ARMSTRONG, William 52*, Ann 44, Isabella 15, Jane 6, William 4, Elizabeth A. 1
GUNDRY, Joseph 40*
HERRINGTON, James 25*
PERRY, David 55, Mary 45
MASON, Joseph 40
KEZEE, Lewis 36*, Lydia 28, John 12, Pamilia 10, Benjamin 8, Mary J. 6, Matthew 3, Jeremiah 2
MAYHEW, William 45*, Mary J. 6
WEST, Matthew 38*, Charlotte 24, James R. 8, Elizabeth 6, Judea A. 4, George W. 3/12
MAYHEW, Elizabeth 13*
WARD, William 23, Elizabeth 20
TANNER, George 49*, Elizabeth 42, Mary A. 23, John 21, Eliza J. 18, Jacob E. 15, William A. 12, Martha E. 10, Robert P. 8, Isabella 5, George H. 1
JONES, William C. 15*, James 1

1850 Census Greenup County Kentucky

Schedule Page 182

COLLINS, Robert 27*, Mary 26, Ann 9/12, Ann 57
WISE, Wesley 14*
WISE, James 30, Hannah 29, David 9, John 7, Merinda 5, Peter 3
POAGE?, John 74*, Margaret 36
KINKEAD, Mary 15*, William 13, Andrew 11, John 11, Caroline 7
HORN, John 45, Lucretia 35, Catharine 15, Nancy 13, Sarah 12, Frederick 11, Benjamin 11, James 9, Polly 7, Sarilda 4, Elvira 1
SHEELER, Jacob 50, Susan 22, Margaret 18, Catharine 16, Ewin 11, Mary 6
JONES, John P. 25, A. A. J. 22 (f), Ann P. 2, Sally 10/12
PICKEREL, Henry 28, Susan 28, Marinda 6, Peyton 5
FITCH, Isaac 45, Mary 36, Susan 15
PICKEREL, Bazel 50*, Lucy 47, Mildred 33, Rebecca 22, Jane 18, Charles 16
JOURDAN, John 23*
KEZEE, C. H. 7 (m)*
MARTIN, Hester A. 4*
ASHMORE, Thomas 35, Eliza 39, James 15, Jacob 13, Richard 11, Thomas 7, Benjamin 6, Jane 3, Margaret 1
SHEELER, Jeremiah 23, Mary 22, Jacob 1
SHIPTON, Barnabas 58, Mary 50, James 18, Robert H. 10, Martha B. 8
SUMMERS, John 49, Clemanza 42, Ellen 17, Henry 14, Alfred 12, Nancy 9, Andrew 7, Morris 5, Joseph 1
POGUE, William L. 56*, Caroline A. 30, Henry E. 23, Robert 9, William L. 7, Harriet 5, Mary E. 2

Schedule Page 183

JONES, William B. 30*
MCCARTY, Henry 35, Susanna 24, Josephine M. 6, Sarah E. 4, Eliza J. 3
BOBBETT, William 43, Nancy 48, Elvira 23, James W. 20, Thomas 18, Henry 15, William 13, Eilzabeth 12, Clay F. 7, Judy A. 5, Calvin 2, Sophia 42
BLACK, Madison 25 (B), Mariah 20, Mary 4, Rachel 2, Clarissa 7/12
OCCOMAN, Samuel 25, Sarah 19, Matilda A. 4/12
IRONS, Solomon 27, Ruth 22, Sarah A. 19, Elias 17
BROWN, William 55, Catharine 51, John T. 21, Mary L. 14, David 18
DIXON, Thomas W. 29*, Tabitha 23, William 5, Caroline 1
FALKNER, Thomas 7*
PRICE, Benjamin D. 61, Nancy 56, James 24, Aladin 22, Benjamin 20, Kendall 18, Jane 17, Olive 16, Elvira 14
DEAN, George 26, Catharine 22, Samuel E. 2
BROWN, William 46, Delila 35, Lorena 14, Caroline 11, John 9, Amanda 7
BRADSHAW, Robert 40, Jane 38, Mary J. 15, Samuel 13, Mariah 10, Nancy 8, Martha A. 7, George 4, James W. 1
WORLEY, Sarah 42*, Henry 16, John 12
WILSON, Elizabeth 70*
DIXON, Meridith 56*, Angeline 24
HEDGES, Catharine 18*

1850 Census Greenup County Kentucky

BLAIR, Harmon 14*
FITCH, Champlin 33, Mary 32, Caroline 12, James 10, Catharine 6, John 4, Charles 2

Schedule Page 184

HOLD, Jabez 43, Catharine 39, Nancy A. 18, Margaret J. 15, Mary K. 13, Jehu R. 11, Lucretia 8, Sophia 6, Elonora 1
FINN, Martin 51*, Elizabeth 48, John B. 26, Martin 19, Jacob 17, Frany A. 15, James H. 12, Willis 10, Arthur R. 7
KIZER, Frany 19*
FINN, Evan 24*, Nancy 29, Docia Ann 4/12
KIZER, Jacob 85*
STARKEY, Sherod 47, Judy 44, Robert 20, Mary 17, Elias 15, Charles 15, John 11
DEEGINS, William 36*, Amanda 33, John 16, Mary A. 11, Thomas 8, Henry 5, Harrison M. 3
MAINARD, Thomas J. 3*
MCINTYRE, James 20*, Jefferson 14
SUTHERLAND, Nelson 40, Samuel 12
COON, Christopher 65, Rebecca 31, Mariah L. 13
ARTHUR, Coleman 47, Mary 51, Josiah 22, James 21, Mary A. 15, Benjamin 13, Sarilda 12, Ellen 10, America 7
HULL, Moses 45, Rachel 28, Thomas J. 11, John D. 8, Elizabeth 4, Ben F. 8/12
COLEMAN, John 30, Edith 28, Thomas 4, Catharine 3, Huldah 1
COLEMAN, Thomas 50*, Hulda 50, Phoebe 26, Thomas 24, Hulda 22, Jacob 19, Susan 17
BLEVINS, John 22*
FERGUSON, A. W. 45 (m), Caroline 33, Henry C. 10, Sarah A. 8, Thomas J. 5, Benjamin F. 2, Amanda J. 4/12
RIFFE, Lexius 31*, Julia 27, Lucretia 9, William H. 6, Osburn D. 3, Coonrod 1

Schedule Page 185

ARTHUR, Sarah 67*, Pickly 28 (f), George D. 9
HART, Sarah 53*, Jackson 23, Margaret 25, Hannah 19, Henry 15, George 12, Martha 10
MURPHY, Emily 17*
MAYBERRY, Josiah 23*
ARMS, Theodore 57, Jane 45, Henry 21, Nathaniel 18, Abigail 15, Andrew J. 12
BAILY, David 39, Elizabeth 38, Archibald 15, Nancy 13, Samuel 11, Sarah A. 8, Elizabeth 5, Susan J. 3, Sylvia 6/12
VICKERS, Jacob 22, Emily 20, Marcus L. 6/12
WEBB, Alexander 50, Margaret 45, Phoebe J. 16, Stephen E. 22, Rosanna 19, John A. 14, Elizabeth P. 11, Sarah A. 8, David 7, Nancy E. 6, Margaret 5
VANBIBBER, Ezekiel 36, Susan 36, Hester A. 14, Elizabeth 12, Sarah 10, Hardin 8, David 6, Rebecca 3, Mary E. 6/12
JOHNSON, William S. 28, Deborah 24, Wartman 5, Sarah C. 4, M. Marcellus 2
SHAFER, Larkin 23, Ann 21, William H. 6/12
JOHNSON, John T. 25, Elizabeth 20, Joseph W. 2, Robert L. 4/12
NEWMAN, Lemuel 38, Matilda 24, George W. 9, John 6, James S. 3
RIFFE, Daniel 29, Elizabeth 36, Patterson L. 2, Madison 3/12

1850 Census Greenup County Kentucky

KOUNS, David 34*, Mager Ann 32, Christian 14 (m), Thomson 10, Eveline E. 5, Fena Ann 1, Marinda A. 13
HENRY, William 23*

Schedule Page 186

FULTS, William 24, Judy 23, Hiram 5, Mary J. 4, Hezekiah 2, Matilda A. 6/12
FULTS, Hezekiah 53, Jane 52, Obadiah 22, James 18, Matilda 15, Milton 12, Martha Jane 11, Delila 2
MARSHALL, Moses M. 33, Elizabeth 23, William 5, Thomas 2, Nancy J. 3/12
GILLEY, Joseph 22*, Hannah M. 22
CAULY, George 32*
FRALEY, James 45*, Nancy 39, Edmund 14, Martin 10, Cloey A. 7, Harvey 6, Jackson 4, Elizabeth A. 1
KEATON, Elizabeth 87*
OSBURN, Paul 35*
GRAY, Marium J. 27*, Emily E. 15, Benjamin 7, Hiram C. 5, James C. 4
WINEKER, Christian 33 (m), Christena 32, Louisa 3, Gertrude 1
SCHLOVOM, Henry 40, Mary 32, Williamena 3
HARTLONG, Charles 43, Lotta 40, Josta 10 (m), William 8, Lewis 6, Frederick 4, August 3/12 (m)
ELLISON, Mary 61*, Harvey 28, Mary 12, Elizabeth J. 10, Sena J. 8
HERELD, George W. 18*, William J. 14, John W. 12
HOLT, James 29, Ann 30, Mildred A. 9, Frances 7, Abner 5, Catharine 3, James 1
WALLACE, George 34, Cintha 28, Hiram 13, William R. 11, George W. 10, Charles H. 8, Elizabeth 6, Nancy E. 4, Eliza J. 2
TEO?, William 27*, Matilda 27, Edmund 7, Richard C. 6, George F. 3, Frances A. 1
SUMPTER, Caziah 64 (f)*, Mary E. 15, Andrew J. 19

Schedule Page 187

NORTH, John 47, Frances 34, Richard 14, Mary 12, John 7, Elizabeth 6, Sarah 2
PASSLEY, Polly 45, Nancy J. 11
WEST, Joel 23, Eliza 16
ROACH, Griffin 52, Mary 53, John W. 27, Mary R. 15, Ann E. 10, Barney 13
WEST, Bluford 31, Lucinda 24, James W. 5, Joel 3
STEWART, James 54*, Elizabeth 52, William M. 25, Sarah A. 18, John H. 16
FERGUSON, Elizabeth 21*, Hiram 29
DIXON, John W. 57, Jane 59, John 20, Griffin 18, Harvey 12, Shepherd 10, Elizabeth 15
RIFFE, Coonrod 56, Mary 52, George W. 21, Phoebe 23, Gordon C. 18, Jeremiah A. 13, Polly A. 12, Anthony A. 10, Sarah 75
RIFFE, Gabriel 33*, Susan 33, George W. 7, John 6, Peter 4, Mary J. 2
GLOVER, J. R. 11 (m)*
ARTHUR, Isam 18*
WEST, Joseph 66, Ann 66, Caroline 25, Judy 20
BELLAMY, Bennet 40, Jane 40, Matthew 18, Nancy A. 15, Elizabeth S. 14, Jesse 12, Sarah 13, Thomas 10, Columbia 9, Joseph 6, Eliza 4, Cleopatra 2
WEST, Joshua 32*, Nancy 33, Harriett 6
MAYHEW, Melinda 20*
STEWART, Jackson 30, Mary A. 28, Sally J. 6, Martha A. 4, John 3, William L. 1, Samuel 3/12

1850 Census Greenup County Kentucky

BARBER, William H. 20, Amanda 16, William H. 9/12
WALLACE, James 25*, Elizabeth 26, Joseph E. 7, James G. 10/12, James 80

Schedule Page 188

CARREY, David 24*
CHANEY, John 21, Elizabeth 21, Mary A. 11/12, Eliza A. 11/12
SUMPTER, Christopher J. 27*, Susan 21, James Robert 2
GILKY, Margaret 40*
PALMER, Samuel 45*, Martha 45, James H. 20, Mary A. 18, George W. 16, Minerva J. 14
VANDOVER, Nicholas 14*
HARRISON, George 58, Matilda 58, George J. 17, William H. 13, John H. 8
RICE, Benjamin 45, Matilda 42, Abdalla 22 (m?), Thomas 21, Eliza 18, Elizabeth 14, Juli Ann 12, Polly 10, William 7, Samuel 4, Harriett 2
KEZEE, Benjamin 58*, Pamelia 40, Benjamin 30, Jonathan 20
MAYHEW, Frances 12*
RILEY, John 25*, Darcus 19, George W. 4, James 2, Mary E. 5/12, Eliza J. 18
MCGRAW, Lorana 13*
NELSON, Rowland 30*
BARBOUR, Pleasant 45, Jane 39, James 18, Reuben 16, John 14, Elizabeth 13, Robert 8, Susan E. 6, Alexander 5, Thomas 3, Josiah 2
SMITH, John P. 25, Mary 25, Susan A. 1
RUNNELLS, Archibald 32, Sarah J. 29, Sarah C. 5, Malinda C. 3, Phoebe A. 1
CHASE, William D. 34*, Mary Ann 30, Mary J. 5, Wm. H. H. 8/12
MOORE, William 28*
POLLARD, A. C. 24 (m), Elizabeth 24, John W. 2, Richard B. 1
WILKS, James F. 41*, Elizabeth 34, Mary 69
BLAIR, James L. 13*
WISE, Francis 40, Mary 35, Jacob 12, Anthony 8, Joseph 5, John 2

Schedule Page 189

CROOKS, Abraham 62, Mary A. 32, Robert 19, Edward 17, Elizabeth 14, Abraham 9, Margaret A. 7, George W. 5, Juliet 3, Arabel 1
BATES, John N. 39, Martha A. 31, Patison C. 12, William H. 10, Samuel B. 7, Virginia A. 4
DIXON, Augustus 21, Amanda J. 18
CRUM, Thomas 39, Wilmoth Ann 31, William G. 11, Eliza K. 10, Unity Ann 7, Thomas J. 3, John A. 2
RUNNELLS, James 37, Sidney 35 (f), Samuel 14, Malissa A. 7, John P. 5, Jehu 2
KETCHUM, Philander 38, Sophia 35, Jerimiah 9, Philander 6, Mary A. 2
DIXON, William 48, Eliza 33, Samuel H. 13, Margaret 11, Mary F. 9, William J. 5, Eliza J. 3, James H. 6/12
POLLARD, Henry B. 40, Sophia T. 37, Margaret A. 16, George B. 15, Thomas O. 14, Edward Y. 12, John C. 10, William H. 8, Milton B. 6, Emma J. 4, Sophia E. 2, Green F. 6/12
MAUPIN, D. G. 28 (m), Margaret C. 22, Sarah M. 2
SPEARS, Paul 41, Patsey 35, Sally 14, Catharine 12, John 9, Nancy 6, Isaac 4, William H. 2
FULLER, George W. 23, Mary L. 20, James L. 1

1850 Census Greenup County Kentucky

BUCKLEY, Joel T. 40, Sarah 43, Franklin 16, John R. 14, Mary E. 11, Malinda 9, Joseph 9, Winton 5, Francis M. 2
JONES, Samuel 45, Margaret 42, John 14, Mary 13, Elizabeth 9, Edward 7, George W. 4, Martha 3, Richard 1

Schedule Page 190

MARTIN, Ezekiel 45*, Nancy 42, William 19, Hiram 15, George 9, Thomas 6, Ezekiel 3
HEDGE, Eliza 14*
HOWELL, Thomas 42, Sarah 40, Andrew 17, Melissa J. 14, William W. 12, James K. 5, Susan 9, John T. 2, John 69
HOWELL, John A. 30, Mary 27, Martha 12, America 7, Harrison 1
HOWELL, Alexander D. 54, Nancy 48, Ottoway Ann 20, Emily J. 18, Celia F. 15, George W. 12, Alexander C. 8, Hiram L. 6
CROOKS, John C. 25, Lucy E. 23, Hiram L. 12
FULLER, James 50, Nancy 23, William 5, Thomas J. 3, John C. 10/12
RICE, Joseph W. 50, Catharine 48, Matilda 17, James H. 15, Mary A. 11
RIGGLE, Daniel 38*, Nancy 32, George A. 9, Catharine 7, Arabella 4, Helen 2, Daniel E. 5/12
HADDOX, Ann 14*
HAWKINS, Isaac T. 36, Zelpah 30, Mary K. 3, Sarah M. 1
POWER, Francis 65, Alice 50
POWER, Francis jr. 31, Lucina 22, Sophia A. 2, Mary L. 9/12
JACOBS, William A. 40*, Polly 36, William H. 16, Jonathan 14, Harrison 13, Frances J. 9
GUARD, Sarah 70*, Sarah 16
CRANTS, Sarah 40, Mary 20, Thomas 16, Jacob 13
DIXON, William 59*, Unity 56
ARTHUR, Piety 28 (f)*, George B. 9
FULLER, Frances 25*, Piety J. 25 (f), Piety J. 3, William A. 2

Schedule Page 191

DIXON, William 17*, Virginia 15
THOMPSON, John H. 35, Eliza W. 32, Ann J. 15, Catharine S. 13, Margaret P. 11
CLEAR, Ezekiel 49*, Nancy 44, George 22, Robert 18, Mary P. 17, Ellen 16, Susan F. 14, Darius 9, Elizabeth 8, Phoebe 6, William H. 3
KAZED, Nelson 2*
MARTIN, Labon 22*
MARTIN, Labon sr. 25, Ardena 24, Elizabeth 4, Jehu 3, John D. 11/12
SHY, Jeremiah 37, Frances O. 40, William H. 12, Louisa 9, Elizabeth S. 7, Thomas E. 6
CREASEY, B. M. 49 (m), Elusty 43 (f), Emily A. 23, William D. 12
NEWMAN, Thomas 28, Tabitha J. 25, Islander 5 (f), J. C. 22 (m)
MCCROSKY, Margaret 65, James D. 29, Flora 24, Thomas J. 10/12
MCCROSKY, John 35*, Ann 30
GOBLE, Lewis 10*
ARTHUR, John 26, Frances 22, Sarah A. 3, James 11/12
SNOW, Thomas 42, Sarah 47, Sarah 17, David 16, Joseph 14, George W. 12, Simon 10, Mary 6, Elizabeth 2

1850 Census Greenup County Kentucky

HACKWITH, John 41, Sarah 40, William T. 22, Tabitha 18, James 13, Reuben 12, Charles 8, Joseph W. 5, Elias 7/12, Thomas 85
ARTHUR, James 25, Sophonia 20, Green S. 2, Milton A. 5/12
ARTHUR, Robert 34, Sarah 30
HOWELL, Mainard 48, Matilda 52, John C. 16, Elizabeth 13, Thomas E. 10
DIXON, John 54, Narotha S. 31, George W. 9, Matilda S. 6, John G. 5, Joseph H. 2, Reuben B. 3/12

Schedule Page 192

TOLER, William 38, Frances 43, Frances A. 15, Amanda 11, Aramatha 8, William A. 6, Adelaide J. V. 4
TOLER, Elijah 50, Diannah 32, Mary 15, William T. 13, Elizabeth 11, Margaret 7, Lewis 5, Columbus 3, Columbus 7/12
STEVENS, John M. 37, Bethaniah 32, Mary T. 12, John W. 10, Cyrus 2, Calvin 3/12
KEITLY, William 30, Mary 30, Leonard 7, Mariah 5, John 2
CLUNN, Dudley 63, Ann 42
TOLER, Caleb 53*, Nancy 37, Martha 17, Caleb 14, James H. 11
JOHNSON, Elizabeth 14*
DIXON, Levi 30, Mary A. 22, Anthony W. 4, Maria E. 2, Allimire S. 3/12
BALL, Wesley 42, Lydia 36, Jesse 18, William 13, Rebecca 12, Mary J. 8, Emily G. 3
DIXON, James 54, Martha 50, Thomas 18, James 15, Louisa J. 12, Martha 10
DIXON, Alexander 27, Lucy 17
ROUS, Samuel 58, Mary 43, Richard 14, Elizabeth 12, Samuel 10, Marshall 8, Spencer 7, Juli Ann 5, Laura 4, Nancy 3
CULVER, John 60*, Charlotte L. 33, Helen J. 3, John 3/12
WILKINS, Sarah 31*
JENNES, John 50*
BOTTS, Alexander 23*
NICHOLS, W. T. 41 (m)*, Frances 35, Drusella 9
PORTER, Caroline 22*
JOHNSON, Isaac 27*, Huldah 23

Schedule Page 193

WALTON, L. D. 32 (m)*
ENNIGER, Jefferson 21*
CLARK, John 49, Jane 34, Lawland 44
HAMPTON, William 42, Sarah 42, George S. 19, William O. 15, Joseph N. 13, Eliza M. 11, John W. 8, Charles H. 5, Wade 2
HAMPTON, Henry 36, Catharine J. 30, William 11, Ann E. 9, Wade 7, John 1
SPURLOCK, Margaret 40*, Francis 20, Frances M. 18
WATKINS, Daniel B. 21*, Hester A. 16, Charles 2
CLOITER, Nancy 20*
POAGE?, Samuel 21*
GRAYSON, John 24*
WILLMAN, Moses 21*
MCCALL, John 24*
PATTERSON, Samuel 30*

1850 Census Greenup County Kentucky

HITE, Erastus 21*
DONALDSON, William 24*
EVERS, James 18*
DAVIS, Daniel 53, James 11, Laura A. 16, Hiram 26, Nancy 18, Laura A. 3, Zachanna T. 2 (m)
WORTHINGTON, J. T. 40 (m)*, Jacob 12, James 10, William 8, Jane 5, America 2, Hannah 35
MEAD, Tolbert 19*
HONAKER, Hugh 23*
HENSLEY, Cornelius 24*
WALTER, Hiram G. 24*, Nancy 18
BRANNUM, John 28*
DAVIDSON, William L. 24*, Barbara L. 23, Samuel W. 4, Napoleon B. 1
HENRY, Amey 21*
KIBBLE, Marcus L. 35*, Elizabeth H. 29, Lewis 9, Emily 7, William 6, Agnes 3, James 1
CAMERON, Elizabeth 18*
KILLEN, James 27, Bethsibba 20, Wellington 4, Mary E. 2
KINCADE, James D. 31*, Leonora 28, Andrew S. 12
CAMERON, Jane 19*
DRAKE, William R. 43, Tabitha 41, Margaret K. 19, James W. 17, Robert 15, Isaac 12, Charlotte 10, Harriett 7, William 5, Winfield S. 2, Clarion A. 2/12

Schedule Page 194

BROWN, Charles L. 30*, Sabina 28, James H. 6, Moses J. 5, Lewis C. 3
BOGGS, Charles L. 12*
CAULBOATH?, Shade 28 (m)*
ULEN, Charles 26*, Sarah 23
GEIGER, John 23*
HAMPTON, Levi J. 33*, Elizabeth 30, Julia 10, Amelia 7, Mary 5, Millard F. 1 (f)
HENDERSON, Mary F. 48*, Mary F. 25, Amanda 18, John 15, Thomas 12
WEGNER, Abram 39, C. O. 35 (f), Cemantha 12, Durtley 10 (m), Harriet 6, Laura A. 4, Mary 2, John 26
ALLAN, Ethan 29*, Patience 29, Charles H. 10, Frances M. 8, George 5, Mary L. 2
RIDGWAY, Ann 23*
APPS, James 60*, Susan 50, Sarah 20
MCCORMICK, Martha A. 23*, Susan 5, Samuel 3, Sarah 3/12
BURTENSHAW, William 21*
YOUNG, Joseph 43, Rebecca 35, James 16, Stephen H. 14, Mary V. 12, William H. 10, Joseph A. 8
MCCULLOUGH, Addison 33*, Eliza 32, Samuel 13, Juliet 7, Catharine 3, John 35
WILSON, John 23*
CATLETT, Letitia 50*
MEANS, Hugh 35*, Esther 33, John 7, Ann 3
PEARCE, Luther 34*
WILLIAMSON, Eliza 24*, Nelly 25
RICKETS, John 26, Jane 23, Thomas 1, Gerrard 23
JUDD, John T. 50*, Dorotha 56, Charles H. 14, Lewis P. 11
SPANGLER, Leonora M. 24*
CUMPTON, James 21*

1850 Census Greenup County Kentucky

TERRY, William 21*
KRING, Henry 40, Sarah A. 33, Polly A. 10, Jonathan 8, Lewellyn 9/12 (f)

Schedule Page 195

WILLIAMS, Marcus 37*, Mordecai 14, James 12
BROWN, James 33*
MCLAIN, Otho 19*
PAYNE, Richard 67*, Jane 50, Hiram 23, Spencer 32
KOUNS, Martha 22*
ARTHUR, Isaac 35, Jemima 25, Martha A. 12, Elizabeth J. 10, Larkey F. 7, Robert Simon 5
PAYNE, Cornilius 33*, Elizabeth 37, Noah 10, Richard 10, JAne 9, Benjamin 6, William 3
STEVENS, Thomas 18*
LEVEY, John 23, Mary 21, Louisa 2
BELLAMY, Bennet 40, Jane 40, Martha 18, Nancy 16, Elizabeth S. 15, Sarah J. 13, Jesse W. 12, Thomas J. 10, Columbia 9, Joseph W. 7, Eliza E. 3, Cleopa T. 1 (f)
POAGE, Eliza M. 53, Mariah 20, Eilzabeth A. 16, Hugh A. 53, Jacob N. 15, Sarah F. 18
POAGE, Nancy 49, Thomas C. 15, John W. 14, Rebecca C. 10
DIXON, Meredith M. 20, Sarah A. 20
POAGE, Pelina 35 (B), Hannah F. 16, George W. 14, Hugh C. 12, William H. 10, John J. 9, Richard M. J. 7, Elias 5, James D. 2, Mary J. 3
DAVIDSON, Thomas 45, Martha 25, Mary J. 8, John W. 5
DIXON, Nancy 30, Newton 11, William 8
DIXON, Benjamin 39, Mary 38, James F. 13, Elizabeth A. 8, Emily J. 5, Hardin R. 3, Eliza 1
CRUM, John 22, Telita 18
RIGGS, John 30*, Mary A. 27, Lucy A. 8
CHADWICK, Lucy 56*
CHINN, Edward 30, Phoebe 27

Schedule Page 196

ARTHUR, James 75, Jane 60, William 40, Terry 45 (m)
HACKWITH, Reuben 62*, Mary 52
HOLIGAN, John 78*
CRUM, Elijah 31, Jane 21, Thomas A. 4, Mary E. 2
CRUM, Gilbert 67, Letitia 67
RUNNELS, Reuben 30, Martha 30
RUNNELS, Thomas 34, Letitia 28, Phoebe E. 5, Reuben N. 4, Talitha J. 1
CREASEY, B. S. 36 (m), Nancy G. 33, James F. 9, John F. 7, George W. 3, Hiram F. 1
SAVAGE, Nickolas 49*, Mary 48, James 23, William 20, Alexander 18, Edward 16, Eliza J. 12, Margaret E. 10, John D. 7, Joseph 4, Elleanor 76, Elleanor 16
WHITE, Andrew 21*, Rufus 14
JONES, Richard 49*, Jane 45, William 22, John 20, Jesse 18, Margaret J. 16, Levinda 15
PITNEY, Levi 24*
PITNEY, William J. 26, Ann 23
BELLAMY, Matthew 51, Elizabeth W. 48, Thomas 20, John 18, William 15, Henry C. 11, Granville N. 10, Pamelia A. 5, Camillus H. 7, Windfield S. 3

1850 Census Greenup County Kentucky

CASE, Abel A. 37*, Martha E. 23, Caroline 26
TUTTLE, James 17*
ROW, Catharine 22*
POAGE, Cyrus 35, Ann 31, James H. 9, Lewella K. 6
POAGE, G. B. 29 (m), Emily R. 26, Samuel D. 30
STUDD, Joshua 23, Elizabeth 20, Caroline 1
TURRY, John 28, Margaret 30, Delila 9, James 6, Elizabeth 3, Abraham 2, Jane 3/12
STUDD, Levi 50*, Nancy 54, Henry 17, Jane 15, George 11

Schedule Page 197

LEIZURE, Marget 22*
SILVERTHORN, John T. 2*
PRICE, John 35, Martha 24, John 2
CANTERBURY, John 45, Elizabeth 50, Jane 22, Marshal 21, Reuben 17
MOMAN, G. W. 35 (m)*, Eliza 35, Jacob 10, Sarah 7, Susan F. 5, Elizabeth D. Q. 2
WELTCH, Jane 34*
WARNER, Larkin 39, Mahala 39, Samuel 16, Isabel 9
KELLAY, Henry 30, Mary A. 22, William H. 1
WALTERS, George 48, Mariah 19, Kasiah 47, Elizabeth 22, William G. 17, George W. 15, Mary E. 12, James S. 9
HENWOOD, Benjamin 29, Ellen 19, Margaret E. 9, Martha A. 6, Sarah J. 4
PEARCE, Harris 56, Anna 56, Joshua 25, Elizabeth 17, Vinton 16, Anna 15
CROW, Joseph 50, Lydia 43, John 21, Adam 19, Sarah 16, Calvin 14, Elizabeth 12, Pelina 8, Catharine 4
HELMS, James 45*, Elizabeth 42
BARNET, Daniel 45*, John 19
SEATES, Michael 25, Frances 28, Sophia L. 10, David B. 5, Mary A. 7/12
RATSY, Adam 62, Susanna 52
HARTSBROOK, John 61, Margaret 62, Polly 39, Elizabeth 21, Inglebert 29, Vilena 8
RUNYON, William 39*, Susannah 35, Harvey 18, George 10, Eliza 7, Margery 5, Elizabeth 3
FERGUSON, Arthur 15*
DIXON, Solomon 31*, Jemima 29, Nicklin 10 (m), Wilson 8, William 6, Isaac 4, Eliza E. 1

Schedule Page 198

RAWLING, Lemuel 23*
FREDERICK, Martin 50*, Ruanna 40, John 13, Rebecca 9
SMITH, Margaret 17*
DIXON, Benjamin 13*
STRAIT, Henry 22*, Eliza 24
CANTERBURY, Jane 23*
ADAMS, Elijah 24, Mary 25, Rhoda 16
PETERMAN, Lavisa 46*, Elizabeth 17, Jacob 15, Eliza J. 14, Malvina 13, Burgess 11
STITH, Nancy 27*, Nancy J. 8
TERRIL, Peter 50*, Ersly 40 (f), George 14
CAMPBELL, Darcus 80*

1850 Census Greenup County Kentucky

MURPHY, Jane 57, Anna 23, Julia 21, William C. 47, Albert 8
WORMAN, Edmund 35, Emma 41, Edward 6
POTEET, Thomas J. 38, Tryphenia 28, Sarah K. Y. 8, William J. 7, Gerrard 4, Alice 2
HITE, William 39, Mary 34, Ann E. 14, Sarah N. 11, Lucretia V. 6
BARRETT, Charles 40, Darcus L. 39, Elizabeth 13, George O. 11, William 9, Charles 7, Thomas L. 2
ADAMS, Nathan 20, Rosanna 22, James T. 1, Levisa 48, Mary F. 11
DISHMAN, John 26, Sarah 26, Julia 5, Robert 3
POWERS, Noah 28, Pamelia 21, James W. 2, Adaline 1
ULEN, Elba 30 (m), Adaline 27
HOGAN, Samuel 48*, Nancy 36, Charles W. 18, John M. 16, Mary V. 10, America J. 7, William H. 4, Samantha E. 2, Samuel 10/12
PERRY, David 28*
WILSON, Charles 70, Priscilla 62
BARTRAM, Solomon 34, Margaret 33, Sarah L. 17, Martha 8, Frederick 6, Allen 5, Henry 2

Schedule Page 199

THOMPSON, Hudson C. 60*, Lucinda 53
VANHORN, Charity N. 9*
GRAY, Jane 83*
SNODDY, John 30, Julia A. 19, Sarah A. 1
HARRISON, Robert J. 49*, Dianna 29, Margaret 19, Elizabeth 18, Juliet 16, Nancy B. 15, Robert J. A. 13, Thomas H. 11, Mary F. 9, Catharine 7, Josephene 2
MCGUIN, Cyntha 7*, Minerva 5
MILES, George 35*, Frances 22, Mary E. 2
GIBBONS, Charles 30*
DEVORE, Margaret 20*
BLANKENSHIP, Farm 30, Anana 23, Sarah 1
TINSLEY, William 43, Mary A. 42, Mary 19, Simon 17, Holbert 15, Emma 13, Henry 11, William 9, Arthur 7, Sarah 5, James 2
CHADWICK, Reuben 38, Mary 37, Sarah S. 5
EWING, Joseph 56, Susan F. 17, Clarissa C. 15, John A. 10, Thomas J. 8, William S. 4
BLANKENSHIP, Hiram 27, Elizabeth 23, William H. 8, Narcissa 5, George W. 2, John R. 4/12
GALLOWAY, James 26, Miranda 20, America 6, Mary J. 4, Nancy A. 3, Elizabeth 6/12
BALLERN, Joseph 23, Merinda 22, Martha J. 6
ALLEY, Jacob 28, Melissa 24, William H. 2, Sarah K. 1, Eliza M. 6/12
ALLEY, John 28, Mary 27, Emily E. 2, George W. 7/12
ALLEY, Mary 59, Polly 19, Lindsey 17 (m), Casey 35
BROWN, John 30, Matilda 33, Andrew 8, Lorinda 6

Schedule Page 200

SMALLEY, John 41, Rebecca 40, George 12, Deborah 10, Hannah 8, Angeline 6, John 4, Hiram 2, Jane 1
WOOD, William 30*, Sarah 27, James 7, Thomas 4, William 2
JONES, Robert 18*
ALLEY, James 25, Sarah 23, Mary E. 7, Martha A. 6, Nancy J. 4, Leonora F. 2

1850 Census Greenup County Kentucky

BARTRAM, Samuel 27, Levina 33, Leonard 3, Martha 2, Mary H. 7/12
BARTRAM, Van 21, Polly 16, John A. 1
SNODDY, Jacob 40, Margaret 35, William 12, Sarah J. 10, Susannah H. 7, Abner 5, Margaret E. 1
DIXON, John 29, Martha J. 19, James A. 3, Meredith M. 7/12
RIPATOE, Sophia 34*, Mary A. 18, Peter 14, Thomas D. 11, Elizabeth 6
STOTH, Margaret 63*
PRICE, Neally 37 (m), Susan 27, Amanda 12, Edmund 8, Elizabeth 6, Eveline 4, Thomas 8/12
PRITCHET, Zecheriah 29, Elizabeth 28, Polly 8, Sarah A. 6, Abigail 4, William 1
SCOTT, Richard 56, Mary 55, John 23, Andrew 22, Stewart 20, Maryann 18, Mary J. 16, Richard 13, Eleanor 11
DAVIDSON, Thomas 49, Frances 39, Sarah F. 14, Elizabeth 11, Matilda 8, Margary A. 7, Lucretia 1
GARD, John 54, Jane 51, Mahala 22, Norah 13, Isabel 12, Hiram 8
POWELL, Abel 45, Frances 34, Elizabeth J. 12, Lucy A. 11, John Tho. 9, Robert 7, Rachel 3

Schedule Page 201

MULLIN, James 44, Mahula 34, Lydia M. 9, Polly W. 8, Angeline 6, William L. 4, John 3, Solomon 1
CHANDLER, William 45, Lydia 38, Jane 12, William 11, Thomas 9, Elizabeth 8, Benjamin 6, Masery A. 4 (f), Juely? 1 (f)
KELLY, William 22, Sarah 19
THOMAS, William 38, Harriet 35, Louisa 15, Mary J. 14, Tarica L. 13, James 10, William H. 8, Ellen 3, Lavinda 4/12
MAINARD, James 25, Elizabeth 26
STEWART, James 45, Sarah E. 18, Agnes A. 16, Hannah 10, Rosannah 6, Jeremiah 5
MAINARD, William 45, Hannah 60
MAINARD, David 29, Mary 19, Harrison 8, James 6, Martha 1
DOBYNS, Henry T. 36, Eliza 34, Joseph 15, Gracy J. 10, Martha 3, Mary 3, Henry T. 6/12
LOWES, John 41, Sarah 41, Moses 20, Aaron 18, Bide 16 (f), Abigail 15, Eve 12, Elizabeth 10, Sarah J. 6
STATEN, Solomon 30, Elizabeth 22, George T. 5, James 4, Sarina 1
KITCHEN, John 36*, Judy 25, Elizabeth 4, John F. 1
PARISH, James 20*
DUVALL, Martin 53*, Harriett 33
ARTRESS, Rebecca J. 1*
ARTRESS, Jesse 34*, William 13, Mary H. 11, John 9, James 7
DEWEY, William 23*, Jackson 16
TURNEY, Rebecca 50*

Schedule Page 202

BROOKS, James 38, Susan 30, Jane 8, Angeline 7, Henrietta 5, Warren 6/12
PRICE, Addison 29, Martha 24, Cyntha 8, William 4, Mary 1
POWELL, Skelton 57*, Nancy 62
HUFFMAN, George 22*
POWELLS, Bartholomew 25, Matilda 19, Casirey 1 (m)
WELKER, James 48, Eliza J. 24, Matilda 14, Nancy 13, James 10, Harriet A. 8, Theodore 2, Nicey 3
WELKER, John 20, Bridget 30, Joseph 18

- 118 -

1850 Census Greenup County Kentucky

ROUS, James 53, Vashta 34, Harriet 16, Christina 14, Clifton 12, Mardula 11 (m), Tharus 6 (m), Samuel 28
BRYAN, Thomas 22*, Ellen 25
SLOAN, Lawrence 8*
BRUNTON, Robert 53, Fanny 14, Robert 12, James 11, Newton 9, Theodore 7, Lewis 5
PATTERSON, William 33, Mary L. 20, Mary T. 7/12
LEWIS, Stephen 38, Judah 40
STEVENS, Jacob 22, Mary T. 20
FLINN, Michael 24, Mary 20
STEVENS, Stephen 52, Cyntha 25, Susan 16, Gilbert 13, Sarah 11, Elizabeth 9, Daniel 7, John 6, Jesse 3, Sarah 2
DIXON, Elisha 29, Frances 23, George 3, James 2, Rease 1 (m)
ODOR, William S. 37*, Frances A. 30, Susan 13, William L. 11, John T. 8, George W. 6, Mary E. 4, Samuel R. 2
MILLER, George W. 20*
DUNNIVAN, John 40*
RICE, James 62, Tabitha 40, Nancy 19, George 17, Jackson 15, Rachel 13, Ann 11, Polly 9, Roxe 7 (f), Joseph 1

Schedule Page 203

SCOTT, J. R. 23 (m), Hannah 23, Armena 1
WELLS, Peter 45, Mary 36, Amanda 17, Jackson 14, Elizabeth 13, Martha 10, George W. 6, Albert G. 3, William P. 11/12
SPARKS, William J. 22, Elizabeth 29, James H. 8/12
YOUNG, Gabriel C. 34, Rebecca 21, Indiana 2, Andrew 6/12
JOHNSON, Ambrose 39, Elizabeth 32, William J. 13, Jesse V. 10, Harrison B. 7, Andrew J. 4, Mary L. 4/12
MAY, Elizabeth 46*, William 34, John 30, Ralph 26, Greenville 24, German 21, Charles 18, Westley 16, Meredith 13
SMITH, Ann B. 28*
SCOTT, John 26*, Mariah 24, James 1, William 6/12, Robert 12
MAYHEW, Rebecca 63*
MCCORMICK, Samuel 56, Elizabeth 55, Matilda 18, Stephen 24, Elizabeth 14, William 10, Samuel 8
BROWNLEE, David 28*, Eleanor 20, William 2, Samuel 1
BETTS, Jacob 12*
GAY, Thomas 33*
COFFIELD, Alexander 35, Mary A. 25, Mary T. 4, Mahala 2, John 1
FINN, Willis 41*, Christiana 43, Elizabeth 18, Frances A. 16, Martin 9, Mary A. 6, Caroline 3, Christiana 3/12
KIZER, Harvey 22*
HOLT, Nancy 65, John 22
HAMMOND, John 34, Sarah A. 30, William 7, Rachel 5, Mary 4, John 2
BETTS, Samuel 42, Edith 38, Eveline 20, Justine 16 (f), Jacob 17, Jane 12, Margaret E. 9, Louisa 6, Angeline 5

1850 Census Greenup County Kentucky

Schedule Page 204

BARBOUR, Reuben 48, Frances 33, Pleasant 23, Jeremiah 17, Henry 14, William 11, Reuben 7, Taylor 3, Eliza 9, Frances 6/12

MOSELEY, Prston 34, Catharine 27, Julian C. 12 (f), John 10, Susan 9, Samuel 7, Ellen 3, Foster 1

LOCY, James 21, Elizabeth 18, Mary C. 1

KOUNS, Henry 42, Mariah 37, Elizabeth A. 12, John A. 9, Ellen C. 6, William 5, Lurina 2, Amanda 6/12

SMITH, David 46, Rebecca 43, Elijah 23, John 21, Polly R. 20, Aramatha 18, Sophia 14, Nancy 13, Josephene 11, William 9, Thomas 7, Susannah 4

MORRISON, William H. 35, Susan 29, Catharine 14, John 12, William 10, Sarah T. 7, George 5, Christopher 3, Julia A. 2, Simon 9/12

DAVIDSON, Joseph 22, Margaret 20, Hamilton 2, Harriet 4/12

HOOD, Lucas 35, Elizabeth A. 24, Charles 8, John 5, Nancy J. 3

HOOD, Albert 26, Elizabeth 17

HOOD, Hiram 30*, Sarah A. 24

THOMAS, James 2*

CALLAHAN, Charles 38, Nancy 38, Robert 16, Malvina 14, Clifton 13, Otho 12, William H. 9, Henrietta 7, Charles W. 6, Milton 3, Leonidas 1

Schedule Page 205

HOOD, Thomas 35, Minerva 35, William 13, Mary J. 10, Charles 8, Sarah A. 6, Eli R. 3, Martha F. 1

CALLAHAN, Sarah 65, John R. 23, Arney 13

DAVIDSON, Jesse 54, Matilda 44, Nathaniel 15, Mary 12, Matilda 6, Jesse 3

CLARKE, Richard 57, Nicey 50, Reuben 25, Joseph 20, John 19, Vina 12, Jesseru 9 (m)

CALLAHAN, Sarah 47, Mary A. 17, James N. 14, Samuel S. 12, Benjamin 7

PRATT, George 27, Eliza J. 19, Julia A. 2

DETMORE, Lucas 40*, Catharine 32, Catharine 11, John 7, Dinah 4, Mary 2

WESTPOLE, Inglebert 40*

RINKES, Benjamin 30*

MORMON, Joseph 30, Mary 30, Eliza 3, Anna 1

MARTIN, Alexander 63, Ann 43, Robert 13, Virginia 3

KERREL, James 26, Sarah 26, William 7

WAMOCK, William 60*, Mary 62, Francis W. 26, Nancy 18

MORRIS, Alcey J. 16*

HOWE, Edward 29*, Rebecca 49, Winfield S. 7, Theodore 6, Elizabeth A. 4

TAYLOR, George 14*

TACKETT, Charles 28*

DAVIDSON, Hannah 53*, John 19, Charles 17, Amy 80

FITCH, Minerva 32*, Champlain 12, Vashta 10 (f), George 8, Sarah 6, Leander 4, Julia 7/12

DAVIDSON, James 24*, Eliza J. 20, Margaret A. 4/12

RICE, Joseph C. 7*, Sarah A. 11

STEWART, Lerenzo D. 44, Catharine 25, Polly A. 9, Andrew 8, Charles 5, Jesse D. 4, Thomas J. 2, Elizabeth F. 5/12

1850 Census Greenup County Kentucky

Schedule Page 206

DAVIDSON, George 29, Elizabeth 23, Minerva 5, John 4, Sophia 1
ADAMS, John 35*, Amy 24, Susan 2, Mary F. 1
MCGUIN, John 16*
CLARKE, Anthony G. 26, Martha A. 22, Theresa 4/12, Ambrose M. 28
DOUGLASS, Thomas 47, Cassander 40, Charles 20, John W. 16, Amanda 18, Mary 12, Thomas 10, Rachel 8, Stephen 6, Lewis N. 4, Sophia 10/12
COLEGROVE, Nathan 34, Sarah 25, Henry 10, Samuel 9, Levina 7, Jesse 3, Lanica 5/12
CALLIHAN, Nancy 39*, Sarah J. 20, Charles W. 18, Amey 15, America 12
SHINGLETON, James 23*
CALLAHAN, Jonathan 25, Catharine 26, Isabel J. 4, John R. 1, Julian 11/12 (f)
EVANS, Griffith 43, Ann 38, Davis L. 15, Henry 12
CLARK, Jesse 22, Mary E. 18, John W. 9/12
CLUTS, Archibald 40, John W. 15, James H. 14, Robert 10, A. A. 7 (m), Isabella 12, Mary E. 5, Margaret 2
PICKET, Eli 39*, Thomas P. 18, Sarah J. 17, John H. 15, Eliza M. 9, Hiram 7, William A. 4
FLINN, George A. 2*
PAYNE, Noah 30*, Sarah 38
EASTHAM, John 18*, Syntha A. 16, Robert 13, Henrietta 11, Hartwell 7, Mary 4
CLARK, Enoch 30, Lean 22 (f), Eliza 6, Reuben 3, Pamelia 1
CARRINGTON, Jesse 50, Jane 40, John 19, Amelia 16, Lucinda 13, Nathaniel 11, Hiram B. 9, Margaret A. 7, Joseph 5, Henry C. 4, Jane 4/12

Schedule Page 207

ABRAMS, Thomas 44, Rose 35, Massa A. 21 (f), Esther A. 18, Isaac 16, William 14, Cassander 13, Aramatha 11, Elizabeth 8, Matilda 6, Jefferson 4, Victoria 2
MATTHEWS, James 44*, Nancy 44, Isaac 17, Margaret 15, Sarah A. 7, Nancy A. 5, James 9, Mahala A. 2
DEFOE, William 13*
EVANS, John H. 35, Elizabeth 29, Shelburn 4 (m), Nancy J. 1
STEWART, Sarah 46, Margaret 20, James A. 17
DOUGLASS, Stephen 39, Elizabeth 29
WAMSLEY, Uriah 62, Jane 62, William 30
DILLON, Robert 54*, Elizabeth 33, Jane 18, Amanda C. 16, Thomas 13, Abram 11, John 7, George W. 7, Vincent 3
CASSIDY, Thomas 82*
BURNFIT, Alpheus J. 46, Ann M. 47, Sarah 23, Hamilton 21, Mary 13, Charlotte 10
EVANS, Green B. 62, Nancy 75
EVANS, Henry 49, Rina 48, Nathaniel 26, Isaac 23, Cracy 15 (f), Mary A. 3
EVANS, David 29, Frances 24, Greenbury 7, Polly A. 5, William H. 3, James C. 1, Martin B. 10
KERBY, John 40*, Eliza 35, Cirkus 18 (m), Cyntha 13, Juliet 12, George A. 8, John 6, Charles 2
MURDOCK, Elijah 28*, Sidney 19 (f)
SIMS, Lydia 47*, George W. 12, Wealthy A. 8, Silas 6, Mary 4

1850 Census Greenup County Kentucky

Schedule Page 208

LOCY, Mary 57*
TWYMAN, James 35*, Lydia 26, William 5, Franklin 3, Samuel 1
VOLUNTINE, Nancy J. 12*
SULLIVAN, Voluntine 47, Pricy 27, John 2, Michael 11/12
MCCARTY, John 32, Mary 28, John 11, Susan J. 10, Caroline 8, William H. 5, Frances 4
SKELTON, Peter 47*, Frances 39, Cissely 12 (f), Sarilda 11, Malissa 9, David 8, Anthony 6, Frances 2
KIZER, David 33*
ROBINSON, John 30, Barilla 30, George D. 7, Elizabeth 4, John L. 3
BELLAMY, William N. 48*, Sophia 36, Minerva J. 21, Eliza A. 18, Matilda F. 16, William H. 11, Adaline 10, Martha 7, Walter 3, Nancy A. 11/12
HIGGINS, James 10*, Daniel 7
COUPLEBARGER, Nich. 57*, Lydia 54
COOLEY, Samuel 16*
SWEET, Benjamin 32, Mary A. 25, Mary A. 7, Catharine 5, Aramatha 3, Margaret 6/12
CLUTZ, Robert 32*, Mary A. 35, Adeline 8, Lydia 7, Thomas 3, Elizabeth 2
BRYAN, Stephen 41*
ABRAMS, Elias 48, Sarah A. 30, Elizabeth 16, Polly A. 15, Samuel 13, Angeline 11, Rhoda 1
BLANKENSHIP, Susanna 38, Ezekiel 18, John 16, Elizabeth 12, William 10, Joseph 8, Mary 6, Lorena 1
ARTIS, Samuel 28, Nancy 27, James 7, Elizabeth J. 6, Evaline 3, Jemilla 6/12, James C. 10

Schedule Page 209

STEWART, James 26*, Mary 17, Joseph 24, Charlotte 23
HEDLEY, George 25*
STRAIT, John 26*
MAY, John 30*
LEWIS, Charles 25, Eliza 22
ROADS, John 28*, Louisa 25
MARKS, James 19*
BLACKBURN, Jeremiah 38*, Sylva 37, Mary 15, Martha 15, Elizabeth 14, William 12, Solomon 9, Jeremiah 7, Persus 6 (f), Charity 4, Irene 3, Nancy 1, Solomon 23
BROOKS, Calvin 18*, John 23
SHELTON, Hardin 44, Mary 38, Morris 17, Shadrach 15, James 13, Joseph 11, Pricy 9 (f), America 6, Frances 1
JOHNSON, Sylvester 40, Rebecca 20
MILLER, John 35, Hannah 33, George 10, Mary S. 8, Abraham 5, Ann E. 2, Amanda 4/12
SMILEY, Uriah 26*, Sarah 23, Edward 2, Mariah 9/12
CONNEAR, William 27*
DAVIS, Joseph 45, Polly 43, Vilotte 22 (f), Edith 17, Robert 12, Jeremiah W. 11, Prudence 9, Emily 6, Frances J. 1
GREEN, John 35, Martha 38, Angeline 4, _____ 4/12 (m)
CLARK, Enos 58, Anna 55, Enos 17
MCMAHAN, Jesse 30, Letitia 26, Mary J. 11, Julia A. 9, William J. 2
MARK, Joseph 32*, Catharine 27, Caroline 1

1850 Census Greenup County Kentucky

HUFFMAN, Joseph 35*
MCINTYRE, Harrison 36, Amelia 30, Sarah A. 9, George W. 7, John W. 5, Mary E. 3, William H. 1

Schedule Page 210

CAMERON, Duncan 40*, Elizabeth 35, John A. 11, Marcellus 8, Narcissas 5 (f), Sarah V. 3
PHILBURN, Thomas 25*
EDWARDS, E. 30 (m)*
FULWIDER, William 28*
BARKES, William 18*, George 20
MARTIN, Peter 25*
PENNINGTON, H. 21 (m)*
RHODES, A. 21 (m)*
CALLAHAN, D. 23 (m)*
MCGEE, Michael 23*
CULL, Hugh 35*
LAFFERTY, Daniel 25*
RAY, William 23*
MCMAHAN, John 25*
MAGOVERN, Daniel 35*
OBRYAN, Henry 26*
LOGUE, Patrick 25*
MARANDA, Isaac 18*
HURSLY, Lewis 30*
MOSELEY, James 22*
SULLIVAN, Patrick 24*
CONNER, Hugh 24*
PENDLETON, H. 19 (m)*
WARD, T. 20 (m)*
PARKER, J. 23 (m)*
MURRAY, M. 21 (m)*
PERRY, J. S. 36 (m)*, Eliza J. 24
BEESOM, Rachel 22*
GEIGER, D. D. 29 (m)*, Ann 20, Mary 2
PATTERSON, Samuel 31*
FULNER, John 40, Martha 37, Margaret 13, Mary E. 11, Theodore 7, Milton 6, John 4, Leander 3
GIBBONS, Richard 50*, Ann 29
OBRIAN, John 25*
GILL, Edward 25*
GREEN, William 27, Nancy A. 25, George W. 8, Elizabeth 5, Frances M. 2
MAYHEW, James H. 23, Rebecca E. 22, John W. 4/12
CAMPBELL, James 53, Nancy 44, Henrietta 25, William R. 21, Charles 17, James 10, Johnson 6, Thomas 1
EVANS, Henry J. 24, Elizabeth 23, Malinda 5, William R. 3
FAIRY, Michael 23, Margaret 24, Mary 1
BROWN, William 50, Catharine 39, William 15, Thomas 13, Henry 11, Alexander 9, Robert 7, John 5, Catharine 3, James 1

1850 Census Greenup County Kentucky

Schedule Page 211

KELLAY, Samuel 27, Rebecca 24, Eliza J. 3, James A. 1
DARBY, Caroline 25, Richard 6, George Ann 2
DARBY, Hugh 32*, Ursula 28, George 10, Mary 8, Martha 5, William 4, Ann 2
MCLARKEY, Samuel 28*
HUNT, William 20*
CARR, James 37, Nancy 19
DAY, William 45, Elizabeth 44, Ann 14, Caroline 13, Edith 12, Emily J. 10, Thomas 8, George J. 6, Elizabeth 2
ABRAMS, Basil 45, Rhoda 47, Thomas 19, Milton 17, Jonathan 14, Elizabeth 13, Nancy 10
BOYD, Henry 30, Nancy 25, Marcus L. 6, Isaac 2, John W. 8/12
COLLINS, Isaac 36, Elizabeth 31, William 15, Cyntha 13, John 11, Joseph 7, Nancy 4, Sarah J. 3
COLLINS, Luan 23 (f), Susan 2, Wealthy A. 8
COLLINS, Ann 65*
FULTS, Harrison 22*, Arty 22 (f), Delana A. 3 (f), John W. 3/12
GULLET, Christy 26 (m), Sarah 24, Nancy A. 9, Roxe A. 7 (f), Adeline 4, Mary J. 2, Henry H. 4/12
HART, William 26*
RODGERS, Roland 19*
MAYHEW, William 18*
JENKINS, Isaac 35, Eleanor 33, Joseph 15, John 12, Archibald 8, Elizabeth 6, Eliza 1
EVANS, Greenbury 32*, Mary A. 28, James G. 4, Henry C. 2
PARTON, Cintha 16*
WOOD, Jackson 36*, Margaret 20, Joseph 8, Harriet 3, Noah 23
WELCH, _____ 1 (m)*
PATTERSON, James 55*

Schedule Page 212

BARTON, George 26*
MCCLURG, Alexander 19*
NUTTER, Levi 22*
CANE, John 23*
BAILY, Andrew 26, Chloe 23
ANDERSON, John 75, Julian 54 (f), Alexander 25, Benjamin 20, James 19, Julian 17, Robert 11
MILLER, William 61, Elizabeth 51, William 22, Elizabeth 18
MILLER, Stephen 20*, Delila 22, Nancy E. 4, Joseph 2, David 3/12
TACKETT, Henry 25*, Rebecca 26, John W. 7, Lewis 4
MCGEE, Coonrod 46, Mary 46, Hannah 18, Mary E. 15, Calvin 10, Sarah J. 7, Louisa 5
SAXTON, John 37*, Barbara 42, Levi J. 8, Barbary A. 6
SCALF, Aggy N. 18*, Patsey 16, William L. 11
STEWART, Sandford 31, Louisa 26, Cintha A. 1, Sophia E. 19, James 27
WELCH, Walter 50*, Jane 52
HIGGINS, Sarah 74*, John 16, Lewis 15
DEVORE, Martha 30*, Richard 10/12
RIGG, Joseph 40, Jane 39, Jefferson 21, John 18, William 16, Martha A. 14
ROBINSON, Elizabeth 40, Cintha 16

1850 Census Greenup County Kentucky

JILES, Nancy 43*, Edwin 23, Rebecca 20, Arematha 14, Mary A. 9, Samuel H. 5
BROWN, Austin 36*
WILLIAMS, Roxe A. 45 (f)*, Thomas W. 29, George 27, James 23, William 21, Leven 17 (m), Lewis 14
JUSTICE, Harrison 22*
THORNSBURY, Martha 48, Nancy 47, Marietta 16, Nancy A. 14, Eliza 10, Mahala 8, Amos 5
SIMPSON, Margaret 53, Samuel 21, Elizabeth 19, Margaret 17, Alexander 15

Schedule Page 213

MCWURTER, Harvey 33, America 27, Ellen 10, James 8, Charles H. 6, Benjamin 4, John C. N. 1
FISHER, William 21, Mary 23, Elizabeth 2, Eli 4/12
NUNLEY, William 33, Elizabeth 30, John 6, Lewis 4, Ibby 2 (f), Robert F. 1
MUTTER, Isaac 26, Elizabeth 41, John 17, William 16
MARTIN, George 66, Priscilla 56, Samuel 34, Lewis 25
MARITY, William F. 46, Mary A. 35, Benjamin F. 14, Elizabeth 12, Martha 10, Jesse 8, Dorotha 6, William 4, Charles 2
WOODWARD, Silas 35*, Jane 34, Sarah F. 7, Almeda 5, John 2
KOUNS, John 12*
EASTHAM, James 32, Christiana 73, Elizabeth 42
MARTIN, James 30, Polly 28, Armazinda 11, Wallace 9, Lauretta 7, James 5, Jane 2, Silas 1
GUSTIN, Robert 42, Christian 44 (f), Orpha 14, Amanda 12, John 10, James 8, Amasa 9/12
BARBECK, Adam 43*, Eliza 44
CALVIN, Vincent 29*
HENSLEY, Joel 26, Pelina 17, John W. 10/12
EASTHAM, Elba 47 (f), Edward 19, George N. 14, William 12, Christiana 9
MORRIS, William 55, Polly 43, David 18, William 16, S. J. 22 (m)
HENSLEY, George 62, Rutha 50, Susan 17, Nancy 14, Tabitha 10, Jacob 7
HENSLEY, William 32, Matilda 30, Martha 15, Samuel 10, Julian 9 (f), Jefferson 6, Emily 2

Schedule Page 214

LITTLE, Henry 21, Sarah 20
HENSLEY, George W. 26, Sarah 19, Matthias 3, Solomon 1
HENSLEY, Milton 23, Polly 21, Malinda 2
JOHNSON, William 45, Isabella 27, Eliza 8, James 6, Angeline 4, America 1, Booker 14, Calvin 20
CLEVENGER, John 23, Cyntha 21, Edmund 1
COOLEY, John 23, Louisa 21, Edmund 2, Isam 1
LITTLE, Allen 80, Polly 36, Mary J. 15, Cornelius R. 17, Susannah 11, Naomi 8, Garret P. 6, Mariah 2
JOHNSON, George 59, Rachel 66
JONES, Charlotte 45, Linton 19 (m), Obadiah 13, Henry 10, Austin 7, Hiram 4, Charlotte 2
SLOAN, Joab 50, Rhoda 44, Enoch 15, George W. 17, Eleanor 21, Manerva 15, Emeline 14, James 12
HALLEY, Thomas 33, Nancy 27, Edmund 8, John 6, James 5, Thomas 2, Patrick 4/12
BLOOMFIELD, William 26, Polly 23, Edmund 2, Louisa 1
LAMBERT, Fannin 34 (m)*, Sarah 32
MCGINNIS, William 5*
SCOTT, Crawford 49, Mahala 44, James 7, Abraham 5, Elizabeth 3
SCOTT, Catharine 55*, Luther 22, Thomas 19

1850 Census Greenup County Kentucky

STERLING, Abraham 31*
STERLING, Clarinda 33*, Charles W. 7, Hugh M. 6, Mary A. 4, Sirus 1 (m)
SCOTT, John 2*

Schedule Page 215

BELTS, John 88*, Nancy 70, Jefferson 18, George W. 15, John W. 13
BRYANT, Sarah 12*, Jenny 6, Isaac 3
GEIGER, William L. 30*, Esther 25, Henry 4, Mary 2, Sidney 18 (f)
CALVIN, James 27*
TUPLETT, Lurana 56, Lurana 23, Joseph 21, Thomas 18
BLACK, J. G. 26 (m)*, Catharine 26, Theodore 10, Elizabeth 8, Nancy 6, James 4, Laura 2, George W. 22, Thomas 23
HILES, William 21*
HERN, Mary 30, George W. 9, Benjamin F. 7, Elizabeth 6, Margaret 4, Samuel P. 4/12
FORD, John H. 38, Amanda 28, C. W. 7 (m), Susannah R. 5, Tandy L. 4 (m), Martha L. 2
ADAMS, E. E. 43 (m)*, Calfurna 29, Roselle 14
DAVIS, Eliza 15*
LOCY, Abrel 19 (m)*
NUNLEY, Daniel 35, America 37, Jane 13, John 9, William 7, Benjamin 3, Easter 1
KIZER, John 35, Cassander 33, America 5
CHAPPEL, George W. 29, Mary 29, Juliet 5, Georgianna 3, William 1
WILLIAMS, William 44*, America 22, Polly 20, Foster J. 11, Sarah 10, Easter 2
JOHNSON, Levi 33*
HYATT, ___ 30 (m)*
BRANNUM, Wiley 25*
MUTTER, Franklin 22*
BURTENSHAW, Bernard 25*, Mary 19, Elleanor 1
ADAMS, Abraham 33, Lorena 26, Montgomery 12, Sarah J. 10, Cyrus 6, Alice 11/12
BURTENSHAW, Thomas 55, Frances 51, Alford 16, Mary J. 12, Frances 10

Schedule Page 216

DUNFIELD, Charles 38, Elizabeth 35, Ahas 16 (m), James 12, Margaret 10, Eliza 8, Harriet A. 6, Leana M. 2
TUBLETT, Francis 32, Mary 32, Samuel 8, John 8, Joseph 7, Thomas 4, Francis 2, John 24
BURGRASS, John 32*, Hester A. 22, John 4, Catharine 2, Louisa 9/12, George 22
BINTLENPANTES, Jacob 40*
MOULDER, William 23*
ROOS, John 28, Catharine 22, John 10/12
TANNER, Pearce L. 42, Mary A. 36, Julia 18, Elizabeth 14, Laura 11, William J. 9, Asa J. 6, John 5, Emeline 2
MEAD, Albert G. 47*, Elizabeth 27, John 18, Mary 16, Richard 9, William 7, Abinda 5, Pearce 11/12
HORNBUCKLE, Luke 21*, America 21, Mary E. 4/12, Margaret 64
COOLY, Edmund 53, Polly 54, Jenny 19, Patsey 17, William 16, Maraba 15, Thomas 13, Matilda 10
CARR, James 35*, Sarah 24
ULEN, Elizabeth 12*, Benjamin 9, Catharine 6

1850 Census Greenup County Kentucky

DAWSON, Ellen 24*
CARR, Canady 63 (m), Jane 61, Margaret 38, Isaac H. 20, Mary E. 18
SHELL, George 28, Emily 22
CAMPBELL, George W. 49*, Sarah 40, Frances M. 4/12
KOUNS, Jasper 16*, Jacob 14, Ire 12 (m), Abraham 8, Marinda 6
MCCROSKEY, William 35, America 31, Mary A. 11, Nancy J. 9, Alexander 6, John 5, Eliza 1

Schedule Page 217

FOSTER, William 38*, Sarah H. 24, James D. 9
CLARKE, Nancy A. 43*
DAVIS, Alexander 50, Eliza 46, John 23, Nathaniel 19, James 17, Mary 14, Aaron 11, Job 9, Ellen 6, Gerard 4, Alexander 2
GARMER, Joshua 66, Elizabeth 64, Catharine 41
KOUNS, Christian 36 (m), Elizabeth 21, John L. 12, Letitia 11, William 8, Mary A. 6, Frances V. 4, Abraham 2, Christian 1
FARMER, Mordecai 28, Abegail 38, William 5, Josephene 3, _____ 1 (m)
FARMER, Jeremiah 30, Catharine 24, John 10, Elizabeth 7, Sarah A. 5, Mary J. 3
GILKERSON, John 43*, Cassander 50, Mary 18, Henry 17, George 11, Elizabeth 15, Julia 6
SPANGLER, Ann H. 11*, Charles W. 10
NEAL, Jonathan 21*, Luanda 18, Augusta J. 1
KRING, Elizabeth 33*
RODGERS, George 18*
DAVIS, Harriet 61
BROWN, Benjamin F. 23, Susan 23
SHUBERT, Samuel 38, Catharine 34, Sarah 131e

Schedule Page 218

WARING, Y. G. 35 (m), Jane 34, Darcus 16, Margaret 14, Richard 12, Frances Mary 10, Windfield 3
GREENSLATE, Mason 33, Mary 45, Margaret 12, Mary Jane 5
LAWSON, Jacob 45*, Elizabeth 32, Ann 19, Thomas 16, Sidney 11 (m), Joshua 8, William 6, Jacob Adney 4, Taylor 2
PARKER, Eliza 13*, James 9
LAWSON, James N. 33, Sarah 24, Mary V. 2
FRIER, A. W. 24 (m), Hannah 17, Mary Catharine 1
PIERCE, John 45, Sarah 37, E. J. 14 (f), Benjamin 9, Sarah 7, John 5, George 1
POST, A. C. 37 (m), Clara 6, Mary Jane 34, William 3, Robert 1
HUNT, Carlisle 35, Rebecca 35
MORAN, William 49, Sophia 44, Joseph 18, William 10, Emly 4, Margaret 6
HILL, John P. B. 43*, Rubey 35, J. M. 14 (m), Amos 12, Electa 10, Joseph 8, James William 4, Samuel 1
SEELEY, Samuel 71*, Electa 67, Electa 40
BEAVERS, Andrew 30, Elen 28, Jacob 8, Thereca 6, Elizabeth 3, Sarah J. 1
DAWSON, John 53, Polly 18, Jane 16, William 14
HOWELL, William 60, Catharine 48, Belinda 24, Samuel 22

1850 Census Greenup County Kentucky

PIERCE, Dixon 43, Mary 37, Hiram 18, Amanda 15, Alfred 13, Cyntha 9, Richard 8, Ruhama 4, William 2
RICHARDS, M. 23 (m), Matilda 22, Decature 1

Schedule Page 219

DUNAWAY, James 32, Rachiel 34, J. N. 10 (m), J. M. 8 (m), Martha 6
BROWN, Lawson 25*, Barbery 29, Nimrod 5, Louisa 4, Martha 1
SALLARS, Sarah 15*, David 14
LAWSON, John Y. 30
LAWSON, Catharine 61, Sarah C. 22
MORTON, Hezekiah 53, Hannah 47, Letecia 21, William 20, Margaret 17, Ann 14, Elenora 9, Hezekiah 3, David 50, John Q. 21
CULVER, Mary A. 38, William 14
GRAY, John L. 54*, Elizabeth 47, John 19, Elizabeth 16, S. J. 14 (f), Lucey 10, Charles L. 7, Bird 21
BIRK, Idea 2 (f)*
FAGAN, Henry 21*
GRAY, Loyd 25, C. E. 18 (f)
BROWN, John 48*, Nancey 46
HUNT, Melvina 15*, Sarah 13, Amanda 9, Cyntha 7, Eliza 4, Reuben 1
PHILLIPS, E. L. 35 (m), Martha 25, Thomas S. 8, William B. 6, N. M. 1 (f)
BUSH, Aaron jr. 38, Catharine 48, John 17, Vilette? 13 (f), Marshal 9, Lewis 6
BUSH, William 28*, Ann 22, Sarah Jane 2, N. L. 1 (m)
JOHNSON, Thomas 23*
CONNER, William 53, S. K. 40 (f), Mary 19, William 17, Amanda 13, Thomas 13, Samuel 8, Lydda H. 6, Rebecca 3
PUTHUFF, John 27*, Frances 30, Silas 7
DRAKE, N. Jane 5*, Mary 3
PUTHUFF, J. B. 37 (m)*, Rhoda 24, Elizabeth 10, Melvena 8, J. W. 6 (m)
WARNER, N. S. 60 (m)*

Schedule Page 220

JAMESON, John 42, Susan 38, M. A. 18 (f), S. J. 15 (f), Elizabeth 10, Emily 8, Martha 4, James R. 3
DORCH, John 46, Sarah 48, E. B. 9 (f), Susan 16, amanda 8, William 24, John 22
RICHARDS, Zachariah 45, Ruth 36, James T. 17, Mary A. 14, Irena 12, Heylin 10 (f), Sarah 8, Riley 6, Zimri? 4 (m), Nathan 2, Calforna 1
WARING, R. W. 36 (f)
BRYAN, James 44, Mary Jane 29, William H. 9, Sarah C. 6, Martha 2
CAMPBELL, Thomas 36*, Emsa 30, Mary L. 13, John 12, William H. 10, Jeremiah 4, James M. 1
MIFFORD, George 25*, Susan 20, Sally Ann 2
RANKINS, Alexander 49*, Elizabeth 42, John 18, Louisa 16, James 15, Alexander 13, Elizabeth 11, Frances 9, Richard 7, M. M. 4 (m)
MIFFORD, Nathan 18*
BOYD, Samuel 54, Fernata 36, E. Y. 1 (m), N. W. 1 (m)
VANBIBBER, Adney 38 (m), L. 80 (f)
THORN, N. F. 35 (m), Lois 29, Rhoda 9, John 6, Edward 3, Alitha 1

1850 Census Greenup County Kentucky

RAWLINGS, Joshua 62, Hannah 50, Aletha 34
MORTON, George 26, Cloey 24, James W. 1
BRADSHAW, Stephen 26*, Matilda 23, C. A. 2 (m)
VALANCE, Carter 30*, Sarah 4
PIERCE, William 39, Mary 32, E. A. 13 (f), Nancy 11, Sidney 8 (m), William 6, James 4, Richard 2

Schedule Page 221

LONG, Martin 69, Mary 69, George 25, Cyntha 20
LONG, Elijah 30
THOMAS, Abraham 47, Elizabeth 45, R. 21 (f), Lavina 18, Marion 16 (m), Amanda 15, Jasper 13, Sarah 12, Malissa 8, Josephine 4
LONG, Elisha 30, Cyntha 22
ROBERTS, Clabourn 60, Susan 55, John 22, Susan 16, William 13, Claborn 10
HARPEREE, Elias 51, Jemima 46, Aaron 17, Hamilton 15, William R. 11, Elias 10, Windfield 5
SONGER, Nancey 42, Jackson 19, Shelton 14, Gemima 11, Mary J. 8
SMITH, John 34*, Mary 13, Alsa 28 (f), J. P. 11 (m), Margaret 9, Martin 7, Thomas 5, Phebey 2
THOMAS, A. 11 (f)*
HINKLEY, Silvester 28*
BIGGS, William 49, lucey 37, R. W. 20 (m), Thomas 18, Susan A. 16, James 14, Ann E. 12, R. 7 (m), George 5, Lucey 1
GALLIHER, John 51*, Mary 44, Samuel 24, Teresa 22, Richard 20, Manassa 18 (m), Mary A. 16, John 14, Matilda 13, Marilda 9, Obediah 5, Clarissa J. 3
BRADSHAW, William C. 21*
JONES, Mary 45, Elizabeth 21, William 17, Thomas 19, Filena 14, Rachiel 11, Afire 8 (f)
BURT, William 31, Mariah F. 23, Mary Ann 7
TEGARDEN, John M. 33*, Manerva 28, E. E. 5 (m), J. B. 3 (m), Ala A. 1 (f)
SNYDER, C. 58 (f)*

Schedule Page 222

INGLAND, William 50*, Sarah 28, Edward 12, William H. 1
SMITH, Melvina 5*
NEACE, John 63*, Elizabeth 50, Sarah 24, Thomas 16, C. G. 8 (m)
STEWART, Charles A. 27*
GRIFFIN, Andrew 60, Lucinda 48, John G. 24, A. J. 21 (m), Elizabeth 17, G. A. 10 (f), H. W. 7 (m), James 5
GRAY, Mary 90, Nancey 52, John 13, Elzaphin 10 (m), Jerusa 8 (f)
GREGORY, Richard 26, Priscilla 24, Mary S. 2, Nancy 1
TRAYLOR, David 25, Elizabeth 24, Thomas 4, Angaline 2, M. S. 1 (f)
GRAY, Joseph G. 47, Delila 39, Mary Ann 16, Carlin 11, Margaret 9, Susan 8, Lewis 5, Lucy E. 2, J. F. 1 (m)
SERGANT, Elijah 29*, E. G. 28 (f), J. L. 5 (m), J. Y. 3 (m), L. E. 1 (f)
BIGLEY, L. J. 10 (f)*
BRADSHAW, George 30, Eliza 31, S. S. 8 (m), J. L. 7 (m), Julian 4 (f), R. W. 3 (m), E. A. 1 (f)
BUSH, Z. 28 (m), Mary 22, Viletta 3, Z. 1 (m)
REED, A. L. 25 (m)*, Heneretta 25

1850 Census Greenup County Kentucky

ROACH, Ruth 81*
GREGORY, Joseph 54, Elila 53, Elizabeth 19, Elenor 17, A. J. 14 (f), Joseph 10
WARING, C. H. 69 (m)*, Mary 67, James L. 24, William 26, Susan 18, M. B. 1 (f), Daniel 17
POWELL, John 15*
RIGG, Townley 51, Susan 44, Robinson 16, Catharine 4
SMITH, H. C. 22 (m)*, Harriet 22
STEWART, Sarah 15*
LITTERAL, H. S. 11 (m)*

Schedule Page 223

BROWN, William 22*, Samuel 18, Elizabeth 17, Peter 13, J. H. 10 (m), Susan J. 2
MEDDAUGH, James 39*, Elen 39, James 7, Susan 5, Ann E. 4
DUVALL, Mary A. 22*, Martha J. 20, John 16, Sarah E. 15
BROWN, John J. 14*
TONG, William 50, Mary K. 50, Nancy C. 24, William H. 22, John 17, Mary J. 12
DUNCAN, Joseph 60, Jemima 63, Emly 24, Albert 20
MEDDAUGH, Benjamin 18*, Sarah A. 40
GORE, James 27*
DOOLEY, Harrison 22*
QUALL, George 29, Cyntha A. 29
BLAIR, Joseph 49, Nancey 31, William 15, Josiah 12, Polly A. 4
MEDDAUGH, Charles 47, Jane 36, Ruth 15, Henry 13, Sarah J. 11, James 9, Martha E. 8, Jerusa A. 7 (f), Melissa 5, P. M. 3 (m)
STEVENSON, Matthew 63*, Elizabeth 40, Demarius 13, Amanda 10, Elizabeth 6, Benjamin 4
BOUSER, Clinton 21*
LONG, Charles 38, Mary 37, Nancey 12, Sarah 11, Lucey 9, James W. 6, Mary 4, G. W. 2 (m), J. P. 1 (m)
BERRY, William 32*, Freelove 28, William W. 8, Lucey 6, Nathaniel 5, Ann E. 2
OSBORN, Silas 23*
MERRIL, Albert 22*
BRADSHAW, Alexander 39*, Nancy 35, J. H. 14 (m), George 13, Mary A. 7
LAWSON, William B. 25*, Fletcher 22
MERRILL, J. P. 24 (m)*, Iula 24 (f), J. M. 1 (m)
MONROE, Jacob 28*, Eliza A. 25, William 2

Schedule Page 224

BRAGG, Moses 75 (B), Chaney 60 (f)
HILDRITH, Uriah 48, Nancy 49, David 23, John 22, Frasier 14, William 8, Nicholas 4, Ann 20, Mary 18, Lavina 12, Sarah E. 10, Susan 9, Rebecca 6, Vincent 21, Margaret 22, Perry 4, John 2
FLANAGAN, George 30*, Suca Ann 30, Richard 7, Lifelet 6 (m), Nathaniel 4, Sarah E. 2
DAVIS, J. C. 14 (m)*, Joseph 7
PATTINGALE, Stephen 37, Lydda 33, James 12, Smith 10, John O. 8, Thomas J. 6, Oscar 4, Lucetta 3, Lorenzo 1
REED, James 30, Josephine 27, Marion 7 (m), Mary 5, Windfield 3, Mariah 1
REED, Rodney 26*, Roxeny 55 (f), Caroline 23, Calvin 15

1850 Census Greenup County Kentucky

RIDENOUR, John 12*
HORNBUCKLE, William 45, Sharlotta 36, Harden 15, Mary 13, Nada 11, Margaret 6, Sarah A. 4, Susan 2
HART, Counsel 44, N. J. 44 (f), J. M. 16 (m), Martha _. 13, Joseph 9
MORTON, John A. 34, Catharine 27
BROWN, James 54, Martha 49, Robert 21, William 17, Rebecca 13, Charlton 12, Samuel 10, Henry 6
SHOEMAKER, John 27, Mary E. 25
SHOEMAKER, Isaac 25*, Margaret 23
BROWN, Matthew 58*
BROWN, Piercol? 42 (m)*, Margaret 36, Marion 8 (m), Adalada 4, Jackson 4
CLAREY, Thorndike 35*, Sarah W. 42, Levina 4
BROWN, Charlton 40*, Roney 32 (f), Julian 9 (f), George W. 7, Perlina 5, Nancy M. 2, B. F. 1 (f)

Schedule Page 225

BOUSER, Temperance 18*
OSBORN, Squire 25*, Mary E. 18
PICKENS, William 44*, Margaret 38, Moses 17, Eliza 14, Jane 11, Robert J. 10, Sophia 4, Nancy M. 2
HART, Angaline 28*
COX, David 47*
WALKER, Robert 52, Margaret 43, Richard D. 21, James W. 17, William 16, Nancy E. 14, John 12, Willis 8, George 6, Robert 4, Ann 1
PARKER, Hannah 44*
BARTLET, Thomas 22*, Trevanion 19, Martin 18, George 16
SMITH, William 23, Martha 21
BRYANT, Benjamin 67*, Sarah 47, Thomas 12, Elizabeth 9, Samuel 18
HARNWELL, Elizabeth 52*
WALKER, Elizabeth 38, Hannah 12, John W. 10, James E. 7, S. W. 4 (m)
RICHARDS, John 29*, Mary A. 22, Elizabeth 3, Judith 1
APPLEGATE, James 20*
WALKER, James 42, Nancey 38, Mary 6, Aaron 5, Samuel 3, Sarah A. 1
LONG, Benjamin 33, Eliza 17, Taylor 3, Judith 2
STEPTER, John 34, Mary A. 27, Elizabeth 7, Martha 5, Lockwood 1, William 68
LEE, Richard 28, Jane G. 30, Ann E. 6
LEE, Green 25, Lucinda 23, Sarah J. 4, William S. 1
FORD, John 28, Sarah J. 20, William H. 1
PUTMAN, Michael 47, Malinda 37, John 18, Elizabeth 17, Jane 15, James 12, Benjamin 9, Moses 4, Nancey 2, Henry 50

Schedule Page 226

MCKOY, Obediah 42*, Casander 37 (f), J. A. 12 (m), Sarah 9, Ella 6, C. H. 4 (m), James R. 1
KING, William P. 9*, Mary 7, Thomas 4
BROWN, William 21*
THOMPSON, Anthoney 34, Mary 34, Cyntha A. 5, Sarah C. 3, Louisa 1
FUQUA, J. C. 37 (m), Amanda 23, Martha 1, Cyntha 63
CRAYCRAFT, Charles 47

1850 Census Greenup County Kentucky

CRAYCRAFT, Ada 51*
BIVINS, Martha 5*
FRAZEL, George 25*
SUTTLE, John 40, Sarah 45, Rufus 19, Amanda 17, Harriet 15
KELLEY, Pagneman? 46 (m), Sarah 26, John 6, Martha 4, Thomas 1
MONTGOMERY, John 50, Margaret 50, Samuel 17, William 16, Joshua 13, Stephen 10
MCKEE, John 65, Elizabeth 64, Elizabeth 24, Easter 18, Thomas 15
MCKEE, John 27, Nancy 26, Eliza 5, Nancey 4, James 7, Mary J. 3, John 1
CROSSET, John L. 25, Mary 26, Sarah J. 3
COOPER, William 28, Martha 24, Adoniram 4 (f), Aretmus 2, Valentia 1 (f), William J. 1
RAWLINGS, Franklin 35*, Mary 42, Letticia 11, Harriet 8, Eliza A. 4, Jonathan 1
TRAYLOR, Ransom 21*
TRAYLOR, Jesse 22, Lucresa 24
PATRICH, Emanual 25, Cathrine 25, Sarah J. 2, _____ 1 (m)

Schedule Page 227

CALDWELL, John 48, Mary 40, Thomas 23, William 21, Elizabeth 15, John 18, Mary J. 14, Hannah K. 11, Jams 8, Eliza 5
WILSON, Guy 42*, Deborah 44, Charles 13, Sarah E. 8, Guy 6
TRAYLOR, Nancy 13*, John 14, William 7
SWEARINGEN, William 21, Elizabeth 20, Mary E. 1, G. W. 1/12 (m), George 23
JACOBS, Shelton 39, Ann E. 28, John W. 11, Rachiel 9, Cassa 5, Adaline 3, Ann E. 1
GARRET, Thomas J. 73, Nancey 63
COX, Jesse 30, Sarah 25, William 2, George 7/12
BLACK, Henry 31, Eliza 33, William C. 8, S. S. 7 (m), R. A. 4 (m), R. J. 5 (f), James H. 2
VALANCE, Samuel 28, Margaret 22, Rebecca 3, J. C. 1 (m)
VALANCE, Harvey 35, Sarah 25, Samuel 10, Henry 8, America 5, C. W. 3 (m), James 4/12
VALANCE, Samuel 70, Delila 56, Delila 19, Henry 26
HORSLEY, James 89*
COCHRAN, Barbery 30, Mary 14, Jane 11
BRILHART, Jacob 41, Louisa 41
CRAYCRAFT, Charles 67*, Sarah 56
OLIVER, Cyntha 23*, John G. 10
ROBERTS, Mark 40, Adaline 35, Benjamin 14, Susan 12, Lewis 10, Cassa 8, Mark 6, James 5, Adaline 4, Helen 3, Alfred 5/12
JONES, John 57, Mary 48, Rachiel 28, Rebecca 20, John 17, Ursley 15 (f), Daniel J. 12

Schedule Page 228

ALEXANDER, Susan 39, Jesse 19, Jackson 13, Susan 9, Polly A. 7
THOMPSON, William 68*, Elizabeth 60, Matthew 36
HOWLAND, Milley 20*, L. A. 1 (m)
VEACH, Nancy 38, Frank 7, Jesse 3
NEACE, William 21, Elizabeth E. 17
THOMPSON, James 25, Clarissa 25, J. W. 2 (m), M. A. 6/12 (m)
SIMPKINS, George 60, Fanny 62, James 22

1850 Census Greenup County Kentucky

THOMPSON, Alfred 31, Hannah 19, William R. 27, Mary E. 18
ALLIN, M. H. 47 (m), Priscilla 81
TRUET, Mary 52*, George 21
GIBBS, Sarah 60*
HOWLAND, Mary L. 3*
WHITE, Jonas 50, Mildred 26, James G. 14
DAVIS, Alfred 44, Matilda Jane 34
LOGAN, Abraham 36*, Julian 32 (f), Minerva 15, Charlotta 14, William 12, James 10, Tobias 8, Abner 2
DAVIS, Alfred 9*, James W. 5/12
ALLIN, Beverally 39 (m), Martha 40, Benjamin 10, G. W. 8 (m), Beverally 6, Nancy J. 4, Margaret 2
BASSET, Isaac 58, Elizabeth 35, John 28, Elizabeth E. 13, A. W. 11 (m)
LOWDER, William 37, Barbery 36, Christena J. 13, Matthew 12, Joyce A. 10 (m), Mary A. 9, James 5, Nathan 4, Martha E. 6/12
UNDERWOOD, William 22, Sabina A. 17, James 5/12
LOWDER, James 40, Matilda 38, Lucinda J. 15, Eilza J. 12, William 5, George W. 3, James M. 1
THOMAS, James 65*, Sabina 58
BUTLER, Benjamin 33*
LOGAN, Edward 45*, Minerva 39, Jane 15, Elizabeth 9, Nancy 8, Marshal 4, Sabrina 3

Schedule Page 229

HACKWITH, Thomas 34, Lucresa 28, Jeremiah 10, Sarah 8, Hetta 6, James R. 4, Jesse 2, Margaret E. 2/12
ALEXANDER, Travis 23, Judith 30, Randal 3, Vilella 2
TINGLER, Solomon 25, Catharine 23, Margaret 3, John 2
BRIGHTS, B. B. 5 (m)*, Louisa 47
BUTRAM, Polly 25*, Mary 3/12
VANBIBBER, James 7*
SMITH, Nancey 58*
STEERUP, Nancy 23*
ANDERSON, J. N. 13 (m)*, Levina 12
STUMP, Sarah 1*
WILLS, James 71, Mary 69, James 31
BUTRAM, W. E. 26 (m), Elizabeth 24, Sarah E. 8, Sylvester 6, Nancey 4, Silvira 1
SITH, George 25, Catharine 23, Matilda 5, William 3, J. T. 1 (m)
DEWIT, William 54, Angaline 45, Francis M. 15, Mary E. 13, John H. 10, R. A. 9 (f), S. J. 8 (m), G. W. 5 (m), S. N. 2 (m)
ELISON, J. B. 79 (m), Elizabeth 57
SMITH, Charles 40*, Mary A. 40, Robert 14, J. L. 12 (m), Martha 11, Malinda 10, Elizabeth 8, Mary 6, Charles 4, William 2, Elvira 2, Bird 3/12
KEETLEY, Evaline 17*
BUTRAM, Westley 51*, Sarah 52, Reding 21, Jacob 18, Crocket 15, Elizabeth J. 14, A. J. 8 (m), Marshal B. 3
WARING, J. W. 5 (m)*
FISHER, Isaac 32, Sarah A. 24, Ursley 7 (f), Michael 7, Mary S. 2

1850 Census Greenup County Kentucky

Schedule Page 230

BRADBURN, Jackson 26, Jane 24, Elizabeth 4, William 1
BUSH, Nathan 30*, Mary 21, Martha E. 4, Frances M. 3/12
CLIFTEN, James 21*
RATCLIFF, James 24, Rudelea 22, James W. 5, Sarah R. 3, Samuel 3/12
HOUGHMAN, Allen 52, Sarah 40, George 19, Polly 17, Eliza 15, Henry 13, Solomon 11, Samuel 9, Joseph 7, Betsey 5, Lydda 3
WARNOCK, William H. 37, Emma 33, J. W. 14 (m), Samuel 12, Matthew 10, James 9, Francis M. 8, Lindsey 5, Rebecca 3, Taylor 1
RATCLIFF, Jer. 45 (m), Malinda 40, John 57
GRAY, Elias 62*, Joana 49, Math A. 18, Tomazine 16 (f), Thomas 14, Eliza M. 12, William 10, Zachariah 7, F. M. 5 (m)
BUSH, William 2*
BRADBURN, Mark 48, Mary 44, Alexander 22, Barnabas 18, Clinton 14, Mark 10, Mary 6, Martha 4, James D. 1
SLOANE, W. C. 37 (m), Harriet 28, Elizabeth 13, Mary E. 8, Thomas W. 6, Margaret 3, Martha 1
WARNOCK, J. W. H. 39 (m)*, Grace 34, J. H. 15 (m), E. G. 13 (m), Matthew 11, William W. 9, B. F. 6 (m), Betsey A. 3, Rebecca 10/12
GILKEY, John 23*
BRADBURN, M. 25 (m), Elizabeth 26, James 1, Jane 4, Sarah 3
BARNET, Elias 25*, Luanna 27, Noah 3, A. J. 2 (m)
RAWLINGS, A. 30 (m)*

Schedule Page 231

MEEK, Samuel 37*, Hannah 39, Sarah 9, Mary 7, Lewis 6, Samuel 4, Godfrey 1
LOVEJOY, Margaret 14*, Emily 14
ANDERSON, Jacob 37, Eliza 33, Sarah J. 13, Matilda 10, Amos 8, William 6, Lucinda 4
HUNT, J. S. 32 (m), Mary A. 27, Thomas O. 8, Emly 10, Harriet 6, Elvira 3, Jackson R. 3/12
HOWLAND, Benjamin 50, Priscilla 49, William 28, Ursley 22, Mahala 18, James 17, Charles 12, George 10, Sarah 8
ALLIN, Thomas J. 42, Minerva 24, Jonathan 6, Benjamin 4, Isabella 1
HOW, John 24*, Susan 21, Nancey E. 2, Nelsena C. 4/12
MORRIS, Calvin 10*
CLARK, Daniel 37, Sidney 20 (f), Lemuel 14, Jonas 5/12, Catharine 1
SHAMBAUGH, J. H. 48 (m), Catharine 48, Frank 10, Levina 8, Sofronas 5
LEE, Wilson 51, Sarah 46, Emma 19, David 17, Sarah 15, James 11, John 5
HOXWORTH, J. M. 26 (m), Isabella 20
PUGH, James G. 40*, Cinderella 40, Frances S. 14, M. H. 10 (m), H. C. 8 (m), James N. 6, Thomas E. 3, Mary A. 11/12
RICHISON, Lydda 19*
BROWN, John 61*, Emma 53
MORRISON, Emma B. 12*
MEEK, James 24, Eliza 23, Thomas E. 1, Mary F. 4/12
CRISP, David 44, Tabitha 38, Samuel M. 16, William 14, Susan 12, Joel 11, Jane 8

1850 Census Greenup County Kentucky

Schedule Page 232

SMITH, William R. 45, Sarah 37, Matilda 17, Margaret 13, Evaline 11, Jackson 10, John M. 8, Sarah 4, Samuel A. 20, Rasana 17
UNDERWOOD, Samuel A. 55, Sally 50, B. F. 27 (m), D. H. 25 (m), Elizabeth 20, Sally 18, Samuel A. 15, Nancey 14, J. D. 10 (m)
MARTIN, John 50, Christena 48, Edward 24, James 22, Calvery 18 (m), David 15, Emly J. 14, Otta 12 (f), Amanda 10, Margaret 17
BAKER, Ewin 33, Mariah 31, Henry 8, Minerva 6, George 4, Hiram 2
SMITH, G. W. 30 (m), Jane 26, Caroline 7, Henry 4, Margaret 2
JAMESON, Wilkshre 25, Nancey 19
JAMESON, David 65, Margaret 62
LOGAN, James 22, Nancy 17
UNDERWOOD, Matthew 50 (B), Lucey 50
HORSELY, James 55, Elizabeth 51, Lear 28 (f), Elizabeth 19, Sarah A. 17, Telitha 15, Basheby 12, Ruhama 10, Jonathan 8, James D. 6
MADDEN, Jonathan 44, Elizabeth 35, James 16, John 14, Eliza J. 11, Isaac 9, D. R. 5 (m), Samuel S. 2, William M. 1, Martha 19
ZORNS?, Philip 33, Rachiel 26, Rebecca J. 10, Elizabeth D. 6, William P. 5, Philip 3, Asa 1
ZORNS?, Thomas 30, Nancy 24, G. W. 6 (m), J. P. 4 (m), Rachiel 2, Lucinda 2/12
HORSLEY, William 39, Catharine 37, Clarinda 18, Lucinda 15, Taylor 10, Sarah C. 8, Philip 5, Delphia 3, Rachiel 1, James 34

Schedule Page 233

ZORNS?, Elizabeth 40, Nancey A. 21, John 19, Malinda 17, Philip 15, Isaac 13, Isam 10, Martin 7, Eliza J. 4, J. R. 1 (m)
DERMIT, Henry J. 21, Elizabeth 1
DERMIT, George 50*, Eliza 32, George 10, John 18, Cortney 16 (f), William T. 9, Sanders 7, E. J. 2 (f)
SARTIN, Jane 14*
STONE, John 67, Delila 65, Margaret 22
STONE, James 47, Betsey 35, John 15, Mary 13, Solomon 11, Martin 9, John 6, Thomas 4
HORSLEY, William 55, Nancy 30, William 18, Joana 21, Rhoda 17, Perry 15, W. A. 12 (m), H. C. 12 (m), Lear 9 (f)
HORSLEY, Matthew 25, Mary 20, Nathan 1
LAWHORN, J. B. 43 (m), Rachiel 22, Thomas 25, William B. 19, John 13, Daniel 11, Rebecca 9, Lear 2 (f), Joseph 1
COOPER, Eli 45*, Rachiel 46, Louisa 24, Sarah A. 21, Lutecia A. 19, John 14, Fletcher 11, Casanda 8, Mariah J. 7, R. W. 5 (m)
DRUZAN, Elizabeth 84*
MACLEESE, Daniel 69, Sarah 22, Martin 25, Martha 16, John L. 1, William 14, Lewis 10
MACLEESE, Daniel 41*, Frances 8, Susan 25, Mary 7, J. P. 5 (m), B. F. 3 (m)

1850 Census Greenup County Kentucky

Schedule Page 234

CRISP, David 3*
ROBINSON, William C. 22*
CRAYCRAFT, John 34, Charlotta 25, Jeremiah 5, Cyntha 2
VEACH, J. W. 51 (m), Nancey 23, Daniel W. 20, Julian 16 (f), Sofia 4, Caroline 2
GRICE, Elias 27*, Mary 25, Joshua 9, Elener 8, Mary 6, William 1
GALLIHER, Neal 28*
KINGSBURY, Charles 37, H. N. 31 (f), Charles 13, Oriana 9, G. F. 5 (m), Elen 3, Harriet 11
FERRIN, J. C. 40 (m)*, Mary 33
NELSON, James 10*
BERRY, Samuel 34, Serena 25, Ann 10, William Y. 7, Susan M. 5, Hannah S. 11/12
SLOANE, James 29*, Martha 26, Mary A. 3, Charlotta 1
PUGH, E. W. 21 (m)*
FOSTER, William 32, Kazier 30 (f), Harriet 14, J. T. 12 (m), Jas.? 10 (m), William 9, Dysa 6, E. J. 5 (f), Matilda 3
JONES, John 33*, Cytha 39, G. H. 11 (m), William 3
BARNEY, J. R. 18 (m)*, Elizabeth 15, Lucinda 13
WARNOCK, Jackson 35, Sarah A. 36, B. F. 8 (m), A. E. 6 (f), J. S. 5 (m), E. S. 2 (f)
VANKIRK, John 32, Eliza 32, W. C. 11 (m), Sarah 9, Lydda 4, R. S. 1 (m)
STEWART, William 27, Mary A. 20, J. T. 1 (m)
SLOANE, John 65*, Charlotte 54, Peter 21, Albert 16, George 16, Nathan 9
BYSEL, Hannah 24*, John 7, C. A. 3 (m)
CONLEY, Sampson 58, Mary 50, Susan 18, Mary 16, Nancy 9, Hetta 6

Schedule Page 235

BALLARD, William 57, Susan 36, Sanders 13, Eliza 12, James 6, Carlisle 5
ALEXANDER, John 29*, Mary 37, Martin V. 8, J. C. 7 (m), G. 5 (m), Cyntha 5/12
INGRAM, Jane 13*
MEEK, Joseph 54, Dysey 27
SHIELDS, W. W. 47 (m), L. S. 47 (f), William 15
JONES, R. D. 53 (m)*, Mary 53, Martha 23, Louisa 22, Rival 21, Samuel 18, Henry 15, John 13, John W. 16
AMES, Samuel B. 53*
THOMPSON, Jackson 34*, Wina 32, Alfred 13, Elizabeth 7
TRAYLOR, Jane 17*
STEVENSON, John 21*, Nathan 18, Elizabeth 19, Sarah 13, Martha 11, Priscilla 8
BALLARD, J. W. 1 (m)*, Emly 6, Pheba 5, Edward 3
SMITH, John 24*, Mahala 50, Theresa 7
CROOKS, H. G. 23 (m)*
SMITH, William 38, Cela 40, Betsey A. 16, John 14, George 12, Sarah 10, Charles 8, Priscilla 7, William 3
COMER, John 34, Eliza 30, William 12, Malinda 10, Henry 7, George 5, Susan 3, Sarah C. 7/12
ROBERTS, Absalom 67, Mary 40, Matilda 6, D. B. 4 (m)
ROBERTS, A. 30 (m), Mary J. 22, David A. 5, W. L. 2 (m)
CONLEY, John 26, Martha 20, William 2, Susan 2/12

1850 Census Greenup County Kentucky

ZORNS?, William 29, Elizabeth 23, Matilda J. 5, Mary E. 2, Rosana 8/12
ARTHUR, Joseph 55, Manutha 38, Tompkins 19, Elen 15, Albert 13, Marshal 11, David 8, Jonathan 8, James 6, John H. 4, Sarah E. 2

Schedule Page 236

BRIGGS, Jacob 60, John 25
MALONE, William 26, Mary 16
CHRISTMAN, Charles 51, Ann E. 13, James P. 10, F. M. 8 (f), Harriet E. 6, Charles H. 5
GREENSLATE, Susan 36, Susan J. 14, Elizabeth 12, Neoma 11, Calista 8, B. A. 6 (f), James W. 4
JENNINGS, Lacey 40 (m)*, Elizabeth 37, Jonathan 8, Calvin 6, Cyntha 3, Reason 5/12
YOUNG, William 16*, Catharine 14, Ibba 9
LITTLEJOHN, Webb 28, William 52, Grace 55
GRIFFEY, Houston 23, Martha 16
FOSTER, John B. 54, Sarah 43, Elizabeth 24, Isaac 22, Cornelus 20, Harrison 18, Nancy 15, Catharine M. 12, M. L. 9 (m)
MEEK, John 30, Elizabeth 28, Mary C. 8, Thomas 1, William 20, Julian 21 (f)
MEEK, Suter 27 (m), Mary 25, J. W. 3 (m), Mary A. 3/12
MEEK, James 76, Mary 57, Mary 15, Abigal 25, Amanda 13
BUSH, George 26, Amanda 25, G. W. 1 (m)
NELSON, David 35, Virginia 26, Mary J. 6, James R. 4
MOULDER, John 58, Mary 39, Rebecca A. 7, E. J. 4 (f)
SUTERS, John 81, Mary 56, Lucinda 25, J. H. 7 (m), Mary 3
MCCLAVE, G. W. 34 (m), Sarah 26, E. 5 (f), Alis 3, E. 1 (f)

Schedule Page 237

ALLIN, Joseph 24, Louisa 20, Ann? E. 2
MOULDER, John 21, Mary A. 15
ALLIN, Adison 24*, Nancey 24, Fielder 8, Mary 7, Jane 5
NELSON, John 24*
COLEMAN, Lafayett 22, Mary C. 21, M. J. 11/12 (m), J. W. 23 (m)
ALLIN, F. C. 33 (m)*, Matilda 22, Lavina 4, Philena 2, Martha 10/12
CRAYCRAFT, H. C. 20 (m)*
JONES, William 25*, Sarah J. 21, Elizabeth S. 8/12
KING, Benjamin 53, Mary 47, Lawrence S. 85, Jane 85
DUNAWAY, Samuel 37, Frances 40, G. W. 8 (m), Elijah 5, Sarah 3
WILLIAMS, Charles 31, Nancey 28, Lucey 9, Ann 5, Martha 4, George 1
BRIGGS, Isaac 24, Lucey 30, James 25, Betsey 59, Robin 10 (m)
HARE, Joshua 30, Polly 26, Nancey 8, Jonas 5, Eliza 4, Limri? 1 (m)
GREEN, Alexander 45, Susan 35, Mary E. 14, Charles 12
HARE, Thomas 28, Nancey 25, Elenora 5, John F. 3, D. E. 1 (f)
HARE, Ferman 38*, Tomazine 33 (f), Thomas 10, Sarah 8, Elizabeth 6, Caroline 3, Joana 9/12
MATTHEWS, Anderson 22*, Louisa J. 16
MATTHEWS, A. A. 50 (m), Mary 48, Catharine 13, Carlisle 11, R. J. 11 (f), Lucinda 8, Ann E. 7, John 5

1850 Census Greenup County Kentucky

POWELL, Reason 39*, Laney 36 (f), Angaline 16, Cyntha C. 13, James R. 11, Lucinda P. 9, H. A. 7 (m), Sarah J. 5, Mary L. 2, Theofolis 27

Schedule Page 238

JOHNSON, Ann 14*
RICHARDS, Thomas 56*, Susan 34, William 15, Hiram 13, Harris 11, Rebecca 18, Bazel 20, Thomas 2, Nancy 5/12
WINDFIELD, John G. 32*
APPLEGATE, Jeremiah 48, Mary 47, Lucinda F. 17, Victora 11, Nancey 9, Lucey 9, R. F. 8 (m), Mary C. 4, Adaline 3, Calferna 11/12
MAGLONE, John 48, Lucresa 20, Percival 18, Frances 15, Elizabeth 14, Jacob O. 10, Sarah 8, Joseph A. 4, Jonas L. 11/12
FOX, Benjamin 23, Nancey 22
HUNT, Harrison 35, Sarah A. 28, Hannah F. 11, Nancey 8, Sarah 4, A. J. T. 2 (m), G. W. D. 1/12 (m)
STEWART, Molissa 23, Elijah 5, Elen 6/12, Reuben H. 2
BRYSON, Houston 24, Martha 23, P. J. 2 (m)
ANDERSON, Noah 30, Hulda 34, William 8, G. W. 6 (m), Martha 5, Benjamin 3, James A. 2/12
HALL, John 28, Jane 30, William 5, Margaret 1
HUNT, A. J. 25 (m)*, E. F. 24 (f)
JOHNSON, Jeremiah 16*
JONES, David 51*, Shepard 20, Julian 17 (f), Angaline 11
GAMMON, George 15*
JONES, Allin 24, Mary A. 17
NELSON, John 28, James 26, Morris 23, Margaret 22, Anderson 18, Elizabeth 12, Margaret 58
CLAREY, Timothey 34, Sarah 28, Sarah 6, James 5, Richard 1

Schedule Page 239

WARNOCK, William H. 27, Ann 22, Louisa 3
GREENSLATE, Silas 41, Elizabeth 36, J. M. 14 (m), R. S. 12 (m), James C. 10, S. C. 8 (m), J. B. 4 (m), G. D. 1 (m)
CRAYCRAFT, J. M. 38 (m), Thereca 25, William 11, Sarah 7, Hugh 6, John 5, Joshua 3, Louisa 2, Susan 1
CRAYCRAFT, William 26*, Eliza 23, Mary E. 4, L. F. 3 (f), V. A. 1 (f)
ROE, George E. 22*
GREENSLATE, George 34, Cyntha 35, Sarah J. 14, Cyntha A. 10, G. W. 7 (m), Wilson 5, J. M. 4/12 (m)
CRAYCRAFT, William 44*, Sarah 45, E. M. 14 (f), Virginia 12, Sarah 65, Thomas 3
SPENCE, Archibald 31*
DUPUY, William 41*, Ann 41, Richard 14, Mary A. 12
RAY, G. W. 46 (m)*
ADAMS, Richard 22*
PUGH, Samuel 30, Mary A. 28, Martha 8, James R. 5, Mary 3, Samuel 5/12
PRATT, Eliza 47, W. F. 23 (m), Mary E. 17, Sarah J. 14, John 12, James 9, Samuel 7, Cassius 4
BROOKS, Edward 38, Amanda F. 25, John 7, Thomas R. 5, William F. P. 1/1

1850 Census Greenup County Kentucky

SPRAGG, N. B. 46 (m), Rhoda 41, Caleb 22, John 19, David 16, William 12, Margaret 10, Mary 7, Charles 5
HAYNES, Martha 36, Jackson 17, Mary A. 15, Elizabeth 12, Solomon 9, Geo.? 7, Jane 5, John 5/12
STEWART, Charles 72*, Rebecca 53, Sarah 11, Jane 8

Schedule Page 240

PHILLIPS, Gabriel 21*
BENTLINGER, Henry 30, Elizabeth 25, Louisa 4, E. E. 2 (m)
BISHOP, J. M. 60 (m)*, Jane 28, Betsey 40, Emeline 20, Jacob 18, Richard 15, Susan 10, Eliza 7, Catharine 1
BROWN, Mary J. 10*, John 1
ARNOLD, Andrew 21*
VANDEGRIFF, James L. 40
DUPUY, Richard 25*, Martha A. 19
TOMILSON, Rhoads 17*
DUPUY, M. F. 50 (m), Phebey 56, Albert 21, Martha 22, Mary J. 15, Louisa 4
JONES, N. 27 (m), Martha 25, M. 3 (m), R. N. 4/12 (m)
BUSH, Henry 35*, M. 25 (f), L. L. 2 (m), C. 1 (m)
STOCKUM, William 49*
CRAYCRAFT, Hugh 41, C. 23 (f), J. 18 (m), M. 11 (m), Hugh 2
SHIERER, Joseph 31, C. H. 22 (f), J. F. 5/12 (m)
GAMMON, Martha 52, William 30, John 27, Sarah 25, Mary 23, Lavina 14, Samuel W. 10
COOPER, John 57, Rebecca 54, F. M. 21 (m), William P. 20, M. A. 17 (f), H. C. 15 (m), Martha 12, John 10
GLOVER, Sarah 35, Johnsa 13 (m), Richard 7, Samuel 5
MCALISTER, Joseph 54*, Elizabeth 52, Mary 38, Mary 25, William 20, Sarah 17, Joseph 13, Charlotta 2
MEDDAUGH, Elijah 38, Mahala 23, J. A. 2 (m), Ira 2/12
RUNNELS, J. 25 (m), S. S. 24 (f)
HORN, Jonathan 27, Eliza 24
HITCHCOCK, S. F. 41 (m), R. 38 (f), J. 15 (m), M. 13 (m), Matilda 10, Susan 8, Smith 5, L. 3 (f)

Schedule Page 241

WARE, A. 35 (m), Sarah 34, J. 10 (m), Eliza 7, Mary 5, Elias 3, F. 6/12 (f)
BLANKINSHIP, J. 57 (m), M. 58 (f), S. 19 (m), L. 16 (m), J. 15 (f)
REEVES, R. 50 (m), M. 44 (f), A. 19 (f), Thomas 17, Richard 13, B. F. 11 (m), Peter 7, A. E. 3 (f)
LAWSON, John 50, Hannah 30, Barbary 18, Thomas 16, James 13, Milton 7, Mary 10, Newton 6, Sofia 5, John 3
SMITH, R. 45 (m)*, Cyntha 39
OLIVER, Betsey 22*, Elias 17
DEATLEY, James 23*
BRYSON, William 45, Betsey 36, Lawson 15, James 13, Catharine 10, William 6, Jane 6/12
KING, B. F. 39 (m), Nancey 37, S. M. 13 (f), Virginia L. 10, John 8, B. F. 6 (m), Z. T. 3 (m)
JACKSON, Charles 61, E. 55 (f), Nancey 18, Martha 16
MORTON, Richard 27, Martha 24, H. M. 1 (f)

1850 Census Greenup County Kentucky

LAUGHLIN, Robert 46, Judith 44
KENDLE, Smith 40, Nancey 35, M. V. 9/12 (f)
WEATHERS, E. 47 (m), Sarah 30, E. 15 (f), Edward 10, Charles 6, William 1
DOVIL, Isaac 38, Easther 33, S. M. 15 (f), G. W. 13 (m), M. C. E. 11 (f), L. J. 10 (f), J. R. 7 (m), C. F. 5 (m)
WARNER, H. 50 (f), E. S. 18 (f), G. W. 14 (m), Frances 13, N. S. 6 (m)

Schedule Page 242

LAWSON, B. 21 (m), Mariah 18
FOSSET, Charles 60* (B), Cloey 56, William 13
JOHNSON, William 55*, Isaac 22, John 20
CARNAHAN, Polly 50*
GAMMON, J. S. 51 (m), Harriet 38, F. M. 16 (f), George 14, Ann 12, Madison 11, Martha 9, Thomas J. 5, Harriet 2
STEPTER, James 32, Rebecca 43, S. A. 11 (f), M. E. 7 (f), R. M. 5 (m)
ALLIN, John 45, Sarah 45
DILLON, Thomas 54, Sarah 47, Mary 15, Fielden 14, James 12, Martha 10, Eletha 8, John 4
COLEMAN, Nancy 60
ANDERSON, Westley 33, Nancey 32, M. J. 13 (f), J. W. 11 (m), Matilda 4, Jonathan 9, Cyntha 1, James 22
CONLEY, Carter 31, Elizabeth 31, George 9, R. E. 6 (f), Mary Ann 3
APPLEGATE, Jacob 40, Lucinda 22, M. J. 4 (f), J. E. 1 (m)
BAKER, John 40, Rachiel 39, Susan 20, Mary J. 12, Elizabeth 10, William 8, Israel 6, Martha 3
FARROW, Mary 42*
SQUIRES, Betsey 16*, Harriet 15
SPENCE, Henry 7*
SAYER, J. 22 (m)*
SMITH, George 28*, Catharine 65, Nancy 23
ASHER, Sarah 30*, Margaret 8
GOODWIN, James 46, Patiance 41, James M. 13, Nancy J. 13, Josiah 8, Bluford 7, M. A. 1 (f)
SMITH, John 25*, Sarah 25, Catharine 5, Daniel 4, S. A. 1 (f)
WALKINSHAW, H. 58 (f)*
APPLEGATE, Smith 22, Elizabeth 23, Harriet 4, William 3, Thomas 1

Schedule Page 243

BUSH, Elizabeth 49*
HOW, Milton 25*, David 23, Minerva 19, Amanda 18, Henry 16
SMITH, Anthoney 41, Pheba 40, Sofiah 14, Jacob 13, George 11, Isaac 9, America 10, William 8, Nancey 5, Wilson 2, Rachiel 1
RICHESON, Mary 64
ANDERSON, James 57, Hilica 57, Mary 21, Richard 19, Jacob 17, Matthias 15, Lucinda 12, Jesse 12, Thomas 10, Elijah 7
SAYER, Asa 68, Nancy 55, Margaret 17, Nancy J. 14
DARAGAN, Edward 47 (B), H. M. 41 (f), Martha 6, Mariah 4, D. 2 (m)
GAMMON, John 52, Hannah 42, Martha 20, James 18, Jackson 16, Nancey 14

1850 Census Greenup County Kentucky

SMILEY, William 40*, John 15
WEEKS, J. C. 30 (m)*, M. J. 22 (f)
ARNOLD, S. 35 (m), E. B. 32 (f), Almira 7, Mary 5, J. F. 3 (m), J. W. 9 (m)
APPLEGATE, Richard 35, Rebecca 20, P. A. 2 (f), J. 10/12 (m)
MORTON, James 28, C. J. 28 (f), L. A. 5 (f), Benjamin 4, Alvin B. 2, Lavina 1
SAYER, Charles 31, Margaret 22, Jeremiah 8, Jesse 6, James 10/12
MARTIN, William 26, Julian 21 (f), Henry 3, F. 1 (m), _____ 1/12 (m)
THOMPSON, Thomas 19
WILLOBY, Harden 28, Emly 21, D. H. 11 (m), J. S. 8 (m), L. 3 (m), F. M. 1 (m)

Schedule Page 244

MCKOY, Moses 50, Hannah 47, John 19, Henry 15, Moses 7, Thomas 35
MORTON, John 60, Mary 57, M. K. 8 (f), John D. 7
BUCKNER, James 28, Sarah 27, M. E. 4 (f), Sarah E. 2, N. B. 1 (f)
THOMPSON, Reuben 37, Catharine 12, Amos 10, Sarah 5, Anthoney 3, James H. 2
MORTON, Willis 30, Caroline 22, Leander 6, Nat 4
HUDDLESON, Able 36, R. 36 (f), M. A. 10 (f), C. 9 (f), Agnes 6, L. 3 (m), L. 1 (f)
THOMPSON, H. 39 (m)
GABLE, N. 28 (m), Mary 22, Mary 2, A. M. 7/12 (f)
DRUZAN, E. 50 (m), Nancey 34, Elen 1 (m)
RODGERS, John 52, A. 21 (m), R. A. 19 (f), J. Q. 17 (m), Augustus 13, Sarah 11, George 5, James 3
DORCH, George 50, Elizabeth 48, Mary 26, Martha 24, J. Y. 22 (m), Rebecca 20, NEwman 18, F. 16 (m), Nancy 14, Hulda 12, Eliza 10, C. J. 5 (f)
KINNEY, Charles 24, E. W. 24 (f), Charles 3/12
COOPER, George 23, Mariah 19, Richard 2/12
SHUFFLE, Jane 42, Edward 16, M. M. 14 (f), James 12, S. J. 11 (f), Emanual 10
ARNOLD, P. 28 (m), S. 25 (f)
BOWCOCK, W. J. 45 (m), E. A. 26 (f), A. 14 (f), G. 11 (f), W. 10/12 (f)
HOYT, W. B. 27 (m), Charity 25, C. A. 4 (f), Levina 10/12
DEGEER?, Daniel 24, Lucinda 24

Schedule Page 245

WISHON, C. 30 (m)*, M. J. 26 (f), F. N. 7 (m), M. C. 5 (f)
DELMAN, Elias 25*
SLACK, Samuel 22, Ruth 30, Charles 4, Mary 7, Nancey 4/12
APPLEGATE, Andrew 54, Sarah 44, James 21, Jacob 19, Sarah 17, Richard 15, Martha 12, Joan 10, Andrew 7, Parthena 5, Charity 1
MESSE, Richard 22, Sarah 26, J. E. 2 (m)
TIMBERLAKE, Thomas 43, Catharine 41, Pleasant 12, Charles 9, M. F. 6 (f), Louisa 4, J. E. 1 (m)
WIMER, George 36, Emly 25, Daniel 13, M. E. 12 (f), M. J. 8 (f), W. 4 (m), Jesse 6, Z. T. 8/12 (m)
TELEY, John 41, Rebecca 36, James W. 17, G. F. 15 (m), Sarah E. 9, Charles W. 6, M. E. 4 (f), R. A. 2 (f), Z. T. 2/12 (m)
WILLS, John 46*, Nancey 39
GILKEY, Mary 13*
SHOEMAKER, Amassa 27, Elen 22, J. J. 1 (m)

1850 Census Greenup County Kentucky

COCHRAN, Samuel 37, Emly 27, W. O. 3 (m)
MORTON, Richard 52*, Hannah 53, H. C. 20 (m), Judith W. 15
HIGLEY, L. M. 24 (m)*, Elizabeth 18
DUPUY, Margaret 74*
DUPUY, Jesse L. 32*, Ann 37, Lewis 9, John 7, William E. 5
WILLIAMS, Risey 17 (f)*
EAST, John 33, Druzilla 33, M. L. 6 (f), James D. 4, C. L. 4 (f), J. A. 3 (f)
CARAGEE, James 35*, Betsey 53
DUFFEY, Rachiel 9*
THOMPSON, W. 41 (m)*, P. 37 (f), N. 17 (m), L. 14 (f), F. 12 (f), G. W. 9 (m), M. 7 (f), Sarah 4

Schedule Page 246

ALEXANDER, Thomas 23*
HEAD, John 18*
BURT, Benjamin 22*
FRANK, C. W. 26 (m)*, Catharine 22
KENDLE, F. 17 (m)*
MYER, Antone 30*
JONES, Thomas 65, Martha 61, John G. 30, William 34, Samuel 28, Thomas 22, Mary 30
BOOKNER, Jacob 61, Elizabeth 50, Charles 21, F. 19 (m), John 14, Elizabeth 7
TEGARDEN, J. M. 40 (m), Margaret 23, J. 5 (f), Louisa 3, Harriet 1
GAMBLE, B. F. 49 (m)*, T. 26 (f), Isabella 11, Jane 6, T. C. 2 (f)
ROACH, Daniel 15*
HUMPHRIES, Charles 25, M. J. 26 (f), E. A. 6 (f), Charles 3
THOMPSON, Anderson 25, Catharine 20, Amanda 1
THOMPSON, David 23*, Elizabeth 17, Wina 1, Sarah 8/12
OLDFIELD, J. M. 35 (m)*
MCQUILLON, Thomas 46, Elizabeth 46, Catharine 22, Samuel 20, John 19, Hannah 16, William 14, James 12, N. S. 9 (m), E. A. 1 (f)
LEE, Derius 42, Matilda 38, Mary A. 12, Elizabeth 9, Lucinda 7, Catharine 4, Thomas A. 1
DEEVERS, George 40*, Jinetta 38, Emly 15, J. W. 14 (m), E. A. 12 (f), Thomas 8, William 5
THOMAS, John 76*, Elizabeth 76
BOOK, William 22, Julian 24 (f), Thomas 6/12
COOPER, Jonathan 27, Charity 26, Melvina 8, Lavina 8, William 6, Hannah 4, Judith 8/12
DUEY, Oliver 59, Harriet 58, Oliver 15

Schedule Page 247

LEE, Harvey 45*, Clarinda 45
BOND, Lucinda 13*, Matilda 14, William H. 9
ALLIN, Christena 6*
BROWN, Allin W. 32, Cyntha A. 28, Nancey M. 7, William A. 5, J. R. 3 (m), M. R. M. 3 (f)
CRUMP, John 69, Malinda 38, Mary A. 18, Teresa 16, William F. 14, Thomas J. 12, Sarah M. 9, M. L. 8 (f)
OSBORN, James 59, Margaret 38, Silas 23, Moses 19, Manoah 17, Owen 16, Ashley 11 (m), Thomas 8, Charles 5, Lucinda 15, Malissa 13, Amanda 12, Sarepta 9, Elen 3, Milander 2 (f), America 6

1850 Census Greenup County Kentucky

ANDREW, Peter 46*, Julian 41, Marcellus 10, Sophia 17, M. A. 16 (f), Alis 6 (f)
OSENTON, J. T. 21 (m)*
PATTON, J. 26 (m)*
MCKEE, John 79*, Elizabeth 62, Henry 26, Samuel 23
SHOVER, Andrew 28*
CASTER, Lewis 24*
DUNLAP, James 21*
LEWIS, Enoch 20*
DEEVERS, James 18*
BREWER, Justus 45, Mary 32, David 10, Mary M. 8, Ann M. 6, James 3
GLASMER, William 27, Sarah 20, John W. 1
MONTGOMERY, John 24*, Sarah 23, G. W. 2 (m)
SWEED, Thomas 35*
BALEY, Joseph 27, Alfred 4
FLICK, Valuntine 45*, Elizabeth 30, Martha 19, Margaret E. 16, Rebecca 13, Mary E. 9, John C. 5, James D. 3, Zelpha 7
CAMERON, Robert 16*
DANIELS, John 21*
SIMPKINS, James 21*
ARTIS, David 22, Elizabeth 20

Schedule Page 248

TRAYLOR, Lewis 32, H. 25 (f), Rosina 2, Marion 3/12 (m)
SPRIGGS, Benjamin 38, Mary J. 32, J. D. 16 (f), Leeter A. 14 (f), Benjamin 12, Lafayat 8, Joseph 6, Martin 4, John 3/12, William 10
LANCE, Peter 26*, Matilda 28, W. A. 4/12 (f)
VANDERVERT, James 22*, Alison 19
CARTER, Nathan 22*
DANIELS, Jonathan 18*
HENSE, Joseph 34*
HUSMAN, E. 20 (m)*
SUDBROOK, P. 28 (m), E. 25 (f), H. 9 (m), E. 4 (f), M. 5/12 (f)
PEARPOINT, Lot 40*, Nancey 39, Ann 13, L. 5 (f), J. 3 (f), J. 1 (m)
MOORE, Timothey 23*
PORTER, Zepheniah 49*, Polly 33, William 14
SPRAGG, Elen 7*
HARVEY, John 31*, Julian 24 (f), Albert 6
RICE, George 22*
MARTIN, Henry 33*, M. 31 (f), M. 7 (m), F. 5 (m), Eliza 3
MESSER, Daniel 24*
HAMILTON, Thomas 33*, Matilda 33, German 11, David 8, Thomas 7, Sarah 6, Samuel 2
WENER, Lao 28 (m)*
SPRIGGS, C. 18 (m)*
TORRENCE, James 22*
ARTIS, Henry 24*, Easter 20 (f), Mary A. 3/12
GALLIHER, John 24*, C. 29 (m)
STEWART, P. H. 19 (m)*

1850 Census Greenup County Kentucky

PENDLETON, A. 34 (m), L. 22 (f), J. 5 (m), A. 1 (m)
COLGROVE, E. 46 (f)*, Nancey 6, George 4
MITCHEL, Jane E. 12*, Samuel 10, Rebecca 9
CONLEY, Joseph 52*, Susan 43, Carter 22, Elizabeth 19, James 16, Nancey 16, David 14, Susan 12, Joseph 9, John 6, William 4

Schedule Page 249

BEAVANER, Adam 33*
BURKHURT, M. 24 (m)*
HOUSER, Philip 27*, Polly 27, John 1
SMITH, John 52*
GEHRON, Jacob 30*
WRENER, Leo 28*
REEVER, Powles 35*
SHAFFNET, Henry 26*
MOORE, Charles 42*
FRIAMOUTH, Nicholas 36*
KOUGH, Mathias 40*
POWELL, T. 23 (m)*, E. 27 (m)
MCNEALAN, William 21*
CLACK, John 21*
BEATTY, R. C. 37 (m)*, E. H. 34 (f), Robert 10, A. C. 6 (f), M. J. 4 (f), H. T. 1 (m)
PROFIT, William 31*
CANE, Henry 65 (B)
HUNT, Hannah 54, Lucetta 18, Ambrose 16
MOSLEY, D. P. 66 (m), Mildred 54
CAMERON, S. 45 (m)*, Amanda 43, Mary 18, Catharine 16, Allen 14, Elizabeth 12, Stephen 10, Amanda 9, William 7, Edmond 2
VANDERVORT, James 22*, Alison 19 (m), Ann 18, Evan 6, P. 4 (m)
HAMILTON, B. 23 (m)*
LEATH, David 25, Amanda 22, Mary 2
PLUMBURG, J. 29 (m)*, Catharine 31, C. 6 (f), J. 4 (f), E. 10/12 (m)
FISHER, Henry 32*
MCPHERSON, Jesse 24*
SMITH, James 21*
HOUSER, Philip 26*, Mary 25, John 10/12
SMITH, John 59*
MILLER, John 14*, Martha 14
GLASS, W. H. 24 (f)*
CORTNEY, Joseph 21*
ARTIS, Joseph 20*
TANAHILL, Joseph 30*
PIERCEFIELD, V. 44 (m), Jane 35, Jackson 17, John 17, Mary 12, Margaret 12, William 14, N. 11 (f), Susan 10, George 6, Betsey _
ARTIS, Thomas 27, Elizabeth 28, C. H. 3 (m), Alis 3/12 (f)

- 144 -

1850 Census Greenup County Kentucky

Schedule Page 250

BRADSHAW, George 66*, George Ann 35, J. C. 10 (m), Rosean 7, J. W. 5 (m)
GORE, Mary 17*
WIATT, Jacob 23, Letecia 45?, Louisa 1/12
JACOBS, J. H. 33 (m), Jane 24, H. C. 7 (m), Martha 4, Isabella 1
MORRISON, N. B. 50 (m)*, Rachiel 50
ARTIS, Rebecca 13*, R. A. 2 (f)
PRICHARD, John 69*, B. 60 (f), James 24
DYZARD, H. S. 19 (m)*
DANIEL, Joseph 53*, Milly 43, George 23
VOLUNTINE, John 21*, William 19?
BARTRAM, Leonard 30, Sarah 16, Lucey E. 3/12
DANIEL, George 25, Eliza 21
COFFEE, Reuben 36, Emly 26, M. J. 9 (f), Susan 6, John 3, William 1
HYSE, John 38*, Fanny 20
COFFER, E. 31 (m)*
CAMERON, Oscar 2*
JONES, Robert 47*, Mary J. 28, James 15, Nancey 13, Joseph 11, Emly 3, Elvina 1
KING, William 26*
NUNLEY, Elijah 22, Lavina 22, Eliza 2
SWEARINGER, Samuel 44, Sarah 42, L. L. 21 (m), John M. 18, Samuel 14, F. M. 10 (m), Jane 7, C. 5 (m), C. 1 (m)
FULTZ, A. 54 (m), Rachiel 19
COLVIN, Joseph 42*, Lydda 35, Louisa 18, Emly 17, Clark 15, Harrison 14, Ruhama 12, Joseph 8, William 6, Rachiel 4, Cansander 2 (m), John 3/12
COFFEE, Ambrose 7*
SWEARINGER, Clem 41, N. C. 37 (f), William R. 14, Wills 10, James 4, N. H. 6 (f), Clem 6, H. H. 1 (f)

Schedule Page 251

BOYLE, John 56, S. 10 (f), James 15, Mary 13, J. W. 11 (m), Susan A. 8, joseph 5
RABORN, Henry 25, Elizabeth 21
WOOD, William 30, Julian 27 (f), C. W. 7 (m), H. E. 4 (m)
SARO, Joseph 27*, Emly A. 22, Elizabeth 1, Cornela 1/12, Peter 30
TRAYLOR, William 12*
JACOBS, Shelton 39, A. E. 28 (f), J. W. 10 (m), R. L. 8 (f), Cassa 5, Adaline 3, A. E. 1 (f)
KEETON, William 56, Elizabeth 56, Shelton 20, Mahala 22, Jackson 16, Julian 10 (f), Albert 8, Susan 1
PETERSON, William 34, E. 26 (f), J. W. 11 (m), M. M. 8 (f), G. F. 5 (m)
PETERSON, John 41, Nancey 41, S. A. 18 (f), J. W. 15 (m), J. A. 12 (m), M. E. 8 (f), David 5, Isaac 2, Mary 58
BRYANT, Lewis 25, Jane 25, Polly A. 10, Frances 8, Lewis 6, Adison 4, Jane 3, S. A. 2/12 (f)
GILES, Edmond 23, Nancey 40, Remathey 14 (f), Mary A. 10, S. H. 4 (m)
COFFEE, Ambrose 26*, Pelitha 3, William 24, Andrew 1
ABRAMS, Bazel 18*
HULL, David 30, Margaret 22, Clara 1
BELL, John 25*, Clarinda 26

1850 Census Greenup County Kentucky

WORMAN, F. 29 (m)*, Leonard 25, Cor. 23 (m), Garret 21
LEWELLING, William 21*
FLIN, John 20*
PRICHARD, Willis 24, Mary 18, Eliza 3/12
LOCEY, John 28, Margaret 24, J. W. 2 (m), Mary 1
252 DYZARD, Isaac G. 47, Elizabeth 15, Jane 20, William 17, Harriet 13, Sarah A. 11, Angaline 7, Rebecca 5

Schedule Page 252

OSBORN, Edward 24*, Mary 20, Amanda 1, Jonathan 20
GARDNER, James 26*, Catharine 21
BRADFORD, Jesse 20*
MORRIS, Thomas G. 18*
EASTEP, William 20*, Henry 18
HOOP, James 26*
SIMPKINS, George 18*
SIMPKINS, Hiram 34, Betsey 21, Daniel 11, George 9, Henry 6
MORRIS, Benjamin 33*, Seely 28 (f)
BIGGS, M. J. 11 (m)*
ARCHER, Naoma 2*
MUSIC, Charles 21, Mary 20
PATTERSON, James 23, Nancey 35, James 9, Surena 7, F. M. 4 (f)
OSBORN, James 51, Letta 30, John 22, David 20, Elijah 18, James 17, Elliot 15, Wilks 13, Cytha 11, Ann 9, Lewis 7, William 4, Mary 3
POND, Samuel 19, Nancey 17
MCCLELAND, John 27, Martha 23, William 6/12
THOMPSON, Moses 35*, Jane 25
HAMMONS, M. J. 13 (f)*
FANNING, B. 25 (m)*
MORRIS, Martin 28, P. A. 35 (m)
COFFEE, Ambrose 65, Margaret 65, William 25, Rolla 21 (m), James 22, Alsa 18, Cyntha A. 16, Susan 12
RILEY, William 45, Betsey 42, William 20, Joseph 16, Thomas 14, Jane 13, Lucey 11, John 9, James 7, Archibald 4, Taylor 2
ABRAMS, Thomas 22, Sarah 26, Daniel 8, Mary 6

Schedule Page 253

ABRAMS, Robert 25, Julian 20 (f), George 2
ABRAMS, Joseph 27, Mary 25, J. W. 8 (m), Susan 5, Bazel 4, Elias 3, B. J. 8/12 (f), Bazel 1
ABRAMS, Bazel 60, Susan 60, Elizabeth 19, Bazel 17
COFFEE, Elijah 52, Margaret 50, Ambrose 25, Jesse 16, Amanda 12, Rebecca 11
GULLET, Reason 28, Mary 28, Melvina 10, Amanda 8, Clarinda 6, Robert 5, Susan 1
INGLAND, John 30*, Surena 27, Mary A. 10, Hulda 7, James R. 6, Nancey 4, W. O. 2 (m)
ELLIS, John 52*
CHASE, Ambrose 70*, Sarah 70

1850 Census Greenup County Kentucky

EASTEP, Fanny 37*, William 19, Henry 18, Lilburn H. 15, Martin V. 10, Sarah 7, Ambrose 5
DRAKE, Ephriam 26, Sarah 20, Mary 1
ROSS, L. D. 39 (m), Catharine 22, John A. 3/12, Hollister _
BROWN, Samuel 27, Elizabeth 22, Cambridge 1
ARMES, William 28, Lutecia 17, Eliza E. 1
PHETTA, Samuel 24*, E. J. 23 (f), Charles 2, Simon 3/12
MUSIC, Martha 11*
PUTHUFF, John 27*, Frances 30
DRAKE, Silas 8*, Nancey 6, Mary 4
MUSIC, Lucinda 42, Sarah A. 17, Malinda 13, Eliza 10
COOK, John 38, Elizabeth 39, Elizabeth 12, Lucinda 10, George 4, Sarah J. 3, Indiana 6/12
LANSDOWN, Hiram 38*, Nancey 36, Sarah J. 18, Abrad 16, Elizabeth 14, Susan 13, Thomas J. 11, James W. 7, Mary A. 5, M. E. 3 (f), Z. T. 1 (m)

Schedule Page 254

SPARKS, Richard L. 19*
COLVIN, Easter 49, Patiance 15, F. M. 10 (m), M. E. 7 (f)
WOODROW, W. G. 33 (m), Tereca 30, Elizabeth 11, Serena 9, Juliet 4, Sarah 2
GREEN, Evaline 50
DARLINTON, G. W. 53 (m)
GILKEY, William 42, Harriet 33, Solomon 16, Lindsey 14 (m), Edward 11, Grace 8, Charles 4, John 6, Elizabeth 2, Harriet 1
DIGINGS, Austin 27, Jane 21, James 2
STEWART, John G. 46, Elizabeth 42, Mathew 18, Cyntha 16, Henry 14, Robert 13, John 11, Sarah 9, Charles 7, Mary Jane 5, James 4, Judith A. 2
STEWART, Matthew 52, Elizabeth 77, Susan 47
ARCHER, John 36, Mary Jane 21, David 11, Charlotta 9, Margaret 7
STAGG, William 24, Elizabeth 17, John 10/12
NICHOLS, B. B. 43 (m), Mary 23, Melcina 3, James 2, Orman 2/12
CALLAHAN, Charles 22, Elizabeth 17, J. W. 1/12 (m)

Schedule Page 255

POYNTER, Edwin 31*, Deborah 24, Z. T. 2 (m)
DYZARD, Milton 23*, Arminta 20
CALLAHAN, Horatio 28, Indiana 25, G. W. 6 (m), Charles 4, H. C. 1 (m)
POYNTER, Jesse 66, Elizabeth 50, John D. 33, Jesse G. 29
PUTTHUFF, Henry 62, Mary 57, Simpson 25, Margaret 20, Harriet 14
PUTTHUFF, B. F. 32 (m), Elizabeth 33, Mary 12, Willis 10, Henry 8, Franklin 6, Ancil T. 4, Elizabeth 2
RUSSEL, Charles 49, Martha 48, John 18, Martha 16, Sarah 13, Charles 11, Mary Ann 9, George 7
PUTTHUFF, James M. 22, Elizabeth 15
CARTER, Joseph 37, Elizabeth 33, William D. 3, Susan A. 6/12
POYNTER, J. K. 40 (m), Mary 35, Emly C. 14, Margaret K. 12, Susan 10, Edwin L. 5, George W. 3, Jesse G. 1
MCALISTER, John 64, Sarah 45, Henry 26, Nancey 20, Mary Ann 18, E. J. 13 (f), Emly 11
HANNER, George 53, Mary 38, Milton 17, James A. 13, Elizabeth 18, Gallahue 9, Sarah 7, Emma 3/12

1850 Census Greenup County Kentucky

NORRIS, Abraham 23, Mary 22, Luceford 5, Nancy 3, Elizabeth 1
HANNER, Judith 83
HANNER, Mary 76
HANNER, Gabriel 27, Mary A. 28, William 8, W. 7 (f), Sarah 1
KOUNS, William 48, Nancey 51, John W. 20, Sarah 15, Samuel 12, Nancey 10, G. W. 9 (m)

Schedule Page 256

STEWART, Robert 42, Margart 38, E. A. 15 (f), Mary J. 13, William J. 11, Nancey F. 9, Sarah 7, Hiram 2
DUNCAN, William T. 32, Frances 27, Elizabeth A. 8, Caleb T. 3, Leroy 1
WOOD, William 29, Julian 28 (f), Charles W. 6, H. E. 5 (m)
POWELL, John M. 28, Dartha 19, Ellis 5/12
HARTLEY, John 23, Elizabeth 29, Sarah 6/12
DOWNS, James 42, Mary A. 25, Franklin 21, John W. 19, Juley F. 17, George H. 15, Henry L. 13, David L. 11, Sarah 5, James G. 2
CAMPBELL, Jesse 24*, Emsey 22, Thomas 1
VIRGIN, Samuel 17*
MCGINNIS, William 66*, Jane 52, Franklin 30, John 19, Thomas 17, Stephen 15, Elsey 13 (m), Caroline W. 10
BROWN, Nancey 15*
CAMPBELL, Hiram 25, Rachiel 25, Mary 3, Elizabeth 1
WARING, Thomas T. G. 70, Nancey 67, Francis 24
BROWN, Berry W. 56*, Fanney 54, Joseph 21, Jane 18, Rhodey 16, John 14, William 12
CONLEY, William 22*
JONES, Franklin 25, Sarah 23, Joseph 2
MEDLEY, Johnson 60*, Jane 49, James 19, Asbury 14, David 12, Lurina 9
LAMASTER, Elijah 18*
JAMESON, James 33, Jane 35, John R. 10, George W. 9, Sarah J. 7
MOORE, Jeremiah 39*, Clarissa 30, John 20, Eliza J. 15, Elizabeth 12, George 10, William 8, Charles 7, Nancey 5, Abigal 4, Levey 2/12

Schedule Page 257

COOLEY, Lucresa 13*
PERKINS, William 23, Malinda 21, Mary 1
ANDERSON, Cornelus 55*, Mary 54, Levey 24, Mary 20, Cornelus 17, Harriet 17, Martha 12, America 8
BUSH, Thornton 8*
MAGINIS, Harvey 25, Sarah A. 20
BUSH, Edward 32, Elizabeth 35, William 10, Thomas 7, Martha 4
SPENCE, John 37, Elizabeth 40, William 13, Ann 11, James 9, Margaret 8, Samuel 5
MEDOWS, Abraham 42*, Sarah 42, Malinda 22, Franklin 15, Washington 14, Lydda 11, Elizabeth 5
MAGINIS, David 21*
JACKSON, Iven 50, Elizabeth 48, Gideon 21, Samuel 20, Eliza J. 16, Mariah 14, J. W. 12 (m), Thomas 9, Joen? 7 (m), Emly 7
SMITH, Peter 37, Paneila 34, William 17, Marion 14 (m), John 9, Henry C. 7, Mary 4, July Ann 2

1850 Census Greenup County Kentucky

SCOWDEN, Solomon 36, Lavica 40, Joen 11 (m), George 8, Sarah 6, Emly 5, John 4, Delila 3
SPARKS, Solomon 25, Angeline 23
BUSH, Aaron 74, Mary 63
BUSH, Nathan 69, Barbery 67, Jacob 41, Elizabeth 28, Andrew 13, Nancey 10, William G. 8, Lewis 4, Catharine 75
WARING, Humphrey 69
WARING, Sarah W. 49, Francis 76
WARING, Tabitha 43, Mary 15, Edward 13, Sarah 8, Agnes 6

Schedule Page 258

TIMMONS, Emly 33*, Ella 2
GARDNER, Virginia 13*, Mary 11, G. A. 6 (f), H. G. 9 (m)
BLOOMER, Daniel 75*
DIGINGS, B. B. 61 (m), Delila 58, C. C. 15 (m)
TRAYLOR, John 67, Nancey 53, Nancey 13, Benjamin 8
BURTEN, Joshua 49*, Mary 39, John 16, James 15, Bednego 12, Ada 10, Wilson 8, Thomas J. 6, K. 4 (m)
DIGINGS, Joseph M. 21*
PATTEN, Alexander 34, Susan 28, John 10, Elizabeth 9, Ellen 7, Sarah 5, Samuel 1
SMITH, William 59, Elizabeth 35
PHILLIPS, William 29, Elizabeth 21
BUSH, Nathan 30, Mary 22, Martha E. 3, William 2, Francis 3/12
WARING, Bazel 49, Mary 42, Francis 20, Jane 14, Lydda 10, Mary H. 7, Bazel 4, Ella M. 6/12
WARING, Jane 52 (B)
WARNOCK, Matthew 43, Lydda 41, Elizabeth A. 20, Rebecca 19, James F. 17, Mary 14, Margaret 12, John W. 10, Bazel 8, Charles W. 6, America 4, M. S. 2 (m)
BAKER, Allin 54, Lucina 23, Susan E. 5, J. A. 3 (f), Mary Ann 10/12, Susan 75
CURRY, Hugh 39, Margaret 28, Adaline 8, A. 6 (f), W. 4 (f), Nancey 2, Famis 2/12 (m)
CURRY, Henry N. 32, Nancey 33, Johnson 11, L. A. 5 (f), Henry S. 3, John 2
WILLIS, Ambrose 37, Mary Ann 22, J. 1 (f)

Schedule Page 259

WILLIS, Joshua 36, Mary 25, William 2, John 1
MILLER, Uriah 41, Mary 47, Hiram 21, A. 15, Louisa 13, Mariah 11, Harriet 9, Rebecca 7
CANIFAX, Calvin 47*, Kisa R. 30, John 14
MILLER, Adrian 22*
STARK, Nancey 55
STARK, C. F. 28 (m)*, Elizabeth R. 40, Nancey 6, Elizabeth 4, Frances 4
LYONS, Ann E. 15*, Jane 14, Casander 13, Mary S. 11
TACKET, Charles 33*
WOMAC, William A. 22*
HALEY, Louisa 17*, John 26, Alfred C. 15
CROOKS, C. F. 27 (m), Mary 22, Charles 3/12
GREER, William C. 30*, Clarinda 28, Nancey J. 6
MORRIS, Allin 8*

1850 Census Greenup County Kentucky

DUNCAN, Harmon 26*
BAKER, Marshal 39*, Mary Ann 41, Sophia 14
HANKS, Louisa 17*
GILKEY, Robert 14*
BATMAN, Henry 34, Mary 34, Emma 15, Sarah 13, George 11, Francis 9, Rebecca 7, America 4, Mary 1
GIBBS, John O. 54, Sarah 50, Nancey 21, James 16, Robert 14
WAMOCK, James 69*, Rebecca 65, Cyntha A. 34
HANEY, Sarah 61*
ALEXANDER, Sarah 46, Susan 19, Rebecca 16, Nancey 14, America 12, Charles 8, Martha 6
WESLEY, James 28, Martha 25, Robert 8, Elizabeth 6, James 5, Windfield 3
RATCLIFF, Samuel 55, Mary 33, William 27, Parker 21, Melvina 18, Thompson 13, Frances 11, Isaac 9, Hamilton 7, Martha 5, Rebecca 4

Schedule Page 260

CARPENTER, Fielden 22, Mary 21, John W. 1, Patterson 2/12
DOWDY, Samuel 35*, Nancey 24, H. 14 (f), John 11, Mary 6, George 5, Marion 3/12 (m)
DANIELS, Wilder 26*
LAMASTER, Lewis 23, Nancey 15
ABDEN, John 24, Malinda 19, James W. 8/12, Rachiel 53
WEBB, Grandvill 26*, R. 25 (f), Mary 4, Martha 2
RATCLIFF, William 20*
WILLIAMS, Hiram 27, Ann 22, Louisa 2
FOX, Ransom 30*, Sarah A. 31, Cyrus 10
PIERCE, Hannah 25*, George 3
STARK, Jeremiah 33*, E. A. 26 (f), Nancey E. 5, J. W. 3 (m), John F. 1
KING, Benjamin 43*, Ann 41, Samuel W. 17, Marinnus 15, Rebecca A. 14, Morris W. 11, Sarah R. 6, Mary E. 10/12
TWYFORD, John B. 23*
WURTS, William 32*
FLOYD, Hickman 46*, Elanor 31, David 22, Thomas 17, William 15, Hickman 8, Elizabeth 13, Eleanor 6 (f), Martha 2
BURRIS, William 38*, Wilson 30
KELLEY, John 31*
HANEY, Martin 32*
LINDSEY, Walter 40*, Elizabeth 40, Rachiel 16, Jesse 14, Elizabeth 12, William 9, John 7, Edward 4, George 2
CARLAN, Thomas 25*
KAPLER, William 20*
MYER, Henry 25*
FRACKER, Augustus 20*
GAPPS, William 35*
DECKER, Christain 23 (m)*
BRANARD, Isaac 22*
THOMPSON, Samuel 47*, Catharine 46, A. J. 21 (m), William 20, James 18, Bazel 14, Eliza 9

1850 Census Greenup County Kentucky

Schedule Page 261

MARTIN, John 19*
ARMSTRONG, Jer. 55 (m)* (B)
HICKS, Charles 55* (B)
KIMMONEY, Anthoney 22*
HANEY, Martin 35*
KELLEY, John 40*
ONEAL, Patrick 30*
MURRY, Patrick 25*
MCDONALD, Thomas 28*
WEBB, William 24*
PUGH, David 36, Genetta 27, Joseph E. 8, David 6, Noah G. 4, Martha 2, Charles 7/12
MEYER, John 50, Mary 40, Mary 13, Charles 10, John 8
RIGGLE, Jackson 28, Eliza 19, A. 3/12 (m)
FISHER, Francis 48, Jane 49, Henry 23M
WEST, Jordan 53, Matilda 41
NEWMAN, Henry 30, Eliza 28, William 5, Mary 3, J. W. 1 (m)
SHORES, Daniel 32, Mary 32
NUTTY, William 29, Ramatha 26, Walter 10/12, Martha 3
GLIN, William 40, Mary 36, Andrew 13, Sarah 11, Catharine 9, Mary A. 7, William 5, Francis 2, Nancy 1/12
MCGOWN, John 38, Sarah 35, Harriet 15, Charles 12, Daniel 10, William 8, Thomas 6, Mary A. 3, Alfred 1
QUICKS, George 40, Drusey 23 (f), Samuel 8, Martha 5, Lavena 3
CARVER, Richard 40, Ama 35, Mary 11, Harriet 9, Caroline 7, John 5, Richard 10/12
PALMER, John 23, Matilda 24
ENGLAND, Samuel 37, Rebecca 36, Sarah 15, John 11, Mary 9, Matilda 6, Samuel 4, Margaret 1, John 76
MOSIER, Henry 35, Mary 25, Malissa 10, A. E. 2 (f)

Schedule Page 262

JOHNSON, Joseph 29*, Sarah 36, Mary 16, Emaline 14, margaret 11, Elizabeth 8, Delily A. 6, Holiver 2
ENGLAND, Sarah 69*
MARTIN, Joseph 28, Nancey 22, John 5
BILLINK, M. 29 (m), L. 22 (f), Berry 40
WARD, Daniel 51, Elizabeth 50, Elen 21, H. 20 (f), John 18, R. 13 (f), Eliza A. 7
HOUGHMAN, Solomon 50, Elizabeth 43, Francis 20, Mary 17, Robert 15, Ambrose 13, Melvina 11, Jacob 9, Aaron 7, Benjamin 5, James 4
RILEY, John 47, Caroline 48, John 19, Nancey 18, Andrew 16, David 14, Susan 12, James 10, Barbery 9, Mariah 6
TRICK, Frederick 40, Easter 39, Sarah 20, Frederick 16, Cristena 14
KILE, Peter 26, Easter 23, Sarah 6, Nancey 4, George 2, Lucey 2/12
RAMEY, Byram 44, Mariah 33, Fidella 13, Emsey 11 (f), Mary 8, M. 6 (f), Franklin 4, Melvina 2
HARTLEY, John 65*, Sarah 55, William 21, James 19, Green 17, Hannah 34
FANING, Hannah 7*, Thomas 3
TANNER, M. 5 (m)*

1850 Census Greenup County Kentucky

HARTLEY, Abraham 35, Elizabeth 26, Sarah 9, John 7, Nancey 5, Elen 3
SELLARDS, Andrew 44, Mary 37, Sarah 18, John 16, William 15, Elias 13, A. 11 (m), Elizabeth 9, W. 7 (m), Archer 5, Lewis 3

Schedule Page 263

RATCLIFF, Charles W. 30, Mary A. 22, Elizabeth 4, Sarah 2
WILLIS, Joseph 68, Elizabeth 62, Sarah 17
STARK, Henry 27*, Adaline 26, Martha 6, James 4, John 1
STEWART, Paull 60*, Allin 17
BOYCE, Richard 21, Jane 35, Margaret 14, Cyrus 10, Elizabeth 8, Martin 6, Sophia 2
CLIFTON, Daniel 50, Elizabeth 46, Nelly 19, John 16, Martha 14, Murcey 12 (f), Daniel 10, William 8, Rebecca 6, Emly 1
ADAMS, Church 50 (B)
WOMACK, A. L. 34 (m), Lucey 28, Samuel S. 6, James W. 1
SWEARINGER, Van 58, Mary 54, George 23, Thomas 21, F. M. 18 (m), Mary 13, Joseph 12, A. 10 (m)
KICKER, Paull 47
DAVIS, James 58, Levina 57, Sarah 19, Margaret 16, Henry 14, William 11, James 8, Mary 5
FETTY, Charles 30, Sarah 19, David 1
STEWART, William 27, Amanda 24, Evaline 1
CURRY, James 42, Myram 12 (m), Amanda 10, H. 6 (f), Sarah 5
OSENTON, Samuel 68, E. 53 (f), Samuel 16, George 11
HOWE, Martha 66, R. 32 (f), James 23
LAMBERT, James 53, Elizabeth 48, Harriet 17, Benjamin 14, John 11, James 9, Lindsey 7 (m)

Schedule Page 264

MARTIN, George 59, Martha 55
MARTIN, Joseph 26, Nancy 24, Martha 6, John 1
CURRY, Robert 35, Isabella 23, John 4, N. 1 (f), James 1/12
CURRY, Nancey 69, Mahala 44, Minerva 34, Margaret 27, Jane 24
WILLIAMS, Shedrick 35, Dicey 35, B. 16 (f), Martha 14, James 12, Andrew 9, George 7, Mary 5, John 2, William 2/12
CRUMP, Turner 71, Susan 58, Benjamin 22, Turner 20, Lucinda 18
MESSER, Benjamin 25*, Mary 18, Eliza 3, Martha 1, David 1/12
CONLEY, David 19*
ALEXANDER, William 22*
MESSER, William 32, Mila 28, Margaret 11, Preston 9, Andrew 7, Mary 5, Henry 3, William 1
SIMPKINS, John 34, Malinda 32, Elijah 12, William 1
STATON, Solomon 27, Elizabeth 22, James 5, George 3
MORAN, John 26, Mahala 24, Mary 6/12
WALLIS, Mary 51*
WALLACE, Mary 23*
CHANDLER, William 10*
WALLACE, Otha 28 (m), Martha 18
LAVINDER, Lewis 41, Mary 34, Virgina 11, Caroline 9, Jackson 5, Martha 2
CRUMP, Willis 46, Marey 46, John 14

1850 Census Greenup County Kentucky

FLOYD, Peter 45, Sarena 47, James 21, Nancey 15, Reubin 13, Solomon 10, Amanda 5
PRATT, Nelson 35, Eliza 24, John 6, Jane 4, James 2, Lott 10/12

Schedule Page 265

GILMORE, Henry 28, Nancy 20, Richard 2, Mary 1/12
BAILEY, Rachiel 38, Elizabeth 20, Joshua 14, John 10, Charles 9, Thomas 6, David 4
BROWN, William 37, Rachiel 28, Sarah 14, Jackson 12, Mary 10, Elcaney 8, Rachiel 1/12
WARING, J. H. 33 (m), Sarah A. 28, Thomas 9, Mary 6, Tabitha 2, Leonard 19

1850 Census Johnson County Kentucky

Schedule Page 80

HARRIS, Kelsey N. 41*, Louisa P. 29, Robert P. 7, Eleanor M. 4, Nancy J. 2
HURT, Garland 30 (m)*
HORN, Edward 24*
HAGER, Henry G. 26, Nancy J. 24, Mary H. 31, William J. M. 1
FRANKLIN, Martin 38, Eliza 37, John 15, Louisa M. 3, Susan 1
FRIEND, Samuel K. 49, Martha 43
SMITH, William M. 26, Mary M. 47, James M. 22
FRANKLIN, John 76, Permelia 63
WALTON, Charles 56, Sarah 39, Mary 12, William H. 10, Evelina 7, Louisa 4, Lucinda 3
SELSOR, George 40, Agness 30, Richard P. 10, Joseph 9, Martha H. 6, Malissa A. 2, Louisa K. 1
STRONG, Hiram F. 30, Phebe J. 31, Warren M. 8, Julius C. 6, James C. 4, Ann 2, no name 1/12 (f)
ROBERTS, Horrace 40, Mary K. 40, John W. 19, George W. 16, Ellen J. 12, James H. 10, Emily K. 8
TODD, Lewis 35, Nancy 34, Sarah E. 10, Catharine 6, Martha 4, James C. 2
BORDERS, David 28, Elenor M. 23, Elenor J. 2, Mary J.? 9/12
WELLS, Dennis B. 28, Nancy K. 25, Martha J. 3, Mary A. 1
HUGG, Jerman 36, Dicy 36, Matilda J. 11, James 9, Sarah A. 7, John W. 5, Henry C. 3
VAUGHAN, John 48, Isabelle 45, Henry S. 26, Alexander J. 16, Rebecca E. 4, William W. 24, Rachel 18
HOUSE, John 39, Jane 34, Permelia 13, Amy K. 8, Nancy J. 5, Melissa 4, Charles J. 3, John E. 5/12

Schedule Page 81

KELLER, John W. 29, Matilda 22, Theophalus 5/12
PRESTON, Moses sr. 53, Nancy M. 38, Martin 22, Moses jr. 20, Franklin 14, Henry 9, Winfield S. 3
STAFFORD, John 45*, Celestia 40, Lucina 15, Marion 12, Melissa 8, Thomas 6, Mary 3
PORTER, Henry 20*, Irena 18
WALES, Caleb P. 46*
HOW, John W. 42*
DAVIS, John 30*
SPRADLIN, Benjamin 54*, Martha 48, James H. 20, Benjamin F. 18
RULE, Andrew W. 35*, Angelina 23, Martha J. 3, Mary 1
OBRYAN, James 77, Mary 26, Elenda 20, Rachel 16
OBRYAN, James 30, Mary 28, James 12, Emely 9, Susanah 7, William 2
GIPSON, Spencer 35, Agey 26 (f), Fanny 10, Andrew J. 8, Lavona 5
BROWN, Daniel G. 39, Elizabeth 24, Rosella 7, Thomas K. 5, William 3, George W. 1
DICKSON, Henry 28, Jane 18
STAFFORD, Ralph 22*, Amanda 15, Sarah E. 5/12
HAGER, Elizabeth 56*
BALDWIN, Thomas 36, Charity 36, Fanny 10, George 7, Nancy 4, Sarah J. 2
STAFFORD, James 24, Cynthia A. 21, John H. 3, George W. 2, William K. 8/12
NOTT, Arbuth A. 57 (m)*, Lydia 47, Eliza J. 16, Lydia M. 13, Lucetta C. 11, Manford A. 6, Jesse 3
AUXIER, Willis 18*
MORTON, William A. 38, Lorinda B. 34, Thomas W. 12, Catharine 10, Florrance 8, Isabela 5, Nancy 3, Isora 1

1850 Census Johnson County Kentucky

Schedule Page 82

LIVINGSTON, Henry A. 59, Mary A. 50, John H. 18, Mary E. 15, Henry R. 12
HARRIS, Littleton Y. 28, Mary J. 21, Amanda J. 6, Julia C. 2, Jone? E. 3/12 (f)
STAPLETON, Bazle 49, Mary 38, William 18, Lydia 16, Eli 15, Zion 11, Marinda 10, Isaac 9, John 7, Miranda 2, Alfred 1, Edward 30, Margarett 80
LEMASTER, Daniel 30, Anna 28, Fanny 8, Marcus 6, Sally 3, Ellen 1
BURKETT, James R. 25, Elizabeth 27, Garland H. 4, Rosannah 2, William O.B. 2/12
DAVIS, Michael 24, Anna 19, Epperson 2, Joseph 4/12
DANIEL, William 24, Catharine 20, Mariah 1
FLETCHER, Alexander 34, Lodema 33, Violet 8, Winston 6, Sylvester 5, Walter 2
CASTLE, Ira 30, Nancy 24, Jackson 4, Paulina 2
PRESTON, Nathan 30, Angelina 18
BALDWIN, Anthony sr. 61, Elizabeth 56, Delila 22, Elizabeth 20, Anthony jr. 26, Sarah 21
SUBLETT, Mathew 32, Jane 30, Frances 1
CASTLE, William 23*, Mary J. 26, Henry 3, Andrew J. 1
DAVIS, Zacheriah 22*
STAMBAUGH, John 63*, Martha 26, Frederick 26, Maurice 29
HARRIS, Luanna 16*
WEBB, Edward 33, Judea 32, William J. 12, Mary J. 11, Clarinda 9, Jacob 7, James A. 5, Margarett 4, Zerilda A. 3, Nancy 1, Saraiah 1/12 (m)

Schedule Page 83

SPRADLEN, Evan 28, Emeline 18, Charlotte 7/12
ABSHER, Allen 55*, Classa 55, Mary A. 12, William 10, Jane 8, Allen 6
BROCK, Nancy 18*
BAILEY, William 32, Sarah 34, John 4
WHEELER, Jesse 38, Lucina 25, Catharine 9, Mary 8, Jane 6, Lydia 1
DANIEL, Isom 26, Elender 25, Henry J. 6, Polly 5, Plymon 3, Daniel J. 1
CHANDLER, James 33, Catharine 28, Henry C. 13, Lydia A. 10, Sarah J. 8, Martin L. 5, Peter M. 1
PRESTON, James W. 28*, Delila 25, Artha J. 12, Lydia 10, Shadrach 8, Jesse 7, Eliphus E. 5
GILMOON, Perry 6*, Caroline 5
DANIEL, Andrew 36, Elizabeth 32, Polly 12, Jonathan 10, Sarah A. 9, John W. 7, Susy 5, Thomas W. 4, Winfield S. 3, William C. 3/12
WHEELER, William R. 40, Elizabeth 35, Catharine 18, Stephen 17, Daniel 14, Henry J. 12, Jemima 11, Jane 9, Darcus 6, Fanny 5, Mary 3, Lucina 1, Sarah 10/12
WHEELER, John B. 19, Nancy 22, Elizabeth 11/12
DANIEL, John O. 21, Margarett A. 21, Mary J. 1
DICKSON, Andrew F. 49, Abagail 42, Farmer 15, Isaac 11, Joseph 4, Sarah M. 2, Andrew J. 7/12
ROWLAND, Armstrong 45, Polly 46, Sally A. 18, Joseph 15

Schedule Page 84

MARSHALL, Reuben 39, Delila 38, John 17, Elizabeth 14, Rachel E. 6
FRANKLIN, James 45, James M. 19, John H. 14, Julia F. 10, Nancy M. 7

1850 Census Johnson County Kentucky

CONNELLEY, John 29, Margarett 31, James H. 9, Thomas J. 7, Tempa J. 5, William 3, Julia 1
WARD, Hezekiah 47, Elizabeth 40, Sarah 25, Matilda 17, Adam 15, Solomon 14, Mahalah 12, Susan 11, Jonathan 9, Marion 6, Washington 6, Celia 4, Hezekiah 2
DICKSON, Martin B. 45*, Ruth A. 27, Mary J. 9, Edda E. 7, John H. 4, Isaac B. 1, Richard S. 1
ROWLAND, Peggy 20*
ROBERSON, William 45, Evelina 44, John 21, Sarah 20, Nathaniel 15, Araminta 14, Polly 11, Washington 10, Elizabeth 7, William 5
ROBERSON, James H. 36, Sally 30, William M. 10, Clarinda 9, Margarett E. 7, Samuel W. 5, Celia 3
BURK, John 59, Mary 52, Wesley 23, Charles 20, Gabilla? 16, Mary 13
HARMON, Aquilla 49, Rebecca 42, William B. 17, Adam 15, Daniel 14, Lucinda K. 12, Aquilla 10, Rachel 7, Mathias 5, Robert 3, Henry 2
BLAIR, John 33, Susannah 32, Andrew 9, James R. 8, Francis J. 5, Elizabeth A. 3, Louisa N. 1
STURGELL, Jesse 35, Malinda 34, James L. 5, John W. 4, Patience J. 3, Amay F. 2/12, William 20, Polley A. 17

Schedule Page 85

HOUSE, James M. 29, Jane M. 23, Marcus L. 6, William E. 4, Elizabeth S. 2
SHORT, Granderson S. 26, Mary 21, Angelina 6/12
JENNINGS, Abram 30, Nancy 30, Cynthia A. 4, Elizabeth A. 2
FITZPATRICK, James 37, Sarah 25, Clarinda 12, Sampson 10, Elizabeth 8, Mahalah 6, Abraham 4, Henry 8/12
ABSHER, Jacob 25, Rebecca 26, Rhoda M. 1
FITZPATRICK, Jerry 38, Lucinda 38, Margarett 15, James M. 12, Rhoda 8, Miram 7 (f), John 4, Elizabeth 2
BROWN, Thomas S. 35, Emelina R. 26, George W. 14, Julian J. 12 (f), Amanda M. 10, Angelina R. 8, Arther W. 5, Tabitha 3, no name 6/12 (f)
BUTLER, Samuel 40, Anna 40, George W. 18, William J. 14, Elenor 12, Samuel 10, Isaac H. 5, David C. 3, no name 4/12 (m)
BLAIR, Levi 37, Rachel 39, John L. 18, Mary M. 16, George N. 15, Lydia M. 10, Berton L. 8, Martha J. 5, James H. C. 3, Levi 10/12
MURRY, Samuel 33, Jane 28, Exer 11 (f), Frederick 9, Samuel 6, Sarah A. 2, Elizabeth 4/12
CRAFT, Tillman 37, Sarah 37, William 14, Aaga 12, Henderson 10, Elizabeth 8, Mary J. 5, Wiley 2
HORN, Thomas 56*, Nancy 42, Susan 30, James 6, Thomas 5
BARNETT, John 11*, Pricy 7

Schedule Page 86

VANHOOSE, Bracken 30, Mary 29, Nancy 8, Elizabeth 6, William 4, Lydia 1
VANHOOSE, James 27, Elizabeth 21, Sarah J. 2, Marion 4/12
DANIEL, Thomas 61*, Winney A. 33, Thomas 18, Francis 16, Wyatt 13, Julius 12
BRYANT, Sarah 13*
VANHOOSE, James sr. 59, Elizabeth 51, Henry J. 15, Eliphus P. 13, Nathan 21, John 18
ROBERTSON, Samuel 37, Martha 32, George 12, William M. 10, Robert 8, Delila 6, Adaline 4, Victoria 2, John W. 19
HORN, John 19, Mary 21
BURKETT, Frederick 76, Churiah? 29 (f), Marion 7, Sally 5, Garland 1

1850 Census Johnson County Kentucky

CASTLE, Isreal 26, Susannah 24, Mary 2, Elizabeth 1, Andrew 19
STURGELL, Joseph 28, Letitia 19, Isabell 4/12
CASTLE, Henry 30, Susan 28, Francis M. 7, Charles J. 5, Angelina 3, Lucina 1
LAVENDER, Edward P. 21, Eliza A. 26, Marthaa? 5 (m)
ALLEY, Simeon 26*, Edy 21 (f), John J. 3, Emy E. 2, William J. 1
STURGELL, Amy 60*
LEE, Simeon 4*
SALYER, Henderson 25, Nancy 25, Luana 1, Joseph 1
OBRYAN, Stephen 34, Mary 26, Edwin 3, John J. 1
HANNA, John S. 50, Anna 44, Ebenezer 27, George W. 19, Jackson 17, Wallan 15, Elizabeth 13, Rebecca 11, Celia 9, Isaac 6, Minerva J. 2
SIMER, Andrew P. 24, Martha 19, Francis M. 8/12

Schedule Page 87

SIMER, Nathaniel P. 48, Lurana 50, Francis M. 16, Philip 10
MCKENZIE, Seargant N. 25, Margarett 28, George W. 5, James H. 4, Samantha 2
SIMER, John P. 22, Catharine 20
KIMBLER, William 27, Nancy 24, Lurena 5, Nathaniel G. 3, Jackson S. 1
SIMER, Emely P. 51*, Abram 20, George M. 14, Julia 16, Mahalah 32, Sarah E. 7, Elizabeth J. 3, Mary A. 1
KIMBLER, Solomon 23*, Lucinda 18, Andrew J. 8/12
REMY, Nancy 64, Tempy 13
REMY, Daniel 31, Frances 33
CLAY, Temperance 32, Henry M. 6, Malissa A. 4, Daniel J. 3, Nancy E. 1
LEMASTER, James 48, Sarah 55, Eleazer 18 (m), George W. 16, Sylvester 15, Ellen 20, Elizabeth 6, James 2
LEMASTER, William 28, Newcarius 18 (f), Levi W. 1/12
SALIERS, David J. jr. 22, Elender 18, Levi F. 2, Levica 1/12
SALIERS, Joseph 40, Sarah 36, Marshad S. 15, Sirava? 11 (f), Resee 9 (m), Hardy 4, no name 1 (f), Asa 21, Samuel 20
SALIERS, Benjamin 52, Frances 49, Margarett 22, Rebecca 20, Neoma 12, Samantha 7, Benjamin H. 4, John H. 18
OSBORN, Jesse 70*, Elizabeth 60
SPARKS, Dinah 23*, Elizabeth 1
LEMASTER, Eleazar 90*
OSBORN, Henry 22, Nancy 20, Clarinda 2, Angelina 1
WINKLE, John 35, Polly 28, Andrew J. 13, Elizabeth 11, Julia A. 9, Lavina 5, Louisa 3, Jesse 1

Schedule Page 88

OSBORN, Lewis 40, Phebe 39, Rachel 17, John 15, Elizabeth 13, Jesse 11, James L. 9, Lavina 6, Martha J. 4, Solomon 2, Nancy E. 11/12
OSBORN, Andrew 24, Susan 21, Samantha 4, Evelina 3, Jonathan 1
BURCHETT, Leonard 26, Letta 28, Enoch 9, Nancy 7, Sally 5, James 4, Robin 2 (m)
EVANS, Thomas 40, Nancy 36, Ursley 15 (f), Elizabeth 13, Mary 11, Jedediah 8, Benjamin 5, David J. 1
LEMASTERS, Thomas 20, Mary 17, Harvy 1

1850 Census Johnson County Kentucky

BLEVINS, Wiley 30, Nancy 27, John R. 12, Elizabeth 10, William 7, Jesse 5, Sarah 16
BLEVINS, Elisha 41, Alsey 44, William 22, Lewis 20, Solomon 18, Mary 14, John 12, Martin 7
WILLIAMS, Robert R. 39*, Elizabeth 39, Andrew J. 19, Noah H. 15, John B. 14, William R. 11, Kelsey E. 9, Amanda J. 5, Malissa M. 3, Lafayette S. 1
FAIRCHILD, John 26*, Sarah A. 18
BLEVINS, William 64, Avey 54
BLEVINS, Daniel 22, Nancy 21, Malinda 1
PENNINGTON, David 29, Malinda 26, Avey 8, Milton 5, Armacinda 3, Daniel 1
WEBB, John 62, Nancy 55, Nancy A. 6
WEBB, Jonathan 33l, Mary 24, George W. 6, Peggy A. 4, John 2, James 1/12

Schedule Page 89

CANTRELL, John 19, Sarah 22, Milissa 4, Nancy 1
SPENCER, Jourdon 31, Malinda 19, George W. 5, Andrew J. 3, Elizabeth 2
PRESTON, Eliphus jr. 26, Nancy 20, Jefferson 3, Charles 2
LEMASTER, Joseph 48, Elenor 37, Stephen 17, Frances 15, Mary 13, Isaac 11, Catharine 9, John 7, Jesse 5, Daniel 1, William 3/12
PORTER, Samuel 55*, Anna 49, Nancy 22, Martha 19, John M. 17, William 14, James 11, Henry C. L. 7, Jane 5
VICARS, Thomas 23*
SMITH, John 18*
RICE, Martin M. 41, Sarah 40, John 17, Martin 15, Francis 12, Delila 9, Catharine 7, Minerva 5, James 3, Servillan? 1 (m)
ROBERTSON, John 42, Elizabeth 35, Susannah 18, William 16, Eliza 14, Elizabeth 12, Thomas J. 10, John 8, Nancy A. 5, Henry 4
FITZPATRICK, John 72, Frances 47, Servillan 23 (m), Nancy 27, William 21, Henry 18, Charles 16
WARD, Stephen 23, Mary 23, Jesse 3, William 1
WARD, William sr. 58, Elizabeth 46, Ali 23 (m), John 19, Dicey 17, Jackson 16?, Jonathan 14, Elizabeth 11, Angeline 8, Solomon 19, Mahalah 15
WARD, William jr. 31, Lucinda 28, Sarah 5, Celina 3, Lovina 3, Frances 8/12
SAYNE, Daniel 48, Civiller 44 (f), William 16, Jane A. 15, Henry 13, Darcus 12, Cynthia 10, Civiller 8, Daniel J. V. 6, Andrew J. 4

Schedule Page 90

LEMASTER, William 34, Sarah 31, Daniel 15, Jane 10, Anna 8, Catharine 6, Lewis 4, Elenor 1
WELCH, James 45, Isabella 36, Eliza J. 20, Margarett 18, Mary E. 16, Thomas 13, James 10, Peter 7, William 6, John 3, Nancy K. 3/12
BLAIR, George W. 30, Matilda 30, Delila 8, Amos B. 7, Samuel R. 5, Jane H. 4, George W. 1
TACKETT, Hiram 27, Lucinda 19, Isaac 2, Lewis 1
TACKETT, Levi 30, Susannah 19, William 5, John 4, Letta J. 3, Christhana 10/12
PELPHREY, William 28*, Mary 26, Daniel 8, Lewis 6, Joseph 5, Francis 1, Elizabeth 3/12, Lydia 65
CURTIS, Margarett 19*
HITCHCOCK, Parker 20*
DAVIS, James McHenry 22, Naomi J. 15

1850 Census Johnson County Kentucky

DAVIS, Elias 45, Elizabeth 46, Anna 20, Susannah C. 15, Lydia 14, Bracken L. 11, Davidson 9, Elizabeth J. 6
BLANTON, James 30, Mary 25, Elias 6, George W. 4, Martha J. 2, Anna 1
BLANTON, George sr. 75, Martha 75, George W. 5
PELPHREY, Stephen 32, Sarah 31, Isaac 8, Rebecca 5, John 3, Martha J. 2, Lydia 6/12
BLANTON, William E.? 23, Elizabeth 17
WILLIAMS, Joseph 40, Elizabeth 38, Lewis 21, John 19, James 18, Lydia 15, Martha J. 13, Sarah 12, Mary 10, Eliphus P. 8, Rachel 7, Joseph 4

Schedule Page 91

MCKENZIE, Hugh 32, Martha 25, Elias H. 8, Emely J. 6, Elizabeth J. 4, Louisa 1
CANTRELL, Henry 44, Rachel 40, Elizabeth 25, Martha 22, Elijah 15, Cynthia 14, Alsey 11, George 9, Henry 6, Rachel 4, William 3, James 1/12, William 1
SPARKS, Allen 55, Elizabeth 55, Daniel 21, Mathew 20, Andrew 18, Thomas 15, Peter 13, Allen 10
JAYNE, William 74
LEMASTER, Francis 56, Elenor 52, Catharine 26, Margaret 22, Francis 18, Sarah 16, Lydia 15, Alsey 14, Christina 12, Rhoda A. 11, Sirena 9, Archebald 7
SPARKS, Reuben 24*, Elizabeth 19
DIAL, Lucy 44*
SPARKS, Nicholas 48, Darcus 33, Elizabeth 11, Bethina 8, Robert 6, Margarett 4, David 2, Nicholas 1, Darcus 1/12
WEBB, George W. 38, Elizabeth 42, Ellen 16, Aaron 15, Lydia 12, Emely 11, Minerva 8, Laurance 6, Crayton 3, Arta C. 1
FAIRCHILD, Aaron 27, Darcus 22, Thomas A. 4, William H. 1
SAGRAVE, Thomas 28, Alineda 27, Mereda G. 2, Milley M. 1
WILLIAMS, Thomas 37*, Susannah 40, David 13, Robert 11, Margaret 9, Lucus 7, William W. 1

Schedule Page 92

ROSS, Mary 23*, Catherine 22, David 25
HAMILTON, Thomas 29, Polley 24, James H. 4, John E. 2, Louisa K. 1/12
ROSS, Robert 29, Alsey 19, Walter 2, Elizabeth 8/12
REMY, William 30, Nancy 24, Hiram 9, Benjamin 4, Henry 2, Mary 1
SALIERS, Elizabeth 35, Nancy J. 5, Frances E. 4, Malissa 2, Thomas J. 1
SALIERS, Mary 43*, Joseph 16, Wiley 14, Benjamin 11, Levi 11, Lucinda 9, Mary A. 7, Riley 5, William W. 3
CURTIS, John 23*, Abagail 17
PRESTON, Redeford 24, Elizabeth A. 21, Rue H. 3 (f), Martha 5/12
WARD, James M. 32*, Irena 31, Alafair 8 (f), Mary 6, Elizabeth 4, Ransom 2
MOORE, John W. 74*
BOWEN, Henry 28, Mary 30, Fanney 5, Elizabeth 3, John A. 1, Adam 67, Rhoda 62
CASTLE, Inmon 49, Hezekiah 17, Charles 15, Mary J. 13, Thomas 11, Jefferson 9, John E. 26, Mary 23, Nancy 5
WEBB, William 35, Frances 36, Henry O.? 9, George W. 7, Francis M. 7, Nancy J. 4, Joicey F. 2 (f), John W. 4/12

1850 Census Johnson County Kentucky

ROBERSON, John sr. 69, Nancy A. 63, Walter M. 19, Thomas J. 17, Martha A. 17, Henry J. 22, Frances 22, Samuel 1
WARD, John H. 26, Nancy 24, Lovina 1, Virazino 7/12 (m)

Schedule Page 93

CASTLE, Drury 29, Sarah 30, Epperson 7, Regina A. 5
TURNER, James W. 54, Anna 40, Mary 21, Priscilla 19, Samuel 16, Joseph 13, Redmund 12, John 9, Rachel E. 8, Cynthia E. 6, Nancy K. 2
DAVIS, John 28, Jemima 34, Elizabeth 9, Darcus 7, Daniel 6, John W. 4, Catherine 10/12
WITTEN, George H. 26, Martha 22, Martha J. 1
OBRYANT, Harrison 28, Elizabeth 22, James V. 22, Luanna 15
BAILEY, Joseph 30, Elizabeth 28, Sandford 6
WEBB, George J. 30, Mary A. 26, John R. 5, Eliza J. 3, William T. 1
OWENS, Elijah 31, Eliza J. 32, Elizabeth M. 8, James M. 6, Samuel P.? 3
HARRIS, John 27, Elizabeth 24, Nancy E. 9, William J. 5, Sarah A. 3, Rachel 1
MARTIN, Morgan 32, Sarah 24, Davis S. 2, Amanda 2/12
HAWES, Elkijah 54, Easther 40, James H. 20, Jane 18, Freelove 16, Matilda 14, Rachel 8, Samuel 6, Easther 10/12
STAMBAUGH, James 24, Martha 23, Benjamin 21
HARRELL, Robert 62, Lucinda 61
GREEN, David 24, Lucinda 19
CHANDLER, Henry 34, Jemima 32, Elzabeth 13, James 12, Nancy 11, Paulina 9, Lovina 9, Catherine 7, William 4, Isaac 2, John 10/12
CHANDLER, Abraham 48, Susan 48, William 24, Thomas 16, Sarah J. 11, Hannah 8, Lydia 6, George 4

Schedule Page 94

WRIGHT, James 30*, Anna 30, Rebecca 9, Elephas 7, James 4, Nancy 2, Samantha 2/12
HELTON, Benjamin 65*, Nancy 68
GREEN, Giles 50*, Margarett 43, Elias 19, William 17, Judea 15, John 12, George W. 9, Enoch 3, Marcus 1, Judea 91
YATES, George 9*
BOTTNER, Oliver D. 30*, Jane 31, Columbus 5, Lydia 3, Haletea 1
BURGESS, Benjamin 13*, Taylor 11, Mary 10
CANDLE, Jeremiah 26*, Lucinda 19, Russell 2, William J. 1
DUNCAN, Absalom 13*
REMY, Owen 32, Lavina 31, Permelia 10, Mary 8, Susannah 5, Rachel 4, Henry C. 7/12, Mary 52
RICE, John 30*, Nancy 27, William M. 9, Julia A. 7, Lydia A. 5, Samuel 2, Henry W. 1
MULLETT, Nathan R. 64*, Rutha A. 48
DANIEL, James 39, Elizabeth 42, Amos 18, Anna 16, Isom W. 14, Mary M. 12, Katherine 10, Darcus 9, James J. 5, John R. 3, Jesse 2
JUSTICE, Abyram 41, Ehod 18 (f), Bethalia 16 (f), Duricey 11 (f), Andrew 9, Susanah 5, Savenah 3 (f)
HELTON, Elephus P. 30, Sarah 26, William P. 4, Celina 2, Nancy 9/12
CRAFT, Wiley 29, Dianah 24, Tillman 4, Katherine 2, Thomas J. 3/12, William 23, Pleasant 14

1850 Census Johnson County Kentucky

Schedule Page 95

JUSTICE, Samuel 30, Mary 25, Edmund 6, Sarah 4, Marena 1
CANDLE, John 35, Phoeba 29, Jessa 5 (m), Sarah 4, Winston 2, Araminta 1
SALIERS, Martin 41, Susanah 33, John M. 17, Jonathan H. 15, Eliza J. 12, Katherine 10, Lydia 9, Elizabeth 6, Sarah 5, William H. 3, Susanah 3, Martha 1
SPARKS, Elijah 38, Sarah 38, William 16, Mary A. 15, Sarah 13, Lucy 12, Milley 8, Lamira J. 6, Katherine 3, Elijah 2/12
SALIERS, John 39, Margarett 35, Mahalah 16, Mary 14, William 12, Lucy 10, Sarah J. 4, Noah 1
SALYERS, Benjamin 20, Martha 21, Nancy 8/12
SPARKS, Elisha 38, Susan 31, Lydia 15, Jane 13, William 11, Elisha 9, Paulina 7, Dianah 4, Caty A. 2, Tillman 2/12
SALIERS, Bracken 19, Araminta 16
SALIERS, Thomas 41, Elizabeth 38, Zacheriah 16, Ephraim 10, Rebecca 8, Mary 5, Martha 4, Dicey 1
SPARKS, Thomas 48, Katherine 43, Sarah 19, Eleanor 17, Margarett 15, Thomas J. 13, Henry 11, Daniel 9, Katherine 6, John 4
FAIRCHILD, Isaah 34, Susanah 31, Rebecca 12, David 8, Jesse 4, Mary 2
FAIRCHILD, Hezekiah 23*, Mahalah 34
SHELTON, Mahalah A. 9*
NICHELL, Alexander W. 22, Katherine 19, Samantha 2, Cevillar 1 (f)

Schedule Page 96

LEMASTER, Eleazur 36 (m), Eleanor 39, John R. 17, Francis M. 15, Henry J. 13, Eleazur J. 11, Elizabeth 9, Jemima 7, Rachel W. 5, Eleanor J. 3
LEMASTER, Lewis 25*, Anna 21, Jacob 1
CASTLE, Jane 17*
SAGRAVE, Joseph 38, Nancy 37, William 16, Mary 14, Susanah 12, Zacheriah 9, Sarah 4, Sylvester 2, Jemima 1/12
GHENT, William 41, Frances 41, Nancy 15, Mary 10, Eleanor 8, Serena 5, William 4
LEMASTER, Richard 43, Bexey? 37 (f), Lancaster 18, Rachel 15, Zelphia 13, Judia 12, James 10, Elizabeth 8, Mary 6, Alsey 3
ROSS, David 90, Margarett 58, Joseph 22, Stephan 20
SPARKS, Mathew 40, Isey 35, Allen 17, Jesse 16, Henry 14, Nathan 13, Lovina 10, Elizabeth 7, Sarah A. 5, Daniel 3, Nancy E. 6/12
BAILEY, Daniel 27*, Agness 27, William W. 4, George W. 3, Sarah A. 1
LYONS, James 30*
LEMASTER, John 52, Tamah 35 (f), Sarah 16, Eleazur 15, Rachel 12, Angelina 11, Clarrinda 6
JOHNSON, Martin 20, Martha 19
DEBORD, Joseph 62*, Martha 59, Martha 15
MCDOWELL, Joseph 31*, Aley 26, Jacob 7, Susanah 5, Martha 3, Eveline 2, Elizabeth 1/12
WHEELER, William 52, Elizabeth 57, Elizabeth 23, Rebecca 21, Jemima 20, Jane 17

Schedule Page 97

MCDOWELL, James 23, Avey 19
WHEELER, John 27, Martha 25, Elzira 3, Jiles 2, William 10/12

1850 Census Johnson County Kentucky

SKAGGS, Peter 47, Clarrinda 40, Solomon 18, Nancy 16, Thursey 13, Sarah 11, Thomas 8, Peter 6, Arthur 3
BAILEY, John 52, Susanah 46, Samuel 13, Thomas 10, Elizabeth 7, Wade 4, Stephen 22
MCDOWELL, William 26, Mary 19, Telitha 2
SAGRAVE, William 34, Charlotte 33, Walter 14, Wilbourn 12, Delila E. 7, Nancy E. 5, Susanah K. 2
ADKINS, Henry 49, Jerusia 47 (f), Hannah 23, Sarah 21, Mahalah 19, Charlotte 17, Mary 15, Darius 13, Jarusia 11, Abagail 9, Clarrinda 6
NICHELL, George 19, Savilla 17, Eveline 3/12
FANNON, Henry 22, Mary 17, Christohper C. 1
CHANDLER, Isaac 22, Elzira 24, Martha 1
ESTEPP, Samuel 24*, Abatine? 24 (f), Francis C. 4, Barbary A. 3, Ira W. 2, William C. 1, John M. 6/12
BOWEN, Sarah 10*
TRIMBLE, James 24, Frances 22, Sarah 7, Nancy 4, John 2, Susanah 1
CANDLE, James C. 26, Mary 42, Lucena 2, Martha 4/12
SPENCE, Jobe 37, Sarah 33, Andrew 16, Rhoda 15, Mary 13, Linton H. 11, Alafair 9 (f), Emily 7, Mariah 6, Nancy 4, Arter L. 1 (m)

Schedule Page 98

GULLETT, Ira 29, Lydia 24, Jane 3, Tempa 2, William 2/12
BLANTON, John N. 29, Sarah 26, James 5, Marinda 3, Samuel 2, Benjamine 4/12
WHEELER, John 38, Nancy 37, Elender H. 15, Eliza E. 13, Nancy J. 11, James 9, Andrew 7, John 5, Amos 2, Lutitia A. 3/12
MCKINZIE, James 47, Frances 45, William J. 21, Henry P. 16, Joseph K. 14, Martin B. 12, Francis M. 10, Sarah M. 7, Andrew J. 6
FAIRCHILD, Moses 29, Katherine 19
STAPLETON, Charles 42, Nancy 42, Allen 17, Katherine 16, Edward 13, Asa 9, Joseph 7, Elizabeth 6, William H. 4
JAYNE, Henry 46, Sarah 46, Daniel 19, Martha 16, Elizabeth 14, Mary 12, Phoeba 10, Henry 8, William 6
CONLEY, Thomas 41, Jemima B. 32, Hannah J. 15, Charity M. 14, Thomas M. 13, Rachel 12, Sarah 10, William F. 6, John H. 4, Katherine 3, Daniel J. 2, Ezekiel 1, Easter 1/12
MCKINZIE, John 56*, Easter 45, Thomas J. F. 17, Hetty 14, Stephan H. 11, Anna 8, Margarett E. K. 5, Julia E. 2
HAMILTON, Anna 79*
BAILEY, James 24, Mary 23, Angelina 3/12
GAMBELL, Hargus 28, Cynthia 28, Lynnville A. 5, Louisa J. 4, Eliza A. 3, America 1

Schedule Page 99

LYONS, William 38, Lenna 34, John 13, Amos 11, Amanda 9, Mary 6, Jesse 4, Hayden 1, John 76, Mary 67, Lucina 24
KELLEY, Frederick 49, Patience 43, Mathias 22, Rachel 19, George 17, Nancy A. 16, Martha 14, Jane 12, John 10, Peter F. 6, William H. 5, Wallace 2, Mathias 79
HOLEBROOK, Pleasant 47, Sarah 44, Mary 23, James 21, Martha 18, Fanney 17, Susanah 15, Larkin 13, Judea 10, John F. 8, Malinda 6, Zerilda 1

1850 Census Johnson County Kentucky

HOLEBROOK, William 39, Sarah 35, Fanney 16, Henry 14, Littleburne 10, Hargus 8, Polley A. 6, John 4, Elizabeth 1
ROSE, Thomas 35, Rhoda 36, Elizabeth 14, John 9, William 7, Sarah 6, Anna 3, Thomas C. 3/12
HILL, Lucy 51, Jemima 17, Katherine 16, William E. 14, Henry H. 11, Benjamin F. 6
PRATT, James 86, Rebecca 55, Elizabeth 18
WRIGHT, Bailus 31, Isabella 34, Elizabeth 5, Mary 3, William 1
FIFFE, John 66, Fanney 66
HAMILTON, Benjamin S. 24, Nancy 18, Teressa F. 2
WILLIAMS, Robert 62, Nancy 22, Mary J. 9/12, Philip 15
WILLIAMS, John M. 32, Christina 24, Angelina 5
WILLIAMS, Hardin H. 31*, Elizabeth 29, Sylvester H. 10, Cynthia 6, Henderson A. 4, John H. 2

Schedule Page 100

SIMER, Eilzabeth P. 76*
PRATT, Enoch 22, Genettee? 27 (f), Benjamin F. 2
FAIRCHILD, Aaron 61, Rebecca 56, Rebecca 15
OSBORN, Edward 37, Paulina 23, Jesse 15, Andrew 14, Elizabeth 12, Jonathan 5, William 4, Frances J. 2
FAIRCHILD, Joseph 41, Katherine 40, Abner 19
PENINGTON, James 20, Nancy 16
JENKINS, Robert 35, Rebecca 28, William H. 13, Robert R. 10, Ruth 8, Fanney 5, Francis M. 3, Nancy J. 1
REED, William 30, Lydia 22, John E. 2, Cinda E. 7/12
CONLEY, David M. 33, Mahalah 30, David H. 15, Eveline 13, Lydia 11, William 8, John R. 6, Elizabeth 5, Ellen 1
BLANTON, William 50, Alsey 35, James 17, Rebecca 15, Tempa 11, John 9, William 7, Harvey 6, Katherine 5, Henry 2
BLANTON, George 36, Tabitha 36, Charity 16, Zachery M. 13, Susanah 11, Wayman 10, Bracken 8, Sarah E. 5, James M. 2, no name 1/12 (f)
REED, Asa J. 35, Darcus 37, Isom M. 15, Hannah S. 14, Nancy 13, John A. 11, David N. 9, Frances J. 7, Martha 6, Cynthia E. 3, Katherine 1
WILEY, William 48*, Polley 52, Adam 13, Peggy 11
DORTEN, William 8?*
DORTEN, Joel 29*, Martha 18, Joseph 1
FITZPATRICK, Rosey 8*
DEAN, Joshua 24, Elizabeth 21, Calistia 3/12

Schedule Page 101

WILEY, Andrew J. 19*, Nancy E. 23
TACKETT, Willliam 22*, Nancy J. 21, Andrew T. 1
HOWARD, Moses 27*, Matilda 24, Emiley 6, Mary 2
FIPPS, James 22*
MCLOWERY, Jelson 23, Jane 21, Pynthia A. 2, James M. 8/12
CONLEY, Edmund 22*, Nancy 55
TACKETT, Rachel 18*, Mahalah 15

1850 Census Johnson County Kentucky

ADKINS, Edmund 8*, Hardin 5
LITTERALL, Elizabeth 58, William 18, Milton 16
GULLETT, Tempa 51, Elizabeth 23, William 22, Anna 17, Andrew F. 15
CONLEY, Edmund 25, Elizabeth 22, James 2, Sarah 1
MCCARTY, Thomas 54, Margarett 53, Lydia 24
MCCARTY, John 26, Patsey 26, Nelson 9, Rebecca J. 8, David 6, Minerva 4
WEBB, James W. 27, Edith 27, Palmyra 3, Henrietta 7
JACKSON, James 45, Susan 37
CANDLE, Thomas 57, Jane 37, Mary J. 6, Abner 21, Polley 21
CANDLE, Mathew 26, Tempa 27, Fanney 6, Thomas 5, Nancy 1
CANDLE, Isom 28, Nancy 26, Mahalah 6, Holley 4 (m)
CONLEY, Thomas 43*, Sarah 41, Martha 24, John 19, Isaac 14, Nancy 11
FITZPATRICK, Elizabeth 9*
SALIERS, Henry 33, Elizabeth 39, Clarrinda 14, Elizabeth 12, Keziah 11, Polley 8, James M. 6, Nancy 3, Henry M. 2
SALIERS, Jerry 22, Elizabeth 24, Isaac 4, Malissa M. 1
SALIERS, Jacob 45*, Nincerius? 44 (f), John 21, Mahalah 16, Eveline 14, Abagail 12, Mary J. 10, Jacob 4, Benjamin F. 1

Schedule Page 102

ROWLAND, Richard 11*
WEST, Joseph 32, Sarah 31, Mary A. 9, Zerilda J. 8, Sarah 5, Shadrach 6/12
BROWN, David 26, Mary 27, Mary J. 7, Seana 6, Katherine 2
MEAD, Robert 31*, Lydia 33, Mary A. 12, Levi 10, Frances 7, Samuel 4, Sarah 2
VANHOOSE, John 30*, George W. 6
VANHOOSE, William 28*, Minerva 23, Matilda 5, Elizabeth A. 3, John W. 1
ELLIOTT, Araminta 7*, James 7
PRESTON, William W. 4*
BARNHART, Sarah 44*
PRICE, Andrew J. 30*, Jemima 24, Julia A. 8, Kingston 6, Mahulda J. 3, Jesse W. 1
ACRES, Mary 16*
LEWIS, Elizabeth 44*
PRICE, David 23*, Delila 21, Lyncha J. 4, Louisa 1, William J. 1/12
VANHOOSE, William 10*
WARD, Solomon S. 22*, Elizabeth 23, Valentine 2/12
VANHOOSE, Sirena 13*
MAY, Caleb 27, Sarah 31, Artemissa 5, Ella M. 3, James S. 1
MEEK, William 39, Elizabeth 40, Julia A. 19, Jane 15, James 14, Nathan 12, John 10, Elias 9, Mary 6, Susan 4, Sarah 2
WARD, Solomon 43, Nancy A. 43, Thompson 19, Solomon 17, William 14, Joseph 12, Nancy J. 10, Jerry 3
PRICE, Jesse sr. 60*, Lyrcha 56, Benjamin F. 15, Christopher C. 13
RIDNER, Lucy 13*

1850 Census Johnson County Kentucky

Schedule Page 103

DANIEL, James B. 29, Priscilla 26, Fleming 9, Lovena 6, Washington 4, Martin 1
SHORT, Thomas 55, Rachel 52, Sarah 22, Silas 20, Adison 18, Amanda 14, Isaac 11, Louisa 3
WYATT, Reuben 54, Francis M. 11, Mary 8, Sarah 6
TACKETT, William 54*, Sarah 44, James M. F. 15
SHAVER, Fanny 24*, Elizabeth 3, William B. 1
TACKETT, Thomas 80*, Sarah 80
RICE, Elizabeth 40*
DELONG, George 37*, Mary 34, William 8, Jefferson 7, George 6, Frances 4, Nancy 2
MOORE, Sampson 19*
MCCARTY, John 35, Lydia 35, Rebecca J. 13, Martha 10, Polley A. 9, John W. 4, Abner 1
COLVIN, Abind 38, Susan 33, Martha 14, Lovina 12, Sarah 11, John M. H. 9, William M. 7, Elizabeth 5, James C. 4, Mary 2, Melvina 8/12
KEITH, Sarah 30*
LEMASTER, William 14*, Lydia 4
MELVIN, George 36, Martha 32, Andrew 12, Lewis 9, Cornelius 7, Goerge 5, Delila 3, Elizabeth 3/12
WITTEN, Isaac 24*, Elizabeth 19, Araminta 1
HACKWORTH, William 13*
ROWLAND, John 48, Edith 48, Peggy 19, Jemima 16, Polley 12, Nancy 9, Phinna L. 6 (m)
COLLINS, Clary 34 (m), Frances 34, Amanda 14, Amos D. 11, Eliza J. 6, John 5
RULE, Andrew 63*, Elender 46 (f), Charles G. 17, Elizabeth 15, Cynthia 13, Marion H. 11, Jesse C. 9, French 7 (m)

Schedule Page 104

TURNER, Edwin S. 23*, Nancy J. 22, Martha E. 2, no name 2/12 (f)
CANDLE, William 27, Martha 25, Samuel 6, Mahalah 4, John M. 3, Sylvister 1
SIMER, John P. 42, Mary 43, Delila 15, Clarinda 13, Samuel 11, William 9
CANDLE, Reubin 25, Levisa 19, Araminta 3, William J. 1
PELPHREY, William 56*, Nancy 55, James 18, Lydia 16, Rowland 12
GIBBS, Nancy 5*
SHAVERS, James 42, Cynthia 25, William 9, Missouri A. 1 (f)
RICE, Samuel 54*, Emiley 37, George W. 18, Nancy J. 16, Wallace B. 15, Francis M. 13, Phoeba 2
REMY, Thomas L. 8*, Lucy A. 13, Zerilda 17
BAYES, Margaret 33, Sarah J. 16, Phoeba 14, Joshua H. 12, William R. 10, Samuel 7, Mary E. 3
LEMASTER, Lewis 58, Martha 51, Francis 32, Samuel 25, Daniel 20, Jesse 19, Martha 16, Elijah 13
RICE, Andrew J. 20, Rebecca 23
COLLINS, Isaac 30*, NAncy 24, Mary J. 7, James L. 6, Elizabeth 2, William H. 8/12
LARKINS, Presley 91*
FAIRCHILD, Shadrach 28, Sarah 25, Mary J. 3, Martha A. 1
RATLIFF, Henry 21*, Louisa 23, Riley 2
GREEN, Martha 7*
PELPHREY, Alixander 54*, Alsey 53, Elizabeth 18, Arta F. 15 (f), David 13
TURNER, Rachel 24*, Eleanur? W. 3 (m), George A. T. 1(f)

1850 Census Johnson County Kentucky

Schedule Page 105

HITCHCOCK, Alexander 1*
PELPHREY, James 35, Mary 35, John W. 15, Clarinda 14, Sarah 12, Alexander J. 10, Samantha F. 8, James M. 5, Angeline 3, Mary E. 1
HITCHCOCK, Nimrod 22, Mary F. 17
HARMON, Joseph 25, Susanah 19, Milton L.H. 10/12
REMY, Thomas 23, Sarah 21, Charles G. 3, George W. 1
REMY, John 27, Phoeba 22, William J. 7, Zachery T. 2, James M. 8/12
KIMBLER, Abee 47, Nancy 60, Silas 18
MCKENZIE, William 45, Barbary 43 (f), Andrew J 20, Samuel G. 18, Lucinda J. 15, Sarah M. 14, Rebecca B. 13, David J. 11, Hiram E. 7, Nancy A. 5
MCKENZIE, John 31, Nancy 25, William F. 7, John W. 7, Mary J. 5, Elizabeth A. 4, George W. 11/12
DAVIS, Richard 33*, Elinora 34, Harvey C. 13, John W. 12, Taletha 8, Mary S. 6
REED, Hannah 57*
REED, Mason 25, Sarah 21, Amanda 8/12
RICE, Samuel K. 24, Katherine 27, Jessee 1 (m)
FAIRCHILD, Rachel 34, Cynthia 15, Serena 12, William 10, Jincey 8 (f)
MAWHAN, Johial 23, Rebecca 24, Lucinda 3, Rhoda 2
MAWHAN, Henry 57, Elizabeth 55, Polley A. 17, William 13, Mason 7, Lucinda 2
COLVIN, Sarah 65, Sarah 29, Asa 27, John 36, Minerva A. 11, Allen R. 10, Elizabeth 8, Henry 7, Sarah J. 4
COLVIN, Jackson 31, Mahalah 26, William 8, John 6, Delila 3, Isaac 1, Nancy 1/12

Schedule Page 106

COLVIN, Isaac 24, Delphia 23, Louisa 2/12
COLVIN, Allen 39, Eveline 25, Jehisa 9 (m), Aburd? 8 (m), Margarett J. 5, Sarah A. 3, Elizabeth 1, Henry 2/12
CONLEY, David 43, Polley 37, Andrew J. 18, Sarah M. 14, Elexious 12, Polley E. 10, John S. 7, Nancy 3, Winston 2
CONLEY, Henry 20, Mahalah 18, Mary 9/12
PRICE, George 37*, Sarah 34, Hamilton 16, Loranda 13, Elizabeth 12, Anderson 10, Frances 8, Luther 6, Sophia 4, Julina 1
SALIERS, William 34*
LITTERALL, Hurston 41, Katherine 41, Polley M. 18, Cynthia 17, Harmon 15, Louisa 13, Marion 12, Lydia 10, Fleming 8, Lindsey 6, Katherine 3, Elsey 1 (m)
CANDLE, William 28*, Rebecca 25, Lydia D. 2, Easter 1
HARRIS, Sarah 18*
CANDLE, Mathew 29, Temperance 26, John 7, Stephen 6, Arbuth A. 4 (m), Triphena 3, Russell 1
RATLIFF, Silas 41, Anna 41, Levisa 22, Nancy 17, James 14, Phoeba 12, John 10, Cynthia 8, Sarah 6, William 3
DALE, Reuben 40, Tabitha 35, Berry 18, Frances 13, Pleasant 11, Arter 6 (m), Charity 7/12
DAVIS, Nancy 50, Anna 21, Henry 16

1850 Census Johnson County Kentucky

Schedule Page 107

BURK, Richard 35, Sarah 35, Elizabeth M. 21, Levi 13, Samuel 11, George W. 8, David T. 7, Lewis H. 3, Charles W. 1
RULE, Harrison B. 39, Elizabeth 22, Andrew W. 8, Sarah 5, Margarett 4, Jessee W. 2/12
RULE, James M. 31, Sarah 27, William W. 8, Sarah A. 7, Andrew J. 5, James M. 3, Nancy J. 4/12
LEMASTER, Elijah 62, Eizabeth 62, Lewis 23, Sarah 25, Delphia 7, Miranda 4, Mary A. E. J. 2, William F. 6/12
PSIMER, Rachel 35, John 16, Asa J. 14, Martin 11, Martha 8, William 3, Mary A. F. 1
PSIMER, Nathaniel jr. 22, Susanah 20, Celia 5/12
BAYES, James J. 21, Rachel E. 18, Emily J. 1, Judea A. 15
PSIMER, David 33, Mary 25, Jasper 6, Wallace 4, Asa 2
SALYER, David J. 30, Mary 35, Sophia 10, Ascenith 9, General F. 7, Malissa A. 6, Zacheriah 4, Thomas 3, Dicey J. 1, Mary 6/12
CONLEY, Isaah 36, Susanah 34, Absalom 15, Edmund 13, Temperance 11, Rachel 8, Nancy 6, David J. 3, Polley 2
HITCHCOCK, John 46*, Mahalah 47, John M. 17, Rowland G. 16, Margarett 12, Isaac W. 11, Lucina A. 7, Mahalah J. 6, Eliza 3
CONLEY, Temperance 69*
PELPHREY, Daniel 22*, Sarah A. 21, James M. 1, Arta F. 6/12
ARMS, Elias 16*
HOWER, William W. 22, Mary S. 21, no name 7/12 (m)

Schedule Page 108

COLINS, David 43, Polley 49, Nancy 22, George W. 19, Andrew J. 17, Hiram 15, Peter 12, Malissa 10
HOWER, Elexious 61, Sarah 56, Katherine 27, Claborne 25, Henry J. 19, Louisa 13
SHAVERS, Susan 46, Thomas 29, Jane 18, Ransom 15, Moses 22
WALKER, Deleware 47 (m), Amey 35, George R. 16, Elexious 14, John W. 12, James F. 9, Sarah V. 5
PRICE, Harrison 19, Zena 18
VANHOOSE, Valentine 30, Louisa 24, William J. 7, Martin 5, Harrison 2, Elizabeth 9/12, Moses 19
STAMBAUGH, Sylvester 25, Member 22, Philip 2, Joseph 2/12
CONLEY, Constantine 44, Celia 40, Hiram 20, Wiley J. 17, Hermon 15, Francis M. 14, Asa J. F. 11, Winston 8, Henry J. 6, Amanda 3, Benjamin F. 8/12
CASTLE, Nathan 50, Sarah 50, Nancy 30, James 36, Elizabeth 24, Judea 23, Jacob 22
COLLINS, Joshua 45, Elizabeth 45, William 21, Elijah 19, Elisha 17, Lydia 13, Allen 11, Cynthia 9, Elizabeth 7
HARRIS, William 55*, Aleann 37, Pleasant 17, Lydia J. 12, Henry C. 11, Rachel E. 9, Julia A. 4, Littleton T. 3
NICHOLL, Shelby 18 (m)*
DANIEL, Solomon 31*, Margarett 24, George W. 7, Polley 4, Wiley 2
WILEY, John 19*, Sarah 24, Nancy 1

Schedule Page 109

KISSNER, William 62, Barbary 57, Elizabeth 15
FAIRCHILD, Enoch 44, Frances 47, Levi 18, Nancey 17, William 14, Asa 11, Hannah 9, Rachel 7

1850 Census Johnson County Kentucky

ROWLAND, John jr. 21, Margarett 24, Mary 5/12
DUTTON, James 42, Matilda 36, Elias 18, George 16, Moses 14, Sarah 12, Jackson 8, Mary 6, Richard 4, Susanah 1
PENIX, Allen 45, Sarah 50, Katherine 21, Anna 18, Sarah 17, Isaac A. 14
WALLER, Jacob 52, Katherine 50, Martha A. 18, Margarett 16, Thomas R. 15, Elizabeth 12, Samuel W. 6
MEEK, Isaac 39, Sarah 38, William 19, Zepheniah 17, Paulina 15, Lucina 13, Shadrach 11, Sarah 9, Judea 7, Jesse 5, Granville 3, Lovina 2, Exer 9/12 (f?)
PRESTON, Jeffrey 58, Jane 54, Charlotte 20, Edy 18 (f), Sarah 16, Francis 15, William 13, Benjamin 11, Amanda 7
SHEARMON, Henry 42, Matilda 35, Eliza A. 15, William 14, Jefferson 14, Burgess 12, Nathan 10, Nancy J. 8, Julia A. 6, John M. E. 4, Winfield S. 2 (m)
PRESTON, Eliphus 55, Lucinda 23, Thomas J. 3, Julia A. 2, Mary J. 1, Leah J. 11, Atchison 25
WHEELER, John 36, Mary 30, Henry D. 11, Martin 9, Sarah 4
WHEELER, Katherine 64, Darcus 44

Schedule Page 110

WHEELER, Daniel 32*, Elizabeth 27, Samuel G. 8, Amanda 6, Eleanor 4
BOWEN, Elizabeth 17*
SWEATMAN, Zepheniah 41*, Charlotte 38, Mildred J. 13, Elizabeth J. 11, Amanda M. 9, Francis J. 8, Mary F. 6, Martha P. 2
BURGESS, Elizabeth 80*
WILEY, Richard 24, Cynthia 18, Francis M. 2, Jane 5/12
PRESTON, James 31, Lovina 29, Elizabeth 9, Lafayette 4, Nancy J. 2, Exer 2/12 (f), Montreville 15, John 6, Judea 18
PRESTON, William 23, Susan 22, Martha J. 2, James H. 1, Jefferson 2/12
PRESTON, Greenville 27*, Exer 25 (f), Lovina 5, Araminta 3, Moses 1
WALTERS, Shadrach 19*, Winfrey 16 (m)
VANHOOSE, Jesse 24, Keziah 24, William 2, Levi 1
DANIEL, Edward 31, Polley 28, Jasper 8, Elizabeth 6, Newton 4, George 3, John 1
GREEN, Charles J. 45, Elizabeth 43, John F. 22, Elizabeth 18, Frederick 16, Lovina 16, Charles J. 13, Benjamin 12, Mary 10, William W. 8, America 5, Charlotte 2
WARD, Jesse 30, Mary 28, Amanda 12, Sarah J. 10, Exer 8 (f), Stephan 4, William J. 6/12
LITTERALL, George 35*, Mahalah 38, Elizabeth 14, George W. 12, Sarah 11, Harrison 9, Martha 4, Mahalah J. 3
MANKINS, John 19*
FITZPATRICK, John 15*
DANIEL, John 39, Margarett 30, Mahalah 16, Cynthia 14, James 12, Washington 10, Thomas 8, David 6, John 4

Schedule Page 111

CASTLE, Edward 24*, Mary 20, Jasper N. 1, Katherine 2/12
WILEY, Adam 53*, Mary 52, Andrew J. 16
CHILDERS, Robert 41, Jane 35, James M. 18, Francis M. 16, John 14, Elizabeth 12, William 10, Lucy A. 7, Henry J. 5, Sarah J. 3, Harden 7/12

1850 Census Johnson County Kentucky

STAMBAUGH, Dicey 50*, Sirena 20, John 18, Salley 14, Dicey 12
WARD, William 22*, Mary E. 23, Philip 2
DAVIS, Thomas 53*, Elizabeth 47, Mary A. 26, John B. 24, Margarett 19, Zacheriah 18, Jennette 15, William H. 12, Andrew 11, Hezekiah 9, Thomas J. 5
SELLERD, Elizabeth A. 11*
OSBORN, Calvin 21, Mary J. 15, Wells 1/12
OSBORN, Alford 22, Cynthia 21
WARD, Malinda 39, Jonathan 12
VANHOOSE, Valentine 52, Jemima 44, John 20, Mary 15, Julina 13, Vasti? 5 (f)
HELTON, Nathan P. 34, Frances 27, Charlotte 12, Jeffrey 10, Charles 6, Elizabeth 5, Lavina 3
PACK, Berry 52*, Rebecca 46, Martha 7, Marion 4
BLEVINS, Phoeby 16*
GIPSON, Abraham 52, Mary 35, John 16, Samuel 12, Sarah 11, Abraham 5, Mary 4, Lydia 1
BRADFIELD, John 29*, Gracia 21, Elizabeth 5, Charles 3, Minerva 1
KIDD, Ellen 45*
PRESTON, Thomas 45, Rhoda 32, Samuel 16, Nathaniel 13, Gilbert 12, Oliver 7, Isaac 2

Schedule Page 112

STURGEON, Elijah 39, Rutha 33, Mary 15, Nancy 13, Wilbourne 10, Sarah J. 8, Matilda 5, Elizabeth 3, John 1
KIDD, John 72, Elizabeth 66, Albert 20
WARD, James 55, Lucinda 47, Jackson 24, Washington 18, Nancy 16, James 14, Jonathan 10, William O. 6
DANIEL, Joseph 34, Nancy 25, Mary J. 16, Aladine? B. 11(m), Winston M. 8, William W. 5, Sarah 3
WARD, John 21, Zerilda 18, Nathan 1
PEONIX, William 26, Sarah 24
WARD, Bluford 25, Sarah 20, Zelphia 1
BLEVINS, Samuel 33, Mary 30, Emiley 10, Elias 8, Levi 6, Rebecca 5, Samuel 3, Hamson 1/12
PUCKETT, Joshua 28, Margarett 27, Rebecca A. 8, Olivia 6, Jemima 3, Nancy 2, Sarah 6/12
BUTCHER, James 27, Mary 25, Nancy 3, John J. C. 1
WARD, Shadrach 37, Abagail 26, James 15, Rutha 11, Granville 9, Zena 7, Jane 5, Solomon 3, Susan 65
MULLETT, Elias sr. 65, Sarah J. 57
MULLETT, Elias jr. 35, Susan 23, William 9, James 8, Cynthia 5, Cloa 4, John 3, Mary 1
HAGER, Daniel 48, Violet 46, William J. 24, Mary J. 22, Martha A. 20, Amanda B. 18, Samuel P. 16, Emiley E. 14, Daniel M. 10, Louisa 7, Benjamin F. 4, Violet V. 1

Schedule Page 113

ADAMS, James B. 38, Keziah 38, Barbary A. 20, Joel Q. 18, Jerry D. 16
HAGER, John J. 27*, Rhoda 28, Julia A. 5, Daniel M. 3, Violet H. 2, James H. 6/12
SMITH, Mary 13*
FISHER, John 48*
GODSEY, James H. 23*
WILLIAMS, Jacob 24, Elizabet 20, Samuel G. 1, John J. 3/12
WITTEN, John W. 28, Lydia V. 23, Malissa J. 3, William J. 1

1850 Census Johnson County Kentucky

RICE, William 36*, Mary 33, Clarrinda 13, John P. M. 10, Cynthia E. 8, Louisa E. 6, Samuel W. 5, William M. 2, no name 4/12 (m)
HARMON, William B. 18*
COLE, Raney 23*
STAMBAUGH, Samuel 54, Charlotte 50, Frederick 20, Jonathan 17, Sarah 12, Robert J. 11, Samuel 8
CASTLE, Patterson 34, Letta 24, Mary J. 8, Priscilla 7, Angelina 3, Elizabeth 5/12
DANIEL, George 24, Mary 21, Loudon T. 3, James 2, Matilda 6/12
DANIEL, Sarah 53, Mary A. 21, Paulina J. 13
CASTLE, Benjamin 60, Elizabeth 60, Marcum 23, Eveline 15, Madison 13, Emeretta 11
CASTLE, Johial 38, Easther 26, Rhoda 7, Benjamin 5, Thomas 3, Asa 1
CASTLE, Zacheriah 39, Rutha A. 34, Amos 9, Wilson 7, Willis 4, Arminda 1
WARD, Shadrach 64*, Lovina 57, Jefferson 22, Lovina 14
WALTERS, John 12*

Schedule Page 114

PACK, Balley 33, Elizabeth A. 10, Elizabeth A. 17, Andrew J. 15
WARD, Hiram 41, Mary 39, David 17, Andrew 15, Zerilda 10, William R. 10, Angeline 8, Sampson 6, Delila 9/12
GILISPIE, Alexander 21, Elizabeth 21, Andrew J. 2, George 3/12
PORTER, Benjamin 41, Abagail 42, Clementina 20, Cannada L. 18 (m), James 16, Benjamin 13, Violet 5, Zelphia 3, Samuel 21
MOLLETT, James 30, Margarett 25, Nathan R. 14, Levi 12, Mary J. 10, Elias B. 8, Sarah 6, Emeretta 3, Rily J. 6/12
BOWEN, Daniel 29, Cynthia 24, Emely 9, John 5, Mary J. 3, Elijah 1
BLEVINS, James 29, Elizabeth 29, Zelphia 10, Clementina 7, Wells 5, Araminta C. 2, Alvus 8/12
MOLLETT, John 28, Zelphia 28, James H. 8, Benjamin 6, Angelina 3, Sarah J. 10/12
BLEVINS, Levi 71, Mary 65
JOHNSON, Andrew 58, Martha 56, John 21, Mahalah J. 13, Martha A. 13, Isaac 11, Margaret 5
MOLLETT, David 38*, Susan 35, John 17, Mary 13, David 10, Melvina 9, Juliann 6, Abby 5, Jane 1
DAMSON, Samuel 19*
DANIEL, George 24, Zelphia 25, Susan 1
LOW, Stephen 61, Susannah 48
LOWE, William 31, Marinda 25, Stephen 6, Elizabeth 4, Andrew 2, William 2, James 3/12

Schedule Page 115

JOHNSON, George 28*, Mary 24, William J. 6, Lucinda 5, Phoeba 2
DAMSON?, Elizabeth 21*
WILLIAMSON, William 26, Margarett 23, Mary 5, James 3, Thomas 1
BLEVINS, Thomas A. 21, Ruth 20, Henderson R. 2, Mathew G. 1
BAKER, Ira 25, Thursey A. 22, Martha 3, Benjamin F. 1
SCOTT, Barnabas 28, Matilda 28, William 10, Mary J. 7, Ruth A. 5, John 2, Elizabeth 2/12
CASSADY, Alexander 24, Lucretia 22, Mary 2
CRUM, Reuben 40, Alafair 37 (f), Mary 15, James 13, Elizabeth 9, Sarah 7, Adam 5, William 1
BANISTER, Pleasant 46*, Mary 47, William 16, Barbary 14, Alafair 13, Lydia A. 11, Mary J. 9, Anderson 7

1850 Census Johnson County Kentucky

CRUM, Eli 22*
MURRY, George W. 23, Margania 19, Marion 10/12
WARD, Wells 31*, Cenia 25, Arta 5, Washington 4, Elizabeth 1, Wells 10/12
PRESTON, Clarinda 9*
WARD, Elizabeth 56, Washington 23, Manuel 12
PAWLEY, Skidmore 53, Elizabeth 40, Dicey 16, Lucretia 14, Lucina 12, Louisa 11, Elizabeth 8, Thomas S. 6, Mordica 2 (m)
COSSLEY, Freman 39, Sarah 38, Sarena 18, Elizabeth 15, Charlotte 13, Amos 11, Jackson 9, Margarette 6, Malissa J. 5, Allen 4/12
CLAY, Peter 43, Martha 43, Nancy 17, Alafair 15, Martha 12, Jorden 11, William H. 8, George H. 7, Elizabeth J. 6, Thomas J. 4, no name 1 (m)

Schedule Page 116

STEPP, James 28, Leannah 24, Rebecca 8, Nancy 6, Mary 3, Joseph 11/12
STEPP, Robert 26, Charity 13, Nancy 4, Sarah 2
WARD, James 23, Cynthia 28, Sophia 8, Nathan 6, Mary E. 3, Anderson 1
WILLIAMS, Owen 28, Margarett 30, John E. 6, Richard C. 5, Eveline 3
STEPP, Moses 19, Lucinda 18
MOLLETT, Hiram 33, Elizabeth 33, Mahulda 14, Henry 12, Cynthia 10, Thomas 5, Jesse 2 (m), Nathan 1
MCNEILEY, Benjamin 23, Rebecca 17
MOORE, William 37, Elizabeth 35, Sampson 17, James 15, Margarett 12, Mary J. 10, Susannah 7, Henry 5, Nathaniel 3/12
CASSADY, Benjamin 51, Julian 44 (f), Philip 22, William 14, Matilda 12, Henry 11, Easter 7, John E. 4
MANOR, Jeremiah 19, Elizabeth 17
STEPP, Joseph 54, Nancy 54, Margarett 29, William 23, Joseph 14, Elias 11
MANOR, Jonathan 21, Nancy 20
COLLINSWORTH, Thomas 25, Arty 24 (f), Louisa 6, America 4, Alafair 3, Minerva J. 4/12
COLLINSWORTH, Reuben 55*, Mourning 61
MATHUS, Lucy 42*, John 5, Daniel 1
WERST?, Alexander 56, Lovina 47, William 18, Elizabeth 17, Mary 13, Hiram 9, Henry 1, Susannah 4

Schedule Page 117

MANOR, Isaac 27, Tabitha A. 16, Chana 13, Isaac 9, Rebecca 7
CLAY, James 46, Malinda 32, Yeoman 21, John 16, Mary 31, Mahulda 11, James 8, Andrew 5, Paulina F. 3
CLAY, Jorden 72, Oliva 60
COSSLEY, Elizabeth 42, Julian 4 (f)
PORTER, Benjamin sr. 52, Mary 47, Joseph 17, Elijah 15, Samuel 14, Ann E. 12, Matilda 9
CECIL, Kinsey B. 70*, Elizabeth 39
MULTER, Christopher 15*, Uria 13 (f), Priscilla 12, Mary J. 10, Rhoda 8, Sophia 6, George L. 4
DELONG, Samuel 31, Jemima 27, John 6, Julian 5 (f), David 4, Daniel 1
MCGINNIS, Hiram 41, Sarah 41, George 12, Jackson 11, Angelina 9, James 5, Elizabeth 5
DELONG, Harvey 22, Nancy 18, Minerva J. 4/12, Nancy 38, Cynthia 15, Emery 13
COLLINS, Christopher 43, Cynthia 34, William W. 17, Emeretta 15, Spencer P. 11, Willey M. 11,

- 172 -

1850 Census Johnson County Kentucky

NAncy J. 8, Andrew 7, Samuel J. 4, Rutha 2, Susan A. 1/12
SPEARS, Thomas M. 21, Rebecca J. 20, John W. 2, Amos A. 8/12
BUTCHER, William 25, Mary 25, Amanda 10, Lewis 4, Susan P. 3, Marcus S. 1
WELLS, George 50, Elizabeth 42, James 18, Jemima 15, Martha A. 13, Marion 11, Hiram 9, David 7, Allen 4, George W. 21

Schedule Page 118

HANNA, Ebenezer B. 37*, Susannah 25, Frances G. 3, Andrew J. 1, William R. 2/12
GOBLE, Isaac 19*
SPEARS, Roseann 40*, Harvey 22, Morgan 20, Wiley 19, Susannah 17, Atheya 16, Ruth J. 14, Wells 12, John W. 11, Thomas J. 9, George 7, Moses 5
WELLS, Susanna 71*
DELONG, James 25, Elizabeth 23, John 14, William 13, George W. 10, David 9, James 7, Samuel 4, Sarah 2
MUSICK, Ephram 54, Elizabeth 48, Thomas 15, Celia 13, Moses 11, Ephram 11, Mary 8, Catharine 5, Julian 2 (f)
DICKSON, William 53, Mahalah 25, Nancy 20, Sarah 15, James R. 13, Marlon 10, Isaac 9, Minerva 7, Mahalah 3
PRESTON, Burgess M. 33*, Elizabeth 28, Samuel W. 6, Mary H. 3, Winfield M. 4/12
FRANKLIN, Bird 18*
AUXIER, John B. 33, Angelina 29, Henrietta 5, Benjamin F. 2, no name 6/12 (f), Thomas 39
CASTLE, James B. 30*, Catharine 28, John W. 6, Goerge W. 4, Samuel W. 2, Harvey W. 10/12
PRICE, David J. 25*
MILLER, Philip 45, Mary 45, John S. 17, Sylvester D. 13, Catharine 5, Mary 3
BLAIR, Britton 28, Malinda 27, Sarah A. 3
WARD, James A. 32, Jane 30, William E. 10, Lucina 8, Catharine 6, Shadrach 4, Lovina 2, Elizabeth 6/12
DANIEL, David 23, Sarah 23, Wyatt 3, Henry 1

Schedule Page 119

WELCH, Andrew 24, Sarah 25, Toliver 11, Thomas 10
HANNA, Samuel 48*, Frances 48, Nancy M. 18, Frances E. 16, Samuel 13, John 9
PHILLIPS, Sarah 93*
BROWN, John 53, Catharine 49, William W. 19, Frances 16, John 12
BORDERS, John 56*, Jane 52, Lewis 27, James 6, John 5, Jane 3, Henry 1
WILEY, Lucinda 13*
SPEAR, Enoch 41, Jane 38, Samuel 19, Nancy 17, William K. 15, Elizabeth 13, Thomas 11, Amanda 9, Enoch 7, Violet 4, John 3
FRANKLIN, Joseph 33*, Susannah 35, William J. 6, Frederick 5, Martha 3, Elizabeth 1
FRALEY, Tempa 18*
HICKS, Isaac 30*, Jane 37, Sarah 5, Louisa J. 4, Mary E. 1/12
BALDING, Cynthia A. 22*
ROWLAND, Daniel R. 39, Emely 31, John 7, Armstrong 5, Mary E. 4, Isaac 2, no-name 1/12 (f)
BALDRIDGE, Andrew 36, Martha 35, Minerva J. 14, William 10, Nancy 8, Araminta 7, Clarinda 6, Benjamin 4, Martin 2

1850 Census Johnson County Kentucky

SPRADLIN, James 65*, Rachel 67, Minerva 15, Rachel 14, William 13, James H. 12, Daniel 11, John M. 9, Andrew J. 7
CONLEY, Mary 45*, Jackson 21, Solomon 13
WHEELER, John sr. 40, Anna 38, James 18, Nancy J. 17, William M. 15, John J. 12, Jane 37

Schedule Page 120

AUXIER, Nathaniel 34, Hester A. 30, Samuel L. 11, David 9, George W. 7, Louisa 6, Andrew J. 4, Julia A.? 3, Thomas J. 1
STURGETT, John W. 39, Eilzabeth 37, Lucinda J. 16, Mary H. 14, John J. 12, Amey C. 9, Ann 7, Robert W. 2, Elizabeth 2?/12
NIBERT, James 30*, Amantha A. 18
KENNEDY, Lewis A. 33*, Elizabeth 28, Cornelius W. 6, George W. 3, Minerva 8/12
DAY, Morgan 21*
TYLINGER, Reuben 36*
PRICE, Thomas J. 30, Susan 26, Minerva B. 5, Lynch? J. 3 (f), Clarra H. 2
DANIEL, Mary 54, Peter 17, Wyatt A. 14
MURRY, Jesse 27, Frances 29, Sarah A. 5, Elizabeth 4, John 2, Roderick 4/12
BRADLEY, Cornelius 23, Thursey 22, Emily 2, Mary 1
FANNON, William 53*, Samuel 16, Frances 14, Sarah 10
VANHOOSE, Jane 70*
BORDERS, William 24*, Sarah 18
MEAD, Samuel 20*
DAVIS, Joseph 74, Elizabeth 50, Elizabeth 20, Joseph 16, Mary 14, Julian 11 (f)
MARTIN, James 72, Jandea 60 (f), John P. 15
STAFFORD, John sr. 71*, Mary 61, Davis 23, Lydia 20, Calistia 17, Amanda 14, Julia 10
BOOTH, Elias 25*
RANKIN, Hugh 27*, Elizabeth E. 24, Gertrude W. 2, William B. 1, Lydia S. 1/12
KING, Marcus L. 30, Catharine 27, Mary K. 2
WOOD, Shadrack 21, Nancy H. 20
MURRY, Roderick H. 28, Frances 25, John 6, Exer 5, Jesse 3, Samuel 2, Jane 9/12

Schedule Page 121

BORDERS, Hezekiah 20*, Jemima 21, Jane 2, Elender 8/12
NELSON, Andrew 12*
CASTLE, Henderson 34, Elizabeth 33, John 13, Juliann 12, Emory 10, Henderson 8, Andrew J. 6, Anderson 3, Zepheniah 1, Robert 1/12
BROWN, Archibald 30, Malinda 21
STAMBAUGH, Philip 21, Mary 21, Winfield 1 (f)
MAYO, Lewis 54, Mariah 52, Maranda S. 22, Rebecca 20, Mariah 16, John W. 14, Cynthia 9
SMITH, Jesse 45, Jane 31, David J. 4, Henderson 3, Samuel 5/12
CUNNINGHAM, William 73*, Rachel 59, Mary 34, Peter 22, William 20, Jonathan 17, Timothy 12
COLLINS, Macha? 24 (f)*, Rachel 8, Mary 7, Charles 2, Christopher 10/12
HYDEN, William 28, Margarett 26, Frances 6, Julia 5, Elizabeth 4, Henry 2, Sarah 1/12, Allen 18
MUSICK, John 63, Isabella 60, Mary 25, James K. P. 5
SPEARS, Ruth 60, Samuel 22, Abraham 20, Frances J. 16

1850 Census Johnson County Kentucky

ACRES, Blackburn 45, Elizabeth 40, Rhodes 22, William 20, Robert 17, Mary 15, Nancy 13, John r. 11, Emely K. 6, James H. 3
PORTER, Cornelius H. 28, Sarah 26, Minerva A. 1
WELLS, William G. 32*, Mary 29, Richard 10, Moses 9, Aaron 9, William A. 5, Susannah 4, Narcarius L. 1, Sarah E. 6/12

Schedule Page 122

BUTCHER, Nancy 17*
WEBB, William 34, Mahalah 25, Julyan 13, Cynthia A. 11, William 9, Edmund R. 6, Joseph H. 5, James M. 3, Harvey L. 1, Abel 4/12
WEBB, John 25, Phoeba 22, Eliza A. 3, James A. 1
WEBB, Thomas 20, Nancy 25, John W. 2
LAMBERT, James 54, Mary 39, Elijah 18, Erastus 16, Samuel 13, Lucinda 10, Joseph 7, Mary J. 5, Robert F. 1
WELLS, Moses 46, Margarett 42, John 20, Henry 17, Juliana F. 14, Morgan 12, Nancy 10, Araminta 5
BALDRIDGE, Mary 80, Zacheriah 30, Francis 25
WELLS, William Jun. 24, Mary M. 20
SPEARS, Wiley M. 24, Elizabeth 23, Frances J. 2, Arta 1
ARROWOOD, Garred D. 24, Louisa J. 18, James M. 6/12
WELLS, John 35, Nancy A. 27, Alexander G. 5, William O. 3, Peter F. 1
BUTCHER, Jacob 63, Arta 50, Nancy 18, Hanah 16, Henderson 5
BALDRIDGE, Joseph 32, Nancy 30, Martha 1
MUSICK, James 44, Mariah 40, Mary A. 22, John 18, Andrew 16, Abraham 14, Thereby 11, Archebald 9, Louisa 8, Newton 6, Milton 2
SPEARS, Vincent 27*, Nancy A. 27, Rosey 6, Rebecca 4, George W. 2, Sarah 1/12
AUXIER, Daniel 24*
FLANNIGAR, Drucilla 18*, Alexander 16

Schedule Page 123

STONE, Mary 40, Minerva A. 14, Samuel 13
AUXIER, Samuel 57, Agness 29, Joseph 25, Samuel 23, Martha 21, Thomas J. 16, Margarett 11, Elijah 9, William L. 7, James K. P. 5, Angelina 3
AUXIER, Enoch 55, Mary a. 36, Sarah 15, Lydia J. 14, Samuel 11, Nancy 9, Joseph 4, Emeline 2
BOYD, David 65, Elizabeth 35, Sarah 16, John 13, Mary A. 11, Marion 10, Elizabeth 8, Susan 6, William D. 3, Nancy 1
VANHOOSE, Levi 54, Elizabeth 41, Anna 20, Nancy 18, Henry J. 15, Sarah 13, Rachel 7, Lucetta 4, Moses D. 1
AUXIER, Constance 62*, Lovina L. 19, John J. 18
COBURN, George 18*
BLAIR, James 23, Nancy 21
SETTSER, Abner 36, Sarah A. 24, Minervia J. 7, Julia A. 5, Christopher W. 2
NOBLE, Blair Sen. 70, Mary 70, Hayden 20, Mary 22
COLEMAN, Peter 56, Hester A. 32, John 16, Adam 13, Andrew 11, Victoria 8, Steward 6, Malissa 2
BLAIR, George 61, Mary 61, Marinda 23, John 18, Asa 16
BLAIR, Noble Jun. 33, Talitha 30, Andrew B. 9, William J. 7, General J. 4, Sirena 1

1850 Census Johnson County Kentucky

COLLINS, George 29*, Mary 27, Sanford 8, John W. 3, Melvina 1/12
WORKMAN, Elizabeth 24*
PATRICK, Hugh 45, Ritter 45 (f), Merida 13 (m), Rebecca 12, Louisa 10, Cambridge C. 8, Granberry 6, Hernod 4, Noah 2

Schedule Page 124

BLAIR, William 35, Saml. 35, Wallace B. 14, Elizabeth 13, Nancy 11, Malinda 7
RICE, Martin R. 40, Mary 22, Harrison 18, Elizabeth 16, John 13, Samuel 11, Wiley 9, Nancy J. 5, Catharine 3, Lydia 4/12
RICE, Nancy 63
CONLEY, Henrey 41, Rebecca 35, Constantine 18, Celia 17, William 15, Thomas 14, Mahalah 11, Elenora 10, Mary 9, John 6, Marinda 4, Lucina 3, Amanda 10/12
SPRADLIN, James 26, Temperance 23, Benjamin F. 5, Tryphena 2, Rachel 9/12
FAIRCHILD, Ebenezer 24, Jincey 21
RICE, Andrwe J. 27, Phoeba 25, John H. 4, Martha S. 2, Benjamin F. 10/12
FAIRCHILD, Ely M. 20, Malissa J. 18
FAIRCHILD, Asa j. 49, Nancy 47, Susan 22, John H. 14, George W. 12, Mary J. 10, Martha 7, Amanda 3
RICE, Isaac 27*, Celia 27, Phoeba 10, Alexander 8, Samuel 6, Andrwe 4, James 2, Thomas 1
CONLEY, Susan 70*
PATRICK, Jilson P. 29, Malinda 21, Amanda J. 3, Louisa 1
SPRADLIN, John 20, Elizabeth 22, Reuben 2/12
ARMS, Aaron 37, Elizabeth 42, Elias 16, wallace 13, Sarah 11, Phoeba 9, Elijah 7, Rachel 6, James 4, William 2

Schedule Page 125

KISTNER, Christopher 29*, Harriett S. 24
COLE, Perry 9*
FITZPATRICK, John 65, Martha 70
BUTLER, Arminta 41*, Andrwe 19, Robert 17, George 15, John 12, James 10, Elizabeth 7, Araminta 4
CLAY, Mathew 29*, George H. 4
REMY, James 48, Anna 51, Elizabeth 21, Sarah 19, Mary 17, Thomas W. 13
WITLEN, William 58, Lockey 49, Rebecca 22, Malinda 16, Nancy J. 14, William 11, Thomas F. 9, Francis M. 6
COLLINS, Martha 43*, Lively E. 21, Wiley J. 17, Cordelia 1
DALE, Jemima 75*
DICKSON, Henry 76*, Joicey 76, Elizabeth 42, Sarah 31, John J. 21
FRANKLIN, James M. 19*
YOUNG, Charles 37, Lovina 35, Phoeba 15, Benjamin 13, Nancy 8, Jane 5, John 4, Lear 2
LAYNE, David 41, Lydia 37, Frances 17, Lindsey 12, Sarah 10, James A. 7, Marion D. 3
PRICE, Jesse Jr. 24, Dicey 22
MAYS, Winston 36, Cynthia F. 35, Charles L. 14, Henry H. 13, Susan R. 11, Millard 8/12

1850 Census Lawrence County Kentucky

Schedule Page 50

MARTIN, O. W. 44 (m)*, Julyann 34, James R. 6
ASHFORD, John D. 40*
JOHNSON, Joseph 24*
DEMETT, Shedk. 28*
PIGG, Mary 24*
LARGE, Wm. G. 24, Malissa 20, Mary G. 3, Genl. Taylor 2
BURTEN, Saml. 22, Nancy 19, Sarilda J. 2/12?
FRASURE, Irvin 25, Anna 20, Lewis D. 1
GRAHAM, Benjm. 38*, Margaret 32, Andrew 12, Mary L. 9, Richd. 6, Oliver P. 4, Harden O. 1
MEAD, Susan 18*
MOORE, James 42, Katharine 32, Elizabeth 14, Nancy 11, Wm. T. 8, John B. 7, Benjm. 4, Margaret 2
BERRY, Reuben 27*, Nancy 27, Wm. J. 6, John W. 4, Hugh T. 3, James M. 1
CARNUTT, Elizabeth 22*
BERRY, Wm. 33, Elizabeth 38, Rebecca 14, Nancy J. 13, Lucinda? 10, John M. 8, Sarahann 7, Arameca 5, Reuben F. 4, Isaac 2, Emly C. 9
BURTEN, Rebecca 65, Franklin 23, James 18
ADAMS, John 31, Katharine 30, James 10, Wm. 8, Milly 6, Sarah A. 4, John Jr. 2
WHITE, James 55*, Sidney R. 61 (f)
MEAK, Madison W. 15*
ARONHART, Elizabeth 79*
LARGE, Wm. 38*, Nancy 37, Lucy 11, John F. 6, Wm. Jr. 5, Saml.? H. 3, Nancy 1
YOUNG, Lady? 70*
ADAMS, Isaac A. 33*, Martha 31, Arthur Jr. 7, James 7, Frances 6, Covey 4 (m)
CARTER, Sarah 13?*
BERRY, James 34, Jane 35, Sarah 14, John 11, Arthur 9, Elizabeth 5, Alford 3

Schedule Page 51

ADAMS, Martha 21*, Frances 21
DURIFIELD, Emma 65*
ADAMS, Arthur 61, Frances 51, Mary 19, Perry 16, Reece 14 (f), Martha 14
CARTER, David 60*, Malinda 40, Robt. H. 7, James R. 2
JORDAN, Covey 65 (m)*
ADAMS, Wm. 25*, Elizabeth 25, Mahale 4, Greenvill 2, Martin 1
CARTER, Thomas 8*, Mahale 10 (f)
BERRY, Isaac 29, Jane 29, Sarah 6, Charlotte E. 5, Nancy 4, Alford N. 2, Hiram C. 1
JORDAN, John 31, Martha 25, Alafan 10 (f), Jesse 8, Rebecca 6, Frances G.? 2, Mary L. 7
ROBERTS, Geo. 62, Martha 60, Juliaan 18, Lucy Jane 15, Garner R. 7
BERRY, Thompson 33, Melvina 27, Rece 8 (f), Louisa 6, Nancy 4, Reuben 2, Polly 1
HARRIS, Asbury 28*, Catharine 24, John W. Jr. 4, Elizabeth R. 1
HALL, Mary 57*
SKEINS, Hiram 53, Mary S. 44, Susan 17, James 16, Margaret 14, Ama 12, John 10, Wm. 6, Harvy 4
WHEELER, John R. 29, Rachel 29, James LO. 8, Eleanor 7, Frances 5, Joshua 3, Wm. H. 2, Henry 1/12
ADKINS, Thomas P. 38, Jane 24, Francis M. 5, Sarah 2, John 9/12
CHAFIN, John 65, Elvira 50, James 24, David C. 21, Harvey 18, Elizabeth 16, Sarah J. 14, Francis M. 12

1850 Census Lawrence County Kentucky

Schedule Page 52

CARTER, Jeremiah 43, Celia 37, John 16, Lucinda 14, Deresa 12, James 9, Wm. 7, Landon 4, Mary 2, Benjm. F. 1
CARNETTE, Reuben Jr. 37, Zelpha 37, John 15, David Jr. 15, Mary 13, Derecia 11, Sarah Ann 8, Thursey 6, James 4, Louvina 1
WELMAN, Elisha 66, Sarah 56, David 36, Jeremiah 25, Nancy 21, Elizabeth 19, Lewis T. 18, Geo. W. 16, Sarah 14
BURTEN, Andw. 30, Rachel 30, Wm. 7, Barnett 5, Andrew J. 3, Lydia 9/12
LIONS, David 30, Minerva 32, Wm. L. 11?, Maria J. 7, Susan 3, Mary 1
WELMAN, Bennett 34, Maria 35, Josaphine 8, Elisha F. 6
WELMAN, James 32, Eunice 28
WELMAN, Elisha Jr. 27, Frances 23, Oliver 3, Lewis F. 1
YOUNG, John 48, Luanna 26, Robt. 8, Rachel 10/12, Mary 16
WOODS, Andrew 41, Nancy 32, James 19, Sarah 9, Wm. H. 8, Ephraim M. 5, Rutha 3, John W. 1
YOUNG, Jesse 51, Rachel 46, John Jr. 24, Wm. 21, James 19, Nancy Ann 16, Jesse 14, Thomas 11, Perry C. 9, Sarahan 6, Danl. B. 3

Schedule Page 53

SPELMAN, Hiram 43, Elizabeth 42, Isom 22, Sarah J. 20, Leah 19, John 17, Saml. 15, Elizabeth 14, Rachel 12, Wm. 7, Alexr. 3, James 4/12
YOUNG, Saml. 32, Mary 41, linda R. 13, Anjaline 12, Pricilla 10, Robt. W. 8, Andrew M. 7, Judy 4, Elizabeth 6/12
MEEK, John 60*, Precilla 41, Lorena 5/12
JOBE, Wm. 21*, Nancy 18, Elisha 16, Henry 14, Judeth 13, Mary 11, Sarah 7
MOORE, David 56, Mary 40, Alexr. 20, Elisha 19, Amanda 16, Mary J. 14, David N. 12, Nancy 9, Mahala 7
BLEVENS, Ephraim 45, Letty 50, James 24, Nancy 23, Hannah 21, Emaline 16, Andrew 14, Letty 13, Rebecca 10
CARNETT, David 50, Didemia 45, Dicy 26, Wm. M. 22, Nancy 20, Elisha Jr. 18, Mary 15, Reuben 15, James 12, Sarah J. 10, Benjm. F. 4
SHORT, Andrew 45, Nancy 27, Dicy 19, Elizabeth 16, James 12
LEVETMAN?, Neri? 72 (m), Mildred 72
CLEVENGER, Joshua 51*, Nancy 37, Martha 16, Susan 12, John 14, Joshua Jr. 10, Thos. 10, Alexr. 8, Sarah 6, Sintha 4, Hannah 1/12
LOAR?, Charlotte 19*
PARKER, James 67, Sarah 51, Rachel 27, Martha 21, Nancy 19, Saml. 15, Elizabeth 13, Lucinda 11, Wm. 6, Anna 5

Schedule Page 54

LOAR?, Moses 21*
JUSTICE, Eliut? 35, Serviry 13, John 9, Angaline 6, Corrilda 4
ROSE, James W. 40, Nancy 37, Martha 18, John J. 16, Nancy L. 14, July A. 12, Elizabeth 10, James M. 8, Lydia 5, Saml. 3, Mary F. 1/12

1850 Census Lawrence County Kentucky

WHEELER, James 50*, Elizabeth 49, Wm. 19, James Jr. 17, Stephen 15, Amos 13, Danl. 12, Elizabeth 10
GENT, Jane 14*
YOUNG, Harrison 40*, Henry 12, Robt. 10
BURTON, Polly 25*, Thos. 9, Marien 7, Abram 4, Eliza 2, Manerva 1/12
YOUNG, John Jr. 18, Elizabeth 18
HOLBROOK, Ambrose 52*, Nancy 56, Ralph 26, Louisa 21, Campbell 17, Ambrose 13
GENT, Rachel 10*
MURPHEY, Wm. 29*, Isabel 36, James 4, Deresa 4/12?
GREEN, Elizabeth 15*, Winney 12, Danl. 7
SHORT, James 27*, Matilda 19, Mary 2, Elizabeth 73
CARNETT, Elisha 31*, Derese 22 (f), Nancy 3/12
CARTER, James 25*, Nancy 22, Mary E. 3, Perlina 1
JORDAN, Robt. 20*
ROBERTS, Wm. F. 25, Jane 22, Mary 3, Gasper N. 2, Elizabeth A 10/12
ROBERTS, Geo. W. 36, Julia 36, Rebecca 15, Christian 13, Mary J. 11, Caroline 9, Geo. G. 7, Katharine 5, Rufus 3, Martha E. 1

Schedule Page 55

HALE, Zachariah 58*, Rebecca 54, Mary J. 13
FLAWHOR?, Rebecca 8*
STONE, Ira 7*
PARKER, John 30, Elisa 9
WELMAN, John 40, Hannah 40, Sarahan 19, Elisha 17, Rebecca 15, Frances 14, James 12, Lewis 11, Nancy 8, Noah 6, David 4, Caroline 3, Tilford 4/12
LEVITMANN, E. M. 34 (m), Sintha 25, Serelda 9, Julia A. 7, Pelina 5, Neri Jr. 3, Leander M. 1
LUSTER, Wm. 37, Rutha 37, Harvy 16, David 15, Isaac 13, Margaret 11, Thos. 9, Katharine 6, Nancy 3
BOGGS, David 44, Sarah 45, Mary 23
BOGGS, John 21, Randol 19, Ephraim 16, Alford 14, James 12, Nancy 10, Sarah 9, Wm. 8, Hugh 5, Elijah 2
SPARKS, Wiley 42, James 7, Jarca? A.? 3, Sintha 30, Nancy 16, Mary 15, Lindsey 11, Washington 6, Matilda 9/12
BOGGS, High 48*, Hannah 46, Nelson 14, Matilda 10, Elenor 8, Rena 5
BLEVENS, Lewis 19*, Hannah 90
BOGGS, Elijah 27*, Katharine 22, Washington 5, Demanda 3, Garret 1, Nancy 66
WELLS, Cristena 15*
LION, Jesse 61, Anna 57, Sarah 20, Ransom 20, Marinda 18, Corbin 14, Caleb 11, Frances 70

Schedule Page 56

HOLBROOK, John 65, Mary 64, Mary 23, Thursey 21
HOLBROOK, Wm. L. 30, Elizabeth 20
SCAGGS, Moses 47, Elizabeth 43, Jeremiah 21, Mary 18, Katharine 16, Lydia 13, Randol 11, Lewis 9, Danl. 4, Wm. 2
HOLBROOK, Elizabeth 24, Wm. H. 2, Benjm. F. 11/12
SCAGGS, Christian 42, Elizabeth 39, Martin 18, Martha 16, Peter 15, Miles 14, John 11, Rutha 7, Soloman 4, Doc J. 10/12

- 179 -

1850 Census Lawrence County Kentucky

BURTEN, Detroit 37, Nancy 35, David 17, John 16, Rebecca 14, Maranda 12, Menca 10, Hardin 8, Nancy 7, Marthaan 6, Mary J. 3, Detroit Jr. 1
WALDECK, N. C. 38 (m)*, Maria 37, Mary E. 12, Wm. H. 7, Elizabeth A. 5, James F. 3, John A. 1
DUNLAP, Martha 25?*
RICE, Wm. C. 27, Mary 20, Nelson T. 3, Thos. J. 1, Charles W. 11/12
GRIFFETH, James 48, Elizabeth 43, Walter 21, James Jr. 19, Elsy 17 (m), John 10, Elizabeth 5, Harrison 3, Clarinda 1, John 37
OSBURN, Walter 47*, Sarah 43, Meredith 24, Thos. 23, Elizabeth 13, Edmd. 15, Elisa 11, Chilton 7, Nancy 5, Chilton, 7, Nancy 5, Charles 3, James L. 9/12
SCAGGS, Retha 24*
EDWARDS, Wm. 25, Laura? 20, Meredith 3, Samantha 2, Milly 2/12?

Schedule Page 57

EDWARDS, Isaac 27, Elizabeth 36
GRIFFITH, Abraham 23, Mary 16, Susan 9/12
SWETNIM?, C. L. 43 (m), Dereca 38, Milton F. 11, Sarah J. 9, Emly A. E. 7, Mary E. 5
SWETNIM?, Neri 36
RATLIFF, Zachariah 37*, Mary 26, Sarah 16, David 14, Mary 24, Sarah 16, David 14, Mary 12, Robt. 10
GRIFFITH, Nelly 7*, Johnson 10
GRAHAM, Jesse 41, Eunice 32, Charmalet 16 (f), Gilson P. 14, Elisa 10, Merica 8, Alafair 6 (f), Lear 2, Thos. 1
RUDD, Riley 59, Mary 60
WARD, Wm. 51, Elizabeth 47, Frances 27, James G. 24, Mary 19, Viletta B. 17, Soloman 16, Elizabeth 8, Wm. B. 6
AUXIER?, Jackson 32*, Nancy 31, Elsy 14 (m), John M. 7
ROSE, James 14*
MURPHEY, John 27, Maryan 18, Mary J. 9/12
GRAHAM, James 44*, Mary 40, Louvena 21, Wm. W. 18, Layfayett 16, Martin V. 14, Granville A. 12, Larkin M. 10, Emly 6, James K. 3, Marcus N. 2
MEAD, Martha 17*
BRAMMER, Amoml. 51*, Mary 53
ROSE, Edward 16*
HENSLEY, Sarah 24*, Emanl. J. 1
WALTERS, Wm. 52*, Elizabeth 42
CORDILE, Elanor 22*
JUSTICE, Sarah 5*
LUSTER, Lindsy 37*
KICHEN, James 34, Malinda 33, Maryan 11, Martha J. 10, Wm. R. 9, Elizabeth 7, Lewis 6, John 4, Emaline 11/12
JORDAN, John 30, Druda 25, Fleming 4, Elisha 2, Jeremiah 1, Elizabeth 1/12

Schedule Page 58

JORDAN, Benjm. 30, Milly 36, Wm. 16, Jeremiah 14, Madison 12, Phebe 9, Nancy 6, Geo. 5, John 3, Elisa 9/2

1850 Census Lawrence County Kentucky

KISEE, John 20, Mary 18, Wm. H. 1
HAM, James H. 31*, Sarahan 22, Mary E. 5, Lucyan 1
GOINGS, Harriett A. 10*
YOUNG, James 44*, Jane 43, Louvina 16, Franklin 15, Alford 13, Henry H. 11, Martha A. 8, Elizabeth 6, Jesse 2, Mary R. 1
DUREFIELD, James H. 2*
HOLBROOK, John 42, Rebecca 38, Phebe 19, Wm. H. 19, Campbell R. 16, Jemima 14, David 12, Mary? 6, John H. 4, Dehart 1/12
GAMBLE, Wm. 31, Jemima 29, John J. 7, Henry H. 5, Meredith 3, Leander 1
GAMBLE, John 24, Rena 23, Wm. F. 1
GAMBLE, Martin 34, Mahala 33, Elizabeth 10, W. H. 8, Sintha 6, Nathan 4, Katharine 2
HOLBROOK, Menard 32
LUSTER, Harvey 44, Katharine 44, Thos. 20, David 17, James 15, Lindsey 12, Lewis 11, Nancy 8, Wm. 5, Geo. 3, John 6/12
HOLBROOK, Randol 34, Mary 33, Neoma 14, Filanden 12, Milly 10, Nancy 5
MOXLEY, Henry 34, Phebe 24, Louisa 15, John 11, Ali? 8 (f), Henderson 5, Elizabeth 1

Schedule Page 59

HOLBROOK, Randol 72, Hannah 82
TERRY, Miles 60*, Nancy 58, Rutha 22, Wm. 17
HILL, James 20*
PELFRY, Isaac 31, Martha 33, John 11, Miles 9, Wm. 6, Nancy 3
HILL, Wiley 23, Malinda 19
TERRY, John 32, Sarah 30, Martha 7, Miles Jr. 5, Nancy J. 4, Mary 3, Saml. 7/12
HANNAH, Joseph H. 56*, Nancy 46, John 19, Elizabeth 15, Joseph Jr. 13, David 11
ROSE, Nancy J. 7*
HILL, Wesley 47, Mary 53, James C. 20, David H. 17, Hannah J. 16, Spencer J. 14, Drusilla H. 12, Wesley H. 10
SCAGGS, John Jr. 25, Mary 23, Sarahan 4, Lewis 4, Henry 2
SCAGGS, John 53, Mary 49, Martin 21, Nancy 20, Dicy 17, Mary 15, Andrew 16, Rebecca 11, Emly 9, Letty 3, Martha 74
SCAGGS, James 30
FIFE, Joseph 32, Martha 25, James 5, Mary 3, Frances 1
CONLEY, Ezekial 22, Elizabeth 19
ROSE, Wm. 34, Sarah 22, Wilson 6
SCAGGS, Lewis 31*, Sarah 30, Martha 8, James 5, Layfaette 3, Andrew 1
WILLIAMS, John 6*
ELDRIDGE, sarah 14*, Wm. 18
ROSE, Wm. 65, Elizabeth 55, Sarah 27
DEER, James 26, Elizabeth 28, Angeline 1

Schedule Page 60

FIFE, Wm. 43, Sebre 38, Elizabeth 16, Sarahann 14, Pelina 13, Wm. H. 8, Frances L. 5, Melvin F. 3, John 1
KELLY, James 55, Anna 40, James Jr. 16, Robt. 14, Wm. 6

1850 Census Lawrence County Kentucky

FIFE, John 41*, Anna 41, Wm. 18, John 15, Cambridge 14, Joseph 12, Larue 8 (f), Meredith 5 (f), Miram 2, Henry C. 2/12
OLFORD, Milly 44*
RIGSBY, Drury 48, Nancy 36, Sarah 15, Rhoda 13, Wm. 11, Thomas 9, Larkin 3, John 1
FIFE, Saml. 32, Fama 21, Sarah 6, Jackson 5, Frances 3, Nancy 1
HILL, Wm. R. 27, Nancy 25, John 4, William 2, Wiley C. 1
HAY, James 49, Elizabeth 42, Henry 21, Mary 19, John 17, Thos. 15, James Jr. 13, Wm. 11, Geo. W. 7, Elizabeth 4, Jesse 2
HAY, Thomas 36
SPARKS, Calvin 43, Sarah 43, Alford 19, Mary 13, Pelina 10, Nelson 5, Benton 1
SPARKS, Levi 72*, Sarah 69, John 26
DEBOAD, Louisa 22*
SPARKS, Garred 47, Elizabeth 41, Reuben 21, Eleanor 21, Levi J. 19, Sarah C. 18, Hugh 16, Matheny 14 (f), Nancy A. 13, Jemima 11, Walter W. 9, Rebecca 8, David L. 6, Phebe J. 5, Sidney L. 2 (f)

Schedule Page 61

GAMBLE, Elizabeth 50, Jesse 19, Ederson 16, Mary 14, Renna 7, Susan 20
COLYIER, John 52, Mary 46, Wm. 23, John Jr. 21, David 19, Lucinda 15, Elizabeth 13, Katharine 10, Benjm. 9, Nancy 7
WILLIAMS, Noah 41, Susannah 39, Robt. 20, Kning? 19 (m), Morris 14, Thos. J. 12, James M. 8, Washington 6, Hardin B. 4, Lutia 2, Elizabeth 1
WOODS, James 43, Mary 41, Margaret 21, Andrew 19, Meredith 17, Robt. 15, James 14, Elizabeth 11, Nancy 9, John 6, Mary 5, Greenville 3
PRINCE, Wilson 25, Zelpha 23, Louisa 2, Susan 4/12, Margaret 11
RAINEY, Joshua 45, Nancy 41, James W. 18, Elizabeth 17, John 16, Wm. 14, Eleanor 11, Eleasor 12, Amos 5, Isaac 1
HALL, John 21, Nancy 21, Richd. M. 3, Lucyan 11/12
RAINY, Thadeus 36, Diama 25, Franklin 14, Saml. 12, John 10, Susan 9, Jane 9, Wm. 7, Perry 6, Owen H. 2
BISHOP, Geo. 31, Elizabeth 25, Lucinda 5, Mahala 3, Rebecca 2, Geo. W. 1
CORDILL, James 24, Eleanor 19, Jane 1
CORDILL, Wm. 47, Jane 45, Pherebe 16, Wm. 14, Jesse 10, Jane 8, Ralph 6

Schedule Page 62

WILLIAMS, Lewis 43, Susanah 46, Wm. 19, Sarahan 15, Dicy C. 13, Susan E. 12, John 10, Nancy R. 8, Elisa 5, Clarinda 4, Alice 1
WILLIAMS, Jacob P. 21, Phebe 18
SHORT, Danl. 43*, Diana 33
JUSTICE, Wm. 27*
CHAFIN, Dicy 30*, Susanah 7, Elsy M. 4
WHEELER, Joshua 26*, Kesiah 26, Henderson 4, James M. 2, Geo. W. 2/12
RAINEY, James W. 19*
CAINS, Thos. 63, Candes 67
GOINGS, Geo. W. 22, Mary 23, Alexr. 6/12
FULLER, Obadiah 48, Pricy 33, Wm. T. 13, James L. 11, Elizabeth M. 9, Benton 7, Permelia 5, Jane 1

1850 Census Lawrence County Kentucky

BURK, Evan 46*, Elizabeth 44, James H. 18, Andrew B. 2
MCCALL, Robt. 21*, Elisa 15
DEAN, John 48, Julyann 36, Wm. E. 19, Hester Ann 16, Mary F. 14, Martha A. 12, Marshall 10, Sarah 7, Jacob F. 6, Flora 4, Sinthaan 1, Woodson 21
LEAKEN, John R. 28, Evalins 18, George 2, Julyann 8/12
THOMPSON, John 67*
RUSSELL, Mary 50*
HARDESTY, Geo. 25*
BRADLEY, George 35, Elizabeth 30, James 13, Saulda A. 12, Wm. A. 9, Malinda 7, Granville 4, Nancyan 5/12
SKEINS, Wm. 49, Anna 32, Frances 17, Geo. 14, Amanda 12, Wm. 10, Peter 8, Saml. 4, John 1

Schedule Page 63

LAYNE, James L. 43, Judith 40, Elizabeth P. 9, Nancy Ann 6, Milly 4, James Jr. 1
DORNEY, John 58, Mary 40, Ezekial 11, Caroline 9, Elizabeth 7, Mary 4, Nancy 1
PEERY, Wm. 37, Claricy 29, Louisa 11, Sarah 9, Collumbus 7, Nancy 6, Charles 4, Matilda 2
CAMPBELL, Layne 27*
HATTON, Melville 23*
DAVIS, Hickman 20, Nancy 19
HARRIS, Saml. 33*, Katharine 18, Nathanl. L. 1, Louisa 3/12
CANTERBURY, Elizabeth 46*, Maryan 17, Wm. 14, Henry L. 3
SPERRY, Benjm. 43, Lucinda 23, James M. 2, Elisaan 1, Nancy 81
CHAFIN, Simon 58, Amanda 39, Mathias? C. 16, Anna 15, Clarinda 12, Wm. 10, Nancyan 5, Mary J. 4
SPERRY, Rudelph 46, Nancy 43, James H. 16, Jackson F. 15, Susan 13, Joseph R. 12, Nancy 10, Milton 8, Rudelph Jr. 5, Van D. 3
MORROW, Hiram 23, Maryan 23, John 3, Maria 2
STEWERT, John 27, Merica 22, Serepta 5, Silveter 3
GUSTON, Ashbel 76, Sarah 71, David 38, Alexr. 18
STEWERT, Absalom 45, Rachel 42, Elizabeth 20, David 17, Charles 79
STEWERT, Chales? 43, Sarah 40, Westly 16, Nancy 14, Sarah 12, Mary 9, Rachel 7, Martha 4, Geo. S. 1

Schedule Page 64

THOMPSON, Richd. W. 49*, Elizabeth 53, James B. 18, Elisa Ann 15, Sindalina 10, Landen C. 9
DIER, Nancy 8*
STEWERT, Geo. S. 27*, Sarilda 23, James H. 4, Lavina 2
STONE, Elizabeth 12*
LINDSEY, James 29, Elizabeth 21, Wm. M. 3, Walter 2/12
DUNCAN, A. J. 30 (m), Lucinda 25, H. C. 6 (m), Rebecca J. 4
WOODS, John 55, Mary 52, Sarilda 22, Ira 21, John Jr. 20, Sarah 17, Andrew 16, Amanda 14, Wm. 11, Frances 6
HUFF, H. J. 32 (m), Elizabeth 25, Wm. S. 9, Lucy G. 7, Lydia F. 5, Sarah J. 3, Francis M. 1
POE, Saml. 33, Eleanor 31, Isaac 11, Mary 9, Sarah 7, James 6, Julyann 3, Jacob 1, Mary 26
HAMILTON, David 23, Nancy 23, James W. 5, Sarah J. 3, Amanda 5/12
SHORT, Wm. 38*, Emly 37, Elizabeth 17, Jamima 14, Garred 12, James 9, Saml. 7, Margaret 6, Ira 1

1850 Census Lawrence County Kentucky

REEVES, Holt 18*
BASWELL, Elias 46, Elizabeth 45, Wiley 21, Wm. H. 17, Pelina 19, Martin S. 15, James B. 14, Maraba L. 12, Louisa 43, Elisa R. 16, Elias H. 2
LAMBERT, Sarah 63*, Elizabeth 25, Hiram 23, Maryan 2
FRENCH, Rebecca 21*
CASEY, James 42*, Sarah 31, Danl. J. 14, Elizabeth 12, James W. 9, Charity 7, John N. 4, Martin 2

Schedule Page 65

DIER, Lucyan 17*
LARGE, Wm. 35, Nancy 26, Martin? S. 8, Martha J. 5, Nancy 3, Wm. F. 2, Joseph R. 1
HUCHERSON, Lewis 47, Frances 51, Maryan 24, Eleanor E. 20, Delila 17, Vinson 15, Harry 12, Thos. 10, Geo. 9, Henderson 6
HULETT, J. D. 34 (m), Seletha 23, Elizabeth 12, Wm. 9, Milton 8, Layfayette 5, Sarah J. 3, Susan 1
BRADLEY, Micajah 46, Margaret 38, John 20, Harvy 16, Martha 13, Cornelius 12, Ballard P. 10, Louverna 11, Ausker 8, Elias 5, Felix 3, Delila 1, Wm. 75, Jemima 74
STEWERT, Harvy 37, Sarah 21, Rhoda M. 8
PARKER, H. W. 35 (m)*, Katharine 38, Rhoda J. 10, David W. 6, Mary F. 3, Wm. H. 1
MCKINSTER, Clemintine 22*
GOINGS, Mary 45*, Margaret 17, Lucy 20, Harriet A. 10, Virginia 8, Elisabeth 3
ADAMS, Fisher H. 38*
SHORT, James 32, Martha 20, Adelaid 6/12, Thomas 56, Jemima 52
ELKINS, Miles 24, Maria 23, Elisa J. 2, Wm. F. 6/12, Overton 19
JORDAN, John J. 29, Martha 25, Angeline 5, Mary L. 3, James L. 2, Jesse 27
PRICE, Robt. 50, Nancy 40, Delila 19, Mary J. 15, Stephen 12, Robt. Jr. 9, John 6, Geo. 2, Andw. 2

Schedule Page 66

HUCHERSON, John 22, Almeda 21, Lorenzo 6/12
COOKSY, John 34*, Nancy 32, Greenville 9, Franklin 7, Layfayette 5, Ira 3, Wm. 1
ROSE, Sarah 21*
FOSTER, Jacob 33, Evy 31, Nancyan 10, Lorena 7, Permelia 5, Charles B. 2, Eleanor 5/12
JOHNSON, Elijah 40, Precilla 34, John 16, Sarah 14, Jeremiah 12, George 10, Pricy 8 (f), Martha A. 6, Manerva 3, Silvester 6/12
POE, James 34, Rutha L. 21, Nancy P.? 1/12, Sarah 17
GRUBB, James 36, Elizabeth 30
SERGENT, Stephen 27, Jane 10, Rebecca 6
COOKSY, Andrew 26, Maryann 22, Martha 1
LARGE, Robt. 50, Lucy 46, Sumner 19, Ann A. 17, Andrew 14, James 12, Elizabeth 10, Sarah J. 8, Landaff W. 5
JORDAN, Benjm. 25, Mary 23, Sylvan 2/12 (f)
BROWN, John 42, Elizabeth 36, Maryan 15, Geo. W. 13, John W. 12, Malinda 6, Nancy 4, Anna 2, Elizabeth 1
FERRELL, Charles 26*
JUSTICE, Sarah 23*, Anna 3, Elizabeth 2
COOKSY, Jonathon 53, Elizabeth 52, Soloman 23, Winney 20, Albert 19
THOMPSON, Martin 48*, Anna 43, Andrew L. 20, Flenning 18, David 17, Nancy 15, Mary 10, Melly 9, Martin V. B. 8, Simpson 6, Jane 4, Greenville 1

1850 Census Lawrence County Kentucky

Schedule Page 67

AUXER, Nancy 87*
THOMPSON, James 26*, Mary 4, Wm. 2
BALL, Letty 20*, Thomas 1/12
THOMPSON, John 22, Abagail 22
MURPHEY, Arch 29, Martha 38, Elisa J. 4, Alexr. 2
BOWLING, Delana 26, Matilda 27, Rebecca 5, Diana 1
LITRELL, Johnson 27, Mary 27, Wm. P. 6, Layfayette 4, Martin V. 2
WITHEROW, Wm. 48*, Rebecca 50, Wm. Jr. 18, Alford 16, Malissa J. 13, Henry 11
GRIFFITH, John 8*, Nelly 7
RATCLIFF, Elijah 44, Mary 43, David 18, Susanah 16, Fleming 14, Isaac 13, Mary 9, Francis M. 6, Noah 5, James M. 1/12, John 2
LEMINGS, Wm. 41*, Jane 35, James 16, Anderson 14, Elizabeth 11, Susan 9, Sarah 7, John 6, Mahale 2, Rebecca 6/12, Isaac 6/12, Mary 5
RATCLIFF, Wm. 20*, Elizabeth 34
LEMING, Saml. 69, Nancy 63
GRIFFETH, Jesse 42, Margaret 39, Archabald 21, James 17, Andrew 14, John 12, David 9, Leva ann 5, Robt. 7, Wm. 2, Nancy 2
PENINGTON, Alford 40, Mary 38, Elizabeth 18, Lucinda 14, Abagail 12, John W. 8, Mary 7
PENINGTON, Wm. J. 19, Margaret 17, Abel 27
KICHEN, Geo. 25?, Delila 23, Sarah 9, Nehemiah 7, Levi 6, Mary J. 4, Rebecca 2, Marinda 2/12

Schedule Page 68

HENSLY, Wm. 23, Nancy 21, Saml. 1
KICHEN, John 66, Sarah 61
HENSLY, Rebecca 49, Wesley 21, Thos. 18, Isom 16, Leah 12
KELLY, Rebecca 50, Mahale 21, John 20, James 20, Rebecca 17
HENSLY, James 26*, Jane 26, Elizabeth 8, Rebecca 7, Louisa 4, Nelson 2, John W. 2/12
GRIFFETH, Elizabeth 57*
PERKINS, Agnet 23 (f), Henry C. 7, Milton 4, Isabel 6/12
PRINCE, James 31, Elizabeth 27, William 10, Rebecca 9, Nancy 7, Elisa 5, Isaac 4, Eleanor 2
PRINCE, Zachariah 24, Serilda J. 18, Elisa J. 13, Wm. 2
PRINCE, Thos. 26, Mary 22, Carter H. 1
PRINCE, Rachel 46*, Clary 40
RICE, Susan 7*
WEBB, Elizabeth 58*, Wesley 27, Mary 21, Genl. W. 19
RATLIFF, Isaac 12*
SANDERS, Jesse M. 50, Nancy 46, Nathanl. 21, Mary 19, Ann 17, Juda 14, Patre? 10 (f), Allen 13, Peter 9, Martha 7
PENINGTON, John 54, Rachel 51, Lucinda 8, John W. 6
PENINGTON, John W. 23*, Agnis 23
WEBB, Marthan 5*, Elizabeth 3
PENINGTON, Elisha 34*, Nancy 30, Jemima 13, Abagail 11, John M. 9, Sarah 6
PRINCE, Rebecca 22*

1850 Census Lawrence County Kentucky

PENINGTON, Elijah 36, Elizabeth 36, Didama 17, Nelson 15, Eli 13, James 11, Frances 9, Abel 7, Danl. 4, Elijah 1

Schedule Page 69

PENINGTON, Wm. 43*, Delila 43, Nancy 20, Levi 18, Elizabeth 14, Andrew 15, Frances 10, Alford 8, William 6, Susanah 5
YATES, Thompson 23*
ROBERTSON, Elizabeth 18*
PENINGTON, James W. 51, Eleanor 45, Henry 23, Isabel 20, John 18, James 15, Abagail 13, Benjm. 11, Huse 9, Francis M. 5, Elizabeth 3
LEARS?, Elisabeth 47, Wm. 16, Louisa 14, Maria 9, Verlina 9, Harvey 6
PENINGTON, Elisha Jr. 24, Sarah 24, Mary J. 1
PENINGTON, Wm. 28, Elizabeth 21, Rebecca M. 3, Jane 2, Wm. J. 7/12
MCDAVID, James 35*, Anna 22, Mary 6/12
EASTRAM, Elizabeth 15*
BOOTH, James 26
MARSHALL, James 34*, Mary 29
GILKEY, Greenville 15*
BOGGS, John R. 23, Martha J. 22
PENINGTON, James 30, Sela 21, Soloman 5, Wm. H. 10/12
PENINGTON, Abel 60*, Elizabeth 59
WARREN, John 45*
WELLS, Lewis 25*, Lucinda 17
JOHNSON, Malinda 37*, Alford 13
BLEVENS, Danl. 38, Sarah 34, Wm. 19, James 16, Cynthaan 14, Frances 12, Elizabeth 10, Jane 7, Mary 4, Danl. 2
JACKSON, Thos. 28, Sarah 19
SCREACH, Saml. 46*, Henry 18, Mary 16, Geo. T. 12, Absalom H. 10, Enoch 7, Thos. H. 2

Schedule Page 70

WELLS, Levi 30*
SCREACH, John S. 23, Nancy 22, Louisa? J. 2, Hugh 1, David 21
WADDLE, Jordan 23, Susan 20, Mary 5, Abel 1, Meredith 6/12
WHITLEY, Wm. J. 27, Rachel 31, Danl. 5, Mahale 3
BOGGS, Henderson 27, Mary 26, Nancy 6, Mary J. 4
BOGGS, John 25*, Mahale 22
BLEVENS, Wm. 22*
BOGGS, James 20, Matilda 17, Phebe 8/12?
FIELDS, Jason 60*, Anna 49, Hiram 21, Nancy 16, Celia 14, Preston 10, Jason Jr. 6, Arena 3
JACKSON, Saml. 24*
PENINGTON, Wm. 35, Nancy 28, Abel 9, Susan 7, Frances 5, John K. 2
ROSS, James 30, Sarah 24, David 5, Mary 2
LIONS, Lewis 55, Sena 44, Assel 21, Lewis 19, Narsisa 15, Malinda 13, Lucinda 11, Jesse 6, Frances 10/12
SPARKS, Reuben 33, Margaret 28, Maryam 5

1850 Census Lawrence County Kentucky

SPARKS, Hiram 30, Calvin 8/12
GILLAM, Isom 38*, Anna 28, Lilyann 17, Melburn 11, James W. 7, Charles 4, Wm. H. 1
HICKS, James 19*
SPARKS, Geo. 54*, Nancy 50, Cyntha 22, Levi 16, Lemuella? 11, Caleb 8, Mary 6
HUCHERSON, Nancy 25*, James F. 1/12
SPARKS, Wesley 44, Nancy 28, Mary 14, Richd. 9, Robt. 7, Martin 4, Lena 2

Schedule Page 71

BARKER, John 29, Frances 24, Jason 5, Preston 2
SPARKS, Wm. 38, Mary 34, Nancy 15, Reuben 17, Isaac 10, Joel 8, Wm. H. 6, Geo. W. 4, Francis M. 3, Docr. F. 1
GREEN, Wm. 32*, Sarah 25, Maryan 11, Elizabeth 9, Manerva 6, Nancy 4, Wm. 1
WHITE, Nelson 18*
HICKS, John 18*
BARKER, Harvey 41, Lucinda 32, Sarah 16, Annias 14 (f), Hardin 11, Lewis 9, Nancy 6, John 5, Katharine 3, Mary 1
GILLOM, Chesley 21, Dianna 22, Katharine 8/12
ISON, Arch 70, Ison 27, Isabel 18
STURGEON, Alvin 50, Nancy 32, Lucinda 19, Elizabeth 16, Isaac S. 14, Merica 10, Voxina? K. 7, Alex. 3, Diana 5, Sarah D. 3/12
FRAILY, Isaac 72, Katharine 62, Fairlina 21, Shelvey 34, Emly 9, Marcus G. 6
FRAILY, Alexr. 26, Susanah 24, Isaac Jr. 3, Harvey F. 1 (f)
FRAILY, James 37, Jemima 30, Geo. W. 13, Andrew C. 11, Eleanor 9, David 5, Brittain 3, James F. 1
CONLEY, Edmd. 35, Dulcena 26, Milten E. 4, James H. 2, Corilda 2/12?
ISON, Argalis 29, Mary 38, Isabel 10/12
GILLOM, Martin 73, Elizabeth 55
GILLOM, Isiah 35, Nancy 26, Mary 7, Jesse 5, Howard 3, Elizabeth 1

Schedule Page 72

KISEE, Elias 52, Mary 57, Cyntha 24, Sarah 21, Harvey 18, Elias Jr. 15, Jane 23, Reuben 4, Garred 7, Rufus 1
RUDD, Thos. 27, Annis 19
GRIFFETH, Robt. 57*, Margaret 52, Sarah 28, Nancy 18, Elisa 15
RICE, Wm. 14*
SCAGGS, Lewis 62*, Nancy 54, Nancy 25, Mary 22
SPARKS, Martha 1*, Saml. 24
GARVEY, John 54*, Susan 47, Jackson 7, Geo. W. 5
HAY, Wm. 16*
WALTERS, Robt. 51, Louisa 45, Edford L. 22, Neri 20, Truvilla 17, Wm. M. 15, Louisa Ann 12, John C. 10, Robt. L. 6, Madison 4, Perlina B. 1
GRUBB, Geo. Jr. 32*, Emly 25, Geo. 73, Sarah 69
WETHEROW, James W. 22*
MOORE, David 32, Anna 24, Sarah 7, Martha 5, John W. 3, Jesse 5/12
BERRY, John 57, Kesiah 44, John L. 9, July Ann 7, Wily 5, Bashaba 3, Nelames 1 (m)

1850 Census Lawrence County Kentucky

ADKINS, John 42, Delila 40, Hiram 22, William 17, Frances 14, Anna 12, Juliann 10, John Jr. 7, Jonas 5, Sarah 3
MCCONNAC, Wiley 29, Rebecca 28, Mary J. 3, Eleanor 9/12, Eleanor 56
WILLIAMSON, Wm. 43, Permelia 30, Nancy 15, Evaline 15, John 11, Wm. H. 10, James M. 7, Soloman 6, Magdolan 1

Schedule Page 73

HULETT, H. B. 43 (m)*, Rachel 37, Thos. B. 14, Mildred 16, Mary J. 12, Wm. 11 (f), Alford 9, James 7, Robt. 5, Benjn. 4, Harden B. 2
FORTNER, John 20*, Aron 23
COX, Bennett 36, Frances 18, Jeremiah Jr. 14, Nancy 13, Geo. H. 11, Marion 7, Manerva 5
PETERS, Jacob H. 38, Jane 33, John N. 11, Noah 7, Garred 6, Wm. D. 4, Charles F. 3, Emily J. 2, Jacob Jr. 6/12
VINSON, Lazrus 25, Jane 25
MCKINSTER, Allen 19, Elizabeth 16
LARGE, Joseph 23, Anna 20, Elzira 4/12
CASTEEL, John 28, Mary 24, James R. 6, Matilda 4, Rebecca 3, Susanah 1
LARGE, Andrew 30, Lucinda 29, John W. 5, Marinda 3, Caroline 2/12
MURPHEY, David 69*, Miram 55 (f), Mary B. 17, Isabel R. 14
ROSE, Zachariah 80*
CARTER, Thomas 47, Katharine 44, John W. 21, Jackson 19, James 17, Jacob H. 15, Elizabeth 13, Margaret 7, Amanda 11, Frances 5, Martha 3
KICHEN, Wm. 28, Milly 30, Martha 6, Mary 2
DAVIS, Saml. 41*, Nancy 38
BOYD, Elizabeth 21*
ADKINS, Wm. 20*
CHAFIN, Wm. 35, Nancy 38, John 14, David 12, James H. 10, Martha 8, Sidney 6 (f), Mary 4, Clary 2

Schedule Page 74

MCCLURE, John 46, Nancy 36, Clementine 15, Mardaca 14 (m), Geo. 12, Rebecca 8
MCDOWELL, Jahue 47, Sarah 46, Sarah 21, Nancy 18, Sidney 16 (f), Rebecca 13, Emanl. 9, Margaret 7, Geo. A. 4/12
SMITH, Linsey 24*, Keren 19, Helon T. 1
FERGUSON, Adeline 21*
SMALL, Wm. B. 38, Sarah 42, James P. 15, Katharine 13, Maryan 11, Margaret J. 9, Leanedes 5, Sarah 5/12
BURK, Benjm. 41*, Mary 32, Elisa J. 12, Benton 10, James 8
LOAR?, Susan 22*
ESOM, Robt. 28*, Julyan 25, Hartwell 2
MCCAY, Reuben 22*
MCDEER, John 30, Luverna 18, Martha 5/12
JOHNSON, Abm. 53*, Sarah M. 46, Abm. W. 22, Richd. F. 19, Elisa G. 16, John H. 15, Lydia 10, Sarah 24
RUBEL, Napoleon 27*
WOODS, John W. 23, Amasetta 18, Millard F. 6/12

1850 Census Lawrence County Kentucky

COOK, John M. 30*, Milly 27
GOINGS, Caroline 15*
WEST, James 27*
GRUBBS, Absalom 46, Elizabeth 39, Geo. W. 22, Isaac 14, Sarah 12, Jedediah 10, Rhoda 8, Nancy 6, Josaphine 5, John 3
CHAFIN, Wm. M. 31, Mary 20
BURCHETT, Wm. 27, Margaret 25, Lydia 13, Elizabeth 8, Naryan 4, James 3, John 1
PIGG, John 31, Elizabeth 27, Julyan 5, Mary F. 3, John B. 1/12

Schedule Page 75

BURCHETT, Armsted 32, Rebecca 26, Drury J. 8, Sarah E. 6, Thos. 3, Isabel 1/12
BERRY, Wm. 28*, Pricy 27, John W. 7, Sirena 5, Melvina 3, James W. 7/12
BALL, Soloman 19*
BERRY, Wiley 28, Martha 30, Mary 8, Charlotte 1
HORNE, Michl. 44, Susan 32, Fredk. 11, Christena 9, Katharine 5, Mary 2, Katharine 63
RING, andrew 43, Sarah 34, Mary J. 15, James H. 14, Sarah K. 6, Saml. S. 1
JOHNSON, Wm. H. 31*, Maranda 18, Mary E. 4/12
JONES, Telitha 18*
CRABTREE, John 42*, Elizabeth 40, Adelaide 16, Saml. 12, Wm. 8, Smith 4
GALASPIE, Thomas 23*
BOWE, Wm. 22*
PICKEREL, Joseph 37, Nancy 31, Virginia F. 11, Margaret S. 9, Mary E. 5, James G. 3, Thos. B. 10/12
EVERETT, J.? W. 29 (m), Elizabeth 26, John F. B. 6, Jane 4, Wm. W. G. 3, Laurence C. 1
MOORE, L. Y.? 21 (m), Sarah 22
ROBERTS, C. L. 40 (m), Jane 38, Martha J.? 17, Elizabeth F. 14, John 12, Mary M. 10, Napolean B. 8, Julyan 6, Geo. W. 4, Christian W. 1, Pricilla 1/12
COBURN, Joseph 30, Rebecca 24?, Sarah 5, Elizabeth 3, Leander 1
FUGETT, Solomon B. 33, Lucretia 23, Geo. W. 5, Z. T. 3, Malinda J. 2, Green B. 1
RICE, James M. 47*, Matilda M. 32, Jacob 23, John M. 19, Sarah J. 14

Schedule Page 76

HANNAH, James W. 27*
MCCOMAC, Meredith 32*, Rutha 42, Geo. W. 5, Andrew J. 2
MOREHEAD, Katharine 80*, Bennett 50
PRICE, Henry S. 35*, Elizabeth 35, Jesse 13, Wm. 12, James 9, Malinda 7, Jeptha 5, Lucretia 3, Edwd. 1
MEEKS, Edwd. 22*
THOMPSON, John H. 35, Elisa 36, Pricy J. 10, James H. 9, Wm. M. 7, David T. 5, Clayton 3/12
CHAMBERS, David 38, Sarah 32, Mary J.? 9, Wm. 8, James 6, Richd. 4, Robt. L. 2, Richd. 65
PAGE, Saml. 30, Margaret 26, Edwd. 6, Reuben F. 1
ISAACS, Fielding 39*, Mary 38, Elihue 4, W. T. 3 (m)
SMITH, Elizabeth 16*, Manerva 11
SPERRY, Sarah 23*
MIRES, Wm. R. 38, Matilda Ann 32, Rachel Ann 15, Wm. V. 9, Mary J. 7, Martha F. 5, Romane M. 2
KELLY, Saml. 27, Mary J. 23, Geo. W. 1
HALE, John 34, Jane 29, Greenville R. 6, Caroline 4, Mathew 10/12

1850 Census Lawrence County Kentucky

MARCUM, A. J. 27 (m), Marinda 26, Frances 3, Sinclare 1, James 24
BUSSEY, H. S. 39 (m)*, Christena R. 34, Crecilla 11, Elisa J. 9, Fredk. 4, Fremont R. 1
DEVENPORT, Pitman 19*
WALLACE, Thos. 38*, Mary 33, Elenor R. 17, Elizabeth C. 15, Parmelia A. B. 8, Fredk. R. W. 6, Charity D. 3, Francis T. 6/12
CANTERBURY, R. F. 27 (m)*

Schedule Page 77

THOMPSON, Johnson 38, Sarah 30, Martha J. 11, Granvill 9, Frances 7, James 5, Lucinda 3
FUGITT, B. E. 27 (m)
BAKER, John C. 32, Katharine C. 26, Elizabeth 8, Armasetta 6, Henry F. 4
DODD, Robt. J. Jr. 23, Mary 23, Rebecca 63
SPERRY, James 34, Frances A. 37, Franklin 8, Cyntha 6, Reuben 4, Sarah 2, John 1/12
CALLIHAN, Robt. D. 43, Louvena 36, Josaphene 14, Mary A. L. 12, Leanedas 9, Henretta 7, Caroline 4
MILLER, Danl. 40*, Permelia A. 25
POAGUE, Elizabeth 16*
WELMAN, Lewis 40, Abagail 34, Mary 8, Eunice 5, Davis S. 2
LORVINE?, Henry 68, Mary 62
VAUGHN, D. B. 31 (m), Martha 24, Lucretia 5, James 2
FULKERSON, James 35, Frances 24, Wm. W. C. 6, Crittenden 3, James C. 9/12
CHAPMAN, Wm. 46, Mary 44, Geo. R. 20, Elizabeth 18, Eleanor 16, Sarah 14, Mary J. 12, Elizial? 9 (m), John 6, Welborn F. 4, James 1
GARRETT, Marshall 19, Amanda 16, Juniatta 17
RANDALL, Peres? 46, Mahale 30, Delutha 17, Georgeann 10, Peres? M. G. 1
WORKMAN, Jesse 35*, Elizabeth 30, Alford 15, Wm. 13, Thos. 9, Jane 3
HALL, Mary 17*, James A. 4/12
JACKSON, Richd. 39, Elizabeth 36, James M. 11, Patten T. 9, Nancy J. 8, Henderson 7, Martha A. 6, Mary 4, Elijah 2

Schedule Page 78

WORKMAN, Stephen 19, Celia 16
COFMAN, Martin 41*, Elizabeth 41, Albert 18, Noah 15, Lovel 12, Lunsford 9, Mary 7, Elenor 5, Elisa C. 2
BILLUPS, Robt. 27*, Sampson 21
OBRIEN, John 75*, Hannah 45, Jane G. 16, James 13, Margaret 12, Belvidere 8, Hannah A. 3
DEVENPORT, F. L. 25 (m)*
NOLTE, Wm. 41*, Dolta C. 39, Caroline 10, Charles 8, Amanda 6, Wm. 4, Henrietta 2
CASINBROK, Anthony 27*
GARRED, James 57, Mary 31, Anderson 19, Sarah 9
SHANNON, Joseph 27, Frances 32, Josephine 6/12
MUNCY, Skidmore 50, Jane 52, Elizabeth 22, Rebecca 20, Granville 19, Lucinda 16, Rhoda 15, Manerva 14, Adison 12, James 9
BRIANT, John 33*, Eleanor 36, America 17, David A. 11, Oliver 9, Wm. H. 7, Johnson 5, Mary A. 3
MULINAX, Geo. W. 18*.
BURNS, John L. 40, Nancy 26, James H. 18, Wm. R. 4, Thos. J. 2, Mary 6/12

1850 Census Lawrence County Kentucky

EASTWOOD, Jesse 24*, Hannah 22, Virginia 11/12
BOGGS, Charles 12*
BIGGS, James Jr. 24, Frances 21, Pemelia 1
WELMAN, Jeremiah 65, Anna 55, Elisha 24, Frances 14, Anna 22, Mary 13, Wesley 20
BRADLEY, Jackson D. 30, Sarah 25, Wm. R. 3, Lewis F. 1, Ira G. 17

Schedule Page 79

KISE, Chancy C. 34, Manerva 26, Benjm. F. 9, Thomas B. 7, David G. 5, Elizabeth F. 2, Rebecca J. 1/12, Rebecca 68
REYNOLDS, John 23, Nancy 19, Geo. 1
HODGES, Gabl. 28*, Mahale 32, James H. 4, Thos. W. 11/12
PIGG, John J. 12*
CRAFT, Thomas 30, Nancy 32, Wiley 12, Suletia 11, Robt. R. 9, Zana 7, Wm. 5, Thos. J. 2, Henry J. 21
COFMAN, Zachariah 43*, Susan 26, Sephrona 14, Emly 9, Columbus 2
CROUCH, Sarah 18*
SLACK, Jeremiah 29*
LEE, Garred 64*, Flora 53, John N. 32, Michl. 26, Elizabeth 22, Wm. 21, Flora 16, Garred Jr. 14
BATES, David 9*, Susan 5
YATES, S. J. 34 (m), Ellen R. 24, Amanda 6, Mary 2
SIMPSON, Allen 28, Bethial 26, Geo. A. 4, Riley A. 1
RICE, Wm. 27, Nancy 16
HODGE, Wilson 31, Lurane 26, Maryan 5, Sarah Jane 3, Maunda A. 1
MUNCY, David W. 20, Jemima 25, Ardela E. 1/12
DEMOND, John 32, Acey 27, David C. 10, Elizabeth E. 8, Francis M. 2, Charles W. 1/12
DEMOND, Charles 47, Susan 43, Henry 19, Charles D. 17, Geo. 12, James M. 10, John 7, Christian R. 4
BRADLEY, Levi 36*, Margaret 35, Isaac F. 15, Wm. B. 13, James H. 11, James R. 9, Green V. 6, Mary J. 4, Pemelia A. 1

Schedule Page 80

CRAFT, Keziah 16*
PIGG, James 62, Geo. 21, Wm. 19, Elizabeth 16, Jane 13, Willis 11, Thos. 9, Fleming 6, Sarah 51
COMPTON, Hiram 50*, Margaret 48, Amanda 13, Caroline 11, Jacob 5, John 4, Margaret 11/12
GRANAHAN, L. D. M. 25 (m)*
GOBLE, G. V. 40 (m)*, Rebecca 36, Parelix? G 16 (m), Montraville 13, Mary L. 10, Marthaan 7, Caroline P. 3, Jessie 8/12 (f)
GODSEY, Augustus C. 23*
WILLIS, Isiah 47*, Nancy 64, Harrison 24, Wm. 22, Tabitha 21
WALKER, Amanda 19*
WELMAN, Fleming 26, Nancy 22, Stephen 3, Sarah F. 2, Julyann 1/12
WELMAN, Jarred D. 36, Sarah 24, Yates 2, Eleanor 1, Lucinda 16
FUGETT, Benjm. 59*, Clarinda 35, Wm. H. 25, James 16, Emly 15, Henry? F. 10
ROBERTS, Martha 12*
CASTLE, Ephraim 34, Jane 29, James F. 7, Forrest M. 6, Matilda 4, Eunice 3
CARTER, John 48, Martha 42, Geo. 14, Mary 11, John Jr. 9, Landon 7, Martha 4, David 15

1850 Census Lawrence County Kentucky

ASTRUP, James 46, Deborah 36, Wm. 17, Enoch 12, Mary 10, Nancy 9, Sarah 7, Logan 5, Jane 3
THOMPSON, Johnson 43, Martha 46, Andrew A. 17, Exony 16 (f), Wm. 13, Elizabeth 12, Margaret 8

Schedule Page 81

THOMPSON, Saml. 26, Sarah 24, Angeline 6, Nancy J. 4, Elizabeth 2
CHAFIN, Thomas 26, Rhodaann 25, Robt. N. 4, Sarah J. 3, Martha 9/12
GAW, Joseph 55, Thuresy 37, Mary F. 22
LEE, David 27*, Mary E. 19, Margaret 1
BREWER, Wm. 35*
SLUPER, Henry 57*, Katharine 56, Raburn 21
HITE, Susan 15*
MACKEN, Hiram 50, Sarah J. 32, Mary 11, Martha E. 8, Elizabeth 4
DAVIS, Nathanl. 42*, Lucinda 38, Elizabeth 18, James 16, Sarah F. 11, Wm. 8, Mary 6, Eliza 3, Alice 6/12
LETCHER, John 21*
PATTEN, Westen F. 40, Nancy 37, Ballard P. 11, Amanda L. 8, John S. 6, Wm. R. 5, Amasetta J. 2
STONEBRAKER, Joseph 39, Louvina 29, Wm. M. 14, John 12, Rebecca 10, Mary E. 6, Martha A. 4, James D. 2
CHAPMAN, Andrew J. 47, Cornelus 19, Mary 16, Martha F. 13, Margaret 10, Julyan 8
JUSTICE, Eli 40, Elizabeth 37, Wm. 10
HALE, Harris 19, Nancy 16
MOORE, Saml. T. 26, Tabitha 21, Martin L. 4, Eli 1
THOMPSON, Jeremiah 40*, Martha 40, Nancy 16, Elizabeth 14, Nelly 12, Martha 6, Ulisses 9/12
RICE, Wm. 22*
DIMOND, Henry 44*, Elizabeth 40, Malinda J. 19, Barbara 17, Henly C. 16, Harret P. 12, Miles K. 9, John F. 7, Henretta V. 6, Rufus F. 4

Schedule Page 82

KINKEAD, Wm. C. 19*
JONES, Maryan 38, John W. 16, Elizabeth M. 14, Martha R. 12, Wm. M. 10, Danl. C. 8, Maryan 6
MELMAN, Wm. 37, Martha 22, Permelian 3
GARRETT, Barton 38, Martha 23, Theodore 1/12
STRAILY, Wm. M. 36, Charlotte 22, Louvina 3, Melvina V. 2
BRANHAM, David 44, Elizabeth 42, Henderson R. 19, James W. 17, Benjm. M. 15, Nancy S. 13, Lucinda 10, Margarett 8, Jane 6, Elizabeth M. 5, Danl. O. 3, Thos. J. 1, Jonathan 24
ROBERTS, John C. 42, Hester 40, Sarilda 18, Geo. H. 16, Joseph F. 14, Pemelia F. 12, Strother F. 10, Reuben 8, Allen F. 4, John W. 1
HUGHS, Israel 45, Pemelia 44, Mary M. 18, Sarah 16, Virgina 14, Joseph C. 12, Garred 8, Wm. W. 6, Pemelia C. 3, James H. 1
BURCHETT, John 43, Milly 42, Calvin 21, Fleming 16, Benjm. 14, James 13, Henry 11, Robt. 9, Elisa 6, Rhoda 4, Susan 2
PETRE, Joel 27, Phebean 25
CHAFIN, David 71*, Pemelia 16, David T. 20
MOREHEAD, Mary 57*

1850 Census Lawrence County Kentucky

WOOTEN, Silas G. 46, Julyan 32, Francis A. 22, Geo. W. 10, Rebecca 6, Isaac 4, Julyan 2, Henry 2/12
VINSON, James 35, Sarahan 26, Elias 8, Rhoda 6, Elizabeth 5, Lazrus 3, John 1

Schedule Page 83

MOORE, Paul 30*, Frederick 25, Paul 1
DICTERTEN, Caroline 23*, Robt. 4, Bertha 3, Maria 1
GELLAR, Wm. 29*
CASEY, Danl. 49*, Mary 46
DYER, Sarah 87*, amanda 26, Sarah J. 16, Mary W. 11
GRANT, Warren 40*
SHANNON, Floyd P. 28*, Elizabeth 25, James W. 6, Mary R. 5, Martha M. 4, Arenetta D. 3
BENNETT, Lewis 24*
JORDAN, Jonas 55*, Lydia 26, Hiram 14, Delila 11, Mary J. 2, Green 6, Jonathon 76
LIONS, Martha 2*
HOLBROOK, Caleb 20, Louisa 19, John N. 2/12
FOSTER, Isaac 62, Mary 63
SCAGGS, Peter L. 36, Lucinda 36, Nancy 2, Marthan 4/12
DEAN, Saml. 55, Sarahan 39, Caroline 16, Geo. 19, Preston 14, Wayne 12, Cynthiana 10, Martha A. 8, Henry H. 6, Etna 5, Telitha 4, Perry 10/12
THOMPSON, Russell 39, Frances 37, Wesley 15, Martha 12, Lewis 10, Granville 8, Elizabeth 6, Wallace 4, Frances 2
BURGESS, Gordon C. 42*, Louisa 31, Julia G. 8, Geo. T. 6
MULLINS, Noah 20*
GEORGE, Henry 50*
CHAPMAN, Wm. 21, Nancy 18
BORDERS, Joseph 32*, Julia A. 30, Henry A. 10, Elizabeth E. 8, Frances 6, Moranda 4, Eda 2, Wallace 2/12, Nancy 2/12
MEAD, Gilbert 14*

Schedule Page 84

PACK, George 40, Eliza 32, Arch 15, John W. 14, Newton K. 10, Thos. J. 7, Jesse H. 4, Sarah 2, Leander J. 1/12
BIGGS, Reuben 47*, Katharine 42, James H. 20, Sarah 16, Nancy Ann 13, Jeremiah 11, Maryan 7, Elizabeth B. 3
FOSTER, Charles 20*
BROMFIELD, Mastin 46, Malinda 42, Lucinda 18, Maryan 17, Sarah J. 14, Louvina 12, Wm. 9, Emaline 5
PACK, Isaac 38, Jemima 35, John 18, Wm. 15, Elizabeth 12, Lucinda 10, Geo. 8, Lewis 6, Frances 4, Isaac Jr. 2, Jemima 1
JOHNSON, Arch 37, Margaret 33, James 10, John D. 8, Lewis 7, Danl. 5, Stephen 4, Sarahan 8/12
CHAFIN, John 25, Elizabeth 29, Lourenzo 1
MCKINSTER, Thos. 29, Delila 31, Elizabeth 9, Sarahan 7, Harrison W. 5, Louisa 4, Louisiana 2
MILLER, Edwd B. 52, Charlotte 37, Albert H. 19, Nancy 16, Mahale 5, James T. 14, Garland 35
JORDAN, Jesse 50, Sarah 54, Hiram 8, James H. 16, David C. 13, Elizabeth 11?, Keziah 8

1850 Census Lawrence County Kentucky

TOMLIN, John 35, Sarah 36, Mary 23, Isom 10, Martha 6
BALL, Robt. 33, Nancy 30, David 10, Wm. 8, Geo. 6, Mary 5, Selena 2, Marshall C. 10/12

Schedule Page 85

JUSTICE, David 29*, Margaret 23, Nancy J. 6, Julia 4, Sarahan 2, Sarah 60
DOBYNS, Abner 53*
COX, Flurry 75*, Milly 48, Jeremiah 36
TAYLOR, Isabell 10*
SPALDING, John Jr. 22*, Cyntha 21, Elizabeth 2, Mary J. 1
DOBYNS, Elizabeth 45*, Margaret 20, Wm. 8
VANHOOSE, Reuben 43, Dotia 42, Wm. 19, Elizabeth 17, Valentine 12, Julyan 10, Thomas 5, Martin 3, Louisa 1
SPENCER, James R. 47, Lucinda 47, John 21, Eleanor 13, Jemima 11, Frances 7, Henry C. 6, Andrew J. 2
BALL, Elihue 26, Pricy 20, Louisa 4, Julyan 1
MCCLURE, Strother 44, Jane 41, Wm. 20, Maria 15, Elizabeth 13, Lucretia 12, Carrilda J. 8
WELMAN, Joseph 68, Nancy 60
MCCORMAC, Wm. 40, Lucinda 38, Harret 18, Elia 16, Floyd 14, Clarina 11, Gordon 9, Eleanor 6, Martha A. 4, Hordela 2
MCCLURE, Geo. C. 26, Jane 19
VICKERS, John 25, Louiza 18, Wm. H. 6/12, Wm. H. 20
MANOR, Charles 51, Sarah 32, Lucinda 11, Katharine 9, Francis 8, Jesse 6, Lewis 5, Milly 3, Calmal? 2 (m), Elizabeth 2/12
BALL, James 68*, Nancy 60, Nancy 21, Nancy J. 2, Calvin 20
STEWART, Charlotte 13*
HARRIS, Enoch 37*, Elizabeth 35

Schedule Page 86

NELSON, James 10*
MCCARTY, John 35, Lucy 38, Henderson 18
JOHNS, Danl. W. 34, Ann 76, Isabel B. 3, Clayton 1
SHORT, Saml. 38*, Elizabeth 21
GAVITT, Elliott 21*
DYER, Wm. 15*
LAYNE, Isaac 35, Jemima 37, Wm. 4, Joseph 2
POAGUE, Geo. B. 27*, Lucy J. 25
GOINGS, Mary 13*
FORTNER, Alexr. 38, Henretta 22, Martha J. 2/12, Elizabeth 58
WELMAN, Calvin 27, Lucy 24, Delaware 3 (m), Winney 2
GRUBB, Andrew 21, Teney 45, Julyan 18
CRANK, Jeremiah 28*, Mary 26, John 2, Collumbus 2
SLOANE, Jane 8*
IDE, Timothy 39, Elizabeth 36, Wm. H. 9, Elizabeth 7, George 5, John 3
MORROW, Francis 30*, America 21, Nancy G. 1
AKERS, Rebecca 50*

1850 Census Lawrence County Kentucky

HUCHERSON, Luther R. 26, Mary A. 24, Jesse 3, Margaret 1
HUCHERSON, Geo. W. 42, Sophia W. 43, Irad? B. 17 (m), Elizabeth E. 15, Allen C. 14, Sarah M. 12, Mary J. 9, Ko W. 7 (m), Sophia C. 5, Emly A. 3, Joseph A. 1
HAYS, Alexr. 38, Maryan 28, Charles H. 12, Sarah J. 9, Francis A. 4, John W. 2, Mary E. 1/12
CLAY, James M. 54, Nancy 46, Michl. F. 23, Wm. E. 19, John L. 17, Judeth C. 15, Nancy E. 13, Louisa H. 10
AKERS, Burwell 24, Rachel 20, Nancy E. 4/12
CAINS, Thomas 30, Derece 36, Mary 11, Sarah J. 9, Malinda 4, Mary E. 6/12

Schedule Page 87

RIFE, John 60*, Elizabeth 49, Wm. 23, Elexe? 21 (f), Julianna 17, John Jr. 15, Elizabeth 8
CHAFIN, James 22*
KINKEAD, Andrew H. 42*
CRANK, Preston 37, Manerva 33, Geo. W. 11, Wm. 5, Maryann 7, Cornelus 3, Martha 1
ROSS, John D. 42*, Susan 37, Elizabeth 15, Jacob 14, Taracy 12, Geo. 10, Hannah 9, Deana 7, John S. 5, Wm. J. 3, James T. 1
LASLIE, Andrew 14*
WILLIAMS, Wm. R. 28, Eleanor 35, Henry 5, Julia 7, Sarah 4, David C. 3, John W. 1/12
COBURN, Gordon C. 46*, Clarinda 44, James 17, Thompson 14, Juliann 11, Wm. 9, Gorden jr 5, Alice 7/12
ROYAR, Alford 33*
CAMPBELL, Smith 28*
LAMBERT, Jeremiah 27, Julyan 19, James K. 2/12, Geo. 10/12
AKERS, Wm. 22, Celia 20, Sarah E. 1
HAYS, James 37, Sarahan 16, Mary J. 10, James T. 7, Maryan 35
WILLIS, Ammill 40*, Emly 36, Andrwe B. 15, Richd. H. 12, Abrn. J. 9, Isaac R. 7, Ammill Z/ 1
FUGETT, Geo. 21* (B)
DITTY, James 30, Permelia 22, Ann 8, Grayson 6, John 4, Thomas 6/21, Thomas 66
COBURN, Thomas 39, Julyna 32, Julyann 12, Rufus 10, Louisa 7, Melvina 4, Anderson T. 2
BROWN, Campbell 23*, Jane 19

Schedule Page 88

STANTON, Richd. 46*
WELCH, Thos. 40*
DARION, patrick 27*
HOWE, James M. 27, Evaline 23, Mary E. 5/12
TAYLOR, Edwd. 56, Martha 60
BRUICE, James 44*, Nancy 46, Susan 15, John 12
LASLIE, Orpha 19*, Wm. 15, Robt. 9, James 7
SADLER, Saml. 27, Nancy 21, Bathena 6, Mary J. 4, Andrew J. 2
HERRON, Thos. 39, Elizabeth 38, John 11, Sarah J. 16, Narcese 10, Karan H. 8, Hanah 6, Thos. 1
KELLY, Plesant 44, Gemima 30, America J. 9, Mary A. 8, Sarah An 6, Harrison 4, Noah 3/12
BROMFIELD, Wm. 28*, Nancy 21, Greenville 3, Caroline 10/12, Eleanor 63, Eleanor 20
MCCORMAC, Lorenzo D. 16*, Malinda 14
ROMAN, Isaac 23, Elizabeth 18

- 195 -

1850 Census Lawrence County Kentucky

KIDD, Jesse 46, Hannah 27, Ephraim 18, Thos. 15, Rebecca 13, Ann 8, Asenetta 6, Geo. 4, Elisa 3, Mary 3
FANNIN, John 38*, margaret 30, Lewis P. 14, Charlotte 12, Geo. W. 11, Martha K. 8, Mary E. 6, Thomas L. 4, Nancy E. 2
STUTTER, Francis H. 50*, Frances 30
STEWERT, Clay 32, Mary 27, Kelly 8, Wm. R. 4, Helsy M. 2
ROMAN, Nathan? M. 33, Mary An 24, Melvina E. 9
WILBURN, Wm. 24*
BROWN, Lucinda 20*, Mary 50, Anderson 26
AKERS, Stephen 30, Sarah 17, Nathanl. 18

Schedule Page 89

WEBB, Wm. R. 35, Martha 30, James P. 10, Elizabeth 9, Levi 6, Elisa J. 6, Geo. W. 4, Martha 2, Wm. R. 2/12
CLAY, Charles 26, Caroline 21, Matte L. 5, Wm. R. 3
FOSTER, Wm. A. 26*, Maria 44, Henry H. 18, Genoa 16, Alice 9
GILBRUTH, Irwin 22*
HENSLEY, John 28, Lucretia 23, Lous 2, Geo. W. 6/?12
SPEARS, Geo. W. 30, Mary 28
TAYLOR, Wm. 22, Elisa E. 16
BURTEN, Henderson 31, Rebecca 21, James E. 5, Nelly 50, Ira 17, Benjn. M. 14, Fletcher T. 24
SWERINGIN, Wm. 26*, Frances 24, John P. 4, Melice A. 2, Van 1
HALL, Sarah 10*
ACHERSON, James 25*, Sarah 25, Jane 6/12
GANNON, Jesse 25*
HOOD, Andrew 47, Emly 40, A. J. 16 (m), Mary A. 11, Sarilda 6, James R. 4, Lucinda 1
LYNN, Christian 45, Mary 40, John 15
LASLIE, John B. 21*, Maria 26
MCCOMAC, Malisse J. 7*, Amanda 5
JACKSON, Wm. 30*
DUNDERI, John 45*
RICE, James 65, Elizabeth 46, James jr 19, David 17
ODANIEL, Thos. 20, Elizabeth 22, James H. 1
ROYAR, John B. 41, Elizabeth 32, Mary 21
LONG, John A. 34, Teliayean 30, Wm. H. 1/12
SADLER, Valentine 22, Mary 22
MESSER, Saml. 36, Elizabeth 29, Rachel 12, Lucinda 10, Nancy 7, Wm. 5, Crawsley 5

Schedule Page 90

COBURN, Thos. jr 22, Mary 22, Jesse 2, Frances 1
CLARK, John 34*, Mary 36, Enos 8, Andrew 6, Margaret 4, Wm. 1
LUMDEL, Wm. 24*
BRUMFIELD, Floyd 24, Rebecca 24, John F. 1
CAMPBELL, John 24, Jane 16, Elizabeth 2/12

1850 Census Lawrence County Kentucky

MCCOY, Geo. 46, Arista 46, Bramma 20, Easther 18, Ezekial 15, Caroline 12, Phebe 11, Elisa 8, Lucinda R. 5
COBURN, Madison 23, Sarelda 19, Wm. 1
WOODY, Everett L. 30*, Sarah 28, Maryann 7, Matilda 5, Albert 3, Oliver 1
THOMAS, Tartia 16*
PARECUE, Henry 45*
PRESLEY, James R. 28, Jemima 40, Martha 4, Miram 2, Robt. 14
ROWE, James 29*, Sarah 21, Bell 2/12
CRONE, Hannah 10*
DURIFIELD, John 24*, Mahale 22
LARGE, Milly 95*
BERRY, Alford 27, Hannah 18, Margaret 52, Lucinda 18, Wm. 11
ADAMS, James 23, Anna 21, John 4, Wm. 2
DURIFIELD, Thos. 32, Mary 32, Derescus 8, Silvester 5, Avesta 2
CLAY, Wm. 25, Mary 23, evan 3, Nancy 1
FANNIN, Rebecca 36, Harvey F. 19, Caroline 16, Montraville 12, Mary? E. 11, Wm. 8, Nancy 4
MORRIS, Henry 30, Cntha 27, Marenda 5, Mary E. 4, Martha L. 2
JORDAN, Richd. 49, Milly 37, Sarah 12, Permelia 11, John 8, Nancy 4, Wm. 2, Martha 1

Schedule Page 91

HOLDER, John 35, Rebecca 24, Stephen 5, Matilda 4, Franklin 2, David 1
SECREST, David 47, Mary 49, Lucy 22, John M. 19, Geo. W. 17, Martha 13, Maryan 8, Elizabeth 6, Caroline 5, Fleming 2
WEBB, John M. 33, Elizabeth 27, James F. 9, Andrew 8, Rachel 6, Jemima 4, Elihue 2, Wesly 1
SECREST, Jacob 25, Elizabeth 20, David F. 2
LIONS, Levi 34, Sarah 21, James 13, Wesley 12, Nancy 10, Jesse 8, Louisa 6, John 4
TAYLOR, Ellis 27, Caroline 25, frances 3, Wm. 2, James 4/12
STEWERT, Michel 59, Frances 55, Rebecca 21, Mary 18, Abbert R. 17
HOLBROOK, Winfry 48*, Elizabeth 46, Calvin 21, Robt. 17, Elisha 14, Wm. 6
COOKSY, Jane 26*, Montravill 3, Wm. 1
MCCOY, Geo. 67, Tabitha 50, Bromfield 13, Basill G. 11
DIMOND?, Joshua L. 21, Sarah 18
WELMAN, James 57*, Elizabeth 46, Lewis 14, Ferebe 11, James C. 7
CAUFMAN, John 21*
JOHNS, Harrison 31*, Lucyann 22, James C. 8/12
ALLISON, John 19*
WINCHELL, Henry 21*
THORNHILL, James 24*, Sarah 27, Robt. D. 2
JUSTICE, Elizabeth 45*, Allen 23, Rhoda 19, Nancy 16, Elizabeth 12, Manerva 8

Schedule Page 92

POE, Edmd. 36, Agnes 36, Elijah 16, James 13, Louvisa 11, Julian 9, Reuben 5, Oliver 3
MEEK, Jesse P. 33*, Abagail 29, Henry C. 12, Elisa J. 10, Jacob 8, Julyan 7, Mary F. 5, Emily 2
WEDINGTON, Wm. 22*
WEAVER, Danl. 19*

1850 Census Lawrence County Kentucky

FRANCIS, Mary 18*
STEWERT, Mary J. 30, Henry R. 7, Ametia an 5
GOODWIN, Jane 37, Frances 14, Charles A. 11, Harrison 6
EADS, Temperance 44*, Lurena 8, Wm. 6
MCKINSTER, Mack 20*, Mahulda 16, Eda 13
WALLER, Henry 45, Elizabeth 44, James 21, Pernina 15, Zackariah 13, Pricy 11, Jacob H. 7, Asbury 5, Malinda 1
BALL, John 36, Martha 34, thompson 13, Nancy 12, Wm. 9, Greenville 7, Elisa? 6, Elsa 4 (m), Silvester 2, Sarilda 2/12
MOORE, Wm. T. 35, Delila 30, Elizabeth 10, Landrum 7, Jane 5, Louisa 2
MOORE, John 39, Frances 33, Wm. 15, James 13, Anderson 9, Frances 6, John Jr. 4, Greene 3
MOORE, Saml. 23*, Eunice 23, John W. 1
CARTER, Phebe 15*
JORDAN, Phebe 65, Susan 33, Geo. 28, Elisa 25, Amanda 11, Clarinda 5
CARTER, Covey 19 (m), Sarah 20, John 3/12

Schedule Page 93

JORDAN, Eleanor 35, Richd. 1, Wm. 1
BERRY, William 23, Artha F. 19, Alice 2, Rhoda 1, Rupert 4/12
CASEY, Nancy 19*, Lucindey 16
PACKWOOD, Stephen 21*
JORDAN, Jonas 27*, Mary 23, Amanda D.? 2
DUNFIELD, David 22*
EVANS, Jane 33, James 17, John 15, Fletcher 12, Manerva 13, Mahale 13, Serilda 11, Geo. 8, Wilshire 5
DANIEL, James 34, Susan 27, Jane 8, Thos. 5, David 3
WITHEROW, Saml. 20, Susan 21
GRIFFETH, Evan 35, Mary 33, Melvina 9, Martha 7, Dereca 5, Sarah J. 3, Elisha 1
GRIFFETH, David 67*, Jane 58
RICE, Nancy 9*
GRIFFETH, Robt. 36*, Susan 32, Geo. W. 10, Sarah 9, David 7, Meredith 7, Jane 4, Milton 2
EDWARDS, Susan 64*
GRIFFETH, Reece 36, Margaret 35, Richd. 17, Susan 15, Talifa 10, John 12, Meredith 8, Anna 6, Amanda 3, Sarah 1
PRINCE, John 32*, Louvina 30, David G. 9, Sarah G. 7, Melvina 5, Nancy 3, James 1
RICE, Ellen 14*
KISEE, Avery 44, Elizabeth 40, Sarah 16, Louvica 11, Phebe J. 9, Susan 4, Geo. R. 2
LAMBERT, Wm. 23, Elizabeth 23, Mary 4, Benjm. F. 1
FERGUSON, John P. 31, Anna 30, Meredith 13, Elisha 11, Katharine 9, Mary 7, Margaret 5, Saml. 2, Susan 4/12

Schedule Page 94

SPURLOCK, Wm. 51
DIAL, Alexr. 31*, Sarah 28, Louisa 9, Eli R. 7, Louely 5, Am. A. 3, Sarah E. 1, Wm. 18
GEARHEART, Hansford 17*
OWSLEY, Josiah 35, Elisabeth 29, Evaline 9, John 7, Sarilda 5, Elisha 3, Wesly 1

1850 Census Lawrence County Kentucky

MORRIS, Mathew 19, Margaret 19
RICE, Susan 37, Robt. 18, James 12, Elizabeth 10, Rebecca 8, Anderson 6
CASTEEL, James 60, Elizabeth 48, Sarah 26, Wm. 19, Milly 22, James 16, Simpson 14, Elizabeth 12, Geo. W. 9, Washington 3
EDWARDS, Meredith 37, Sarah 36, Susan 14, Edmd 12, Elizabeth 9, Sarah 3, Isaac 2/12
MORRIS, Elizabeth 65, Richd. 39
MORRIS, Pendin 39, Diana 39, Benjm. 17, Sarah 15, Thos. 13, Elizabeth 11, Richd. 9, Henry 7, Pendin 5, Danl. 3, David 1
MORRIS, Benjm. 32, Frances 24, Sarah 5, Hannah 2, Richd. 3/12
GRIFFETH, Evan 52*, Mary 53, Gabl. 27, Elvina 20, Abm. 2, Evan 6/12
RATCLIFF, Wm. 18*
KISEE, Frances 34, John 12, Arena 10, Malinda 8, Lucinda 5
PRINCE, Nicholas 48, Charity 35, John 16, Temperance 15, Elias 11, Delila 8, James 6, Mary 4

Schedule Page 95

EVANS, John 48, Milly 50, Silly 18 (f), Elizabeth 16, Nancy C. 14, Henry C. 11
PHILLUPS, Iredel 33, Mary 31, Meredith 13, John 10, Sarah 8, Milly C. 6, Wm. P. 4, Henry 1
FIELDS, James 33, Mary 26, Martha 10, Joseph 8, Matilda 6, Stephen 5, Elizabeth 3, Evaline 1
SEGRAVES, Saml. 44, Sarah 43, William 21, Edmd. 19, Louverna 17, Louisiana 15, Nancy 13, Alcy 9, Green V. 7, Jonathon 5, Jesse 2
GAMBLE, Henderson 29, Delphia 22, Elijah 1
LIONS, William 51, sarah 52, James 30, Agnus 27, Wm. 25, Mahulda 19, resin 17, Manon 14, Sarah 12, Sumatta 10
RIGSBY, Lewis 40, Elizabeth 40, Willis 20, Lucinda 18, Henry 16, Nancy 14, Miels 11, Sernetta 9, Wilburn 7, Martha 5, Meredith 3
RIGSBY, Thos. 73, Lericy 28, Thos. jr 10, Sarah 7, Lucinda 3/12
HASLETT, Robt. 46, Margaret 43, Abagail 18, John 16, Sarah 13, Mary 13, Rutha 11, Wm. 9, Julia F. 7, Leander 5, Robt. 2
FITSPATRICK, Burgess 38, Manerva 11, Juliet 10, David W. 8, Ulises 6, James 1

Schedule Page 96

TURMAN, James L. 39, Margaret 27, James R. 3, J. J. C. 2 (m), Belvedore 6/12, Benjn. 42
BURGESS, Reuben 37*, Nancy 29, Strother 11, Wm. 9, Sarah 7, Emly 4, Geo. 2, Elizabeth 6/12
HALL, Elisha M. 22*
COOMPTON, Gasper 21*
WELMAN, Lot 34*, Elizabeth 33, Joseph jr 9, Wm. 8, Van B. 5, Mary J. 3
BRADLEY, Sarah 12*
MILLER, James F. 29*, Eleanor 24, Missouri A. 2, Mary 10
CHAPMAN, Elizabeth 1*
HAYS, Basiel 44*, Ardela 18, Julyan 18, Johnn 16, Delila 15, Frances 13, Maryann 11, Basiel jr 10, Sarah 7, Allen 5, Andrew 3
PUCK, Elizabeth 75*
HAYS, William 22, Elizabeth 20, Saml. 1
HAYS, Isaac 20, Katharine 18, Valentine 2?/12

1850 Census Lawrence County Kentucky

PRICHARD, James 52, Elizabeth 47, Allen 26, Wiley 23, Lewis 20, John 14, Kenez 12, Napolian 10, Noah 8, Gerome 6
BOYD, Andrew 27, Julyan 21, Wm. 3, John 1
SPENCER, John 37, Matilda 33, Mary 15, Frances 14, John B. 10, Katharine 8, Lewis W. 7, Elizabeth 5, Jemima 3, Wm. B. 1
WELMAN, John R. 33, Mary 22
MOORE, Lucinda 47, Amanda 14, Joseph 19, Cornelus 17, Wesley 12, Ephraim 11, Garland 9, Pemelia 7
MEAD, Jesse 47, Nancy 35, Ambrose 20, Robt. 18, John H. 15, Mary 11, Martha 10, Nelly 7, Charles 4, Elizabeth 1

Schedule Page 97

SPENCER, Charles 41, Rebecca 37, Mary 16, Nancy 15, lewis 13, Wm. H. 9, Nelly 6, Matilda 5, Lucy 7/12
JUSTICE, Geo. 45, Martha 50, Geo. T. 14, Kisiah 18, Martha 12, Margaret L. 11, Jesse 9
MORROW, Danl. 34, Nancy 23, John 5, Sarah F. 3, Joseph W. 2, Elisa L. 1/12
BURCHETT, Oliver 22*, Maryann 22, Permelian 1
CHAFIN, Levi 48*
MILLER, Henry B. 49, Elizabeth 38, James M. 18, Thompson 16, Louisa 14, Polly 12, Susannah 9, Mary R. 7, Nancy E. 7
GARRED, Jane 75*, Ulyus 36, David W. 26, Nancy 18, Isadore 1
CARY, Wm. 8*
KISEE, John 30, Susan 22
BISHOP, David 30, Sarah 23, Rutha 12, John 10, Lydia 8, David 5, Elizabeth 3, Rebecca 3, Katharine 6, Martha 15
JOHNSON, John 53, Nancy 38, Mason 19, John 18, Martha 15, Anna 12, Elizabeth 12, Mary 10, James C. 3, Jacob 1/12
BURGESS, Geo. R. 42, Emly 38, Cornelus H. 17, Thos. J. 15, Nancy J. 13, Hesteran 12, Julyan 9, Cynthian 8, Emly J. 7, Isabel 3

Schedule Page 98

BURGESS, Edwd. 47, Elizabeth 40, James E. 20, Wm. H. 17, John F. 15, Francis M. 13, Mary J. 11, Jula? 9, Davis S. 7, Elizabeth W. 4, Edwd. L. 9/12
DEBOAD, Jacob 33, Caroline 30, Wm. 12, Joseph 10, Elizabeth 8, John 6, Martha 5, Milly 4, Jacob 2
DULY, Thos. 58?, Margaret 33, James W. 6, Louisa 3, Mary 2, Sarah 1/12
BURGESS, Henry 77, Mary 36, Elizabeth 14
CARTMILL, Thos. 26, Manerva 21, Caroline 2, Elisha 1
SALYERS, Thos. 26, Frances 21, Ma;ry 2/12
PRESTON, John 48*, Kisiah 27, Hamilton 6, Asbury 4, Zephaniah 1
MEAD, Isabel 20*
NELSON, Elizabeth 34*, Basaline? 12, Asbury 3, James 1
MCDOWELL, Johns 25*
SHORT, John 48, Susannah 32, Nancy 14, Lucinda 11, Judith 7, Isaiah 2
FERSHEE, James 60, Mary 33, Caleb 11, John 9, Danl. 7
PRESTON, Robt. 18, Mahulda 21, Permelia 1/12

1850 Census Lawrence County Kentucky

SALYERS, Nancy 63, Zachariah 18
PRESTON, Stephen 54, Pricy 44, Robt. 16, James 13, Nancy J. 9, John 2
DAVIS, Wm. jr 31*, Katharine 31, Mary 11, John 9, Joseph 7, Amos 5, Jane 3, Elizabeth 2
FRANCIS, Wm. 20*
MICHELL, David 35*, Louvina 33, Martha 11, Miram 6, William 4, Louisa 1

Schedule Page 99

CASTLE, Wm. 26*
PENINGTON, Hardin 30, Elizabeth 30, Maranda 14, Henderson 5/12
BORDERS, Arthur 23
PALMER, Amanl. 29*, Agnus 27, Cyrus 9, Sarahan 8, Reuben 5
TACKETT, Dorcus 21*
BOYD, Wm. 22, Louisa 19, Geo. W. 10/12
NEAL, Andrew 26, Bridget 20, patrick 1
KARKIN, Thos. 26, Bridget 25
PRILE, John 45, Bridget 30, Michell 2
NEWMAN, Henry 44, Agnus 36, Valentine 16, Agnus 13, peter 11
BORDERS, Archabald 52*, Jane 51, Allen 19, Julyan 10
HALL, Richd. 53*
WILEY, Wm. 20*
WARMAC, Wm. 18*
CASTLE, John 5*
AMBUSH, Aron 30*
REYNOLDS, Wm. 26, Katharine 21, James H. 1
HANEY, William 99, Elizabeth 53
WHITE, Francis 34, Nancy 24, Martin 12, Emaline 11, Sarah 10, Calforna 8, Juliaan 2
FAIRCHILDS, Benjn. 53*, Manerva 20, Caleb 2
AMEN, Henry 22*
CARY, Benjn. 53, Hannah 43, lewis 15, Henry 13, Sarah G. 11, Margaret 8, nancy 6, Geo. 3
BORDERS, John 26, Serelda 22, Martin 7, Wallace 5, Matilda 3, Telitha J. 1
PRESTON, Reuben 33, Lucinda 25, Alafair 13, Frances 12, Judy F. 9, Wm. H. 4, Julyan 1/12
BOYD, Greenville 27, Mary 21, Arthur 4, James S. 2, Sarah J. 2/12
PRICE, Richd. 52, Elizabeth 50, Lyncha 19, Hannah 13, Jane 9, Elizabeth 5

Schedule Page 100

JAMES, Soloman 24*, Sarah 21
PRICE, Richd. C. 8/12*
PRICE, James 28*, Emoretta 24, Wm. J. 7, Julia 4, John N. 1
VANHOOSE, Reuben jr 11*
FITSPATRICK, Wm. 67, Martha 50, Jane 16, Vina 14, John 12, Reason 10
BOYD, Isom 24, Mary 21
JONES, Saml. 32, Anna 28, Margaret F. 10
FITSPATRICK, James 28, Jane 26, Julia 6, Peemina 4, Bengess? 2
PRESTON, John 36, Elizabeth 36, James 17, Wallace 15, Henry 12, Cyntha 10, Allen 7, Sarah 5, Vian 7/12

1850 Census Lawrence County Kentucky

FITSPATRICK, Wm. 26, Jane 18, Levy 1
CHILDERS, Russell 23, Pricy 16
PRESTON, Isaac 62, Mary 55, Harrison 20, Bateman 15
PRICE, John 33, Sarah 33, Julian 12, Franklin 10, Telitlha 8, Jesse 5, Batheny 3, Elizabeth 3, David 1
BRIANT, Geo. 29, Elizabeth 22, Julyan 3, Mary J. 1
BRIANT, Wm. 27, Margaret 24, Elizabeth 1
OBRIANT, Herrald 59, Margaret 46, James 26, Isaac 23, Owen 21, Sarahan 16, John 14, Dotia 12, Mary J. 11, Julilan 6, Chistena 4, Delila 2
HINKLE, Wm. 26, Elizabeth 19, Gasper 1
HINKLE, Randal 58, Charlotte 50, Wesley 23, James 17, Haniford 15, Charlotte 12, Lorenzo 8

Schedule Page 101

HINKLE, John 29, Lazabeth? 23, Lorenzo 3, Eli 1
JOHNSON, Joseph 37, Eleanor 44, Francis 16, Margaret 14, James 12, Martha 10, Mahala 8, Joseph 6, Apperson 4
BOYD, James 55*, Sarah 40, Lucinda 18, Julyan 15, Elizabeth 12, Sally 9, Anderson 8, James 6, Lena 4, Lewis 7/12
CALAWAY, Elizabeth 12*, Julena 11
RANDOLPH, Wm. 25*, Mary 29, Burgess 3, Anjeline 1
PRICE, Jane 11*, Kenez F. 8, Moveta 5
PRICE, Moses 41*, Sarah 41, Charlotte 17, James B. 15, Detroit 14, Mirckworth 12, Sumey 10, Martin V. 8, Morgana 6, Cleavland 4, Molenthian 1
VANHOOSE, Thos. 36*, Moses 13, Saml. 8
HICKMAN, Francis 42*, Matilda 22, Nancy 13, Mary 12, Elizabeth 8, John W. 6, Isiah 3, Zach 1/12
SALYERS, Isiah 50*
PRESTON, Arthur 43*, Nancy 42, Hariford 20, Calvin 18, Moses 16, Jane 14, Roxyan 12, Layfayett 10, Pricy 8, Perlina 6, Telitha 2, Arther W. 4/12
MEAD, Noah 16*
CHILDERS, Abram 52, Elizabeth 39, John 24, Moses 16, Arch 13, Sarah 11, Wesly 9, Cornwallace 7, O. H. 5 (m), Sarilda 1

Schedule Page 102

PRESTON, Henry 45, Elizabeth 45, Hiram 20, Martha 16, Setphen 15, Jane 16, Wm. S. 14, Julyan 13, Frances 12, Caroline 11, Sarilda 10, James M. 9, McDonald 8, Amanda 7, Julyan 6
BOYD, Hugh 23*, Lavica 19, McCass 1, Samantha 6/12
HINKLE, Alford 24*
CALEWAY, Cornelus 17*
BORDERS, Hezekiah 58*, Jemima 35, Mary 2
MEAD, Mary J. 14*
BORDERS, Archabald 30*, Emaline 20, Sarha F. 1
CALAWAY, Washington 14*
MURRY, Saml. 60*, Sarahan 53
CALEWAY, Harvey 19*
FANNIN, Jackson 32*, Lucinda 18
CASTLE, Harper 24, Elizabeth 22, Lucinda 4, Precilla 2, Nathan 30

1850 Census Lawrence County Kentucky

DAVIS, Henry 64*, Rachel 61
BOTTOMS, Wm. 15*, Sarahan 14
DAVIS, Saml. 66, lucretia 56
BORDERS, John 29, Elizabeth 33, Hezekiah 11, Maryan 9, David 7, Jane 4, Bartha 2
BORDERS, Wm. 23*, Abagail 24, John 4, Stephen 2, Jemima 1
NELSON, Isaac 10*
NELSON, Emml. 74*, Anna 51
BURTEN, Allen 17*, Susannah 21?, Jemima 9
DAVIS, Joseph 42, Katharine 40, Christena 22, Wm. 21, Michl. 20, Burna 15, Martin P. 13, Hezekiah 12, Jededidah 11, David 9, Saml. 5, Mary J. 3, Frances 5/12
DAVIS, Hezekiah 25, Milly 29, Frances 7, Clarinda 5, Elizabeth 2, Emaline 2/12

Schedule Page 103

BORDERS, Henry 20*, Sarah 17, Ira 10/12
HAIL, Mary 14*
VANHOOSE, John 22, Sarahan 20, Louisa 8/12
LOWE, Hannah 39, Wm. 17, John 14, Margaret 8
DAVIS, Elihue 52*, Rachel 42, Kisiah 20
MULLINS, Hetta 6*
NELSON, Rachel 2*
SPENCER, James 23*
YOUNG, Wm. 52*
GREEN, Mary 26*, Louisa 4, John 4/12
BEVENS, David 44, Jane 45, Anna 24, Manerva 21, Joseph 20, David 18, Elizabeth 14, Jane 12
BORDERS, Michl. 63*, Christena 63
BOYD, James 19*
DURCKIM, Wiley 18*
BURTEN, John 20, Elizabeth 20
BORDERS, Danl. 24, Sarahan 21, Elizabeth 3, Wm. W. 9/12
MILLER, Robt. 39, Susan 38, Silverna 19, David C. 11, Layfayette 9, Nancy J. 8, Elizabeth 6, Amanda 4, Henry C. 2, Selerda 7/12, Philip 78
AUSTIN, Thomas 24, Virginia 17, Mary 50, Francis 20, John 18, Elizabeth 15
MCDOWELL, John 51, Jemima 48, Sintha 21, Danl. 18, nancy 12, Elenor 10, Rachel 7, Arch 4
DAVIS, Wm. sr. 80*, Nancy 53
MCGUIRE, Joseph 12*, Emaline 16
MCDOWELL, John jr 24*, Manerva 21
MEAD, Susan 70, Sarah 23, Jackson 18, John 15
MEAD, Abm. 32, Jane 28, Sarahan 12, Wm. H. 8, Lucy 5, Nancy 4, Elizabeth 9/12
MEAD, Kisiah 35*

Schedule Page 104

NELSON, Kisiah 37*
ROSE, Nancy 24*, Geo. W. 3, Martha 1
BLANKENSHIP, Henry 34, Elizabeth 29, Silvester 14, Rily 11, John 9, Mary 8
WEBB, Rhoda 28, James 10, Calvin 7, Allen T. 5, Wm. 2

1850 Census Lawrence County Kentucky

OWSLEY, Fleming 28, Elizabeth 29, Elizah 3, Margaret 1/12
SPENCER, Charles 22, Margaret 23
THOMPSON, Wm. 29, Milly 32, Michl. 12, Julyan 10, Frances 9, Arch 7, Saml. 5, Christena 2, Amos 1
THOMPSON, John 32, Maryan 36, Sarah 16, Squire 14, Rebecca 13, Susan 12, Preston 10, Harrison 8, Katharine 7, Hannah 5, James 3, John 1
THOMPSON, Eleanor 32*, John 11, Mary 9, Caroline 2, Francis 7/12
DUNCAN, David 60*
HINKLE, Nancy 36*, Mary 18
MILLER, Asher 15*
MILLER, Saml. 20, Elizabeth 15
SPALDING, John 55, Pemelia 30, Thos. 78, Martha 70
THOMPSON, Richd. 45, Mahale 44, Lurena 16
THOMPSON, Saml. 22, Emaretta 18, Richd. 10/12
THOMPSON, Andw. 72, Katharine 75
MOORE, David 26, Lucinda 23, Mary 5, Nancy 3, Exony 1, Harvey 22
MOORE, John 24, Katharine 20, Pricy 8/12
THOMPSON, Andrew 30, Sarah 30, Geo. 10, Mahale 8, Richd. 6, Henson 4, Andrew 1
THOMPSON, Geo. 24, Mary 24, Martin 6, Green 4, Johnson 2

Schedule Page 105

SMITH, Thomas 69, Rachel 60, Falla O. 38, Henry C. 22, Saml. 9, Francis H. 3
ALLISON, John H. 54, Mary J. 40, Emly 20, Adelaide B. 17, Mary J. 14, James L. 12, Danl. J. 10, Louisa 8, Ann 6, Josaphine 3, Richd. A. 1, Robt. C. 1
MARCUM, James 58, Dicy 50, Alford 30, Rebecca 18, Nancy 16, Evaline 12, Julia 10, Dicy A. 7
MARCUM, Fleming 26*, Elizabeth 22, Dicy 8/12
LOWDER, Lewis 22*
FRASURE, Saml. 37*, Pelina 34, Manerva 15, Wm. 12, David P. 10, James 8
HARDY, Henderson 19*
DYER, Cynthiann 30*, John M. 10/12
CRANK, Elizabeth 9*, Nancy A. 6, Richd. W. 3
PRICE, Hansford 24*, Pemelia 23, Nancy G. 2/12
HAYS, Montraville 9*
LIKENS, John M. 29*, Maryan 31, Joseph F. 10, Nancy L. 8, Goodwin 4, St.? Mark 3, Elizabeth 2
BERICH?, Lewis 35*
THOMPSON, Granvill 28, Elizabeth 23, Abagail 5, Louvana 2, Hesterann 1
THOMPSON, David 26, Elizabeth 27, Andrew 4, Eleanor 2, Mary F. 2/12
GRUBB, Isaac 50, Rebecca 37
LEE, James 29, Lucinda 19, John 3, Elizabeth 2
BELCHER, Andw. J. 32, Nancy 22, Martha 3, James 1
HUNTER, Saml. 40, Rebecca 35, Nancy 18
ROBERTS, Sinclare 57*, Anna 48

Schedule Page 106

MORGAN, Saml. 29*
BAILY, Saml. 26*

1850 Census Lawrence County Kentucky

WALLACE, Elizabeth 20*
VANHORNE, John 20, Hilyan 20
ROBERTS, Wm. A. 23*, Elizabeth 22, Wm. O. 3, Sinclar Jr. 10/12
WHITE, Lear 21*
MCCOY, Geo. W. 20*
SIMPSON, Fredk. 25*, Frances 19, Margaret 1
RUCKLES, Elizabeth 13*
HOWE, Geo. W. 40, Sarah 36, Martha K. 12, James 10, John W. 8, Hiram B. 6, Philip H. 4, Sarah ann 2
LAMBERT, Josiah 45, Margaret 37, Elizabeth 14, Abner 11, Perlenos 9, Hiram 6, Benjm. 4, John 2
STEWERT, John 45, Lucinda 35, Elisa 16, Richd. 15, Andrew 8, Sidney 6 (f), Elizabeth 4, Wm. 1
CECIL, John 37, Margret 32, Emorine 14, Margret 11, Eliza Ann 6, Harriel M. 3 (f)
FANNIN, John Sr. 71*, Keziah 66
LAMBERT, Saml. 13*
PITTS, Thos. N. 32*, Mary 28, John N. 3, Ara 10/12
FANNIN, Joseph 48, Achillis 21, Jefferson 19, Isaac 17, Lucinda 15, Mahala 13, Sarah Ann 11
BRANHAM, Rachael 24*, Joseph 4
FANNIN, Bryant 6/12*
BOLT, Greenville 35, Mary 27, Sylvester D. 12, Elizabeth 11, Wm. D. 9, Isaac N. 6, Montraville 4, Katharine 2
BOOTEN, Hiram 46, Emma 32, Ralph 8, Mary 6, Susan 1
LINDNER, Ernest 31*, Caroline 26, Charles W. 5, Mary L. P. 3
CRAWFORD, Elenor 18*
KRAUSS, John 37, Kathrine 28, Luther 6, Mary 8, Rider 4, Lee 2, Franklin B. 1

Schedule Page 107

RIDER, Conrad 41*, Katharine 39, Phillip 16, Mary 14, Jacob 11, Barbara 6
BUTTS, Derotha 63*
BOLT, Montraville S. 34, Patience 34, Mary L. 9, Angeline 8, Elija? 7, Greenville 4, Keziah 1, Oleva 1
QUEEN, John 45, Sarah 37, Emiline 8, Walter 19, John W. 19, Stephen 6, Frances 4, Isaac 3, Hector M. 1
TOMLIN, Solomon 22, Julia An 18, Rebecca J. 5/12
CLAY, Henry 43, Honor 47, Eliza 21, James 18, Nancy 15, John 13, Isaac 11, Mary 8, Henry H. 6
PRICHARD, Geo. W. 29*, Oleva ann 22, Mary E. 6, Leander C. 4, Virgina 4/12
HAYS, Harvey 17*
WEST, Charles 30, Eleanor 22, Elizabeth 5
BOLT, Isaac 60, Elizabeth 54, Alford 24, John M. 20
STEWERT, Absalom Jr. 42, Ama 31, John M. 10, Wm. R. 7, Isaac 5, Kesiah 3, Leander 6/12
FANNON, Briant 24, Louisa 20, Wm. E. 1
FANNIN, Saphira 40, John D. 17, Joseph 16, Kesiah 15, Mary H. 12, Phillip S. 5
KINNER, Greenvill 27, Elizabeth 28, Mary F. 6, Oliver H. 4, Mary E. 2, Samanthe 4/12
LEAKEN, Joseph 52, Miram 44, Saml. 24, Saphira 21, James 20, Katharine 8, Amanda 6, Margaret 3, Susan F. 1, Levi 50

1850 Census Lawrence County Kentucky

Schedule Page 108

BOCOCK, Wm. 30, Sarah 35, Malica 11, Marshall 9, Alford 8, Saml. 7, James A. 6, Martha 3, Collumbia 2, Lydia 5/12
BOCOCK, Elijah 44, Jane 44, Wm. 22, Malinda 19, Elizabeth 17, Rudelph 15, Sarahann 13, Francis M. 10, Allen 5, Columbus 1
ALLISON, Isaac 67*, Katharine 58
BURNS, Rowland 16*, Layfaette 17
BRIANT, Kesiah 7*
CUMINGS, David 25, Hannah 19, Riley 1
LAMBERT, Jobe 24, Clarinda 18, Lindsey 3/12
MCKEE, Geo. W. 26, Sinthaan 26, Eldridge 2, Sarah 4/12
SPERRY, Saml. 74, Lydia 70
BOCOCK, John 24, Martha 30
BOWLING, James 50*, Sarah 40, Jane 9
MURRY, Eleanor 13*
IRONDUFF, Elisha 20*
NEALY, Margaret 17*
LASLIE, John P. 40, Jane 37, Elizabeth 13, Martha 11, David 7, Elisa M. 1
SHOCKEY, Geo. 32*, Mary 44, Leanor 7 (f), Wm. 5, Geo. W. 4
LOVEJOY, Elizabeth 16*, Layfayett 11
LOVEJOY, James 21, Rebecca 17, John 4, Mary 2
BRIANT, Reece 37*, Mary 28, Rachel 10, John 8, Washington 5, Taylor 3/12, Geo. W. 30, Rachel 43
MURRY, Jane 18*
SPENCER, Jesse 18, Mary 18
LOCKWOOD, Elizabeth 43, Wm. 19, David 17, Jacob 15, John 13, Frances 4

Schedule Page 109

HOLIDAY, Wm. H. 40, Katharine 37, Wm. H. 13, Mary P. 10, Charlotte 8, Giles D. 6, Katmahom? 2 (f)
LOCKWOOD, Jacob 74, Jacob Jr. 40, Luette 34, Martha 13, Elizabeth 11, Wm. 9, David 7, James 5
LOCKWOOD, Wm. 45*, Sarah 40, James 16, John 14, Mary 12, David 10, Caroline 8, Benjm. F. 6, Elizabeth 3
WHITE, Sarah 71*
BRIANT, David 38, Arena 33, Sarah A. 11, Helon 9, Elizabeth 4, Mary 1
BECKLEY, James 23, Amatha 20
SYRAS, Levi 26, Elisa J. 22, Elizabeth 1
VANHORNE, John 37*, Indiania 37, Franklin 22, Francis 18, G. 16 (m), Lucinda 6, Pernelia 5, Mary 3
MCVAIN, James 30*
HUCHERSON, Logan E. 37, Susan 40, David 13, Geo. W. 7, Henry L. 5, Nancy 2
GRAY, David 43, Elisabeth 30, Frances 9, Tealy A. 7, John N. 5, Mary E. 8/12
ADAMS, Constantine 50, Frances 40, Lucinda 18, Wm. 15, Sarah 13, John 12, Mary 9, Andy 1/12 (f)
CYRAS, Jesse 37*, Sarah 34, Jackson 20, Barbara 18, Julian 16, Sarah 14, Luala 12, Saml. H. 8, Susan 6, Elizabeth 3, Helon 2/12
DANIELS, Harrison 10*
FORTNER, Wm. 23, Maryan 22
GARVIN, John S. 37, Mary E. 29, Saml. 8, Elizabeth 3/12

1850 Census Lawrence County Kentucky

Schedule Page 110

BURGESS, Geo. R. 35*, Martha 30, Octava M. 13, Strother 11, Sarah F. 9, Goble 7, Susan M. 5, Vergina C. 3, Charity C. 1
SPURLOCK, Wm. 20*
BEAN, Wm. 25*
STITH, Wm. 25*
MARKS, Thos. 29*, Elizabeth 24, Sarahan 8, Edmd. 6, Susan H. 4
BRAGG, Wm. 20*
MCDOWELL, Mary 23*
STEPHENS, John A. 28, Isabel 29, Mary E. 4, Wm. A. 2
DAMRON, Lazrus 30, Eliza 29, Rebecca 9, Wm. 6, John M. 4
BECKLEHIMER, Isaac 50*, Mahala 35, Martha 5, Mary 16, Wm. 14, Adeline 9
MCGRAW, John V. 17*, Caroline 13, Mahale 8
MURRY, Hiram 45, Nancy 38, Melvina 17, Matilda 12, Elizabeth 8, Beely 6 (f), Orrela 5
SCOTT, Sarah 35, Elizabeth 17, Wm. 15, Sarah 11, Maryan 8, Katharine 6, Lucinda 4
CARTER, Calvery 37, Elizabeth 39, John H. 10, Mary E. 9, Octava 7
BROWN, Richd. 35, Katharine 30, Clarinda 12, John 9, Ruhama 5, Mahala 2
STEWERT, Ralph 51, America 36, James E. 17, Elizabeth 16, Layfayette 14, Jeremiah F. 11, Albert 9, Frances 7, Gerard 4, Emma 1
CHADWICK, Geo. E. 50, Dama 45, John L. 23, Sarah 17, Jackson 20, Frances 14, Margaret 12, Wm. 10, James K. 6, Virginia 5, Zac T. 3, Thos. J. 4/12

Schedule Page 111

POWELL, Burr 39*, Nancy 32, Elizabeth 16, Wm. H. 14, John W. 11, James A. 9, Ferebe 6, Eliza F. 4, Perry A. 2
QUEEN, Absalom 20*
NEWMAN, Reynolds 45, Malinda 36, Caroline 18, Ama 16, Peyton 15, John 14, Wm. 12, Virginia 6, Marion F. 4, Isabel 1
GILKERSON, Jeff 28, Rebecca 22, Celia 2
SMITH, Edmd. 30*, Jane 23, John 4, Elizbeth 2, Nancy 7/12
MIKLES, Henry 20*
STITH, James 30, Sarilda 28, Caroline 9, Elizabeth 6, Merica 4, Geo. W. 3
PRICHARD, Lewis 55, Lucy 47, Wm. 23, Jackson 21, Lucinda 17, Joseph 14, Lewis 12, James 10, Thos. J. 8, Robt. 6, John J. 2
PRICE, James 45, Katharine 42, Arch 17, Nelly 16, Edmd. 12, Magean 9, Jances? 6 (f), Katharine 4, James 1
SMITH, Francis 27, Elizabeth 21, John 1
HATTEN, Edmd 35, Sarah 35, Emarine 13, Joseph 10, Elizabeth 5, Melcena 3, Francis 1
MASSY, John 23, Emaline 22, Geo. 4
HARDIN, James 46*, Mary 46
TURMAN, Renee? 80*
CARNUTT, Reuben 57*, Elizabeth 50, Mary 32
WILSON, John 18*
TURMAN, Permelia 15*, James 9

1850 Census Lawrence County Kentucky

Schedule Page 112

MCSORLEY, Edmd. 23, Elizabeth 28, Ralph 13, Margaret 2, James 10/12, Nancy 21
VENTERS, John 27, Elizabeth 23, Geo. N. 6, Plesant 5, James 3
KINNER, David 29*, Mary 47, David Jr. 20, Harvy 18, Layfayette 10, Mary F. 7, Martha 5, Louisa 3
STEWERT, Nancy 68*, Adeline 15
CLAY, Bartly 50, Nancy 45, Evan 25, John 17, Geo. 15, Jane M. 13, Indyan 11
KINNER, Hansford 25*, Mahale 19, Stephen G. 2
CHAFIN, Jeff 27*
LARGE, William 48, Ann 65, Wiley 16
WHITE, Danl. 48*, Mary 48, Ephraim 19, John 16, Barbara 12, Francis M. 8, Alvin 5
PETERMAN, Wm. 23*
STEWERT, Ralph 78, Elizabeth 68?, Elliott 25
BALMORE, Nancy 40, Robt. 22, Lydia 16, Michell 14, Elizabeth 9
MEAD, Malinda 28, Abm. 12, Kesiah 10, Cyntha 7, Henry K. 6, Katharine 4, Lyncha 1
STEWERT, Madison 28, Rebecca 25, Granvill 5, Nancy 2, Marinda 1
BROMFIELD, Madison 37, Malinda 35, Mahale 12, Marshall 11, Smily 9, Absalom 7, Nancy 6, Gerrard 1
MORROW, Francis 38, Nancy 19, Silas 1
TOMLIN, Isom 63, Mary 57, Logan 27, Jameson 24, Joseph 21, Isom 12
BANK, Laney 45, Anna 20, Isom 19, Katharine 18, Elizabeth 16, Thos. 14, Alexr. 11, Nancy 9

Schedule Page 113

TOMLIN, Henderson 32, Polly 32, Lemuel 9, James 6, Gasper 3, Joseph 1
BURNER, Ann 46, Arch 20, Oliver 18, Henry 11, John 7
BRIANT, Zach 44, Susan 48, Jeff 24, Sarah 21, Mary J. 19, Lucinda ;16, Elizabeth 14, Susan 9, Silvester 6, Alford 17, Rouland J. 5
LEAKEN, Thos. 44*, Elizabeth 42, James 23, Levi 21, Julyan 17, Charlotte 15, Sarah 15, Susan 13, George 9, Thos. 7, Elizabeth 5
MCFARLAND, Geo. 15*
BUCHANNON, Wm. 80, Elizabeth 71, Oliver 34, Geo. 21, Louisa 18, Susan 16
BRIANT, John 78, Moarning 50 (f), Rhoda 21
TOMLIN, Alexr. 36, Elizabeth 25, Elisa 12, Geo. 8, Peter 5, Pelina 2
SCISSON, Charles 50*, Sarah 50, Emanl. 17, Hiram 14, Jane 12
SHANNON, Jane 65*
SCISSON, Joseph 20, Elizabeth 18
SCISSON, Miles 23, Sidney 18 (f)
CARNUTT, Stephen 27, Elizabeth 25, Hansford 5, James H. 3, Mary 1
WHEELER, Amos H. 32, Hannah 23, Henry C. 15, Elmena 13, Richd. 11, James A. 10, Margaret 8, Hannah 5, Elizabeth 3, John B. 6/12
MILLER, Wm. 42, Mary 42, Wm. 11, Charlotte 9, Martha 7, Edwd. 4

1850 Census Lawrence County Kentucky

Schedule Page 114

STROAD, Mark? 75, Sarah 70
SPENCER, Thos. 27*, Rebecca 29, Johnson 5, Robt. 3, Ferabe 2
PRICE, Marinda 24*
CORD, Wm. 17*, Sarah 1
BROWN, Andrew 28, Susan 29, Elizabeth 3, John 1
PACK, Wm. 39, Matilda 36, Phebe 17, John 16, Andrew 14, Delila 12, Wm. 6, Geo. W. 5
KELLY, Joseph 24, Elisa 20, Joseph 6/12
VENTERS, Geo. M. 21, Susan 19, Alexr. 3, James 1
LOOTS, John 27, Caroline 21
LOOTS, Nathanl. 55, Sarah 50, Amanda 17, Jane 11, Nathanl. Jr. 9, Sarilda 7
BALL, Minten J. 20, Cyntha 20, Nancy 2, Hardin 5/12
CORDELL, John 21, Jane 22, Jesse 1
CORDILL, Amos 18, Jane 18, Jeremiah 6/12
MCDOWELL, Wm. 61*, Susan 59, Riley 23, Lewis 21, Rutha 16, Henson 15, Diana 2, Meredith 2
SWANN, Resin 38, Mary 37, Elizabeth 14, Pelina 12, Agnes 10, Lewis 8, Lutelia 5
GREEN, Enoch 38, Elizabeth 39, Amasa 19, Andrew J. 18, Geo. W. 16, Burwell 15, Abagail 13, John F. 10
RAINEY, John 45, Rachel 37, Rebecca 19, Wm. 17, Eleanor 15, Henry 13, John Jr. 10, Caroline 8, James 6, Jemima 3, Rachel 1

Schedule Page 115

MATNEY, John 30, Lucinda C. 25, James A. 4, Virginia 2, John M. 1
GREEN, Thos. 29, Jemima 23, Isiah 5, Geo. W. 4, John W. 2, Giles 1
SPARKS, Danl. 43, Sarah 37, Delila J. 15, Henry W. 13, Elisa Ann 12, Mahale 8, Jemima 4, Rachel H. 3
BISHOP, David 68, Elizabeth 67, Thos. 23, Gatha 22 (m), Telitha 12
THOMPSON, Saml. 72*, Roda 47, Frances 1
BOWLING, Robt. 20*, Rebecca 18, Jane 11, Wm. 7
THOMPSON, Wesley 41, Esther 35, John S. 17, Thomas 15, Elizabeth 13, Russell 12, Nancy 11, Isaac 10, Pernelia 8, Mary 6, Allen 5, Asbury 1
MCKINSTER, Elizabeth 45, John 19, Jesse 15, Martha 12, Dotia 7, Saml. 6
MCKINSTER, James 26, Julia 19, Wm. 1
SHANNON, Thomas 46, Rebecca 30, Elizabeth 21, Harvey 20, Wm. 19, Nancy 16, James 15, Jane 13, Harrison J. 9, Andrew L. 7, Isaac J. 5, Julia 3
JUSTICE, Hamilton 22, Martha 17
JUSTICE, Pilot 24, Margaret 19
SCAGG, John L. B. 24, Mary 23, Harvey 6, Lewis 2, Martha 3
WOODS, Walter 27, Mary 23, Sarah J. 2
DIER, Owen 46*, Rebecca 40, Elizabeth 19, Frances 16, Corrilda 14

1850 Census Lawrence County Kentucky

Schedule Page 116

MCKINSTER, Jackson 15*
HAY, Henry 33, Eunice 27, Elizabeth 8, Mary 7, Nancy 10/12
DOBYNS, John 53, Katharine 39, Nancy 18, Dicy 17, Danl. 16, Francis 15, Rebeca 12, Wm. H. 11, Washington 9, Elizabeth 6, Sarah 3, John 1
SPALDING, Francis 76, Dicy 66
SHANNON, Geo. 30, Jane 26, Rebecca 4, John W. 2
CHAPMAN, Michel 37, Henretta 29, Geo. 12, Robt. 11, Cynthan 10, Jane 9, Emly 7, Albert 3, Greenvill 1
UNRUE, Danl. 36, Maryan 27, Rebecca 11, Emly 8, Nancy 5, Malinda 3, Mikonai? 1 (f)
PECK, Joseph 66, Elizabeth 59
PECK, Geo. C. 38, Emly 31, Joseph 11, Rebecca 9, Elizabeth 7, John 5, Mary 2, Lydia 2/12
ALLY, Wm. 36, Mary 40, Louisa 15, Margaret 12, Floyd H. 10, Hiram B. 9, Eleanor C. 5
CHAPMAN, Isaac 60*, Malinda 25, David 23, Henry 21, Lucretia 12
STEWART, Rebecca 7*
SHANNON, James 54*, Jane 54, Nancy 31, Thos. 22, David 21, Cornelus 11, Wm. 77, Martha 5
COMPTON, James H. 1*
MCCLURE, Wm. 60, Lucretia 51, Alzannah 21, Sarahan 20, Strother 18, Nancy 16, Wm. Jr. 15, Julia 12, Albert 9, Stephen 8, Precilla 6, Isaac T. 3

Schedule Page 117

ROBINETT, Wesley 27, Elizabeth 31, Geo. W. 4, John D. 2
GAVETT, Ezekl. 52*, Sarah 43
MEEK, Richard 13*
BRADLY, Margaret 12*
STAFFORD, John 27*, Mary 24, Sarah 4, Ezekl. K. 1
BRADLY, Malinda 8*
COMPTON, James H. 23, Eleanor 20
CHAPMAN, Maria 45, Geo. 19, John 17, Rebecca 12, Wm. 10, Elizabeth 9
BRADLEY, Stephen 42, Mary 42, Wm. 23, Elizabeth 22, Harriet 19, Jemima 17, Andrew L. 15, Silvester 13, Wesley M. 11, Jacob 9, Emaline 6, Amanda 4
CARNUTT, John 25, Amanda 22, Louisa 2, Mary 4/12
CHAFIN, Judy 45*, John 15, Kenez? 14, Washington 11
LARGE, Solaman 21*
CHAFIN, Owen 25*, Mahale 23, Sarah 2, Amanda 5/12
FUGETT, Elizabeth 6*, Mary 4
FUGETT, Benjm. H. 21*, Maryan 27, Frances 1
THOMPSON, Rachel 24*
NELSON, Wm. 45, Nancy 35, Lucy 13, Elizabeth 6, Enoch 3, Lydia 1
YORK, John 34, Sophia 26, James M. 5, Joshua 2, Elizabeth 1
MCGUIRE, N. B. 52 (m)*, Elizabeth 44, Ruthaan 21, John 18, Mary J. 16, James 13, Elizabeth 11, Katharine 8, Luke 6, Geo. 3
MCFARLAND, Wm. 50*
FRASURE, Geo. 48, Charlotte 39, Granville 15, John W. 14, James C. 12, Susan 8, Micajah 6, General W. 5, Andrew J. 2

1850 Census Lawrence County Kentucky

Schedule Page 118

JARRELL, Levi 21*, Sarah 19, Mary J. 4/12
PEREGOE, Jacob 25*
HATCHER, Geo. F. 41, Amanda 43, Nancy J. 17, John 16, James R. 14, Wm. W. 12, N. B. 10, Thos. B. 6, Julia A. 2
CUSHING, Z. 47 (m), Nancy A. 29, Mary 9, M. L. 7 (f), Romane V. 5
HODGE, Mary A. 64*, Marcus 24, Harvey 19
BRADLY, Thos. 40*
CALDWELL, E. W. 41 (m), Elisa 36, Thos. 14, Sarah 12, Ellon 10, James 7, Elisa 5, Wm. W. 3, Robt. 1
SLUSSER, Havey? 24*, Ellenor 22, Mary A. 2, John 3/12
MEEK, Raburn 21*
MCCOMAC, Madison 17*
GREEN, Sarah 40*
FOSTER, Lucinda 35, Mary 15, Jemima 13, George 6, Emaline 10/12
JOHNSON, Saml. 23, Elisa 22, Frances 4, Luverna 2, Mary J. 3/12
WHITE, David 40, Rhoda ;43, Havey 19, Elizabeth 17, Alcey 15, Jemima 9, Jackson 6
JOHNS, Mary J. 30, Martin H. 12, Elizabeth 10
CHAFIN, Agnes 60*
BRADLEY, Mahala 35*, Louisa 6, Katharine 3
HAWS, John W. 30*, Elizabeth 23, Arthur W. 3, John J. C. 1
JOHNSON, Thos. 22*
CHAPMAN, Wm. F. 24*
SHAW, Abm. 54 (B)
MARCUM, Lurena 30, Wm. 10, Many G. 6, Doc 5/12
LAMONDS, John 26, Elizabeth 25, Nancy 8, Flurry 5 (m), Neoma 4, Rowland 2

Schedule Page 119

YORK, Joshua M. 49, Jane 36, Andrew E. 13, Elizabeth 13, Martha 9, Ann 7, John 5, Robt. 2, Joseph 2
HARDWICK, Richd. 47, Susanah 41, Geo. 14, John 12, Nancy 10, Jane 8, Ferebe 5, Richd. 3, Louisa 1
BURCHETT, Oliver 21, Mary 16
HAMONDS, John 55*, Mary 43, Emily 16
FALKNER, Thomas 19*, Lucinda 14, Wm. 10
ROBERTS, Isaac 56, Phebe 55, James 22, Mary 20
BATES, Nathanl. 30, Mary 22, Elizabeth 8/12
ROBERTS, Isaac Jr. 24, Cynthan 20, Elisaan 3, James 2
MARTIN, Wm. 29, Hesther 28, Marsena 5, Benjm. F. 3, Perlina F. 3/12
ENDICOTT, Benjm. 35, Elizabeth 31, Sarah A. 15, Wm. 13, Joseph 11, Saml. 8, Joshua 5, Polly 4, Lourana 2
MANOR, Jesse 27, Polly 27, Celia 7, Alves 5, Lydia 3, Elen 7/12
PACK, John 24, Sarah 25, Elizabeth 4, Saml. 1
CASTLE, John E. 29, Elizabeth 25, Owen 7, Soloman 6, Joshua 5, Glawner 3, Richd. H. 1
HINKLE, Geo. 31, Katharine 25, Charlotte 9, Araminta 7, Pherebe 2
BOWEN, Alford 37, Mahale 36, Malisa 14, Wm. 12, Franklin 10, Julina 8, Mattie 7, Sarahann 5, Sarah 2, Henderson 7/12

1850 Census Lawrence County Kentucky

Schedule Page 120

JUSTICE, Timothy 21, Rachel M. 21, Alford 1, Geo. W. 4
WILLIAMSON, Soloman 49, Richd. 21, Soloman 19, Orpha 16, Joshua 13, Nancy 11, Wm. 9, John 5
WILLIAMSON, Benjm. 22, Jane 18
FITSPATRICK, Arthur 26, Elizabeth 25, Wm. 8, Geo. W. 6, Benjm. H. 4, Evaline 2, Martha J. 2/12
CASTLE, Zedekiah 72*, Ann 50, Isaac A. 22, Zedekiah 16, Caroline 13
SPRIGG, Farris A. 13*, Henry C. 10
SPRIGG, Polly 30, America 6, Amanda 4, Julyan 7/12
CASTLE, Jackson 24, Fanny 20, Maranda 2, Angeline 1
PACK, Cornelus 37, Nancy 35, Leander J. 15, Davis 13, Nancy J. 11, John 9, Ira? 7, Evaline 5, Wm. A. 3, Alven 3/12
CASTLE, Lindsey 35, Phebe 28, Polly 15, Danl. 11, Julia 13, Henry 9, Anna 7, Rhoda 4, Albert 2
PRESTON, Robt. 28, Matilda 25, Malissa 7, Alford 2, Acherson 2/12, James 18
PACK, Geo. 26, Anna 26, Thos. B. 6, Noah 4, Arthur 2, R. G. 7 (m)
BISHOP, Henry 26, Lucinda 23, Geo. W. 6, Harvey 4, Elisha 2
ELSWICK, Bradly 44*, Rebecca S. 38, Pricy 15, Martin B. 13, Wm. T. 12, Name? E. 9 (f), Aramenta 7, Louisa 3, Malias 1

Schedule Page 121

ROBINSON, Rebecca 79*
WILLIAMSON, James 37, Sintha 33, Aly 14 (m), Cassey 12, Elizabeth 10, John 7, Nancy 5, Lofaman 4, James 2, Wiley 4/12
BELL, Abner 51*, Chrisana 24, Robert A. 1
WILLIAMSON, Anthony 25*
WILLIAMSON, Stephen 21, Eleanor 18
WILLIAMSON, Alden 65, Polly 60, Asa 23, Jackson 18, Konez 15, Elizabeth 12, John 8
MOSELY, Martha 38, Katharine 10, Malinda 2, Thos. 2/12
JAMES, Ephraim 31, Sarah 23, John 8, Joseph 7, Milly 4, William 1
JONES, Joshua 77*, Milly 55, Sarah 26, Mary 3
JAMES, Sidney 7/12 (f)*
CASTLE, Joshua Z. 26, Maranda 20, Sarah J. 1
HANEY, John 21, Mary 19, Elizabeth J. 2/12, Neoma 20, Katharine 2
HANEY, Philip 65, Elizabeth 60, Sarah 15, Nancy J. 11
HANEY, Wm. 25*, Rebecca 22, James 4, John B. 2, Wm. H. 1/12
MOORE, John 25*
WILLIAMSON, Elijah 43, Susanah 36, Judith 14, Asa H. 12, Olden 9, Jane 8, Elisabeth 6, Soloman 4
WARD, Nathanl. 25, Minta 22, Angeline 6/12
PREWETT, Rachel 59, Sally 29, Polly 25, Susan 21, Malinda 16, Elijah 14
ALDRIDGE, Francis 43*, Nancy 43, James 16, Owen 14, Aron 11, Harrison 9, Thos. 7, Adelaide 4

Schedule Page 122

PRIEST, Cornelus 24*
RUNION, Adam 30?, Welthy 36 (f), Arena 12, Luesbury? 10, Heriford 8, Alexr. 5, Maria 4, Caroline 2

1850 Census Lawrence County Kentucky

MARCUM, Thos. 20, Jane 18, Elisa 2/12
EVANS, Susan 43, Thophelus 26, Joseph 11, Manerva 21, Sarah A. 5
SMITH, Isaac 35*, Mahale 36
ALEXANDER, Lewis 9*, John 7, Wm. 5, Margaret 3
HENSLY, Sarah 60*, Jacob 18
JEWELL, Nancy 26*, Wm. 5
EVANS, Henry 24*
DAVIS, Henry 40, Nelly 35, Thos. 17, Nancy 14, James 12, Henry 9, Harvey 7, Louisa 5, Jeremiah 3, Polly 1
THOMPSON, Patten 30, Malinda 24, Joseph 1, Lewis 7, Sally 5
BAKER, Nathanl. 33*, Elizabeth 33, Susannah 13, Jonathon 11, Saml. 9, Thos. L.? 5, Maryan 3
STATTEN, John B. 17*
CHAPMAN, John 59*, Sally 59, Wm. 39, John 31, Geo. 25, Thedorick 23, Sarena 19, Lydia 15
STAFFORD, Sally 14*, Lydia 8
ALDRIDGE, James 23*
MUNCY, Sally 34, Polly 13, Louisa 11, Nancy 9, Lydia 7, James 5
STAFFORD, Wm. 33, Fanny 29, Sarah 14, John 13, Thos. 11, Jefferson 2, Julia 8, Lydia 7, Wm. 2, Richd. 7/12
BOWEN, John 43, Elizabeth 38, James W. 16, Polly 15, Sally 14, John R. 13, Lucinda 11, Asa 9, Mason 7, Oliver 6, Percival 5, Lewis 1

Schedule Page 123

WILLIAMSON, Shadrach 30*, Sarah Ann 28, Amos 10, Gasper 8, Asa 4, Joseph 3, Abasha 4/12
MESSER, Jacob 65*
CHAPMAN, James 29, Polly 23, John 3, Melvina 1
CHAFIN, Thomas 27, Jane 28, Arch 8, Katharine 8, James 5, Sarah Ann 4, Elizabeth 3, Wm. 2/12
CRUMB, Fredrick 52*, Naomia 47, Lucinda 15, Frederick 11
SALMONS, Wm. C. 23*
SALMONS, Miles 27, Margret 20, Fredrick 1
HORN, James 23, Jane 20, Katharine 2, Thedk. 2/12
CRUM, Thos. 21, Deanna 19, Neoma 7/12
CRUM, Wm. 45, Polly 40, John 20, Jesse 18, Wm. 16, Jane 12, Susan 6, Elizabeth 4, Katharine 2, Matha 8/12
DINGESS, Wm. 43, Susannah 39, Cloe 22, John 18, Phebe 13, Thedk. 11, Neoma 9, Mary J. 7, Elizabeth 5
MILLS, Geo. 40, Matta 36, Elizabeth 19, Wm. 16, Maryann 13, Martha J. 11, John 9, Ko W. 7, Jesse M. 4, Amanda 2
SMITH, David 26, Mary 19, Mary J. 11/12
MILLS, John 49*, Rutha 28, Martin 23, Thos. 8, Wm. C. 4, James 2

Schedule Page 124

SALMONS, Thos. 26*, Oliver 4, Randolph 23
FRY, David 49, Christena 47, Andrew 27, Anny 16, Polly 13, Bury 8, Serilda 5
FLUTY?, Francis 58, Elizabeth 57, Eveline 19, Marinda 19, Polly 15
FLUTY?, Aron 24, Mary 21, Milly 6, Elizabeth 4, Anna 1

1850 Census Lawrence County Kentucky

FLUTY?, Francis Jr. 22, Ester 17, John 2
MANER, Lewis 25, Catharine 25, Sally 6, Charles 4, Elizabeth 2
ENDICOTT, Samuel 48, Ester 50, Gabriel 18, John 15, Joshua 13, Francis 11
ENDICOTT, Saml. Jr. 23, Rachel 20, Elizabeth 2
HAMMONS, John 30, Elizabeth 26, Elizabeth 4, Frances J. 2, Martha 1
COPLEY, Wm. 59, Nancy 51, Thos. 18, Aley 16 (m), Nichols 12, Marinda 7
SAMONDS, David 21, Mary M. 18
SAMONDS, Rowland 51, Nancy 37, Rowland 18, Wm. 13, James 11, Joel 7, Nelson 6, Jeremiah 4, Elizabeth 3, Bennet 2, A. J. 1/12 (m)
BARTRUM, James 37*, Jane 39, Wm. 15, Polly F. 6, Saml. 3
JONES, Henry 27*
MARTIN, Booker J. 26, Elizabeth 23, Harrison 3/12
LEWIS, Jackson 30, Margaret 30, Elisa 8, Wm. 6, Jane 2

1850 Census Letcher County Kentucky

Schedule Page 125

DAY, William Sr. 62, Jane 62, Jacob 20, William Jr. 16
WHITEKER, Stephen 19, Viny 19
HOGG, Kelly 30, Mary 31, Hiram W. 10, Susanah 7, Stephen 4, Matilda 2
CAUDILL, Henry 29, Susanah 20, David 2, Phebe 4/12
CAUDILL, Henry Sr. 65, Phebe 55, David 19, Jesse 16
CAUDILL, William 27, Sary 20, Becksy 2, Nancy 7/12
GILLY, Preston 31, Priscilla 23, Nancy 4, Marthaan 2
EVRUDGE, Gideon 25, Cely 22, MarthanJane 10/12
CORNETT, Stephen 18, Mary 22
DAY, George 36, Mahaly 37, William 14, John 11, Jane 8, Malinda 7, Lucinda 5, Mary 3, Rebecca 1
WHITEKER, Nelly 37, John 15, Moses 12, Maryan 10, Isaac 8, Sarah 5, James M. 2
HOGG, Stephen 36, Cyntha 36, Silas 13, Elizabeth 11, Marthaan 9, James 7, George 5, Lucinda 4, Kelly 2
MITCHELL, George W. 39, Elizabeth 29, Ransom 8, Hiram 6, Thomas 2
FIELDS, William 52, Lydia 42, Jincy 20, Stephen 18, Davis 16, Sary 12, Elizabeth 10, Nancy 7, Daniel Boone 5, George W. 4
HOGG, James Sr. 73*, Elizabeth 50
HALL, Henry D. 16*
HOGG, James Jr. 24, Dicy 23, Margaret 6, James 4, Squire 2, George 1
CAUDILL, Jesse 32, Mary 23, Watson 5, Benjamin 4, Sarah 2, Susanah 7/12

Schedule Page 126

BANKS, Mary 55, Cassy 25, Polyan 7, Elijah 3, Sarah 2
CAUDILL, Wilburn 38, Nancy 32, Isbella 16, Sarah 13, William 11, Susanah 8, John 6, Rachiel 4, James 2, Frances 6/12
INGLE, Daniel 35, Kezire 30, Emaline 17, Cassa 12, Mary 11, George 9, Andrew J. 7, Susanah 4, Nathaniel 2, Robert 6/12
ADAMS, Randolph 48, Nancy 44, Stephen 20, Elizabeth 17, Lydia 17, Watson 13, Jesse 11, Randolph D. 9, Absalum 5, Nancy 3
HOGG, James 24*, Mary 23, Nancy 1
ADAMS, Nancy 16*
FIELDS, Isaac 41, Alsey 40, Sarah 19, Mosses 17, Ebalina 15, Louisa 13, Annette 11, Robert H. 9, Leroy W. 8, Ambrose J. 7, Joseph 5, Martin 4, Henry 3
BROWN, John S. 57, Elizabeth 50
BROWN, Stephen 32, William 24, George W. 18, Heneritta 16, Esther 13, Jesse M. 9, Hiram 6
CAUDILL, William 25, Maryan 22, George W. 5, William 2
MAGGARD, Henry 29*, Polly 26, Milly 8, Sarah 6, William 4, John 2
BOWMAN, Elizabeth 13*
JOHNSON, Benjamin 65, Nelly 65, John 26, Rachiel 24, Adams W. 1
ESTUS, Bartley Y. 25, Sarah 19, Richard Y. 3, Phebe Jane 2, Adam A. S. 3/12

1850 Census Letcher County Kentucky

Schedule Page 127

BLAIR, Joseph 26, Susanah 26, Stephen T.? 5, Preston M. 3, John P. 1
BANKS, William 36, Nancy 40, James 12, Elizabeth 10, Alfred 8, Zachry 7, Solomon 5, Henry C. H. 3
BLAIR, Elihu 25*, Cely 26, Elizabeth 3, Hiram B. 2, William L. 10/12
ADAMS, Jane 16*
SERGENT, David 41, Christena 38, Mary 18, Nancy 15, Alen 11, Andrew 10, John 8, Wilson 4, Emily 1
BLAIR, John R.? 51, Elizabeth 47, Susanah 16, Hiram 14, Rebecca 12, Lucinda 10, Samuel 7, Elizabeth 5, Ceiley 3
SUMPTOR, Lewis 19, Esther 20
SUMPTOR, Sarah 53, William G. 13
PERKINS, Joshua C. 33*, Sarah 32, Hannahamanda 5, Mary Polina 3, Highly 2/12, Elizabeth 65, Martha 30
DOLPHIS, Benjamin 2*
MAGGARD, James 33, Abigail 32, Sally 12, David 10, Henry 8, Mary 5, James 5/12
GROSS, William 60, Nancy 37, William 9, Edmund 8, Solomon 5, Jemima 10/12
COLLIER, Randolph 23, Arminta 22, James B. 8/12
LEWIS, Wilson 24, Katharine 21, Rebecca C. 2, John J. C. 2/12
COLLIER, William R. 53, Frances 53, John B. 18, Martin D. 16, David 14, Isom W. 12, Elizabeth 9
BLAIR, Charles 43, Sarah 43, Elizabeth 17, Susanah 15, Marion 13, Henry 11, Hiram 9, Sarah 7, Charles 5, Mima 8/12

Schedule Page 128

MAGGARD, Samuel Sr. 76, Rebecca 72
MAGGARD, Rudolph 50, Anny 46, Henry 16, Elizabeth 18, Margaret 13
MAGGARD, Samuel Jr. 36, Rachiel 34, John 15, Moses 13, Mary 11, William 7, Jemima 5, Sarah 4, Samuel 2
MAGGARD, Samuel 20, Elizabeth 22, Freelove 2
MAGGARD, Moses 31, Charlotte 27, John 6, Rebecca 4, Sarah 2
MAGGARD, David 45, Susannah 45, Elizabeth 16, James 14, Moses 13, Sally 13, Frances 11, Silas 9, Susannah 6, David 3
MAGGARD, John H. 24, Surviller 23 (f), David 3, Mary 1
CAUDILL, Samuel 46, Sarah 41, David 19, John 17, Mary 15, Margaret 12, Abner 11, Susanah 8, Abel 7, Samuel 6, James 8/12
CAUDILL, Henry 21, Elizabeth 20, Sarah 1
CAUDILL, Isom 55, Elizabeth 54, Benjamin 20, John 18, Sarah 15, Nancy 13, Fairaby 9, Susanah 6
MAGGARD, Isaac 25, Mahaly 24, John 5, Francis S. 3, Samuel 10/12
CAUDILL, James 22, Mary 16
WILSON, John 49, Mary 46, Patterson 18, Leroy 15, Thomas M. 12, Sarah 9
HALL, Alexander 63*, Rebecca 37, Isom 9/12
STURGILL, James 16*, John 15, Nancy 13, Sarah 11, William M. 3

1850 Census Letcher County Kentucky

Schedule Page 129

STURGILL, Andrew 19, Dicy 19
STURGILL, Francis 42, Ruth 38
STURGILL, John 21*, Clearinda 17, Isaac 15, Andrew 12, Joseph 6, Jemima 3, Mahaly 1
ESTUS, Richard 21*
CAUDILL, Alfred 26, Arra 19, Ruth 2
ESTUS, Micager 24, Viny 17
MUSSELWHITE, Joseph 35, Delily 31, Tamer 12 (f), Mary 9, Elizabeth 6, Lydia 4, Ruth 4/12
STURGILL, David 50, Rachiel 47, James 18, McGuire 16, Jemima 14, Nancy 13, Mathias 10, Samuel 8, Anny 6, Sarah 3
CAUDILL, Henry 23, Mary 16, Ruth 6/12
STURGILL, Francis 21, Delily 18, Joshua 10/12
STURGILL, Jordon 21, Manda 21, Hugh 2, Elizabeth 3/12, Rachiel 3/12
MAGGARD, James 24, Elizabeth 23, Rachiel 6, Anna 3
WILSON, Robert 24, Beneter 25 (f), Felix 6, Martha Jane 4, Morgan 1
COLDIRON, Isaac D. 25, Mary 20, Louisa Jane 2, Francis 1
MAGGARD, Samuel 20, Lucinda 20, Liah 2, Susanah 7/12
BANKS, Henry 65, Nancy 49, Henry C. 18, David 16, Jackson 14, Allen C. 12, James 10, Mary 8
BANKS, Cassa 45, Jane 13, William 9, Lansford 5, John R. 3
POLLY, Stephen 24*, Nancy 20, Elizabeth 1
COMBS, John 5*
BANKS, Alfred 35, Jane 37, Elizabeth 6, Sally 2

Schedule Page 130

FRAZIER, Elizabeth 68
FRAZIER, Solomon 19, Sarah 20
BANKS, Samuel 24, Mary 22, James 3
FRAZIER, Squire 49, Phebe 47, Margaret 25, James 20, Squire 17, Nancy 15, Solomon 13, Lydia 7, John 5
FRAZIER, George 22, Maryhetha 19, Ira 6/12
ISOM, George 40, Lucinda 38, Gideon 20, George 16, Elijah C. 12, Elisha 9, Anna 14, Sarah 6, Lucinda 3, Jesse 4/12
LUCUS, Parker 60, Susanah 45, Mary L. 16, Jane 13, Mima 12, Nancy 10, John 8, Martha 7, James N. C. 4, Margaret 8/12
LUCUS, Emanuel 33, Charlotte 25, Elizabeth 12, Orny 10 (f), Rebecca Berilla 8, Susanah 4, Henry C. 3, Parker 1
LUCUS, Willis 26, Elizabeth 25, Henry N. B. 5, Parker 3, Teague D. 1
COLLINS, Robert; 46, Anny 25, Wilson 18, Mary 8, George 5, Margaret 4, Thomas 4, Larkin 3, Nancy 1
COLLINS, Ely 22, Mary 20
PHIPPS, Isaiah 60, Edy 55, David 14, William 14, Marion 12, Isaiah 10, Louisa A. 3
HUNDLEY, James H. 30, Sarah 25
HOGG, Hiram 49*, Mary 29, Stephen 18, Hiram 16, Henry 14, Edward 12, Nancy 10, Rosey 10, Lucinda 8, Tennessee Ray 6, William W. 4, Maletha 2, Solomon T. 1

1850 Census Letcher County Kentucky

Schedule Page 131

ADAMS, Elizabeth 20*
ADAMS, John C. 46, Elizabeth 40, Nancy 18, Letta 16, Nelson 13, Benjamin 10, John 8, Solomon 6, Elizabeth 3
HOLEBROOKS, William A. 27, Lydia 21, Hiram 8, John 5, Elizabeth 1
BATES, James 27, Elizabeth 26, Henry C. 6, Sarah 4, Nancy 2
SEXTON, Moses 45, Theny 45, Prisciller 26, Richard 18, Olva 15 (m), Wilburn 13, Hiram 11, Eliza 9, Greenbury 6, Paskal 5, Moses 1
BATES, Jesse 29, Elizabeth 25, John B. F. 6, Margaret 2, Saryan 5/12
FRAZIER, Solomon 32, Susanah 25, James 7, Jonathan 5, Hiram 3, Sarah 1
BAKER, Henry 42, Mary 34, Elijah 17, Carline 15, George W. 13, Martha 11, Angeline 10, Frances 6, Rebecca 2, Mary 3/12
HALL, Alfred 35, Bocksanah 29, Cyntha 13, Mary 11, Ira 9, Preston 7, Martha 5, Ruth 3, Sarah 1
ADAMS, Isaac 40, Nancy 40, Spencer 16, Wiley 14, Moses 12, Stephen 10, Matthew 8, Jane 7, Rachiel 5, Nancy 3
ADAMS, John D. 22, Elizabeth 1
ADAMS, Moses Sr. 75, Kizire 37, Rachiel 15, Henry 14, Franky 12 (f), Viny 10, Elizabeth 8, Margaret 5
POLLY, Edward Jr. 24
COMBS, Hacker 22

Schedule Page 132

POLLY, David 40, Elizabeth 16, Nancy 14, Edward 8, Henry 5
POLLY, Randolph 20, Dianah 18, Heneritter 9/12, Mary 85
ADAMS, George 50, Sarah 45, Jesse 16, Nancy 15, Elizabeth 12, Jane 10, George W. 8, Margaret 5, Ezekiel B. 4, Isaac 1
CAUDILL, James 23, Mary 17
WILLIAMS, John 55, Sarah 50, Mariah 29, William 23, Mary 18, Martha 14, Samuel 11, Eliza 16, Bogle 9, Henry 4, Thomas 4/12
WILLIAMS, Isaac 27, Sarah 20, James 2, Sarah 7/12
ADAMS, John 24, Anna 24, Jesse 5, Dianah 3, George 1
CRAFT, Henry 25, Elizabeth 22, Nancy 2, Sarah 2, Shaderick 3/12
CRAFT, Archealous 48, Nancy 45, John P. 16, David K. 14, Reineritter 12, Scena 10, Viny 8, Margaret 6, Martha 4, Joseph 2, Dorinda 8, John F. 5
HAMMONS, Martin 24, Elizabeth 24, David 4, Mary 2
ADAMS, Jesse 22, Mary 22, Elizabeth 4, Nancy 2, Martin H. 6/12
ADAMS, Squire 19, Elizabeth 20
CRAFT, Archealous 96*, Scena 80
PRITCHET, Harvy 15*
CRAFT, Benjamin 24, Jane 24, Nehemiah 2, John A. 1
CRAFT, Drusiller 60, Nehemiah 21
PRITCHET, Charity 40, John H. 19, Archealous 14, Semantha Jane 12, William 9, Audy 7 (f), Nehemiah 3

1850 Census Letcher County Kentucky

Schedule Page 133

AURSBURN, John S. 22, Darcus 20, Pollyemly 2, Marthaan 1
CRAFT, William 43, Rachiel 38, Mary 15, Marthaan 14, America 10, William 8, George W. 7, Nancy 4, Lucinda 2, Christopher 1
HARGIS, Samuel V. 59, Louvicy 53, Henry 17, Cornelia 13
VANOVER, William 56, Jane 55, William 16, Archibald 14
LUCUS, Aaron 23, Eliza 21, Rebecca Eliz. 1, William H. 3/12
ADAMS, John 39, Sarah 35, William 16, Jesse 14, Mary 12, Edward 10, Simpson 9, Spencer 7, Drusiller 5, Manerva Jane 3, John Jr. 1
ADAMS, Spencer 25, Ceiley 23, William G.? 4, Margaret 1, Jesse 35, Kizire 33, Rachiel 12, Mary S. 10, John 9, William 8, Isaac 7, Sarah 5, Jesse 4, Emily 3, Nipper 3/12
CRAFT, Archealous 36, Letta 35, Nelson 16, Drusiller 13, Jason 10, Enoch 8, Jane 5, Joseph 2
ADAMS, Benjamin 56, Nancy 51, Benjamin 22, Simpson 19, Randolph 16, Nancy 14, Heneritta 10
ADAMS, Jesse 29, Margaret 24, Elizabeth 5, Benjamin 3, Nancy E. 5/12
ADAMS, John 32, Sarah 29, Benjamin 10, James 8, Nancy 5, Jesse 3
CAUDILL, Abel 33, Mary 24, Sarah 6, Pleasant 4, Samuel 2, Maryan 7/12

Schedule Page 134

CAUDILL, Sarah 71
HAMPTON, Silvester 30, Elizabeth 34, Sarah 5, Caleb D. 3, Mary 2, Elizabeth 8/12
COLLIER, Richard 53, Mary 49, Stephen 16, William 15, Samuel 12, Sally 11
HAMPTON, Joseph 35, Susanah 30, Abel 12, Mary 10, Sarah 8, Nancy 7, Matthew 5, Solomon 3
QUILLEN, Teague 78, Jane 47, Richard 17, Solomon 16
QUILLEN, Teague 19*, Jane 22
GIBSON, Sarah 63*, Asbury S. 7, William B. 3, Sarah 9/12
MCCRAY, Levicy 43*, Benjamin 10
YONTS?, David 21*, Charles 18, John 14
YONTS?, Solomon 44*, Susanah 49
BAKER, Elijah 18*, Mary 15
YONTS, William 42, Nancy 37, Elijah 19, Katharine 16, Solomon 14, Millyan 12, Mary Jane 10, Nancy 8, Loueasy 6, William J. 1
BENTLEY, Benjamin 62, Elizabeth 58, Simeon 24, John V. 22, Solomon 21
WRIGHT, John 37, Mary 31, Benjamin 12, Andrew 9, Hiram 7, John V. 5, Eliza 2
CAUDILL, Stephen 56, Elizabeth 39, Jane 14, Rachiel 12, Mary 10, Susanah 8, Anny 1
QUILLEN, Henry 27*, Elizabeth 32, Drewry 8, Malen 6, Elizabeth 4, James 2
HALL, Samuel D.? 14*, Richard 11
HALL, Rheuben 32, Mahaly 28, Elizabeth 11, Thomas 9, Benjamin 7, Mary 4, Rheuben 1

Schedule Page 135

WRIGHT, Susanah 65 (wid.), Margaret 47, Susanah 24, George 21, William 20, Sidney 13 (f), Lutia 6, Anna 3
FLEMING, Fredrick 27, Anna 30, Elizabeth 9, Susanah 7, Mary 5, Viny, 3, Janeperlina, 1

1850 Census Letcher County Kentucky

WRIGHT, James 39, Susanah 25, Hulda 16, Joel 14, Docy 11, Matilda 9, James H. 8, Joseph R. 6, Marjarine 4, Henry C. 2
POTTER, Isaac 49, Mary 41, John 20, Janperlina 19, Hanner 17, Mary 14, Abraham 12, Nancy 10, Margaret 7, Isaac 5, Mahaly 2, Manerva 2
HOLEBROOKS, Randolph 21, Jane 18, Enoch 8/12
QUILLEN, William 25, Nancy 22, Louisa 7, Hanor 5, Elizabeth 4/12
HALL, Allen 21, Hanor 20, Solomon 2, Mary 8/12
BENTLEY, John 57, Squire 29, John Q. 22, Benjamin 11, Patty 16
WRIGHT, Andrew 23, Hariet 20, William 3, FreeLove 1 (f)
BENTLEY, Dankiel 27, Marinda 23, Tobitha 5, Didama 3, John 1
BENTLEY, Lewis 60, Nancy 55, William 21, Sally 17, Nancy 15, Dicy 13
BENTLEY, Joseph 24, Anna 24, John 8, Matilda 5, Elizabeth 3, Lewis 5/12
BATES, Sarah (widdow) 57, Robin 25, Sary an 20, Henderson 18, Mary Jane 14, Martin V. B. 12
BATES, Uriah 22, Letta 21

Schedule Page 136

HUGHS, John 32, Matilda 27, Nancy 12, Gabriel 10, Sarah 7, Delily 5, William 2
BENTLEY, Thomas 65, Margaret 55, Sarah 26, Mary 22, Esther 20, Roady 16, S. Davis 14, May 12, Mary 6, James 1
WRIGHT, Joel 33, Eliza 31, Solomon 9, John B. 6, Sarah 3
CRAFT, Joseph 32, Martha 32, John H. 15, Sarah 14, Drusiller 12, James W. 9, William R. 6, Marthamanerva 4, Mary 2, Joseph 6/12
WEBB, Enoch A. 39, Susanah 38, Benjamin S. 20, Edward T. 16, Henry M. 14, Maryan 12, Andy L. 10, Rily 8, Lettyan 6, Saryan 5, Enoch W. 3, David L. H. 3/12
HAMMONS, Larkin 26, Sarah 19, Lydia 5, Henry 2, Nancy 1
WEBB, Benjamin 66, Janea 61, Wiley W. 22
HARRIS, Jacob 45, Janea 43, Nancy C. 20, Frances 18, Squire 16, Mary 14, John 12, William 10, Jemima 8, Enoch asbury 6, George W. 4, Rachiel 3/12
WEBB, Jason L. 30, Elizabeth 26, Mahaly 7, Archealous C. 5, Wiley 3, Mary 1
KINSER, Fredrick 20, Lydia 17
ADAMS, Simpson 28, Sarah 25, Jane 4, Mary M. 1
ADAMS, William 30, Mary 32, Benjamin T. 10, Lydia 5, Jane 3, Sarah 4/12
ADAMS, William 62*, Mary 56

Schedule Page 137

KINSER, David 15*
ADAMS, Simpson 53, Susanah 40, Austin 16, Letta 11, Elizabeth 7, Jane 4
WEBB, Miles M. 28, Mary 23, Benjamin R. 5, Jane 3, Nancy 1
POLLY, Henry 56, Martha 50, Henry Jr. 18, Dicy 16, Lena 13, Richard R. 11, Viny 9
COMBS, Edward 24, Martha 20, William 5/12
ADAMS, Moses 38, Rebecca 38, Mary 18, Gilbert 15, Isaac 13, George W. 10, Lucinda 8, Dianah 5, Marinda 2
ADAMS, Stephen 58, Sarah 38, John 5, Lydia 3
HAYES, Jonathan 75

1850 Census Letcher County Kentucky

ADAMS, William 43, Sarah 25, Jane 22, George 18, Rebecca 16, Stephen 13, William Rily 11, Elizabeth 9, John 5, Frankyan 3 (f), Clearinda 1
ADAMS, Gilbert 23, Perlina 20, Jane 2
HANY?, John 40, Mary 24, John 2, George 5/12
ADAMS, Absalom D. 41*, Nancy 37, Sarah 14, Freaszier 10, Solomon 8, Randolph 4
BRECK, Daniel 1*
MULLINS, Nancy 15*
POLLY, James 26, Margaret 27, Dicy M. 5, Shaderick 3, Jane 4/12
YOUNG, William 68, Jane 58, Fanny 22, Hanner 20, David 22, Louisa 18, Rease 15
POLLY, Edward 48, Jane 40, David 17, Edward 14, Nancy 12, John W. 9, Elizabeth 7, Lucinda 4, Andrew 1

Schedule Page 138

COMBS, Wesley 35, Mary 27, John 9, Elizabeth 8, Shaderick 6, James 4, Lucinda 3, Wesley 7/12, Shaderick Sr. 66, Shaderick Jr. 16
ROWARK, James 65, Elizabeth 41, Tillith 13 (B), Elizabeth 11, Marthaan 9, Jesse 8, Manerva 6, Clarinda 4
COMBS, Shaderick 38, Sarah 28, George W. 8, William R. 6, Mary 4, Lydia 1
ADAMS, Stephen 23, Usly? 20 (f), Rachiel 1
BROWN, Benjamin 28, Mary 22, James W. 3, Martin C. 2, Henry C. 6/12
CORNETT, Joseph E. 36, Sarah 31, John B. 12, Samuel A. 10, Elizabethan 9, Nathaniel W. 7, Rachiel 4, Benjamin 2
CAUDILL, Watson 28, Elizabeth 23, Nancy 5, Sarah 4, Franky 2 (f)
ADAMS, John 22, Franky 20 (f)
FIELDS, Abner 45, Mary 35, Effa 15, Jincy 12, Obeydiah 7, Solomon 4, Fairabe 8/12
FIELDS, Martha 67
ADAMS, Jesse 50, Margaret 44, Stephen 19, Moses 17, Samuel 14, Henry 12, John 11, Sarah 8, Allen 5, Daniel B. 1
RALEIGH, William 28, Mary 23, John 4, James J. 3, Hiram 5/12
COLLIER, James 27, Elizabeth 23, Susanah 3, Hiram 1
DAY, Joseph 33, Dianah 30, Lettitia 8, James K. P. 6, Preston C. 3, Rebecca C. 7/12
DAY, John N. 64, Lettitia 58, Moses 23, Henry 21, Martha 18, Rebecca 16, Lettitia 14

Schedule Page 139

DAY, John B. 26, Susanah 24, Mahaly 4, Randolph C. 2, Elizabeth 11/12
CAUDILL, James 36, Elizabeth 31, Rebecca 14, Nancy 12, Mary 10, Atha 8, William 6, Isom 4, Joshua M. 3/12
MULLINS, Joshua 40, Mary 38, Joseph 16, Solomon 12, Caleb 10, Joshua 8, Anna 6, William 4
MULLINS, John 18, Celey 18
PARSONS, David 31, Emaline 28, Maizy 7, Matilda 5, Altamira 4, Maryan E. 7/12
BOGGS, Abel 37*, Rebecca 29, Jane 17, Elizabeth 11, Susanah 9, Silas 5
MULLINS, Nancy 14*
STAMPER, William M. 29*, Rebecca 25, Jesse A. 6, Milly 4, Margaret 2, Nancy 9/12
SEXTON, Dilly 16*

1850 Census Letcher County Kentucky

CAUDILL, John 52, Rachiel 43, Samuel 19, John D. 15, David J.? 13, Nancy 11, Elizabeth 9, Pollyan 4, Watson 2
CAUDILL?, Chany 8 (f) (B)
CAUDILL, Stephen 24, Elizabeth 24, Manerva 8/12
CAUDILL, William 26*, Margaret 28
THOMAS, Nancy 14*
LUSTER, William 5*
CAUDILL, Benjamin 21, Martha 20, John A. 1
TYRE, David 22, Mary 22, William J.? 3, Hughston 1
BOWEN, Perin Tyre 36 (B)*, Hanner 30, William 9, Lucinda 7, Joseph 3, Rachiel 56
JOHNSON, Mary 5*
JACKSON, Lucy 49, Manda 6
WALLEN, Preston H. 32, Elender 28, Hansford 10, John 8, Rebecca 6, Elisha 4, Joseph 2

Schedule Page 140

MEADDOWS, Darcas 30, Lydia 7, Abatine 4
BOWEN, William 30, Rebecca; 32, John W. 6, Jesse 4, William 2
SEXTON, Samuel 28*, Elizabeth 28
MADDEN, Nancy 23*, Lexious F. 2, Samuel H. 3/12
BLAIR, Henry 39, Nancy 36, Esther 12, Lettitia 10, Ira D. 8, Susanah 6, Joseph 4, Sarah 2, Enoch 2
HOLEBROOKS, William B. 41, Sarah 43, Mary 23, Elizabeth 21, Nancyan 19, Susanah 16, James E. 14, William B. 11, Randolph E. 9, Ransom H. 7, Benjamin W. 5
HOLEBROOKS, Elizabeth 75
HOLEBROOKS, Benjamin a46, Nancy 45, Heneritta 16, Nancy 18, Jesse 13, Christena 10, Margaret 8, Susanah 6
HAUBELL, James 50, Sarah 35
BOWLIN, James 40, Pollyan 24, Newton R. 2, Richmond 1, Jane 6
VERMILLION, Douglas J. 33, Manerva 26, William S. 2, John A. 8/12
STRONG, Thomas 40, Margaret 39, Elizaan 17, Christena 16, George W. 14, Hariet T. 10, Joseph Y. A. 8, Laura 6, Katharine 5, Frances F. 3, Saryan 1, Mary Louisa 3/12
ASTRAP, Jesse 70, Mary 42
HIGGENS, James 54, Ellouisa 8
GILBERT, George 33, Lydia 25, James 5
GRAVES, Hardy 55, Sarah 46
CASADAY, Thomas 38, Louisa 22, Martha Jane 4, Sarah E. 2, Pollyan B. 10/12
BURNS, John M. 24, Keziah B. 24, Rebecca C. 5, Rowland C. 3, Mary E. 1

Schedule Page 141

MADDOCKS, John H. N. 40, Elizabeth S. 40, Marelda L. 13, Clemintine A. 12, Louisa M. A. 10
FAIRCHILDS, Joseph S. 21, Sarah 16, John M. 1
COLLINS, Carter 37*, Susanah 37
BANKS, Susanah 8*
BRASHEARS, Ezekiel 44*, Manerva 29
DAVIDSON, Susanah 6*
COMBS, Elihu E. 19*

1850 Census Letcher County Kentucky

COLLIER, Preston H. 32, Rebecca S. 28, Eliza Comfort 10, William R. 9, James Caar G. 8, Manerva B. Mc. 7, Bivian Kathrine 6, Joseph B. 4, Frances Esther 2

Schedule Page 143

DICKSON, Thos. 53, Sarah 27, Jeremiah 23, Isaac 19, John 28
DICKSON, James 25*, Susanah 25, John 5, Nancy 3, James 1
COOPER, Jeremiah 13*
SUMNER, James 50, Nancy 50, Levi 25, Stephen 16, Polly 20, Eligah 12, John 10, James 8, Sarah 6, Robin 4, Eliza 11/12, Judah 1/12 (f)
PRATT, Henry 41, Sila 38, John 20, Anna 19, Susan 13, Stephen 12, Willarson? 10, William 8, Elizabeth 6, Mariah 4, Nancy 2
HAMPTON, Jeremiah 37*, Mary 36, William? 11
WALTERS, Matilda 16?*, Hiram 13, Polly 8, John W. 7, Jeremiah 6, Henry 4, Turner 2
HAMPTON, William 32, Phebia 31, John S. 12, Solomon 9, Nancy 7, Terry 4 (f), Dolley 2
SUMNER, John 34, Nancy 33, Winny 13, Betsey 11, Judah 9 (f), John W. 7, Polly 5, Peggy 4, Selea 2, Judah 80 (f)
HAMPTON, Calep 23, Elizabeth 20
CAUDILL, James 34, Abba 26, Nancy 6
HAMPTON, Turner 60*, Mary 61, Nelson 20, Solomon 17
BOWMAN, Mahala 10*
CAUDILL, Stephen 40, Elizabeth 35, Rebeca 15, Henry 13, Dicey 10, Rachal 8, Phebia 5
CAUDILL, Henry 21, Palsey 24 (f)
CAUDILL, Isom 21, Judah 20 (f), Mary 2, Henry 1/12

Schedule Page 144

CAUDILL, William 25, Sarah 20, Becksey 1, Nancy 2/12
ELDRIDGE, Wm. 24, Sarah 22, Isaac 1
CAUDILL, Mathew 38, Terry 37 (f), Henry 20, Phebia 18, Elizabeth 15, Rachal 11, Sarah 6, Susan 5, William 2, Nancy 1/12
CAUDILL, Wm. 71, Nancy 63, Sarah 11
CAUDILL, William 23, Nancy 19, James 3, Thomas 2, William 2/12
ELDRIDGE, Levi 44, Easter 42, John 17, Sarah 15, Eliza 13, Jane 11, Elizabeth 9, Lydia 7, Polly an 3, Jesse 1
ELDRIDGE, Benj. 20, Patsey 22, Sarah 2/12
BACK, Henry 65, Susanna 52, Lewis 17, David 13, Sarah 8, James 6, Elizabeth 14
BACK, John 35, Sarah 27, Susan 8, David 6, Nancy 5, Henry 4, William 2, Rebeca 1/12
CAUDILL, Isom 24, Elizabeth 30, Henry 11, Samuel 6, Susan 2, David 4
BACK, Henry 27, Frances 28, Elizabeth 6, Susana 4, Easter 1
DAY, David 28, Rebeca 25, William H. 5, Nancy 1
BLAIR, Preston 23, Elender 20
BACK, Samuel 27, Rodah H.? 24, Henry 8, William 4, Elizabeth 2, David 1
ADAMS, Moses 42*, Sarah 40, Nancy 16, Easter 13, Sarah 11, John C. 9, Benjamine 7, Mary 3

1850 Census Letcher County Kentucky

Schedule Page 145

BANKS, Johnson 50*
INGLE, Enoch 18*
ADAMS, Stephen 34, Nancy 34, William 13, Isaac 11, Polly 9, Manerva 6, Moses 4, Malinda 2/12
STAMPER, Isaac D. 34*, Polly 25, Hiram 9, William 7, Stephen 5, Milly 3, Daniel B. 1, John 14, Daugherty 8
SECTON, Polly 9*, Hatler 18, Eliza 16
PRIDEMORE, Emily 20*
ADAMS, Harrison 28
CAUDILL, James 60, Sarah 60, Miram 35, Emaline 18, Eligha 16, James 11, Sarahan 7, Isaac 2, Rebeca 2
CRAGER, Harvy 30, Polly 37, Elender 17, Margaret 15, Nancy 13, Thomas 11, Rebeca 5
SEXTON, Solomon 42, Leurinda 23, Hatler 18, Campbell 15, Eliza 14, Polly 12, Lucinda 9, Manerva 6, Verlina 6, Lafayette 4, Diletha 1
GIPSON, John 53, Caharity 53 (f), Mahala 18, Eligha 16, Jesse 13, Nancy 13, Julia 12, David 6, Lucy 5
COLLINS, Charles 31, Lucey 26, Sarah 5, Washington 3, Joseph 9/12
SEXTON, Isaac 30, Jane 25
CRAGER, James 25, Louisa 30, Martha 3, Ambrose 11/12
SEXTON, Andrew 40, Sarah 39, Elvira 18, Andrew 14, Henry 12, Jefferson 10, Rosa 8, Cenea 6, Marion 4
BREEDING, Wesley 26, Jane 25, William 4, Eliza 3, Elisha 11/12

Schedule Page 146

SEXTON, William 40*, Nancy 40, Dilley 20, Clark 18, Talitha 15, William 12, Joel 10, John 2, Sarah 7
MOORE, Stuffley 22* (B), Linda 22, William 5, Calvin 2
COLLINS, Nathaniel 35*, Nancy 33, Robert 25, Elizabeth 10, Manerva 4
LOGAN, Stephen 26*
CHILDERS, Goolsby 45, Nancy 36, Dolley 16, Dicey 15, Arta 13, Abram 11, David 9, James 7, George W. 6, Frances 5, Goolsby 2
EWING, Saml. 55, Lydia 44, George 18, Matilda 20, Liza 17, Lucinda 15, Patten 13, Sarah 12, Emley 9
COLLINS, Thos. 30, Thursey 30, Polly 7, Nathaniel 5, Martha 3, Feriba 1
SEXTON, Riley 19, Dicey 19, Matilda 1
COLLINS, Thos. 29, Catharine 29, Grazilda 1
GIPSON, Henry 20*, Cintha 42
COLLINS, Sanders 15*, Finley 11, Mary 11, Wauson 7
GIPSON, John 23, Sarah 24, Lafayette 4, Larkin 2, Manerva 5/12
COLLINS, Berdine 40, Mary 35, Margaret 17, Calvin 16, Henry 14, Cowden 11, Didama 9, Betsey 8, Zilpha 6, Dallas 3, Letcher 6/12
COLLINS, Briant 36, :Polly 34, Carter 13, Nancy 11, Nelly 9, Jesse 7, Fielden 5, Berdine 3, Hugh 1, Nancy 68

1850 Census Letcher County Kentucky

Schedule Page 147

SEXTON, Wm. 35*, Elender 36, Oma 16, Nathaniel 14, Peggy 12, Wm. 10, Elsbury 8, Martha 4, Felany 1
TAYLOR, Elizabeth 19*
KISOR, Naman 29, Thursey 23, LPollyan 5, Elihu 4, Seely 2
BREEDING, Huston 30, Mary 32, John 7, Eliza 6, Jasper 5, Robert 2, Baby 6/12 (m)
THOMAS, Greenbury 30, Ciltania 25, Pollyan 5, Freelin 4, Marshal 3, Phelix 2
SEXTON, Huldy 30, Harker 12, Emaline 8, Helen 2
BENTLEY, Benj. 21, Elizabeth 20
SEXTON, Isaah 38, Jane 32, Samantha 6, Elizabeth 4, Polly 2
HUGHS, Gabriel 30, Patsy 30, John 8, Louisa 7, Solomon 4, Nathaniel 2
ADAMS, Jesse 52, Mary 51, Sarah 28, Sina 13, Diana 6, Mary J. 4, Solomon 1
ADAMS, Moses 31, Margaret 24, Mary A. 6/12
COLLINS, William 27, Eliza 28, James 7, Frances 5, Uley 3, Baby 1 (f)
NIECE, Jackson 25, Malinda 22, Sarah 3, Eliza 1
NIECE, Jacob 26, Margaret 21, Henry 1
COLLINS, James 67, Elizabeth 50, Wesley 25, Uley 39, James M. 23, Tivis 22 (m)
BENTLEY, Solomon C. 23, Susana 19
BENTLEY, Mary 50, Elizabeth 20, Barret 18, Jane 16, Aaron H. 14, Susan 12
BENTLEY, Wm. 28, Elizabeth 24, James 4, Pollyan 3, Baby 6/12 (m)

Schedule Page 148

HALL, James 50, Sarah 45, Arta 22, Anthony 20, David 19, Darcus 15, Wiley 12, Dicy 5, Kernilid 4, Clerinda 8/12
HALL, Alexander 25, Clarinda 21, James 4
TAYLOR, Gideon 24, Fama 22, Wesley 4, John 1
HALL, John W. 42, Henereta 40, Preston 21, Polly 15, Susan 13, Ruth 10, Sarah 8, Geo. W. 4, Wm. 2, Ruth 84
HALL, Alexnder 39, Susan 36, James 12, Reter 9 (f), John W. 4
MORGAN, Wm. 43, Barbrey 21, James 14, Samuel 13, Elizabeth 10, Isom 8, Frank 7, Mary 8/12
MORGAN, James 63*, Eliza 43, Washington 12
BRANHAM, Eliza 9*
FERRIL, Andrew 22*, Malissa 20, John 3, Harvy 2/12
MORGAN, Isom 39, Elizabeth 29, Meriba 12, Elizabeth 10, Harvy 8, Polly 3, Marilda 6/12
BRANHAM, Betsey 34, Susan 15, Isom 14, Martha 8, Milly 5, Wm. 4/12
HALL, Hiram 36, Lucy 32, Alexander 15, Rousey 16 (f), Aldrin 11, John 8, Lucinda 5, Pollyan 2, Clarinda 6/12
ISAACS, Wm. 31, Jane 28, George 9, Rebecca 7, Polly 5, Jonathan 4, Wm. 2, Samuel 7/12
HALL, John 27, Hapick 21 (f), Viny 4, Reuben 2

1850 Census Letcher County Kentucky

Schedule Page 149

HALL, Lucinda 37, Pollyan 18, Nancy 15, Jonathan 13, Rachal 11, Hiram 8, Wm. 6, Lucinda 3
HARGIS, Jacob 23, Lucinda 16, John R. 6/12
HALL, Reuben 26, Nancy 22, Mary J. 4, Baby 4/12 (m), Jane 10
HALL, Randolph 39, Catharine 41, John 18, Drewry 16, Hanah 9, Henry 6, Lewis 3
HALL, Jonathan 51, Mary 52
MORGAN, James 35*, Emily 25, John 8, Riter 6 (f), Patsey 4, Manerva 2
POLLY, Clabron 22*, Nancy 19
ADAMS, Eligha 31*, Polly 25, Stephen 10, Wm. 8, Isaac 6, Nathaniel 4, Elizabeth 2, Spencer 28
PHIPS, Patience 27*
BREEDING, Elisha 56*, Belinda 36, Wm. 16, Eligha 15, John 12, Alcey 10, Nancy 8, Betsey 6, Jasper 7, Milly 3, James H. 11/12
BELCHER, Hardin 23*
KISOR, Nimrod 26*, Polly 18, Eliza 22, Washington 29, Martha 18, Polly 50
BREEDING, Elizabeth 1*
BURGEY, Wm. 63, Lucy 64, Rolin 24, Letta 22, John 16, Robin 7, Nancy 3, Lucinda 1
BURGEY, Alfred 34, Polly 31, Wm. 14, Lucy 7, Thos. 4, Sarah 6/12
JOHNSON, Washington 35, Sarah 35, Samuel 14, Thos. 12, Delpha 10, Lesley 8, John M. 6, Simeon 2, Keziah 5/12

Schedule Page 150

CODEY, John 21, Matilda 17, Alderson 15
MADEN, Arch 18, Rachal 49, James 26, Wesley 16, Washington 12, Jackson 11, Sarah 14, Nancy 9, John 19
MADEN, Wm. 28, Tena 18, Elizabeth 1, Ruth 17
MULLINS, Valuntine 27, Tilda 25, Sarah 3, John 1, Nancy 25, Franklin 18
ASHLEY, Franklin 22, Lucy 25, Jordan 2
SMITH, Wm. 50, Milly 48, Jerry 18, Thos. 14, Nancy 13
MILES, Anderson 35, Susan 33, Wm. 12?, Jane 8, Roda 6, Jacob 4
MULLINS, John 22, Matilda 36, Nancy 15, Lucy 13, Elizabeth 11, Pollyan 9, John 7, Samuel 5, Letty 4, Matilda 2
FRANCE, Simeon 32, Kassey 25, John 18, Elizabeth 9, Samuel 7, Jane 5, Nancy 2
MULLINS, Rachal 48*
SHELL, Samuel 68*
FRANCE, Thos. 77, Lurana 54, Anna 13, Elsybeth 12, Margarcon 8 (f), Lurana 15
HIGGINS, John V. 25*, Jane 27, Linville 2
ADAMS, Rebeca 9*, John 3
AISTROP, Jesse 34, Louisa 35, Loranzo 14, John H. 11, Martha 10, Albert 7, Susan 1
FRANCE, Samuel 39*, Dicy 32, Betsy 16, Dicy 12, John 10, Simeon 8, Rebeca 6, Matilda 4, Marinda 2
EVERAGE, Nicholas 25*

1850 Census Letcher County Kentucky

Schedule Page 151

STAMPER, Lucinda 38, Elizabeth 20, James 18, Hiram 16, Matilda 14, Lucinda 14, John 12, Wm. 10, Milly 8, Peggy 6
SMITH, Wm. B. 52, Elizabeth 47, Eliza 14, Rebeca 13, Wm. 12, Emery 10, Elmer 8, Lucinda 4
HALE, Wm. 27, Nancy 26, Catharine 4, Lilburn 3, Robert 1, Polly 65
SMITH, John B. 25, Sally 25, Wm. 7, Nancy 4, Randolph 2, Stephen 4/12
SMITH, Andrew 21*, Tina 18, Baly 2/12
KELLY, John 67*
PIGMAN, John A. 26, Nancy 30, Jesse 6, John 5, Robin 3, Braxton 3/12
CALIHAN, Silas 26, Hanah 20, Wesley 4, Anjuline 3, Jarusha 1
PIGMAN, Wesley 28, Polly 27, John 5, Jesse 3, Dudley 9/12
HERALD, Reuben? 53, Polly 26, Susan 16, Elizabeth 13, Wm. 9, Mikel 7, Louisa 6, Reuben 2
AMBURGY, Wilburn 46, Elizabeth 41, John 14, Rebeca 12, Susy 9, Nancy 7, Elizabeth 3, Nancy 27
NICHOLAS, Thos. 40* (B), Elizabeth 30
GIPSON, Squire 25* (B)
AMBURGY, Robert 58, Elizabeth 46, Wilburn 17, Elizabeth 15, Eligha 12, Thos. 4, Darkaan 5/12 (f)
AMBURGY, Wm. W. 24, Vina 23, Robin 2, Wm. 6/12
AMBURGY, Jesse 28*, Rachal 20, Martha 3, Manerva 1

Schedule Page 152

SPARKMAN, Elizabeth 7*
PIGMAN, John 56, Rosanna 54, Wilbern 24, Wm. 17
AMBURGY, Elizabeth 84?
PIGMAN, Campbell 21, Mary 18, Madison 2
FRANKLIN, James 30, Eliza 30, Nancy 9, Elizabeth 7, Kelly 5, Sarah 3
PIGMAN, Umphry 23, Elizabeth 20, Mariah 2, John B. 2/12
CHRISTIAN, Thos. 42, Polly 43, John B. 18, Thos. W. 16, Elizabeth 14, Rosana 13, Robin P. 11, Nancy 8, Polly 6, Quintenea 4, Wm. 1
CRAGER, Mikel 69, Elizabeth 62
INGLE, Eliza 41*, John 22, Wm. 12, Richard 9, Mary J. 7
CRAGER, Adam 27*
MUSICK, Eligha 41, Elizabeth 33, Wm. 16, Isabella 16, Eligha C. 15, John A. 13, Vanleeren C. 14, Nimrod 13, Noah 9, Rosana 8, Emanuel 6, Marinda 4, Elizabeth 3, Gen. William 2, Pollyan 10/12
BURGY, Fanny 33, Wm. 16, Ambrose 15, Walker 13, Mahala 11, Anderson 9, Arta 7, Fielden 5, Umphrey 1
REYNOLDS, Joseph 45, Tena 38, Elizabeth 15, Sarah 14, John 12, Nancy 10, Wesley 8, Polly 7, Rebeca 5, Martha 3, Wm. 1
HUGHS, James 40, Jinsa 36, Mathus 18, Mary 17, John 15, Elizabeth 13, Henry 11, Martha 8, Gabriel 6, Jesse 4, Rebeca 1

1850 Census Letcher County Kentucky

Schedule Page 153

EVERAGE, Benj. 26, Elizabeth 25, Wm. 6, Rachal 4, Nicholas 3, Silvania 1 (error on film, beginning of this family found p. 154 of film)
BURGY, Wm. 28, Hanah 25, Lucy 5, Arminda 2
STEWART, Wm. 50, Polly 46, Peggy 16, Martha 14, Mary 12, Luana 9, Sarah 6, Wm. 3
HIGGINS, Gilbert 55, Leah 43, Rebeca 21, Susana 18, Wm. R. 22, Judah 15, Thos. 10, Alen 7
MARTIN, John 32, Pollyan 24, Rebeca 5, Milly 3, Jane 1
KELLY, Nathan B. 50, Elizabeth 43, Joseph 22, Mary 20, Martha 18, Wm. 15, Nancy 12, James 10, Rebeca 8, Cyntha 6, Sarah 1
KELLY, John 25, Louisa 18
THACKER, Jesse 46, Nancy 40, Sarah 26, Betsey 24, Luisa 14, Robert 9, Malisa 3, Baby 5/21 (f)
JOHNSON, Levi 54*, Anny 38, John 18, Levi 17, Nancy 15, Herod 14, Isaac 11, Alexander 9, Betsey 7, Henry C. 6, Lucind 3, Lydia 21
RIFELL, Crisa 22*
GILBERT, Thos. 65, Susa 54, George 20, Roda 14, Rosana 12
DICKERSON, Benj. 26, Feriba 28, Fany 4, Elizabeth 3
CALHOUN, Thos. 28, Jane 19, Mary 1
COMBS, Biram 35, Hanah 26, Minda 10, Fielden 6, Eliza 2
MULLINS, Joshua 33, Polly 30, Joseph 11, John 9, Rachal 7, Duff 6, Elizabeth 1

Schedule Page 154

CALHOUN, Ransom 33, Mary 30, Elizabeth 10, Saml. 7, John M. 5, Jas. M. 2
PIGMAN, Madison 21, Radhel 20, Campbell 1
CALHOUN, David 38, Rachal 30, John C. 10
CALHOUN, David 60, Eda 60, Samuel 18
CALHOUN, B. W. 30 (m), Pracilla 35, Wm. 8, Martha 6, Robert 5, Mary 3, Feiba? 1
MARTIN, Benj. 26, Melvina 24, Elizabeth 5, John 4, Wm. 2
CORNITT, Samuel 47, Polly 35, Wm. 14, Margaret 10, Rachal 7, Joseph 6, Moses 3, Jane 6/12
CALHOUN, Jackson 25, Fanny 19, Wm. 6/12
STONE, Levi 21, Hanah 21, James 3, Shadrach 1
BURGY, Ambrose 27, Elizabeth 27, Abby 10, John 8, Eliza 6, Noah 4, Manerva 1
SMITH, Nicholas 44, Nancy 42, Simeon 15, Wm. 13, Mary 11, Missa 9, Milly 7, Sarah 5, Nancy 3
BALDRIDGE, James 47, Vina 45
JOHNSON, Wm. 33, Nancy 30, Barbry 2
CAUDILL, Wm. 33*, Ticy 30, Peggy 14, James 7, Shadrach 5, Kinick 2
COMBS, Kinick 26*
HICKS, Jesse 36, Betsey 34, John 14, Nancy 12, Charles 10, Kitty 8, Claburn 6, Elihu 4, Betsey 3, Margaret 1

1850 Census Letcher County Kentucky

Schedule Page 155

EVERAGE, John 23, Sarah 18
EVERAGE, Joseph 60*, Sylvania 56, Thomas 18, Benjamine 24
MCKEE, Roda 5*
MULLINS, Daniel 51, Nancy 32, David 9, Daniel 7, Mary 5, Vina 3, Samuel 1
MULLINS, Joseph 21, Catharine 16
BURGEY, Ambrose 58, Rebeca 48, William 21, Elizabeth 15, Umphrey 17, Susanna 9
AMBURGEY, Wiley 28, Dianna 24, Rebeca 4, Peggy 2
CAUDILL, Leticus? 26, Sarah 26, Eligha 6, Benjamine 3, Nancy J. 1
BURGEY, Francis 25, Polly 23, Wiley 4, Washington 2, Eligha 1
MADEN, Peter 58, Jane 50, Eda 16, Vina 14, Jane 8
BURGEY, John 31*, Rachal 24, Ambrose 8, Polly 6, Jane 5, Reuben 3, Rebeca 1
HALL, Reuben 75*, Nancy 70
CORNITT, Jesse H. 55*, Nancy 55, Marinda 17, Wesly 23, Franka 15
HALE, A. D. 38 (m)*, Nathaniel 13, Ruth 11, Joseph 8
CORNETT, W. B. 21 (m), Mary 24, Nancy 6, Susan 4, Polly 2
SEXTON, Stephen 24, Crissa 24, John 2
CORNITT, Davis 26*, Bexey 19
RILEY, Miles 25*

- 229 -

Page 230 Blank

1850 Census Morgan County Kentucky

Schedule Page 86

CASKEY, Thomas H. 39, Martha 24, Sarah 18, Permela 16, Martha 14, Perlina 11, James 4, Samuel 3, Mary 8/12
LYKINS, David P. 31*, Lavisa 28, Peter 10, William 8, Harrison 5, Alfred 3, Joseph 1/12
GENT, Ellen 11*
FERGUSON, Isaac 36, Elizabeth 35, Mary 14, Richard 11, Thomas 6, Martha 1
SMITH, Thomas 32, Mary 28, Eilzabeth 10, Hiram 6
PRUETT, John W. 24, Alce 24 (f), Sarah 4, Matilda 1
CONLY, Moses 30, Nancy 22, Allen 6, Isaac 3, Lyda 1
CONLY, Isaac 24, Elizabeth 15
HOWERTON, James 54, Susan 50, James 24
DAY, Peter 63, Frances 63, Vilet 29 (f), Alfred 24, Matilda 23, Allen 18
MYNHIER, William 28
BOYD, Alexander 25*, Mary 20, Hannah 2, Frances 1/12
SMOOT, Eliza 25*, Marinda 9
WALKER, Wyett 7*, Manerva 4
DAVIS, Benson C. 51, Mary 48, Melvina 25, Cela 22, Reuben 20, Travis 17, Adelia 4, Mary 3
COX, Charles G. 32, Almira 31, Margarett 2
DAY, John W. 32, Lydia 36, Eunice 16, Elizabeth 14, Alfred 10, David 8, Peter 6, Frances 4, Anna 1
LEWIS, Gideon 46, Margarett 42, Jane 19, William 17, Mary 16, Rachael 14, James 11, John 9, Elizabeth 5

Schedule Page 87

LEWIS, Enoch 48, Margarett 45, Rachael 20 (twin), Cyntha 20 (twin), Thompson 18, Sarah 16, Andrew 14, Menifer 11, Stephen 9, Johnson 7, Julia 4, William 3
TRIMBLE, David 31, Mary 30, John 10, Nancy 5, Angeline 8/12
YOUNG, John 38, Nancy 24, Richard 2, Catharine 2/12
MCKENYER, Harrison 36, Garner 35 (f), Andrew 14, Mary 12, Jamima 10, William 7, Sarah 4, Lewis 2, John 1/12
ELAM, James S. 25, Mary 28, Frances 1
DEAL, William jr. 35, Margarett 30, Willis 10, John 6, William 3, Elizabeth 1
BROWN, James sr. 62, Nancy 62
WILLIAMS, Anderson 30, Rachael 25, Mary 7, Thomas 4, Wallis 3 (f), Martha 2/12
MCKENZIE, Henly 27, Celia 26, John 5, William 5/12
PERRY, Thomas D. 53, Martha 45, Thomas 19, Jane 16, Benjamin 15, John 13, Edmund 11, Mary 9, Margarett 7, James 5
BROWN, John 39, Abagail 32, Eveline 16, James 15, William 10, Jessee 8, David 6
NICKELL, John 43, Malinda 42, Henry 20, Clara 18, Clarinda 16, Ambrose 15, Rutha 14, Greenup 12, Richard 11, Alfred 10, Martha 8, Marion 7 (m), Precilla 6, Mary 3, Edy 1 (f)

1850 Census Morgan County Kentucky

Schedule Page 88

PEARCE, William 29*, Sarah 27
GOOCH, Martha A. 10*
LUMPKINS, Frances M. 2*
FUGETT, James jr. 27, Sarah 24, Rebecca 8, William 7, Mary 5, James 3, Frances 1
FULLER, Hosea 50*, Darcus 47, Nancy 27, Elizabeth 19, Robert 17
CYPHUS, James 4*
COTTLE, Uriah 50, Cyntha 50, Edward 25, Joseph 23, John 21, Malissa 16, Ambrose 13, Uriah 10
BROWN, Harvy 31, Huldah 27, James 4, William 3, John 4/12
BROWN, Amanda 36, Elizabeth 15, Mary 8, Permelia 6, James 3
DAY, John H. 22, Susan 21, Mary 3
LEWIS, Francis jr. 33, Mary 31, Lucinda 10, Malinda 9, Francis 8, Daniel 2
WILLIAMS, William F. 38*, Celia 34, Edward 16, Elliott 12, Sarah 8, John 5
PENDLETON, Milly 40*
DAYS, Allen T. 53, Mary 48, Jesse 16, Amanda 13, William 10, Henry 8, Mary 4
ELAM, James sr. 45, Rebecca 45, James 19, William 16, Richard 13, Jesse 11, Rebecca 9, Susan 8, Zerilda 5
HOWERTON, Andrew J. 31, Adelia 26, Matthew 5, Mary 2
ELAM, William H. 30, NAncy 25, Thomas 8, Robert 3
JOHNSON, Israel 35, Vina 34, Franklin 16, Emily 13, Phillip 11, Ellen 9, Anna 6, Rosannah 4, Hannah 2

Schedule Page 89

STAMFUR, George W. 32, Nancy 27, Martha 12, Elizabeth 9, Isabel 7, John 5, Sarah 3, Isaac 1
WELLS, John 26, Anna 20, Queena 5, John 3, Harrison 2
NICKELL, Silas 39*, Susannah 32, William 17, Matthew 15, Andrew 14, Alfred 11, Harvy 7, Thomas 5, Mary 3
LEWIS, Eveline 15*
EASTERLONG, Thomas 46, Joannah 43, Catharine 21, Elizabeth 18, William 16, Rebecca 12, Sarah 11, Susannah 4
MAYS, Sarah 42, Thomas 17, Blair 13, Catharine 10
LACY, John B. 58, Amanda 38, James 20, William A. 18, Harvy 16, John 14, Daniel 12, Sarah 10, Elizabeth 8, Nancy 5, Miles 3, Luellen 3/12 (f)
NICKELL, Matilda 52, Amos 16, Isaac 14, Robert 10, Matilda 5
BROWN, Daniel W. 36, Rebecca 28, Samuel 10, Walters 6, Henry 4, Elizabeth 3, William 2
MCGUIRE, Jesse J. 25, Margarett 23, James 3, Louisa 10/12
NICKELL, John D. 24, Precilla 25, Lucretia 4, Sarah 2
EASTERLING, Henry jr. 26
COFFEE, William 65*, Elizabeth 64, Nancy 21, Amos 20
CANARD, Eliza 21*
BAYS, George W. 29, Sarah 29, Cyntha 10, James 8, William 7, Pleasant 4, Sarah 3, Martha E. 1

1850 Census Morgan County Kentucky

Schedule Page 90

KEETON, Thomas B. 46*, Rebecca 35
WHEELER, George W. 30*
HAVENS, Josiah 37*, Jane 39, William 10, James 7, Samuel 4, Sarah 1
COOPER, Archibald 24*
EVANS, Edwin 39, Mary 29, Emeline 10, James 8, Adeline 5
WILLIAMS, Elijah 44, Elizabeth 38, William 18, Nancy 15, Thomas 10, Mary 6, James 4
EVANS, B. M. 27 (m), Eliza 23, Misouri 3, Wilson 2, Rhoda 6/12
PRATER, Robert 41, Cyntha 29, Emily 15, Nancy 13, John 9, William 7, Archibald 5, Wiley 3, George 2
HAMMONS, Andrew J. 31*, Jane 27, Perlina 8, Thomas 5, Christianna 3, James 2, Mary 10/12
PRATER, Elijah W. 15*
HAMMON, Jilson P. 42, Mary 35, Susan 10, John 8, James 6, Margarett 4, Wiley 3, Thomas 2, Henry 8/12
MONTGOMERY, Joseph 20, Cassa 18, James 5/12
COOPER, Perry 32*, Arena 32, Elizabeth 12, Archibald 8, James 2, Patsey 78
BALEY, Levi 13*
HAMMONS, John 66*, Margarett 62
LUMPKINS, Mary 45*
ELAM, Jeremiah 38*, Elizabeth 37, Meredith 19, Nancy 18, William 16, Shelby 14 (m), James 12, Robert 10, Mary 9, Manerva 7, Andrew 5, Zackary 2
HOLBROOK, William 25*
BROWN, Elijah 45, Alce 38 (f), William 22, John 18, Alfred 15, Nathaniel 13, Elizabeth 12, Samuel 10

Schedule Page 91

PRATER, Thomas 57*, Rebecca 55, Perlina 19, Thomas 12
LEWIS, Thomas 9*
KEETON, Isaac 20*
WILLIAMS, Elizabeth 34, Thomas 16, Lucinda 14, Kelsey 12, Wiley 10, Perlina 8, Emily 6
EASTERLING, Henry sr. 50, Francina 40, Susannah 22, Jeremiah 18, Richard 16, Thomas 14, Agnancy 10
MADDUX, James 44, Dicy 41, William 21, Sarah 19, John 18, Robert 13, Mary 6, Lucy 6/12
ADAMS, Allen 39, Eliza 39, Milton 18, William 15, Perlina 13, Brice 11, Newton 8, Jasper 5, Thomas 4, Louisa 3, James 4, Rebecca 78
MCGUIRE, Samuel W. 28, Frances 19, Louisa 1
KEETON, George W. 41, Cena 40, Thomas 17, Riley 15, Cornelius 13, Catlett 11, George 5, Green 4, Mary 1
BAYS, John E. 25*, Sarah 29
COFFEE, Martha 28*, Pleasant 11, Sarah 9, Alce 5 (f), Martha 1
GULLETT, Ezekiel 49, Ellen 49, Charles 21, Lewis 17, Matthew 14, Allen 12, Nancy 5, Ezekiel 2
COFFEE, Wiley J. 33, Elizabeth 34, Harvy 10, Emily 7, William 5, Daniel 3
PRATER, William D. 32*, Telitha 24, William 4, Thomas 2, Wiley 1
BUFFINGTON, Rebecca 18*

1850 Census Morgan County Kentucky

Schedule Page 92

HOWARD, James sr. 42, Sarah 38, Elizabeth 13, Thomas 9, Frances 6, Elijah 4
HOWARD, William 50, Anna 46, Calvin 19, Lucinda 14
HAMMONS, Joseph 80, Henrietta 20, Joseph 15, John 1
RISNER, John 35, Nancy 26, Andrew 9, Malinda 7, Reuben 5, William 3
HOWARD, Reuben 36, Nancy 33, Richard 10, Clarinda 7, Susan 5, Delana 3, Reuben 2, Harvy 13
HOWARD, Henry sr. 40*, Elizabeth 33, Isaac 17, Alfred 15, Joseph 14, Franklin 12, William 9, Luanna 7, Rebecca 5, Uriah 3, David 1
COOPER, Martha 19*
HOWARD, James jr. 29, Cyntha 25, Berthena 7, Perlina 3, William 3/12, Zerilda 15
HAMMON, Benjamin 50, Sarah 45, Hezekiah 20, Thomas 18, Benjamin 16, Sarah 14, Drucilla 10, John 8, William 6, Jeptha 4 (m), Louisa 2, Nancy 1
WARD, John H. 26, Rutha 22, James 5, NAncy 3, Rebecca 2, Joseph 3/12
PATRICK, Hugh 45, Mary 40, Robert 17, MArgarett 14, Cela 11, Nancy 9, Lucinda 6, Mary 3
SULIVAN, Pryor 25, Mary 23, George 1/12
HOWARD, Thomas 80, Frances 71
HOWARD, William jr. 23, Catharine 20, Henry 3, Letha 1
PERKINS, Isaac 22, Mary 15, Margarett 40, Jilson 11, Sarah 19, Susan 17, Isaac 4, Elizabeth 2

Schedule Page 93

HENSLEY, Stephen 26*, Mary 19, Lear 3 (f), Westly 8/12
PERKINS, Thomas 9*
LYKINS, John 38, Jane 33, JAmes 13, Nancy 9, Mary 7, Richard 5, Eli 4, Mary 1
HYLTON, Samuel 24, Eliza 18, Mary 3, Louisa 2, John 1
HOWARD, Andrew 35, MAtilda 25, Fleming 9, Frances 8, Mary 11/12
HOWARD, Moses 53, Mary 50, Jilson 16, Andrew 14, Margarett 11, Margarett 20, Levi 3, Stephen 1
PERKINS, James 28 (B), Belinda 22, Rebecca 8, Christina 6, William 3, Mary 1
PERKINS, Lewis 25 (B), Mary 21, Eli 1
PHIPPS, John 48, Cyntha 47, James 21, John 16, Green 12, Ailcy 11, Ludena 7, Winny 5
ADAMS, Gilbert 27, America 23, Cela 7, Sabre 5 (f), Preston 1
MCGUIN, Ambrose C. 40, Nancy 37, William 18, John 16, Edy 14 (f), James 12, Joel 10, Jesse 7, Sarah 6, Samuel 3, Leander 1
MCCLANAHAN, Moses 52, Sarah 36, Cornelius 18, David 14, Robert 12, John 11, Amanda 10, Elizabeth 6, William 4, George 2, Sarah 1
OAKLEY, Richard M. 37, Belinda 24, Elijah 14, Joseph 12, William G. 9, John 2

Schedule Page 94

HALL, Isaac 47, Anna 49, George 22, David 20, William 17, Elizabeth 15, Isaac 11, Jane 8, John 6, James 3
AMYX, Peter H. 38, Dama 32, John 11, James 9, Lydia 7, Hannah 3, Nancy 1
CASSITY, John 66*, Elizabeth 66, John 35, William 33, James 29, Henry 6, Elizabeth 4, Sarah 2
ELLINGTON, Martha 21*, Sarah 20
HARDIN, Jackson 16*
CASSITY, Isaac 38*, Lucinda 31, Edmund 12, David 10, Mary 7, John 5, James 8/12

1850 Census Morgan County Kentucky

ELLINGTON, Dorothy 15*
MYERS, Joseph 55, Rachel 49, Sarah 17, Isaac 15, Lydia 14, Nancy 12, Lucretia 10, Joseph 7, David 20
UTTERBACK, Harmon 66*, John 70, Washington 20
STATON, Amanda 14*
UTTERBACK, Paterson 35, Barbara 28, Marsaleta 7, Rosaline 5, Malinda 3
BRADSHAW, John H. 37, Catharine 27, Mary 8, James 6, Sarah 5
CLINE, Samuel 22, Mary 19, Angeline 1
BISHOP, Elihu 28, Nancy 23, Mary 2, Eliza 4/12
EPPERHART, Henry 67*, Christena 55, David 23, Henry 19, Daniel 17, Rebecca 15
CASSITY, Catharine 1*
FANNIN, David 60*, Cyntha 30, Derissa 4, Jane 1
FRALEY, Susan 8*, Sarah 6
KENDALL, James P. 55, Phebe 44, Virginia 16, America 14, Elijah 8, Nancy 6, James 5/12

Schedule Page 95

KENDALL, William jr. 32, Elizabeth 27, James 9, John 8, Phebe 4, Sarah 2
HOWARD, Suddath 21 (m), Sarah 20
CLARK, George B. 51, Elizabeth 46, Eliza 17, John 15, Leonard 14, Samuel 11, Mariah 9, Mary 6, Manerva 10/12
MONTGOMERY, Watson 31, Frances 26, James 10, Celena 7, William 4, Isaac 1/12
JENNINGS, John 30, Rachael 24, David 7, Rosannah 2, Mary 1/12
BROWN, John E. 39, Catharine 33, Francis 12, Samuel 10, Christena 6, Eliza 4, Catharine 3, John 3/12
HUNT, George M. 27, Elvira 25, Martha A. 4, Sarah 3, John 1
KENBELL, James 61, Margarett 45
MCDANIEL, George 35*, Elizabeth 28, William 5, Eliza 3, Moses 1/12
ROYCE, John 80*, Mary 75
JONES, Isaac 29, Jane 26, Lemon 7 (m), Hezekiah 5, Franklin 4, Robert 3, Wells 2, William 1, William 65
SARGENTS, William 73*, Lucy 68, Francis 16, Selena 14, Martha 11
JONES, William 7*
BLAIR, Anderson 32, Clarissa 18, John 2/12, Jesse 70, Rebecca 64
THOMAS, James 55, Sarah 52, Sarah 21, James 18, Amanda 14, Franklin 11
LITREL, Daniel? 39, Elizabeth 25, Cyntha 14, Newcanny 12 (f), Hastin 4 (m), Wyman 3, Samuel 2, John 1/12

Schedule Page 96

CASSITY, George 28, Mary 24, Elizabeth 3, Sarah 5/12
CONLY, John 38, Rachael 37, Sarah 16, Mary 14, Bertholomew 12, William 9, Milton 4, Elizabeth 3, Nancy 2
FERGUSON, John W. 31, Nancy 30, Susan 10, Mary 8, Edy 5 (f), Elizabeth 1
THOMAS, John 30, Pinean 30 (f), James 8, Lydia 6, William 4, Leander 1
TEMPLEMAN, Enoch G. 27*, Miriam 23, Rhoda 5/12
PARKER, Nancy 19*
DAY, Jedediah 29*, Cyntha 29, William 7, David 5, Jacob 3, Sarah 1
FANNIN, Mary 17*

1850 Census Morgan County Kentucky

ADKINS, Levi 26, Price 21, Mary J. 3, Eliza 1
HARRIS, James 23, Susannah 25, James 4/12
FULTYS, John 60, Dicy 45, Scott 17, Clarinda 15, James 10
PERRY, Mitton 22, Elizabeth 27
CHRISTY, Joseph K. 62, Anna 63
KIRK, Alexander 56, Elizabeth 46, Ellen 25, Robert? 23, James 19, Andrew 17, William 15
ROYCE, Benjamin 48, Elizabeth 45, Susan 22, Mary 18, Rebecca 16, Elizabeth 14, Nancy 12, William 10, Campbell 8, Francis 6, James 4, Fleming 2
FRALEY, Wilson 25, Ciler 20 (f), Harrison 2, Washington 1, Jackson 30
DAY, James A. 31, Anna 28, Susannah 6, David 4, Henry 3, James 3/12

Schedule Page 97

FRALEY, Frederick 35, Barbara 25, John 10, Mary 9, Price 7, Eliza 5, Elizabeth 4, Amanda 1
LEE, Matthew 32, Lydia 29, Lucy 10, James 7, William 5
BROWNING, Josiah 42, Elizabeth 37, Joseph 18, James 15, Laura 12, Sidney 9 (m), Louisa 6, Virginia 1/12
NICKELL, Fowler 32, Nancy 29, Clarisa 13, Elizabeth 12, John 7, Rebecca 4, Daniel 2
FOUCHE?, William 23, Eveline 25
SANFORD, Thornton W. 41, Louisa 34
WHITE, George 50, Ellen 47, Jacob 24, Jane 21, Andrew 16, Perry 14, Martha 10, James 6
TOLIVER, Elijah 58, Martha 52, Lewis 20, Joel 18, John 15, Hannah 11 (twin), Susannah 11 (twn), James 8
RAMEY, Samuel 27, Sarah 25, Benjamin 2, Sarah 1, Susannah 2/12
SANDFORD, Augustus 34*, Nancy 29, NAncy 13, John 11, Josephine 9, James 8
MCILHANY, Elizabeth 15*
MCKENZIE, William 20*
CHRISTY, Julius 24*
EDWARDS, James 37, Sarah 36, John 15, James 13, Elizabeth 12, Joseph 10, Thomas 8, Phelix 3, Emily 1
ROYCE, John 43, Anna 33, Lucinda 13, Mary 11, Elizabeth 10, Moses 8, Andrew 7, Louisa 3
PARKER, Joel 56, Julian 45 (f), Thomas 21, Rhoda 17, James 9, Jemima 7, Lewis 5, William 2

Schedule Page 98

JACKSON, William 40 (B), Anna 42, William 14, Victoria 7, Ira 6, Caldonia 5, Josephine 2, Henderson 7/12
JONES, William 24 (B?), Anna 24
NICKELL, James 30, Elizabeth 22, Mary 2, Frances 4/12
MCDANIEL, Hezekiah sr. 66, Sophia 70, William 29, John 21, George 7, Precilla 5, Elizabeth 4
MCDANIEL, Hezekiah jr. 23, Nancy 19
JACKSON, Anderson 41 (B), Jane 40, William 18, Alexander 16, Sarah 15, Lucinda 11, John 7, Nancy 4
DAY, Susannah 45, Isaac 20, William 15, Jilson 14
MCGUIN, James 24, Mary 25, William 1
CRAIG, William 32, Endfield 23 (f), Henry 6, James 4, Mary 2
GOSE, Mason 34, Gilean 34 (f), Rebecca 14, Anderson 12, Elizabeth 10, Henry 8, Mary 6, Delila 4, Elizabeth 2, William 1/12

1850 Census Morgan County Kentucky

BLAIR, William 44, Lydea 42, David 20, Elizabeth 19, Rachael 17, Lucinda 15, Martha 13, Hariett 12, Dorothy 10, Alvin 8, William 6, Ellen 4
SARGENT, Joseph 28, Sarah 22
ELLINGTON, Abram 57*, Mary 47
DOWNING, Mary 15*, Cyntha 12
PERRY, Daniel 53*, Julian 46 (f), Francis 22, James 16, Joseph 15, Gardner 13, Daniel 11, Allen 7, Jane 5, Cordelia 4, Cyrus 2

Schedule Page 99

SUBLETT, James 25*, David 19, Mary 17
CLICK, Parthena 15*
SARGENT, Lovel 41, John 19, William 16, Gabriel 13, Elizabeth 10, Elijah 7, Rebeca 5, Carline 4 (f), Margarett 1 (twn), Martha 1 (twin)
BLANKENSHIP, Henry 60, Druciller 51 (f), Benjamin 27, Nancy 25, Mary 23, Lydia 22, Clea 19 (f), Malissa 17, Linea 15, Henry 13, Julian 9 (f), Joshua 6
CASKEY, Samuel 37, Catharine 37, Isabel 5, Hulda 12, Thomas 9, Mary 7, Hannah 5
MCCLURE, Ezekiel 37, Elizabeth 33, Nancy 14, Matthew 12, William 11, Mary A. 9, Jane 7, Louisa 4, Sarah 1
MCCLURE, James H. 33, lucinda 27, Matthew 7, Margarett 6, John 5, James 4, George 2, William 1
LEWIS, Henry H. 42*, Catharine 34, David 14, John 11, Harrison 9, Thomas 7?, Hannah 4, Mary 2
DYER?, William 10*
LEWIS, Hannah 84*, Sarah 45
COGSWELL, Hannah 23*
MCCLURE, Matthew 70*, Anna 62, Adeline 24
BLACK, Andrew J. 5*
VIST, Thomas 17*
CASSITY, Harrison 36, Mariah 35, Elizabeth 17, Newton 13, Reuben 10, Jesse 8, Allen 4, Martha 1
ELLINGTON, Isaac 28, Matilda 36, James 10, Abram 7, Reuben 4, Carline 1

Schedule Page 100

MCKINZIE, Isaac 86, Rebecca 45, Clarinda 12, Oscar 9, Martha 7, William 2
ARMSTRONG, Rutha 45, James 19, Vianna 13, Eliza 10, William 5
BALEY, Susan 36, Manerva 19, Miles 17, Telitha 15, Berthena 12, Precilla 10
COLE, Harrison 33*, Lucinda 19, Vian 1 (f)
MCGUIRE, Newton 21*
COLE, Samuel 46, Eliza 38, Clarinda 16, Elizabeth 13, James 9, William 7, Cyntha 5, Asberry 1
MURRAY, Dulcena 36, William 11, Jasper 7, Mary 5
COLE, Mary 24*, James 4, Martha 2
DRICKELL, Isabel 64*
CASKEY, Thomas jr. 23, Amanda 16, Malissa 1
HENSON, James jr. 22, Elizabeth 21, Mary A. 5/12
HUNT, Barnet 31, Mary 25
OAKLEY, William 25, Mary 24, Thomas 4, Margarett 1, Austin 2/12
DYER, Gardner 32, Sarah 32, Carline 11 (f), William 9, Mary 6, Lydia 4, Hannah 1

1850 Census Morgan County Kentucky

MCCLAIN, Beverly 42 (m), Lydia 34, Nancy 17, Sarah 15, Hannah 12, Elizabeth 10, William 8, John 6, Joshua 4, Scott 2, Alfred 4/12
KEETON, Samuel 38, Catharine 42, Alean 17, Margarett 13, Mason 12, Rebecca 9, Sarah 8, Nancy 7, Francis 5
LEWIS, William H. H. 37, Elizabeth 32, William 14, Daniel 12, Eliza 10, John 8, James 5, Leander 3, Isaac 6/12

Schedule Page 101

FRALEY, Honor 31 (f), Margarett 15, Emily 10, Marcus 6, William 4, Taylor 1
ELLINGTON, Jacob 24, Martha 23, John 1
LEWIS, John P. 35*, Mary 25, Malinda 6, John 4, Edmund 3, Moses 11/12
PETITT, Benjamin 20*
PEYTON, Daniel 53*, Anna 50, Charles 19
SARGENT, Martha 1*
RATLIFF, John 24, Sarah 33, James 2, John 4/12
RATLIFF, Judy 63, Rebecca 33, Jacob 14, James 6
RATLIFF, Reuben 37, Nancy 33, Elizabeth 13, Sarah 12, Amy 10, John 9, Jesse 7, Ezekiel 3, Phebe 1
DYER, Margarett 28, William 7, Hannah 5, Edmund 3, Mary 1
LEWIS, William 62*, Jane 55, Edmund 26, Nancy A. 1
DYER, Nancy J. 9*
LEWIS, Daniel P. 23, Margarett 26, William 3, Zachary 1
ELLINGTON, John 50, Mary 45, Isaac 19, James 18, John 16, Mary 14, David 12, George 10, Dorothy 8, Frances 6, Amanda 5, Zerilda 3, William 1
RICHARDSON, Lewis H. 42, Rebecca 39, Joel 14, Elizabeth 11, Sampson 8, Rosannah 6, Phebe 4
ANDERSON, Richard 35, Mary 15, Absalum 13, William 11, Edieth 8
COLBERT, William 33, Eliza 20, George 9, John 8, Elias 1
ELLINGTON, Alfred 26*, Hannah A. 26, Mary 8/12

Schedule Page 102

WILBOURN, Mary 22*
HUNT, Lewis 53, Frances 38, Lewis 16, Melvina 13, Manerva 8, Henry 5, Richard 2
TRUMBO, John J. 30, Mary 29, Nancy 8, Louisa 6, George 4, Manerva 3, Mary 1
ELLINGTON, Benjamin 33*, Elizabeth 20, John 8/12
CUPS?, Margaret 2*
MONTGOMERY, James 35, Clarinda 23, James 7, Nancy 5, Evan 3, Mary 2
HUNT, A. D. D. 36, Malinda 28, Malissa 9, Terissa 8, John 6, Joseph 2
DALEY, Alfred 29, Elizabeth 26, John 8, Samuel 6, Margarett 3, William 4/12
DALEY, John 22, Mariah 26
ARMINTAGE, John 41*, Mary 31, William 12, Elizabeth 9, Jacob 7, Mary 4, James 3
KIDWELL, John 21*
HUNT, Joseph 41*, Rebecca 37, Oliver 20, Martha 16, Armelissa 15, Annetta 11, Joseph 1
DENNIS, Green 20*
DUNAHOO, Alfred 37, Mariah 36, Matthew 15, Catharine 13, Lucinda 12, Julia 10, William 8, Mary 7, Louisa 5, Adremoney 3 (f), John 10/12
DUNAHOO, James 35*, Julia 30, Thomas 14, Jesse 13, Joseph 8, Amanda 4, Mary 3/12

1850 Census Morgan County Kentucky

REED, Sarah 16*
DUNAHOO, Alfred 23*, Martha 22, Sarah 1/12
JONES, Rachael 9*
WILSON, Charles S. 30*, Penelope 23, John 1
JONES, Josiah 16*

Schedule Page 103

WILSON, Abijah 24, Catharine 16, Mary 3/12, Dosha 36, William 14, Sarah 12, Francis 8, Louisa 5, Jacob 3
WILSON, Isaiah 38*, Jeremiah 60, Elizabeth 62
SMITH, Robert 22*
HYMER, Asa 21, Catharine 19, Armazilda 1
BRADSHAW, David 76, Rebecca 57, Rebecca 33, Thomas 26
DAY, Isaac 30, Lucinda 29, Martha 8, Elizabeth 5, Permelia 1, James 18
ALFREY, Rachael 59, John 25
ALFREY, Alfred 35, Mary 28, Samuel 9, Carline 7 (f), Bruce 5, Nelson 2
PEARCE, Green B. 25, Susan 27, Mordeica 3 (m), Marcus 1, William 2/12
SADDLER, William 62, Rachael 55
EVANS, Rolly M. 27 (m), Martha F. 26, Mary 4, Isaac 2, America 1
EVANS, John 29, Elizabeth 28, Isaac 9, Mahala 7, Joseph 6, Rebecca 5, David 3
RAMEY, Thomas 38, Malinda 28, Strother 10, Julia 9, Gilean 6 (f), Martha 4, Jasper 8/12
HARBER, Abner 37, Elizabeth 25, Eliza 7, Isabel 6, Thomas 4, Catharine 2, Asa 1
MURPHY, Monroe 27, Louisa 29, John 7, Mary 6, Jonathan 1
ELLINGTON, John W. 30, Hannah 27, Zerilda 7, Jacob 5, Francis 3, Lucinda 11/12
EVANS, Evan 50, Jane 53, Jaley 21 (f), Frances 17, Sarah 13
CASSITY, Isaac sr. 68, Delila 60, Martha 20

Schedule Page 104

ELLINGTON, Jacob sr. 61*, Catharine 45
EVANS, Rebecca 35*
HASTEY, James 19*
ELLINGTON, Isaac sr. 59, Elizabeth 49, Mary 18, Abraham 14, Joseph 11
ELLINGTON, David 86
CRAIG, Thomas 43, Eliza 37, Elizabeth 9, Sarah 6, Catharine 2, John 2/12
BYRAM, Westley 42, Margarett 31, Robert 9, Newton 7, Nancy 5, James 3, Mary 1
ABBOTT, William 66, Mary 58, Henry 20, Arzilda 17
JONES, James jr. 22, Emily 18, Rebecca 9/12
JONES, James sr. 50, Lucinda 49, Mary 27, Sarah 25, William 24, Lucinda 20, David 18, Nancy 15, Josiah 12, John 9, Emery E. 6, William 86, Sarah 75, James 3, Sarah 1
PEARCE, Mordeica 63*, Anna 58, Martha 19
FERAND, Jane 15*
MYERS, Samuel 31, Emily 31, Lueda 11 (f), Joseph 9, Artameca 8, Mary 2
UTTERBACK, Joseph 41, Deborah 29, William 8, James 5, Wingfield 2, Martha 8/12, Washington 20
SMEDLY, Samuel 52*, Mary 58, Samuel 17
HALL, David 20*

1850 Census Morgan County Kentucky

CASSITY, Mary 5*
CHAPMAN, Nathan 80*
GREGORY, Jamison 30*, Henrietta 30, James 5, Jesse 4, Benjamin 1
HARDIN, Amanda 19*
BROWN, Thomas 41*, Nancy 43, John 14, Margarett 11, Davis 9, Martha 7, Harry 1
COFER, Elizabeth 30*, Mary P. 6/12

Schedule Page 105

BROWN, John S. 55, Catharine 46, Lueda 15, John 14, Solomon 13, Dorothy 11, William 10, James 9, Andrew 5
BROWN, James 67, Emily 55, Cisa 23 (f), Delila 17, Emily 16, Matilda 12
FERAND, Thomas J. 23, Martha 20
CASSITY, Margarett 62, John 24, Rebecca 25
HALL, Jacob 44, Nancy 39, Isaac 19, Mary 17, Lucinda 15, Elizabeth 10, John 8, Sarah 5, Adeline 2, Martha 1
CROSE, Adam 50, Sarah 53, John 23, Dorothy 19, Adam 14
HARDIN, Isaac 46, Nancy 37, Martha 12, Brown 6, Isaac 3, Mary 6/12, Isaac N. 14
BROWN, John C. 26, Rebecca 25, Coleman 4
HARDIN, Savel 48 (m), Leodica 27, Lucinda 3/12
CASSITY, Thomas 22, Elizabeth 16
STEPHENS, Benjamin 49, Nancy 49, Lucinda 18, David 15, Rebecca 7
MYNHIER, Solomon K. 45, Anna 41, Jonathan 22, Simon 20, Nancy 18, Sarah 16, Hannah 13, Julia 10, Henry 9, Josiah 8, William 6
MOTT, Almarian 32 (m), Charlotte 35, Belinda 7, James 5, John 3, Samuel 1
BROWN, Coleman 28, Joanna 20, James 6/12
SINK, Simon 42, Mary 39, James 17, John 14, Lucretia 12, Lucinda 10, Thomas 7, Robert 5, Mahala 2

Schedule Page 106

PETITT, Samuel 39, Rebecca 23, Benjamin 19, Mary 18, Lorinda 16, Bluford 15, Preston 13, Elizabeth 11, Louisa 3
ELLIOTT, Samuel sr. 47, Fanny 44, John 19, James 17, Humean? 15 (f), Amanda 13, Mary 11, Benjamin 9, William 4
LAW, Marcus 36, Mahala 33, James 15, Rebecca 12, Amanda 10, Catharine 8, Mary 4, Elizabeth 3, Eliza 1/12
CASSITY, Thomas J. 29*, Amanda 22, John 6, Elizabeth 3, James 1, Elizabeth 52, Jackson 15
HARDIN, John 24*
KID, Edmund 35, Amanda 28, Angeline 12, Carline 10, Aaron 8, Harrison 5, Mary 4, John 1
HAVINS, William 60*, Elizabeth 59, Samuel 21
MANIN, Elizabeth 22*
FRISBY, Jasper N. 6*
FRISBY, John J. 25*, Elizabeth 29, Leander 2, Ledena 1, James 2/12
KING, George J. 11*
FUGETT, William W. 22*, Elizabeth 22, John 2
CARPENTER, Lucinda 20*
WELLS, Richard 27, Emily 22, Jane 2

1850 Census Morgan County Kentucky

CASKEY, John sr. 56, Hannah 52, Miles 24, Mary 21, Elizabeth 19, Robert 17, Mary 13
CASKEY, Thomas sr. 84, Lydia 75, Isabel 15
FUGETT, Mary 43, Sarah 20, James 16, Nancy 14, Elizabeth 11, Louisa 8, John 6, Joseph 4
HENRY, Lewis jr. 28*, Catharine 27, John 6, Phebe R. 4, Mary 2, Nancy 1

Schedule Page 107

BARNETT, Andrew 14*
HAMMONS, James 44, Edy 41 (f), Elizabeth 19, John 17, Martin 14, Lafayett 12, Rebecca 10, Mary 6
OAKLEY, Austin 47, Eliza 40, John 17, Sarah 15, Mary 13, William 10, James 6, Benjamin 4, Eliza 3, Allen 2/12 (twin), Albert 2/12 (twn), Thomas J. 12
FUGETT, William M. 29*, Hannah 29, James 6, Rebecca 3, Lucinda 1
PETITT, Martha 16*
BROWN, Daniel 61, Mary 58, Manerva 18, James K. 20, Harrison 10
BROWN, Stephen 29, Mary 26, Louisa 7, Elizabeth 5, Mary 3, William 5/12, Margarett 31, Julia A. 7, John 10/12
PERRY, Cyrus sr. 38, Elizabeth 23, Huldah 15, Matilda 11, Thomas 10, William 7, John 4
PERRY, Joseph 34*, Lydia 33, John 12, Mary 10, James 8, Daniel 5, Lucinda 3, Samuel 1/12
OAKLEY, George Ann 15*
GIBBS, Milton 34, Jane 29, Lydia 7, Nancy 5, Hannah 3, James 1
CARPENTER, Josiah 31, Nancy 30, Levi 6, George 1
PEYTON, Daniel jr. 23, Frances 17
CARPENTER, Levi 32, Mary 19, Albert 1
GOODPASTER, George W. 39*, Elizabeth 32, Richard 9, Nancy 8, Fountain 6, James 3, John 7/12
COOK, George 15*
COOK, Joshua 28, Juretta 23, Rebecca 3, James 1

Schedule Page 108

COOK, James 23, Edith 21
MCGUIRE, James 56, Hannah 54, Samuel 20, Cyntha 13, Thomas 11
MCGUIRE, Harrison 23, Derissa 26, James 1
SEXTON, Stephen B. 45, Martha 42, Isaac 17, William 8, Enoch 5, Richard 2, Ira 1/12
LAWSON, Joseph 54, Mary 48, Mary 20, Amos 18, Francis 16, Martha 13, Franklin 11, Emily 9, Elizabeth 6
DENNIS, Elizabeth 63, Mary 29, James 27, Angeline 14
PEARCE, Jacob 61, Barbara 56, Samuel 27, Nancy 19, Sarah 17, Jackson 14, John Powers 23, Permelia 23
AMES, Jacob 39, Letitia 29, Elizabeth 9, Anna 7, William 5, John 3, Benjamin 1
COMBS, Richard 28, Mary 27, Sarah 11, Aaron 9, Permelia 7, Rachael 4, Frances 2, Nathan 19
HOWARD, Boon 48*, Amelia 32, John 4, Randall 1, Elizabeth 1/12
DONITHAN, Jamima 26*
GILBERT, Stephen 45*
ROBERTS, Elkana 28, Martha 25, Alva 6 (f), James 3, William 1
YARBOROUGH, Thomas 66, Elizabeth 55, Thomas 25, Berthena 19, John 11, Berthena 1, Elizabeth 23
YARBOROUGH, Randle 43*, Anna 33, Georgean 11 (f), Henry 9, William 7, Thomas 4, Harry 2, Elizabeth 8
GILBERT, George 17*

1850 Census Morgan County Kentucky

Schedule Page 109

POWER, Jeremiah 49*, Lear 43 (f), Silas 22, Edward 17, Saunders 14, Sandford 8, Samuel 6
MONTGOMERY, Lucretia 18*
POWER, Thomas 25, Cyntha 23, Benjamin 4, John 2, Edward 1
WELLS, Richard 46, Sarah 44, George 17, William 15, Elizabeth 13, Hester 10, Samuel 8, Benjamin 4, John 23, Martha 21, James 22
IGO, Daniel 45, Sarah 44, Dulcena 18, Absalum 17, Mary 13, Ira 12, Elizabeth 10, John 9, Daniel 7, Richard 2
CULBERTSON, Cumfort 43 (f), John 17, Jeptha 13, Urena 12, Mary 10, Rebecca 8
WELLS, Oliver P. 24, Elizabeth 20, Benjamin F. 3/12
HUGHES, James 26, Susan 23, Mary 5, Arbell 3, Sarah 6/12
HUGHES, Gabriel 37, Lorinda 32, Nancy 13, Mary 11, Eveline 10, James 8, Carline 6 (f), Roseline 4, John 1, George 11
LAWSON, Edmund R. 29, Casanna 20
BARKER, Hezekiah 63, Rachel 38, Henry 16, Isaac 15, Elizabeth 10, Solomon 7, Lucinda 5, William 1
BARKER, Elijah 19, Sarah 19, John 10/12
WILLS, Shelton 25 (m), Cordelia 25, Nelson 8, James 6, Ellsberry 4, Emeline 1
LUNSFORD, Moses 77, Susan 73
CARTER, Enoch B. 50, Elizabeth 43, Sarah 22, Henry 20, Jane 15, Joshua 14, Briar 12 (m), Nancy 10, Hiram 8, Elizabeth 6, Emily 4, Mary 2

Schedule Page 110

KASH, Levi 28*, Mary 26, Caleb 7, Eli 6
HUGHES, Mary A. 7*
ORSBURN, John P. 35*, Perlina 29, William 8, Elizabeth 5, Louisa 3, Janetta 1
GOURD, Hiram 52*
YOUNG, John B. 32*
HUGHES, Martha 16*
ORSBURN, John 73, Elizabeth 66
LAWSON, William P. 33, Sarah 32, Eveline 9, Carline 8 (f), Nancy 4, Lewis 1
LAWSON, William H. 24*, Huldah 22, Ellen 1
KILGORE, Nancy 14*
NICKELL, James K. 29*, Elizabeth 21, John 3, William 2
HUGHES, Susan 8*
WARD, Nancy 36*, James 14, David 9, Mary 6, Anna 4, Frances 5/12
HUGHES, Elizabeth 36*, Elizabeth 3, Louisa 1
WARD, Mary A. 60, Elizabeth 30, Nancy 22, Vilet 19 (f), William 17
DENNIS, Mathias 52, Martha 47, Mary 22, Greenberry 20, Sarah 14, Samuel 13, Reuben 11, Martha 8, Elizabeth 5
NICKELL, Milton 35, Nancy 32, William 12, James 8, Sarah 4, John 1
DENNIS, Samuel S. 40, Lucretia 31, Mary 10, Zelpha 8, Mary 6, Martha 4, Laurena 7/12
HENRY, John jr. 27, NAncy 27, Daniel 7, Rachael 5, Frances 3
BLANTON, Vincent 58, Sarah 53, John 28, Darcus 26, David 24, Angeline 22, Philander 19 (m), George 16, Elizabeth 14, William 4/12

1850 Census Morgan County Kentucky

Schedule Page 111

GOSE, James 45, Jane 44, Eveline 19 (twin), Eliza 19 (twin), Elizabeth 17, Sarah 15, Stephen 13, Henry 11, Julia 8, Phebe 5
GOSE, John jr. 25, Cyntha 25, Alce 2 (f), James 1
LAWSON, James B. 31, Ellenor 26, Emily 8, Isabel 5, Mary 4, Perlina 1, William B. 25, Emiline 22, Elizabeth 10/12
LAWSON, Travis 37, Frances 27, Carline 8 (f), Nancy 6, Abner 3, Isabel 7/12
SAULBY, William H. 25, Mary 18, John 10/12
PERATT, Eli 32, Gilean 32 (f), Emily 11, Andrew 9, Joseph 7, Eliza A. 6, Mary 4, John 2
NICKELL, Joseph D. 27, Martha 34, Elizabeth 13
KASH, Shelby 23 (m)*, Nancy 19, Miles 1
BROWN, William G. 29*
MAUPIN, William 37, Sarah 37, Mary 13, Elizabeth 11, Richard 10, James 5, John 3, Thomas 1
DIXON, William 45, Teamer? 47 (f), Margarett 17, Armilda 14, William 13
DANIEL, James W. 32*, Louisa 17, Alonzo 1, Alfonzo 1
GILLESPIE, Henry 18*
COAXEREL?, Franklin 13*
INGRAM, Isaac 29, Mary 28, Virginia 5, Letitia 3, Zerilda 1
HARMAN, Daniel 34*, Nice 27 (f)
INGRAM, Mary 50*, Mary 25
DAY, Daniel 21, Mary 19
DENNIS, Jacob 34, Sarah 32, Samuel G. S. 14, John 12, Lafayette 10, Jehu 8, Solomon 6, Lewis 4, Reuben 2, Elizabeth 5/12

Schedule Page 112

INGRAM, Abram 34, Ezera 32, William 11, Mary 9, Sarah 7, James 5, George 3, Emily 1
PERATT, Thomas 30, Elizabeth 29, John 7, Sarah 5, Derinda 3, James 1?
MANNIN, Tube 40 (m)*, Anna 41, Comadore 19, Alfred 17, Berthena 15, James 13, Cyrus 11, Nancy 9, MArtha 7, William 5, Cerina 2, Cyntha 7/12
WARD, Cyrus 65*
HENRY, Michael 30, Frances 27, William 5, John 1
INGRAM, Sarah 49*, Isabel 17, Angeline 15
LAWSON, David 16*
YOCUM, William 31, Phebe 22, Susan 2, Mary 6/12
KASH, James 43, Sarah 42, Angeline 20, Martha 18, Franklin 16, James 13, Samuel 11, Mary 9, Moranda 6, William 3, Sarah 1
BOLING, Baley 24, Louisa 23, Daniel 3, William 11/12
GRIFFETH, John 46, Nancy 52, Sarah 16, Hiram 14, Malinda 12, Nancy 10, Emerine 8, Wilkerson 6
BOLING, Henry 37, Ellen 30, William 13, James 11, Preston 9, Sarilda 6, Eveline 4
DEAN, Elizabeth 65, Daniel 35, Elisha 23
MARTIN, Pleasant 38*, Martha 36, John 16, William 13, George 11, Nancy 10, Lucinda 8, Elizabeth 5, Angeline 1

1850 Census Morgan County Kentucky

Schedule Page 113

JENKINS, Elizabeth 24*
MARTIN, William 41, Elizabeth 30, Andrew 11, Nancy 6, John 5, Alexander 3, Daniel 1
CARPENTER, Harry 41, Cyntha 41, Willis 17, Levi 16, Sirena 11, Lafayett 8, Luan 7 (f), Terissa 4, Louisa 3, Susan 1
OAKLEY, Napolean B. 35, Mary 33, Robert 11, Martha 10, Louisa 7, James 4, John 3, Sarah 5/12
CARTER, Raney 28, Louisa 26, Oliver 1
LOVELESS, Thomas R. 46, Malinda 38, Travis 17, Ananias 13, Mary 12, Milbourn 10, Sarah 8, Perlina 6, Isaac 2, Hannah 1
BARKER, Wiley 25, Elizabeth 20, Thomas 2, John 3/12
MAY, Caleb 25, Louisa 26, William 4, Louisa 4/12
DAY, James W. 29, Rebecca 24, Jesse 8, Lydia 6, Nancy 4, Margarett 2
JENKINS, Solomon 54, Lany 57 (f), Meradith 19, Elis 17 (m), William 15, Samuel 13, Lucy 11, Solomon 7
STRICKLING, Britian 25 (m), Carline 22, Peyton 5, Isaac 6/12
JENKINS, Willis 21, Nancy 23
COMBS, John 65, Rebecca 64
BOLING, Benjamin 56, Nancy 58, William 17
BOLING, Sarah 27, Ellen 8, John 4, Vica 2
COMBS, Shadrick 25, Elizabeth 23, Nancy 8, Jordan W. 6, Rebecca 5, Davis 3, Elizabeth 1

Schedule Page 114

VEST, Hamilton W. 28, Mary 27, David 7, Sarah 5, Eliza 3, Edward 11/12
GIBBS, Ebenezer 34, Sarah 18, John 7, Logan 5
OAKLEY, Margarett 58*, Georgean 19 (f), Eliza 16, Johnston 13
COOLY, Andrew 36*
SAXTON, Preston 20*, Mary 39, Richard 6/12
NICKELL, Georgean 14 (f)*, Frances 13, Lucinda 12, Margaret 10, Holly 8 (m), Napolean 6, John 4
LEACH, Judith 54, John 28, Elizabeth 23, Margarett 20, Nancy 16
PERATT, John 59*, Lydia 22, John 20, Silas 15, Gilean 13 (f), James 10, Anna 7
CULBERTSON, Delila 16*, Raney M. 1
KISEE, Charles 53, Barbara 48, William 25, Richard 24, Susannah 21, Elias 16, Jesse 14, Lorenzo 12
ELAM, Samuel sr. 45, Margarett 38, Nancy 20, Mary 18, Joseph 16, Susannah 14, William 12, uriah 10, David 8, Lorenzo 5, Isaac 3, Robert 1
ELAM, Watters 23*, Jineyan 23 (f), Caleb 6, John 4, James 1
LEWIS, Barbara 12*
DAY, David 51, Eliza 37, Gilean 19 9f), William 15, Margarett 13, John 11, Elizabeth 9, James 6, Anderson 3, Rebecca 4/12
VEST, Edmund 66*, Sarah 56, Samuel 20, Martin 17, Marian 12 (m)
FRISBY, Sarah 12*

1850 Census Morgan County Kentucky

Schedule Page 115

ELLIOTT, James 48, Matilda 46, Rachael 13, George 9, Sarah 4
JACKSON, Samuel 38, Nancy 37, James 16, Elizabeth 14, Eliza 11, William 9, Dorothy 6, Catharine 6/12
ADAMS, Richmond 29*, Susan 50, Charles 22, Mary 21, David 17, Sarah 16
BROWN, Harrison 12*
BARKER, John 50, Nancy 49, Elisha 14, Martin 12, Precilla 8
LYKINS, William 39*, Prudence 39, Elijah 18, David 15, Williamson 14, Eli 12, Clarinda 10, Joshua 9, Joseph 7, Dudley 5, Angeline 10/12
LUMPKINS, Manerva 19*, Carline 10 (f)
RATLIFF, Milford 16*
FANNIN, Travis 31, Nancy 31, David 11, John 9, Benjamin 5, Travis 3, Alford 1
PRUETT, Moses 50, Jane 46, McHenry 14, Crocket 11
PRUETT, John W. 20, Rebecca 24, James 8/12
DAVIS, James 57*, Catharine 56, William 19, Alfred 16, Amos 14, Sanford 12
LUMPKINS, Jane 13*, Perlina 4
PHIPPS, Levi 40, Lydia 24, James 11, George 4, Mary 3, John 2, Sarah 1
LYKINS, David 59*, Hannah 50
RATLIFF, Reuben 83*, Silas 12
DEBOARD, Simpson 28, Nancy 27, James 7, Stephen 5, John 3, William 1
HENRY, John sr. 37, Elizabeth 31, Mary 14, William 12, Eliza 6, Louisa 3, John 8/12

Schedule Page 116

KEETON, Elijah 30*, Rachael 28, Julian 7, Harvy 5, Sarah 3
ELDRIDGE, Druzy 15 (f)*
NICKELL, Andrew 48, Rachael 45, Thomas 22, George 18, John 16, Emeline 15, Martha 14, Lucinda 12, Julian 8 (f), Asberry 5, Josephine 3, Marion 7/12 (m)
GIBBS, James 36*, Delila 33, William 10, Cazanna 8, Samuel 7, John 5, Mary 3, Nancy 2, Sarah 1
PHILLIPS, Henry 26*
KIDD, Mary 50*
PERKINS, Elean 18 (f)*
LEWIS, Gardner sr. 48, Mary 42, Ellen 19, Tilmon 18, Louisa 16, James 13, Darny 12 (f), Francis 9, Hannah 7
HANKS, Cudmelon 35 (m)*, Millyan 33 (f), William 12, Roseline 10, Sarah 7, Christopher 5, Mary 3, Laura 10/12, Fielding 66, Lydia 63
NOBLE, Samuel 19*
RATLIFF, William 34, Nancy 30, Laurinda 1, Nathan 10/12
ONEY, William P. 26, Sarah 23, John 4, Nancy 2, William 5/12
HURST, Samuel H. 50, Sarah 44, William 20, Elizabeth 18, Easter 15, Daniel 12, Dulcena 10, Henry 8, Emily 6
WILLIAMS, Daniel 39, Rebecca 38, Eliza 19, Isaac 16, Clarinda 13, John 8, William 2
MCCLURE, Matthew 29, Mary 21, Alwirda 4 (f), Franklin 2, Ezekiel 3/12
HOWERTON, Perry 24, Sarah 17, James R. 7/12

1850 Census Morgan County Kentucky

Schedule Page 117

CONLY, John jr. 33, Jane 26, Nancy 10, Edmund 6, Frances 4, Matilda 1/12
FUGETT, James sr. 57, Rebecca 48, Joseph 16, Rebecca 14, Luanna 12, Margarett 10, Granville 7, Catharine 5
KENDALL, Jesse 47, Jane 45, James 17, Andrew 15, Elizabeth 13, Martha 11, Mary 9, Wesley 7, Eliza 4, Julian 3 (f)
REID, Ananias 43*, Sarah 26, William 17, Mary 6, George 4, Cyntha 2
MURRAY, Daniel 33*
HORTON, Robert A. 34, Anna 24, Mary 5, Letitia 3, Cornelius 1
GREENWOOD, James 27, Elizabeth 50, Louisa 22, Lila 16, Henderson 13, Sarilda J. 3
DAVIS, James jr. 24, Sarilda 25, Perry 2, Martha 1/12
WILLIAMS, Ambrose 23, Anna 22, William 2, John 4/12
BIRDS, John 48, Anna 37, William 21, Michael 17, Charly 14, Samuel 11, Anderson 9, George 7
COCK, William 48, Mary 46, Mahala 20, Carter 18, George 16, Reuben 13, Franklin 11, Lucy 9, Mary 7, Sarah 5
LYKINS, Caleb 27, Mary 25, Eli 1, Edy 4/12 (f)
MCGUIRE, Samuel 59, Jane 63, Samuel 23, Isaac 21, Washington 17
WILLIAMS, James 46*, Mary 40, John 20, Samuel 18, Elizabeth 16, Jane 13, James A. 11, Nancy 9, Amanda 6, Thomas 3

Schedule Page 118

MCMEAR, James P. 40*
WILLIAMS, John 68*, Phebe 58, James 19, Margarett 17, Alvin 11
FERGUSON, William 52*
TUTT, William 36, Sarah 27, Matilda 11, Cordelia 9, William 6, James 3, Stephen 1
DAY, Thomas P. 46, Margarett 34, Anice 15, Jackson 12, Itera 7, John 4, Clarinda 2, Cale 1 (f)
HAVENS, Thomas 35, Marena 33, Mary 11, Cyntha 9, William 7, Elizabeth 5, John 1
LEWIS, Thomas E. 27, Nancy 30, William 6, John 4, Francis 2
CHAPMAN, Robert O. 38*, Catharine 26, Mary 4, Julian 2 (f)
HARMON, Nancy 10*
LANSAN?, James 38*, Elizabeth 26, Frances 10, Lurinda 8, Mary 6, Easter 4, Sarah 1
WRDS, John 50*
REED, Daniel 45, Martha 43, Lewis 20 (twin), Jesse 20 (twin), James 17, Anna 16, NAncy 13, Eliza 12, Rachel 10, John 8, Wiley 6, Solomon 5, Sarah 4, Phebe 3, William 11/12
UTTERBACK, William 31, Manerva 26, Mary 6, Tazarett 4 (f), William 1
HANEY, William 57*, Cela 53
RATLIFF, Samuel 22*
EASTERLING, William 54*, Susannah 54, Nancy 22, William 20, Susannah 17, James 16, Martha 14, Elizabeth 12, Thomas 10, John 8

Schedule Page 119

ELAM, Walters 70*
DAY, Peter jr. 21*, Edy 22 (f), Andrew 3/12

1850 Census Morgan County Kentucky

WILLIAMS, William 19*
COX, William 45*, Cyntha 50, Milton 20, George 18, Martha 16, William 15, John 14, Elizabeth 13, Juda 12, Mary 8
REED, Martha 86*
DAY, Robert C. 27, Ellen 23, William 1
LEWIS, John P. jr. 29, Clarinda 21, Anna 2, Elizabeth 6/12
FRISBY, Cornelius 28*, Jane 20, Mary 5, Sarah 3, Milford 9/12
RATLIFF, Elizabeth 45*, Silas 20, Milford 16
DAY, William 28, Ellen 25, Nathan 5, Taylor 3, Margarett 1
WILLIAMS, Ambrose 31, Cytha 24, Elliott 5, Spencer 1
WELLS, William jr. 24, Caley 22 (f), James T. 1
WHITT, Richard S. 42, Mary 42, William 17, Nercissa 14, Rhoda 11, Percissa 9
AMYX, Joseph H. 35*, Frances 26, Sophia 6, Elizabeth 5, Alexander 4, Holloway 3, Peter 2, Cyntha 6/12
ROBERTSON, John 22*
CASKEY, Robert 49*, Mary 46, Dyer 21, Catharine 17, John 16, LEaner 12 (f), Richard 10, Henry 8, Benjamin 6, George 4, Mary 2
PERRY, Thomas 20*
CASKEY, Jesse 24, Jane 26, Marcalete 2 (f), Heron 3/12
HUMPHREY, Rufus 35, Catharine 33, Lewis 15, Elizabeth 13, William 11, Eliza 9, Martin 5, John 3, Sarah 1

Schedule Page 120

LEWIS, Joseph 39, Eliza 24, Gideon 7, Lucy 6, Rebecca 4, Sarah 3/12
LEWIS, Thomas L. 28, Catharine 22, Landaff 1 (m), William 1/12
STAMPER, Richard S. 27, Mary 25, Joseph 1
DAVIS, William 26, Berthena 21, Mary 4, James 2, Thomas 6/12
WYETT, Hezekiah 36, Martha 25, Mary 7, Uriah 4, James 2, Farlina 6/12
FERGUSON, James J. 28*, Mary 25, William 11/12
HILL, Sarah E. 20*
PILFREY, John 41, Catharine 38, Richard 21, Martha 18, Edward 17, James? 14, William 11, James 7, John 4, Fleming 1
KEMPLETON, John H. 27, Elizabeth 26, Frances 7, Preston 2, Sarah A. 2/12
YATES, Mary 76, Mary 43, Nancy 23
FANNIN, James 39, Elizabeth 36, Sarah 15, Cyntha 13, William 11, Margarett 9, Milton 6, Delila 4, Louisa 2
DAY, James P. 41, Elizabeth 37, John 19, Isaac 16, Jane 11, Mary 9, Emily 7, William 4, Henry 2, Allen 4/12
HUNTER, Spencer 30, Elizabeth 22, Cyntha 3, Sarah 1
HUTCHESON, Franklin 29, Margarett 31, David 11, Peter 9, Henry 6, Anna 4, John 2
HUTCHESON, Peter 61, Elizabeth 52, James 66, James H. 20, Benton 6
MASON, James 38, Sarah 32, Mary 14, Hariett 12, Sarah 9, Jamima 7, Jesse 5, Rachel 3, Thomas 1

Schedule Page 121

ADKINS, Absalum 40, Delila 38, Meraby 18, Miles 17, Vice 15 (f), Eli 13, Lewis 11, William 9, Margarett 7, Peter 5, Cela 3, Thomas 2, James 5/12

1850 Census Morgan County Kentucky

ADKINS, Lewis 30, Margarett 30, Prica 14, Mary 12, Amanda 10, William 8, Dulcena 6, Milly 4, Owen 3, Delila 4/12
CONLY, William 41, Catharine 40, Sarah 19, Elizabeth 17, Lear 15 (f), John 13, Bride 11 (m), Isaac 9, William 7, Eli 5, Nancy 3
FANNIN, George 45*, Mary 40, Brant 20, Peter 18, Thomas 15, Elizabeth 13, Eve 10, Rosannah 8, John 6, George 3, Henry 7/12
MUMBOWER, Eve 71*
FANNIN, William 24, Eunice 16
BARKER, William 40, Elizabeth 38, Henry 18, John 16, Peter 13, Mary 12, George 9, Sarah 8, William 6, Verlina 3, Eve 1
CONLEY, John sr. 66, Lear 65 (f), Henry 13, Lear 26
KEMPLIN, Henry 39, Penivia 30, William 6, Lemuel 3, Anna 11/12
FERGUSON, John jr. 19*, Anna 23, William 3/12
HAMILTON, Elizabeth 11*
CONLEY, David 44, Celitha 38, Sarah 16, James 13, John 12, Elizabeth 10, Drusilla 8, William 4, David 2, Celitha 1

Schedule Page 122

ISOM, Isaac 44*, Anna 39, Susannah 16, HAmilton 12, Mary 10, Archibald 8, Doctor 6, William 4, Elliott 1
ELDRIDGE, James 3*
COTTON, Jobe 63, Easter 21, Ellen 26, Milly 9, Phebe 5, Susan 3, Campbell 1/12
COTTON, John 23, Martha 20, John 1
ELDRIDGE, Jesse 44, Mary 30, Lear 12 (f), James 11, Rachel 8, Susan 6, Mary 5, Nancy 2
COTTON, James 21*, Susan 29, Mary 5, Elizabeth 1
HURST, John 67*
HURST, Campbell 35, Anna 23, George 10, John 8, Isaac 6, Anna 4, Susan 2, Malinda 1/12
ELDRIDGE, James 38, Jane 36, Jesse 13, Joshua 11, Isaac 9, Samuel 7, Nancy 5, Mary 1
HAMILTON, Benjamin 44, Elizabeth 43, Isaac 21, Sarah 18, John 17, David 14, Susan 12, Elizabeth 10, Benjamin 7, Martha 5, Nancy 1
KEETON, Nelson 68, Sarah 51
HAMILTON, Benjamin jr. 23, Julian 25 (f), Wallace 1
KEETON, Joseph 29, Mary 29, James 6, Celena 4, Julian 1 (f)
KEETON, William 25, Kesiah 30, John 6, Julian 4, Nelson 2
BROWN, Wallace W. 32, NAncy 29, Celena 7, Edward 4, Sarah 3, Francis 1

Schedule Page 123

BORDERS, John 26*, Isabel 26, Emeline 5, Wallace 3, Nathan 1
BROWN, Nathan A. 22*
FERGUSON, William 40, Nancy 36, Richard 17, James 15, Haden 9, Nancy 5, Phebe 2, Cyntha 8/12
TRUSTY, William 70, Anna 66, Masean 23 (f), Hiram 18
BROWN, William 44, Julian 32, John 20, Frances 18, Mary 16, Edy 14 (f), Elizabeth 12, James 9, Thomas 6, Sarah 4, William 1
SMITH, Elijah 84, Mary 60, James 22, Lucinda 19, Elijah 2, Aaron 1, Rachel 80, Mary 55
SMITH, David 32, Susan 24

1850 Census Morgan County Kentucky

SMITH, Elijah jr. 39, Lucinda 39, David 18, Elijah 16, Mary 14, John 12, Hiram 10, Peter 8, Cove 7 (m), Sarah 6 (twin), Elizabeth 6 (twn), Susan 3, Augustus 2/12
SMITH, Elisha 30*, Mary 30, David 10, Catharine 8, Ibby 6, James 4, John 1
DYER, William 20*, Rebecca 26
SMITH, Lewis 27, Elizabeth 18, Tobitha 9/12
KEETON, Edmund 37, Catharine 38, Greenberry 16, Mary 14, James 13, Lydia 11, Elizabeth 9, Edmund 6, Lucinda 4, Elisha 1
HILL, Spencer 31, Cyntha 29, Edward 10, Phebe 7, Sarah 5, Elizabeth 3, Nancy 2
RIGSBY, Travis 47, Ave 49 (f), Cala 16, Susan 13, Rebecca 11, John 10, Mary 8, Thomas 6, Tobitha 1

Schedule Page 124

HAMILTON, John 57, Mary 45, John 23, Mary 17, David 16, James 14
HAMILTON, Samuel 30, Cyntha 25, Jackson 5, William 3, John 1
HILL, William 25, Martha 24, Louisa 4, Cetha 2
DYER, William 20, Rebecca 23
HILL, Edward 56, Sarah 55, Elliott 23, Elizabeth 14
DYER, Francis 55, Jamima 52, Francis 25, Wiley 22, Joseph 17, Nancy 14, Joshua 12, Sarah 10, David 7
HUFF, Hiram 25, Cela 19, Armilda 20
GILLUM, Peter H. 16, Anna 16
GILLUM, Jesse 22, Margarett 25, Peter 1
JENKINS, Robert 62, Fanny 58, Henry 21, Rosannah 16
PENDLETON, Hiram 25, Sarah 24
LAMASTERS, Lancaster 45, Rachel 53, John 25, Martha 21, Francis 17, Daniel 15, Elizabeth 13, Sarah 10, Alexander 20
JENKINS, Isaac 29, Almira 23, Emiline 6, Nancy 2
PENDLETON, Joshua 57, Nancy 57, Levi 17, Jesse 15, Margarett 10
PENDLETON, William 33, Martha 34, Claboum 12, Rachel 9, Rebecca 7, Joshua 5, George 3, Levi 9/12
MONTGOMERY, William 28, Elizabeth 26, Citha 2, John 8/12
GEORGE, Alexander 60, Elizabeth 45, James 15, Mahala 11, Elias 8, Thomas 4, Susan 1

Schedule Page 125

SMITH, Hiram 23, Sarah 24, Elizabeth 5, Thomas 1
CANTRELL, Mary 28, Susan 9, Levisa 7, Nancy 5
SMITH, Henry 46, Elizabeth 30, Thomas 15, Elisha 13, Mary 10, Margarett 7, Elijah 4, James 2
CANTRELL, John 52, Margarett 49, Cale 18 (f), Frances 15, James 11, Elizabeth 7, Sarah 4, Julian 2 (f)
CANTRELL, John 20, Elizabeth 18
LAMASTERS, Richard 22, Catharine 23, Benjamin 1
CANTRELL, Henry 25, Frances 19, Benjamin 1
GILLUM, Isaac 34, Mary 28, John 8, Jesse 4, Henry 2, Margarett 1/12
HUFF, James 58, Arian 58 (f), Washington 23, Armilda 20, Lucinda 18
COFFEE, Mason W. 39, Martha 37, William 14, Richard 12, Emily 10, Isaac 7, Nancy 5, Amos 2, Mary 2/12
FERGUSON, Elizabeth 32, Henry 12, William 6, Miles 2, Martha J. 15, Henry 12

1850 Census Morgan County Kentucky

SPARKS, John A. 29, Mary 26, William 7, Nancy 5, Hannah 3, Allen 1
DYER, Preston H. 22, Manerva 22, Henry 7/12
WILLIAMS, Jane 57, Nancy 34, Richard 23, Haden 22, Amanda 21, Daniel 17, Ambrose 15
PENIX, Henry 36, Rachel 35, Gilbert 14, Manerva 11, Robert 9, John 7, William 6, Elizabeth 4, Nancy 1, George 11/12

Schedule Page 126

MONTGOMERY, Elizabeth 60*, Elizabeth 34, Sarah 14, William 14, Eveline 8, Nancy 2
JENKINS, William 23*
MONTGOMERY, Margarett 32, John 9, William 9, Francis 7, Thomas 4, Matilda 2
HOWARD, Thomas 34, Mary 28, Thomas 7, Rhoda 5, Mary 3
DULIN, Bazel 25, Berthena 27, David 7, Mary 4, Henry 2, Nathan 5/12
LEWIS, Francis 64, Ellen 43, William 20, Gardner 18, Charlotte 17, James 15, Ellen 13, Francis 10, Benjamin 6, Henry 6, Isaac 3, Wiley 2, Dial 2 (m)
ELLINGTON, E. Wells 33, Jane 39, Rachel 11, Elizabeth 10, Thomas 7, Lucinda 5, John 2
WALSH, David 36, Mahala 36, Sarah 16, James 13, Mary 10, Lucinda 9, William 6, Nancy 4, John 1
MUCKMELON, John 27, Eliza 29, William 5, Lewis 3, Amanda 1
MUCKMELON, William 60, Susan 50, Susan 17, Peyton 15, Sarah 13, Catharine 9
HOWARD, Cornelius 46, Mary 47
ADKINS, Straley 45 (m), Andocia 44, Elisha 18, Preston 16, Pratte 14 (f), William 12, Straley 8, Spencer 7
BLACK, William S. 31*, Margarett 26, Susan 6, Mary 4, Nancy 1, John 19

Schedule Page 127

ADKINS, Jane 48*
HOWARD, Jesse K. 23, Lockey 20, Carline 2
ADKINS, William 26, Alce 26 (f), Carline 4, Matthew 1
HORTON, Daniel 40, Susan 35, William 18, Julian 16 (f), Mary 14, Lorenzo 12, Travis 9, Lettrice 7, Elizabeth 4, Elizabeth 4, Robert 2, James 4/12, Lucy 4/12
HOWARD, Dyer 27, Cela 24, Edy 6 (f), Hulda 5, William 4, Henry 2, Sarah 9/12
ADKINS, Nathan 23, Amanda 16
MAYS, Ehud 47 (m), Sophia 16, Elizabeth 15, William 13
WHITT, Martin 35, Eveline 28, Allen 12, Nancy 10, Alfred 8, Caswell 4, Margarett 2, Lydia 8/12
MAYS, Nathan 33, Rachel 30, George 13, Mary 11, Sarah 10, James 6, Elizabeth 5, Amanda 4, Clarazene 3, Margarett 2, Mahala 1
WHITT, Richard jr. 28, Margarett 25, Piety 9, Nancy 7, William 4, Cornelius 3, Vice 7/12 (f)
JARREL, Parks 49, Jane 48, George 20, William 19, Amos 15, Julian 13 (f), Elizabeth 5
WHITT, Miles 22, Maryan 18, Sarah 4/12
ADKINS, Harrison 33, Rebecca 27, Melvina 5, Amanda 4, Margarett 1
ADKINS, Moses 42, Cloa 40, James 17, Eliza 15, William 13, Vina 11, Noton 8 (m), Jacob 6, Sarah 2
STEAGALL, Mastin 45, Mary 44, Lydia 17

1850 Census Morgan County Kentucky

Schedule Page 128

BUMGARDNER, John 36, Sarah 40, Elizabeth 14, Margarett 12, Austin 10, Celena 8, William 7, Mary 5, Robert 3, Eliza 2
WHITT, Moses 34, Perlina 32, James 14, Hamilton 11, Washington 5, William 2, Mitchel 10/12
CLICK, William H. 35, Sarah 25, Susan 9, John 7, Jane 5, Carrol 3 (m), Meradith 2
WHITT, Richard sr. 52, Vice 51 (f), Meradith 20?, Susan 17, Clara 15, Queen 12
ADKINS, William 48, Nancy 44, Wyett 21, Pricy 18, Frances 14, Anna 12, William 10, Nancy 8, Almeda 4, Clarinda 1
ADKINS, Westley 28*, Mary 23, John 2, Nancy 7/12
WHITT, George W. 22*
BARKER, Phillip 40, Elizabeth 33, Mary 16, Jeremiah 13, Louisa 12, Jane 11, Sarah 9, William 7, John 5, Allen 3, Abagail 1
HOWARD, Phillip 27, Hulda 21, Jacob 2, Mary 8/12
ROBERTS, Hiram 37, Jane 31, Rachel 9, James 7, William 5, Martha 3, Mary 1
HORTON, Rhoda 34, Catharine 32, William 13, James 10, Sarilda 8, Jacob 6, George 4, Sarah 2
DEHART, Thomas 26, Patience 26, Martha 3, Jesse 1
HOWARD, Joseph 33, Margarett 20, Vice 9 (f), James 11, Sarah 7, Rachel 3, Eliza 1, Mary 1/12

Schedule Page 129

DEHART, Stephen 31, Jamima 73
STEAGULL, George S. 75, Catharine 80
HOWARDS, Gideon 30, Jala 58 (f)
BROWN, Nicholas 34, Malinda 30, Samuel 11, Jefferson 8, Martha 6, Judge 6, Mastern 5 (m), Susan 3, Nicholas 1
BROWN, Moses 67*, Lydia 52, Moses 25, Miram 21, Moses 16
JOHNSON, Zachariah 20*
FRALEY, Phillip 26*, Catharine 21, Lydia 7/12
STEAGALL, Jesse 22*
STEAGALL, Drinkard 47, Precilla 44, Cornelius 17, Louisa 15, Joshua 13, Mastin 11, Martha 9, John 3, Rufus 2, Gabriel 19
BROWN, Stephen 40, Mary 34, Jamima 16, John 14, Sarah 13, Thomas 9, Susan 8, Nancy 6, Elizabeth 2
THOMPSON, Matthew 66, Martha 38, Catharine 21, Eliza 15, Samuel 11
CON, Jesse 62, Mary 63, Josiah 25, Mary 14, Jackson 12, Rosannah 7, Washington 6
CON, John 40, Ursley 40 (f), Hiram 22, Mary 19, John 16, William 12, Louisa 10, Jesse 8, Melvina 6, Benjamin 4, Josiah 1
CARTER, Milton 45, Rosannah 38, Morning 18, James 13, Greenville 11, Lucinda 8
FLANNARY, Huston 28, Manerva 27, Nancy 5, William 4, Eliza 2, John 1/12

Schedule Page 130

EVANS, Drew 50, Mary 31, Susan 7, William 5, Milly 3, Jamima 1, Ursley 75, Mary 30, Milly 13
BRYANT, Jesse W. 44*, Sabina 39, James 20, Isaac 15, Joseph 9
BARNETT, Rachel 20*, Sabina 2, Jesse 6/12
BRYANT, John 28, Elizabeth 28, Jesse 10, Mary 8, Calvin 7, Lilly 5, Malissa 3, James 2, Sabrina 2/12

1850 Census Morgan County Kentucky

CRUMB, Henry 26, Sarah 25, Dolly 4, Mary 2
NICKELL, Reuben 36*, Rebecca 40, Ary 14 (f), Nancy 13, Enoch 11, Joseph 10, Solomon 8, John 7, Eli 6, Gilbert 5, Daniel 3, Jesse 1
STEPHENS, Andrew 21*, Milly 15
GRAY, James M. 30, Elizabeth 27, Mary 7, James 4, William 2, Malinda 1/12
COCK, Tobias 44, Fanny 45, Mathew? 23, Susannah 21, Jane 20, Annice 18, John 16, Rhoda 14, Andrew 12, Manerva 9, Lydia 7, Rodon 6, Mary 3, Vina 1
CRISP, Elizabeth 48, Jane 25, Joel 23, Jackson 20, Sylvester 16, Columbus 14, Francis 11, George 9
CON, Harrison 29, Elizabeth 23, Freeland 4, Eliza 3
CON, Wilson 30, Emily 26
MAYBERRY, Levi 26, Mary 20, Nancy 2
GOODMAN, Calvin 34, Elizabeth 28, James 10, William 8, Louisa 6, Mary 4, Santafe 1 (m)

Schedule Page 131

RAMSEY, John H. 31*, Frances 27, Malissa 8, Lafayette 6, William 4, James 1
BARNETT, James R. 21*
CHANDLER, George R. 13*
CON, John 16*
ROE, David 39*, Cyntha 39, Timothy 15, Martha 13, Sidney 11, Lorenzo 8, Jesse 2
MAYO, Elisha 22*, Elizabeth 20, James 2
STEVENSON, John 59, Mary 64, Nancy 21, Noa 15, Joseph 15, Margarett 13, Mero 11 (m), Isabel 5
STEVENSON, William 33, Sarah 34, Nancy 13, Martha 12, Mary 10, Greenville 5, Melsina 2, Caleb 7/12
BLANKENSHIP, Permela 45, Matilda 17, Mary 11, Jesse 10, Henry 6
PORTER, John W. 24, Emeletta 20, John 6/12
PORTER, John P. 52*, Elizabeth 21, Mary 18, Rachel 14, James 10
BLANKENSHIP, Amanda 10*
BRYANT, Allen R. 22, Mary 23, Martha 7/12
BRYANT, Squire D. 24, Sarah 22, Catharine 2
SKAGS, John T. 33, Margarett 31, George 6, Nancy 4, Hannah 3, Levisa 1
SKAGGS, Peter 40, Mary 38, Nancy 16, Margarett 13, Nelly 8, Hannah 5, William 2
SKAGGS, Amos 39*, Rutha 39, Martha 7
KISEE, Anderson 64*
HOLBROOK, Braddock 54, Judy 48, William 19, Pleasant 17, Richard 15, Sarah 14, Cova 12 (m), Mary 10, Lewis 8, Delila 7, Amos 6, James 4, Martha 2, Simeon 1/12

Schedule Page 132

SKAGGS, Squire 32, Mahala 30, Lewis 12, Malinda 10, Epperson 7, Sarah 5, Susan 2
PORTER, William 48, Rebecca 43, Louisa 18, Daniel 17, Jackson 14, James 11, Levi 9, Henry 7, Gabrel 4, Amanda 3/12
SWANSON, Levi 95, Elizabeth 76
DAVIS, Davidson 28*, Mary 28, John 2
BINYAN, Lincoln 28*
TACKETT, John H. 42, Elizabeth 35, Jesse 21, Mary 16, Helen 5, Leander 2

1850 Census Morgan County Kentucky

WAGGONER, Daniel 32, Nancy 32, Mary 13, Henry 10, David 8, James 6, Daniel 3, Elizabeth 1/12, Hannah 1/12
LIDDINGHAM, Jesse 26, Eliza 20, Walter 2, Terman 4/12 (m)
STAFFORD, James 35, Huldah 34, Eliza 16, Jesse 14, Abagail 11, Mary 9, Joseph 8, Margarett 6, Emesetta _/12, John 7/12, Elvira 1/12
MOCKABY, Murte? 70 (m)*
LUNTS, Dicy 50*, Mahala 23, Reuben 6
VANSANT, William H. 30*, Lavisa 29, James 7, Elizabeth 4, Mary 2, John 5/12
BROWN, Isaac 13*
EVANS, Wilson 35*
FLANNARY, John jr. 35, Ellen 33, Sarah 11, Elizabeth 9, Henderson 7, William 5, Martha 3, Singleton 6/12
STEVENS, John 27, Mary 27, William 6, Fanny 5, Susan 4, Andrew 6/12

Schedule Page 133

MURRAY, Reece 43, Lucinda 38, Eliza 22, Anderson 19, Ellen 14, Augustus 12, Elizabeth 10, William 2
STEVENS, Jesse 24, Mary 23, Amanda 2
STEVENS, Andrew 49, Susan 49, Nancy 19, Solomon 16, William 14, Robert 11, Lurena 7, Sarah 5, Hamilton 1
BOLING, Jarrett W. 42, Nancy 36, Reece 17, David 15, James 13, Isaac 10, Harris 8, Eveline 6, Wilbourn 3
ADKINS, Bartlett 65, Mary 59, Wyett 21
FLANNARY, John 71, Elizabeth 63
ADKINS, Franklin 26, Lavisa 24, William 2, James 2/12
DEHART, John 38, Nancy 35, James 8, Martha 7, Susan 4, John 2
DEHART, Elizabeth 42*, Letha 16, Louisa 20
WHITE, Nathan 52*
SHELTON, John 35*, Mary 26, Angeline 4, Montgomery 2
GRAY, Gatsey 47 (f)*
MAYS, William sr. 73, Frances 70, David 26, Susannah 29, William 8, Davidson 7, Moses 5, Rosannah 1
MAYS, William jr. 37, Anna 35, James 14, Frances 13, Nancy 10, Rebecca 9, William 7, John 5, Elizabeth 3, Thomas 1
ROE, James 46, Agness 41
GRAY, Durin C. A. 35, Arminda 31, William 12, Susan 8, Mary 7, David 2
ALLEN, Samuel 24*, Rosetta 28, William 6, George 4, John W. 2

Schedule Page 134

CLICK, Eliza J. 15*
BARKER, William 41, Jane 34, John 16, Mary 15, Sarah 13, Cloa 11, Abagail 9, Elizabeth 7, Westena 4, Amanda 1
ADKINS, Nathan 52, Huldah 53, Westena 23, Jane 20
CLICK, John 22, Amanda 17, Alexander 1
HOWARD, Thomas 28, Nancy 27, Emeretta 11, Cornelius 2, Serena 8/12

1850 Census Morgan County Kentucky

CLEVENGER, Pleasant 26, Margarett 27, John 6, Mary 5, Alexander 3, Elizabeth 1
HOWARD, George 69, Sarah 65
BLAIR, David 43, Rebecca 36, James 16, William 14, Travis 13, Jesse 10, Sarah 8, Mary 4/12
HALL, Lewis 32, Letty 31, Rachel 12, Sarah 9, Riley 7, James 5, Nancy 4, Martha 6/12
QUILLON, Anderson 30*, Charlotte 26, Catharine 12, Elizabeth 10, Mary 7, Rebecca 4, Ira 1
CON, Hiram 22*
HUNTER, Sylvester D. 31, Mary 27, Arminda 10, Squire 7, Martin 4, Milly 2, Emerine 1
ADKINS, Joel P. 46, Mary 42, Elizabeth 21, Myrena 18, Westena 16, Agness 13, Huldah 11, Susan 8, William 6, Joel 80
ADKINS, Wyett 26, Matilda 24, Charles 6, Francis 3, Wilson 4/12
DAVIS, Henry 70, Cela 68, Harden 41, Elizabeth 24
ADKINS, Howard 53, Mary 47, Howard 21, Braxton 15, Green 13, Joseph 10, Lurena 6

Schedule Page 135

ADKINS, Owen 27, Fanny 22, Mary 1
ADKINS, Frederick 23, Rosannah 18, Rufus 1
ADKINS, Joseph 45, Elizabeth 42, Hawkins 13, Milly 9, Amanda 7, George 6, Lindsey 4, James 1
ORSBURN, Wilkerson 30, Mary 24, Jackson 5, Samuel 3, Hannah 1, Rebecca 4/12
ORSBURN, Alexander 22, Sarah 23, James 3/12
HENSON, James 60*, Mary 54, Margarett 17, John 16, Daniel 13
WILLIAMS, Lucy 14*
TERRY, Rebecca 55, Margarett 22, Miles 21, Hannah 16, Leonard 15, Jesse 12, Isaac 10
LEWIS, Solomon 32, Sarah 30, Howard 10, Andrew 8, Rachel 5, John 3, Daniel 1
LEWIS, William 48, Sarah 45, William 22, Rachel 15, Enoch 12, Martha 9
ISOM, Ira 39, Scina 38, Sarah 15, Argalus 14, Nelson 12, Emily 10, John 8, Ira 7, Martin 4, David 1
WATSON, Rolly 38 (m), Turena 28, Sarah 15, Frances 9
SARGENT, Bales 34*, Elizabeth 28, Mary 10, Hiram 8, Stephen 4, Bales 4, Judy 3/12, Neoma 48
THOMPSON, Adrom 16 (m)*
MASON, Jefferson 40, Susan 45, Elizabeth 12, William 9, Martha 8, David 5, Dulcena 2

Schedule Page 136

WHITE, James 22, Mary 24
JOHNSON, James 28, Sarah 20, William 3/12
ISOM, Bird 34, Cyntha 31, Citha 10, Doctor 7, Sarilda 2, Elizabeth 2/12, Cyntha 8
LEWIS, John 68*, Rachel 67, Nathan 22
BROWN, Hannah 12*
ISOM, Doctor 33, Elizabeth 30, Anderson 3, Samuel 2, Phebe 3/12
LEWIS, John jr. 36, Susan 34, JAmes 12, John 10, Andrew 8, Phebe 4
BROWN, George D. 50, Mary 39, Julia 18, Elizabeth 14, Wilkinson 11, Susan 8, Allen 6, Zerilda 3, Daniel 10/12
KENDALL, Lewis 42, Louisa 34, Perlina 13, John 11, James 5, Jacob 3
STEPHENS, Jesse 30, Winney 30, Nancy 6, Mary 5, Sarah 3, Elizabeth 2
BURTON, John 35, Sarah 56, John 16, Jesse 15, Ransom 12, Susan 10, Rachel 8, Sarah 5
HENSON, Lewis 36, Sarah 35, Pricy 12, Jamima 10, Squire 7, Vica 6, Abagail 3, Catharine 2, James 1/12

1850 Census Morgan County Kentucky

STEPHENS, Daniel 34, Nancy 28, James 14, Daniel 12, Stephen 10, Margarett 6, Amanda 5, Solomon 4, Charlotte 1
BINYAN, William 27, Susan 22, Cora 2, Isaac 3/12
STEPHENS, James 81, Sarah 52, Malinda 6
STEPHENS, Stephen 38, Phebe 34, James 16, Hamon 13, Mary 12, Gabrel 10, Nancy 8, Sarah 7, Drusilla 4, Margarett 3, Daniel 1

Schedule Page 137

STEPHENS, Gilbert 91, Nancy 84, Mary 28, Gilbert 12
STEPHENS, Solomon 39, Nancy 36, Andrew 14, John 10, Henry 6
SELVAGE, Isaac 30, Louis 24 (f)
DEAL, Jonier 9 (m)*, Harriett 26, Stephen 1
MASTERS, William 9* (B), Jackson 5, Henry 3
COLLINS, Elijah 35 (B), Darcus 32, Elizabeth 13, Sidney 8 (m), Phebe 5, John 4, Elijah 2
HUNTER, Francis 58, Elizabeth 50, James 18, America 16, Manerva 14, Nancy 12, Kency 10 (m), William 9, Louisa 7
DEAL, William 88, Isabel 96
FOSTER, James S. 22, Penelope 22, Benjamin 2, Nancy 5/12
FOSTER, Hampton 56, Jamima 47, Andrew 18, William 15, Susan 11, Nancy 9
ADKINS, Milly 58, Frederick 22, William 16, Green 13
WEDDINGTON, Jacob 73*, Phena 46, William 4
HUNT, Charles 16*, Francis 12
DAVIS, Catharine 30*
ADKINS, Hezekiah 49*, Susan 46, Christian 17 (m), Frances 16, Locky 13, Prety 9 (f), Hezekiah 8, James 5
TACKET, Nancy 4*
KENDALL, William H. 52*, Susan 52, Samuel 30, Louisa 18, Alvira 14, Amanda 12, William 10, Sarilda 4, James L. 26, Elizabeth 20, William 2, Susan 6/12

Schedule Page 138

JONES, Benjamin 18*
DOWEN, Larkin 20*
ADKINS, Caswell 49, Margarett 32, Tanzy 12 (f), Washington 8, Sarah 7, Sampson 4, Dolly 1, Oliver 70
ADKINS, Wiley 22, Sarah 17, Nancy 1
ADKINS, Mitchell 25, Sarah 24, Martha 4, Caswell 2
JENKINS, Samuel H. 23, America 21
ADKINS, John M. 44, Sarah 43, Sylvester 25, Virginia 17, Queena 14, Samuel 12, Carline 10 (f), Amanda 7, James 5, Eliza 1, Harvy G. 23, Ellen 19
SMITH, William B. 45*, Sabre 41 (f), Mary 15, Margarett 13, James 11, Huldah 9, Adeline 7, Lucy 3
HAMON, John 18*
ELLIOTT, Jackson 34, Elizabeth 38, Allen 13, Cornelius 10, William 8, James 7, Richard 5, Milbourn 5
ELLIOTT, James sr. 79, Mary 55, Richard 23, George 21, Tennessee 20, Nancy 16, Hannah 2, William 6/12
HOWARD, William 47*, Darcus 41, George 19, Sarah 14, Elisha 12, John 11, Mary 8, Eliza 5, Green 2
ADKINS, Archibald 20*, Amanda 16

1850 Census Morgan County Kentucky

PARSONS, Robert 40*, Tobitha 37, James 16, Elizabeth 14, Eliza 12, Margarett 9, Wilbourn 7, Eveline 4, Mary 1
SARGENT, Elijah 73*, Elizabeth 64
BROWN, Sophiah 39, Catharine 20, Matilda 8, Mary 7, William 4, Gideon 9/12, Squire 2

Schedule Page 139

STEAGALL, Lewis 25, Mary 24, Susan 3, Nathan 2, George 6/12
BROWN, Isaac 26, Mary 27, Andrew 12, William 6, Dulcena 4, George 2, Zachariah 1
ADKINS, Anna 26, Jasper 6, Nancy 5, Mary 2
GRAY, Mary 45, Sylvester 21, Stephen 19
ADKINS, Elisha 37, Delila 35, Filada 17, Malinda 15, Daniel 10, Gilbert 8, Wilbourn 6, Panuda? 4, Delila 1
ADKINS, Joseph 20, Elizabeth 20, Wyram 3/12 (f)
GILLUM, Charles 43, Winny 42, Judith 19, Rachel 17, Richard 13, John 11, William 9, Mary 7, Sarah 3, Elizabeth 1
KEETON, John 86, Sarah 47, Nelson 12, Stephen 11, Jamima 10, Rebecca 5
DEHART, Gabriel 43, Martha 35, Phebe 14, Susan 13, James 10, Mary 9, Joshua 7, Thomas 5, Martha 4, Jesse 2, Catharine 6/12
ELAM, Walters W. 52, Elender 43, William 23, Nancy 22, Suffrona 20, Martha 18, Amos 16, John 14, Richard 12, Eveline 10, Barbary 9, Ellen 5, Walters 1
ELAM, William W. 45, Mary 30, James 11, George 8, Margarett 6, Nancy 4
ELAM, William 22, Lamanda 23, Ralph 2/12, Nancy 24
DAY, Jesse 48, Margarett 45, John W. 17, Cyntha 15, Allen 13, Ellenor 9, Trumbo 4 (m), Rebecca 85

Schedule Page 140

CARROL, Lemuel 25, NAncy 28, William 3, John 2
CARTER, Joseph 58, Elizabeth 55, Margarett 18, Francis 14, Benjamin 9
OLDFIELD, Jesse 72*, Elizabeth 56, Joseph 22, Rezin 19 (m), Jesse 16, John 14
ROSS, Elizabeth 21*
MANNIN, John 24, Rebecca 24
HAVENS, Joel 29*, Susan 25, Joseph 5, William 3, Elizabeth 9/12
MANNIN, John W. 29*
GRIGSBY, James A. 23*, Eveline 19, Nancy 3
GRIFFY, Sarah 17*
KASH, James sr. 77*, Phebe 73
NICKELL, Caroline 20*, Emerine 1
GILMORE, Enoch 49, Elizabeth 47, Saviller 24 (f)
PRATER, William C. 22, Margarett 25, Rosaline 1
FORTNER, Jacob 46, Rachel 44, Delfa 13, Alexander 12, Jacob 9, Benjamin 6, John R. 20, Nancy 25
MITCHELL, Leonard 28, Sarah 26, Gracy 8, William 6, Rachel 4, Charles 2, Sarah 6/12
NEEDHAM, Christian B 26(m), Lucinda 26, Deborah 3, Laurara 8/12
MURPHY, Miles 31*, Sibby 30, William 11, John 10, Calvin 8, Michael 7, Eliza 5, Matilda 3, Simpson 1
OHORIN?, Sidney 25 (f)*

1850 Census Morgan County Kentucky

GILLESPIE, Alexander 45, Mariah 26, Mary 17, Elizabeth 14, William 12, Granville 7, Harry 4, Sarah 3, Marinda 2/12, John 19
MAXEY, Raney 44, Mary A. 42, John 18, Frances 16, Rebecca 14, Elizabeth 12, Ruan 10 (f), Raney 9, Margarett 7, Silas 3, Eliza 2

Schedule Page 141

MANNIN, Charles 54, Susannah 52, Frances 25, Meradith 23, William 22, Asberry 20, Cornelius 17, Eliza 16, Lucinda 15, Mary 9, Samuel 22
MANNIN, John D. 30, Ludema 18
MONEYPENNY, Frederick 21, Martha 18
HOLDERBY, James P. 38*, Sarah 34, Frances 4, JAmes 1
MAXEY, Christopher C. 20*
KASH, Caleb 49*, Mary 47, Eveline 22, James 19, Andrew 17, William 15, Joseph 13, Mason 11, Elizabeth 9, Rice 7
WILSON, Sarah 16*
POWERS, Lewis 30, Emily J. 18, Sarah 6/12
TUTT, John 48*, Jane 36, Thomas 18, Nancy 15, Jackson 9
BROWN, Stephen 59*
SYFERS, Jeritta 4*
LOCK, James A. 31, Malinda 32, William 7, Sarah 4, Nancy 2
GILLESPIE, John P. 34, Nancy 31, Mary 10, Nancy 8, William 4, Archibald 2
COX, John 66*, Judy 68
TOLIVER, Nancy 22*
RICHARDSON, Nelvin 17*
COX, Benjamin 33*, Zerilda 33, Harrison 4/12
ELLINGTON, Elizabeth 15*
WILLS, Thomas 59, Mariah 52, Abraham 21, James 14
JOHNSON, John P. 26, Mary 26, Richard 7, William 4, Frances 2
COX, Joshua 63, Nancy 67
DAY, Archibald 36, Anna 25, Benjamin 3, William T. 1, John 11/12

Schedule Page 142

NICKELL, Joseph 57*, Rachel 56, Miles 22, Andrew 17, Joseph 13, Asa 12
GILLESPIE, William 17*
STAMPER?, James C. 38, Derinda 36, John 14, Rosaline 12, George 8, Sarah 5, Lewis 2
MORGAN, Johnson 35, Nancy 35, Emeline 14, James 12, Elizabeth 9, John 7, Paris 5, Sarah 2
CHILDERS, John W. 24, Julian 23 (f), Samuel 1
GILLMORE, James 52*, Fanny 49, Robert 26 (B)
LITTLE, Phillip 44*, Sarah 43, Charles 18, George 13, Ellsberry 12, Savannah 9, Lucy 7, Viny 5, Mary 2
WILSON, Wiley 22*
LAWSON, John 56, Elizabeth 36, Travis 36, David 17
COX, Solomon 54, Louisa 46, James 23, Preston 19, Elizabeth 16, Martha 12, Lucinda 10, Louisa 8
WOOD, Washington 57, Sarah 60
WOOD, Hiram 32, Lamira 27, John 6, Jasper 4, Francis 3, Lewis 3/12

1850 Census Morgan County Kentucky

STAMPER, George W. 40*, Jane 32, Perlina 8, Rosannah 6, Miles 4, Thomas 1
LACY, Paris 25*
LITTLE, Peter 32, Perthena 32, Ellen 11, William 9, Sarah 7, Eliza 5, Harrison 1

JOHNSON, Tilmon 35, Elizabeth 30, Rachael 12, Mariah 9, Abraham 8, Mary 5, Deborah 3, Rosannah 9/12
NICKELL, John 31, Elizabeth 27, Precilla 10, Frances 8, Robert 6, Mary 4, Andrew 1

Schedule Page 143

DENNIS, David C. 29, Sarah 23, Leander 2, William 5/12
SWANGO, Stephen 30*, Carline 31, Nancy 10, Emily 7, Greenberry 4, Zerilda 2
HARMON, Mary 25*
ROBINSON, John 64, Mary 60, Nancy 27, Elizabeth 24, Peter 16, John 5
LAWSON, Jere 42 (m), Nancy 37, William 19, Hannah 17, John 15, James 12, Phebe 10, Solomon 6, Lucinda 4, Louisa 2, Sarah 3/12, Martha 80
LUNDA, Elisha 25*, Anna 28, Columbus 5, Louisa 5/12
PUCKET, Gardner 16*
BROOKS, Archibald H. 26, Isabella 23, James 4, Saribela 3, William 8/12
BROOKS, James C. 53, Mary 50, John 15, Augustus 13, Rufus 13, Charles 11, Leonidas 9
GILLESPIE, Calvin S. 25*, Catharine 25, James 3, Edward 1
DOUGHERTY, Isaac K. 18*
SWANGO, Harrison 34*, Anna 33, Deborah 12, David 10, Abraham 7, James 5, William 3, Asberry 1
DUNN, William 20*
COLDIRON, Henry F. 23, Sarah 22, Mark 1, Huldah 2/12
CORNWALL, William 27, Mary 25, Emily 12, Marion 10 (m), John 8, Deborah 5, Elizabeth 1
STACY, Claboum 38, Dorothy 36, Sarah 15, Samuel 13, Anna 11, James 9, William 7, Elizabeth 5, George W. 3, John 6/12

Schedule Page 144

OHAIR?, William 43*, Mary 33, James 17, Michael 16, John 14, William 11, Greenville 9, Marion 7 (m), Huston 5, Taylor 2, Ellen 1/12
CYPHIRS, Aaron 50*, Mary 21, Patsy 14, Amos 16, Emily 12, Elizabeth 6, James 3
CLEAR, Riborn 21*
TRIMBLE, William 63*, Ellen 53, Asberry 23, Elizabeth 16, Nelson 14, James 10
MASON, John 43*
JONES, George 19*
HENSLY, Campbell 23*
CLEARER, William T. 24, Hannah 22, Ellen 6, Susan 3, John R. 21
TRIMBLE, James G. 26, Nancy 25, Mary 3
GIBBS, Nathan 56*, Nancy 54, James 20, Nancy 16, Eveline 13, Huldah 11, Hannah 96
BROOKS, James 20*
PATRICK, Robert J. 24, Talitha 27, Rebecca 6/12
RATLIFF, James 23*, Mary 24, Lucinda 2, William 8/12
MANNIN, Meradith 70*

1850 Census Morgan County Kentucky

PECK, Isaac 38*, Mary 41, Andrew 12, George 9, Greenberry 6
THOMAS, Catharine 60*
CORNWALL, William 62, Rachael 67
WELLS, William 44, Sarah 40, Elijah C. 19, William 18, John 16, James 14, Nancy 12, David 11, Elisha 8, Benjamin 7, Rebecca 5, Mary 4, George 2, Daniel 8/12
HEWETT, Lydia 60 (m?), Madica 19 (m)
BARNES, David 22*, Mary 21
SYPHERS, William 3*
CASKEY, William 35*, Rebecca 31, James 12, Elizabeth J. 10, John 8, Lydia 6, Daniel 5, Louisa 3, William 2

Schedule Page 145

LONG, Solomon 25*
GILLMAN, William 29*, Jane 31, Hannah 8, Mary 6, Margarett 5, Nancy 3, Rebecca 1
RATLIFF, James 22*
FALLEN, Gabriel 23, Frances 24, Mary 2, Eveline 6/12
EASTERLING, Walters C. 24, Eliza 23, Mary 3, JAmes 1
COOK, Wiley 20, Delila 17
BROWN, Samuel W. 30, Cyntha 29, James 8, Martha 5, William 4, John 3, Daniel 2/12
COX, James 39, Anna 39, Andrew 14, Joshua 9, Felan 6, John 3, Nancy 3/12
GILLESPIE, John G. 31, Eliza 28, Matthew 9, James 7, William 5, Susan 3/12
MONTGOMERY, William 41*, Lydia 33, James 13, Stephen 10, Artheima 8, Elizabeth 6, Emeline 4, Adeline 1
CLEAR, Reuben 19*
PERKINS, Squire E. 25*, Deborah 55
GARDNER, Perlina S. 32*, Mary 5, Eveline 9
GRIFFING, Louisa 25*, John 4, Mary 1
ALCORN, Greenville 6*
WINKLE, James 50*
STAMPER, Eli 23, Angeline 22, John 9/12
JOHNSON, Jefferson H. 31*, Mary 19, Oletha 3, Thomas 1
EASTLEY, James J. 24*
SYPHERS, John 22*
LUNTS, Archibald 20*
WARD, James 26, Martha 23, William 5, John 3
GEORGE, John M. 32, Rhoda 25, George 5, Artheia 3, James 1/12
BUCKHANNON, William 41*, Lurena 40, Archibald 16, Alexander 14, James 9, Margarett 7, George 4, William 2, Martha 4/12

Schedule Page 146

WARD, John 52*
TRIMBLE, David S. 28*, Mariah 27, Robert 7, Taylor 5, Kelsey 1 (m)
BROWN, Young 21*
SMITH, Wiley 45, Nancy 35, Elizabeth 16, William 15, Frances 13, Emeline 11, Morgan 7, Elmer 6, Nancy 3, Rosannah 2, Wiley 1/12

1850 Census Morgan County Kentucky

JOHNSON, Elijah 55, Anna 55, Elizabeth 28, Ellen 21
JOHNSON, George W. 24, Nancy 27, Manerva 5, Lavisa 2, Elizabeth 1
BROOKS, James C. 52, Mary 51, James 20, Catharine 18, John 16, Rufus 14, Augustus 14, Charles 12, Leonidas 10

NICKELL, William P. 35, Sarah 40, Francis 14, Benjamin 12, James 11, Elizabeth 9, Martha 6, Fowler 4, Wheeler 1
COX, Western G. 21, Elizabeth 19, Luellen 3/12 (f)
NICKELL, William 73*, Martha 63, William 20
WILLIAMS, Thadeus 9*, Sarah 7
ORSBURN, Samuel 22, Mahala 20
ADAMS, Samuel J. 25, Mahala 21, John 3, Cyntha 4/12
PATRICK, Hiram 28, Elizabeth 21, Corilda 6, Susan 2, William 4/12
SEXTON, John 75*, Elizabeth 80
MCLAIN, Nancy 28*, Melvina 6, Mary 1
NICKELL, William K. 35, Phebe 44, Levingston 12, Jeremiah 9, Robert F. 12, Margarett 6, Joseph 4

Schedule Page 147

DOWNING, John 22, Nancy 22, James 3, Joseph 1
MCCLAIN, Charles 50, Cumfort 50, Elizabeth 21, Cumfort 19, Judy 17, Mariah 14, William 10
MAY, Samuel 34*, MArgarett 67, Margarett 37
ADAMS, William 15*
KILKANNON, Franklin 26, Rhoda 28, Mary 4, William 3, Rhoda 2
MCKINNEY, Shelton 30, Magdaline 26
PERATT, Volentine 32, Dulcena 32, James 10, John 8, Phebe 6, Gilean 4 (f), Asa 1
PATRICK, William 31, Nancy 21
CARTER, David 54, Virginia 47, Nancy 17, Elijah 15, Elizabeth 14, Joel 12, Mary 9, Mariah 7
TUTT, James B. 36, Easter 33, Mary 17, Elizabeth 16, William 14, Henry 13, Eveline 12, Easter 11, James 9, America 7, Matilda 3
ROBINSON, William 40, Nancy 30, Mahala 20, Anna 18, Westley 17, Mary 14, Milton 11, Sarah 6
GILLESPIE, Elijah 49, Mary 40, Harvy 20, William 18, Henry 16, Hemazilla 13 (f), Rebecca 12, Rufus 8
AMYX, Matthew J. 28*, Alicy 21, Savilla 8/12
BIRD, Michael 21*
LUCY, Frances 50, William 33, George 28, Moses 23, Rachael 20, Franklin 16, Newton 14, Stewart 12
JOHNSON, Benjamin 55, Fanny 45, Tenmi? 19 (m), Elias 17, William 14, Jedadaih 4, Benjamin 3

Schedule Page 148

SANDSAN, Lorenzo D. 37, Susan 39, Lavina 17, Mary 15, Elizabeth 13, William 11, Susan 9, Nancy 7, Sidney 5 (m), McKinley 3, John 2
GILLMORE, Daniel 23, Lucinda 21
ELY, James F. 27, Elizabeth 29, MArgarett 5, Werden 3, Jane 1
PEYTON, Western 35, Elizabeth 37, Mary 14, Franklin 13, Carline 12, Eveline 7, Daniel 6, Joseph 5, Matthew 3
STAMPER, Margarett 60, Lodena 28, Carline 26, Nancy 21, Julian 18 (f), Carline 16

- 260 -

1850 Census Morgan County Kentucky

STAMPER, Jackson 32, Matilda 32, Campbell 16, Mary 12, Martha 11, Nancy 9, Benjamin 7, George 6, Perlina 4, Francis 3, Rosella 3/12
MUSICK, James 38*, Martha 37, Robert 14, Cansena 7, Charles 3, Campbell 2
FRANKLIN, Thomas 67*
ASBERRY, George 48, Nancy 51, Catharine 19, Thomas 17, Alexander 14, Mary 12, Henry 6
SWANGO, Abraham 59*, Deborah 56, Samuel 24, Jesse 19, Nancy 17, Ellen 15, Henry 12, Miles 58, Thomas 48, Rebecca 12
COCKMAN, Humphrey 26*
LINDON, David 50*, Elizabeth 40, James 15, Miles 14, Robert 12, William 9, Andrew 7, Mary 6, David 3, Elizabeth 2
SMOOT, Barton 55*
MURPHY, William 57, Matilda 48, Lewis 27, Isaac 21, Martha 21, Michael 18, Lucretia 16, Jeremiah 14, Francis 12, Logan 7, Elizabeth 4, Jonathan 1

Schedule Page 149

MURPHY, William jr. 24, Sarah 18, Matilda 3/12
MURPHY, John 39, Sarah 28, Ellen 8, James 7, Nancy 3, Sarah 3/12
PERKINS, Elizabeth 38, Ellen 18, George 7, Eliza 2
CHILDERS, Archibald 22, Mahala 22, Lurena 5/12
PEYTON, John 28, Berthena 23, Francis 4, William 3
JONES, William 40, Rachael 44, John 18, Jacob 16, William 15, Adeline 13, Harvey 10, Giles 6
KASH, Andrew 30, Frances 26, Artecia 6, Robert 4, Sarah 3, Berthena 2
LITTLE, John F. 38, Peter 16, James 15, Emeline 13, Elizabeth 10, Charles 6, Hannah 4, William 1, Hannah 62, Charlotte 9
LITTLE, Charles 44*, Charlotte 40, Phillip 16, Sibby 15, Joseph 11, Greenville 8, Rosilla 7, Precilla 6, Franklin 5, Charles 3, Eveline 1
LYONS, John 21*
SWEATNAM, John J. 38*, Rebecca 29, James 8, Elizabeth 6, Isaac 4, Laura 2, America 2/12
CULBERTSON, Jane 20*
NICKELL, Isaac 23*, Sarah 20
HUGHES, Emily 4*
CRAINS, James T. 64, Nancy 55, Nancy 22, Nathaniel 19, Elizabeth 14, John 9
CRAIN, Robert 31, Denice 23, Telitha 1, David 1

Schedule Page 150

ORSBURN, James 65, Sarah 53, James 15, Cela 12, John 10
ORSBURN, Stephen 37, Maranda 29, John 9, William 7, James 6, Rebecca 4, Sarah 1
TRIMBLE, Lewis 37, Phebe 39, William 8, James 7, Nancy 6, Silas 4, Elizabeth 2
LAWSON, Joseph jr. 25, Mary 18
CRAIN, Richard 29, Elizabeth 23, John 2, Andrew 1
NICKELL, Mary 51, Elizabeth 19, Mary 17, George 16, Miles 14, Jane 13, Frances 11, Robert 9
LEWIS, Edmund P. 46*, Cyntha 41
FRISBY, William 8*
LEWIS, John C. 24, Lucinda 21, Sarah 5, James 3, Mary E. 3/12
LEWIS, James C. 21*, Prudence 23, Cyntha 2

1850 Census Morgan County Kentucky

BARKER, Abraham 16*
TEASTER?, Benjamin 48, Mary 46, John 21, William 20, Rachael 16, Eveline 12, Jacob 10, Elvira 7, Benjamin 5
HACKWORTH, Joseph 20, Tobitha 28
CONGLETON, Margarett 68*, James 27
LUCKY, John M. 14*
FULTZ, Calvin 22, Melvina 18, Isaac 6/12, Nancy 46, James 19, John 16, Nicholas 15, George 12
TAULBY, William 20, Mary 22
CORNWALL, Jefferson 29, Margarett 28, Charles 8, Rachael 7, Thompson 5, Ellen 1
STAMPER, Matilda 41*, Dicy 20, William 19, Milly 17, Lucinda 12, James 3
BOWMAN, Bradford 19*

Schedule Page 151

BARKER, Vachel 61 (m), Sarah 54, Elizabeth 13, Thomas 10, Daniel 8
KID, Harrison 35, Letty 30, Sarah 10, Edward 8, Louisa 6, Citha 4, Ellen 2
WISEMAN, Jacob 55, Nancy 43, Bunyan 15, Nancy 13, William 11, James 9, Jackson 7, Sarah 4
WISEMAN, John 32, Elizabeth 21, Sylvester 2
HANKS, George 33*, Jamima 22, Fielding 3, Jacob 2, Lydia 1
MILLER, Hiram 70*
LAMASTERS, Benjamin 32*, Elizabeth 25, John 11, James 9, Jamima 7, Elizabeth 3, Nancy 1
GARRETT, Elkana 34*, Sarah 26, William 6, Elizabeth 4, Mary 2, Milly 3/12
HOLLAND, Elisha 9*
ANDERSON, William 50, Jane 50, Samuel 19, Jane 16
CHAMPERS?, Jasper 21, Susan 19, Alvin 4/12
SPENCER, Marion 20, Sarah 19
SPARKS, James 40, Tempa 40, John 15, Phebe 13, Charlotte 11, Nancy 9, Ephraim 7, Cordela 5
ADKINS, Hiram 35*, Elizabeth 30, William 3, Goldman 1
PATTON, Charles 9*
SPENCER, William 35, Louisa 24, Lydia 1, William 12, James 10, Mary 8
DAY, Allen 33, Nancy 29, Malissa 11, George 8, Newton 6, Lucinda 4, Sarah 5/12
HAMMONS, James sr. 62, Susan 58, JAckson 20, Margarett 16, Lucinda 11
HAMMONS, Silas 28, Louisa 17, Nancy 2, Susan 1/12

Schedule Page 152

SWANGO, Washington 38, Lucinda 38, Andrew 17, Fanny 15, Stephen 13, Greenville 10, John 9, William 6, Ambrose 4, Phebe 2, Calvin 8/12
BALEY, Mary 47, Eveline 21, Miles 14, Jefferson 10, Lavisa 7
BANKS, James 24, Sarah 16
ROSE, John 59, Mary 56, Robert 22, Elijah 19, Mary 12, Jefferson 10
ROSE, William B. 35, Nancy 28, Elizabeth 9, Powel 7, Sarah 5, Isaac 3, John 8/12
ROSE, John D. 24*, Nancy 24, Joseph P. 31
JOHNSON, Woodson 18*
NICKELL, Jane 13*
ROSE, David 62*, Sarah 58, William 15, Robert 14
DUN, Andrew 15*, Mary 13

1850 Census Morgan County Kentucky

HOGG, Silas 22, Eliza 22, David 4/12
ROSE, Bowen 25, Martha 22
ROSE, David jr. 22*
PERRY, Andrew 42*, Susan 35
ROSE, James N. 20*
CYPHERS, Overly 18*, Susan 46
COX, Calvin 40, Keturah 35, Adeline 12, Virginia 11, Malinda 9, John 7, Nancy 5, William 3, James 1
PHILLIPS, Abraham 44, Elizabeth 58, George 19
LACY, Edy 44 (f), George 20, Ellen 15, Wilbourn 13, Phebe 12, Carline 8, Frances 7, Armstrong 6, Jasper 5
ODEL, Henry 35, Martha 23, William 7, Eliza 5, Elizabeth 3, Georgean 8/12
SMITH, Elijah 28, Elizabeth 28, William 8, Lacy 5 (m), Emily 2, Nancy 10/12

Schedule Page 153

LACY, Harvy 40, Sarah 34, Sibby 11, Elizabeth 9, Louisiana 4, Henry 2
LACY, William 61*, Sibby 56, Rosannah 13, Phillip 48, Moses B. 48
LEETON, Elizabeth 38*
MORRIS, Jamima 30*
LACY, Mark 56, Sarah 54, James 23, John 21, Alexander 15, Sanford 11, Eliza 10, Greenville 9, Andrew 12
LITTLE, John 22, Sarah 16
WINKLE, William P. 29*, Sarah 27, Angeline 6, Josephine 3, William 1, James 8
KASH, Caleb 22*
ELY, Martha 47, Isaac 19, William 14, Alfred 10, Frances 7
ELY, Woodson B. 21, Emily 24, William 1
BROWN, Braxton 59, Rebecca 40, Thomas 17, Mordeica 15, Peter 12, Robert 9, Precilla 7, Elisha 3
MANES, Thomas 21, Elizabeth 20, Taylor 6/12
RIFFET, William 34, Patsy 24, Rebecca 12, Nancy 10, Mary 6, Daniel 1
HAMPTON, Elijah 37, Lucy 36, James 18, Menella 15, Lydia 13, Malissa 10, Letha 4, Lucy 1
COCKEREL, McKinly 24, Emily 23, Luellen 2, Mary 2/12
NICKELL, Perry A. 29, Hannah 25
WILSON, Joseph 51, Mary 46, Andrew 24, Wiley 22, Rebecca 20, Gillean 18 (f), Emily 15, Miles 14, Rosilla 10, Joseph L. 5, Leander 2, George 15, John 12

Schedule Page 154

STAMPER, James 52, Rebecca 35, James 15, Malinda 14, Mary 13, John 8, Isom 7, Matilda 12, Hiram 17, George 18
TAULBY, John 46, Nancy 46, William 16, Citha 13, John 8, Eliza 5, James 4
NICKELL, Andrew B. 56, Elizabeth 52, Saviller 23 (f), James 19, Morrison 16, Joseph 14, Rachael 12, Nancy 11, Holloway 8
NICKELL, Stewart 32, Nancy 34, Rachel 9, Mary 6, Andrew 4, Kelsey 1/12 (m)
WILSON, Andrew 52, Easter 52, Samuel 22, Elizabeth 16, Richard 12
LONG, George 22, Hannah 23, Cyntha 10/12, Solomon 27, John 17
WILSON, Jackson 24, Margarett 16

1850 Census Morgan County Kentucky

WILSON, Shelby 37 (m), Rebecca 37, Elvin 18, George 15, Milton 14, David 11, Logan 9, Preston 8, Holloway 7, Carline 4, Thomas 2, Shelby 10/12
NICKELL, Andrew P. 25, Elizabeth 25, Sarah 4, Mary 4, Moranda 2
NICKELL, Caleb 24, Lucretia 21, Franklin 3, Frances 1
GIBBS, Mason 24, Melvina 19, Ellen 2, Hezekiah 3/12

BANKS, John 45, Hannah 29, Easter 9, Edy 7 (f), Anna 5, Jane 4, Henry 11/12
CHILDERS, William 33, Eliza 31, Carline 10, Madison 8, William J. 6, Martha 3, Leander 1

Schedule Page 155

NICKELL, Thomas sr. 84, Elizabeth 58, Nancy 25, George 15, Mahala 14
TERREL, Timothy 21, Nancy 20, Emily 1
TERREL, Hezekiah 46, Ellen 40, John 18, Sarah 16, Angeline 14, Cyntha 12, Charles 10, Lee 6, Jane 5, Rosaline 2
LYON, John 23, Clarissa 18, John 1
MINTON, Evan 32, Margarett 26, William 8/12
LYON, Francis 58*, Mary 59
ELY, Michael M. 14*, Mary 13
LITTLE, Harrison 22, Mary 26
ORSBURN, Joseph 31, Matilda 23, William 2, Nancy 3/12
ORSBURN, William 38*, Nancy 25, Emily 8, David 5, Samuel 3, Sarah 1
MAY, Mary 22*
HADDOX, Samuel 34, America 29, Richard 11, Perlina 8, Nancy 6, Roseline 4, Henry C. 9
MCQUINN, James 31, Margarett 22, Julian 1 (f), John 3/12
DAVIS, John 25, Mary 24, Richard 7, Mary 5, Henry 2
WILSON, Robert 42, Rebecca 41, Joseph 20, Mary 17, Marshall 14, Easter 12, James 10, Sarah 7, Miles 6, William 2, Pethana 1
WALTERS, Matilda 44, Franklin 23, Felix 20, Berthena 18, Thomas 16, Mary 14, Oliver 11, Eveline 9, Francis 7
WALTERS, Andrew 26, Manerva 25, Thomas 2, Charles 3/12

Schedule Page 156

MCQUINN, Alexander 62, Lavisa 52, Lucinda 16, Daniel 13, Carline 10
WILSON, Preston 26*, Louisa 23, Henry 2
RATLIFF, Solomon 16*
LONG, Benjamin 57, Cyntha 47, Rosaline 14, Catharine 7, Noah 5, Isom 4
JOHNSON, John W. 38, Ellen 34, Goodson 7, Matthew 1
PERRY, John 24, Sarah 27, Sarah 2, Nancy 1
KENDALL, Allen 45, Elizabeth 41, William 18, John 16, Louisa 15, Travis 10, Robert 8, Samuel 6, Daniel 3, Angeline 1/12
ROBERTS, David 24*, Nancy 23, Mary 1, Elizabeth 6/12
WALSH, Lucy 33*, John 1
HENRY, Jacob 25*, Elizabeth 30
LUMPKINS, Joseph 15*
LYKINS, John C. 34, Cyntha 31, Aaron 13, William 11, Louisa 4

1850 Census Morgan County Kentucky

JOHNSON, John 40, Susannah 36, James 14, Sarah 13, Martin 10, Oscar 9, William 7, Leticia 5, Susannah 4, Joseph 2, Rachael 1
HENRY, Lewis sr. 59*, Sarah 38, David 20, William 18
LUMPKINS, Wiley 6*
KILLGORE, Jane 19*
KENDALL, Jesse jr. 23, Elizabeth 19
TRIMBLE, Mark 74, Nancy 64, William 14
WELLS, Benjamin F. 48, Elizabeth 48, Jane 22, Melvin 21, Edmund 17, Thomas 15, Daniel 11, Sarah 9, Melicient? 19 (f)
HANEY, James 31*, Jane 50, John 12, Rebecca 10, Asberry 8, Louisa 4

Schedule Page 157

WELLS, Thomas 32*
EASTERLING, Walters 32*, Susannah 36, William 16, Rebecca 8, Jeremiah 6, Rhoda 4, Raney 1
ELAM, Elizabeth 21*
FANNIN, Bryant 59, Hannah 37, Nancy 15, William 12, Elizabeth 10, John 8, Francis 6, Catharine 2
WILLIAMS, James H. 30, Temperance 19, Ezekiel 1
CASKEY, Gardner 53, Elizabeth 45, Robert 19, Elizabeth 9, Jane 7, Thomas 5
ADAMS, Charles T. 31, Elizabeth 26
BROWN, James jr. 22, Fanny 23, Alce 1 (f)
HENRY, William 43*, Eliza 38, Sarah 14, Nancy 13, John 9, Daniel 20
LUMPKINS, George 13*, Thomas 7
HOOLBROOK, Nancy 25*
MONTGOMERY, George 27*
BISHOP, Elizabeth 55*, Stephen 22, David 20, Johnson 16, Anna 14
BLANKENSHIP, Cela 18*
BISHOP, Elisha 30, Elizabeth 26, Easter 6, Henry 4, Elisha 1
HENRY, Isaac 34*, Mary 28, Thomas 6, James 4, John 3, William 2
FUGETT, Rutha 85*
PRATER, James 65, Phebe 54, Eli 19, Harry 14, Louisa 12
QUICKSELL, Aaron 32, Elizabeth 34, Matilda 7, Miner 5, James 4, Louisa 3, Emazilla 3/12
WILLIAMS, Mason 70, Sarah 68, Dial 26 (m)
COTTLE, Robert C. 36*, Hannah 32, Thomas 14, Mary 12, David 10, Lucinda 8, Martha 6, Mitton 5, Malinda 3, Rebecca 1

Schedule Page 158

KISER, Richard 27*
CASSITY, Jesse 61, Margarett 5, Edward 17, Diannah 14, John 12
MCGUIRE, Elijah C. 33, Sarah 30, Stewart 12, Gilean 8 (f), Elizabeth 6, Matilda 3, John 1
WELLS, James 19, Cary 18 (f)
CYPHERS, Susan 37, Obadiah 18
MCGUIRE, John 27*, Elizabeth 26, Samuel 7, James 5, Emily 2
LOGGINS, Joseph 75*, Susan 65
SAUNDERS, Nancy 46*
QUICKSELL, James 38, Matilda 45, Jonathan 15, Rebecca 12, Lemuel 7, John 4

1850 Census Morgan County Kentucky

LYKINS, Milton 31, Elizabeth 26, Carline 8, Mahala 6, Louisa 4, Willis 1
LYKINS, Isaac 28, Rachel 27, Rosaline 7, William 5, Mary J. 1
LYKINS, Peter 49, Winney 45, Nancy 23, Elizabeth 21, Isaac 19, David 14, Edy 12, Peter 10
ALLEN, Daniel W. 29*, Susannah 28, Perlina 7, Arena 6, Greenberry 3, John 1
DUNN, Isaac 15*
LYKINS, David K. 29, Mahala 23, Rosannah 5, Elizabeth 3, Nancy 2, Rebecca 2/12
TAULBY, John D. 23, Phebe 19, Cela 11/12
ALLEN, Elijah 27*, Martha 26, Richard 6, William 4, Susannah 2
BARKER, Nancy 16*
KILGORE, Charles 29, Catharine 27, John 5, James 3, Isaac 7/12
FERGUSON, William 29*, Alcy 26, Milton 8, John 6, Emily 4, Isaac 2

Schedule Page 159

HANEY, Jariel 18 (m)*
STACY, John 52, Margarett 48, Lizana 17, Nancy 15, Mashack 13, Salathael 11, Riley 8
STACY, Allen 27, Nancy 24
BURTON, John 30, Elizabeth 27, William 6, Eli 4, Elizabeth 1, Margarett 2/12
WHITELY, Timothy 40, Jane 30, Elizabeth 4, Jacbo 50, Margarett 80
HANEY, Paschal 32, Matilda 32, Almeda 6, John 4, Nancy 3/12
PRATER, James W. 21, Lucinda 19, Cary 2 (f), Selvina 9/12
PRATER, George W. 35, Sarah 31, Henry 13, Elisha 11, Nancy 10, Margarett 8, Darcus 6, John 3, Wiley 1
PERCELL, Quinton 42, Sarah 34, James 13, John L. 12, Marinda 11, Phebe 10, Floyd 4, George 3, William 1
MCCLAIN, Archibald 30, Nancy 23, James 4, Rebecca 1
LEWIS, Harmon 27, Darcus 27, Mary 4, Benjamin 2, James 2, John 4/12
PHILLIPS, William W. 32*, Malinda 31, James 3, John 1
BRANNUM, Mary 23*
OLDFIELD, George W. 33, Jane 28, William 10, Sitha 9, Mary 7, James 6, Jesse 3, Elizabeth 1
RATLIFF, Richard 47, Elizabeth 44, Cela 15, John 13, Emily 10, William 8, Isaac 6, Mary 4
PHIPPS, Eli 24, Mahala 26, Francis 8, William 5, Silas, Amanda 1

Schedule Page 160

STAMPER, William 29, Jane 21, Jesse 4, Margarett 1
PRATT, Henry 30, Rachael 24, Adeline 4, Roseline 3, Margarett 1
KILLEN, Morgan 18, Elizabeth 19
BARKER, Williamson 52, Margarett 34, William 17, Hiram 9, James 7, Lucinda 5, George 1
JIVEDEN?, Joseph 24, Martha 21, Berthena 1, Virginia 2/12
JIVEDEN?, John jr. 27, Nicy 21, Anderson 4, Nancy 3, Gilean 1 (f)
JIVEDEN?, John sr. 62, Eilzabeth 37, Joshua 16, Jackson 7, Magdaline 29, Elizabeth 1
ELAM, Frances 49, Mary 27, Elizabeth 25, Robert 22, Mason 17, Easter 16, Richard 11, Matthew 10, Meredith 20
MAY, John 48*, Elizabeth 49, Catharine 26, Delila 18, Allen 15, Elizabeth 8, Rebecca 6
LEWIS, Washington 12*
COMBS, Mason 37, Malinda 30, James 5, Perlina 5, Thomas 3, Martha 2, Edy 4/12 (f)

1850 Census Morgan County Kentucky

PRATER, ARchibald 40*, letitia 36, John 19, Sophronia 16, Eliza 13, Catlett 8, Margarett 5, Robert 4, James 2
BURTON, William 20*
BROWN, Jackson 22*
NICKELL, Martha 40, Andrew 18, Fleming 16, Jane 13, Matilda 10, Julean 8, Louisa 4, Elizabeth 2
STACY, Hugh A. 25, Anna 28, Nancy 6, Greenville 4, Rosaline 3, Auldin 1
STACY, John jr. 25, Anna 21, Aylvania 4, Lezera 1

Schedule Page 161

STACY, George 49, Mary 35, John 16, Wilbourn 15, William 13, Elizabeth 11, Asberry 10
WATSON, Teryan 45 (m), Mray 39, Michael 16, Jackson 14, Margarett 12, Lucy 10
COLLINGSWORTH, David 38*, Elizabeth 39, Julian 12 (f), Mary 3, John 1
WILLIAMS, Malinda 17*
AMYA, James F. 27*, Wyaha 25, Mary 2, Sophia 1
ADAMS, Simpson 10*
DAVIS, Jeremiah 38, Jane 37, Louis 17 (f), David 16, Sarah 13, Amos 12, Franklin 10, Eli 8, James 4, George 2
PERKINS, Joshua 47, Rebecca 37, William 19, Rachael 18, James 16, Wallace 14, George 12, Spencer 10, Mary 8, Andrew 6, Sarah 3, Lewis 2
BAYS, Joshua 47*, Mary 30, William 12, Margarett 8, Rebecca 7, Elijah 6, Daniel 3/12
RILEY, James C. 8*, John 6
COOPER, Thomas 26, Mary 21, John 2, David 2/12
MEADOWS, Matthew 36, Susannah 33, Tyre 16, Melvina 14, George 12, William 10, Louisa 8, Thurston 6, Virginia 4, James 2, Marion 3/12 (m)
BALEY, Elisha 34, Lucinda 30, Mashack 12, Melford 11, Mary 9, Vina 8, William 5, Alfred 3, James 6/12
ADAMS, Jackson 31, Latha 21, Clarinda 12, Jane 10, Daniel 8, Fielding 6, Lydea 4, Joseph 2, John 6/12

Schedule Page 162

MAY, Harvy 28*, Margary 34, Samuel 7, Martha 5, William 3, Elizabeth 1
WILLIAMS, winney 16*
EASTERLING, Silas 27, Rebecca 27, Louisa 7, Henry 6, Rebecca 4, William 1, Thomas 23
DAVIS, Joel 31, Martha 26, Henry 9, William 7, Sandford 5, James 3
DAY, Thomas P. 34*, Perlina 31, Peter 9, Elizabeth 8, Louisa 4, Joseph 20
TAYLOR, Joseph 23*
DAY, Travis 63, Anna 58, David 27, John 17, Rebecca 15, Martha 13
COTTLE, Isaac 46*, Lucinda 36
BURTON, Isaac 15*
NICKELL, Martha 8*
CARR, Isaac 25*
COOPER, Catharine 14*
COTTLE, David N. 41*, Belinda 39, Henry 18, James 15, Elizabeth 13, Cyntha 10, Isaac 8, John 6, Robert 3, Lucinda 1
EASTERLING, Lucinda 29*

1850 Census Morgan County Kentucky

CASSITY, Stephen 58, Margarett 49, Ashby 32, Sarah 30, Margarett 24, John 22, Mary 20, Thomas 18, Elizabeth 12
COTTLE, James 28, Elizabeth 27, Mary 6, Daniel 4, Lucinda 1
LEWIS, Thomas 32, Mary 29, Lucinda 5, Jesse 2
LEWIS, John sr. 61*, Elizabeth 50, Gardner 22
PETITT, Jackson 4*
ELAM, Jeremiah sr. 70*, Jane 56, Robert D. 23, Washington 15, Margarett 13
MASON, Susan 15*

Schedule Page 163

EASTERLING, William M. 25, Sarah 28, Miles 3/12
NICKELL, Greenup 25, Dulcena 24, Franklin 3, Angeline 2
MCGRAW, Martin 23, Sarilda 21, Susan 1
MONTGOMERY, John 42, Letty 48, Benjamin 21, Charles 16, Marion 13 (m), William 10, Louisa 7
RISNER, John 27, Elizabeth 27, Delila 9, Charlotte 7, Rebecca 5, Rosannah 3, Tennessee 2
KENNARD, David 43, Nancy 32, Elizabeth 22, Elias 19, Mason 14
PATRICK, Emily 35, William 18, Robert 16, Elizabeth 14, Jackson 10, Nancy 7, Rebecca 5
GULLETT, Jesse 34, Elizabeth 32, William 8, Telitha 6, Tempa 5, James F. 1
NORMAN, Thomas 27, Margarett 23, Sarah 5, William 4, James 1
MCGUIRE, James C. 20*, Mary 26
PRATER, William T. 9*, Rebecca 7, Elizabeth 4
COOPER, Lee 24*, Catharine 18, Jefferson 3/12
FITZ, Jerry 12*
KIMBERLING, John W. 31, Elizabeth 21, Manerva 1
ADAMS, Loth 33 (m), Rebecca 26, Malinda 9, Sarah 7, James 5, Elizabeth 3, Stephen 1
PATRICK, John 36, Charlott 31, William 11, Wiley 10, Rebecca 8, Elizabeth 7, Amos 5, Mary 3, Martha 1
CONLY, Edmund 34, Jane 45, Nancy 19, Isaiah 16, Henry 14, Wallace 11, Hasten 7, Mearies? 21 (f), Nancy J. 1, Sarah 3/12

Schedule Page 164

BAYS, John 88, Sarah 74
PRATER, James W. 27*, Elizabeth 22, Rebecca 2, Nancy 7/12
PERKINS, Margarett 9*
CORDELL, Abagail 46, Stephen 27, Rebecca 19, Elizabeth 18, Nancy 15, Mary 13, Lydia 11, Benjamin 9, Rachael 7, John 4, Rachael 27, Sarah 6, Benjamin 4, Abagail 1
ADAMS, William 47*, Lucinda 17, Manerva 14, Smith 12, Isaac 9, Elizabeth 7, Stephen 70, Mary 75
LANE, Lewis 35*
SANDYS, Hendrick 35, Nancy 19, Alice 1
GARDNER, Benjamin F. 40*, Sarah 32, Benjamin 10, Mary 8, Emily 6, Eliza 3, Joseph 14
FRIEND, Charles W. 24*
MONTGOMERY, Wiley 19*
RISNER, Michael 60*, Sarah 60, Catharine 23, Abraham 17, Amanda 4
BARKER, Elijah 21*
REED, Sandford 46*, Mary 38

1850 Census Morgan County Kentucky

GARDNER, Joseph H. 29*, Mary 19, Hamilton 8/12
BAYS, Wiley 17*
PENIX, Daniel 22*
STACY, Elizabeth 16*
BAYS, Eliza 18*
BAYS, James 42, Elizabeth 60
REFFIT, John 24, Mary 50, Mary 18, Daniel 16, Joseph 14, Luanna 12
MAY, James jr. 38, Matilda 40, Eliza 18, Gildean 16 (f), William 14, Fleming 12, Thomas 8, Franklin 5, Mary 3
NICKELL, Joseph D. 19, Freelove 19, Stewart 1
BROWN, Nancy 25, John 6, William 4
HANEY, James 48*, Anna 46, Louisa 18, Granville 16, Gilean 13 (f), Lilbourn 11, Myram 8, Elizabeth 2

Schedule Page 165

STACY, William 18*
STACY, Mashack 59*, Vilett 53, Nancy 17
ROSE, James 21*
STACY, Henderson 28, Virginia 30, Emily 6, Benjamin 5, Mary 4, Cary 3 (f), James 1
PRATER, Samuel 39, Lucinda 38, William 12, Robert 10, Sarah 8, Mariah 6, James 4, Isaac 2
HANEY, William jr. 28, Elizabeth 20, James 2, Absalum 3/12
LYKINS, Peter D. 30, Eveline 29, Isaac 11, Milton 9, Peter 6, Mason 4, NAncy 2, William 2/12
FERGUSON, Isaac W. 22*, Silva 23, Henry 1
KILGORE, John 23*
BURTON, Andrew 51, Susan 46, David 20, Daniel 17, Hannah 15, Jonas 13, William 11, Jarrett 10, Andrew 2, Franklin 6/12
WALLACE, Major L. 23, Ellen 21, Lear 1 (f)
SIMMONS, William 28, Amy 27, Martha 5, Sarah 4, Margarett 2, William 1/12
ARENHART, Mary 43, Elizabeth 21
MAY, James sr. 52*, Mary 48, Noah 19, Easter 17, Preston 15, Haney 13
HARRIS, Nancy 70*
ELAM, Elizabeth 3*, Easter 1
NICKELL, Isaac 23, Nancy 25, Louisa 4, Rhoda 2
BALEY, Pryor 53, Sarah 55, Holloway 21, Elizabeth 17
GULLETT, Franklin 36, Martha 30, Samuel 14, William 7, Cyntha 5, James 4, Thomas 1

Schedule Page 166

MAY, Campbell 23, Easter 25
HAMMON, Ephraim 48, Lucinda 31, Eveline 1, Thomas 17, Lucinda 14, Letty 7
GULLETT, John 87, Mary 50, James 23
COOPER, David M. 48, Cela 42, Lucinda 20, Nancy 18, Gilean 16 (f), John 13, William 11, Rebecca 10, David 8, Milton 4, Mary 1
PATRICK, Lewis 34, Lucy 33, Levi 12, Precilla 11, Harrison 9, Nancy 8, Irvin 6, Sirena 4, Green 3, Harmon 1
COOPER, William 60, Roxanna 40, Jacob 17, David 13, Elizabeth 12, John 8, Joel 7, Sanford 6, Mary 3, William 2/12

1850 Census Morgan County Kentucky

RICE, George W. 32, Elizabeth 31, John 9, William 7
COOPER, Joseph 30, Julian 25 (f)
GULLETT, Daniel 28, Nancy 26, Lucinda 12, James 10, John 7, Moses 6, Daniel 4, Henry 3, Mary 1
WILLIAMS, Eli 24, Violett 22, Richard 3, Rhoda 1
HAMMONS, George W. 24, Louisa 22, Delfa 2
HAMMONS, Josiah 22, Gilean 20 (f), Sarah 5/12
GOSE, Phillip 25, Mary 25, Susan 1
ARNETT, Ambrose 32*
RAY, Susan 20*
PRATER, Elijah 30, Frances 24, Mary 5, Sarah 4, Martha 1
PATRICK, Charlotte 57, Clabourn 24, Jeremiah 21, Samuel 18, Emeline 16, Elizabeth 14

Schedule Page 167

GOSE, John 75, Elizabeth 55, John 15
POWER, Archibald 36, Rhoda 30, Lucinda 13, Jilson 11, Fleming 8, Lewis 6, Charlotte 4, Elizabeth 1
GULLETT, Mason 30, Mary 34, Mahala 8, Gilean 4 (f), James 1
BURTON, JAmes 36, Mahala 36, Cyntha 15, John 12, Hannah 9, Thomas 5, Elizabeth 3
GULLETT, Andrew 33, Anna 28, Elizabeth 9, Dial 8, James 6, Margarett 3, Mahala 1
PATRICK, Henry 50, Lucinda 40, Mary 17, Samuel 13, Elijah 13, Allen 10, John 7, Hiram 5, Margarett 3, Brice 1/12
GULLETT, Nancy 50*, Harvy 21, Asa 16, Lucretia 13
BOMAN, Susan 40*, Alexander 4
DYER, Nelson 53, Clarissa 38, James 9, Nancy 8, Henderson 6, Wiley 4, Martin 1
DUNN, Asa 26*, Eliza 27, Rebecca 5, Jeremiah 3, Letha 1
ADAMS, Solomon 16*
WAGES, Moses 55, Rebecca 66, Harrison 19, Wilson 19, Anna 16
WAGES, Alfus 22, Martha 19, Herod 11/12
WAGES, Benjamin 24, Nancy 24, Elizabeth 2, Nancy 10/12
WAGES, William 29*, Moses 7, Thomas 5, Marion 3 (m)
DAVIS, Elizabeth 22*, Andrew 19, Angeline 10/12
KEETON, Harvy 22, Sarah 20, Madison 1
WILLIAMS, Caleb 40, Malinda 40, David 13, Isaac 10, Perlina 8, Daniel 6, James 4

Schedule Page 168

LAMASTERS, William 36, Eliza 22, Sarah 2, Caleb 1
WILLIAMS, Isaac 52, Elizabeth 46, Margarett 17, James 15, Miles 13, Isaac 10, Elizabeth 10, John 8, William 6
WILLIAMS, James H. 26, Sarah 26, Lucinda 3, Telitha 1
LYKINS, John 39, Martha 37, Mary 20, Sarah 18, Susannah 17, James 14, Nancy 12, Andrew 11, George 6, William 4, Rebecca 2, Elizabeth 1/12
LAMASTERS, John 36, Elizabeth 34, Winston 15, Amanda 9, Meredith 5, Francis 4, Sarah 1
ELAM, Joshua 25, Nancy 25, Rebecca 5, Samuel 4, Louisa 2, Mary 8/12
ELAM, Daniel 28, Nancy 26, Joshua 8, Sarah 6, Perlina 4, Emily 8/12
ELAM, Gilbert 54, Catharine 48, Joel 31, Francina 22, John 19, Catharine 16, Martha 14, Gilbert 12, Benjamin 8, Elizabeth 6

1850 Census Morgan County Kentucky

GULLETT, Westley 24, Milly 24, Dial 6, Rebecca 4, Wiley 2, Manerva 7/12
LYKINS, William S. 53, Rebecca 54, Eli 18, John 16, James 13, Greenville 11
LYKINS, Rolly C. 20, Sarah 18, William 6/12
PATRICK, Archibald 22, Docia 17
PATRICK, Jesse 43, Mary 40, Elizabeth 20, Jamima 18, Andrew 16, William 13, Nancy 11, Susan 9, Delila 7, Rhoda 4, Meradith 2, Sarah 7/12, Franklin 4

Schedule Page 169

WILSON, Joshua 47, Elizabeth 48, Mahala 14, Rebecca 9, Emily 6, Lydia 3
WILSON, Harvy 20, Elizabeth 19, William 1
DAVIS, John 72, Mary 72, Thomas 29, Eveline 26
WHITELY, George 46, Rebecca 45, Hiram 20, Lucinda 17, Mary 15, Margarett 14, Isom 10, William 7, Elizabeth 6
WHITELY, John 24, Eliza 21, White 8/12
WHITELY, Robert 22, Margarett 21, Elizabeth 2/12
DAVIS, Ephraim 42, Nancy 33, Eveline 16, Rebecca 12, Lucinda 10, David 8, Mary 6, Emily 4, Jackson 3, Louisa 2/12
REED, Lewis 20, Sarah 20
LAMSTERS, John 35, Rebecca 35, Benjamin 12, Sarah 10, Micha 8 (f), James 6, Joseph 4
KEETON, Vina 48, Miles 14, Elizabeth 12, Caleb 10, Harrison 4
KEETON, Madison 20, Clarissa 19, James 1/12
MCGUIRE, Jilson P. 35*, Sarah 31, George 11, Malissa 10, William 7, James 5
KEETON, Jane 71*
LYKINS, William 55, Hannah 55, Joseph 17
AMYX, Peter 64, Sophiah 58, William 33, Nancy 20, Elizabeth 14, Andrew 11, Angeline 8
WHITELY, Alexander 65, Elizabeth 60, Edy 18 (f)

Schedule Page 170

WHITELY, Moses 29, Jane 28, Pleasant 4, Robert 3, Thomas 1
WHITELY, Thomas 24, Anna 22, Emerine 1
HOLLIDAY, Martha 35, William 17, Jilson 14, Alexander 12, Mary 10, Elizabeth 10, Ellen 7
KILGORE, John 51, Isabel 25, Cyntha 5, Isaac 2
RATLIFF, Robert 24, Sarah 20, William 2, Samuel 4/12
RATLIFF, Sarah 40, Ellen 14
ALLEN, Richard 53, Edy 47 (f), Frances 19, George 15, Darcus 13, Nancy 11, Rachael 8, Joseph 21, Rebecca 20
SPENCE, Joseph 55, Sarah 53
BURTON, Daniel 29, Perlina 23, Lucinda 3, Nancy 2, Mary 1
LYKINS, William V. 25, Vilet 24, Elizabeth 3, Nancy 1
SEBASTIAN, John 35*, Margarett 35, Emily 14, William 11, Louisa 8, Susan 5, Gilian 4 (f), Hezekiah 1
TAULBY, Lurena 16*
STEEL, Jeremiah W. 24, Martha 24, Nancy 4, Sarah 2
HANEY, Absalum 55, Elizabeth 52, John 24, Almeda 22, Johisa 21 (m), Herscal? 18, Jariel? 16, Martha 7

1850 Census Morgan County Kentucky

BARKER, Morgan 46, Ludema 35, Henry 17, Lucinda 16, John 14, Elizabeth 12, Harvy 8, Allen 6, Franklin 4, Margarett 2
SANFORD, Meese 70*, Elizabeth 60, Jerome 21
DEWITT, Cela 26*
WARREN, Allen 24, Lucretia 26, Reuben 1

Schedule Page 171

WARREN, David L. 32*, Maryan 27, Julian 5 (f), Sarah 4, Joel 3, Lydia 8/12, Harmon 28
PARKER, Lydia 33*
WARREN, Hugh 26, Reuben 61, Sarah 62, William 42, Cyntha 33, Eliza 17, Elizabeth 15, Joseph 14, Sarah 12, Phillip 10, William 6, Hugh__ 1
CHRISTY, Phillip 34*, Nancy 36, Joseph 7, Taylor 5, Scott 3
DAY, Elbert 13*
WELLS, David 50, Nancy 44, Sarah 24, Elizabeth 22, Edward 12, Rachael 9, Jacob 5, Sarah 74
BAYS, Joel C. 34, Lucinda 17
CARTER, Willis G. 28, Frances 23, Martha 4/12
STEEL, George S. 36, Catharine 32, Emerine 16, Maland 12, Sarah 10, Mary 8, John 6, Rosannah 4, Cyntha 8/12
ROSE, Winney 30*, Carlisle 12, Dillard 10, Ann 8, Nancy 6, Mary 4
WALSH, Mary 25*, Sarah 8
HOWERTON, John 56, Barbary 48, James 28, MArtha 22, Cordelia 20, Phebe 15, John 13, Jane 11, Ambrose 18
HOWERTON, Preston 32, Cyntha 25, Mary 2
CASSITY, Elizabeth 43, Leander 17, Peter 16, William 9, John 6
DOWNING, William 27, Rebecca 25, William 4, Mary 2, Eliza 1
JOHNSON, John 29, Almeda 28, Huldah 11, Elizabeth 8, Samuel 7, James 5, Perry W. 1

Schedule Page 172

FULTZ, Morgan 32, Mary 31, Daniel 15, Barbary 11, Jesse 10, Nancy 8, Precilla 5, John 4, Charles 1
PERRY, Cyrus jr. 29, Dorothy 27, Thomas 6, Jesse 4, Francis 3, Anderson 1
TURNER, Samuel R. 43, Mary 43, James 18, Thomas 13, Moses 12, George 6, Menefee 3, John 1
FLETCHER, Alexander 31, Jane 24, James 2, Thomas 1, Elizabeth 66
BARBER, Jesse 36*, Nancy 28, andrew 8, Margarett 6, Sarah 4, John 1
ABBOTT, Elizabeth 32*
CASKEY, Alvin 28*, Jesse 21
HENRY, Cincinnatus 29, Sarah 26
WILLIAMS, Richard F. 33*, Rebecca 20, Andrew J. 4, Susan 1
HARRIS, John 23*
GORDON, Joel W. 39*, Neoma 40, Margarett 17, Alfred 15, Elizabeth 10
BARNES, Mary J. 19*
TAYLOR, Joseph 22*
JONES, John 56, Sarah 44, Alvin 18, Telitha 16, Marion 13 (m), Gardner 9, Mason 6, Dial 4, Perlina 1, Gilean 28, Thomas 23

1850 Census Morgan County Kentucky

FERGUSON, John 56*, Elizabeth 54, Elizabeth 20, Mary 18, John 16, James 13, David 9
BURTON, Mary 25*, Elizabeth 6, Emily 4
MCGUIRE, JAmes sr. 70, Nancy 62
JONES, Henry C. 27, Elizabeth 19, Roena 2, Mary 1
PUGH, Joseph 37, Jane 33, William 12, Colonel 10, Martha 8, Sarah 6, Fanny 4

Schedule Page 173

ELLIOTT, Perry 21, Mary 17
ADAMS, William 47, Rachael 43, Sarah 16, William 10
FARISH?, Stephen M. 63, Sarah 50
WOMACK, Samuel W. 36, Susan 27, William 12, James 8, Andrew 4, Samuel 1
ADAMS, Matthew 45, Mary 41, Rhoda 16, Franklin 12, Doctor 5, Matthew 4
WALSH, John 40*, Sarah 36, Nancy 18, Mary 17, William 15, James 14, Lucinda 11, Malinda 10, Norman 8, Franklin 5
REED, Newton P. 30*
HAZELRIGG, John W. 40*, Albert W. 22
SPRADLIN, Henry J. 29*
GARRETT, Francis 50*, Andrew 20
CASSITY, Shelton 29*, Carline 27, Mary 6, Martha 4
BARKER, Clarinda 22*
FARISH, William E. 26*, Jane 24, Colvit 1/12 (m)
MAXEY, Clark 12*, Armilda 6
WILLIAMS, John T. 26*, Rebecca 24, Ann 3, Henry 1
DUKE, Edward E. 29*
BARKER, Jane 18*
VAUGHN, Jane 31, James 7, Alice 5, John 3, Janoah 2 (f)
GARRETT, Henry 53, Elizabeth 42, Samuel 13, David 11, James 9, Estes 7, Agness 5, Mary 3, Virginia 1/12
MARPLE, John 32*, Sarah 48
BARNES, John V. 31*, Wellington 3
ELLINGTON, John M. 14*
WARD, William 26, Phebe 23, Mary 8/12
LYKINS, Eli 48*, Frances 37, Martha 2
HENRY, Susan 18*, Edwin 16, Patrick 11, Thomas 9, Walters 9

Schedule Page 174

CARTMILL, William H. 32, Lucy 24, Sarah 5, Ellis 3, Lucy 1
WALDICK, Alexander S. 36*, Rhoda 28, James 9, Sarah 5, Luellen 2
MAXEY, Jacob 19*, Thomas 17
PHILLIPS, George D. 39*, Mary 40, George 5, Mary 3
CASSITY, Thomas 16*, Margarett 15, Josephine 7, Peter 16
HENSLEY, Edward A. 26, Rosanna 18, Harvy 21
CASKEY, William 23*, Isabel 25, Elizabeth 1
KENDALL, Elizabeth 63*

1850 Census Morgan County Kentucky

SWEATNAM, Hamilton 32, Mary 22, Cordelia 1
TURNER, Andrew W. 47, Berthena 38, Joseph 13, Margarett 8, Clay 5, Bruce 6/12
BURNS, William H. 33*, Mary 31, Harrison 16, Wallace 14, Oliver 12, Ann 10
WILLIAMSON, Willis 26*, Ann 16
DUKES, Dean 23*
PAUL, Doctor 28*
RICE, John 20*

1850 Census Perry County Kentucky

Schedule Page 397

GULLETT, William 29, Ann 29, Elisa 5, Minerva 4, Henry C. 2
STACY, Calvin 80, Phebe 30, Elizabeth 12, Margaret 11, Sirena 7, Anderson 5, Irvin 4, Nancy 1
COMOS, Ira 26*
MARILLER, Cinda 26*, Lavina 9, Elvira 8, John 5, Andrew 4, Ira 1/12
COUCH, John 38, Rachel 27, Polly 10, Henry 9, Nancy 7, Matthias 6, Ezekiel 3, Alfred 1
BAKER, Isack 37, Elisa 34, Lurena 12, John 10, David 8, Minerva 5, Cynthia 4, Martha 6, William 3
COMBS, Bluford 24, Winney 28, William 4, Elizabeth 1
COMBS, Jeremiah 62, Elizabeth 52, Eveline 22, Ephram 19, Polly 15, Ceely 1
COMBS, Margaret 31, Stephen 18
COUCH, Joseph 45*, Mary 29, Sally 13, John 11, Samuel 9, Martha 7, William 5, Mary 2
HALL, David 28*
COMB, Stephen 45, Francis 45, William 16, Jackson 15, Lucinda 13, James 11, Nancy 9, Wilson 4, Hugh 1
STACY, Felix 3, Cynthia 23, Polly 34, John 1, Calvin 21
YOUNG, Lucy 45, Chany 25 (f), Polly 17, Nathan 16, Mahulda 15, James 13, William 11, Larkin 9, Louisa 8, John 7
FIELDS, William 9*
FOLER, James 3*, John 1

Schedule Page 398

MORGAN, John 35*, Rebecca 30, Elisa 13, Martin 12, Johnathan 10, Nancy 18, Sally 4, John 2
HOUR, Joseph 22*
BAKER, Wilson 40, Sarah 37, Isack 17, Mary 15, William 12, Polly 10, Roderick 6, James 4
STACY, Sally 40, Benjamine 16, Elitha 13, Feelix 4
MILAM, Lewis 54, Nelle 37 (f), Preston 16, Marinda 14, William 17, Mahala 4, Lewis 7/12?
COUCH, Martin 65*, Sarah 65
HALL, Rebecca 9*, John 7
COUCH, Ira 25, Parmenia 23, Couch? 12, Eli 9, Wiley 7 (f), Jane 6, Abigail 3
COUCH, Thomas 38, Elizabeth 36, William 20, Cassey 19, Sarah 17, Lucinda 15, John 13, Anderson 11, Malinda 9, Rachael 7, Clinton 5, Elizabeth 3
WOOTON, Polly 53, Ceiley 23, William 7, Rutha 3, Polly 1
LIGHT, Anderson 23, Matilda 36, Polly 8, Sarah 3, Heviss? 2 (m), Malinda 1
MCINTOSH, William 29, Syrena 22, Nancy 4, Elizabeth 2, John 2/12
MCINTOSH, Roderick 67, Polly 40, Susan 23, James 20
HYDEN, John 34, Elizabeth 3_, Mary 3, Nancy 1
FELKNER, Moses 46, John 15, William 11, Polly 9, Nancy 5
FELKNER, Adam 35, Henry 13, William 10, Irvin 8, Jackson 5, Leander 5, Russell 2, James 3

Schedule Page 399

VANOVER, Eli 27, Clarissa 25, Margaret 4, Alexander 1
FELKNER, William 25, Candice 25, Eliseann 7 (f), Sylvania 5, Sarah 2
JACKSON, John 27, Martha A. 27, Julia 11, Elisha 9, James 7, Robert 5, John 3, Elizabeth 1

1850 Census Perry County Kentucky

JACKSON, Larkin 48, Elizabeth 66, David 28
JACKSON, Elizabeth 24, Jasper 8, Nancy 5, Sarah 4, Judah 2
ROBERTS, Thomas 25, Margaret 22, Elisabeth 2/12
ROBERTS, Sympfield 50, Samuel 22, John 15, Susan 13, Martha 8, James 8, Lucinda 6
MUNDY, John 22, Marinda 17
MORGAN, Adrian 27, Polly 25, Maddison 3, Josephine 1/12
MORGAN, Jesse 46, Rebecca 44, Samuel 21, Polly 20, Hanah 18, Wilson 16, Rachel 15, Nancy 13, Jesse 7, Emily 5, Rebecca 4, Hiram 1
EASTRIGE, William 38, Sophiah 35, John 21, Charity 19, Betsey 17, Wade 15, Martha 13, Eli 11, Polly 9, Becca 7, Zachariah 5
EASTRIGE, Ephragm 34, Susan 33, Matilda 19, Hiram 17, Sally 15, Malinda 10, Polly 8, Isom 6, Betsey 4, John 2
MORGAN, David 50, Jane 50, John 7, Andrew 4, Sylvania 1/12

Schedule Page 400

MORGAN, Elisha 30, Mary 27, Joseph 3, Edmund 4, Hughs 2
MORGAN, Able 34, Sarah 32, Mary 12, Rebecca 10, Margaret 8, Martha 6, Nancy 8, John _/12
HOSKINS, Thomas 40, Elisa 39, Sarah 18, Irvin 15, Andrew 12, Julia 7, Malinda 5
HOSKINS, John 29, Lucinda 29, Nancy 10, Catharine 9, Elizabeth 6, Minerva 5, Syrena 2, Leonidas 8/12
COLDIRON, John 22, Martha 20, Zachary 2, Nancy 1
MORGAN, Washington 26, Martha 28, Abigal 8, Elkannon 5, Henderson 3, John 1
MINCY, Elizabeth 49, John 22, Joshua 26, Elizabeth 17, Luther 12, Marion 9
LEWIS, Daniel 27, Nancy 26, Polly 7, Martha 4, Irvin 2, John 1/12
CRIP, Henry 34, Nancy 21, James 10, William 9, Perry 8, Barbary 7, Elvira 5, Charlotte 1/12
NAPIER, Patrick 34, Elizabeth 27, America 9, Crittenden 7, Martha 5, Lesly 3 (m), Leonidas 1/12
ELDRIGE, William 31, Gussey 27 (f), James 6, Carter 2
SHEPPARD, Calvin 26, Nancy 31, Sarah 5, Riley 3
PACE, John D. 32, Lavina 25, Robert 4, Martha 3, Elisa 1/12, Martha 65
HIXON, James 52, Rutha 50
HIXON, Wilson 26, Elizabeth 24, Elisa 4/12

Schedule Page 401

SHEPPARD, Huriah? _1, Franer 16 (f), Eli 1/12
COOTS, William 50*, Amy 30, Henry 30, Jane 29, Judah 26, James 24, Sylvester 22, Cloa 18, Rosamine 16, Lavina 12, Alexander 10, Nancy 7
FRANCIS, Hansperd 17*, Milly 10, Ira 7
LEWIS, Gideon 29, Sarah 23, Jane 2, Mathias 1
LEWIS, Kadern 65*, Mary 65
WILLIAMS, Margaret 3*
PAMINGTON, Levi 40, Winney 38, Rebecca 14, Timmothy? 12 (f), William 8, Anny 7, Felix 4, James 2
SHEPPARD, William 53, Sarah 50, Thomas 21, William 13, Alexander 17, John 15, Rebecca 13, Ira 10, Sarah 8, Henry 6
WELLS, Elihu 31, Elisabeth 31, Rebecca 12, Larkin 10, Ira 8, Mary 5, Nancy 4, William 2, Sarah 2/12

1850 Census Perry County Kentucky

BAKER?, John 54, Rachel 42, Henderson 21, William 19, Polly 16, James 14, Abby 12, Lucinda 9, Rachel 5, Tabitha 5, Rebecca 3, Winney 1
BAKER, William 24, Elisa 24, Rachel 24, Nancy 5, Polly 4
PENNINGTON, Ephraim 57, Matilda 39, Martha 17, Anna 17, Nancy 14, William 12, Anna 10, Aaron 8, Isaac 3, Levi 6/12, Malinda 7
COOTS, Henry 29, Malinda 29, Sarah 18, William 6, Nancy 2, Lucinda 3/12

Schedule Page 402

COOTS, James 22, Tabitha 21, Elizabeth 1/12
YOUNG, John 39, Rebecca 37, Abbigal 17, Ellender 15, Brarbary 13 (f), Timothy 9, John 7, Francis 5, Henery 3, Thomas 1/12
BAKER, John 22, Sarah 16
SHEPPARD, Levi 37, Sarah 37, Martin 15, John 12, Nancy 9, Lavina 7, Elizabeth 5, Polly 3, Sarah 1, Rebecca 1
LEWIS, Timothy 33, Nancy 30, Levi 9, Christly 7, Jesse 2
BAKER, Mary 55, Larkin 14
SHEPPARD, Elizabeth 26, Jane 7, Rebecca 4, Wilson 2
MAGGARD, John 53, Sarah 48, Sammuel 22, Jesse 21, John 18, Gilbert 14, Rheuben 12, Nancy 5
MAGGARD, Moses 27, Elizabeth 21
SHEPPARD, Anderson 23, Sarah 17
HENDERICKS, James 29, Ellendar 30, William 9, Joel 7, Phebe 5, Polly 3, Elizabeth 2
LEWIS, Samuel 56, Kesiah 52, James 24, Juder? 22 (m), John 19, Samuel 17, Lucretia 15, Winney 14, Andrew 11, Polly 7
WOOTON, Hiram 50, Sarah 78, Polly 23, Sarah 3
MILTON, Terry 59 (f), Sarah 53, Jane 19, John 16, Terry 12 (m), Nancy 11, Sarah 9
BARLEY, James 35, Elizabeth 33, Reuben 15, John 13, Nancy 11, Jane 2/12, Harrison 11, Susanna 9, James 7, Minter 5 (m)

Schedule Page 403

MILTON, William 22, Charlotte 25, Abner 1
THOMAS, James 59, Polly 56, David 27, Bora 15 (f), George 13, Preston 11
MILTON, Preston 27, Polly 22, David 4, Jane 3, Terry 7/12 (m)
WOOTON, Davis 47, Amy 25, Allison 10/12
HOWARD, John 40, Jane 40, Nancy 20, Jarnett 16 (m), Julia 14, Rosanna 12, Sarah 9, Rebecca 7, Anderson 5, John 3, Polly 1
LEWIS, Joseph 55, Sarah 58, Felix 22, Syrena 19, Minerva 17
WOOTON, Charles 42, Jane 33, Jarvis 14, William 12, Hiram 12, Elias 7, Irvin 5, Catharine 3, Emeline 1, James 1/12
ARA, Watson 51, Nancy 62
BEYLY, Pleasant 40, Anna 40, Henry 14, John 13, Russell 11, Polly 8, Russell 7, William 6
BEYLY, Pharis 31, Polly 31, Leander 12, Nancy 10, Sarah 8, Malinda 7, Rebecca 5, Elizabeth 3, Leonidas 1/12
BEYLY, Eligah 22, Mary 16
MCLEMORE, Hiram 70?, Margaret 22, Harrett 7, Benjamin 5, Josiah 4, John 4/12

1850 Census Perry County Kentucky

BIZLY?, John 36, Jane 15, Alrqut? 13 (m), Bradford 10, Adella 4, Lafayett 1
LANGDON, Isaac T. 35*, Maranda 28, John 11, Martha 3, Elizabeth 7, William 5, Letha 4, Mary 2

Schedule Page 404

EADIN, William 19*
FELKNER, Henry 73, Jane 53, Moses 23, Russell 18, Elizabeth 15
COMBS, Henry 53*, Nancy 53, Wiley 24, Hugh 22, William 15
FORNERS?, Nancy 15*
WILLIAMS, James 35, Jane 33, Sarah 18?, Anderson 12, Hardy 10, Nancy 5, Nathaniel 4, Mary 2, Hebe 6/12 (f)
OWAN, Harvy 24, Polly 24, James 5
WILLIAMS, John 26, Polly 20, Amanna 2, Robert 1
WILLIAMS, Robert 26, Susanna 22, Polly 4, Anna 1
WILLIAMS, Samuel 29, Elizabeth 29, Sarah 8, Rebecca 6, James 1
WILLIAMS, Hardy 54, Sarah 49, George 15
WILLIAMS, Andrew 19, Sarah 17
WILLIAMS, Phillip 21, Jane 24
EVERSON, Irvin 18, Elisa 17
BAKER, Christopher 27, Sarah 24, Dorcas 7, Hanah 5, Timothy 4, Mary 3, William 6/12
CALDWELL, Morris 42, Sarah 42, Henderson 20, James 18, Mary 12, Rebecca 8, Samuel 10
FRUMDEN?, Hiram 26 (B), Eady 28, Amanda 9, Arusellen? 7 (f), William 5, Abner 3, Robert 2
DUFF, Colvon 40, Elizabeth 30, John 13, Alexander 11, Daniel 9, Henry 7, Sarah 5, Susanna 3, Bardumine 2 (f)
DAVIDSON, Daniel 27, Sarah 25, John 8, Amanda 7, Nancy 5, Ellender 4/12

Schedule Page 405

LYTTLE, Edmund 76, Sarah 47, Elizabeth 19, William 16, Anna 13, Daniel? 11, Catharine 8, Sarah 4
SPENCER, John 81, Zoranene 88
SPENCER, Isac 43, Polly 55, John 20, Reason 17, Elizabeth 15, Joanna 11, James 9, William 7, Joseph 5
WILLIAMS, Joseph 57, Elizabeth 40, Isac 17, John 16, Marion 12 (m), Louisa 9, George 7, Orena 5, Jeptha 3, Eilzabeth 5/12
MULLINS, Burgandin 24 (m), Levina 18
HILTON, George 27, Leanner 21, James 2, Peggy 7?/12
HUFF, Daniel 26, Margaret 24, George 8, Mary 6, Nancy 4, Jussee 3
OSBORNE, Jesse 25, Elizabeth 29, Bambaner? 13 (f), Mima 7, Ephram 7, Lucy 5
BOLING, Justice 60*, Hanah 60
AMY, Thomas 15*
WILDER, Wilson 35, Elizabeth 24, Minerva 9, Abizut? 6 (m), Martha 5, Lucinda 4, Joseph 2, Kempsones? 8 (m)
WILDER, Joseph 80, Hanah 40, William 19, Washington 17, John 16, Harrison 13, Ewell 9, David 6
BOLING, Robert 36, Polly 36, William 10, Nancy 13, John 9, Jesse 7, Rebecca 5, Hanah 3, Huram 1
BREWER, Howel 23*, Elizabeth 23, Hanah 3, George 3, Polly 2, Martha 16
BARGER, Polly 62*

1850 Census Perry County Kentucky

Schedule Page 406

BARGER, Jesse 39, Elizabeth 34, Abraham 18, Marinda 15, Dulana 13 (m), Andrew 11, Nelson 3, Henry 7, Samuel 2
HEYNIGHT, Joseph 24, Nancy 21, William 2
GAY, Nelson 37, Hanah 30, Margaret 12, Abraham 10, Henry 8, Jesse 6, Joseph 7, Polly 6/12
BOLING, William 40*, Elizabeth 34, Lucy 15, John 13, Robert 11, Wolery 9 (m), Julia 7, Nancy 4
RICE, Jacob 22*
RICE, Jeremiah 49, Polly 49, Margaret 21, John 17, William 14, Jesse 12, Lavica 7, Henry 5
BOLING, Justice 29, Sarah 23?, John 7, Alfred 6, Polly 2/12, Elizabeth 3, Jesse _/12
LEWIS, Juder 48 (m), Nancy 40, Lavisa 10
LEWIS, James 24, Cloa 20, William 6/12
MILLER, Sarah 22*, Rebecca 33
DAVIDSON, Nancy 10*, William 6, James 1
GYLEY, Henry 35, Elizabeth 30, Granville 11, Jane 7, Sarah 3
GAY, Henry 45*, Hanah 40, Edward 11
COMB, James 20*
CORNETE, Samuel 22, Margaret 24, Christiana 5, Mary Ann 3, Martha 1
RICE, Fereler 55 (f), Lidia 23, John 3, William 2
FARRIS?, George 26, Mahala 23, Thomas 7, Mary 6, Julius 4, Rhoda 2
ARND, Andrew 43*, Elizabeth 26, Amelia? 5, Elizabeth 3, Elisa 2

Schedule Page 407

HAMLET, Wade 7*
MCCRARY, John 75, Ceiley 60, Lavina 5, Bartin 1
LANGDON, Samuel 69, Mary 40, Minerva 7, Mariah 5
HIGHNIGHT, Peter 40, Rachael 39, Joseph 24, Jane 22, James 20, Ballenger 18, Margaret 16, Eilzabeth 14, Moses 12, Nancy 10, Susan 8, Olivia 4
CAMPBELL, James 36, Polly 36, Jane 16, Zorda 14, Jeremiah 12, William 10, Hancel? 8, John 4
BEYLY, Henery C. 58, Elizabeth 58, Malinda 28, Sympfield? 20 (m), Nancy 16, Sarah 14
HUGG, John 41*, Hala 33, Pleasant 27, Polly 15, Ann 15, William 13, Catharine 6, John 11, Elizabeth 11, Edward 8, Winney 6, Hiram 4, Harrison 2, Taylor 1
BEYLY, Edward 42*, Nancy 40?, Hiram 18, Polly 14, Hamil 12, John 13, Sally 7, Asa 5
BEYLY, Russell 41, Elizabeth 30, Mary 16, ancy 10, Susanna 8, Sarah 7, Jackson 5, John 4, Armilda 4
BEYLY, Hiram 48, Cryarthera? 33, Felix 16, Jackson 14, Hiram 12, Ira 9, Mary 7, Sarah 5, William 3, Susanna 3, Allan 1
BEYLY, William 79, Winney 78, Margaret 78
SAWVILER?, John 82, Hydya 41, Harlus? 10, Nelson 8, Ed. 8 (m), Martin 6, Maricy 4, Elisa 2

Schedule Page 408

FEELUS, Jacob 40, Sarah 40, Rebecca 18, Elizabeth? 16, George 14, Hanah 12, James 10, Cromwell 8, Carter 6, Polly 4, Louisa 2, Jamison 1
FIELDS, James 38*, Elisa _8, Matilda 13, Wisely 11, William 9, Granville 7, Lewi 5, Jacob 3, Doctor 2
STANDEFORD, William 40*, Sarah 40, Samuel 8, Stephen 6, Elisha 4, Martin 2

1850 Census Perry County Kentucky

COMBS, William 44, Elizabeth 40, Malinda 19, Franklin 17, Larkin 15, Rebeca 13, Armena 11, Jesse 9, Ama 7, Jesse 5, Mary 3
COMBS, Granville 28*, Marinda 22, Robert 18, Elizabeth 1
STACY, James 24*
OWENS, William 28*, Francis 27, John 21, Jane 10, Wane? 9 (f)
HOSKINS, William 48, Rebecca 40, William 14, Jefferson 18, Thomas 14, Nancy 11, Martha 8, Louisa 1
COUCH, Charles 25*, Elizabeth 38, Allen 12, Andrew 10, Thomas 6, Mary 5, George 1
RICHARDSON, Thomas 46, Elizabeth 49, Daniel 19, Lucy 15, Amis 13, Elcana 12, Elizabeth 9, Mary 3
CAMPBELL, James 27, Rachel 23, John 26, Elizabeth 6, Abner 4, Elizabeth 2, Polly 16, campbell, Francis 48, Margaret 46, Susanna 11, Joseph 3, Thomas 7

Schedule Page 409

BAKER, Jackson 45, Sarah 54, Rebecca 15, Mary 10, Martha 7
FELKNER, Jacob 21, Nancy 29, Lewis _/12
COMBS, Francis 34, Elizabeth 34, Mathew 10, Shadrick 8, Hamil? 6, Rachel 4, Franklin 2
CAMPBELL, John 55, Cassey 50, Elihu 12
CAMPBELL, William 25, Elizabeth 30, John 13, Abigal 11, Martha 9, Rachel 5, Cassey 2, Jeremiah 1
HITCHUM?, Jeremiah 34, Prissilla 33, Thomas 13, Samuel 10, Jackson 8, Sarah 1, Hezekiah 5
MORRIS, Joseph 63, Rebecca 38, Morris 13, Louisa 8, James 6, Mary 7, Martha 5, Joseph 4, Lucind 2
MORRIS, Larkin 22, Margaret 22, Withat? 4 (f), Joseph 2, John 1
STEDHAM, John 25, Margaret 24, Jackson 7, Sally 6, Henderson 5, Leonidas 1
STEDHAM, Samuel 65, Sarah 66, Martha 20, William 23
OLIVER, Joshua 64, Rachel 53, Rettie? 27 (f), Shadrick 22, Matilda 20, Henry 18, Rachael 12, John 11
EVERSOLE, Elijah 23, Catharine 23, Sarah 4/12, Sarah 24, Emeline 6, William 2
CAMPBELL, Elijah 49*, Rebecca 40, Adam 16
MCINTOSH, Sarah 22*, William 4
CAMPBELL, John 21, Sarah 23, Rebecca 2/12
NAPIER, Edmund 23, Poly 22, Hiram 2, Elisa 1

Schedule Page 410

CAMPBELL, William 50, Hanah 44, Olivia 21, Haniel? 18 (m), Susan 15, John 12, James 9, William 6, Lewis 2
CAMPBELL, Samuel 36, Narcissa 35, John 16, Christly 14, Elisha 12, Louisa 9, Samuel 7, John 5, Sally 2, Polly 4/12
CAMPBELL, John 87, Polly 78
CAMPBELL, Jesse 27, Elizabeth 24, MArtha 5, Polly 3, Narcissa 2, Isac 5/12
CAMPBELL, Isac 44, Polly 42, John 20, Mariah 16, Hiram 13, Polly 7, Hirdin 5 (f), Ellen 1
CAMPBELL, Hiram 42*, Susanna 38, Preston 16, Stephen 16, Elizabeth 13, Lucinda 11, Worley 7 (m), Isaac? 5, Rebecca 1
LAD, Martha 63*
EVERSOLE, Woolery 25, Jane 22, Thomas 4, Alfred 2/12
EVERSOLE, Joseph 50, Rittie 46, Lucy 21, Wilson 18, Henderson 11, Elisha 9. William 21, Jane 21, Robert 6/12
LEWIS, Juder 30 (m), Matilda 27, Polly 9, Joseph 7, Abigah 5, Lucy 2

1850 Census Perry County Kentucky

OLIVER, James 41, Lethe 40 (f), Elizabeth 22, Thomas 21, James? 17, Wiley 15, Sally 10, Polly 8, James 6, Alfred 2
EVERSOLE, Woolery 56, Lucy 54, Joseph 10, Elizabeth 1/12
EVERSOLE, John C. 21*, Nancy 22, Sarah 23, Elizabeth _

Schedule Page 411

WHITAKER, Susanna 17*
COLLINS, Archabald 25, Nancy 30, John 5, MArgaret 3/12
BOLING, Polly 50*, Polly 10, Polly 3
LEWIS, James 74*
WHITAKER, Peter 45, Delila 45, Elisha 21, Sarah 15, Isac 16, Charlotte 18, Mary 10, Jane 7, Lavenia 5, Clarinda 1
WHITE, Simeon 20, Cloe 25, Jane 4, Patrick 2, Allen 1
EVERSOLE, William 34, Barbara 26, Sally 14, Nancy 13, George 10, Martha 6, Mary 1
CAMPBELL, William 25*
EVERSOLE, Joseph 31*, William 13, Anderson 9, Abner 7, Lucy 5, Polly 3, Elizabeth 1
MURRELL, Thomas 43, Polly 45, Joel 20, Alfred 20, Sarah 18, Lucy 14, Nancy 12, Mary 11, Thomas 9, Wiley 7, Elizabeth 5, Margaret 3
BEYLY, Jesse 29, Polly 25, Justice 6, Hiram 3, Hanah 1
GAY, Joseph 30, Sarah 24, Nancy 5, James 4, NElson 1, Margarett 70
WHITEBEARD, Washington 46, Nancy 43, William 22, Jackson 19, Joshua 15, Hetty 12, Elizabeth 10, Jane 6, James 5, Mary 2
SMITH, Jeremiah 52, Elizabeth 51, Huston 31, Sylvester 22, Sarah 18, Polly 15, Lewis 8
RILEY, Samuel 45, Sylvania 36, Elisann 15, Jeremiah 13, Preston 11, Huston 8, Sylvester 7, Rebecca 5, Elizabeth 3

Schedule Page 412

RILY, James 34, Luvina 28, Margaret 28, Mary 9, Ira 4, Alexander 3, Elliott 3, Marinda 6/12
RILEY, James 40, Elisdence? 28 (f), Lewis 5, William 3, Margaret 2
COWLES, William 27, Lethe 24, Henry 3, Jasper 1
AMES, Wells 38, Elizabeth 31, John 12, Robert 10, William 8, Alfred 6, Anderson 4, Nancy 2, Polly 8
RILEY, James 24, Nancy 21, Justice 1
FARMER, Samuel 25, Sarah 22, Mallissa 2
WHITEHEAD, Wiliam 23, _____ 18 (f)
JOHNSON, Campbell 39, John 1/12, Sarah 32, Franklin 13, Nancy 12, Susan 10, John 7, Elizabeth 3, Edward 1, Thomas 19
STANFIELD, Jackson 21, Nancy 21, Mahala 1
BEYLY, Granville 24, Nancy 22, Rebecca 1, Mahala 4/12
BOLING, William 44, Debora? 42, Olivia 13, George 12, Elizabeth 10, Charlotte 8, Molutt? 6 (f), McCoy 3, Henry 17
BURTON, Robert 27, Polly 28, Ira 1
MAY, Thomas 27, Tabitha 30, William 10
JOHNSON, James 30, Margaret 40, Henry 21, John 19, Samuel 17, Able 15, Amis 14 (f), Janus 12, Granville 11, Robert 8, Polly 6, __son 4 (f)
ALLEN, Johnathan 28, Rhoda 30, Susanna 13, Nancy 12, Elizabeth 5, Joseph 3

1850 Census Perry County Kentucky

Schedule Page 413

JOHNSON, Elizabeth 40, Thomas 17, Abby 19, Samuel 13, Polly 11, Charity 8
FUGATE, Levi 21, Delila 21
HACKER, Samuel 45, Nancy 4, Massa 16, Alfred 15, Armelda 14
DANIEL, Kenis 26 (m), Ellender 19, Maxaline 1
GROSS, Peter 21, Dorcas 23, Lucinda 6/12
MCINTOSH, Peter 30, Candella 30, Rebecca 5, Jeremeus? 4, Sarah 3, Nathan 7/12
MCINTOSH, Levi 35, Margaret 25, John 9, Darcas 5, Polly 4, Henry 3, Jeremiah 2, Susanna 1
HUNT, William 40, Susan 37, William 16, Nancy 15, Lucinda 7, Easter 6
GILBERT, Isac 28, Rebecca 37, Henry 17, John 14, Morzenia 12, Emely 9, Margaret 7, Ira 5, Rebecca 3, Ezekiel 1
MCINTOSH, Samuel 23, Polly 19, Elijah 2, Sally 1/12
SMITH, Preston 33, Margaret 29, Mary 8, Abigah 7, John 5, Lewis 3, Abraham ?/12
DUFF, John A. 48, Polly 45, Shadrick 17, Eligah 14, Louisa 11, Daniel 9, Orlena 7, Mary 9, Joel W. 2
FIELDS, Henry 23, Louisa 20, Mary 2
COMBS, Samuel 30*, Elisa 34
MORGAN, Washington 12*, Nicholas 3, Granville 2

Schedule Page 415

GODSEY, A. C. 34 (m), Mary 27, Ann 7, James 5, Minerva 3, Drewrey 1, Francis 3/12
DAVIDSON, Joseph 27, Alisy 21, Susanna 5, Sarah 3, Ira 1/12
COMBS, Jesse 53*, Polly 48, Josiah 17, Jesse 14, John 12, Margaret 10, Nancy 7
BOLING, Lucy 19*
COMBS, Elijah 80*, Sally 75
ELLIS, Polly 50*, Jacob 10
NAPIER, Samuel 31, Susan 21, Daniel 9, John 20, Polly 15, Sarah 1
MORGAN, Zachariah 24, Louisa 22, Eligah 10/12
COMBS, Biram 37, Mariah 32, Minerva 14, Anderson 10, Milton 8, Claborne 6, Stephen 4, Lidia 3, Nancy? 12
COMBS, Matilda 40, George 17, Jackson 7
HACKER, John 82*, Lidia 75, Margaret 8
MORGAN, John 5*
CORNETT, Eligah 25, Cinthia 21, Jane 3, Daniel 1
SIZEMORE, Harvey 26, Willey 25 (f), Nancy 5, Polly 4, Sally 3
COMBS, Lurena 29, Elisa 12, Robert 10, Alexander 8, John 6, Virgil 4, Mary 4/12
COMBS, William D. 60
COMBS, Alexander S. 25, Polly 23, Silas 3, Crittenden 2
COMBS, Biram S. 32, Serebe? 26 (f), James 5, Jesse 3
COMBS, Rachael 54, Jesse 22, Louisa 19, Margaret 17
BUTLER, David K. 42, Martha 25, Martha 6, Julia 5, Elizabeth 4, William 2, Margaret 1

1850 Census Perry County Kentucky

Schedule Page 416

COMBS, Robert C. 28, Elisa 25, Henry 7, James 5, Martha 3
HURT?, Washington 26, Susan 17
COMBS, Jeremiah C. 68, Sally 25, Jeremiah 11, Bettia 7, Rany 4 (f), Harrison 2
COMBS, Nicholas 58, Elizabeth 55, Elkanon 19, Kindrick 16, Lorenso 13, Mararet 10 (f), Nicholas 7
COMBS, Nicholas 86
CRAWFORD, James M. 30, Elvira 26, Thornton 1
SUTHERN, Henry 29*, Haney 27 (f), Jane 4, William 1
MESSER, Eligah 9*, Alexander 7
GRIGSBY, William 38, Jane 31, John 14, Dorcus 11, Wesley 8, Andrew 6, Cynthia 2, Martha 3/12
OWENS, James 25, Rachael 25, Cynthia 4, Nancy 3, Martha 2/12, William 87
NAPIER, Micager 57, Leanner 51, Jerome 18, Micager 16, Margaret 14, Martha 12, Mehala 6
JACKSON, James 36, Nancy 33, Franklin 11, Mary 9, Sarah 7, Nihala 5, Cynthia 3/12
NAPIER, Patrick 46, Mehula 39, James 19, William 17, Sarah 14, Elizabeth 9, Michager 7, Gabriel 4, Leanner 2
NAPIER, Elizabeth 50, Michager 18
GRIGSBY, Thomas 35, Frances 31, Sally 9, William 7, John 5, Nancy 3, James 1
COLLANWORTH, William 52, Rachel 47, Isac 21, Edmund 18, Thomas 15, William 14, John 10, Malinda 6

Schedule Page 417

COLLANWORTH, Reuben 23
MERRIDD, William 71, Malinda 77
COMBS, Wesley 30, Nancy 23, Margaret 7, Granville 4, Elizabeth 2, Milly 3/12
BUSH, Aaron 40*, Elizabeth 37, Polly 9, Malinda 6, Catharine 4, George 1
SUTHERS, Andrew 10*
ALLEN, James 26, Nancy 24, Samuel 6, John 5, Granville 4, Harrison 2, Susan 3/12
MILLER, Andrew 51, Martha 34, Frances 17, William 16, Nancy 14, Wiley 13, Andrew 11, Polly 10, Mason 9, Malinda 7, Lette 6 (f), Milton 2, Preston 1
CONAWAY, Thomas 35, Elizabeth 60, David 16
HOWARD, Elizabeth 43, Andrew 18
GWIN, William 51, Nancy 46, Elizabeth 21, James 18, Charlotte 13
PARKER, Matilda 40, Andrew 17, William 15, Camel 12 (m), Franklin 10, Lotte 7 (f)
CONAWAY, Wesley 26, Catharine 45
FRANCIS, Sally 40, Jackson 9, Harrison 9, Hiram 20
FRANCIS, Hiram 25, Judah 23, Jefferson 3, Jane 7/12
NAPIER, James 29, Mary 22, Mickager 6, Francis 4, Martha 2, Calop 9/12 (m)
CAMPBELL, Zachariah 28, Rebecca 21, Elizabeth 2
CAMPBELL, Caleb 47, Frances 46, Andrew 18, John 16
CAMPBELL, William 21, Polly 18
FRANCIS, James 70*, Rebecca 51, Lawson 19, Wesley 13
COMB, Wiley 16*
JONES, John 40, Elizabeth 16, Andrew 14, Sermanthia 13, Letha 11, Susan 5, William 1

1850 Census Perry County Kentucky

Schedule Page 418

ALLEN, Samuel 44, Susan 43, Andrew 19, Sarah 15, Emery 15, Malinda 13, Irvin 12, George 11, John 10, Ira 9, NAncy 6, Winney 3, Samuel _/12
CAMPBELL, Lewis 25, Rachel 22, Samuel 4, Elvira 2
HALL, John 30, Sally 26, William 7, Mary 6, Henry 3, Elisa 1
WILLIAMS, Jeremiah 23, Ibby 25, Ann 6, Eligah 4
JONES, Polly 25, Delpha 8
SMITH, Joshua 31
HOLLIDAY, William 23, Polly 22
HOLLIDAY, Tolbert 24*, Rachel 22, John 9, Elisa 7, Elisha 5, Eligah 3
JONES, Peggy 8*
SMITH, Elisha 70*
DAVIS, Larkin 3, Prudence 35, Casander 23
HOLLIDAY, Abley? 48 (f), Amy 52, Raney 17 (f), Green 14, Sarah 12, John 10, Walter 7, John 1
SMITH, Isaac 29, Sythia 25, Catharine 5, Shade 2 (m)
COMBS, George 52, Nancy 48, Francis 19, Mathew 17, James 15, Nickolas 13, Rachael 11, Isaac 9, Loranso 7
SMITH, Samuel 41, Nancy 39, Minerva 17, William 15, Daniel 11, Isaac 9, Seathe? 7 (f), John 5, Samuel 3, Newton 1
STACY, James 59, Polly 48, James 21, William 17, Shadrick 15, Frances 13, Joseph 11, Octavia 9, Nancy 7

Schedule Page 419

WILLIAMS, Nicholas 35, Ann 34, Rebecca 13, Polly 11, Elisa 7, Darcus 4
WILLIAMS, John 68, Rebecca 55
WILLIAMS, John 22, Frances 22, James 2, Preston 4/12
SMITH, Lorenso D. 33, Sarah 36, Letta 11
STACY, John 26, Synthia 25, James 5, Isaac 3, Manfred 1
FUGATE, Martin 30, Elizabeth 25, Polly 9, Levi 6, Charles 4, Henry? 1
FUGATE, Levi 55, Nancy 60
FUGATE, Zachariah 33, Polly 35, Mary 16, John 14, Gabriel 12, Martha 11, Daniel 8, Zachariah 5, Martin 3, Minerva 1
WILLIAMS, Pleasant 35, Elizabeth 30, Patsey 14, Jackson 12, Nathaniel 10, Susan 4
RICHIE, James 40, Hanah 39, Martin 21, Gabriel 19, Crockett 12, Andrew 12, Samuel 10, Zachariah 7, John 5, Hanah 6/12
FUGATE, Henley 25, Rittia 20
PATRICK, James 25, Elizabeth 21
RICHIE, Jurem? 37 (m), Martha 37, Hiram 14, Gabriel 13, Ephraim 11, Hugh 9, Barbara 7, James 4, Miles 9/12
RICHIE, Crockett 60
RICHIE, Nicholas 25, Nancy 26, John 12, Martha 10, Irvin 8, Silvia 5, Hanner 4, Mahala 13
WALKER, Alexander 32, Polly 32, Nancy 13, Elizabeth 12, Mary 10, Marth 8, Cynthia 6, James 4, William 1

1850 Census Perry County Kentucky

Schedule Page 420

COMBS, John L. 42, Polly 42, Shade 16, Polly 13, John 13, Susanna 6, Julia 3
COMBS, Hezekiah 25, Mehala 21, Susan 28, Wesley 25
JOHNSON, Preston 24*
COMBS, Milley 30*, Wesley 11, Jeremiah 15
FULLER, Elijah 60, Jeptha T. 15, Robert 13, Leviticus 12, ARchibald 11, Martha 7, Mary 6, Elijah 5
COX, Sally 40*
COMBS, Elijah 14*, Jane 12, Nicholas 9
WALKER, James 51*, Hanner 51
OWENS, Jane 9*
WALKER, Cristopher 24, Elizabeth 23, Milton 4, Permelia 1
MESSER, Reuben 25, Sally 24, John 9, Sytha 8, Milly 6, William 3, Preston 1
WALKER, John 33, Polly 31, Elizabeth 13, Wayne 11, Elisa 9, Jeremiah 7, Mary 5, Sila 3, Sulla 4/12
GEARHEART, John 46, Florrence 32, Lewis 23, Sylvester 20, Allen 14, Sally 17, Elizabeth 15, Catharine 13, Polly 11, John 9, Robert 7, Joseph 5, William 9/12
MORRIS, Ezekiel 60, Polly 55, Zachariah 25
MORRIS, Elizabeth 24, Nancy 22, Sylvester 8, John 17, Isamanda 11
DOBSON, William 39, Winney 38, John 16, William 12, James 11, Juda 10, Pressilla 8, Henry 6, Polly 3

Schedule Page 421

GIBSON, Joel 39, Nancy 39, Susanna 18, Allen 16, Thomas 14, Linsey 12, Martha 10, John 8, Mary 6, Sally 4, Rebecca 2, Roda 5/12
HAMILTON, James 35, Polly 23, Roda 6, William 5, Jackson 3, John 1
MULLINS, James 64, Agnes 58, Sarah 12, Booker 88
MULLINS, Elijah 26, Sarah 6, George 3, James 1, Joel 21
STEWART, Bird 19, Nancy 1, Mary 28
STEWART, James J. 26, Synthia 31, Araminta 19, John 20
GEARHEART, Richard 42, Rebecca 35
GEARHEART, William 17, Malinda 17, Falta? 15, Roda 17, Adaline 13, Christena 11, Jackson 9, Arta 7, Johnathen 5, Rutha 3
RICHIE, Hira 35, Phebe 30, Alexander 15, Elizabeth 12, Lucinda 10, Mark 9, Yernty? 6 (f), Christopher 5, Selta 3, Elias 6/12
HICKS, Charles 55, Rebecca 60, Charles 7
HICKS, Rebecca 21
HICKS, Caleb 25, Sally 30, Isaac 4, Elizabeth 2, John 7/12
JACOBS, William 28, Rachael 28, Lenard 8, Orena 5, Jackson 1
GIBSON, Hiram 66, Ann 36, Nancy 13, Racher 11 (f), Martha 9, Rebecca 7, Mary 5, George 3
TERREY, Jirel? 38 (m), Ginsy 38, Polly 11, William 12, Ann 10, Jesse 8, Elizabeth 5, Thomas 3, Elisha 2, John 1

1850 Census Perry County Kentucky

Schedule Page 422

NOLUND, Nathaniel 45, Ann 45, Nancy 19, Rachael 17, William 15, Polly 13, Silvester 11, Susan 9
CORMITT, Nathaniel W. 39, Lidia 34, Joseph 14, Rachael 12, SAlly 10, Roger 8, Nancy 2, Mary 6
WALKER, John 60, Polly 45, James 10
WALKER, Alexander 21, Elizabeth 16, William 6/12
SMITH, James 45, Roda 46, Nicholas 21, William 16, Frances 14, John 11, Isaac 9, Rebecca 5, Louisa 4/12
COX, Joseph 16
MESSER, Moses 22
MASSY?, Henderson 40, Polly 35, Lewis 17, Nelson 16, Kelsey 13 (m), William 11, Camerel? 9 (m), Frances 7, Martha 4
GEARHEART, Joseph 49, Catharine 46, Catharine 19, Joseph 17, William 18, Riley 13, Salley 11, Abigal 8, Mortin 6, Alexander 4, Lidea 7/12
INGLE, William 40, Nancy 31, Henry 10, Brick 8 (m), Hulda 7, Sampson 6, Jane 3, Ann 1
COMBS, Moses 44, Leta 44, Jeremiah 18, Thelix 23 (m), Susanna 21, William 2, Dianna 5?/12
CAMPBELL, Nancy 46, Hiram 8, Martha 5
GRIGSBY, John 59*, Patsey 57, John 26, Lewis 16
CAMPBELL, Nancy 88*
HONEYCUTT, Nancy 45*
CAMPBELL, Nancy 21, Elisa 4/12

Schedule Page 423

GRIGSBY, Samuel 18, Elisa 20
NAPIER, Stephen? 31, Polly 30, Leanner 6, Micager 4, Ably 3 (f), Stephen 1
HURT, William 80, Lucy 54, Jackson 23, Elizabeth 22, William 21, Isaac 18, Sally 14, Polly 10, Robert 14
HALL, Phillip W. 27, Elizabeth 27, Elevender? 2 (f), Mary 6/12, Wesley 12
GRAY, Mellender 39 (m), Catharine 42
SMITH, William 40, Elizabeth 43, Jacob 14, Catharine 5
MESSER, Sally 40, Thomas 17, Jesse 15
INGLE, Henry 34, Ann 28, Winney 9, Hudah 8, Benjamine 4, William 3, Nancy 1
GRIGSBY, Benjamine 28, Winnie 49, Polly 25, Thomas 22, John 20, Edward 16, Nancy 14, Bales 12, David 8, Gabriel 8, Benjamin 7
GRIGSBY, Edward 76
RICHIE, Gabriel 37, Nancy 30, Alexander 14, Alcy 12, Squire 11, Andrew 9, Gabriel 6, Henery 4, Manford 1
COMBS, Samuel 22*, William 25, Hanah 28, Patsey 6, Silvana 2
MILLER, Henly 26*
OWENS, Hardin 69, Levisa 29, John 28, Harvey 8, Granville 6
SIZEMORE, Ephraim 3, Omer? 38 (f), George 34, Jackson 15, Lera? 12 (f)
MILLER, Samuel 8, Nancy 5, Hiram 3, Russell 1
SMITH, John 29, Willey 22 (f), William 3, Jeremiah 1

1850 Census Perry County Kentucky

Schedule Page 424

MARTIN, William 24, Nancy 33, Polly 10, John 7, William 5, Sally 1
KELLEY, Washington 23, Sarah 21, Thomas 3, Jackson 2, Louisa 4/12
SMITH, Richard 24, Mary 24, Milly 1
OWENS, William 25, Frances 26, John 11, Jane 9, Polly 7, Jasper 6, W. 5 (m), Matilda 15
COMBS, Levi 22, Silver 23 (f), Mariah 1
GRIGSBY, Benjamine 21, Mary 22
JENT, Joshua 74, John 60, Susanna 22, Nancy 16
RICHIE, Thomas 45, Hesiah 38 (f), John 19, Benjamine 16, Armelda 14, James 13, Samuel 10, Elizabeth 8, Joshua 6, William 4, Thomas 1
HAMMONS, Esau 38, Elizabeth 37, John 15, Morgan 13, Nancy 11, Polly 9, Joshua 7, William 5, Mehala 3, Robert _/12
RICHIE, John 35, Silvia 34, Justin 17, Vina 15, Roda 12, Ann 9, Nicholas 7, Elizabeth 5, Alexander 1
RICHIE, Polly 40, Samuel 15, Henry 12, JAmes 7, Nancy 4, Susanna _/12, Lewsanna 3/12
RICHIE, Alexander 21
FELKNER, Jacob 38, Nancy 30, Polly 12, John 10, Lewis 8, Elizabeth 6, William 4, Martha 2, Catharine 3/12, Stephen 30
COMBS, Nicholas 28, Peggy? 26, Sytha 7, Elizabeth 5, David 10, Jeremiah 5, Nancy 1/12

Schedule Page 425

CORNITT, Robert 52, Louisa 47, Polly 13, John 11, Henry 9, Nancy 7
COMBS, Washington 4, Sally 50, Peggy 41, Jane 17, Jefferson 15
EVANS, William 13, Vena 28, Aley 19 (f), Samuel 3
COMBS, Clinton 41, Elizabeth 40, Hiram 29, Martha 20, Newlson 12, Hugh 11, Sidudema 9 (f), Emeline 7, Susan 5, Adrian 3 (m)
EVERIDGE, Solomon 6_, Catharine 55, John 45, Sampson 21, Synthia 20, Elisha 16, Polly 15, Abner 13, Greenville 10, Elizabeth 8
COMB, John D. 25*, Sytha 25, Lafayett 25
CORNITT, Sally 2*, Runine? 1 (m)
COMBS, Elsey D. 24 (m), Clinton D. 21
COMBS, Martha 40, Elizabeth 36, Jane 24, Eliza 22, Gilbert 21, Alcy 16, Preston 14, Massingal 12, Feribe 10, Washington 8, Handbelle 6 (m), Clinton 4, Bonapart 2, Polly 1
JENT, Elias 33, Rachael 33, William 70, James 5, Elizabeth 3
COMBS, Polly 46, Hiram 18, Nancy 16, Polly 15, Minerva 19, Eligah 6, John 16
DAVIDSON, Benjamin 28*, Sarah 29, Leonidas T. 1
COMBS, Dicy 11*
MCINTIRE, Benjamin 66, Sally 51, James 22, Alexander 16, William 12, John 10
STACY, Shadrick 38, Sady 38 (f), Elizabeth 15, John 13, James 11, Shade 9 (m), Nancy 6, Simms 4, Leander 1

1850 Census Perry County Kentucky

Schedule Page 426

COMBS, William 40, Peggy 35, Washington 11, Thomas 9, Dyanner 8 (f), Martha 6, Sampson 4, Isabell 1

COMBS, Jeremiah L. 35, Sally 35, Jackson 14, Washington 12, Price 10, Huldon 8, Andrew 6, James 4, William 1

CORNITT, John 56, Rachael 50, Robert S. 24, John 22, Mary 18, Nancy 15, Elizabeth 13, Russell 10

CORNITT, Archibald 31, Polly 26, Martha Ann 9, Minerva 7, Hardin 5, Louisa 4, Marion 2 (m), Mariah 5/12

JENT, Henry 27, Manda 23, George 7, Robert 4, Elias 2, Vina 6/12

KINSER, Harvy 24, Polly 33, Susanna 12, John 3, Elihu 3/12

MADDEN, Nancy 60

MADDEN, William 24, Polly 22, Minerva 2

MADDEN, Reese 27, Arra 29, Mary 7, Orna 5, Russell 4, Anderson 3, William 4/12

ASHLEY, Jordan 49, Barbara 45, Jesse 16, Sheppard 13, Hilliard 9

SMITH, William 24, Martha 18

ASHLEY, William 26, Christiana 25, Jourdan 2

SMITH, Alexander 22, Mary 16

WATTS, Enoch 42, Sally J. 36, Gery 18, Susanna 16, John 13, Sally A. 5, Theophilus Z.G. 1

BELCHER, John W. 35, Ann 35, George 16, Isaac 15, Polly 13, William 9, Levi 8, John 6, Elizabeth 3, Jourdan 1

Schedule Page 427

CHRISTIAN, Allen 46, Abbey 46, Polly 14, William 9

WILLIAMS, Joseph 54 (B), Henry 12

STEPHENS, Jane 24, Polly 3, Lurena 1

COOPER, John 60

CRACE, Peter 52, Rebecca 23, Wilson 4, Andrew 2, George 5/12

LINK, Samuel 66, __ly 38 (f), William 29, John 24

CHRISTIAN, Barnabas 25, Elfa 25, Nancy 7, Silas 3

STEPHEN, George 33*, Susan 30, Dorcas 12, George 10, William 8, James 5, Mariah 3

CORNITT, Roger 45*, Polly 40, Nancy 20

CORNITT, William 17, Sally 14, Samuel 17, Nathaniel 5, Hudly A. 2 (m)

CORNITT, Charles L. 21, Polly 16

BRASHEAR, Isaac 33, Jane 30, Margaret 18, Sampson 6, Mary 4, Louisa 1

BIRCHFIELD, John 35, Polly 32, Adam 13, Nancy 11, Samuel 8, William 7, Louisa 5, James 2

COMBS, Alexander 34, Mary 27, Almira 5, Robert 3, William 2, Elizabeth 7/12

BRANSON, Lenard 30, Elizabeth 26, Hanah 4, Louisa 2, Lurinda 4/12

BRASHAR, James N. 50, Elizabeth 42, Eli 23, Robert S. 19, Adaline 17, James N. 15, Sampson 12, William 9, Elizabeth 6

ROBERTS, James 64, Nancy 38, William 7, James 3, Obediah 2

1850 Census Perry County Kentucky

Schedule Page 428

CANDELL?, Robert 14*
COMBS, Elias 22*, Lucinda 22
HAMILTON, Jabez L. 27
COMBS, James 42, Elizabeth 35, Caleb 20, Edward 17, Henry 14, Martha 13, Polly 11, Sylvia 7, Mary 5, Sally 3
COMBS, Andrew 38, Polly 35, Elisa 14, Wane 12, Allen 9, Simpson 7, Elizabeth 4, Daniel 2
COMBS, Jackson G. 34, Martha 33, Polly 14, Lesley 12 (m), Eligah 10, Sally 9, James 8, Jackson 7, John 5, Casseus 2
FOSTER, John 28
FOSTER, Alexander 32, Roxa 29, William 10, John 9, Sally 6, Henry 4
FIELDS, Stephen 55, Elizabeth 50, Polly 25, Nancy 20, James 16, Elisa 14, George 12, Minerva 10, Rachael 8
FIELDS, Malen 32, Mary 28, Martha 10, Hulda 8, Anderson 6, Rachael 3
FOSTER, Farris 60, Sally 55, Polly 24, Milly 22, Farris 21, Nancy 16, Matilda 12, Sally 8
MILLER, William 30, Rebecca 28, Stephen 4, Mary 2, Elizabeth 1
YOUNG, Thomas 69, Elizabeth 68
YOUNG, James 20, Emeline 17, Elisha 12
YOUNG, Thomas 28, Lucinda 23
YOUNG, Isaac 31, Polly 25, Jesse 8, Jeremiah 6, Thomas 3, Arminda 1
LEWIS, William 35, Rutha 33, Mary 6, David 5, Abby 3

Schedule Page 429

HALL, Ezekiel 39, Cloa 35, Henry 16, Sally 14, Elizabeth 11, Synthia 9, Cloa 5, Joseph 3
GILLUM, John 30*, Elender 28, Louisa 8, Emaline 7, George 5, Ruhania 4, Wilburn 2, Lucinda 5/12
CANDELL, Rebecca 40*
BRASHAR, Sampson 69, Peggy 53, Ezekiel 23, Sampson 21, Robert 18, Louisa 16, Harvey 14, Jesse 12, William 10, Hezekiah? 8
BRASHAR, Robert S. 57*, Mary 53, Joseph? 19, William 16, Martha 12, Samuel 9, Thomas 6, Margaret 87
CORNITT, Mary 78*
COADY, Thomas 31, Elizabeth 27, Syna 3, Ira 1
COADY, Thomas 60, Molley 66, Ira 22, Lisa 21, Anderson 14, Carter 14
CORNITT, Anderson 30, Susan 30, Judah 6, Mary Ann 4, Matilda 3, William 2, Archabald 1
HULCOMB, Linsy 45*, Polly 50, William 21, John 18, Polly 15, Hardin 13
WEBB, Polly 35*, Sally 11, Nancy 11, Gudie? 9 (f), Elias 6
SHEPPARD, Elias 45, Patsy 46, Levi 16, John 12, Elias 9, William 7
SHEPPARD, Hugh 20, Sally 20
BUTLER, Edward J. 30
HOLLEDAY, Eligah 65
BURTON, Robert 39, Elizabeth 36, June 15, Polly 13, Lucinda 17, Isaac 5, Martha 4, Rebecca 1
CALLEHAN, William 45, Ann 45, Edward 19, William 17, Nancy 16, Marry 11, Hiram 9, Eli 7, Jackson 5

1850 Census Perry County Kentucky

Schedule Page 430

CALLEHAN, Isaac 24, Polly 24
BRASHEAR, James 29, Elizabeth 28, Alzira 4, Polly 1, John 30, Rebecca 27, Lethe 4 (f), Polly 6/12
CORNITT, William 25*, Nancy 33, Juda 11, Archabold 9, Louisa 7, Polly 6, Elizabeth 4, John 2, William 11/12
ELLIS, Mary 18*
CORNITT, Archabald 61, Judah 61, Archabald 21
CORNITT, Robert 32, Peggy 21
CORNITT, Hiram 25, Jerusha 24, Larkin 5, Preston 3, John 1
CORNITT, John 34, Elizabeth 25, William 8, Judah 6, Robert 4, Randolph 8/12
WILSON, Andrew 50, Tabitha 47, Poper? 26 (m), June 24, Andrew 22, Elizabeth 20, Julian 18 (f), Polly 16, Judah 14, Dorcus 14, Adaline 10, Ozine 8 (f), Margaret 6
LEWIS, Bazel M. 25, Rebecca 20, John 3, Elizabeth 1
SMITH, Johnathan 23, Florris? A. 17, Elizabeth 49, Polly 50, John 20
CORNITT, Clarke 17, Malvina 30, Joseph 28, Silas 7, William 4
HOLTCOMB, Hardin 52*, Polly 48, Polly 25, Jane 30, Ira 20, Judah 18, Paris M. M. 17, JEsse 14, Susan 12, Lynsa? 8 (m), John 5
SMITH, Andrew 4*, William 2, Hardin 6/12, Monroe 9, Thomas 3

Schedule Page 431

HOLTCOMB, Henderson 28, Matilda 23, Mary 3, Mary 1, Susan 30
SPARKMAN, Rear? 24 (m), Hanner 22, Jane 1, William 53
HOLTCOM, Henderson 46, Sally 40, Samuel 16?, Joseph 19, John 17, Henderson 15, Martha 12, Olivia 10, William 8, David 3?, Sally 38
CORNITT, Samuel 36, Lucy 17, Hiram 39, Pegg 15, William 13, Samuel 11, Joseph 9, Syra 6 (m), Doctor 4
HITCHCOCK, Sarah 40*
MCDANIEL, Joshua 27*, Malinda 35, Johnathan 15, Lucy 12, Judah 5, William 4, John 3, Peggy 2
DAY, John 33, Lavisa 23, Thomas 20, Martha 16, William 13, Sally 11
INGRAM, John 52, Elizabeth 52, Goodson 20, Hardin 17, Catharine 15, Clark 13, Cynthia 12, Archibald 8, Garrard 6, Susanna 4
INGRAM, Alexander 26, Mehala 26, Louisa 6, Ann 1
INGRAM, Washington 24, Mary 18, Susanna 2/12
CORNITT, James 36, Mornam 36 (f), Hiram 14, Clark 13, June 10, James 8, Samuel 7, Irvin 5, Blacksone 3, Elizabeth _/12
ISOM, Gideon 47, Machael 47, John 22, George 20, Bonapart 17, Eligah 16, Moses 13, Jonas 11, Daniel D.? 8, Gideon 6

Schedule Page 432

HALL, Elias 41, Mary 38, Hanah 17, Nancy 13, Phillip 8, Pherebe 5, Charlotte 2
FARLEY, Thomas 8, Sarah 32, Elisa 13, Marion 10 (f), Martin 7, Hanah 4, Martha 1
ISOM, Ann 60
WHITAKER, Isac 72, Susanna 69

1850 Census Perry County Kentucky

WHITAKER, Isac 41, Susanna 42, William 15, Milly 13, Nancy 12, Lucinda 10, Wilson 8, Enoch 6, Mulza 6 (m), Eligah 3
ISOM, Isac 68, Rebecca 60, Isaac 17, Ustly 15 (f), Scott 13
ISOM, Welson 22, Frances 18, Susanna 4/12
WATTS, Thomas 35, Nancy 27, George 11, Masutt 9 (m), Malvina 7, Squire 5, John Vin_ 3, Jeptha? 7/12
WHITAKER, Esquire 37, Arnett 31 (f), Samuel 15, John 12, Lurana 10, Nancy 8, Frances 6, Hiram 4, Susanna 2, Thomas 3/12
STAMPER, Isam 43, Sarah 43, Ira 20, Enock 18, John 16, Sarah 14, Elizabeth 12, Synthia 16, Alexander 8, Susanna 5, Lemuel 3, Wiley 2, Polly 4/12
CAMPBELL, William 56, Elizabeth 55, Seely 22, Louis 20, Elizabeth 17, Judah 14, John 12
CAMBELL, Woolery 32, Ceela 30, Enock 4, William 3, Thophilus 7/12
PRATT, Hiram 22*, Roda 24, Henry 6/12
SMITH, Rheuben 58*, Sarah 38, James 13, Turner 12, Lucretia 10, Sampson 7

Schedule Page 433

GODSEY, Clinton 25*
COMBS, Tarleton 46*, Elizabeth 40, Mary 20, Nancy 18, Catharin 15, Ustla 13, Carlo 11, Harrison 9, Ira 6
EVANS, John 27*
STACY, William 25*
MESSER, Agness 20*
BRASHEARS, John 45, Nancy 44, Samuel 23, Margaret 17, John 18, Ruth 16, Ezekiel 11, Benjamine 7, Polly 4
COMBS, John S. 28*, Ceilee 28 (f), Milly 11, Nicholas 7, Asa 3
DAVIDSON, Daniel 22*
MESSER, Jinsey 20 (f)*
GODSEY, John J. 31*, Margaret 24, Josephine 6, Arminta 4, Belbvadora 2
REMINE?, John W. 20*

1850 Census Pike County Kentucky

Schedule Page 434

ADKINS, William 39, Sarah 27, Darcus 9, Spencer 7, Thomas 5, Louisa A. 3, Daniel H. 2
SLONE, James 35*, Rhoda 37
ADAMS, Henderson 16*, Rhoda 12
PASSONS, Richard 40*, Lydia 38, Nancy 17, Sarah 16, Mary 10, Jefferson 9, Elizabeth 4, Susannah 2,
  Sarah 80
FAULKNER, William 46, Mary 37, Tabitha C. 14, Sarah Phina 11, John C. 10, Albert W. 7, William J.
  6, George R. 4/12
CAMPBELL, William W. 36, Mary 34, Nancey 15, David 10, James M. 8, Richard 5, Mary 3
CHANEY, Thomas G. 36, Sophia 32, Abner 15, John 13, Nancy J. J. 10, Harvey G. 6, Arminta 4,
  Thomas jr. 2
CAMPBELL, Nancy 75
ROBBINSON, John 24, Susan 17, Thomas G. 3/12
JUSTACE, George 45, Nancy 37, George W. 18, William 16, Abner 14, James 11, Mary 5, David 3
RATLIFF, Silas 27*, Mary 33, John 5, Mary A. 4, William 2, Nancy 8/12
JUSTACE, Nathan 12*
FULLER, Calvin 32, Margaret 37, Apperson 14, Irvin 11, Marion 10 (m), Thomas 8, Arveline 5,
  Elizabeth 3, Jefferson 1/12
GIBSON, Joel 40, Mary 56, Lavina 18
ROBBINSON, David 48*, Frances 50, Henery 26, David 23, George 22
ROBERTSON, John 17*, Richard 12, Caroline 20, Pricey 16 (f)
HOPKINS, Cornelius 72, Darcus 52, Cozey 21 (f), John? 16

Schedule Page 435

HOPKINS, Columbus 20, Mary E. 17
JUSTACE, William 18, Almeda 22
CAVENS, Anna 52, Samuel 11
JUSTACE, Peyton 59*, Mary 53, flemming 21, America 13, Jeferson 10, Peyton A. 4
ADAMS, Elijah 11*
POWELL, George 37?*, John W. 20, James H. 18, Elizabeth A. 16, David A. 14, Lavinia J. 12, Thomas
  H. 9, Frances A. 7, Susan V.? 3, Frances 87
CHILDRES, Miles 19*
BEVINS, James 41*, Elizabeth 31, James M. 14, Mary A. 12, Elizabeth C. 9, Sarah F. 7, John 4, Rebecca
  1
SLONE, Randolph 26*
SLONE, Mitchell 27, Pricey 16 (f), Peyton A. 4, William G. 4/12
KINDRIE, Milton G. 4, Elizabeth 24, William H. 11, George 9, James 7, Jefferson T. 5, Lylburn 3,
  George 9/12
THACKER, Absolom 24, Mary 20, Nancey 4, Vicey J. 3, Nathaniel 2/12
KINDRIE, Harvey 26, Sarah 21, Martha J. 3, Perlina 15
SPEARS, George W. 26*, Mary 26, Christopher 6, Mary S. E. 2/12
CAVINS, Katherine 27*, George W. 3
GUESS, John 33, Sarah 27, Victoria T. 8, James A. 6, Joseph N. 5, Zachary T. 3, Mary E. 3/12
SLONE, Mary 79*, Eliza M. 76, Mary J. 4 (B)
POLLY, Spencer 21* (B)

1850 Census Pike County Kentucky

POLLY, John 24 (B)
SLONE, Archibald 33, Nancey 33, William 15, Elizabeth 13, Mary 11, Simeon 5, Sarah J. 2, Greenville 1
JUSTACE, Thomas 25, Mary 16, Edward 1

Schedule Page 436

ADKINS, Milton 41, Sarah 38, Margaret A. 10, Amanda G. 9, Millinton 5
JUSTACE, William A. 40*, Lucinda 11, Richard 9, Hutson 7, Thomas 4
ROBBINSON, Elizabeth 56*
JUSTACE, Gillmore 18, Mary 17
CHANEY, Abell 50*, Agness 50, Johnithan 7, Mahala 5, John 11
SLONE, Thomas 23*
SLONE, James 35, Mary 29, Mahala 1
THACKER, Absolom 26, Mary J. 25, Jefferson 5/12
THACKER, Elisha? sr. 67, Judy 62, Joseph 18
THACKER, Greenville 21, Darcus 23, John W. 1
THACKER, Elisha jr. 33, Florina 37, Pirtey 11, Reuben 9, Hiram 8, Timmothy 6, Greenville 5, Piety 3, Willburd 3/12
SMITH, Aron 28, Jenny 22, William 6, John 2
THACKER, John 34, Malinda 27, Harrison 19, George W. 9, Darcus 7, Sarah 4, Judy 2
SLONE, Milley 50, Joab 35, Morgan 19, John 13
SLONE, Elijah 30*, Nancey 25
CONNOWAY, Sarah 15*
BLACKBURN, Thomas 51, Sarah 48, Harmon 20, John 17, Mary 16, George 14, Nathaniel 12, Delilah 10, Nancey 8, Elizabeth 3
ADAMS, Bartholomew 65, Elizabeth 60
SLONE, Archibald 25, Malinda 3, Amia 23, Mary 2
SLONE, Amos 30, Sarah 30, James H. 10, Elizabeth 9, Nancey 7, Louzina 3
JUSTACE, Abner 25, Martha A. 25, James M. 4, John W. 2

Schedule Page 437

JUSTACE, Nancey 70, MArgaret J. 29, Lewis 32, Linsey 3 (m)
THACKER, Abner sr. 70, Sarah 66, Elizabeth 18
THACKER, John 34, Emiline 30, Elizabeth 14, Nancey 12, Perlina 10, Absolam 6, Anthony 4, Mary 2
THACKER, Randolph 38, Martha 37, Millinton 16, Sarah 14, Marilda 12, Lydia 10, Elizabeth 8, Mahala 6, John 5, Harrison 3, Joel 2/12
ADKINS, Nathaniel? 28, Elizabeth 24, William 5/12
THACKER, William 30, Ruth 25, Martha J. 3/12
JUSTACE, William 29, Mary A. 28, Jenny 9, Sarah 7, Nancey 5, Absolom 3, George 1
THACKER, Reuben 45, Malinda 39, John 24, Simon 17, Elisha 15, Jackson 13, James M. 11, Farrell 9, William A. 7, Mahala 1
JUSTACE, Peyton 38, Elizabeth 35, Pricey 11, Nancey 9, Alexander 7, Elizabeth A. 4, Rhoda 2
JUSTACE, Simeon 62, Mary 59, Simeon 25, William 21, Mary 19, Milla 16, Arta 15
JUSTACE, Booker 40, Giddey 37 (f), Comely 17 (m), Harlan 15, Elisha 11, Mary 10, Judy 8, Berrill 5, Rhoda 1

1850 Census Pike County Kentucky

JUSTACE, Absher 25 (m), Sarah 28, Hibbard 4, Tolberd R. 2
JUSTACE, Harvey 27, Rebecca 22
JUSTACE, Claiborne 30, Frances 25, Vica 3, Mary A. 2, Arta 5/12

Schedule Page 438

KEEN, Joseph H. 28, Elizabeth 26, Sarah 6, Clarinda J. 4, William T. 2, Pricey 1
ADKINS, James 65*, Nancey 55, Andrew 28
ROSS, Henely 20*
HACKNEY, Ruell 20, Westina 18, Clark T. 9/12
ADKINS, Susannah 43, William R. 18, Squire 15, Flemming 12, Surilda J. 3
ADKINS, James 30*, Nancey 22
KEENE, James 4*
SLONE, Shadrack 70, Winna 70
SLONE, Shadrac jr. 38, Susan S. P. 36, Bethena 16, McPharlan 11, Spottswood 8, Elizabeth 6, Arretta 3, Thompson 10/12
ADKINS, Jeone? 44 (m), Janee M. 42, Linsey 14 (m)
BELCHER, John M. 27, Cela 33, James H. 9, William A. 7, Leonard 5, Louisa 1
JUSTACE, Hiram 31, Nancey 28, Levi 11, James H. 9, Miles 7, Mary 5, Pleasant 2
ANDERSON, David 33, Jenny 30, George W. 11, Pricey J. 10, Miles J. 5, James F. 3, William H. 1
JUSTACE, Rhoda 58, Roda 23
JUSTACE, Andrew 33, Rachel 29, John 9, Elizabeth 8, Sarah 6, Ambrose 5, Pricey 3, William T. 1
BLEVINS, Daniel 22, Mary 23, James L. 2, Arminta J. 1
BLEVINS, Jacob 24, Elizabeth 22, Almeda 3, George 7/12
BLECHER, Margaret 63
JUSTACE, Joab 35, Elizabeth 25, Rebecca J. 7, Richard 5, Simion 2
ROWE, Charles 45*, Pricey 36, Ellen 19, Nancey 17, Milla 15, Henderson 13, Apperson 11, Jefferson 8, Jackson 6, Mary J. 3

Schedule Page 439

SLONE, Isom 25*
BISHOP, William 39, Mary 38, Uriel 16, Rhoda A. 14, Pricey 12, Marion 9, Miles 5, James 4, Lavina 1
BELCHER, James D. 21, Nancey 18
ROBBINSON, James 30, Rachel 20, Elizabeth 2, Eliza 4/12, Reda 82 (m), Frances 62, Sarah M. 24
BLAKELY, Wiley 40, Reedy 38, Saddy 13 (f), Frances 11, Hiram G. 9, James A. 7
ROBERTSON, Nathaniel 41, Lucy 45, Martha 15, James 14, Frances 12, Richard 11, Mary 9, Elizabeth 7, Nancey 5, William A. 3, Pleasant 1
CLEVINGER, Levi 32, Nancey 26, William A. 7, John W. 5, Pleasant 3, Judy A. 10/12
ROWE, Franklin 32, Lotta 23, Louisa 9, Martha 6, Miles A. 4, Sarah J. 2
ROWE, John 21*, Mary 19
EPLINE, Isaah 20*, Nancy 20, William L. 2, Martha 11/12
EPLINE, Isaac 45, Alla 41, Hiram 20, Henery H. 19, Margaret 16, Elizabeth 14, James 12, Amanda 9, John 7, Louisa 5, Sarah 3, Mary 1
SLONE, Archibald 45*, Elizebeth 35, David 21, Arminta 17, Gordon D. 13, Archibald 11, Robert 8, VanBuren 6, Dicey 5

1850 Census Pike County Kentucky

LOW, Sarah A. 15*
HAMILTON, James 40*, Martha 25

Schedule Page 440

YATES, Richard 19*
CHILDRES, Mary 16*
MILLER, John 28, Nelly 23, Lydia 5, Martha 3, Lutha 1
YATES, James 32*, Perlina 29, Louisa M. 8, Howard 7, George J. 4, Sarah 2, Margaret 3/12, James R. 5/12
PAYNE, Mary 56*
MORTRIDGE, William 16*
HACKNEY, John 30, Frances 24, George W. 7, Sarah M. 5, Andrew J. 10/12
HACKNEY, Thomas 54, Precilla 50, Ephraim 18, Jane 16, Syndesta? 14, James 11, Pricey 9 (f)
HACKNEY, Charles 27, Mourning 22, Thomas 2
MORGAN, James 31, Nancey 32, David 11, Mary J. 8, Elizabeth 6, Lavina 3, Pricey 7/12 (f)
SLONE, John 40, Jane 28, Francis M. 4, Mary E. 2, Flemming 13, Andrew 10, Villa 8 (f), Vesta 5, Columbia 17, Hannah 16
TAILEN, Edward 55, Janey 40, Isaac 18, Andrew 14, Marion 12 (f), John 10, Samuel 8, Clara 6
ROWE, Elizabeth 64*
SLONE, Spencer 21*, Elizabeth 23, Nancey J. 1
MUTTER, John 45, Mary 40, Thomas 22, Almeda 18, George W. 15, Mary 12, James H. 10, John W. 8, Charlotta 4, Sarah 1
KEAN, Lewis 25, Susannah 20, Isreal H. 4/12
GRIFFEY, James 64, Letha 56
GRIFFEY, David 19, Jane _. 18, Matilda 1/12
GRIFFEY, Richard 22, Lavina 18, Nancey 1
KEAN, John 21, Charlotta 18

Schedule Page 441

GRIFFEY, Wesley J. 24, Hulda 21, Jane 2, Louisa 3/12
THORNSBURY, Martin 64, Milla 60, Lewis 27, Walter 24, Martin 22
HYLTON, William 41, Katherine 37, Jessee 18, Julina 13, James 11, Marion 9 (m), Telitha 6, Washington 4
THORNSBURGY, John 37*, Elizabeth 35, James M. 11, Nancey P. 9, Ruthy A. 7, Milla J. 4, Louisa E. 2
TAILOR, Elizabeth 20*
GRIFFITH, Susannah 16*
HUNT, George 44, Cely H. 38, John 21, William 19, Mary A. 17, Jane 16, Elizabeth P. 12, George W. 13
KING, Lewis 44, Mary 38, William 19, Elizabeth J. 18, Pricey 14 (f), Ellen 13, Rachel 10, Mary 10, Minerva A. 5
HUNT, John 45, Dica 39, Mary 15, John 10, Vancey 8 (f), Elijah 3
HUNT, Moses 37*, Mary 30, Aron 12
CARTER, July A. 29*, Mary E. 4
GOODE, John 9*

1850 Census Pike County Kentucky

LANE, Alexander 53, Anna 43, Alfred 22, John 17, David 14, Susannah 12, Alexander 10, Henery 5, Miller W. 2, Lydia A. 1
ROW, Wiley 20*, Synthia _. 19
HYLTON, James 23*
ADKINS, Allen D. 43, Matilda 37, Lackey E. 16 (f), Lavinia C. 13, Orpha A. 11, Elizabeth A. 8, Mary J. 6, Matilda E. 5, Oliver W. W. S. 3
WILLIAMS, William 22, Sylvia 23, Malinda J. 1
HUNT, Henery 28*, Sarah 30, Louis F. 6, Mary E. 6, Sarah A. 2

Schedule Page 442

GOODE, Andrew M. 13*
STANTON, Malinda 32*
SLONE, William 40, Sarah 47, Braxton 18, Pricey 16 (f), Morgan 14, Jane 12, Nancey 10
ROWE, John 44*, Sarah 23, Borillis 5, Aquillis 5
SLONE, Wimea 17 (f)*
SOWARDS, Lewis 37*, Olla 37 (f), Morgan 16, Thomas J. 14, James M. 13, America 11, Kentucky 6, Henery C. 5, William H. 3
PHILLIPS, Merrida 20*
MEAD, William 21*
JUSTACE, Edward W. 25*
RAMSEY, Letitia 67*
SWORD, Lucas B. 43*, Malinda 42, Francis M. 21
ROBINSON, Elizabeth J. 19*, William H. H. 9
WILLIAMS, Eli 26*
LAWSON, Hezekiah 30, Malinda 27, George W. 11, Eliza J. 8, Elizabeth M. 6, Melvina F. 4, Abijah 13
CLEAR, James M. 34, Tabitha 32, Henery H. 8, Phoeby J. 7, Sarah H. 6, Orleana R. 5, David R. 3, Margaret E. 1
PORTER, Elijah 45, Nancey 41, Frances 15, Elijah 7, Lorenzo D. 5, Colbert C. 2, John 13
JOHNSON, William 26*, Elizabeth J. 21, James R. 4, Louisa J. 1, William 22, James 26
RAMSEY, Margaret 19*, Ann 17
RAMSEY, John 23, Mary 21, Tamsey 3 (f), William R. 6/12
ADKINS, William 53, Nancey 49, Jefferson 20, Jackson 18, Samuel 16, Sarah A. 9, Spurlock 7, Elizabeth 3
EMILEY, Alexandre 32, Sarah 28
ADKINS, George W. 23, Mary 23
FORD, Rebecca 49*, Jackson 20, Harrison 19

Schedule Page 443

MORGAN, Mary A. 26*
FORD, William 29*, Malinda 24, John H. 8, John W. 7, Harrison 5, Elizabeth 3, Nancey P. 8/12
GIPSON, Pricey A. 19 (f)*, Causbey 16 (f)
CAMPBELL, Nathan 20* (B)
ROBBINSON, James H. 27, Sarah 23, Mary T. 1
MCGEE, James 60, Elizabeth 50, Mary 21
MAY, Henery 26*, Rhoda 24, Nancey D. 1

1850 Census Pike County Kentucky

KEEL, Marshall G. 18*
COLEMAN, Lucy 39, Pheeby 16, Sarah 13, Matilda 12, Moses 9, Winright 9, Delilah 7, Druzilla 2
ADKINS, Wenright 75, Sarah 70
ADKINS, Jessee 35, Elizabeth 27, Hiram 9/12
ADKINS, Henery 51, Elizabeth 48, Winston 21, Owen 18, Henery 15, Judy 12, Jessee 9, Reubin 4
ADKINS, Winright 25, Sarah 24, Clarinda 5, Henery 3, Elizabeth 1
GARDINER, Joseph 56
COLEMAN, Abraham 42, Rebecca 35, Nathaniel 8, Riley 5, Nathaniel 3, Elizabeth 1
ADKINS, Elizabeth 64, Riley 17, Elizabeth 19, Willend 6/12 (f)
ADKINS, William 29, Anna 20, Nathaniel 5, Sarah 3
ROBINSON, John 25, Nancey 24, Richard 66
THACKER, Nathaniel 47, Delilah 47, Emanuel 21, George 17, Sarah 14, Elizabeth 13, Thomas 10, Joseph 9, Mary A. 6
ROWE, Joseph 34, Elizabeth 32, Nancey 16, Milley 14, Sarah 13, Winna 11, Horatio 9, Henderson 5, Mandona 3, William H. 4/12

Schedule Page 444

JUSTACE, Geenville 25, Rebecca 27, Sarilda 6, Peyton 5, Mary 3, Pricey 1
ADAMS, John 26, Pricilla 20, William 3, James 3
ROBINSON, Sarah 24, Elizabeth A. 3, Mary J. 1
HOPKINS, Elisha 35, Pheeby 35, Elizabeth 16, Bethena 15, Darcas 12, George 10, Mary J. 5
FIELDS, Richard L. 35, Nancey 36
FIELDS, Thomas 25, Eliza 21, Elenor 2, Nancey A. 10/12
FULLER, Jessee 45, Hessie 44 (f), Sarah 21, John 15, Hawkins 12, Elizabeth 10, Nancey 4
FULKERSON, Martin 31*, Elizabeth A. 20, Susan A. 2
CHILDRES, Harvey 21*
COLLINS, Jacob 26*
ROW, Johnithan 43, Elizabeth 36, Guy J. 18, Dulcena 17, John A. 15, Louisa 13, William H. 9, Louanne 6, Henery J. 4, James H. 2, Sophia J. 2
BOLING, Henery 24*, Susannah 32, Lewis 3
ADKINS, George W. 13*, Minerva J. 11, Rebecca V. 9
POLLY, Anna 35, James 20, John 17, Pricey 14 (f)
ROW, James 73*, Sophia 72
COOLEY, Katherine 60*
LOUKS, Anthony P. 26, Barbary 29, Syrena 10, Sarilda 2, Elizabeth S. 2/12
ADKINS, Winston 45, Hannah 44, Stephen 17, Peeter? 15, Winright 13, Joseph 11, Mary 9, John H. 7, Moses 6, Elizabeth 2
ADKINS, Eli 19, Margaret 18
ROWE, Hyram 37, Anibal 24, Mary J. 8, Nancey 5

Schedule Page 445

MAY, James 45, Ann E. 26, Mary A. 13, David A. 10, William 8, Francis M. 6, George W. 4, James K. P. 2, Nathan 4/12
CASTLES, James 27, Synthia 24, Dianna 6, Maryinda 4, Lucyinde 2
CASTLES, Henery W. 29, Oma 26, Louisa 6, John 5, Miles 2, Henery 1/12

1850 Census Pike County Kentucky

FIELDS, Samuel 35, Esther 30, Rebecca 13, Nancey 11, Susannah 8, Pricey 6, Jenny 3, James 1
RATLIFF, John 26, Tamsey 26, Nancey 9, James 6, Sarah 3
RATLIFF, Sparley 23 (m), Nancey 23, Louisa 4, William P. 3
MURPHEY, John 30, Rachel 30, Harvey 8, Gabriel 6, Alexandre 4
RAMEY, John 30, Arminta 29, Mary 14, Rebecca 8
WHITE, Nancey 68, Robert 27, Sarah 33, Crockett 8
WHITE, Horatio 49, Delilah 44, John D. 18, Rachel 16, Harrison 13, Hensly 11, Clara 7, Lewis 2
CHILDRES, Flemming 42, Charity 40, L. 15 (m), Alexandre 13, John W. 11, William 9, Walter 7, Francis M. 5
CHILDRES, Nathaniel 20, Syrlena 16
LOONEY, John 23, Mary A. 18, Joseph 9/12
ADKINS, Anderson 39, Nancey 35, William J. 11, Levi 8, Lewis 6, James D. 4, Louisa 1, Sarah 21, Mary E. 4/12
ROWE, Loyd 22, Ryena 17, Louanna 1/12
MATNEY, Alex. 25*, Jane 20

Schedule Page 446

HAMILTON, Susan 55*
ROWE, Jacob 50, Sarah 45, Jacob 16, Emaletta 13, Mary A. 11, Clementine 8, Reuben 7
ROWE, Stephen 20, Frankey 20 (f), Henery 2, Harris H. 6/12
SNOW, Fielding 40, Mary 45, John 15, Elizabeth 12, Daniel 10, Nancey 8, Matilda 5, Sarilda J. 3
TAILOR, Burgess 49, Frances 48, Alexandre 14, Sarah 13, Thomas 10, Louisa 7, Isaac 4
RAMEY, Moses 40, Jane 28, Lavicey 9, William 6, Berry 5, Marinda 3, Nancey 1, Sherod 4/12
POTTER, Richard 50, Mary 47, Andrew 22, Mary 17, George 16, Henery 15, Anna 12, Tammaree? 11 (f), Malinda 8, James H. 5, Didema 3, Noah 5/12
STUART, Abraham 30, Esther 29, Nancey 10, Mary 8, Ann 6, William 4, Jenny 3, Thomas 4/12
RAMEY, William 67, Anna 66, William 24
RAMEY, Daniel 40, Lucinda 30, Henery 8, Jackson 7, Rebecca 5, Martha 4, Mary 2, Washington 7/12
BENTLEY, Benjamin 27, Anna 21, Jenny 4, Elizabeth 2, Mary 2/12
HOGSTON, John 28, Susannah 25, William J. 5, Frances 3, Salina 1
CARTER, Sarah 52, Henery 18, Granville 12, Catherine 11
RAMEY, Tabitha 50*
OWENS, William 19*, Anna 19

Schedule Page 447

MCCOLLEY, James 44, Mary 44, Colbert C. 10, Nancey 7
RATLIFF, Nathan 34, Matilda 33, James 15, Rebecca 13, William A. 11, Samuel 10, Paul 6, Silas 6, Marion 4 (m), Matilda 2, Victoria 7/12
SWEENEY, James 45, Sarah 43, Spencer 16, Willis R. 13, Moses 12, Tabitha 11, Elizabeth 7, Martha 5, Anna E. 3, James 4/12
ROWE, Charles 20, Katherine 20
ROWE, Reuben 36, Clara 42, Stephen 17, William 14, Barbary 12, Sarah D. 9, Clara J. 8, Reuben H. 4
HOWELL, Samuel 42, Katherine 40, Charles R. 15, Rebecca 14, Samuel G. 12, John 10, Martha 8, Henderson 7, George 5
GIPSON, Elijah 25, Delilah 21, James M. 10, John 8, William 6, Elizabeth P. 4, Charles 9/12

1850 Census Pike County Kentucky

GIPSON, William 80*, Elizabeth 80, David 16
SWEENEY, William 13*
CASE, Rebecca 40*, Vanburen 12, Henery C. 9, Malinda 3
GIPSON, Isom 19*
RATLIFF, Alexandre 32, Elizabeth 31, Harrison 12, William H. 10, Elizabeth 8, Colbert C. 7
CASE, James 33, Jane 23, Jasper 5, Mary 2, Eveline 1, Margaret 62
MAY, Gideon 44*, Malinda 42, David 18, Susan 16, Martha 14, Gideon 12, America 9, John W. 7, James 4, Jacob 2/12, Elizabeth 2
HYLTON, Patton 11*, Lorenzo D. 12

Schedule Page 448

CANTRELL, Abraham 76*, Lucy 55, Isaac 18, Reuben 16
ANDERSON, James 22*, Lydia 18, Nancey 17, Thomas 15, John 13, Lucy 12, Moses 10, Aron 10
MAY, Johnethan 31, Eliza 24, Charles M. 7, Harrison 5, James 3, Elizabeth 2, Emilene 1/12
RATLIFF, Silas 36, Mary 34, Elvira F. 15, William 13, Emiline 11, Joell 9, John 7, Rebecca 4, Elizabeth 2
POTTER, Levi 32, Sarah 37, Elizabeth 10, Mary 9, Benjamine 5, Levi 4, William 3, Caroline 8/12
POTTER, Benjamine 54*, Susannah 50, Reuben 21, Anna 19, Mary 17, Susan 15, Esther 12, Isaac 10, Elizabeth 8
HOLLINGSWORTH, Susan 4*, Squire 2
CANTRELL, John 45*, Agness 44, Caleb 20, Winna 19, Hiram 14, Elizabeth 12, Lucy 7, William 3
FIPPS, James 85*
ELZIC, Johnethan 22, Nancey 23
MCPEEK, James 20*, Elizabeth 16
MOORE, William 40*
SWEENEY, Joshua 25*, Martilda 17
MCCOINE, Joshua 10/12*
MOORE, Isaac 60, Rebecca 29, John 6, Moses 6, Ollivia 5, Solomon 3, Rebecca 1
MOORE, Ananias 40, Susannah 37, Nancey 18, Isaac 16, Mary 15, James 13, Ananias 10, Andrew 7, William 5, Preston 2
OSBORNE, J. W. 25 (m), Cene J. 24, Sherwood 5, Mary 3

Schedule Page 449

CLAY, Henery J. 32, Mary 34, Hyram 11, Elizabeth 9, Marston 7, Lucy C. 4, Solomon 1
ANDERSON, Charles 29, Hannah 27, Abigal 9, Alfred 7, Shadrack 5, Tabitha 3, Jeptha 1
ENGLAND, Ruele 21 (m), Pricey 19 (f)
MOORE, Isac 30, Mary 25, Alexandre 8, Aron 6, William 4, George W. 2
GREENE, James P. 35, Unis 26, Mary A. 4, Melvina 2, Emeline 1
MOORE, Aron 35*, Lydia 30, Katherine 9, Merriba 7, John W. 6, Joseph F. 4, Hulda E. 2?
HILTON, Ellen 15*
JOHNSON, Martin 26, Susan 23, Lucy 5, Chrissa 4, Nancey 2
ANDERSON, Jessee 23, Sarah A. 21, Hansford 2, Marinda E. 4/12
MCPEEK, James 63*, Sarah 61
MILLER, Sarah 45*
CLEVINGER, Alex. 55*, Elizabeth 58

1850 Census Pike County Kentucky

LUNSFORD, Alexandre 12*
MCPEEK, George 32, Malinda 27, Elizabeth 8, Elisha 6, William 4, James 2
JOHNSON, Isaac 28, Mary 29, William 3, Elizabeth 10/12, Lucinda 20
OSBORN, Jerremiah 36, Mary 31, Zarilda 12, Hulda 11
HOLLINGSWORTH, Beasley 60, Jerremiah 15, Susan 14, Matilda 11
CLAY, John 49*, Amilia 41, Marston 20, John H. 17, Bradley A. 12, Katherine 10, Maribee 7, William J. 4, Henery W. 2
ELZIE, Bradley 22*
SAUNDERS, Greenville 27, Rhodica 26, Levi 7, Onica 5 (f), James H. 3

Schedule Page 450

MULLENS, Booker 31, Nancey 34, Susannah 14, Sherwood 12, Mary 11, Sarah 9, James 7, Martha 5, Nancey 3, Rhoda 1
MULLENS, Elijah 25
BLANKENSHIP, Barnabus 39, Jenny 38, Henery 14, Preccilla 12, Mahala 10, John 8, Margaret 6, Charrity 5, Elizabeth 3, James H. 3/12
BENTLY, George 31, Loucinda 28, Moses 9, Lucy 7, Malinda 5, Vincent 4
STEEL, Andrew 22, Winna 20, Nancey 1
BENTLEY, Samuel 26, Mahala 20, John 4, Elizabeth 2, Lavinia 1
STEEL, Samuel 50, Nancey 42, Reuben 19, Sydney 17 (f), William A. 14, Mary A. 11, Samuel 6, Levi 3, Matilda 8/12
BENTLEY, William 35, Rebecca 30, Pricey 6, Elizabeth 4, Marybee 2, Gilbert 1
BENTLEY, Moses 30, Martha 30, Darcas 12, Anna 10, William 7, Hyram 6, Sarylda 2
CRASE, Campbell 36, Mahala 32, James 15, Peeter 13, Elizabeth 11, Nehemiah 9, Drucilla 7, Ciney M. 5 (f), Noah 1
STEWART, Thomas 30*, Sarah 31, Isaac 7, Abraham 4, Andrew 3, Jenny 2, Benjamine 6/12
LUNSFORD, Eliza 11*, James 35
POTTER, Abraham 46, Martha 35
POTTER, Richard 18, Nancey 18
STUART, John W. 21*, George W. 3, Sophia 3/12

Schedule Page 451

SMITH, Margaret 65*
COOLEY, James 21*
PLYMALE?, Isaac 44, Mary 34, Hugh 18, Barbary 16, Eveline 14, Elizabeth 12, John 9, Mary E. 7, James H. 5, William H. 3, Sophionia 1, Delcena 15
ROANE, Barbary 69, Matilda A. 30, Frances S. 26, James H. 3, William H. 3, James S. 4/12
ROWE, Huffman 21, Louisa 19
RATLIFF, Richard 51, Sarah 46, Thompson 20, Tiry 18 (m), William 16, James 15, Aldaree 12 (m), Mary 10, Eliza 8, Richard 3
ADKINS, Nolen 60, Elizabeth 55
COLEMAN, Daniel 25, Bethena 24, Miles 7, George 4, Syndesta 3, Pricey 2 (f), John 1
COLEMAN, John 26, Elizabeth 33, Louisa J. 12, William A. 10, Melvina 8, Elizabeth 5, James K. P. 2/12, Harvey E. 2
COLEMAN, Peeter 74, Sarah 52, Mathias 16, Stephen 13, Pricey 12 (f), Moses 10, Hannah 8

1850 Census Pike County Kentucky

COLEMAN, David 24, Anna 20, David C. 3, John A. 10/12
COX, Dixon 25, Charlotta 22, Nancey 3, Lilburn 1
FRY, Andrew J. 24, Katherine 57
RATLIFF, Robert 30, Mary 26, John A. 9, Mary J. 7, Arminta E. 5, William B. 2, James M. 5/12
FULLER, John 35, Cela 33, Hiram 8, Thomas 7, James 5, Nancey 3, William J. 1, Thomas 71, Christena 19, Mary 2, Reuben 3/12

Schedule Page 452

HOLLINGSWORTH, Squire 29*, Margaret 40, Rhoda 10, Samuel 8, Susan 5, Squire 4, Joseph 2
LUNSEE?, Elizabeth 24*
LUNSFORD, Thomas 10/12*
BRANTHAM, John 28, Mahala 27, Elizabeth 7, Joseph 4, Richard 3, Charrity 1
MULLINS, Smith 40, Margaret 39, Booker 16, John 13, William 11, Mary 9, Nancy 5, Smith 4, Henery 3, Owen 1
HENSLEY, Nelly 50, Delilah 25, Charrity 17, William 15, Mary 12, Paul 12, Susan 7
RIGHT, Samuel 30, Elizabeth 28, George 12, Clarrissa 10, Joel 8, Charritey 4, Andrew 2, Samuel 3/12
ADAMS, William 62, Christena 55, Sidney 16 (f), Martha 13, Mary 13
MULLINS, Booker 46*, Mary 43, William 19, Smith 18
BURKS, John 12*
MULLINS, Owen 23, Jenny 22, Judy 5, William 3, Booker 2, James 10/12
ELKINS, James 20, Marinda 18
ELKINS, Harvey 21, Mary 18, Jack 15, Mary 17, Elizabeth 12, Matilda 10, Oda 4 (f), Booker 2
HOUKS, Jesse 40, Sydney 27 (f), George 9, Isaah 7, Sydney 4, Samuel 3, Frances 1/12
MULLENS, Solomon 21, Matilda 20, Andrew J. 1
MULLENS, Aelxandre 40, Margaret 38, Robert 19, Nelson 18, Spencer 16, Alexandre 14, Jefferson 11, Lavindy 8 (f), William 6, Sarah 3, Matilda 1

Schedule Page 453

EDWARDS, John 60, Eda 51, John 15, Benjamine 11
WILLCOX, Samuel 29?, Barbary 33, Francis M. 8, Elizabeth 5, Isaah 3, Hambleton 2/12
FLEMMING, William 27, Elizabeth 21, Tabitha 7, Diannah 5, Preston 3, Lucinda 2, John N. 1/12, Robert 77
FLEMMING, Jefferson 25*, Letta 23, Margaret 5, Philip 3, James 1
HABE?, Lewis 17*
FLEMMING, Elizabeth 65
VANOVER, Nealus 25, Margaret 21, Tenna 4, David 2, Lucinda 1
MULLENS, Elizabeth 56*
HALL, Eliza 10*, Katherine 8
MULLENS, John 53*, Lucinda 40, Esther 8, Eliza 8, Lucinda 6
ELIOT, Michael 17*
BAKER, Jenny 35*
SAUNDERS, Wade H. 29
SAUNDERS, Ichabod 21, Elizabeth 23
ELZIC, Jacob 24, Anicca 21, Elizabeth 3, Mary 1/12

1850 Census Pike County Kentucky

AUNDERS, Thomas J. 49, Elizabeth 48, Susannah 18, Arta 16, William R. 14, Hannah M. 12, Jacob 9, Sarah 4
MULLENS, John 27, Mary 21, Eliza 7
JOHNSON, Thomas 26, Mary 20, Rosaline 4/12
JOHNSON, Elisha 48, Martha 45, Amey 24, Elisha 21, Madison 19, William 13, Walter J. 8, Sarah 7
EDWARDS, Isom 28, Emma 24, William W. 8, Mary E. 4, John B. 2, Lydia A. 1/12
EDWARDS, Humphrey 23, Jane 21, Sarah A. 1

Schedule Page 454

SMALLWOOD, Elijah 31, Mary 32, John 8, William H. 6, Miles 2
JOHNSON, William 35, Susannah 20, NAncey 12, Mary 9, Elizabeth 7, Sarah 5, William 1
JOHNSON, James 35, Nancey 34, Elizabeth 13, John 11, Hannah 6, William 4, Mary 1, Grace 55, Lucinda 17
DAMERON, Elisha 27*, Sarah 30, William J. 4, Mary J. 2
ELZIE, George W. 13*, Katherine J. 11
DAMERON, John 47, Nancey 42, Elizabeth 16, Spurlock 14, Sarah 12, Frances 10, Alesey 5, James 1
DAMERON, Jackson 24, Spicey 19, John 2
NEWSOM, Henry 43, Martha 35, Elizabeth 18, William 16, David 14, Washington 11, Margaret 9, Usley 6 (m), Henery 3, Mary 2/12
BRANKAM, John H. 26*, Usley 29 (f), Louisa 6
HILTON, Daniel 15*
BRANHAM, James 46*, Frances 45, Henery 16, Mary 19
SWEENEY, Anna 16*
BRANKAM, Edward 23, Elizabeth 21, Nancey 4, James 1
BRANKAM, Reuben 26, Harriet 21
BRANKAM, David 32, Katherine 27, Alfred 10, William 9, Elisha 5, Leonard 4, David 1
KINNEY, William 34*
ROBERTSON, Sarah 37*
BRANKAM, Elizabeth 70*
ROBERTSON, Harvey 16*
BRANKAM, William 42*, Elizabeth 41, Wesley 19, Lewis J. 17, Hulda 15, Elizabeth 13, James 11, William 9, Nancey 6, William 4, John 1

Schedule Page 455

JOHNSON, Mitchell 26*, Matilda 21
ROBERTS, John jr. 40, Nancey 41, Daniel 19, Malinda 11, Marinda 9, John P. M. 7, Dica 4, Hulda 2
ROBERTS, James 78, Nancey 75
ROBERTS, Niel 22*, Winna 28
HAMMONDS, Elizabeth 8*
DAMERON, Richard 48*, Elizabeth 50, James 26, Willson 22, John W. 16, Harvey C.? 15, William 13, Walter 9
DRAWDAY, Margaret 37*
LITTLE, William 31, Mary 26, Reuben 9, Sythia 7, Louiza 3, Sylvinia 1, Nancey 2, John 21
NEWSOM, Harrison 38*, Mary 32, Margaret 14, Harrison 11, Samuel 9, Spicey 5, Harmon 3, Riley 10/12

1850 Census Pike County Kentucky

HALL, Riley 21*
TACKETT, Philip 53*, Charity 45, William 12
BRANKAM, Elias 20*, James W. 17
PAINE, James 36*, Elizabeth 26, Narcissus 4 (f), Rebecca J. 3, Noah 11/12
HARRISON, Nelly 13*
TACKETT, Isaac 33, Judy 26, Louisa J. 8, Mary 6, Lucy 5, Ola 4, Judy 2
MULLENS, John 33, Darcus 30, John H. 12, Jenny 10, Nancey 8, Mary 5, Alexandre 2
ELZIE, Bradley 65, Katherine 58, Bradley 21, Henery S. 17, Richard 13
ELZIE, James W. 26, Margaret 22, Marabee 4, Joseph 3/12
MULLENS, William 65, Delilah 52
MULLENS, Richard 32, Lucinda 25, Angeline 6, William 5, Burrell 1
ELZIE, William 36, Nancey 33, Caroline M. 14, Sarah A. 12, John 10, Elizabeth 8, Tolbert 7, Margaret 5, Mary A. K. 2, William R. 4/12

Schedule Page 456

HALL, Samuel sr. 53, Spicey 54, Harmon 19, Nancey 17, Rebecca 15, Louisa 12
TACKETT, George 46*, Hannah 47, Greenville 18, Hiram 17, Benjamine 15, Harvey 13, Sarah 11, Rachell 9, George W. 7, Stephen 1
OSBORNE, Solomon 82*
AUSTIN, Robert 38, Aly 23 (f), Lydia 11, Nancey J. 9, Prudence 7, Mary 6, Margaret 1
TACKETT, William 20, Nancey 21, Tapley 1/12 (m)
TACKETT, Solomon 20, Angeline 18
HALL, Richard 42, Sarah 37, William 16, Marybee 13, Pernetta 11, Lousina 9, Maylen 7 (m), Lavina 5, Willburn 1
TACKETT, William 72, Amey 74
JOHNSON, William 38, Matilda 37, Harvey 17, Margaret 14, Sarah 11, Tandy 8 (m), Jenny 7, Katherine 4, William 1
BENTLEY, Thomas 23, Delcena 18, John 4/12
TACKETT, William 41, Sarah 37, Martha 21, James 19, Abell 17, Elizabeth 14, George 12, Mathew 10, Rebecca 8, Abner 5, Enoch 3, Enos 1
BURKS, John 48, Rachel 37, Owen 19, Elizabeth 15, David 12, Rebecca 8, Ann 6, Matilda 3
HALL, William 33, Elizabeth 35, Ellen 13, Lucy 12, Thursday 10, Richard 7

Schedule Page 457

JOHNSON, Pleasant 31, Anna 20, Jeptha 1, Solome 6/12 (f), Lucy 65
JOHNSON, Paine 44, Margaret 36, Sarah J. 14, Eliza 12, William 10, Margaret 8, Lucy A. 6, John W. 4, Uriah 1
JOHNSON, Robert 40, Esther 26, Richard 8, William 7, Lucy 3, Lorenzo 2/12
BRANHAM, Turner 22, Malinda J. 21, David C. 2
BURK, Isaac 42, Nancey 37, Bailey 18, Clarinda 16, William 15, Bethena 13, Nathaniel 11, Pleasant 9, Lucy 7, Margaret 5, Jarvis 3, Elbert 1, Ellen 1
JOHNSON, Bailey 29, Rebecca 27, Abigal 7, Martha 6, Sebastian C. 3, Humphrey M. 1, Thadeous S. 3/12
AUSTIN, Samuel W. 26, Christena 19, Nancey S. 3
ROBERTSON, Richard P. 23*, Martha J. 20, Nancey V. 1

1850 Census Pike County Kentucky

ROBBINSON, Samuel 28*, Hannah S. 24, Mary E. 2
GILBERT, Ellen 65*
OWENS, Thomas 70*, Mary 69, Pheeby 13
RUST, Henery M. 23*
JONES, Nathaniel 20*
MCCALISTER, Louisa 29, Rachel 17, James W. 15, Mary A. 12, George W. 11, Arminta 3, Robert H. D. 4/12
OWENS, Robert S. 26, Darcas 24, John J. C. 2
OWENS, Rhodes M. 26
GILBERT, Samuel 23, Mary A. 20
WEDDINGTON, Jacob 38, Sarah 28, Henery 13, William 12, Marietta 10, Nancey 8, Loudena 4, French 3 (m), Elizabeth 2

Schedule Page 458

REYNOLDS, Thomas 65, Pheeby 63, Harvey 23, Susan 18, Malinda 16, Mary 9, James 6
CECIL, Colbert 35*, Thomas 19
DAMERON, Solomon 24*
RATLIFF, William F. 24*
DRAPER, James N. 44*, Alpha R. 43, James M. 20, Josephine 11, Robert T. G. B. 9
STARK, Caroline L. 24*, Fielding 28
OWENS, Thomas J. 24, Mary H. C. 22, Eveline A. 1
PATTERSON, Erastus J. 32, Hellen A. 26, Mary E. 5, John W. 3, Elbert S. 1
DILSO, John jr. 31, Ann 28, Georgeann 6, Mary E. 4, Augusta 2
RICHARDSON, John N. 38*, Caroline M. 34, Marybee 9, Jane 7, James 5, William 4, Katherine 3, John C. 1
RATLIFF, Lucinda 38*, Marybee 76
MCGUINE, Elizabeth 29*, Ellen J. 29, William R. 5, Victoria A.L.M. 3, Thomas J. 10/12
LEWIS, Johnson 34*
BOYER, Thomas H. 39*, Sarah T. 38, Synthia A. 16, Joseph 10, Mary 12, Elizabeth 10, Moses 8, John 4, Matilda 1
HURT, Robert 27*
ROBINSON, Isaac 45, Nancey 45, Daniel 22, Mary 21, William 17, John 16, Rachel 14, Andrew J. 13, Hannah 12, Virginia 7, Sylvia 4
DYER, Calvin F. 31, Tabitha 37, Tennessee W. 5(m), Elizabeth 2
DAMERON, Solomon 23, Frances M. 18, Moses 1/12
SMITH, Preston 30, Mary J. 25, Elizabeth J. 5
HATFIELD, Raptre? 22 (m), Elizabeth 22, Thomas W. 5, Hannah A. 3
SWORD, William 30, Christena 26, John W. 8, Elizabeth 7, Moses 5, William 4, Enos B. 3, James M. 2, Marinda J. 4/12

Schedule Page 459

WARRICK, Thomas 26, Susannah 27, James W. 10, Lucy 8, Calvin C. 7, Nancey R. 5, William J. 3, John P. 5/12
JOHNSON, John 23, Rebecca _. 21
JOHNSON, Lucinda 46?, Willers 15 (m), Solomon 7, Mathew 3

1850 Census Pike County Kentucky

IRICK, William 30, Lydia 23, John 5, William 3, Elizabeth 1
SWORD, John 53, Rebecca 45, Martha 22, Mary 16, Rebecca 19?, Malinda 9, Virginia 6, Eliza 2
SWORD, Richard P. 26, Pheeby 23, Rebecca 4, Nancey 4, Arminta 2, Hellen 10/12
HINTON, Richard 45*, Nancey 35
NICHOLS, James 5*
COMPTON, Lee 33, Alesee 27 (f), James T. 11, John W. 8, Pheebee 6, Hulda 4, Malinda 1
DAMERON, James 55, Mary 43, Moses 13, Sarah 75
MCGEE, James 25, Rebecca 23, Mary E. 3, Nancey J. 1
MAY, John 27, Martha J. 22, Solomon 4, Margaret E. 2, Mary D. 1
MANOR, James 22, Elizabeth 22, William 8/12
MAY, Samuel jr. 29, Mary 24, Solomon 6, Darcus 5, David 3, Elizabeth 6/12
MULLENS, Elijah 23, Elizabeth 22, Martin 4, James 2, William 6/12
HOPKINS, Joseph 25, Lucinda 25, Victoria 7, Mary A. 6, Elizabeth 3, Louisa 1
DAMERON, William 25*, Ruthy 31, Mary J. 2, Elizabeth 1/12

Schedule Page 460

RAMSEY, James W. 14*, George W. 12
RAMSEY, Daniel 61, Sarah A. J.? 25, William 1, Sarah 1
MARRS, John 36, Synthia 33, Alexandre 15, Thomas 14, Sarah A. 11, Samuel 10, HEnery 8, James 6, John 1
HARRISS, William 33, Lucy 22, Thomas H. 5/12
IRICK, John 64, Elizabeth 63, Amanda 19, Johnethan 23, Joseph 21
LITTLE, David 21, Lydia 17
MAY, Thomas sr. 63*, Darcas 60, David L. 22, Adaline 4
HAMBLETON, Jessee 19*, William 22
LITTLE, John 24*
KINNEY, John 35, Mary 32, Eliza 15, Henery 13, Mary A. 11, William 9, Washington 7, Drury 4, Usley 3 (f), David 2
TACKETT, Francis 66, Martha 53, Thomas 29, Alex 18, Mary 22, Ferina J. 15, John 12, Robert 11
MCCOWAN, William 34, JEmima 21, Martha A. 8, Louisa J. 6, James K. P. 5, John W.? 1, Melvina 4
MCCOWAN, John 28*, Mary 25, James M. 5, Thursday A. 4, Hugh 1
OSBORNE, Hannah 84*
HALL, Riley 25, Lucinda 24, John 7, Rebecca 4, Nancey 3, Mary 7/12
HALL, Morgan 19, Litta 18, Henery 8/12
HALL, Johnethan 17*
COOK, Mary 17*
HALL, Henery 30, Anna 29, David 9, Samuel 8, Amey M. 5, William M. 4, William R. 8/12, Samuel 23

Schedule Page 461

CASEBOLT?, John J. 50, Mary 36, Charlotta 15, David 13, Matilda 11, Hiram 9, William 7, Darcas 5, George W. 3, Andrew J. 1
OSBORNE, Hiram 51, Nancey 53, Lewis 23, Jessee 20, George W. 19, Nancey 15, Ruthey 12, Rachel 9
ANDERSON, Hiram 26, Spicey 23 (f), Elizabeth 5, Preston 2, Harvey 6/12
OSBORNE, Salsbury 27, Jenny 19
OSBORNE, Stephen 31, Naney 25, Sherwood 8, Booker 6

1850 Census Pike County Kentucky

OSBORNE, Louisa 52, Cornelius 21, Delilah 15, Candasa 14 (f)
TACKETT, William 26, Sarah 18, Shadrack 2, Adaline 6/12
OSBORNE, Shadrac 23*, Elizabeth J. 22, William J. 3, Jerramiah 2
COOK, Jenny 16*
MCKINNEY, Mary 52, Leonard 18
RHEA, John W. 43*, Rebecca 37, Milla 14?, Synthia 15, Reubin 12, Matilda 9, Rowena 7, Jackson 5, Martha 4, William T.L. 2
KEELS, Samuel 23*
MCCOWAN, Hugh 65, Milla 55, Mary 26, Sarah 20, Elizabeth 17, Thomas 14
NEWSOM, Fredric 36, Agnes 30, Davenport 14, Lackey 12 (m), Robert 11, Jarvis 10, Sytena M. 8, General Jackson 6, Rosannah 4, Anah 1
NEWSOM, Davenport 34, Marinda 25, Mary 72, Fredric 10, VanBuren 8, Anza C. 5 (f), Rebecca 3, Henery 1
NEWSOM, Hartwell 47*, Sarah 35, Rachel 18, Margaret 16, Daniel 14, William 10, George W. 8, Elkaney 2

Schedule Page 462

TOLLEY, Elkaney 97*
LITTLE, William 63, Elizabeth 45, Marion 17 (m), Cornelius 14, Henry 13, Elizabeth 11
KEETHLY, Sympkins 46, Martha 38, Willis 18, William R. 16, Mary A. 15, Henery R. 13, Rebecca 12, Sympkins 9, Susan M. J. 5, Ewell S. 3, Martha L. 8/12
ACRES, Andrew 43*, Mary 38, James W. 21
CLAY, Andrew 15*, Matilda 14
ROTEN, Mary 33, Rebecca 12, Elizabeth 5, Malinda 2, John 1/12
ACRES, John 69*, Rebecca 60
CLAY, Susan 10*
RHEA, Pheeby 19*, Lucinda 21
RHEA, Linsey 45 (m), Nancey 40, Elizabeth 13, Ely 10 (m), Margaret 7, James L. 4, Amey 3
THORNSBURY, Levi 29, Charlotta 27, Rebecca 6, James M. 4, William H. 1
RATLIFF, William jr. 56*, Eilzabeth 57, Katherine 19, Thomas J. 18, James L. 16, Joseph E. 15, Hammond 25
OWENS, Ann E. 4*
FORD, Mary 58, William B. 31, Ann 22, Rebecca 19
HUFFMAN, James 29, Amanda 25, Giles M. 5, Nancey T. A. 2
RATLIFF, Harrison 34*, Margaret 31, Nancey E. 9, Virginia 7, William 6, Mary J. 1
STURGEON, John 19*
CHADWELL, John A. 43, Tamsey 35, Alexandre 17, John E. 12, Nancey 10, Lavernia 8, Mary J. 5, Elizabeth 2
WOLFINGTON, Jeffery 29, Sarah A. 25, Leonidas M. 2
LANE, Austin 29, Katherine 25, William 10, Barbary 5, George 3, Solomon 1

Schedule Page 463

LANE, William 23, Sarah 2, Nancey 6, John N. 4
HELVEY, Henery 40, Miram E. 35, William M. 12, NAncey J. 10, Jacob 9, Mary 7, Susan 5, Barbary 1
SPARKS, Etheldred 34, Elben 36 (f), Martha J. 9, Margaret A. 8, Josiah 4, Mary 3

1850 Census Pike County Kentucky

SPARKS, Martha 50, Keziah 21, George L. 17
RATLIFF, Squire 36, Rosannah 31, Matilda J. 13, Andrew 10, Lavicey 8, Thomas 4, Washington 1
RATLIFF, Nathan 22, Adiline 16
DEBOARD, Ira 42, Martha 36, HArriet 17, Euphema 15, Diannah 12, Jefferson T. 11, Lavicey 8, Andrew J. 6, Colbert C. 5, Caroline 3, Marion 8/12, James F. 9/12
PEYTON, John 29*, Barbary J. 2/12
GREEN, Nancey 76*
THOMPSON, William 40, Nancey 40, Samuel 21, Albert 15, Barnabas 12
SPENCE, Stephen 26, Nancey C. 22, NAncey S. 7, Williams 4, James J. 2
MCCOY, Randolph 49, Anna 41, Malinda E. 19, Louisa 17, William E. 12, Marion 8 (m)
CECIL, Nancey 52*, Richard T. 17, Samuel M. 16
HIBBARD, John W. 28*
SMITH, Jeremiah 70, Susan 46, David 21, Fredric 17, Chaney 15, William 12, Tennesse? 9 (f), Elizabeth 7, Jeremiah 6, Milton 3, Mark 6/12
BEVINS, John 64, Mary 60, Rebecca 27, Louisa 22, Jefferson 19

Schedule Page 464

DAUGHERTY, Francis M. 23, Rhoda A. 17, Phatima 2
HURT, Absolom 47, Elizabeth 55, Mukin 17 (m), Nancey 16, Creed F. 12, Sarah 10, Absolom 7, Minerva J. 5, Synthia J. 5
HOWELL, James 60, Susannah 18, Dulaney 17 (m), Louisa 14, Harvey 6
HENKLE, William 61, Elizabeth 63
ONEY, John A. 21, Arminta 21
PINSON, Allen 65, Elizabeth 39, Eliza J. 16, Robert 13, John 10, Henery C. 8, Nancey 6, Susannah 5, Sophia 3, Malinda 2/12
SHORTRIDGE, Andrew 40, Sarah 33, Ann M. 12, Martha 11, George 10, John 9, Robert 7, Joseph 6, Jefferson 4, Levi 2
PINSON, Aron 42, Ellen 21, Harrison 1
BEVINS, James 33*, Mary 35, Mary A. 12, Margaret 9, John W. 6, Allen P. 4, Rebecca 1
PINSON, Thomas 22*
WILLIAMSON, Farrell 24, Sarah 27, Esther 3, Marion 3/12 (m)
KING, Franklin 51*, Ellen 45, Harrison 19, Andrew J. 16, Mary 12, Matilda J. 9, Franklin 6, Samuel M. 4
PATRICK, Greenbury 20*
KING, John 54, John 14, Jemima 11, Sophia 8, Barbary 5
WILLIAMSON, Hibbard 24, Mary A. 23, Barbary E. 4, Sarah 3
ARNOLD, Benjamine 56*, Elizabeth 40
NICHOLS, Elizabeth 2*
BEVINS, Lydia 52, William R. 14, Marybel 12, Richard P. R. 10, Lydia 8, Malinda 26

Schedule Page 465

BEVINS, Madison 20, Nancey 19, Sarah A. M. 4/12
KENEDAY, Harrison 18, Reecey 19 (f)
MORRIS, Ambrose 33, Mary 30, James M. 10, Nancey 8, Tenis F. 7 (m), Elizabeth 6, Louisa 3, Malinda 1

1850 Census Pike County Kentucky

PINSON, George 33, Sarah 24, Thomas B. 7, Aron H. 5, Louisa A. 3, Elizabeth 2
KENADAY, Thomas 48, Delilah 40 (f), Lavicey 18, Greenviller 15(m), Andrew 13, George H. 11, Sarah J. 10, James Q.? 7, Robert 5, Ruthey 2?
BEVINS, Thomas 35, Elizabeth 42, Lydia 14, John H. 12, Lucinda 9, Nancey J. 5, James M. 3, Pricey 1/12 (f)
WILLIAMSON, Richard 35, Susannah 28, Nancey 13, Jane 11, James W. 9, Elijah 6, John 4, Moses 1
FIELDS, Chason 25, Margaret 22
FIELDS, Preston 55, Elizabeth 55, Joseph 20, John 16, Reuben 14, Harrison 10, Elisha 9, Elijah 8
REED, Dowe 24, Judy 21, Jane 5/12
FIELDS, William 28, Frances 26, Amey 8, Jane L. 6, Parthena 5, Lucinda 1
REED, Humphrey 71, Naney 60, Mahala 21, Simon P. 17
FINKLE, Harvey 31, Sarah 31, Eveline 8, George 6, William 2, Elizabeth 1/12
BEVINS, George 42, Nancey 45, James 16, Louisa 12, Keenis? A. 8 (m), George M. D. 6, Rebecca 2
RUTHERFORD, Robert 48, Gincey 47 (f), Sarah 23

Schedule Page 466

REED, Gilbert 33, Lydia 27, Elizabeth 7, Amos A. 5, Milton A. 3
FRANCES, James 24, Lucy 25, John 5, Morgan 2, David 1/12
MEAD, Robert 36*, Mary 40, Alexandre 2
HOLT, Oma 13*
MANOR, William 24, Mary 25, James A. 2
FRANCES, William H. 54, Delilah 53, Elizabeth 17, Andrew 14
FRANCES, Elijah 21, Charrity 16, Matilda 10/12
YOUNG, Absolom 95, Susan 56, Milla 27, John J. 20, George W. 16, Perlina 10, Nancey J. 8
YOUNG, John 35, Nancey J. 16, Elzira 15, James E. 14, Elvira J. 9, George W. 7, Andrew J. 7, Elizabeth O. 5
LOWE, Nathaniel B. 39, Rebecca A. 34, Fountain B. 15, Larkin 10, Aron 7, John H. 5, George W. 4, Orrison P. 2
TAILOR, Allen 38, Jemima 41, Kelsey 16 (m), Mary 14, James 11, Arta 9, Alessa 8, Nancey J. 2, Henery F. 1/12
ALLEY, Benjamin 21, Elizabeth 22
MILLER, Timmothy 47, Mary 27, Rebecca 5, John 3, William H. 2
BLANKENSHIP, Hiram 35, Elizabeth 36, Obediah 17, Jenny 14, John 12, Daniel 9, Margaret 8, Solomon 5
FREDRIC, John 37, Pricilla 37, Sarah 16, Mary 14, Martin 12, Joseph 8, Hiram 6, Dicey 5, Nancey 3, Mary A. 6/12
FREDRIC, Nathan 21, Mary 19

Schedule Page 467

STEPLER?, John 32*, Susannah 30, Mary 12, Hiram 8, Thomas 6
JUDE, Sarah 15*
LOW, Orrison R. 42, Jane 46, James F. 21, Lawyer T. 19, Dotia A. S. 16, Orrison B. M. 10, Nancey J. 8, Perlina A. M. 6
BURGETT, John 44, Sarah 51, Nancey 26, Anna 20, Elizabeth 17, Rachel 14, John 12, Sarah 10, Moses 8

1850 Census Pike County Kentucky

BURGETT, William 24, Martha 23, Oma 3, Nancey J. 1
STEPP, Nancey 57, Moses 36, Aron 25, Nancey 22, David 21
JONES, John 39*, Sarah 30, Elizabeth 2/12
SNEED, Henery 19*
DESKINS, Rebecc 53, Harrison 16, Jackson 12
ROSA, Jareal 27 (m), Sarah 50, Lewis 13, Isaah 11, Emeline 9, Thomas 2
HENSLEY, William 30, Nancey 26, John H. 2, James L. 1
ROBERTS, Samuel 52, Matilda 29, George A. 3, John L. 2, Darcas E. 6/12
DESKINS, Lewis 18*, Martha J. 18, John W. 8/12
MILES, Emily 80 (m?)*
RUSSELL, Henery 25*
TAILOR, Jessee 45, Frances 55, Levi 16, Greenville 14, Jackson 12
HENSLEY, Aron 21, Martha 22, Elizabeth 6/12
HENSLEY, Abraham 25, Jane 25, Lorenzo 10/12
STARE, Samuel 44, Nancy M. 39, LEvi 23, William 20, Rebecca 10, Nancy 7, Henery M. 6, Lydia 4, Samuel S. 2
PRAGMORE, Mary 40, Louisa 4
MUNSEY, Levi 45
DAVIS, John 37*, Nancey 21, Mary 12, James 9, John 6, William 4, George 2, Sarah 10/12

Schedule Page 468

MCQUIN?, Andrew R. 51*
COLLINS, George 51*, Sarah 22, George 19
RIGHT, Elizabeth 60*
ADAIR, Mary 7*
ADAIR, Samuel 39, Nancey 35, Perlina 13, Katherine 11, James 9, William 6, Mary 3, John 2
MUNSEY, William 45, Margaret 45, Thomas 21, James 16, Daniel 13, Richard 12, William 7
HARDIN, John 65, Dicey 25, Harvery 15, Amanda 11, Vicey 7
DESKINS, James 28*, Isabella 29, Lorenzo 8, Nancey 6
BLANKENSHIP, William 25*
ALLEY, Paul 51, Rebecca 44, Peeter 24, Elizabeth 17, Thomas 10?, Sarah 8, Rebecca 4
EVANS, Lowery 30, Hannah 39, Francis M. 13, Elizabeth 10, Susan 9, Martha A. 7, Hasting 6 (m)
CHAPMAN, Thomas 69*, Mary 49, Thomas 20, Andrew J. 11, James B. 8
LAWSON, Sarah 24*
SLATER, William 38, Elizabeth 36, Josephine 11, James 8, Martha 6, Mary 6, Virginia 9/12
FURRELL, Clay 29*, Mary 21, Martha A. 2, Elizabeth 1
RUNION, Lewis 19*
MAINOR, Rhoda 36, William F. 16, John H. 14, Elizabeth 8, James M. 6, James E. 1
MAINOR, Edward 52, Katherine 45, Mark 16
MAINOR, William 26, Andrew 6, Malinda 3
WILLIAMSON, Moses 20, Elizabeth 18

Schedule Page 469

WILLIAMSON, John 28, Nancey 26, Jerremiah 8, James 6, Jane 4, Matilda 2, Jonah 17
MILLARD, Elijah 25, Mary J. 22, Abraham 2, Hiram H. 3/12

1850 Census Pike County Kentucky

WILLIAMSON, Benjamin 70*, Susannah 40, Freeman 14, Hammond 13, Eva 11, Julius 7
LOWER, Katherine 45?*, Eva 80
HARRIS, Thomas H. 25, Rebecca 20, John C. 3, Emily A. 1
REED, Hiram 43, Lucy 39, George 19, Johnethan 18, Hannah 16, Susannah 13, Humphrey 11, Amos 9, Miram 7, Lydia 5, Willis 3, MAhala 1
REED, Reuben 21, Mary A. 18
HARRIS, Thomas 34, Hellen 36, Mary 5, Henery C. 3
HARRIS, James 30, Margaret 20, Thomas 2, Josephine 8/12
SLATER, Mary 28, Narcissus 5 (f), William 2
SMITH, Aly 38 (m)*, Sarah 32, Mary 15, Charlotta 11, John 10, Hawkins F. 8, James M. 7, Syrus 5, Henery 2
WALLACE, Solomon 30, Lucinda 25, Martha 7, Richard 5, Katherine 4, James 3, Apperson 1, Sarah 3/12
MCGINIS, Leonidas 19*, Ira 18
FERRILL, Richard 19*
GOOSLING, Hammond 23, Jenny 19, Barnabas 6/12
MAINARD, Alvis 42*, Harriet 42, Mary A. 20, Matilda J. 17, Lavicey 12, Andrew J. 10, John B. 9, Sarah 7, Alvis 6, William 4
TAILOR, Syrus 37*
MAINARD, Moses 34*, Lavicey 26, Rosannah 6, Matilda J. 3, Sarah 8/12

Schedule Page 470

TAILOR, Mary A. 10*
BROWNING, William 48, Sarah 45, Francis 22, Mary M. 18, Adaline 12?, Elias 12, John B. 9, Susan 5, Eveline 2
MCCOY, Samuel 66*, Nancey A. 57, Jane 17
WILLIAMSON, Jonah 16*, Louisa 15, Jerremiah 11
MCCOY, Pierce 25, Malinda 17, Martha 2, Pricey 1/12 (f)
MAINARD, Henderson 30, Lucinda 29, Tabitha 7, Elizabeth 5, Caroline 4, Semanthia 3, Lewis 1/12
MCCOY, Allen 25*, Elizabeth 23, Sylvestre 7, Esther 6, Jane 3, Henson 2
BALL, Ens. 20 (m)*
STAFFORD, Compton 45, Ellen 35, Sarah A. 12, Harrison 11, Thomas 7, Montville 5, Lavicey 1
SANSOM, John jr. 38, Perlina 38, Elias 13, John C. 11, Nancey 9, Hiram 7, Sarah A. 5, Elizabeth E. 3, Causbey C. 1 (f)
SANSOM, John sr. 90, Elizabeth 70, Riley 19
FARRELL, Moses 25, Jane 19, Barbary 12, Martha J. 8/12
HATFIELD, Joseph 63, Martha 63, Pheeby 33, Joseph 26, Smith 21, McGinnis 17
HATFIELD, Thomas 24, Elizabeth 19, Nancey 2/12
HENSLEY, Stephen M. 21, Pheeby 23, Sarah 3, Karless 1 (m)
CAREY, John 35, Barbary 25, Benjamine 8, Mary A. 7, William N. 5, James K. P. 3, Joseph 6/12
HATFIELD, George 46, NAncey 35, Ransom 20, James 19, Elexius 17, Andrew 14, Johnson 12, Bozwell 10, George 9, Jerremiah 7, Lydia 5, Wallace 3, Nancey 3/12

1850 Census Pike County Kentucky

Schedule Page 471

HATFIELD, John 33*, Mary A. 24
NEW, David 19*, John 12
CRABTREE, Rachell 15*
HATFIELD, Valentine 28, Mary 26, Leah 2, Albina 1 (m)
HATFIELD, Jeremiah 41, Rachel 40, NAncey 18, Hellen 17, Mary 14, Ephraim 12, Lavicey 10, John 8, George 6, Jacob 5, Elizabeth 2, Anna 95
KENADAY, Andrew 48, Margaret 45, Ephraim 22, Charles 20, Pricey 16, Rachel 14, Pheeby 12?, Joseph 10, Elexius 2
KENEDAY, Aly 25 (m)*, Christena 17, Mary 1
WITT, Mary 15?*
RUTHERFORD, Eliot 29, Isabella 23, Eliza 2, Louis 7/12, Louisa 19
DAVIS, Henery T. 39, Rebecca 45, William G. 18, Francis E. 17, John M. 15?, Thomas C. 14, Nancey A. 12, Henery S. 8, Joseph M. 2
ROBINET, Nathan 56, Nancey 61, Pheebee 22, Mary 18, Nancey 15
STAFFORD, Flemming 36, Elizabeth 28, Elexius 8, John T. 6, Phebe? 5, Hammond 3, Compton 2, Lewis 3/12
EVANS, Farrell 66, Pheeby 50, Hammond 25, Pheebe 19
COLEMAN, Peeter 35, Mahala 26, Sarah J. 6, David W. 5, Louisa O. 4, Abigal J. 3, Daniel H. 1, Jacob R. 4/12
HATFIELD, Madison 22, Nancey 21, Harrison 2, Fulton A. 1/12

Schedule Page 472

DANIELS, Rachel 27, Lewis 7, Floyd 5, Richard 4, Comfort 2 (f), Margaret 1, Elizabeth 6/12, Elizabeth 60
MOUNTS, Elijah 41, Comfort 35, Charles 15, Sarah 13, Susannah 10, Nancey 8, Asbury 5, Charlotta 3, Ellen 2
MOUNTS, Michael 30, Matilda 30, Harrison 9, Lavicey 8, Jackson 6, James 4, David 1
STEEL, John 28, Martha 25, Raphael 4, Margaret 3, Nancey 2
DANIELS, Richard 32, Margaret 26, Jenny 11, David 10, William 7, Samuel 4, George 1
PRATER, William 27, Sarah 25, Mary E. 11, Pleasant M. 8, Vicey 6, Mary A. 4, John H. 3, James 2, William H. 3/12
BLANKENSHIP, John 30, Milla 33, Lucinda 13, Jenny 12, John W. 9, Francis M. 7, Sarah 5, Mary 3, Ezekiel 8/12
BLANKENSHIP, Priestley 29, Mary 32, Dicey 13, James A. 10, William W. 8, Rachel 6, Bird 4, Richard 2, Mary 4/12
BLANKENSHIP, Ezekiel 37, Anna 27, Olover 12, Elizabeth 10, Mary 8, Nancey 6, Alexandre 3, Priestley 1/12
MCCOY, Richard 50
MCCOY, William 25, Lucinda 30, William H. 15, Silkerk 12 (m), Amanda 9, Louisa 7, James 6, Lucinda 2, Linsey 3/12 (m)

1850 Census Pike County Kentucky

Schedule Page 473

GIPSON, Buck 20*
MCCOY, Barbary 19*, Sarah 1
PATTEN, Daniel 19, Mary 23, Emeline 3, William 1
BLANKENSHIP, William 25, Judy 21, Henery 3, JAcob 1
MITCHUM, William A. 30, Susannah 35, Hiram 7, David 5, Reece? 3, Matilda 1
LANE, William 56, Abigal 57, David 18, Marybee 16
BAKER, Elisha 48*, Sarah 45, Thomas 18, William 15, Edward 13, James 13, Matilda 12, Hicey? 5 (f), Elizabeth 3, Calvin 21, Andrew 21
FRAZER, John 45, Sarah 44, David 15, Boyle 12, Matilda 14, Stump 8
MCCOY, Mary 35, Frances 14, Nancey 12, Margaret 8, James 5, William 8/12
SLONE, Franklin 21, Margaret 18
LAINE, John 21*, Elizabeth 20, Mary J. 4, Malinda 8/12
MCCOY, Eliza J. 2*
CHURCH, Joel 36, Nancey 29, Abigal 11, William 8, Sarah 4, Jacob 7, David 1
COLEMAN, Curtis 40, Matilda 36, Daniel 13, Mary 11
ESTEP, Isaac 55, Charlotta 45, Alfred 18, Andrew J. 14, Martin V. B. 14, Charlotta 10, William H. 5
ESTEP, Sampson 28, Mahala 23, Bethina 2, Benjamine 1
MCCOY, Benjamine 27*, John R. 10, Ellen J. 5, Ulysses 4
PRATER, Letta 24*, Daniel 3, James E. 2, Lynsee 1 (m)
CHARLES, John 61*, Nancey 45
MCCOY, John 11*
WILLSON, Henery 25, Sarah 22, James H. 3, Jenny 1

Schedule Page 474

CARTER, Henery 55*, Patience 50, Rachel 13
CAMPBELL, Edward 16*, Mary 12
ESTEP, Ellen 30, Joseph 3, Emanuel 1
CARTER, Charles 36, Rhoda 25, George 1
SMITH, Henery 22*
CARTER, Elizabeth 25*
MCCOY, Nancey 11*
CARTER, John 33, Hesther 26, Henery 5, Louiza 2
COLEMAN, Abigal 29, Mary J. 6, Tolbert 6/12
CHARLES, Michael 58, Elizabeth 49, Pricey 13, Elizabeth 16, Mary 11, Nancey 9
DOTTSON, John 23, Sarah 19, Rebecca 4/12
WOLFORD, John 63*, Mary 50, Daniel 22
CHARLES, John 21*
ROBINET, Nathan 27, Alice 25, Nathan 6, William 4, Phebee 2
ROBINET, William 25, Mary 23, Nansey 6 (f), Daniel 4, Peeter 2
MCCOY, Acy H. 23, Martha 20
CLINE, William T. 24, Margaret 26, Lavicey 2, Jacob 3/12
WOLFORD, Fredric 24, Margaret 18, Johnithan 1/12
WOLFORD, George 33, Surrey 20 (f), Daniel 14, George 11, Mary 6, John 2, Ellen 1

1850 Census Pike County Kentucky

CHARLES, David 25, Rachel 23, Pricey 15, George 7
COLEMAN, Isaac 34, Mary 34, William F. 14, Elexius 11, Joseph 10, Moses 6, Daniel 4, Doctor L. 3, Pheeby 2, Richard D. 6/12
DOTTSON, Jordon 46, Mary 40, Reuben 20, Elijah 17, Sarah 15, George 13, Rachel 11, Elizabeth 9, Jordan 7, Mary 5, Ransom 2

Schedule Page 475

COLEMAN, Daniel 63, Sarah 62, Matilda 15
MAY, James 22, Sarah A. 19, William J. 5/12
COLEMAN, Moses 23, Louiza 17
COLEMAN, Daniel 24, Sarah 18, Curtis 1
WILSON, Abraham 30, Rachel 33, George W. 6, Reuben 5, Elizabeth 2
SCARBURY, Robert 20, Mary 20, Elizabeth 6/12
SCARBURY, David 52, Sarah 46, Thomas 18, William J. 16, John H. 14, Nancey 12, Jacob 9, Sarah 6, Ollivia 4
HATFIELD, Richard 29, Verlina 24, William A. 5, Isabella 2, Thomas New 16
HATFIELD, Ephraim 37, Pheeby 32, James 15, Joseph 13, Martha 10, Thompson 8, Mary 7, Sarah 4, Mathew 2
MAY, David 31, Amanda M. 25, Nancey 10, James M. 8, Milla A. 6, Amanda V. 4, Leah 2, Emeline 10/12
MAY, Daniel 28, Mary 24, Sarilda J. 3, Elizabeth 2, James F. 4/12
MUSIC, Elevius 22, Mary 21
HATFIELD, William 41*, Sarah 35, John F. 17
DAVIS, Zatto 14 (m)*, James W. 9
HATFIELD, Farrell 39, Judy 33, Marietta 11, Sophia 9, Marion 7 (m), Lewis 4, Smith 1
DYLES, John 35, Sarah 30, George W. 15, James P. 13, Moses 9, Elizabeth 7, Martha 5, Andrew 3, Mary 58
BLACKBURN, Hutson 38, Katherine 33, Nancey 14, Farley 12, Jenny 11, Henderson 9, Causley 7 (f), Jerremiah 4, Sarah 1, Anna 1/12

Schedule Page 476

HATFIELD, Richard 29*, Perlina 25, William 6, Isabella 2
MEW?, Thomas 15*
MAY, Daniel 65, Nancey 60
MAY, Elizabeth 34, Henderson 18
BALL, Moses 63, Elizabeth 47, William 20, Martin 18, Marinda 16, George 12, Pricey 7, Wesley 4
BALL, James 31, Nancey 22, Mary J. 1
MAY, Mary A. 28, Washington 17, William J. 15, Harvey 12
RANION, Mitchell 20, Margaret 20, Lewis 1
BALL, Jessee 49, Rebecca 36, Moses 18, Silas 17, John F. 16, Melvina 12, Syrenna 10, Malissa J. 7, Almeda 3, George W. 1/12
MAY, James M. 24, Nancey 25, Telitha 6, Moses 4, William J. 2
VARNUM, John 34, Anna 33, William A. 15, Mary 14, Alexandre 12, Henry C. 9, Cela A. 6, Flemming 5, James 2, Melvin 2/12

1850 Census Pike County Kentucky

BLACKBURN, John 34, Lydia 33, Nancey 14, Jenny 13, Henery 12, Gilbert 8, Rebecca 5, Lydia 3, William 1
WHITT, David 47, Margaret 40, Mary 21, William 19, Charles 15, Sela 13, Orrena 11, John 9, Elizabeth 7, Eliza 4, Sarah A. 2
MAY, William 50, Susannah 50, Rebecca 25, Mary 22, Joseph 18, Alexandre 16, William C. 14, Sarah 13, Martha 80, Sarah 75, Joseph 1

Schedule Page 477

BLACKBURN, James 33, Margaret 27, Granville 9, George 8, Eliza 7, Esther 5, Isom 3
TAILOR, William A. 44, Sarah 36, Lydia 17, Tabitha 14, Alvis J. 12, John D. 9, Pricey 7 (f), Jane 4, Sarah A. 2
RUNION, Moses 22, Eliza 18
RUNION, William 36, Nancey 31, Greenville L. 12, Lucretia P. 10, Mary E. 8, James H. 5, Sarah A. 1
RUNION, Henery 62, Hannah 60
TAILOR, Mary 21, Allen 3, July A. 1
HUNT, Moses 24, Rebecca 24, Nancey 2, Allison? 2 (m)
HUNT, Thomas 50, Clarissa 30, Thomas 17, Henery 15, Maria 14, Sarah 13, Penelope 12, John 10, Franklin 9, William 6, Pheebe 2, Lavicey 3/12, Judy 6
MCCOY, William 27, Sarah 22, James A. 6, Lavicey 4, Walter 3, Albert 3/12
RUNION, Adron 49, Jane 41, Asa H. 19, John C. 17, Arminta 15, Lavicy 14, Mary 12, Elizabeth 9, Thomas W. 7, William A. 4, Charrity 3, Adron 2/12
MCCOY, Uriah 24, Elizabeth 21
RUTHERFORD, Reuben 52, Mary 47, Barsheba 15, John 14, Matilda 12, Lucy 9, Emeline 8, Lydia 6, Reuben 4, Andrew 2

Schedule Page 478

LOW, James 27, Mary A. 24, William 3
LOW, Aron 75, Sarah 75
FRANCISCO, Jacob 60, Jane 53, Nancey 39, Synthia 26, George 24, John 23, Evans 22, Franklin 17, Rachel 15, Oscar 13, Patrick 11, Saminel 9 (m)
BURRIS, James 21, Isabella 19, George W. 8/12
BLACKBURN, Jacob 20*, Elizabeth 17, Nancey J. 2
STAFFORD, Nancey 50?*
SCOTT, Daniel 35, Nancey 34, William C. 13, Lavicey 11, James M. 9, Thomas 7, John H. 6, Elizabeth 5, Andrew 3, Apperson 1
SCOTT, Thomas 25, Lavenia 20, Elizabeth 6, Nancey 4, William 2, John 1
FARLER, Jessee 22, Elizabeth A. 20, William T. 1/12
MURPHEY, Alexandre 23, Keziah 22, John 1, Lucinda 15
MCCOY, John 45, Margaret 35, William T. 19, Samuel 17, Mary J. 15, Pheebe 13, Jemima 12, Addison 10, Lucinda 8, Mary 6, Daniel 4, Ellen 1
FARLER, Samuel 26, Matilda 28, Granville 11, Harriel 9, Mary A. 7, Aly 5 (m), Nancey 3, John F. 2, William 8/12
MCCOY, William 39*, Mary 30, Elizabeth 12, Pleasant 10, James H. 9, Rachel J. 7, Careless 5 (m), Anderson 3, Robert 1
BURRESS, Rachel 73*, Daniel 40

1850 Census Pike County Kentucky

BURRESS, Elizabeth 53, Harrison 14
VARNEY, Alexandre 53, Susannah 53, Madison 20, Asa 17, Matilda 14

Schedule Page 479

VURNEY, Andrew 30, Nancey 28, Alexandre 10, Mary A. 8, Louis J. 5, Perlina C. 4, Harrison 2, Henery 1/12
RUTHERFORD, Joseph 54*, Milla 40, Spicey 19 (f), Diannah 18, Elizabeth 14, Sarepta 12, Judy 11, Nancey 8, Joseph 6, Milla 3, Richard 2
COZEE, Judy 78*
COZEE, Booker 31, Mary 31, Sarah 9, Orrison 7, Judy 5, Nancey 3, Richard 5/12
STANLEY, Moses 50, Ellen 47, William 20, Nancey A. 18, Sarah E. 16, Joseph 14, George H. 11, Amerrica 8, John O. 6, Mahala 3, Rebecca 3/12
CHAPMAN, Edward 38, Elizabeth 24, Thomas 7, Moses 6, Jane 5, John 4, Robert 3, Clark 7/12
HUNT, Mary 23, Judy 5, Rebecca 2
GOOSLING, John 29, Synthia A. 17, Jessee 6/12
WHITE, Bethena 38 (B), Thomas M. 9, Juley A. 2, Joseph 1, James T. 14, Charles 10, Nancey 12
SLATTEN?, Charles 64, Nancey 50, Richard 25, Joseph 22, Arminta 18, Pietey 15, Booker 13, Avery 10, Judy 8
RUTHERFORD, James 58*, Sarah 55, Roxsalena 22, Sarah 20, Mary 10, Mourning? 13, Margaret 12
LAWSON, Amanda 18*
FREDRIC, John 19*
SMITH, Jacob 28, Lucinda 26, Sarah A. 10, Elizabeth A. 8, William H. 6, Cela J. 4, Melvin 2, Nancey 1

Schedule Page 480

WILLIAMSON, James 27*, Mary 24, Louisa 6, Amey 5, Charlotta 2
MILLER, Charlotta 23*
BLACKBURN, William 66, Elizabeth 35, George 15, Thomas 10
SCOTT, Axton 36*, Ruth 29, Sarah A. 11, Mitchell 8, Rebecca 6, Emeline 4, Peeter 2
SHEPPARD, Louvina 16*
SHEPPARD, Sarah 45, Jane 20, Elizabeth J. 1
WHITT, Jesse 45, Mary 45, Nancey 17, Eda 10, Louisa 7
WILLIAMSON, Benjamin 33, Mary 32, Nancey 13, Perlina 10?, John B. C. 9, Sarah A. 7, James M. 5, Hammond 3, Benjamine 1
WEST, John 41, Mary 40, Uri? 16 (f), Violetta 14, John T. J. 11, Thomas F. 9, Amos A. 7, William J. P. 5
WEST, Greenville 22, Sela 17
GRIFFEY, George 21, Nancey 18
SMITH, Henery 26, Lucretia 17, Malinda 2, James M. 3/12
SMITH, James 24, America 20, John 1
SMITH, Jesse 25, Esther 18
SMITH, John 37, Eliza 24, Alexandre 6, NAncey 4, Findlay 2 (m), Mary 12
SMITH, Henery 33, Mahala 31, George H. 12, Sarah A. 10, John W. 8, Hiram J. 6, Nancey 4, Joseph 3, Eliza 2, Cressa 8/12
SMITH, John 63, Nancey 60, Isaac 22, Isaac 18, Cristena 31, July A. 2
HARRISON, George 33, Dicey 25, Daniel 4, Lorenzo 2

1850 Census Pike County Kentucky

Schedule Page 481

CHARLES, Fredric 44, Elizabeth 39, Thomas 20, David 18, Greenbury 17, Andrew J. 16, Harvey G. 14, Lavicey 12, Nancey 8, Elizabeth 6, Fredric 4, Allen C. 2
MCCOY, Thomas 50, Nancey 42, William 23, Lockey 20, Samuel 19, Elijah 16, Elizabeth 14, Nancey 12, Leannah 10, Rebecca 7, John 4
MAINER, Allen 27*, Nancey 38, Colbert Q. 7, Louisa J. 9, Thomas J. 4, David A. 4, Nancey 1
CAIN, Mary E. 17*, Olover W. 14
FLETCHER, John S. 45, Sarah 32, Barbary? 14, Joseph 12, Selah? 9, James W. 7, Louisa C. 5, Colbert C. 3, John 1
MCCOY, Joseph 55, Mary 50
CHARLES, John jr. 23, Elizabeth 26, George W. 2, Thomas J. 8/12
GOFF, Edward 46, Isabella 45, John 26, William 21, Charlotta 16, Elizabeth 13, Isabella 11, Martin V. B. 10, Edward 4
GOFF, George 18, Nancey 18
ROBERTSON, Samuel 28, Synthia 26, Mary J. 7, Rebecca 5, Leandre 3 (m), Amanda A. 2
DINSMORE, James 23, Mary M. 22
CONNOWAY, James 29, Lucinda 20, Sarah 2, Noah 6/12
CONNOWAY, John 32, Mary 32, Charlotta 13, Sophia 10, William 9, Lydia J. 5, Thomas 3
CHARLES, George 87, Charlotta 65
RAINS, John 45, Sarah 44, John 20, Charles D. 19, Charlotta 17, Christopher 14, Elizabeth 13, Isabella 10, Nancy 9, Martha 8

Schedule Page 482

CHANY, Charles 23, Elizabeth 19, John 8/12
LANE, Marideth 39, Margaret 35, Thomas J. 11, James M. 10, Martha 7, Henderson 4, Sarah 3, John N. 10/12
PHILIPS, Elizabeth 63
MURPHEY, Gabriel 25, Frances 20, Lorenzo D. 1, William 12
PHILIPS, Thompson 35, Anna 32, Milla 15, Harper 13, Zachariah 10, Elizabeth 7, Nancey 5, Sarah 3, Frances 3/12
WILLIAMS, William 65, Mary 58, Mary 20
HESS, Mary 34, Elizabeth 16, Milla 14, William P. 6, Nancey J. 4
SLONE, Lucinda 35?, Preston 21, Jessee 18, Speede 16 (m), Snode 14 (m), Ellison 12, Causbey 10 (f), Dawson 6, Shadrac 2
PHILIPS, Zachariah 24, Clarinda 22, John W. 3?, Elizabeth 2, Francis M. 1
SMITH, Martin 50, Nancey 44, Nancey 16, William 14, Davidson 12, Marion 10, Colbert C. 8, Martin 5
SMITH, George 22, Elizabeth 21
SMITH, Johnethan 24, Levaniah 20
WHIT, Henery 36, Matilda 32, Nancey A. 14, Selecia E. 12, Isaac M. 11, John H. 5, Mary J. 3, Samuel M. 3/12
SMITH, Isaac 30, Mary A. 20, Willburn 12, Curtis 10, Sarah 7, Elizabeth A. 6, Matilda J. 4, William N. 1
PHILLIPS, Jessee 39, Nancey 46, William 15, John 13, Sarah 11, Franklin 9, Telitha J. 7

1850 Census Pike County Kentucky

Schedule Page 483

DAUGHERTY, Hiram 46, Keziah 45, Hiram M. 17, Daniel J. 15, Keziah V. 13, Marian L. 10, Nancey J. 7, William H. H. 5
STUMP, George 33, Elizabeth A. 32, James H. 13, Mary J. 7, Rhoda M. 4, Clark T. 3, Victoria A. 4/12
BEVINS, Joseph 38, Mary 37, Sela A. 16, Orrena 15, Rebecca 11, Thomas J. 6, John W. 4, James G. 1, George W. 17
WILLIAMS, John W. 28, JEmima 25, Louisa E. 6, Martha R. 4, Orpha A. E. 2, Jefferson K. 2/12
WILLIAMS, Achilles 24, Nancey 20, William J. 2
COLLINS, Andrew 26, Elizabeth 23, Amanda J. 4, William M. 2
MAINER, Thomas 21, Sarah 23, Richard K. 2, Elizabeth 1
MAINER, David 60, Margaret 30, George W. 17, Jane 14, Decatur 6
SMITH, Isaac 48, Elizabeth 50, Jacob 38, Martin 24, Sarah 22, Callihan 17, John 16, LAvinia 14, Eda 11
GANNON?, Barnabas 27, Elizabeth A. 23, Johnethan 8, Martha J. 2
GANNON?, Daniel 56, Orpah 56, Johnethan 23, Elizabeth 21, Sarah A. 13
ALLISON, James 24*, Mary 16
GANNON?, Robert 1*
WILLIAMSON, Anna 36, Pricey 18 (f), Abner T. 16, James F. 14, Sarah A. 10
WILLIAMSON, John 69, Sarah 65
WILLIAMSON, John 35, Anna 35, Hiram 14, Mary 12
WILLIAMS, James Y. 35, Perlina 32, Gordon F. 13, William H. 10, Achilles M. W. 8, Victoria M. 5, Nancy A. 4, James M. 1

Schedule Page 484

SHORTRIDGE, John 34*, Sarah 35, George W. 13, Emeline 11, William 9, Sarilda 7, Nancey J. 6, Thomas B. 3, Esther 1
DAVIS, Esther 59*
STACEY, James T. 29, Malinda 24, Rebecca 9, Jemima 6, William 4, Lavicey 3, Mary E. 8/12
JOHNSON, Barnabas 74*, Barbary 71
SLONE, Samuel 65* (B)
CARTER, Morgan 22, Mary 24, Telitha 3, William 2, Mary 1/12
MEAD, William 33*, Barbary 24, Mary 7, Elizabeth 5, Barbary 3, Thomas 2
LEEDY, Randolph 21*
ADAMS, Margaret 18*
PINSON, Jarrett 65*, Dilla 27, Elizabeth 18
WALTERS, Nancey 38*
ADAMS, Milla 15*
JONES, Johnethan 70, Keziah 60, John 25
COLLINS, Margaret 30*, John 8
JONES, Decind? 13 (f)*, Sophia 6, Keziah 3, Henery 30
MAINOR, Marcus 58, Charity 57, Elizabeth 25, William 22, Susannah 18, Tenessee 14
RHEA, James 33, Mary 36, Sarah 11, Nancey 9, Edward 7, Jerremiah 6, Joseph 5, William 2
FRANCIS, John 28, Malinda 26, Allen 4, Elizabeth 3, Susannah 1/12
MAINOR, Moses 35, Chlora 28, Elizabeth 10, Delilah 8, Charritey 6, William 2
MAINOR, Edward 26, Amia 24, Charrity 5, Elizabeth 3, John 2

1850 Census Pike County Kentucky

Schedule Page 485

SICK, James 27, Sarah 29, William H. 7, Elizabeth 6, Charrity 4, Mary 2
LACKINS, John D. 21, Lydia 23, Susannah 1
LACKINS, John 58, Elizabeth 48, William 26, Jacob 22, Nancey 16, Moses 13, Susannah 12, Joseph 9, Elizabeth 6
SMITH, Charles 23, Sarah 20, Crittinden 1
MAINOR, Christopher 36, Eva 34, Barnabus 13, George W. 11, Stephen 10, John 8, Elisha 6, Rebecca 4, Diannah 2, James 1
DYLES, Absolom 40, Nancey 44, Tabitha 18, Elvirey 16, Mary 14, Moses 12, Barnabus 10, Elizabeth 8, Nancey 4, Edward 2
MAINOR, Lewis 30*, Jane 23, Amaria 4, Alfred 2
YOUNG, Nancey 24*
FINDLAY, Nancey 56?*, Samuel 21, Elvira 19
MEAD, Margaret 28*, Tamsey 8 (f)
ROBBINET, John 25*, James M. 6, John W. 1
PINSON, Hiram 19*
DAVIS, John 36, Rebecca 25, William H. 9, Mary A. 5, James H. 4, Elizabeth 2
MAINOR, Stephen 33, Mary 32, James 11, Nancey 9, Rebecca 7, Mary A. 6, Leannah 4, Sarah 2
MAINOR, James 77, Rebecca 56, Jarrett 17, Eva 16
BLACKBURN, Hatson 53, Mary 53, Lucinda 17, Allen 14, Mahala 25, Willburn 22, Mary A. 3
BLACKBURN, George 28, Sarah 24, Moses 6, George W. 3, Wesley 1

Schedule Page 486

BLACKBURN, Daniel 30, Nancey 22, Lavicey 4, Willburn 2
JUSTACE, William 23, Mary A. 31, Madison 8, James A. 1
HINKLE, Lorenzo D. 33, Mary P? 30, Thomas J. 2
TAILOR, William 40, Nancey 37, Elizabeth 18, Nathan 15, Henery 14, James 12, John 10, Rebecca 8, Hiram 6, Louisa M. 2, Sarah J. 6/12
MAINOR, Benjamine 34*, Elizabeth 25, Elvina 9, John D. 8, Rebecca A. 7, Amos L. 5, Esther M. 2, William H. 8/12, Lucretia 19
MULLENS, James 21*
JACKSON, Hawkins 30*, Elizabeth 30, Sarilda J. 4, William J. 2, Isaac E. 4/12
KEETH, Norman T. 12*
JACKSON, James M. 27, Maomi 35, Martin G. 4
SKATH?, Telitha 49, John 23, Elizabeth 21, Archibald 17, Mary A. 14, Levi 12, Hezekiah 9, James 7
COLLINSWORTH, Moses 40*, Mariaret 40 (f), Mary 20, Thomas 18, Ammariah 15, Nancey 13, John 11, Susannah 9, Lydia 7, William J. 5, Joseph 2
WILLIAMSON, Peeter 35*
RUNION, Henery 29, Mary 25, Alfred 6, Calvary 4, Alpha 2, Henery 1
SMITH, William 28, Marinda 23, Madisen 3, Raleigh 2, Joseph 3/12
MORRISON, Mary 50, Benjamine 20, Thomas 18, John 16, Mary 13, Sarepta 10
NICHOLS, Elizabeth 38, Flemming 23, Louisa 17, Lavinia 14, Serenia? 12, Hiram 9, Greenville 7

1850 Census Pike County Kentucky

Schedule Page 487

MATHES, Thomas 61*, Synthia 60
MORRISON, Raleigh 22*
BEVINS, Hiram K. 33, Leenia 40, Martin D.W.C. 13, John J. 11, Layfayett A. 9, Winfield P. 7, Mary E. 5, Montville 3, Esther J. 1
COMPTON, James 64, Mary 56
MILLS, William 45, Mary 49, Columbus 16, George 14
THOMPSON, William 23, America 18, Andrew 1
BLANKENSHIP, Riley 35, Nancey 25, Amanda M. 7, Martha J. 5, John M. 3, William A. 1
DEAN, James R. 24, Job 65, Margaret 51, Solomon 15, William 12, Jefferson 12, Thomas 9, Josephine 9
STRUTTEN, Solomon 35*, Nancy 35, Hiram 38
CASSADAY, James 25*
MCGUIRE, James B. 14*
ELKINS, William T. 22, Elizabeth 21, Arminta J. 8/12
JACKSON, Elizabeth 59, Robert 12
TAILOR, John 35, Mary 30, Elizabeth 6, Eveline 5, Henery 4, Alexandre 2
CECIL, Samuel 39, Mary J. 23, Albert S. 3, Thomas M. 9/12
LITTON, James 55, Mary 39, John T. 10, Margaret E. 7, Augustus W. 5
AUCTIER, George W. 30*, Nancey 34, Mary 10, Emeline 8, Martha R. 6, Samuel M. 4, Amanda A. 2, William B. 9/12
HALE, John 17*
MAINER, James 28, Sophia 27, Isabella 10, George T. 9, Unis 7 (m), Martin W. 6, Jemima E. 2
ELKINS, James 47, Elizabeth 43, Rhoda J. 18, Allisa A. 15, John H. 16, Charles A. 13, Louisa A. 10, James H. 8, Lorenzo D. 6, Samuel J. 3

Schedule Page 488

BALL, Jessee 25*, Jane 23, William B. 2, James T. 2/12
KEETH, Louisa E. 10*
LASLEY, Martin 42*, Sarah 29, Thomas J. 8, John W. 6, Rebecca E. 4, Amos S. S. 5/12, Jemima 49, Esther 47
MILAM, Esther 25*
PORTER, Joseph 30, Mary A. 27, Amanda 11, Drury 7, Mary J. 4, Arminta 2
WALKER, Henery W. 19, Ona 39
LASLEY, Allen 57*, Elizabeth 56
LEE, Sarah A. 13*
MAY, Thomas P. 34*, Elizabeth M. 26, Synthia 7, Allen J. 5, Mary T. 2, Sarah 9/12
BURRIS, Marion T. 22*
LASLEY, Pharmer 47, Mary J. 37, Robert W. 18, John E. 17, James K. 15, Esther M. 13, Addison N. 12, Elizabeth 10, Feenis F. 8 (f), Samuel 4, Victoria A. 2
LASLEY, James H. 28, Mary J. 24, Nancey M. 5, Amos P. 4, Thomas J. 2
CLARK, Edmond 49*, Malani 43 (f), Delilah 25, Daniel R. 18, Andrew J. 15, William 13, Reuben 10, Lydia 8
KING, Milla 6*
ADAMS, William D. 75, Mahala 35, John T. 12, William B. 10, Robert C. 7, Henery E. 4, Thomas R. 2/12

1850 Census Pike County Kentucky

ETTER, Henery 53, Nancey 46, Sarah F. 20, Elizabeth A. 16, William H. 13, John H. 11, Nancey K. 8, Emory D. 6
SCOTT, John 36, Mary 35, William M. 15, Matilda J. 13, Andrew J. 9, Henery A. 7, Barbary 5, Elizabeth 3, Nancey P. 6/12

Schedule Page 489

SCOTT, William 64*, Elizabeth 63
STEEL, Henery 25*
BLACKBURN, William 25, Rebecca 22, Barnabas 5, Peyton 4, Andrew 2
KANES, Jackson A. 35, Charlotta 32, Sarah 10, walter 9, Richard A. 7, Martha 5, Syrena 2
STRUTTON, Harry 43, Martha 41, Nancey A. 20, Richard 18, Mary J. 16, Muldon N. 14 (m), Harvey 12, Tandey 10 (m), Henery 8, Laviney 4, Lucinda R. 1
STRUTTON, Hiram 38, Rhoda 35, William 14, Alexandre 9, James H. 7, Jane 5, Margaret 4, Una 5/12
MCGUIRE, William 24, Jane 23, John W. 6, William P. 3, Elizabeth 1, Sarah 22
GRIFFET, John 100, Nancey 60, Rachel 22
SCOTT, Evans 28, Martha 25, William W. 7, Henery C. 3, Anna 2
PINSON, Henery 70*, Mary 46, Russell 13, Malissee 15, Anna 9
SMITH, Tempa 45*
BLACKBURN, Peyton 34, Malinda 24, John 3, George 2
SPARKS, Richard 24, Mary 21, Susannah 4/12
JOHNSON, William 48, Nancey 36, Joseph 21, Nealey 18, Margaret 13, Sarah 11, Adelaid 9 (f), Elizabeth 7, George 5, Amanda J. 1
SCOTT, Andrew 41, Margaret 36, James H. 15, John 12, Henderson 9
PINSON, John 38, Synthia 39, James T. 10, Moses W. 8, William R. 6, Mary A. 4, Elizabeth T. 1

Schedule Page 490

PINSON, William 59
HONAKER, Thomas D. 33*, Nancey P. 36, Belvadora 5, Louisa K. 1
LION, Humbros 20*
DOTTON, John 42 (B), Causbey 21, Ellen 4, Louisa 2
RATLIFF, William sr. 70*, Martha 60
MORGAN, William 7*
MCCALISTER, Susan 20*, ____ 1/12 (m)
RATLIFF, William 21*, Katherine 24, James 2
SORD, Sena 21*, John 1
JUSTACE, Simeon 27*, Barbary 28, Elizabeth 5, James 3, Louisa C. 1
WILLSON, Robert 12*, Pricey 8 (f), Arminta 7
JUSTACE, Simeon 29, Susannah 26, Mary A. 7, Mark M. 5, George W. 3, William T. 3/12
LAWSON, Mark 53*, Martha 52, Henery 3/12
HALE, Caroline 21*
JOHNSON, John 28*, Mary 29
LEE, Elizabeth 7*
KEETHLEY, Henery 55*, Nancey 32, Sarah A. 14, James A. 13, Clover G. 10 (m), Christopher C. 8, William T. 6, John F. 5, Margaret J. 3, Thomas J. 11/12
NICOLS, Rebecca 12*

1850 Census Pike County Kentucky

KEETHLEY, William 75*, Susannah 76
TERRY, Joseph P. 42*
DAMERON, Lazerius 45*, Jenny 30
MAY, Rebecca 20*, Jackson 7
ADKINS, Elisha 21, Seerena 16, Mary E. 2, Martha J. 1/12
DIMERON, Moses 35, Charrity 30, Mary C. 10, Louisa 9, Sarah M. 4?, Olla J. 1
COLEMAN, Henery 45*, Sarah 40, Aron 9, Pharmer 7, Harvey 5, Rebecca 3/12
MAY, David T. 25*, John 17, Martha 16, Roland 12
CRABTREE, Ritta 45, John 20, Elizabeth 16, Wilson 15, William 12, Winna 10, Henery 8, Harvey 6

Schedule Page 491

BALDRIDGE, John 50, Elizabeth 50
REPHIT, James 23, Elizabeth 20, John 6, Elizabeth 4, Katherine 2
DAMERON, Spurlock 35*, Sarah 35, John 15, Christiane 13 (m), Louis 11, Rebecca 8, Arminta J. 5, William 3, Solomon K. 1
COMPTON, William 23*
DAMERON, Abraham 43, Robert 10, Elizabeth 69
HANNEARD?, Fredric 26*, Veronica 22, Fredric 8/12, Charles 20
SUCHER, Julia 9*, Eliza 14
WEDDINGTON, James 46*, Katherine 44, William M. 21, James W. 19, Henery 16, Jackson 11, Kanis 9 (m), Thomas 7, Susan 6, Nancey 5, David 3
FOWLER, William 27*
GAUSE, Alex 31*, Barbary K. 25
BECKWIT, Stephen 17*
FURGURSON, Stephen 26*, Lucinda 22, Mary 3, William D. 8/12
MCINTOSH, William 24*
WILLIAMSON, Franklin 26, Louisa 25, John H. 8, Samuel R. 7, Hellen 3, Zachariah T. 1
MARRS, Samuel 59, Sarah 53, Harmon 20, Caroline 18, Samuel 16, Sarah A. 14, Reece T. 11
MACE, Stephen 57, Rebecca 50, Louisa 26, Olover P. 24, Stephen D. 22, Sarah 18, Christopher 16, John 14, Rebecca 12, Hellen 7
WALTERS, Zachariah 47, Margaret 40, Sarah 18, Barnabus 17, Barbary 14, Thomas 13, Arminta 10, Lavinia 9, John E. 7, Louisa 4, Causbey A. 2 (f)
HEYTON, Jacob 28, Hannah 33, Martha 14, Elizabeth 8, Parazeda 5, John 2, Nancey 1

Schedule Page 492

MEAD, Rhodes 44, Sarah 42, Jane 17, Katherine 14, Samuel? 11, McDonald 8, Robert 6, Rhodes W. 4, John P. 2
YATES, John 38, Eliza 40, Susannah 17, Elizabeth 14, John 11, Matilda 8, Sarah 7, Emiline 5, Rhodes W. 2
WEDDINGTON, William 43, Mary 41, James M. 19, Rhodes M. 18, Elizabeth P. 15, Robert H. 13, Harrison 11, Mary K. 10, Angeline 8, Colbert C. 6, Alpha D. 3, Nancey M. 1, Elizabeth 70
HEYTON, John 35, Mary 30, Jane 6, Joseph 4, Mary J. 1
SAUNDERS, John 26, Mary 30, Mary J. 6, Nancey _/12
SAUNDERS, Elizabeth 42, William 21, Charles 17, Elizabeth 16, Jacob 13, Barbary 11

1850 Census Pike County Kentucky

PRICE, Thomas 67, Nancey 54, Mary R. 31, Pricilla A. 27, Marriba F. 24, James R. 22, John W. 20, Caroline M. 14
PRICE, William C. 30, Elizabeth 23
GILLISPIE, James J. 24, Lucinda 24, Russell 5, Lucy A. 3, John H. 6/12
MCCOWAN, Linsey 24 (m), Mary A. 26, Christena 1/12
GILLISPIE, Mathew 58, Lucinda 58, Susan 21, Martha 15, Mathew W. 16, Lavicey 12
RATLIFF, Silas 33*, Margaret 30, John S. 9, Vincent D. 6, Susan J. 4, William D. 1
DAWSON, Jane 55*, Tamsey J. S. 15

Schedule Page 493

RATLIFF, Susan 61*, Susan 25, Anna 24, John 22, Lucinda 17
ROBINSON, Joshua 50*
GILLISPIE, William H. 22, Nancey 21, Mary 1
DAWSON, Vincent 24, Lydia 23, Jane 1
NUNNERY, John 58, Malinda 57, Stephen 24, Ann E. 18, Thomas 12
NUNNERY, Mitchell 19, Elizabeth 21
RATLIFF, Richard 37, Louisa 25, Jane 5, Ann 4, Henery C. 3, Causbey A. 2, Isaah 1
MEAD, Benjamine 28, Martha 27, Rhodes 11, Arnold 9, Keenis? 7 (m), Mary 5, Martha J. 2
HARGAS, Thomas 41, Jane 38, Elizabeth J. 16, John P. 14, Jacob 12, Sanniul? 10 (m), James K. 9, Louisa 7, Nancey 5, Jessee 1
MEAD, Reuben 37, Martha J. 26, Jacob 11, Ely 9, Thomas H. 7, James 4, William J. 2, Elizabeth P. 4/12, Greenville 23, Ely 57
RATLIFF, William 43, Lydia 25, Addison 16, George 14, Susannah 8, Samuel C. 3
ISABELL, William 30, Marinda J. 22, David 1/12
FIFE, Edmond 38, Margaret 31, George W. 13, John 10, Thomas 8, Mary E. 6, Martha J. 5, Granville 2
WEDDINGTON, Jacob 45, Nancey 43, Jacob 21, Marry J. 19, John T. 14, James H. 6
BLANKENSHIP, Benjamine 35, Izabella 24
RATLIFF, Silas 74, Anna 72
DAWSON, William 34, Susannah 30, Elizabeth 9, John 7, Benjamine K. 7, Perlina 1

Schedule Page 494

BOWLING, John 56*, Lucy 51, Charles R. 24, John R. 22, Frances 19, William A. 17, Joseph R. 14, Benjamine F. 11, Lucy A. E. 8
MCCOWAN, Mitchell 30*
ROTEN, Luvicey 16*
SMITH, Henery 40*, Matilda 32, Sarah A. 15, Nancey 13, Emeline 11, Mary J. 8, Caroline 5, Bartholomew C. 2
BURRESS, George W. 17*
HONAKER, Louisa 56*, Saul 25, Isabella 20, James 18
BURK, Charles 22*
OWENS, William F. 30*, Louisa J. 21, Robert F. 3, William H. 1
BRANHAM, Grandison F. 19*
BURK, Elizabeth 35, Alvina 9
RATLIFF, Thomas 50, Deborah 49, Silas 23, John 21, Lourisa 19, Susannah 17, Mary 15, Pricilla 13, William 11, Lucinda 9, Freeland 7

1850 Census Pike County Kentucky

BRANHAM, Samuel 32*, Milla 26, Reevis P. 11/12
RATLIFF, Thursday 22*
RATLIFF, Jarrett 33*, Anna 31, Eliza 6, Nancey A. 5, Thursday 3, Martha 4/12, Mary 4/12
CECIL, Elizabeth 46*
REYNOLDS, John H. 41*, Synthia 32, John W. 15, Pheebe 13, Anna 11, Elizabeth 8, Jane H. 5, Frances 2, Layfayett 4/12
COLLINS, Harvey 17*
COLLINS, Amey 54, Martha J. 13
CLEVINGER, Russel 53, Elizabeth 56, Silas 22, Pinson 20, Barbary 18, Synthea 16, Margaret 15
CLEVINGER, Levi T. 25, Sarah 21, William R. 3
REYNOLDS, William M. 30, Anna 27, Elizabeth 8, Scotch McD. 6, William J. 4, Pheebe 2, James P. 1?

Schedule Page 495

SICK, William 35*, Elen 37, Sarah 13, Robert F. M. 10, John 9, Arminta 7, Lucas W. 5, Richard C. 3, Jacob L. 1
CLEVINGER, Nancy A. 16*
REED, James 40*, Elizabeth 21, James W. L. 4
BROWNING, John B. 8*
SWORD, Francis 50, Susan 47, Malinda 24, William J. 23, Elizabeth 18, Sarah 14, Mary 11, Louisa 8, Sarelda A. 4
BUCKLEY, Willburn 23*, Frances 17
BROWNING, Francis 23*
RATLIFF, John sr. 58*, Nancey 60, Lebalina 21, Jacob 18, Jefferson 16
LEEDY, Randolph 20*
MIMS, Abigal 45, Frances 19, Jenny 12 (m?), Anna 7, Robert 4, Mary E. 2
CECIL, William 47, Colbert 13, Perlina 11, John P. 6, Crittenden 4
BROWN, George N. 28, Sophia S. 21, Nancey F. 2, Margaret M. 10/12, Richard 20
MIMS, John D. 42*, Arminta D. 33, David A. 17, Victoria P. 10, Charles R. 8, Theodore 6, Alonzo 4, Mary L. 1
WHITE, Martha 25*
HUFFMAN, Anderson 25, Caroline M. 16
FORD, Nancey 40, Robert E. 4
FORGUSON, James 45, Rachel 36, Mary E. 17, Emeria J. 15, Malinda M. 12, Dida M. A. 8 (f), John M. 6
SICK, Jacob 39*, Mary 43, Richard 16, Sarah A. 14, George W. 12, Daniel W. 9, Perlina 7, Malinda 4, John 1
LAWSON, Dailey A. 17 (f)*
CONNOWAY, Michael 23*, Barsheba 21, John 2
RATLIFF, Elizabeth 26*, Robert 2

Schedule Page 496

BILLITER, Charles 37, Mary 33, John W. 11, Susannah A. 10, William C. 9, James N. D. 6, Tabitha 5, Mary J. 1
HAMILTON, Nelson 31, Almeda 35, Pricey 10, Mary J. 7, Arveline 5, Nancey 3, William 5/12
FIELDS, Joseph 40, Rebecca 25, Alpha C. 10/12

1850 Census Pike County Kentucky

RATLIFF, Mary 45, Noah 10
THOMPSON, Elizabeth 65
FURGURSON, Joseph 39*, Eliza 32, Arematha 14, William M. 12, July A. 10, Elizabeth J. 7, Alexandre 4, Louisa 1
MANIER, Linsey 24*
LANE, John N. 33, Mary A. 21
HUFFMAN, Solomon 50*, Sarah 52, Archibald 23, Pheebe 17, Guarlend 16 (f), John F. 11
CLAY, Mitchell 25*
JOHNSON, Andrew J. 27, Margaret J. 21
ROBINSON, Richard P. 54, Mary 40, Katherine 30, Louisa 24, James W. 18, Mary B. R. 15, Mary P. 14, Lucinda 12, Caroline M. 10, Amerrica 6, Virginia 3
HUFFMAN, Albert 21*, Hannah E. 26
MOORE, Langford 24*
RIDER, Martha J. 20, William L. 3, Thomas J. 1
EMMERT, John W. 24, Frances 24

Page 326 Blank

Index

ABBOTT
  Elizabeth 32* (MG-172)
  William 66 (MG-104)
ABDEN
  John 24 (GN-260)
ABDON
  Lucinda 18* (GN-181)
ABRAMS
  Basil 45 (GN-211)
  Bazel 18* (GN-251)
  Bazel 60 (GN-253)
  Elias 48 (GN-208)
  Elizabeth 67* (GN-169)
  Joseph 27 (GN-253)
  Robert 25 (GN-253)
  Samuel 30 (GN-168)
  Thomas 22 (GN-252)
  Thomas 44 (GN-207)
ABSHER
  Allen 55* (JO-83)
  Jacob 25 (JO-85)
ACHERSON
  James 25* (LW-89)
ACRES
  Andrew 43* (PI-462)
  Blackburn 45 (JO-121)
  Burrell 26 (CT-273)
  Edward 50 (CT-245)
  John 69* (PI-462)
  Mary 16* (JO-102)
ADAIR
  Mary 7* (PI-468)
  Samuel 39 (PI-468)
ADAMS
  Abraham 33 (GN-215)
  Absalom D. 41* (LE-137)
  Allen 21* (FO-431)
  Allen 39 (MG-91)
  Arthur 61 (LW-51)
  Bartholomew 65 (PI-436)
  Benjamin 56 (LE-133)
  Charles 26* (CT-282)
  Charles T. 31 (MG-157)
  Church 50 (B) (GN-263)
  Constantine 50 (LW-109)
  Daniel 50 (FO-458)
  E. E. 43 (m)* (GN-215)
  Eligha 31* (LE-149)

Elijah 11* (PI-435)
Elijah 24 (GN-198)
Elizabeth 20* (LE-131)
Fisher H. 38* (LW-65)
George 50 (LE-132)
Gilbert 23 (LE-137)
Gilbert 27 (MG-93)
Gilbert 35 (FO-457)
Green 8* (BE-19)
Harrison 28 (LE-145)
Henderson 16* (PI-434)
Isaac 40 (LE-131)
Isaac A. 33* (LW-50)
Jackson 31 (MG-161)
James 22 (CT-270)
James 23 (LW-90)
James B. 38 (JO-113)
Jane 16* (LE-127)
Jesse 22 (LE-132)
Jesse 29 (LE-133)
Jesse 50 (LE-138)
Jesse 52 (LE-147)
Joel 36 (FO-448)
John 22 (LE-138)
John 24 (LE-132)
John 26 (PI-444)
John 31 (LW-50)
John 32 (LE-133)
John 35* (GN-206)
John 39 (LE-133)
John C. 46 (LE-131)
John D. 22 (LE-131)
Johnson 21 (FO-448)
Johnson 22 (FO-442)
Loth 33 (m) (MG-163)
Margaret 18* (PI-484)
Martha 21* (LW-51)
Matthew 45 (MG-173)
Milla 15* (PI-484)
Moses 31 (LE-147)
Moses 38 (LE-137)
Moses 42* (LE-144)
Moses Sr. 75 (LE-131)
Nancy 16* (LE-126)
Nathan 20 (GN-198)
Pleasant 47* (CT-270)
Priscilla 28 (FO-428)
Randolph 48 (LE-126)

Rebeca 9* (LE-150)
Richard 22* (GN-239)
Richmond 29* (MG-115)
Robert 53 (CT-246)
Samuel J. 25 (MG-146)
Simpson 10* (MG-161)
Simpson 28 (LE-136)
Simpson 53 (LE-137)
Solomon 16* (MG-167)
Spencer 25 (LE-133)
Squire 19 (LE-132)
Stephen 23 (LE-138)
Stephen 34 (LE-145)
Stephen 58 (LE-137)
Thomas 24 (CT-245)
Wiley 23* (FO-456)
William 15* (MG-147)
William 23 (CT-270)
William 23* (CT-272)
William 28 (FO-458)
William 30 (LE-136)
William 43 (LE-137)
William 47* (MG-164)
William 47 (MG-173)
William 62* (LE-136)
William 62 (PI-452)
William 80* (FO-451)
William C. 22* (CT-270)
William D. 75 (PI-488)
Wm. 25* (LW-51)
ADKINS
  Absalum 40 (MG-121)
  Allen D. 43 (PI-441)
  Anderson 39 (PI-445)
  Anna 26 (MG-139)
  Archibald 20* (MG-138)
  Bartlett 65 (MG-133)
  Caswell 49 (MG-138)
  Edmund 8* (JO-101)
  Eli 19 (PI-444)
  Elisha 21 (PI-490)
  Elisha 37 (MG-139)
  Elizabeth 64 (PI-443)
  Franklin 26 (MG-133)
  Frederick 23 (MG-135)
  George W. 11* (CT-280)
  George W. 13* (PI-444)
  George W. 23 (PI-442)

Index

ADKINS
  Harrison 33 (MG-127)
  Henery 51 (PI-443)
  Henry 49 (JO-97)
  Hezekiah 49* (MG-137)
  Hiram 35* (MG-151)
  Howard 53 (MG-134)
  Isaac 47 (CT-225)
  James 30* (PI-438)
  James 65* (PI-438)
  Jane 48* (MG-127)
  Jeone? 44 (m) (PI-438)
  Jessee 35 (PI-443)
  Joel P. 46 (MG-134)
  John 42 (LW-72)
  John M. 44 (MG-138)
  Joseph 20 (MG-139)
  Joseph 45 (MG-135)
  Levi 26 (MG-96)
  Lewis 30 (MG-121)
  Milly 58 (MG-137)
  Milton 41 (PI-436)
  Mitchell 25 (MG-138)
  Moses 42 (MG-127)
  Nathan 23 (MG-127)
  Nathan 52 (MG-134)
  Nathaniel? 28 (PI-437)
  Nolen 60 (PI-451)
  Owen 27 (MG-135)
  Straley 45 (m) (MG-126)
  Susannah 43 (PI-438)
  Thomas P. 38 (LW-51)
  Wenright 75 (PI-443)
  Westley 28* (MG-128)
  Wiley 22 (MG-138)
  William 26 (MG-127)
  William 29 (PI-443)
  William 39 (PI-434)
  William 48 (MG-128)
  William 53 (PI-442)
  Winright 25 (PI-443)
  Winston 45 (PI-444)
  Wm. 20* (LW-73)
  Wyett 26 (MG-134)
AIKMAN
  Abner 21* (BE-42)
  John 71 (BE-42)
  John Jr. 27 (BE-43)
AISTROP
  Jesse 34 (LE-150)
AKERS
  Burwell 24 (LW-86)
  Daniel 28 (FO-411)
  David 49 (FO-412)
  Jonathan 35 (FO-415)
  Levi 25 (FO-412)
  Randle 41 (FO-441)
  Rebecca 50* (LW-86)
  Stephen 24 (FO-413)
  Stephen 30 (LW-88)
  Tolbert 50 (FO-414)
  Valentine 23* (FO-412)
  Wm. 22 (LW-87)
AKINS
  Elizabeth 14* (GN-168)
ALCORN
  Greenville 6* (MG-145)
ALDRIDGE
  Francis 43* (LW-121)
  James 23* (LW-122)
ALEXANDER
  Fleming 18 (CT-265)
  Greenup 44 (CT-269)
  John 29* (GN-235)
  John 52* (GN-167)
  Lewis 9* (LW-122)
  Louis 45 (CT-237)
  Mary 52* (CT-269)
  Sarah 46 (GN-259)
  Susan 39 (GN-228)
  Thomas 23* (GN-246)
  Thompson 24 (CT-269)
  Travis 23 (GN-229)
  William 22* (GN-264)
  William 23* (GN-168)
  William 28* (CT-216)
ALFREY
  Alfred 35 (MG-103)
  Rachael 59 (MG-103)
ALLAN
  Ethan 29* (GN-194)
ALLEN
  Adam 41 (FO-438)
  Cynthia 65 (FO-438)
  Daniel W. 29* (MG-158)
  David W. 43 (FO-464)
  Elijah 27* (MG-158)
  Felix 35 (FO-440)
  George 18* (BE-12)
  George 32 (FO-441)
  George 42 (BE-9)
  George J. 32 (FO-438)
  James 22 (BE-10)
  James 26 (PE-417)
  James 28 (BE-22)
  James S. 25* (CT-217)
  John 20 (FO-438)
  John 42 (FO-421)
  Johnathan 28 (PE-412)
  Joseph 27 (BE-12)
  Nancy 19* (BE-8)
  Polly 31* (BE-31)
  Richard 53 (MG-170)
  Samuel 24* (MG-133)
  Samuel 29* (FO-441)
  Samuel 44 (PE-418)
  Thomas 25 (BE-28)
  William 32 (BE-11)
  William 67 (BE-10)
ALLEY
  Benjamin 21 (PI-466)
  Jacob 28 (GN-199)
  James 25 (GN-200)
  John 28 (GN-199)
  Mary 59 (GN-199)
  Paul 51 (PI-468)
  Simeon 26* (JO-86)
ALLIN
  Adison 24* (GN-237)
  Beverally 39 (m) (GN-228)
  Christena 6* (GN-247)
  F. C. 33 (m)* (GN-237)
  John 45 (GN-242)
  Joseph 24 (GN-237)
  M. H. 47 (m) (GN-228)
  Thomas J. 42 (GN-231)
ALLISON
  Eliza 32* (GN-169)
  Isaac 67* (LW-108)
  James 24* (PI-483)
  John 19* (LW-91)
  John H. 54 (LW-105)
ALLY
  Elisha 23 (FO-414)

Index

ALLY
  Jonathan 26* (FO-410)
  Turner 32 (FO-415)
  Usly 50 (f)* (FO-415)
  William 60* (FO-415)
  Wm. 36 (LW-116)
ALSOP
  Joel 45 (FO-436)
  Robert 22 (FO-452)
AMBURGEY
  Wiley 28 (LE-155)
AMBURGY
  Elizabeth 84? (LE-152)
  Jesse 28* (LE-151)
  Robert 58 (LE-151)
  Wilburn 46 (LE-151)
  Wm. W. 24 (LE-151)
AMBUSH
  Aron 30* (LW-99)
AMEN
  Henry 22* (LW-99)
AMES
  Jacob 39 (MG-108)
  Samuel B. 53* (GN-235)
  Wells 38 (PE-412)
AMY
  Thomas 15* (PE-405)
AMYA
  James F. 27* (MG-161)
AMYX
  Joseph H. 35* (MG-119)
  Matthew J. 28* (MG-147)
  Peter 64 (MG-169)
  Peter H. 38 (MG-94)
ANDERSON
  Andrew 28 (GN-169)
  Charles 29 (PI-449)
  Cornelus 55* (GN-257)
  David 33 (PI-438)
  Hiram 26 (PI-461)
  J. N. 13 (m) (GN-229)
  Jacob 37 (GN-231)
  James 22* (PI-448)
  James 57 (GN-243)
  Jessee 23 (PI-449)
  John 24* (GN-173)
  John 75 (GN-212)
  Noah 30 (GN-238)

Richard 35 (MG-101)
Westley 33 (GN-242)
William 50 (MG-151)
ANDREW
  Peter 46* (GN-247)
ANGEL
  Adrain 42 (m) (BE-24)
  Arch. 27* (BE-29)
  Delila 26* (BE-26)
  James 87* (BE-34)
  John 30* (BE-32)
  Joseph 21* (BE-20)
  Mathena 50 (BE-19)
  Nicholas 36 (BE-25)
  Philip 28 (BE-25)
  William 34 (BE-26)
ANGLIN
  Abram 32 (CT-215)
  Gabriel 37 (CT-214)
  John Sr. 65 (CT-215)
ANTIS
  Hiram 40 (GN-171)
  Samuel 32 (GN-171)
APPLEGATE
  Andrew 54 (GN-245)
  Jacob 40 (GN-242)
  James 20* (GN-225)
  Jeremiah 48 (GN-238)
  L. V. 28 (m)* (GN-171)
  Richard 35 (GN-243)
  Smith 22 (GN-242)
APPS
  James 60* (GN-194)
ARA
  Watson 51 (PE-403)
ARCHER
  John 36 (GN-254)
  Naoma 2* (GN-252)
ARENHART
  Mary 43 (MG-165)
ARMES
  William 28 (GN-253)
ARMINTAGE
  John 41* (MG-102)
ARMS
  Aaron 37 (JO-124)
  Elias 16* (JO-107)
  John 23? (CT-277)

John 68* (CT-275)
Mary 70* (CT-271)
Moses 35 (GN-170)
Theodore 57 (GN-185)
William 25* (GN-167)
ARMSTRONG
  Jer. 55 (m)* (B) (GN-261)
  John 40 (CT-284)
  Rutha 45 (MG-100)
  William 27* (CT-256)
  William 52* (GN-181)
ARND
  Andrew 43* (PE-406)
ARNETT
  Ambrose 32* (MG-166)
  Ambrose 37* (FO-453)
  David 38* (FO-453)
  Hiram 30* (FO-453)
  Juicy 20 (f)* (FO-448)
  Reuben 40 (FO-447)
  Reuben sr. 64 (FO-454)
  Stephen 18 (FO-453)
  Stephen 3rd? 44 (FO-453)
  Stephen 68* (FO-448)
  Wiley 35* (FO-451)
  William 40 (FO-453)
ARNOLD
  Andrew 21* (GN-240)
  Andy 49 (GN-173)
  Benjamine 56* (PI-464)
  John 80* (FO-447)
  P. 28 (m) (GN-244)
  S. 35 (m) (GN-243)
ARONHART
  Elizabeth 79* (LW-50)
ARROWOOD
  Garred D. 24 (JO-122)
ARTES
  Mary 37 (GN-175)
ARTHUR
  Coleman 47 (GN-184)
  Eli 29* (CT-222)
  Isaac 35 (GN-195)
  Isam 18* (GN-187)
  James 25 (GN-191)
  James 75 (GN-196)
  John 26 (GN-191)
  Joseph 55 (GN-235)

Index

ARTHUR
  Piety 28 (f)* (GN-190)
  Robert 34 (GN-191)
  Sarah 67* (GN-185)
ARTIS
  Daniel 33 (GN-173)
  David 22 (GN-247)
  Henry 24* (GN-248)
  Joseph 20* (GN-249)
  Rebecca 13* (GN-250)
  Samuel 28 (GN-208)
  Thomas 27 (GN-249)
  William 28* (GN-173)
ARTRESS
  Jesse 34* (GN-201)
  Rebecca J. 1* (GN-201)
ARTRIP
  John 38 (CT-274)
ASBERRY
  George 48 (MG-148)
ASHER
  Sarah 30* (GN-242)
ASHFORD
  John D. 40* (LW-50)
ASHLEY
  Franklin 22 (LE-150)
  Jordan 49 (PE-426)
  William 26 (PE-426)
ASHMORE
  Thomas 35 (GN-182)
ASTRAP
  Jesse 70 (LE-140)
ASTRUP
  James 46 (LW-80)
AUCTIER
  George W. 30* (PI-487)
AUNDERS
  Thomas J. 49 (PI-453)
AURSBURN
  John S. 22 (LE-133)
AUSTIN
  Robert 38 (PI-456)
  Samuel W. 26 (PI-457)
  Thomas 24 (LW-103)
AUXER
  Nancy 87* (LW-67)
AUXIER
  Constance 62* (JO-123)
  Daniel 24* (JO-122)
  Daniel jr. 27* (FO-463)
  Daniel sr. 64 (FO-463)
  Enoch 55 (JO-123)
  John B. 33 (JO-118)
  Margaret 40 (B) (FO-445)
  Nathaniel 34 (JO-120)
  Samuel 57 (JO-123)
  Samuel jr. 23 (FO-474)
  Willis 18* (JO-81)
AUXIER?
  Jackson 32* (LW-57)
BACK
  Alfred 43 (BE-32)
  Alfred 46 (BE-13)
  Henry 27 (LE-144)
  Henry 65 (LE-144)
  Isaac 33 (BE-26)
  Jacob 57* (GN-176)
  John 35 (LE-144)
  John 40 (BE-13)
  John Jr. 21 (BE-43)
  John sr. 75 (BE-26)
  Joseph 48* (BE-26)
  Lewis Sr. 52 (BE-6)
  Lewis jr. 43 (BE-18)
  Samuel 27 (LE-144)
  Solomon 38* (BE-13)
BAGBY
  James 32 (CT-232)
BAILEY
  Alfred 25 (FO-456)
  Daniel 27* (JO-96)
  Elijah 20* (FO-453)
  James 24 (JO-98)
  James 30* (FO-453)
  John 35 (FO-447)
  John 35 (FO-453)
  John 52 (JO-97)
  John sr. 62* (FO-447)
  Joseph 30 (JO-93)
  Lemuel 58* (FO-453)
  Martin 29 (BE-3)
  Mary 5* (GN-171)
  Nancy 73* (CT-230)
  Patsy 100* (FO-455)
  Rachiel 38 (GN-265)
  Samuel 25 (FO-447)
  Walis 46* (FO-456)
  William 32 (JO-83)
BAILY
  Andrew 26 (GN-212)
  David 39 (GN-185)
  Saml. 26* (LW-106)
BAKER
  Alexander 30 (BE-5)
  Allin 54 (GN-258)
  Christopher 27 (PE-404)
  Elijah 18* (LE-134)
  Elisha 48* (PI-473)
  Ewin 33 (GN-232)
  George 36* (FO-473)
  Helton 18* (FO-471)
  Henry 42 (LE-131)
  Ira 21* (BE-40)
  Ira 25 (JO-115)
  Isaac 32 (BE-40)
  Isack 37 (PE-397)
  Jackson 45 (PE-409)
  James 25* (GN-167)
  James 28 (FO-430)
  James 30* (CT-267)
  Jenny 35* (PI-453)
  John 22 (PE-402)
  John 38 (BE-24)
  John 40 (GN-242)
  John C. 32 (LW-77)
  Marshal 39* (GN-259)
  Mary 55 (PE-402)
  Nathanl. 33* (LW-122)
  Robert 52 (CT-214)
  William 23 (BE-23)
  William 24 (PE-401)
  Wilson 40 (PE-398)
BAKER?
  John 54 (PE-401)
BALDING
  Cynthia A. 22* (JO-119)
BALDRIDGE
  Andrew 36 (JO-119)
  James 47 (LE-154)
  John 28 (FO-424)
  John 50 (PI-491)
  Joseph 32 (JO-122)
  Mary 80 (JO-122)
  Robert 22* (FO-435)

- 330 -

Index

BALDRIDGE
  Robert 39 (FO-463)
  William 13* (FO-463)
  William 40 (FO-465)
BALDWIN
  Anthony sr. 61 (JO-82)
  Mary E. 20* (GN-163)
  Solomon 40* (FO-412)
  Thomas 36 (JO-81)
BALEY
  Elisha 34 (MG-161)
  Henry 23 (CT-285)
  James F. 56* (CT-279)
  Joseph 27 (GN-247)
  Levi 13* (MG-90)
  Mary 47 (MG-152)
  Pryor 53 (MG-165)
  Samuel R. 27* (CT-277)
  Susan 36 (MG-100)
  ___ 26 (m) (CT-268)
BALL
  Elihue 26 (LW-85)
  Ens. 20 (m)* (PI-470)
  James 31 (PI-476)
  James 68* (LW-85)
  Jessee 25* (PI-488)
  Jessee 49 (PI-476)
  John 36 (LW-92)
  John C. 43* (CT-215)
  Letty 20* (LW-67)
  Mansford 37 (CT-278)
  Mary A. S. 6* (CT-285)
  Minten J. 20 (LW-114)
  Moses 63 (PI-476)
  Robt. 33 (LW-84)
  Soloman 19* (LW-75)
  Wesley 42 (GN-192)
  William D. 38 (CT-215)
BALLARD
  J. W. 1 (m)* (GN-235)
  William 57 (GN-235)
BALLERN
  Joseph 23 (GN-199)
BALLOO
  Garrett 32 (GN-177)
  Lincy 26 (m) (GN-177)
BALMORE
  Nancy 40 (LW-112)

BANFIELD
  John 51 (CT-222)
  Thomas K. 27* (CT-269)
  Zedakiah 55* (CT-278)
BANISTER
  Pleasant 46* (JO-115)
BANK
  Laney 45 (LW-112)
BANKS
  Alfred 35 (LE-129)
  Cassa 45 (LE-129)
  Danl. 27 (BE-1)
  David 46 (FO-462)
  David 47 (BE-5)
  David sr. 65 (FO-420)
  Henry 65 (LE-129)
  James 24 (MG-152)
  John 26 (BE-1)
  John 41* (BE-5)
  John 45 (MG-154)
  Johnson 50* (LE-145)
  Mary 55 (LE-126)
  Nimrod 18* (FO-407)
  Samuel 24 (LE-130)
  Samuel 31 (FO-420)
  Susanah 8* (LE-141)
  William 36 (LE-127)
  William Sr. 73 (BE-5)
  Wm. W. 39 (BE-5)
BARBECK
  Adam 43* (GN-213)
BARBER
  Jesse 36* (MG-172)
  Nancy 72* (GN-166)
  William H. 20 (GN-187)
BARBOUR
  Pleasant 45 (GN-188)
  Reuben 48 (GN-204)
BARE
  Peter 48 (CT-283)
BARGER
  Jesse 39 (PE-406)
  Polly 62* (PE-405)
BARKER
  Abraham 16* (MG-150)
  Annis 9* (CT-262)
  Clarinda 22* (MG-173)
  Elijah 19 (MG-109)

Elijah 21* (MG-164)
Hardin 50 (CT-261)
Harvey 41 (LW-71)
Hezekiah 63 (MG-109)
Jane 18* (MG-173)
John 29 (LW-71)
John 50 (MG-115)
John 61 (CT-260)
Morgan 46 (MG-170)
Nancy 16* (MG-158)
Phillip 40 (MG-128)
Solomon 50 (CT-256)
Vachel 61 (m) (MG-151)
Wiley 25 (MG-113)
William 28 (CT-256)
William 40 (MG-121)
William 41 (MG-134)
William 55 (CT-262)
Williamson 52 (MG-160)
BARKES
  William 18* (GN-210)
BARLEY
  James 35 (PE-402)
BARNALL
  Nelson 40 (FO-444)
BARNARD
  Joshua 80 (FO-418)
BARNES
  David 22* (MG-144)
  John V. 31* (MG-173)
  Mary J. 19* (MG-172)
BARNET
  Daniel 45* (GN-197)
  Elias 25* (GN-230)
BARNETT
  Andrew 14* (MG-107)
  Harmon 24 (BE-22)
  James 28 (CT-277)
  James 36 (FO-440)
  James 40 (BE-42)
  James R. 21* (MG-131)
  John 11* (JO-85)
  John 35 (FO-458)
  Mary 63 (BE-29)
  Notty 58 (FO-418)
  Rachel 20* (MG-130)
  William 33 (FO-451)
  Wilson 42 (BE-16)

Index

BARNEY
 Benjamin 19* (GN-160)
 J. R. 18 (m)* (GN-234)
 Jacob 33 (GN-157)
 John R.? 34* (GN-159)
 Thomas sr. 55 (GN-163)
BARNHART
 Sarah 44* (JO-102)
BARNS
 Elizth. 15* (BE-34)
 James 13* (CT-217)
BARRETT
 Charles 40 (GN-198)
 David 33* (BE-23)
 Isham 60* (BE-34)
 Isham Jr. 22* (BE-34)
 James 38* (BE-34)
 Joshua 35 (BE-24)
BARTEE
 Thomas 17* (CT-246)
BARTLET
 Thomas 22* (GN-225)
BARTLEY
 James 62 (GN-162)
BARTON
 George 26* (GN-212)
BARTRAM
 Leonard 30 (GN-250)
 Samuel 27 (GN-200)
 Solomon 34 (GN-198)
 Van 21 (GN-200)
BARTRUM
 James 37* (LW-124)
BASH
 Nancy 21* (BE-20)
BASSET
 Isaac 58 (GN-228)
BASWELL
 Elias 46 (LW-64)
BATES
 David 9* (LW-79)
 James 27 (LE-131)
 Jesse 29 (LE-131)
 John 36 (FO-430)
 John N. 39 (GN-189)
 Nathanl. 30 (LW-119)
 Sarah (widdow) 57 (LE-135)
 Uriah 22 (LE-135)

BATMAN
 Henry 34 (GN-259)
BATTEN
 James P. 56* (CT-223)
BAYES
 James J. 21 (JO-107)
 Margaret 33 (JO-104)
BAYS
 Charles 65 (FO-472)
 Eliza 18* (MG-164)
 George W. 29 (MG-89)
 Isom 55 (FO-457)
 James 42 (MG-164)
 Joel C. 34 (MG-171)
 John 37* (FO-462)
 John 88 (MG-164)
 John E. 25* (MG-91)
 Joshua 47* (MG-161)
 Judah 15 (f)* (FO-452)
 Lucy 7* (FO-452)
 Margaret 54* (FO-461)
 Robert 38 (GN-177)
 Rufus 30* (FO-450)
 Samuel E. 22 (CT-226)
 Seana G. 17* (CT-265)
 Wiley 17* (MG-164)
 William 20* (CT-228)
 William 44 (FO-461)
 William 52 (CT-277)
BEAN
 James 41* (GN-160)
 Wm. 25* (LW-110)
BEAR
 Ambrose J. 29 (CT-283)
 Avery 34 (CT-256)
 Elias 26 (CT-283)
 George 50* (CT-283)
 Henry 65* (CT-283)
 Reuben C. 22* (CT-283)
 Richard 37 (CT-283)
BEASON
 John 30* (GN-175)
BEATTY
 R. C. 37 (m)* (GN-249)
BEAVANER
 Adam 33* (GN-249)
BEAVERS
 Andrew 30 (GN-218)

BECKLEHIMER
 Isaac 50* (LW-110)
BECKLEY
 James 23 (LW-109)
BECKNEL
 Jane 75* (BE-36)
 Wm. 32 (BE-37)
BECKWIT
 Stephen 17* (PI-491)
BECKWITH
 Arthur C. 35 (CT-243)
 Matilda 58 (CT-244)
BEESOM
 Rachel 22* (GN-210)
BEGINBACK
 John 36* (GN-172)
BELAMY
 Townley H. 19* (CT-252)
BELCHER
 Andw. J. 32 (LW-105)
 Hardin 23* (LE-149)
 Isaac 21* (CT-278)
 James D. 21 (PI-439)
 John M. 27 (PI-438)
 John W. 35 (PE-426)
BELEW
 John L. 27* (BE-33)
BELL
 Abner 51* (LW-121)
 Archibald 24 (FO-473)
 John 25* (GN-251)
 Samuel 20* (CT-228)
 Sarah 55 (CT-271)
BELLAMY
 Bennet 40 (GN-187)
 Bennet 40 (GN-195)
 John 22* (GN-173)
 Matthew 51 (GN-196)
 William N. 48* (GN-208)
BELLOW
 Asa 42* (CT-228)
BELTS
 John 88* (GN-215)
BENNETT
 Lewis 24* (LW-83)
BENTLEY
 Benj. 21 (LE-147)
 Benjamin 27 (PI-446)

Index

BENTLEY
  Benjamin 62 (LE-134)
  Dankiel 27 (LE-135)
  John 57 (LE-135)
  Joseph 24 (LE-135)
  Lewis 60 (LE-135)
  Mary 50 (LE-147)
  Moses 30 (PI-450)
  Samuel 26 (PI-450)
  Solomon C. 23 (LE-147)
  Thomas 23 (PI-456)
  Thomas 65 (LE-136)
  William 35 (PI-450)
  Wm. 28 (LE-147)
BENTLINGER
  Henry 30 (GN-240)
BENTLY
  George 31 (PI-450)
  Thomas 20* (FO-470)
BENTON
  William T. 24* (CT-268)
BERICH?
  Lewis 35* (LW-105)
BERRY
  Alford 27 (LW-90)
  Isaac 29 (LW-51)
  James 34 (LW-50)
  John 40 (FO-439)
  John 57 (LW-72)
  Reuben 27* (LW-50)
  Samuel 34 (GN-234)
  Thompson 33 (LW-51)
  Wiley 28 (LW-75)
  William 23 (LW-93)
  William 32* (GN-223)
  Wm. 28* (LW-75)
  Wm. 33 (LW-50)
BETTS
  Jacob 12* (GN-203)
  Samuel 42 (GN-203)
BETTYS
  Mary 8* (CT-226)
BEVENS
  David 44 (LW-103)
BEVERLY
  Jacob 30* (BE-25)
  Jacob 30* (BE-29)

BEVINS
  George 42 (PI-465)
  Hiram K. 33 (PI-487)
  James 33* (PI-464)
  James 41* (PI-435)
  John 64 (PI-463)
  John M. 32* (GN-174)
  Joseph 30 (FO-449)
  Joseph 38 (PI-483)
  Lydia 52 (PI-464)
  Madison 20 (PI-465)
  Thomas 35 (PI-465)
BEYLY
  Edward 42* (PE-407)
  Eligah 22 (PE-403)
  Granville 24 (PE-412)
  Henery C. 58 (PE-407)
  Hiram 48 (PE-407)
  Jesse 29 (PE-411)
  Pharis 31 (PE-403)
  Pleasant 40 (PE-403)
  Russell 41 (PE-407)
  William 79 (PE-407)
BIAS
  Berry 24 (CT-223)
BIGGS
  Andrew 22* (CT-272)
  James 19* (CT-279)
  James Jr. 24 (LW-78)
  James P. 20* (CT-273)
  Jeremiah 48 (CT-243)
  M. J. 11 (m)* (GN-252)
  R. M. 43 (m)* (GN-163)
  Reuben 47* (LW-84)
  William 49 (GN-221)
BIGLEY
  L. J. 10 (f)* (GN-222)
BILLINK
  M. 29 (m) (GN-262)
BILLITER
  Charles 37 (PI-496)
BILLUPS
  Robt. 27* (LW-78)
BINGOM
  Elijah 15* (FO-453)
BINION
  James 23 (CT-261)

BINTLENPANTES
  Jacob 40* (GN-216)
BINYAN
  Lincoln 28* (MG-132)
  William 27 (MG-136)
BIRCH
  Oliver 22* (CT-264)
BIRCHFIELD
  Adam 57 (BE-32)
  John 35 (PE-427)
  John 38* (CT-267)
  William 39 (BE-13)
BIRD
  Michael 21* (MG-147)
BIRDS
  John 48 (MG-117)
BIRK
  Idea 2 (f)* (GN-219)
BISHOP
  David 30 (LW-97)
  David 68 (LW-115)
  Elihu 28 (MG-94)
  Elisha 30 (MG-157)
  Elizabeth 55* (MG-157)
  Geo. 31 (LW-61)
  Hannah 52* (CT-263)
  Henry 26 (LW-120)
  J. M. 60 (m)* (GN-240)
  William 39 (PI-439)
BITTERWATER
  Joseph 112* (B) (CT-246)
BIVINS
  Martha 5* (GN-226)
BIZLY?
  John 36 (PE-403)
BLACK
  Andrew J. 5* (MG-99)
  Andy 30* (B) (GN-171)
  Charlotte 41* (B) (GN-166)
  Daniel 30* (B) (GN-180)
  David 19* (B) (GN-164)
  Henry 31 (GN-227)
  J. G. 26 (m)* (GN-215)
  Madison 25 (B) (GN-183)
  Robert 50* (B) (CT-246)
  Sarah 27* (GN-160)
  Washington 45* (B) (CT-265)
  William S. 31* (MG-126)

Index

BLACKBURN
  Daniel 30 (PI-486)
  George 28 (PI-485)
  Hatson 53 (PI-485)
  Hutson 38 (PI-475)
  Jacob 20* (PI-478)
  James 33 (PI-477)
  Jeremiah 38* (GN-209)
  John 34 (PI-476)
  Peyton 34 (PI-489)
  Thomas 51 (PI-436)
  William 25 (PI-489)
  William 66 (PI-480)
BLAIR
  Anderson 32 (MG-95)
  Britton 28 (JO-118)
  Charles 43 (LE-127)
  David 43 (MG-134)
  Elihu 25* (LE-127)
  George 61 (JO-123)
  George W. 30 (JO-90)
  Harmon 14* (GN-183)
  Henry 39 (LE-140)
  James 23 (JO-123)
  James L. 13* (GN-188)
  John 33 (JO-84)
  John R.? 51 (LE-127)
  Joseph 26 (LE-127)
  Joseph 49 (GN-223)
  Leann 7* (CT-274)
  Levi 37 (JO-85)
  Noble Jun. 33 (JO-123)
  Preston 23 (LE-144)
  William 35 (JO-124)
  William 44 (MG-98)
BLAKELY
  Wiley 40 (PI-439)
BLANKENSHIP
  Amanda 10* (MG-131)
  Barnabus 39 (PI-450)
  Benjamine 35 (PI-493)
  Cela 18* (MG-157)
  Ezekiel 37 (PI-472)
  Farm 30 (GN-199)
  Henry 34 (LW-104)
  Henry 60 (MG-99)
  Hiram 27 (GN-199)
  Hiram 35 (PI-466)
  John 30 (PI-472)
  Obediah 69* (CT-216)
  Permela 45 (MG-131)
  Priestley 29 (PI-472)
  Riley 35 (PI-487)
  Sarah 69 (CT-273)
  Susanna 38 (GN-208)
  Thomas 53* (CT-222)
  Vincent 8* (CT-273)
  William 25* (PI-468)
  William 25 (PI-473)
  Wm. 60 (FO-413)
  Wm. R. 28 (CT-275)
BLANKINSHIP
  J. 57 (m) (GN-241)
BLANTON
  George 36 (JO-100)
  George sr. 75 (JO-90)
  James 30 (JO-90)
  John N. 29 (JO-98)
  Vincent 58 (MG-110)
  William 50 (JO-100)
  William E.? 23 (JO-90)
BLECHER
  Margaret 63 (PI-438)
BLEDSOE
  Sampson W. 26* (FO-419)
BLEVENS
  Danl. 38 (LW-69)
  Ephraim 45 (LW-53)
  Lewis 19* (LW-55)
  Ryal 33 (CT-261)
  Wm. 22* (LW-70)
BLEVINS
  Alexander 5* (FO-411)
  Daniel 22 (JO-88)
  Daniel 22 (PI-438)
  Eli 25 (FO-442)
  Elisha 41 (JO-88)
  Jacob 24 (PI-438)
  James 29 (JO-114)
  James 38 (CT-262)
  John 22* (GN-184)
  Levi 71 (JO-114)
  Phoeby 16* (JO-111)
  Samuel 33 (JO-112)
  Sarah 65 (CT-261)
  Thomas A. 21 (JO-115)
  Wiley 30 (JO-88)
  William 35 (CT-262)
  William 64 (JO-88)
BLOOMER
  Daniel 75* (GN-258)
BLOOMFIELD
  George 28 (CT-229)
  Reuben 33 (CT-229)
  William 26 (GN-214)
BOAL?
  William K. 18* (GN-169)
BOBBETT
  William 43 (GN-183)
BOBBIT
  Absalom 24* (GN-164)
BOCOCK
  Elijah 44 (LW-108)
  John 24 (LW-108)
  William W. 65 (CT-234)
  Wm. 30 (LW-108)
BOCOOK
  John 40* (CT-252)
BOGGS
  Abel 37* (LE-139)
  Bryant 33 (CT-281)
  Charity 32 (CT-281)
  Charles 12* (LW-78)
  Charles L. 12* (GN-194)
  David 44 (LW-55)
  Elijah 27* (LW-55)
  Frances 58 (CT-279)
  Henderson 27 (LW-70)
  High 48* (LW-55)
  James 20 (LW-70)
  John 21 (LW-55)
  John 25* (LW-70)
  John R. 23 (LW-69)
  Mary A. 27* (CT-279)
BOGS
  Cathrine 16* (CT-274)
  Hugh 36 (CT-259)
  James 39 (CT-261)
BOGUS
  Reuben 37* (CT-273)
BOHANNON
  Henry C. 33 (BE-28)
  Robert 70 (B) (BE-23)
BOLEY
  William B. 38 (CT-215)
BOLIN
  John 20* (GN-177)

Index

BOLING
Baley 24 (MG-112)
Benjamin 56 (MG-113)
Dulaney 26 (BE-38)
Elijah 52 (BE-38)
George 40 (BE-38)
Henery 24* (PI-444)
Henry 37 (MG-112)
Jarrett W. 42 (MG-133)
Jesse 27 (BE-38)
Justice 29 (PE-406)
Justice 60* (PE-405)
Lucy 19* (PE-415)
Polly 50* (PE-411)
Robert 36 (PE-405)
Sarah 27 (MG-113)
William 40* (PE-406)
William 44 (PE-412)
William jr. 25* (BE-39)
BOLLING
William P. 19 (GN-173)
BOLT
Greenville 35 (LW-106)
Isaac 60 (LW-107)
Montraville S. 34 (LW-107)
BOMAN
Susan 40* (MG-167)
BOMWARS
Henry C. 23 (BE-20)
BOND
Bazel Sr. 36 (CT-237)
Lucinda 13* (GN-247)
BONDURANT
Isaac 22* (B) (CT-272)
BOOK
William 22 (GN-246)
BOOKNER
Jacob 61 (GN-246)
BOOTEN
Hiram 46 (LW-106)
BOOTH
Elias 25* (JO-120)
Harris 24 (FO-409)
James 26 (LW-69)
BOOTHE
Wm. 25* (BE-33)
BORDERS
Archabald 30* (LW-102)

Archabald 52* (LW-99)
Arthur 23 (LW-99)
Danl. 24 (LW-103)
David 28 (JO-80)
Henry 20* (LW-103)
Hezekiah 20* (JO-121)
Hezekiah 58* (LW-102)
John 26 (LW-99)
John 26* (MG-123)
John 29 (LW-102)
John 56* (JO-119)
Joseph 32* (LW-83)
Michl. 63* (LW-103)
William 24* (JO-120)
Wm. 23* (LW-102)
BOTTNER
Oliver D. 30* (JO-94)
BOTTOMS
Wm. 15* (LW-102)
BOTTS
Alexander 23* (GN-192)
James R. 29* (CT-244)
BOUSER
Clinton 21* (GN-223)
Temperance 18* (GN-225)
BOW
Argus 33 (CT-273)
Joel 49 (FO-473)
BOWCOCK
W. J. 45 (m) (GN-244)
BOWE
Wm. 22* (LW-75)
BOWEN
Alford 37 (LW-119)
Daniel 29 (JO-114)
Elizabeth 17* (JO-110)
Henry 28 (JO-92)
John 43 (LW-122)
Lewis 24* (GN-167)
Perin Tyre 36 (B)* (LE-139)
Sarah 10* (JO-97)
William 30 (LE-140)
BOWLIN
James 40 (LE-140)
BOWLING
Delana 26 (LW-67)
Hannah 41 (CT-223)
James 50* (LW-108)

John 56* (PI-494)
Robt. 20* (LW-115)
BOWMAN
Bradford 19* (MG-150)
Elisha W. 35 (BE-21)
Elizabeth 13* (LE-126)
Henry 34 (BE-19)
John 40 (BE-30)
Joseph 42 (BE-21)
Mahala 10* (LE-143)
Nicholas 53 (BE-20)
Wesley 19* (BE-41)
Wm. 30* (BE-31)
BOYCE
James 28 (GN-171)
Richard 21 (GN-263)
BOYD
Alexander 25* (MG-86)
Andrew 27 (LW-96)
David 65 (JO-123)
Elizabeth 21* (LW-73)
Greenville 27 (LW-99)
Henry 30 (GN-211)
Hugh 23* (LW-102)
Isom 24 (LW-100)
James 19* (LW-103)
James 34 (FO-408)
James 55* (LW-101)
John 32* (FO-416)
Joseph 51 (FO-461)
Milton 20* (CT-228)
Samuel 54 (GN-220)
William 49 (FO-419)
William 70* (FO-416)
Wm. 22 (LW-99)
BOYER
Thomas H. 39* (PI-458)
BOYLE
John 56 (GN-251)
Martin 27* (CT-227)
BOYLS
John 46 (GN-175)
BOZE
Jane 14* (CT-282)
BRADBURN
Jackson 26 (GN-230)
M. 25 (m) (GN-230)
Mark 48 (GN-230)

Index

BRADFIELD
  John 29* (JO-111)
BRADFORD
  C. S. 14 (f)* (GN-168)
  Jesse 20* (GN-252)
  John 44* (CT-218)
  Sarah 55* (CT-218)
  Saunders C. 27 (BE-18)
  William 31 (CT-228)
BRADLEY
  Cornelius 23 (JO-120)
  David 26* (GN-176)
  George 22* (BE-8)
  George 35 (LW-62)
  George 68 (BE-10)
  Jackson D. 30 (LW-78)
  James 38 (BE-8)
  Jesse 63 (CT-217)
  Levi 36* (LW-79)
  Mahala 35* (LW-118)
  Micajah 46 (LW-65)
  Sarah 12* (LW-96)
  Stephen 42 (LW-117)
  William H. 35 (GN-166)
BRADLY
  Elias 31* (FO-444)
  Malinda 8* (LW-117)
  Margaret 12* (LW-117)
  Thos. 40* (LW-118)
  William 33 (FO-443)
BRADSHAW
  Alexander 39* (GN-223)
  David 76 (MG-103)
  George 30 (GN-222)
  George 66* (GN-250)
  John H. 37 (MG-94)
  Robert 40 (GN-183)
  Sarah J. 21* (CT-218)
  Stephen 26* (GN-220)
  William C. 21* (GN-221)
BRAGG
  Moses 75 (B) (GN-224)
  Wm. 20* (LW-110)
BRAMMER
  Amoml. 51* (LW-57)
  John 16* (CT-252)
  Joseph 56 (GN-162)
  Joshua 20* (CT-241)

  Samuel 50* (CT-251)
  William 23* (CT-240)
  William 28 (CT-253)
BRANARD
  Isaac 22* (GN-260)
BRANHAM
  Betsey 34 (LE-148)
  David 44 (LW-82)
  Elisha 46* (FO-415)
  Eliza 9* (LE-148)
  Grandison F. 19* (PI-494)
  Isom 57 (FO-410)
  James 46* (PI-454)
  Jonathan 45 (CT-283)
  Rachael 24* (LW-106)
  Samuel 32* (PI-494)
  Turner 22 (PI-457)
  Turner 90* (FO-415)
  Turner jr. 21 (FO-415)
BRANKAM
  David 32 (PI-454)
  Edward 23 (PI-454)
  Elias 20* (PI-455)
  Elizabeth 70* (PI-454)
  John H. 26* (PI-454)
  Reuben 26 (PI-454)
  William 42* (PI-454)
BRANNUM
  Edward 77 (CT-227)
  John 28* (GN-193)
  Mary 23* (MG-159)
  Wiley 25* (GN-215)
BRANSON
  Lenard 30 (PE-427)
BRANT
  Michael 47 (GN-172)
BRANTHAM
  John 28 (PI-452)
BRASHAR
  James N. 50 (PE-427)
  Robert S. 57* (PE-429)
  Sampson 69 (PE-429)
BRASHEAR
  Isaac 33 (PE-427)
  James 29 (PE-430)
BRASHEARS
  Ezekiel 44* (LE-141)
  John 45 (PE-433)

BRECK
  Daniel 1* (LE-137)
BRECKENRIDGE
  James 5* (GN-181)
BREEDING
  Elisha 56* (LE-149)
  Elizabeth 1* (LE-149)
  Huston 30 (LE-147)
  Wesley 26 (LE-145)
BREWER
  Frank 18 (BE-44)
  Howel 23* (PE-405)
  Justus 45 (GN-247)
  Wm. 35* (LW-81)
BRIANT
  David 38 (LW-109)
  Geo. 29 (LW-100)
  John 33* (LW-78)
  John 78 (LW-113)
  Kesiah 7* (LW-108)
  Reece 37* (LW-108)
  Wm. 27 (LW-100)
  Zach 44 (LW-113)
BRIEN
  Daniel 31* (FO-471)
BRIGGS
  Isaac 24 (GN-237)
  Jacob 60 (GN-236)
BRIGHTS
  B. B. 5 (m)* (GN-229)
BRILHART
  Jacob 41 (GN-227)
BRINEGAR
  Jacob 54 (CT-253)
BRINIGER
  Morgan 37 (CT-236)
BROADDUS
  Wm. 30 (BE-20)
BROCK
  Joshua 50 (BE-19)
  Nancy 18* (JO-83)
  Wm. 46 (BE-39)
BROMEGAR
  William 22 (CT-258)
BROMFIELD
  Madison 37 (LW-112)
  Mastin 46 (LW-84)
  Wm. 28* (LW-88)

Index

BROOKS
  Archibald H. 26* (MG-143)
  Calvin 18* (GN-209)
  Edward 38 (GN-239)
  James 20* (MG-144)
  James 38 (GN-202)
  James C. 52 (MG-146)
  James C. 53 (MG-143)
  John 45 (CT-256)
BROWN
  Allin W. 32 (GN-247)
  Amanda 36 (MG-88)
  Andrew 28 (LW-114)
  Archibald 30 (JO-121)
  Austin 36* (GN-212)
  Benjamin 28 (LE-138)
  Benjamin F. 23 (GN-217)
  Berry W. 56* (GN-256)
  Braxton 59 (MG-153)
  Campbell 23* (LW-87)
  Charles L. 30* (GN-194)
  Charlton 40* (FO-224)
  Clarissa 39* (B) (GN-181)
  Clerinda 16* (FO-458)
  Coleman 28 (MG-105)
  Daniel 61 (MG-107)
  Daniel G. 39 (JO-81)
  Daniel W. 36 (MG-89)
  David 26 (JO-102)
  David 40 (FO-446)
  Deborah 35* (CT-242)
  Delila 10* (CT-253)
  Elihu 24 (CT-255)
  Elijah 45 (MG-90)
  Elizabeth 20* (FO-459)
  Francis 64 (FO-460)
  Geo. A.F.Co. --* (BE-41)
  George 54 (CT-238)
  George 67 (FO-443)
  George A. 45 (BE-41)
  George D. 50 (MG-136)
  George N. 28 (PI-495)
  Hannah 12* (MG-136)
  Harrison 12* (MG-115)
  Harvy 31 (MG-88)
  Irvin 32 (CT-226)
  Isaac 13* (MG-132)
  Isaac 26 (MG-139)
  Jackson 22* (MG-160)
  James 21 (FO-458)
  James 31* (CT-238)
  James 33* (GN-195)
  James 38 (FO-459)
  James 54 (GN-224)
  James 67 (MG-105)
  James jr. 22 (MG-157)
  James sr. 62 (MG-87)
  John 30 (GN-199)
  John 39 (MG-87)
  John 42 (LW-66)
  John 48* (GN-219)
  John 53 (JO-119)
  John 55 (GN-157)
  John 61* (GN-231)
  John C. 26 (MG-105)
  John E. 39 (MG-95)
  John J. 14* (GN-223)
  John S. 55 (MG-105)
  John S. 57 (LE-126)
  Lawson 25* (GN-219)
  Lewis 40 (FO-425)
  Low 55* (CT-248)
  Lucinda 20* (LW-88)
  Mary J. 10* (GN-240)
  Matthew 58* (GN-224)
  Moses 67* (MG-129)
  Nancey 15* (GN-256)
  Nancy 25 (MG-164)
  Nathan A. 22* (MG-123)
  Nicholas 34 (MG-129)
  Peggy 40 (FO-455)
  Piercol? 42 (m)* (GN-224)
  Richd. 35 (LW-110)
  Samuel 18* (FO-459)
  Samuel 27 (GN-253)
  Samuel W. 30 (MG-145)
  Sophiah 39 (MG-138)
  Stephen 29 (MG-107)
  Stephen 32 (LE-126)
  Stephen 40 (MG-129)
  Stephen 59* (MG-141)
  Thomas 41* (MG-104)
  Thomas C. 91 (FO-460)
  Thomas S. 35 (JO-85)
  Wallace W. 32 (MG-122)
  William 21* (GN-226)
  William 22* (GN-223)
  William 26* (FO-409)
  William 37 (GN-265)
  William 44 (MG-123)
  William 46 (GN-183)
  William 50 (GN-210)
  William 55 (GN-183)
  William A. 22* (CT-248)
  William G. 29* (MG-111)
  Wilson 22* (FO-460)
  Young 21* (MG-146)
BROWNING
  Francis 23* (PI-495)
  John B. 8* (PI-495)
  Josiah 42 (MG-97)
  William 48 (PI-470)
BROWNLEE
  David 28* (GN-203)
BRUER
  Dennis 27 (BE-1)
  Forrest 25* (BE-24)
  Isham 20* (BE-2)
  Thomas 25 (BE-1)
BRUICE
  James 44* (LW-88)
BRUMFIELD
  Floyd 24 (LW-90)
BRUNTON
  Robert 53 (GN-202)
BRYAN
  James 44 (GN-220)
  Stephen 41* (GN-208)
  Thomas 22* (GN-202)
BRYANT
  Allen R. 22 (MG-131)
  Arney 4* (GN-172)
  Benjamin 67* (GN-225)
  David 46 (FO-429)
  Elijah 56 (BE-21)
  Evin 35 (BE-3)
  Hiram 27* (BE-21)
  Hurum 23 (BE-21)
  Isaac 45* (GN-172)
  Jesse W. 44* (MG-130)
  John 28 (MG-130)
  Julian 10 (f)* (GN-174)
  Lewis 25 (GN-251)
  Martha 13* (BE-1)

Index

BRYANT
Sally 9* (BE-5)
Sarah 12* (GN-215)
Sarah 13* (JO-86)
Sarah 48 (BE-21)
Squire D. 24 (MG-131)
BRYSON
Houston 24 (GN-238)
Isaac 75 (CT-218)
James 40 (CT-218)
William 45 (GN-241)
BUCHANNON
Wm. 80 (LW-113)
BUCKHANNON
William 41* (MG-145)
BUCKLEY
A. J. 34 (m) (GN-174)
Joel T. 40 (GN-189)
Willburn 23* (PI-495)
BUCKNER
James 28 (GN-244)
Mack 60 (CT-233)
Overton M. 38 (CT-233)
BUFFINGTON
Ailsey 13* (BE-13)
Rebecca 18* (MG-91)
William 23* (CT-269)
BUMGARDNER
John 36 (MG-128)
BUNYARD
James 40* (CT-249)
BURBY
Matthew 44 (GN-157)
BURCHETT
Armstead 55 (FO-418)
Armsted 32 (LW-75)
Benjamin 36 (CT-216)
Burrell 45 (CT-216)
David 39* (CT-276)
David F. 30* (FO-466)
Drury 60 (FO-419)
James 33* (CT-216)
John 43 (LW-82)
Leonard 26 (JO-88)
Oliver 21 (LW-119)
Oliver 22* (LW-97)
Thomas 54* (FO-466)
Thomas jr. 23 (FO-462)

William 33 (FO-463)
Wm. 27 (LW-74)
BURD
Thomas 36 (CT-254)
BURGESS
Benjamin 13* (JO-94)
Edwd. 47 (LW-98)
Elizabeth 80* (JO-110)
Geo. R. 35* (LW-110)
Geo. R. 42 (LW-97)
Gordon C. 42* (LW-83)
Henry 77 (LW-98)
Reuben 37* (LW-96)
Robert 55* (GN-178)
BURGETT
John 44 (PI-467)
William 24 (PI-467)
BURGEY
Alfred 34 (LE-149)
Ambrose 58 (LE-155)
Francis 25 (LE-155)
John 31* (LE-155)
Wm. 63 (LE-149)
BURGRASS
John 32* (GN-216)
BURGY
Ambrose 27 (LE-154)
Fanny 33 (LE-152)
Wm. 28 (LE-153)
BURK
Benjm. 41* (LW-74)
Charles 22* (PI-494)
Elizabeth 35 (PI-494)
Evan 46* (LW-62)
Isaac 42 (PI-457)
James P. 56 (GN-164)
John 59 (JO-84)
Richard 35 (JO-107)
William 60 (GN-175)
BURKETT
Frederick 76 (JO-86)
James R. 25 (JO-82)
BURKHURT
M. 24 (m)* (GN-249)
BURKS
John 12* (PI-452)
John 48 (PI-456)
Rolling 23 (FO-429)

BURNER
Ann 46 (LW-113)
BURNETT
John 31 (FO-472)
William 88 (FO-425)
BURNFIT
Alpheus J. 46 (GN-207)
BURNS
Benjamin 39 (GN-161)
John L. 40 (LW-78)
John M. 24 (LE-140)
Rowland 16* (LW-108)
William H. 33* (MG-174)
Wm. B. 30 (BE-34)
BURRESS
Elizabeth 53 (PI-478)
George W. 17* (PI-494)
Rachel 73* (PI-478)
BURRIS
James 21 (PI-478)
Marion T. 22* (PI-488)
William 38* (GN-260)
BURRISS
Ridgway 50 (CT-231)
Sanders 24 (CT-232)
BURROUGHS
Thomas 25* (CT-257)
BURT
Benjamin 22* (GN-246)
William 31 (GN-221)
BURTCHETT
Robert 42 (CT-232)
William 33* (CT-223)
BURTEN
Allen 17* (LW-102)
Andw. 30 (LW-52)
Detroit 37 (LW-56)
Henderson 31 (LW-89)
John 20 (LW-103)
Joshua 49* (GN-258)
Rebecca 65 (LW-50)
Saml. 22 (LW-50)
BURTENSHAW
Bernard 25* (GN-215)
Thomas 55 (GN-215)
William 21* (GN-194)
BURTON
Andrew 51 (MG-165)

Index

BURTON
  Daniel 29 (MG-170)
  Eleanor 54* (CT-270)
  Isaac 15* (MG-162)
  Isaac 42 (CT-245)
  JAmes 36 (MG-167)
  James 28 (FO-469)
  John 30 (MG-159)
  John 35 (MG-136)
  Margaret 18* (CT-274)
  Mary 25* (MG-172)
  Polly 25* (LW-54)
  Robert 27 (PE-412)
  Robert 39 (PE-429)
  Samuel 66* (CT-280)
  William 20* (MG-160)
  William 24 (CT-280)
BURTONSHAW
  James 23* (CT-272)
BUSH
  Aaron 40* (PE-417)
  Aaron 74 (GN-257)
  Aaron jr. 38 (GN-219)
  Edward 32 (GN-257)
  Elizabeth 49* (GN-243)
  George 26 (GN-236)
  Harmon 21* (BE-22)
  Henry 35* (GN-240)
  Hugh 35 (BE-43)
  James 39 (CT-273)
  James 42 (GN-169)
  James 43* (BE-31)
  John 45 (BE-43)
  John 67 (CT-232)
  Nathan 30* (GN-230)
  Nathan 30 (GN-258)
  Nathan 69 (GN-257)
  Sanford 36 (CT-232)
  Telitha 35 (B) (CT-271)
  Thornton 8* (GN-257)
  William 2* (GN-230)
  William 28* (GN-219)
  Z. 28 (m) (GN-222)
BUSSEY
  H. S. 39 (m)* (LW-76)
BUTCHER
  Jacob 63 (JO-122)
  James 27 (JO-112)
  Nancy 17* (JO-122)
  William 25 (JO-117)
BUTLER
  Arminta 41* (JO-125)
  Benjamin 33* (GN-228)
  David K. 42 (PE-415)
  Edward J. 30 (PE-429)
  James 35 (GN-176)
  Samuel 40 (JO-85)
BUTRAM
  Polly 25* (GN-229)
  W. E. 26 (m) (GN-229)
  Westley 51* (GN-229)
BUTTENSHAW
  Bernard 25 (CT-272)
BUTTS
  Derotha 63* (LW-107)
BYRAM
  Westley 42 (MG-104)
BYRNE
  Peyton 41 (GN-161)
BYSEL
  Hannah 24* (GN-234)
CAIN
  Ann 55* (GN-168)
  Anthony 50* (GN-163)
  Anthony 50* (GN-168)
  Charles H. 16* (GN-179)
  Mary E. 17* (PI-481)
CAINS
  Hiram 40 (GN-167)
  Thomas 30 (LW-86)
  Thos. 63 (LW-62)
CALAWAY
  Elizabeth 12* (LW-101)
  Washington 14* (LW-102)
CALDWELL
  E. W. 41 (m) (LW-118)
  John 48 (GN-227)
  Morris 42 (PE-404)
  William 24 (CT-223)
CALEWAY
  Cornelus 17* (LW-102)
  Harvey 19* (LW-102)
CALHOUN
  B. W. 30 (m) (LE-154)
  David 38 (LE-154)
  David 60 (LE-154)
  David A. 15* (FO-434)
  Evins 23 (BE-12)
  Jackson 25 (LE-154)
  James 47 (BE-12)
  Lister 21* (BE-32)
  Ransom 33 (LE-154)
  Thomas 65 (BE-13)
  Thos. 28 (LE-153)
CALIHAN
  Silas 26 (LE-151)
CALLAHAN
  Charles 22 (GN-254)
  Charles 38 (GN-204)
  D. 23 (m)* (GN-210)
  Daniel 36 (GN-178)
  George 24 (GN-178)
  Horatio 28 (GN-255)
  Jonathan 25 (GN-206)
  Sarah 47 (GN-205)
  Sarah 65 (GN-205)
  Thomas 36 (GN-170)
CALLEHAN
  Isaac 24 (PE-430)
  William 45 (PE-429)
CALLIHAN
  Nancy 39* (GN-206)
  Robt. D. 43 (LW-77)
CALLOWAY
  Mary 15* (B) (GN-158)
CALVIN
  Aquilla 40* (GN-171)
  James 27* (GN-215)
  Vincent 29* (GN-213)
CAMBELL
  Woolery 32 (PE-432)
CAMERON
  Duncan 40* (GN-210)
  Elizabeth 18* (GN-193)
  Jane 19* (GN-193)
  Oscar 2* (GN-250)
  Robert 16* (GN-247)
  S. 45 (m)* (GN-249)
CAMP
  James 18* (GN-170)
CAMPBELL
  Alexander 30* (BE-16)
  Caleb 32 (BE-16)
  Caleb 47 (PE-417)

Index

CAMPBELL
Charly 47* (BE-38)
Darcus 80* (GN-198)
David 19* (CT-270)
Edward 16* (PI-474)
Elijah 49* (PE-409)
George W. 49* (GN-216)
Hiram 25 (GN-256)
Hiram 42* (PE-410)
Isac 44 (PE-410)
Jackson 58 (BE-16)
James 27 (PE-408)
James 36 (PE-407)
James 53 (GN-210)
Jesse 24* (GN-256)
Jesse 27 (PE-410)
John 21 (PE-409)
John 23 (BE-30)
John 24 (LW-90)
John 55 (PE-409)
John 87 (PE-410)
Layne 27* (LW-63)
Lewis 25 (PE-418)
Lewis 50 (BE-32)
Nancy 21 (PE-422)
Nancy 46 (PE-422)
Nancy 75 (PI-434)
Nancy 88* (PE-422)
Nathan 20* (B) (PI-443)
Richard 30 (FO-472)
Riley 20* (CT-274)
Samuel 36 (PE-410)
Smith 28* (LW-87)
Thomas 36* (GN-220)
William 18* (GN-171)
William 21 (PE-417)
William 25 (PE-409)
William 25* (PE-411)
William 50 (PE-410)
William 56 (PE-432)
William W. 36 (PI-434)
Willis 42 (GN-170)
Zachariah 28 (PE-417)
Zechariah 26 (BE-29)
CANARD
Eliza 21* (MG-89)
CANDELL
Rebecca 40* (PE-429)

CANDELL?
Robert 14* (PE-428)
CANDLE
Isom 28 (JO-101)
James C. 26 (JO-97)
Jeremiah 26* (JO-94)
John 35 (JO-95)
Mathew 26 (JO-101)
Mathew 29 (JO-106)
Reubin 25 (JO-104)
Thomas 57 (JO-101)
William 27 (JO-104)
William 28* (JO-106)
CANE
Henry 65 (B) (GN-249)
John 23* (GN-212)
CANIFAX
Calvin 47* (GN-259)
CANNON
Susan 14* (CT-244)
CANTERBURY
Elizabeth 15* (GN-174)
Elizabeth 46* (LW-63)
Jane 23* (GN-198)
John 45 (GN-197)
R. F. 27 (m)* (LW-76)
CANTRELL
Abraham 76* (PI-448)
Henry 25 (MG-125)
Henry 44 (JO-91)
John 19 (JO-89)
John 20 (MG-125)
John 45* (PI-448)
John 52 (MG-125)
Mary 28 (MG-125)
CARAGEE
James 35* (GN-245)
CARDWELL
Danl. 24* (BE-33)
John 60 (BE-18)
John O. 25 (BE-24)
CAREY
John 35 (PI-470)
CARLAN
Thomas 25* (GN-260)
CARNAHAN
Polly 50* (GN-242)

CARNETT
David 50 (LW-53)
Elisha 31* (LW-54)
CARNETTE
Reuben Jr. 37 (LW-52)
CARNUTT
Elizabeth 22* (LW-50)
John 25 (LW-117)
Reuben 57* (LW-111)
Stephen 27 (LW-113)
CARPENTER
Benjamin 21 (BE-8)
Felix 75 (BE-8)
Fielden 22 (GN-260)
Fielding 26 (BE-11)
Harry 41 (MG-113)
Josiah 31 (MG-107)
Levi 32 (MG-107)
Lucinda 20* (MG-106)
Samuel 23 (BE-9)
Sarah 36* (BE-5)
Wilson 20* (BE-8)
CARR
Canady 63 (m) (GN-216)
Isaac 25* (MG-162)
Jacob 38 (GN-165)
James 35* (GN-216)
James 37 (GN-211)
Miles 30* (CT-271)
Willis M. 30* (GN-176)
CARRELL
Daniel 26 (CT-262)
Daniel 54 (CT-262)
Nelson 26 (CT-263)
CARRELL?
Patsey 23* (CT-258)
CARREY
David 24* (GN-188)
CARRINGTON
Jesse 50 (GN-206)
CARROL
Lemuel 25 (MG-140)
CARROLL
John 22* (CT-269)
CARSIN
Elijah 25* (CT-271)
CARSON
Elijah 28* (CT-270)

Index

CARTER
Calvery 37 (LW-110)
Charles 36 (PI-474)
Covey 19 (m) (LW-92)
David 54 (MG-147)
David 60* (LW-51)
Elizabeth 25* (PI-474)
Enoch B. 50 (MG-109)
Frank 23* (B) (GN-171)
Henery 55* (PI-474)
James 25* (LW-54)
Jeremiah 43 (LW-52)
John 33 (PI-474)
John 48 (LW-80)
Joseph 37 (GN-255)
Joseph 40 (FO-413)
Joseph 58 (MG-140)
July A. 29* (PI-441)
Milton 45 (MG-129)
Morgan 22 (PI-484)
Nathan 22* (GN-248)
Phebe 15* (LW-92)
R. G. 50 (m)* (CT-266)
Raney 28 (MG-113)
Sarah 13?* (LW-50)
Sarah 52 (PI-446)
Thomas 47 (LW-73)
Thomas 8* (LW-51)
William 30* (GN-176)
Willis G. 28 (MG-171)
CARTMILL
Thos. 26 (LW-98)
William H. 32 (MG-174)
CARTRIGHT
Elizabeth 18* (GN-167)
Jesse 40 (GN-166)
Moses 66 (GN-166)
CARTY
David 30 (FO-454)
CARVER
Frances 20* (CT-270)
George 32 (CT-221)
Jackson 12* (CT-230)
Jackson 5* (CT-230)
Morgan 66* (CT-242)
Percival 8* (CT-229)
Richard 40 (GN-261)

CARY
Benjn. 53 (LW-99)
Wm. 8* (LW-97)
CASADAY
Thomas 38 (LE-140)
CASE
Abel A. 37* (GN-196)
James 33 (PI-447)
Rebecca 40* (PI-447)
CASEBOLT?
John J. 50 (PI-461)
CASEBOTT
Nancy 52 (FO-407)
CASEY
Danl. 49* (LW-83)
James 42* (LW-64)
Nancy 19* (LW-93)
CASINBROK
Anthony 27* (LW-78)
CASKEY
Alvin 28* (MG-172)
Gardner 53 (MG-157)
Jesse 24 (MG-119)
John sr. 56 (MG-106)
Robert 49* (MG-119)
Samuel 37 (MG-99)
Thomas H. 39 (MG-86)
Thomas jr. 23 (MG-100)
Thomas sr. 84 (MG-106)
William 23* (MG-174)
William 35* (MG-144)
CASSADAY
James 25* (PI-487)
CASSADY
Alexander 24 (JO-115)
Benjamin 51 (JO-116)
CASSIDA
Enoch 21 (CT-283)
CASSIDY
Thomas 82* (GN-207)
CASSITY
Catharine 1* (MG-94)
Elizabeth 43 (MG-171)
George 28 (MG-96)
Harrison 36 (MG-99)
Isaac 38* (MG-94)
Isaac sr. 68 (MG-103)
Jesse 61 (MG-158)

John 66* (MG-94)
Margarett 62 (MG-105)
Mary 5* (MG-104)
Shelton 29* (MG-173)
Stephen 58 (MG-162)
Thomas 16* (MG-174)
Thomas 22 (MG-105)
Thomas J. 29* (MG-106)
CASTEEL
James 60 (LW-94)
John 28 (LW-73)
John 32* (GN-178)
John J. 64* (CT-230)
CASTER
Lewis 24* (GN-247)
CASTLE
Benjamin 60 (JO-113)
Drury 29 (JO-93)
Edward 24* (JO-111)
Ephraim 34 (LW-80)
Harper 24 (LW-102)
Henderson 34 (JO-121)
Henry 30 (JO-86)
Inmon 49 (JO-92)
Ira 30 (JO-82)
Isreal 26 (JO-86)
Jackson 24 (LW-120)
James B. 30* (JO-118)
Jane 17* (JO-96)
Johial 38 (JO-113)
John 5* (LW-99)
John E. 29 (LW-119)
Joshua Z. 26 (LW-121)
Lindsey 35 (LW-120)
Nathan 50 (JO-108)
Patterson 34 (JO-113)
William 23* (JO-82)
Wm. 26* (LW-99)
Zacheriah 39 (JO-113)
Zedekiah 72* (LW-120)
CASTLES
Henery W. 29 (PI-445)
James 27 (PI-445)
CATLETT
Letitia 50* (GN-194)
CAUDELL
Abijah 25 (FO-428)
Abijah 33 (FO-428)

Index

CAUDELL
Abner 53 (FO-428)
Benjamin 25 (GN-162)
CAUDILL
Abel 22 (FO-455)
Abel 33 (LE-133)
Alfred 26 (LE-129)
Benjamin 21 (LE-139)
Henry 21 (LE-128)
Henry 21 (LE-143)
Henry 23 (LE-129)
Henry 29 (LE-125)
Henry Sr. 65 (LE-125)
Isaac 28 (FO-458)
Isom 21 (LE-143)
Isom 24 (LE-144)
Isom 55 (LE-128)
James 22 (LE-128)
James 23 (LE-132)
James 25 (FO-455)
James 34 (LE-143)
James 36 (LE-139)
James 60 (LE-145)
Jesse 32 (LE-125)
John 52 (LE-129)
Leticus? 26 (LE-155)
Mathew 38 (LE-144)
Samuel 46 (LE-128)
Sarah 71 (LE-134)
Stephen 24 (LE-139)
Stephen 40 (LE-143)
Stephen 56 (LE-134)
Watson 28 (LE-138)
Wilburn 38 (LE-126)
William 23 (LE-144)
William 25 (LE-126)
William 25 (LE-144)
William 26* (LE-139)
William 27 (LE-125)
Wm. 33* (LE-154)
Wm. 71 (LE-144)
CAUDILL?
Chany 8 (f) (B) (LE-139)
CAUDLE
Henry 27 (BE-35)
Jesse 35 (FO-429)
John 54* (BE-34)
Polly 21* (BE-35)

CAUFMAN
John 21* (LW-91)
CAULBOATH?
Shade 28 (m)* (GN-194)
CAULY
George 32* (GN-186)
William 39* (GN-159)
CAVENS
Anna 52 (PI-435)
CAVERN
William 35 (FO-442)
CAVINS
Katherine 27* (PI-435)
CAZELL
Joseph 33* (GN-174)
CECIL
Colbert 35* (PI-458)
Elizabeth 46* (PI-494)
Harvy 31 (FO-417)
James 36 (FO-409)
John 37 (LW-106)
Kinsey B. 70* (JO-117)
Nancey 52* (PI-463)
Samuel 39 (PI-487)
Thomas 60 (FO-416)
William 37* (FO-416)
William 47 (PI-495)
CHADWELL
John A. 43 (PI-462)
CHADWICK
Geo. E. 50 (LW-110)
James 16* (BE-34)
Lucy 56* (GN-195)
Reuben 38 (GN-199)
CHAFEN
John 39 (CT-280)
CHAFIN
Agnes 60* (LW-118)
David 71* (LW-82)
Dicy 30* (LW-62)
James 22* (LW-87)
Jeff 27* (LW-112)
John 25 (LW-84)
John 65 (LW-51)
Judy 45* (LW-117)
Julia A. 15* (CT-267)
Levi 48* (LW-97)
Owen 25* (LW-117)

Sally 25* (CT-222)
Samuel 20* (FO-434)
Simon 58 (LW-63)
Thomas 26 (LW-81)
Thomas 27 (LW-123)
Wm. 35 (LW-73)
Wm. M. 31 (LW-74)
CHAIN
John 28 (CT-254)
CHAMBERS
David 38 (LW-76)
Elijah 46 (BE-20)
CHAMPERS?
Jasper 21 (MG-151)
CHANDLER
Abraham 48 (JO-93)
George R. 13* (MG-131)
Henry 34 (JO-93)
Isaac 22 (JO-97)
James 33 (JO-83)
William 10* (GN-264)
William 45 (GN-201)
CHANEY
Abell 50* (PI-436)
John 21 (GN-188)
John 35 (BE-27)
Thomas G. 36 (PI-434)
CHANY
Charles 23 (PI-482)
CHAPMAN
Andrew J. 47 (LW-81)
C. P. 33 (m) (GN-160)
Edmund 53 (BE-18)
Edward 38 (PI-479)
Elizabeth 1* (LW-96)
George 25 (BE-33)
Isaac 60* (LW-116)
James 29 (LW-123)
John 59* (LW-122)
Maria 45 (LW-117)
Michel 37 (LW-116)
Nancy 39* (CT-264)
Nathan 80* (MG-104)
Robert O. 38* (MG-118)
Thomas 69* (PI-468)
Wm. 19* (CT-264)
Wm. 21 (LW-83)
Wm. 46 (LW-77)

Index

CHAPMAN
  Wm. F. 24* (LW-118)
CHAPPEL
  George W. 29 (GN-215)
CHARLES
  David 25 (PI-474)
  Fredric 44 (PI-481)
  George 87 (PI-481)
  John 21* (PI-474)
  John 61* (PI-473)
  John jr. 23 (PI-481)
  Michael 58 (PI-474)
CHASE
  Ambrose 70* (GN-253)
  William D. 34* (GN-188)
CHILDERS
  Abram 52 (LW-101)
  Archibald 22 (MG-149)
  Goolsby 45 (LE-146)
  James M. 31 (BE-2)
  John W. 24 (MG-142)
  Robert 41 (JO-111)
  Russell 23 (LW-100)
  William 33 (MG-154)
CHILDERSTON
  George W. 38 (GN-158)
CHILDRES
  Flemming 42 (PI-445)
  Harvey 21* (PI-444)
  Mary 16* (PI-440)
  Miles 19* (PI-435)
  Nathaniel 20 (PI-445)
CHINN
  Benjamin 66* (GN-165)
  C. C. 32 (m)* (GN-166)
  Edward 30 (GN-195)
  Sophia 36* (GN-164)
CHOCKEY
  John 75* (CT-222)
CHRISMAN
  Ira G. 34 (CT-272)
CHRISTIAN
  Allen 46 (PE-427)
  Barnabas 25 (PE-427)
  Jackson 21* (CT-246)
  Thos. 42 (LE-152)
CHRISTMAN
  Charles 51 (GN-236)

CHRISTY
  Joseph K. 62 (MG-96)
  Julius 24* (MG-97)
  Phillip 34* (MG-171)
CHURCH
  Joel 36 (PI-473)
  Joseph 22 (BE-13)
CLACK
  John 21* (GN-249)
CLANCY
  Nancy 54* (GN-163)
CLAREY
  Thorndike 35* (GN-224)
  Timothy 34 (GN-238)
CLARK
  Daniel 37 (GN-231)
  Edmond 49* (PI-488)
  Edward 34* (FO-460)
  Enoch 30 (GN-206)
  Enos 58 (GN-209)
  George B. 51 (MG-95)
  James 24 (CT-281)
  James 39 (CT-215)
  Jesse 22 (GN-206)
  John 34* (LW-90)
  John 40 (CT-281)
  John 47* (FO-465)
  John 49 (GN-193)
  John W. 30* (FO-422)
  Joseph 28 (CT-281)
  Joseph 29 (CT-225)
  Joseph N. 32 (CT-252)
  Joshua 44 (CT-281)
  Lorenzo Dow 43* (FO-410)
  Lucinda J. 27* (CT-251)
  Mitchel 30 (CT-217)
  Morgan 33 (FO-465)
  William 48 (CT-252)
CLARKE
  Anthony G. 26 (GN-206)
  James 30 (GN-162)
  Margaret 54 (GN-168)
  Nancy A. 43* (GN-217)
  Richard 57 (GN-205)
CLAVIS
  Coonrod 37* (GN-180)
CLAY
  Andrew 15* (PI-462)

Bartly 50 (LW-112)
Charles 26 (LW-89)
Elijah 35 (BE-41)
Henery J. 32 (PI-449)
Henry 43 (LW-107)
James 46 (JO-117)
James M. 54 (LW-86)
Jane 45* (FO-414)
John 49* (PI-449)
Jorden 72 (JO-117)
Mathew 29* (JO-125)
Matthew 34 (FO-421)
Mitchell 25* (PI-496)
Peter 43 (JO-115)
Robert 30 (FO-469)
Solomon 80* (FO-421)
Susan 10* (PI-462)
Temperance 32 (JO-87)
Wm. 25 (LW-90)
CLEAR
  Ezekiel 49* (GN-191)
  James M. 34 (PI-442)
  Reuben 19* (MG-145)
  Riborn 21* (MG-144)
CLEARER
  William T. 24 (MG-144)
CLEMMONS
  Richard 40 (BE-12)
CLEMONS
  Benjamin 53 (BE-7)
  Francis 28 (BE-7)
  John C. 28 (BE-6)
  William 37 (BE-12)
CLEVENGER
  John 23 (GN-214)
  Joshua 51* (LW-53)
  Pleasant 26 (MG-134)
CLEVINGER
  Alex. 55* (PI-449)
  Levi 32 (PI-439)
  Levi T. 25 (PI-494)
  Nancy A. 16* (PI-495)
  Russel 53 (PI-494)
CLICK
  Alexander 24 (FO-422)
  David 42 (FO-440)
  Eliza J. 15* (MG-134)
  James 50 (FO-422)

Index

CLICK
 John 22 (MG-134)
 Parthena 15* (MG-99)
 William H. 35 (MG-128)
CLIFTEN
 James 21* (GN-230)
CLIFTON
 Daniel 50 (GN-263)
CLINE
 Levi 40* (CT-253)
 Levi W. 24* (CT-254)
 Samuel 22* (CT-254)
 Samuel 22 (MG-94)
 William 21* (CT-253)
 William T. 24 (PI-474)
CLOITER
 Nancy 20* (GN-193)
CLUNN
 Dudley 63 (GN-192)
CLUTS
 Archibald 40 (GN-206)
 Mary 32* (GN-172)
CLUTZ
 Robert 32* (GN-208)
COADY
 Thomas 31 (PE-429)
 Thomas 60 (PE-429)
COAXEREL?
 Franklin 13* (MG-111)
COBOURN
 David 41 (FO-437)
 John P. 26? (FO-437)
 Samuel jr. 40 (FO-437)
 Samuel sr. 67* (FO-437)
COBURN
 George 18* (JO-123)
 Gordon C. 46* (LW-87)
 Jeremiah 76* (FO-444)
 Joseph 30 (LW-75)
 Madison 23 (LW-90)
 Thomas 39 (LW-87)
 Thos. jr 22 (LW-90)
COCHRAN
 Barbery 30 (GN-227)
 Samuel 37 (GN-245)
COCK
 Tobias 44 (MG-130)
 William 48 (MG-117)

COCKEREL
 McKinly 24 (MG-153)
COCKMAN
 Humphrey 26* (MG-148)
COCKRAM
 Danl. 24* (BE-41)
 James 19* (BE-29)
COCKRELL
 Emilia 68 (BE-24)
 Harrison 22 (BE-25)
 James 33* (BE-25)
 Jereme 62 (BE-12)
 John 40 (BE-24)
 Simon 78 (BE-25)
COCRELL
 William 60 (BE-1)
CODEY
 John 21 (LE-150)
COFER
 Elizabeth 30* (MG-104)
COFFEE
 Ambrose 26* (GN-251)
 Ambrose 65 (GN-252)
 Ambrose 7* (GN-250)
 Elijah 52 (GN-253)
 Martha 28* (MG-91)
 Mason W. 39 (MG-125)
 Reuben 36 (GN-250)
 Wiley J. 33 (MG-91)
 William 65* (MG-89)
COFFER
 E. 31 (m)* (GN-250)
COFFIELD
 Alexander 35 (GN-203)
COFMAN
 Martin 41* (LW-78)
 Zachariah 43* (LW-79)
COGSHELL
 Levina 38* (GN-173)
COGSWELL
 Hannah 23* (MG-99)
 William 55 (CT-240)
COHEN
 Harrison 35* (GN-162)
COLBERT
 Jonathan 49* (GN-167)
 William 33 (MG-101)

COLDIRON
 George 22 (BE-3)
 Henry F. 23 (MG-143)
 Isaac D. 25 (LE-129)
 John 22 (PE-400)
COLE
 Allaniah 49 (m) (GN-163)
 Charles 24 (B) (FO-445)
 George 22 (FO-451)
 Harrison 33* (MG-100)
 Isaac 24 (BE-27)
 Jemimah 26* (FO-457)
 Jeremiah 22 (CT-245)
 John 42 (FO-450)
 Mary 24* (MG-100)
 Perry 9* (JO-125)
 Raney 23* (JO-113)
 Samuel 46 (MG-100)
 William 59 (FO-449)
COLEGROVE
 Edwin 30* (CT-215)
 J. D. 39 (m)* (GN-172)
 Jeremiah 65 (GN-172)
 Nathan 34 (GN-206)
COLEMAN
 Abigal 29 (PI-474)
 Abraham 42 (PI-443)
 Curtis 40 (PI-473)
 Daniel 24 (PI-475)
 Daniel 25 (PI-451)
 Daniel 63 (PI-475)
 David 24 (PI-451)
 Henery 45* (PI-490)
 Isaac 34 (PI-474)
 John 26 (PI-451)
 John 30 (PI-184)
 Lafayett 22 (GN-237)
 Lucy 39 (PI-443)
 Moses 23 (PI-475)
 Nancy 60 (GN-242)
 Peeter 35 (PI-471)
 Peeter 74 (PI-451)
 Peter 56 (JO-123)
 Thomas 50* (GN-184)
COLGROVE
 E. 46 (f)* (GN-248)
COLINS
 David 43 (JO-108)

Index

COLLANWORTH
  Reuben 23 (PE-417)
  William 52 (PE-416)
COLLIER
  James 27 (LE-138)
  Preston H. 32 (LE-141)
  Randolph 23 (LE-127)
  Richard 53 (LE-134)
  William D. 32* (GN-169)
  William R. 53 (LE-127)
COLLINGSWORTH
  David 38* (MG-161)
COLLINS
  Amey 54 (PI-494)
  Andrew 26 (PI-483)
  Ann 65* (GN-211)
  Archabald 25 (PE-411)
  Berdine 40 (LE-146)
  Briant 36 (LE-146)
  Caroline 17* (CT-254)
  Carter 37* (LE-141)
  Charles 31 (LE-145)
  Christopher 43 (JO-117)
  Clary 34 (m) (JO-103)
  Elijah 35 (B) (MG-137)
  Elizabeth 46? (FO-427)
  Ely 22 (LE-130)
  George 29* (JO-123)
  George 51* (PI-468)
  Harvey 17* (PI-494)
  Isaac 30* (JO-104)
  Isaac 36 (GN-211)
  Jacob 26* (PI-444)
  James 67 (LE-147)
  John 42 (GN-161)
  John 45* (FO-466)
  John L. 38* (GN-162)
  John W. 30 (CT-246)
  Joseph D. 51* (GN-159)
  Joshua 45 (JO-108)
  Luan 23 (f) (GN-211)
  Macha? 24 (f)* (JO-121)
  Margaret 30* (PI-484)
  Martha 43* (JO-125)
  Nathaniel 35* (LE-146)
  Robert 27* (GN-182)
  Robert; 46 (LE-130)
  Sanders 15* (LE-146)
  Shepherd 38 (BE-10)
  Simpson 33 (FO-425)
  Thos. 29 (LE-146)
  Thos. 30 (LE-146)
  William 27 (LE-147)
  William 30 (FO-466)
  William 40 (BE-7)
COLLINSWORTH
  Anderson 44* (CT-222)
  Mason 40 (FO-451)
  Moses 40* (PI-486)
  Reuben 55* (JO-116)
  Samuel 26 (FO-458)
  Thomas 25 (JO-116)
  Thomas 65 (FO-456)
COLLINWORTH
  John 23 (FO-457)
COLVIN
  Abind 38 (JO-103)
  Allen 39 (JO-106)
  Easter 49 (GN-254)
  Isaac 24 (JO-106)
  Jackson 31 (JO-105)
  Joseph 42* (GN-250)
  Sarah 65 (JO-105)
COLYIER
  John 52 (LW-61)
COMB
  James 20* (PE-406)
  John D. 25* (PE-425)
  Stephen 45 (PE-397)
  Wiley 16* (PE-417)
COMBS
  Alexander 34 (PE-427)
  Alexander S. 25 (PE-415)
  Alfred 36* (BE-14)
  Andrew 38 (PE-428)
  Benjn. 57 (BE-34)
  Biram 35 (LE-153)
  Biram 37 (PE-415)
  Biram S. 32 (PE-415)
  Bluford 24 (PE-397)
  Buonapart 40 (BE-35)
  Clinton 41 (PE-425)
  Dicy 11* (PE-425)
  Edin 21 (BE-19)
  Edward 24 (LE-137)
  Elias 22* (PE-428)
  Elihu E. 19* (LE-141)
  Elijah 14* (PE-420)
  Elijah 80* (PE-415)
  Elsey D. 24 (m) (PE-425)
  Francis 34 (PE-409)
  George 52 (PE-418)
  Granville 28* (PE-408)
  Hacker 22 (LE-131)
  Hardin jr. 35 (BE-36)
  Henry 23 (BE-23)
  Henry 31 (BE-15)
  Henry 53* (PE-404)
  Hezekiah 25 (PE-420)
  Hugh 17* (CT-239)
  Isaac B. 27 (BE-18)
  Jackson G. 34 (PE-428)
  James 12* (BE-15)
  James 42 (PE-428)
  Jeremiah 62 (PE-397)
  Jeremiah C. 68 (PE-416)
  Jeremiah L. 35 (PE-426)
  Jesse 53* (PE-415)
  John 5* (LE-129)
  John 65 (MG-113)
  John L. 42 (PE-420)
  John S. 28* (PE-433)
  Joseph 24 (BE-35)
  Kinick 26* (LE-154)
  Levi 22 (PE-424)
  Lurena 29 (PE-415)
  Margaret 31 (PE-397)
  Martha 40 (PE-425)
  Mason 37 (MG-160)
  Mason 55 (BE-43)
  Matilda 40 (PE-415)
  Matthew 60* (BE-26)
  Milley 30* (PE-420)
  Moses 44 (PE-422)
  Nicholas 21* (BE-38)
  Nicholas 28 (PE-424)
  Nicholas 58 (PE-416)
  Nicholas 86 (PE-416)
  Polly 46 (PE-425)
  Preston 46* (BE-36)
  Rachael 54 (PE-415)
  Richard 28 (MG-108)
  Robert C. 28 (PE-416)
  Saml. 51* (BE-34)

Index

COMBS
- Samuel 22* (PE-423)
- Samuel 30* (PE-413)
- Shaderick 38 (LE-138)
- Shadrick 25 (MG-113)
- Simon 16* (BE-15)
- Sira 26* (BE-35)
- Stephen 45 (BE-23)
- Tarleton 46* (PE-433)
- Tarlton 24 (BE-36)
- Washington 4 (PE-425)
- Wesley 30 (PE-417)
- Wesley 35 (LE-138)
- William 40 (PE-426)
- William 44 (PE-408)
- William D. 60 (PE-415)
- William M. 22 (BE-18)

COMER
- John 34 (GN-235)

COMOS
- Ira 26* (PE-397)

COMPTON
- Hiram 50* (LW-80)
- James 64 (PI-487)
- James H. 1* (LW-116)
- James H. 23 (LW-117)
- Lee 33 (PI-459)
- William 23* (PI-491)

CON
- Harrison 29 (MG-130)
- Hiram 22* (MG-134)
- Jesse 62 (MG-129)
- John 16* (MG-131)
- John 40 (MG-129)
- Wilson 30 (MG-130)

CONAWAY
- Thomas 35 (PE-417)
- Wesley 26 (PE-417)

CONGLETON
- Margarett 68* (MG-150)

CONLEY
- Caly 25* (FO-454)
- Carter 31 (GN-242)
- Constantine 44 (JO-108)
- David 19* (GN-264)
- David 43 (JO-106)
- David 44 (MG-121)
- David M. 33 (JO-100)
- David sr. 63 (FO-437)
- Edmd. 35 (LW-71)
- Edmund 22* (JO-101)
- Edmund 25 (JO-101)
- Elijah 28 (FO-449)
- Elizabeth 33* (FO-452)
- Ezekial 22 (LW-59)
- Henrey 41 (JO-124)
- Henry 20 (JO-106)
- Henry 55 (FO-455)
- Isaah 36 (JO-107)
- John 25* (BE-10)
- John 26 (GN-235)
- John sr. 66 (MG-121)
- Joseph 52* (GN-248)
- Mary 45* (JO-119)
- Sampson 35 (FO-437)
- Sampson 58 (GN-234)
- Susan 70* (JO-124)
- Temperance 69* (JO-107)
- Thomas 41 (JO-98)
- Thomas 43* (JO-101)
- William 22* (GN-256)

CONLY
- Edmund 34 (MG-163)
- Isaac 24 (MG-86)
- John 38 (MG-96)
- John jr. 33 (MG-117)
- Moses 30 (MG-86)
- William 40 (FO-455)
- William 41 (MG-121)

CONN
- Ira 25 (FO-417)
- William 23 (FO-417)

CONNEAR
- William 27* (GN-209)

CONNELLEY
- John 29 (JO-84)

CONNER
- Hugh 24* (GN-210)
- William 53 (GN-219)

CONNOWAY
- James 29 (PI-481)
- John 32 (PI-481)
- Michael 23* (PI-495)
- Sarah 15* (PI-436)

COOK
- Angeline 8* (CT-274)
- Eliza 19* (FO-456)
- Fielding B. 31 (CT-236)
- George 15* (MG-107)
- George 40* (CT-272)
- Hiram 35* (CT-217)
- James 23 (MG-108)
- James 7* (CT-246)
- Jenny 16* (PI-461)
- Joel 59* (CT-265)
- Joel 83* (CT-275)
- John 38 (GN-253)
- John M. 30* (LW-74)
- Johnson 62 (CT-218)
- Joshua 28 (MG-107)
- Levi 30 (GN-173)
- Mary 17* (PI-460)
- Peter 45 (GN-177)
- Weley 28 (CT-244)
- Wiley 20 (MG-145)

COOKSY
- Andrew 26 (LW-66)
- Jane 26* (LW-91)
- John 34* (LW-66)
- Jonathon 53 (LW-66)

COOLEY
- David 42* (FO-473)
- James 21* (PI-451)
- John 23 (GN-214)
- John 38* (CT-230)
- Katherine 60* (PI-444)
- Lucresa 13* (GN-257)
- Richard 21* (CT-230)
- Samuel 16* (GN-208)

COOLY
- Andrew 36* (MG-114)
- Edmund 53 (GN-216)

COOMPTON
- Gasper 21* (LW-96)

COON
- Christopher 65 (GN-184)

COOPER
- Archibald 24* (MG-90)
- Catharine 14* (MG-162)
- David M. 48 (MG-166)
- Eli 45* (GN-233)
- George 23 (GN-244)
- Jeremiah 13* (LE-143)
- John 57 (GN-240)

Index

COOPER
 John 60 (PE-427)
 Jonathan 27 (GN-246)
 Joseph 30 (MG-166)
 Junius 23* (GN-170)
 Lee 24* (MG-163)
 Malinda 21* (CT-230)
 Martha 19* (MG-92)
 Perry 32* (MG-90)
 Rebecca 37* (BE-27)
 Thomas 26 (MG-161)
 William 28 (GN-226)
 William 60 (MG-166)
 Wyatt 45 (CT-230)
COOTS
 Henry 29 (PE-401)
 James 22 (PE-402)
 William 50* (PE-401)
COPE
 A. C. 22 (m) (BE-18)
 James D. 51 (BE-13)
 James P. 64 (BE-27)
 Wiley 31 (BE-26)
 William 27 (BE-27)
COPLEY
 Robert 30* (GN-175)
 Wm. 59 (LW-124)
CORD
 Wm. 17* (LW-114)
CORDELL
 Abagail 46 (MG-164)
 John 21 (LW-114)
CORDILE
 Elanor 22* (LW-57)
CORDILL
 Amos 18 (LW-114)
 James 24 (LW-61)
 Wm. 47 (LW-61)
CORLEY
 David 27 (BE-9)
CORMITT
 Nathaniel W. 39 (PE-422)
CORNETE
 Samuel 22 (PE-406)
CORNETT
 Eligah 25 (PE-415)
 Joseph E. 36 (LE-138)
 Stephen 18 (LE-125)

W. B. 21 (m) (LE-155)
CORNITT
 Anderson 30 (PE-429)
 Archabald 61 (PE-430)
 Archibald 31 (PE-426)
 Charles L. 21 (PE-427)
 Clarke 17 (PE-430)
 Davis 26* (LE-155)
 Hiram 25 (PE-430)
 James 36 (PE-431)
 Jesse H. 55* (LE-155)
 John 34 (PE-430)
 John 56 (PE-426)
 Mary 78* (PE-429)
 Robert 32 (PE-430)
 Robert 52 (PE-425)
 Roger 45* (PE-427)
 Sally 2* (PE-425)
 Samuel 36 (PE-431)
 Samuel 47 (LE-154)
 William 17 (PE-427)
 William 25* (PE-430)
CORNWALL
 Jefferson 29 (MG-150)
 William 27 (MG-143)
 William 62 (MG-144)
CORTNEY
 Joseph 21* (GN-249)
CORUM
 Jesse 40 (GN-157)
 Martha 57 (GN-159)
 William 39 (GN-157)
COSSLEY
 Elizabeth 42 (JO-117)
 Freman 39 (JO-115)
COTTLE
 David N. 41* (MG-162)
 Isaac 46* (MG-162)
 James 28 (MG-162)
 Robert C. 36* (MG-157)
 Uriah 50 (MG-88)
COTTON
 James 21* (MG-122)
 Jobe 63 (MG-122)
 John 23 (MG-122)
COUCH
 Andrew 42 (BE-24)
 Charles 25* (PE-408)

Elijah 40 (BE-40)
Ira 25 (PE-398)
John 38 (PE-397)
Joseph 45* (PE-397)
Martin 65* (PE-398)
Thomas 38 (PE-398)
COUNTS
 Christopher 33 (CT-263)
 George W. 26 (CT-265)
 John S. 23* (CT-263)
 Samuel 20* (CT-273)
 William 29 (CT-265)
COUPLEBARGER
 Nich. 57* (GN-208)
COURTNEY
 Robert 26* (FO-471)
COVEY
 Nixon 59* (BE-22)
COWLES
 William 27 (PE-412)
COX
 Benjamin 33* (MG-141)
 Bennett 36 (LW-73)
 Calvin 40 (MG-152)
 Charles G. 32 (MG-86)
 David 47* (GN-225)
 Dixon 25 (PI-451)
 Flurry 75* (LW-85)
 Henderson 22* (BE-38)
 Henry 29 (CT-259)
 James 39 (MG-145)
 Jesse 30 (GN-227)
 John 16* (CT-286)
 John 66* (MG-141)
 John F. 27 (CT-268)
 Joseph 16 (PE-422)
 Joshua 30* (CT-227)
 Joshua 63 (MG-141)
 Mrk 36 (CT-248)
 Odom 30 (CT-256)
 Rebecca 62 (CT-256)
 Sally 40* (PE-420)
 Solomon 54 (MG-142)
 Western G. 21 (MG-146)
 William 21 (CT-256)
 William 45* (MG-119)
COYLE
 Sarah 67* (GN-172)

Index

COZEE
  Booker 31 (PI-479)
  Judy 78* (PI-479)
CRABTREE
  John 42* (LW-75)
  Rachell 15* (PI-471)
  Ritta 45 (PI-490)
CRACE
  Peter 52 (PE-427)
CRAFT
  Archealous 36 (LE-133)
  Archealous 48 (LE-132)
  Archealous 96* (LE-132)
  Benjamin 24 (LE-132)
  Drusiller 60 (LE-132)
  George 6* (FO-449)
  Henry 25 (LE-132)
  John 54 (FO-451)
  Joseph 32 (LE-136)
  Keziah 16* (LW-80)
  Thomas 30 (LW-79)
  Tillman 37 (JO-85)
  Wiley 29 (JO-94)
  William 28* (BE-26)
  William 43 (LE-133)
CRAGER
  Adam 27* (LE-152)
  Harvy 30 (LE-145)
  James 25 (LE-145)
  Mikel 69 (LE-152)
CRAIG
  Stewart 25* (CT-227)
  Thomas 43 (MG-104)
  William 32 (MG-98)
CRAIN
  Richard 29 (MG-150)
  Robert 31 (MG-149)
CRAINS
  James T. 64 (MG-149)
CRAME
  William 16* (CT-270)
CRANE
  James 14* (CT-274)
CRANK
  Elizabeth 9* (LW-105)
  Jeremiah 28* (LW-86)
  Preston 37 (LW-87)

CRANTS
  Sarah 40 (GN-190)
CRASE
  Campbell 36 (PI-450)
CRASE?
  Alfred 32 (FO-457)
  Henry 30 (FO-455)
  Stephen 30 (FO-455)
CRAWFORD
  Archibald 78* (BE-20)
  B. F. 43 (m)* (CT-265)
  Benjamin 27* (CT-279)
  Clabourn 45 (BE-22)
  Elenor 18* (LW-106)
  F. B. 18 (m)* (BE-2)
  George W. 40* (CT-217)
  Gideon 62 (BE-1)
  Harrison 31 (BE-21)
  James M. 30 (PE-416)
  John 33 (GN-167)
  Katharine 55* (BE-2)
  M. N. 30 (m) (BE-41)
  Milton 42* (GN-168)
  Oliver 35 (BE-21)
  Owens 33 (BE-20)
  Robert 31* (CT-243)
  Sanders 37* (CT-243)
  Valentine 39* (BE-20)
CRAYCRAFT
  Ada 51* (GN-226)
  Charles 47 (GN-226)
  Charles 67* (GN-227)
  H. C. 20 (m)* (GN-237)
  Hugh 41 (GN-240)
  J. M. 38 (m) (GN-239)
  John 34 (GN-234)
  William 26* (GN-239)
  William 44* (GN-239)
CREASEY
  B. M. 49 (m) (GN-191)
  B. S. 36 (m) (GN-196)
CREECH
  Hiram 23 (BE-18)
CRESSEL
  Martha A. 28 (GN-180)
CRETZER
  Samuel 32* (GN-160)

CRIDER
  John 54* (FO-467)
  Resso? 25 (m) (FO-469)
  William 31 (FO-466)
CRIP
  Henry 34 (PE-400)
CRISP
  David 3* (GN-234)
  David 44 (GN-231)
  Elizabeth 48 (MG-130)
  Joel 49 (FO-420)
  William 25 (FO-423)
  William sr. 53 (FO-423)
CROAN
  Thomas 52 (CT-269)
  William 30 (CT-269)
CROFT
  Susan 47 (BE-11)
  William 27 (BE-11)
CRONE
  Hannah 10* (LW-90)
CROOKS
  Abraham 62 (GN-189)
  C. F. 27 (m) (GN-259)
  H. G. 23 (m)* (GN-235)
  John C. 25 (GN-190)
CROSE
  Adam 50 (MG-105)
CROSSET
  John L. 25 (GN-226)
CROUCH
  Sarah 18* (LW-79)
CROW
  Joseph 50 (GN-197)
CROWDER
  Coonrod 28* (GN-171)
CRUM
  Eli 22* (JO-115)
  Elijah 31 (GN-196)
  Gilbert 67 (GN-196)
  Henry 33 (FO-417)
  Henry 47* (FO-441)
  John 22 (GN-195)
  John 51 (FO-422)
  John jr. 35 (FO-407)
  Jonathan 34 (FO-441)
  Matta 30 (f)* (FO-422)

Index

CRUM
  Michael 56 (FO-417)
  Michael 9* (FO-441)
  Reuben 40 (JO-115)
  Susan 31 (FO-417)
  Thomas 39 (GN-189)
  Thos. 21 (LW-123)
  William 24* (FO-418)
  Wm. 45 (LW-123)
CRUMB
  Fredrick 52* (LW-123)
  Henry 26 (MG-130)
CRUMP
  John 69 (GN-247)
  Simpson 48 (GN-161)
  Turner 71 (GN-264)
  Willis 46 (GN-264)
CRUTCHER
  Robert 33* (FO-471)
CULBERTSON
  Cumfort 43 (f) (MG-109)
  Delila 16* (MG-114)
  E. D. 45 (m)* (GN-175)
  Jane 20* (MG-149)
  Samuel 48* (GN-174)
CULL
  Hugh 35* (GN-210)
CULVER
  John 60* (GN-192)
  Mary A. 38 (GN-219)
CUMINGS
  David 25 (LW-108)
CUMMINS
  William 27* (FO-470)
CUMPTON
  James 21* (GN-194)
CUNDIFF
  Joseph 26 (BE-25)
  Stephen 22* (BE-23)
CUNNINGHAM
  James 36 (GN-170)
  William 73* (JO-121)
CUPS?
  Margaret 2* (MG-102)
CURRINGTON
  Rosan 22* (GN-179)
CURRY
  Henry N. 32 (GN-258)

  Hugh 39 (GN-258)
  James 42 (GN-263)
  Lena 34* (CT-217)
  Nancey 69 (GN-264)
  Robert 35 (GN-264)
CURTEEL
  William 45* (GN-175)
CURTIS
  John 23* (JO-92)
  Margarett 19* (JO-90)
CUSHING
  Z. 47 (m) (LW-118)
CYPHERS
  Overly 18* (MG-152)
  Susan 37 (MG-158)
CYPHIRS
  Aaron 50* (MG-144)
CYPHUS
  James 4* (MG-88)
CYRAS
  Jesse 37* (LW-109)
DALE
  Jemima 75* (JO-125)
  Reuben 40 (JO-106)
DALEY
  Alfred 29 (MG-102)
  John 22 (MG-102)
DAMEREL
  Moses 30 (FO-426)
DAMERON
  Abraham 43 (PI-491)
  Elisha 27* (PI-454)
  Jackson 24 (PI-454)
  James 55 (PI-459)
  John 47 (PI-454)
  Lazerius 45* (PI-490)
  Richard 48* (PI-455)
  Solomon 23 (PI-458)
  Solomon 24* (PI-458)
  Spurlock 35* (PI-491)
  William 25* (PI-459)
DAMRELL
  Saml. 37 (BE-4)
DAMRON
  Hiram 43* (CT-269)
  Joseph Sr. 64 (BE-44)
  Joseph jr. 38 (BE-24)
  Lazrus 30 (LW-110)

  Nancy 20 (BE-24)
  Samuel 37 (FO-441)
DAMSON
  Samuel 19* (JO-114)
DAMSON?
  Elizabeth 21* (JO-115)
DANBY
  Henry 24* (FO-471)
DANIEL
  Andrew 36 (JO-83)
  David 23 (JO-118)
  Edward 31 (JO-110)
  George 24 (JO-113)
  George 24 (JO-114)
  George 25 (GN-250)
  Isom 26 (JO-83)
  James 34 (LW-93)
  James 39 (JO-94)
  James B. 29 (JO-103)
  James W. 32* (MG-111)
  John 39 (JO-110)
  John O. 21 (JO-83)
  Joseph 34 (JO-112)
  Joseph 53* (GN-250)
  Kenis 26 (m) (PE-413)
  Mary 54 (JO-120)
  Sarah 53 (JO-113)
  Solomon 31* (JO-108)
  Thomas 61* (JO-86)
  William 24 (JO-82)
DANIELS
  Harrison 10* (LW-109)
  John 21* (GN-247)
  Jonathan 18* (GN-248)
  Rachel 27 (PI-472)
  Richard 32 (PI-472)
  Wilder 26* (GN-260)
DARAGAN
  Edward 47 (B) (GN-243)
DARBY
  Caroline 25 (GN-211)
  George 29* (GN-174)
  Hugh 32* (GN-211)
  James 64 (GN-177)
  John 26* (GN-177)
DARION
  Patrick 27* (LW-88)

Index

DARLINTON
  G. W. 53 (m) (GN-254)
DARNELL
  William 31 (CT-257)
DARTER
  Alexander M. 23 (BE-18)
DAUGHERTY
  Francis M. 23 (PI-464)
  Hiram 46 (PI-483)
DAVIDSON
  Benjamin 28* (PE-425)
  Daniel 22* (PE-433)
  Daniel 27 (PE-404)
  George 29 (GN-206)
  Hannah 53* (GN-205)
  Isom 35 (CT-273)
  James 24* (GN-205)
  Jeremi 21 (BE-32)
  Jeremiah 34* (GN-158)
  Jesse 54 (GN-205)
  John 25 (BE-42)
  Joseph 22 (GN-204)
  Joseph 27 (PE-415)
  Nancy 10* (PE-406)
  Robt. 47 (BE-42)
  Samuel P. 50 (FO-462)
  Susanah 6* (LE-141)
  Thomas 45 (GN-195)
  Thomas 49 (GN-200)
  William L. 24* (GN-193)
DAVIS
  Aaron 34 (CT-224)
  Agnes 9* (GN-168)
  Alexander 50 (GN-217)
  Alfred 44 (GN-228)
  Alfred 9* (GN-228)
  Asa 22* (FO-430)
  Benjamin 23* (GN-174)
  Benson C. 51 (MG-86)
  Betsy 20* (BE-40)
  Catharine 30* (MG-137)
  Daniel 53 (GN-193)
  Daniel 6* (FO-470)
  David 57 (CT-224)
  David J. 40 (FO-470)
  Davidson 28* (MG-132)
  E. P. 40 (m)* (CT-257)
  Edmund Sr. 46 (CT-224)

Eilza 45* (GN-167)
Elias 45 (JO-90)
Elihue 52* (LW-103)
Eliza 15* (GN-215)
Elizabeth 22* (MG-167)
Elizabeth 65 (BE-7)
Ephraim 42 (MG-169)
Esther 59* (PI-484)
F. W. 5 (m)* (GN-157)
Harriet 61 (GN-217)
Henery T. 39 (PI-471)
Henry 23 (BE-28)
Henry 30 (BE-16)
Henry 33* (GN-175)
Henry 40 (LW-122)
Henry 64* (LW-102)
Henry 70 (MG-134)
Hezekiah 25 (LW-102)
Hezekiah 41 (CT-214)
Hickman 20 (LW-63)
Isaac 28* (CT-245)
J. C. 14 (m)* (GN-224)
James 57* (MG-115)
James 58 (GN-263)
James McHenry 22 (JO-90)
James jr. 24 (MG-117)
Jeremi 25 (m) (BE-16)
Jeremiah 38 (MG-161)
Job 62* (CT-244)
Joel 31 (MG-162)
John 25 (MG-155)
John 28 (JO-93)
John 30* (JO-81)
John 36 (PI-485)
John 37* (PI-467)
John 40* (CT-227)
John 40 (CT-272)
John 72 (MG-169)
John 98* (BE-13)
Jonathan 38 (GN-171)
Joseph 42 (LW-102)
Joseph 45 (GN-209)
Joseph 74 (JO-120)
Larkin 3 (PE-418)
Mary Ann 14* (GN-160)
Michael 24 (JO-82)
Nancy 50 (JO-106)
Nathanl. 42* (LW-81)

Peggy 80* (GN-176)
Pleasant 26 (BE-25)
Reece 33 (FO-435)
Richard 33* (JO-105)
Saml. 41* (LW-73)
Saml. 66 (LW-102)
Sarah K. 13* (CT-242)
Thomas 26* (FO-471)
Thomas 35* (GN-176)
Thomas 49* (FO-430)
Thomas 53* (JO-111)
William 14* (GN-158)
William 21* (CT-214)
William 26 (MG-120)
William 29 (CT-224)
William 31* (BE-8)
William 40 (BE-2)
Wm. jr 31* (LW-98)
Wm. sr. 80* (LW-103)
Zacheriah 22* (JO-82)
Zatto 14 (m)* (PI-475)
DAWSON
  Ellen 24* (GN-216)
  Isaac 23 (FO-466)
  James 56 (CT-244)
  Jane 55* (PI-492)
  John 53 (GN-218)
  Joseph 33 (FO-466)
  Larkin 55* (CT-257)
  Olive 49* (CT-214)
  Vincent 24 (PI-493)
  William 34 (PI-493)
  _____ 45 (m)* (GN-164)
DAY
  Allen 33 (MG-151)
  Archibald 36 (MG-141)
  Daniel 21 (MG-111)
  Daniel 23 (CT-248)
  David 28 (LE-144)
  David 51 (MG-114)
  Elbert 13* (MG-171)
  Eli 28 (CT-248)
  George 36 (LE-125)
  Isaac 30 (MG-103)
  James A. 31 (MG-96)
  James P. 41 (MG-120)
  James W. 29 (MG-113)
  Jedediah 29* (MG-96)

- 350 -

Index

DAY
Jesse 48 (MG-139)
John 33 (PE-431)
John 53* (CT-250)
John B. 26 (LE-139)
John F. 38 (GN-157)
John H. 22 (MG-88)
John N. 64 (LE-138)
John W. 32 (MG-86)
John W. 39 (CT-249)
Joseph 33 (LE-138)
K. B. 44 (m) (GN-157)
Morgan 21* (JO-120)
Peter 63 (MG-86)
Peter jr. 21* (MG-119)
Robert C. 27 (MG-119)
Susannah 45 (MG-98)
Thomas P. 34* (MG-162)
Thomas P. 46 (MG-118)
Travis 63 (MG-162)
William 28 (MG-119)
William 45 (GN-211)
William Sr. 62 (LE-125)
Willoughby 41 (BE-42)
DAYS
Allen T. 53 (MG-88)
DEAL
Jonier 9 (m)* (MG-137)
William 88 (MG-137)
William jr. 35 (MG-87)
DEAN
Elizabeth 65 (MG-112)
George 26 (GN-183)
James R. 24 (PI-487)
John 16* (FO-473)
John 48 (LW-62)
Joshua 24 (JO-100)
Saml. 55 (LW-83)
DEATLEY
James 23* (GN-241)
DEATON
Bryant 25* (BE-44)
Isaac 25 (BE-42)
John 21* (BE-41)
John 41 (BE-14)
Lucinda 22* (BE-7)
William 22 (BE-42)

DEBELL
Alfred 48 (CT-241)
DEBOAD
Jacob 33 (LW-98)
Louisa 22* (LW-60)
DEBOARD
Ira 42 (PI-463)
Jeptha 50* (CT-261)
Simpson 28 (MG-115)
DEBORD
James 50* (CT-265)
Joseph 62* (JO-96)
DEBOW
Eliza 9* (GN-178)
DECKER
Christain 23 (m)* (GN-260)
DEEGINS
William 36* (GN-184)
DEEL
Thomas 90 (FO-414)
DEER
James 26 (LW-59)
DEERING
William 57 (GN-177)
DEEVERS
George 40* (GN-246)
James 18* (GN-247)
DEFOE
James 8* (CT-245)
William 13* (GN-207)
DEGEER?
Daniel 24 (GN-244)
DEHART
Elizabeth 42* (MG-133)
Gabriel 43 (MG-139)
John 38 (MG-133)
Sarah 40* (CT-252)
Stephen 31 (MG-129)
Thomas 26 (MG-128)
DELANEY
Margaret 30* (BE-30)
Thomas 32* (FO-471)
DELMAN
Elias 25* (GN-245)
DELONG
George 37* (JO-103)
Harvey 22 (JO-117)
James 25 (JO-118)

Samuel 31 (JO-117)
DEMETT
Shedk. 28* (LW-50)
DEMOND
Charles 47 (LW-79)
John 32 (LW-79)
DENNIS
David C. 29 (MG-143)
Elizabeth 63 (MG-108)
Green 20* (MG-102)
Jacob 34 (MG-111)
John L. – (CT-241)
Mathias 52 (MG-110)
Samuel S. 40 (MG-110)
DERBY
Mary 23 (CT-269)
DERMIT
George 50* (GN-233)
Henry J. 21 (GN-233)
DEROSSETT
James 51 (FO-473)
DEROSSETTS
Tolbert 24* (FO-473)
DESKINS
James 28* (PI-468)
Lewis 18* (PI-467)
Rebecc 53 (PI-467)
DETMORE
Lucas 40* (GN-205)
DEVAN
Hester A. 18* (GN-167)
DEVENPORT
F. L. 25 (m)* (LW-78)
Pitman 19* (LW-76)
DEVORE
Alfred 39* (CT-228)
David 41* (CT-271)
John 52 (GN-172)
Margaret 20* (GN-199)
Martha 30* (GN-212)
DEWEY
William 23* (GN-201)
DEWIT
William 54 (GN-229)
DEWITT
Cela 26* (MG-170)
DIAL
Alexr. 31* (LW-94)

Index

DIAL
 Lucy 44* (JO-91)
DIALS
 Eli 21 (GN-174)
DICKERSON
 Absailom 32* (CT-252)
 Benj. 26 (LE-153)
 Levi 34 (CT-259)
DICKSON
 Andrew F. 49 (JO-83)
 Henry 28 (JO-81)
 Henry 76* (JO-125)
 James 25* (LE-143)
 Martin B. 45* (JO-84)
 Thos. 53 (LE-143)
 William 53 (JO-118)
DICTERTEN
 Caroline 23* (LW-83)
DIER
 Lucyan 17* (LW-65)
 Nancy 8* (LW-64)
 Owen 46* (LW-115)
DIGINGS
 Austin 27 (GN-254)
 B. B. 61 (m) (GN-258)
 Joseph M. 21* (GN-258)
DIKES
 Wm. 26 (BE-32)
DILLION
 George 21 (FO-417)
 James 24* (FO-441)
 James 47 (FO-420)
DILLON
 Robert 54* (GN-207)
 Thomas 54 (GN-242)
DILSO
 John jr. 31 (PI-458)
DILY
 Lewis C. 30* (FO-473)
DIMERON
 Moses 35 (PI-490)
DIMOND
 Henry 44* (LW-81)
DIMOND?
 Joshua L. 21 (LW-91)
DINGESS
 Wm. 43 (LW-123)

DINKINS
 James 22 (BE-18)
DINSMORE
 James 23 (PI-481)
 Wm. F. 21 (CT-255)
DISHMAN
 John 26 (GN-198)
DITTY
 James 30 (LW-87)
 Nathaniel 22* (GN-169)
DIXON
 Alexander 27 (GN-192)
 Augustus 21 (GN-189)
 Benjamin 13* (GN-198)
 Benjamin 39 (GN-195)
 Elisha 29 (GN-202)
 George 32 (GN-174)
 James 54 (GN-192)
 John 29 (GN-200)
 John 54 (GN-191)
 John W. 57 (GN-187)
 Levi 30 (GN-192)
 Meredith M. 20 (GN-195)
 Meridith 56* (GN-183)
 Nancy 30 (GN-195)
 Solomon 31* (GN-197)
 Sophrona 24* (CT-222)
 Thomas W. 29* (GN-183)
 William 17* (GN-191)
 William 45 (MG-111)
 William 48 (GN-189)
 William 59* (GN-190)
DOAN
 Sally 46* (BE-29)
DOBSON
 William 39 (PE-420)
DOBYNS
 Abner 53* (LW-85)
 Elizabeth 45* (LW-85)
 Henry T. 36 (GN-201)
 John 53 (LW-116)
DODD
 Robt. J. Jr. 23 (LW-77)
DOLPHIS
 Benjamin 2* (LE-127)
DOLTON
 Peter 41 (BE-22)

DONALDSON
 William 24* (GN-193)
DONITHAN
 Jamima 26* (MG-108)
DOODY
 William 27* (GN-176)
DOOLEY
 Harrison 22* (GN-223)
DOOLY
 Nicholas 45* (CT-244)
DORCH
 George 50 (GN-244)
 John 46 (GN-220)
DORNEY
 John 58 (LW-63)
DORTEN
 Joel 29* (JO-100)
 William 8?* (JO-100)
DOTSON
 Mitchell 30 (FO-442)
DOTTON
 John 42 (B) (PI-490)
DOTTSON
 John 23 (PI-474)
 Jordon 46 (PI-474)
DOUGHERTY
 Isaac K. 18* (MG-143)
 Mary J. 14* (GN-169)
DOUGLASS
 Stephen 39 (GN-207)
 Thomas 47 (GN-206)
DOVIL
 Isaac 38 (GN-241)
DOWDY
 Samuel 35* (GN-260)
DOWEN
 Larkin 20* (MG-138)
DOWNING
 John 22 (MG-147)
 Mary 15* (MG-98)
 William 27 (MG-171)
DOWNS
 James 42 (GN-256)
DRAKE
 Ephriam 26 (GN-253)
 Hulda 23 (CT-245)
 N. Jane 5* (GN-219)

Index

DRAKE
  Silas 8* (GN-253)
  William R. 43 (GN-193)
DRAPER
  James N. 44* (PI-458)
DRAVENSTOT
  Tobias 15* (GN-178)
DRAWDAY
  Margaret 37* (PI-455)
DRICKELL
  Isabel 64* (MG-100)
DRUGIS?
  Peter 21* (FO-444)
DRUZAN
  E. 50 (m) (GN-244)
  Elizabeth 84* (GN-233)
DUEY
  Oliver 59 (GN-246)
DUFF
  Alexander 29 (BE-25)
  Colvon 40 (PE-404)
  John A. 48 (PE-413)
DUFFEY
  Rachiel 9* (GN-245)
DUKE
  Edward E. 29* (MG-173)
DUKES
  Dean 23* (MG-174)
DULIN
  Bazel 25 (MG-126)
DULY
  Thos. 58? (LW-98)
DUN
  Andrew 15* (MG-152)
DUNAFIELD
  John 63* (CT-222)
DUNAHOO
  Alfred 23* (MG-102)
  Alfred 37 (MG-102)
  James 35* (MG-102)
DUNAWAY
  Caleb 34 (BE-41)
  James 32 (GN-219)
  Samuel 37 (GN-237)
DUNCAN
  A. J. 30 (m) (LW-64)
  Absalom 13* (JO-94)
  Alamander 73* (CT-218)

Allen 29* (CT-244)
David 60* (LW-104)
Edward R. 27* (CT-220)
Eli 43 (CT-219)
Harmon 26* (GN-259)
Joseph 60 (GN-223)
Leroy 71* (CT-219)
Lewis 24 (CT-272)
Marshall 55 (CT-246)
William T. 32 (GN-256)
DUNDERI
  John 45* (LW-89)
DUNFIELD
  Charles 38 (GN-216)
  David 22* (LW-93)
DUNLAP
  James 21* (GN-247)
  Martha 25?* (LW-56)
DUNN
  Asa 26* (MG-167)
  George 42* (GN-176)
  Isaac 15* (MG-158)
  Jesse 35 (BE-2)
  John 37 (BE-18)
  Julian 19* (BE-3)
  William 20* (MG-143)
DUNNIVAN
  John 40* (GN-202)
DUNWAY
  Joseph 54 (CT-255)
DUPUY
  Jesse L. 32* (GN-245)
  M. F. 50 (m) (GN-240)
  Margaret 74* (GN-245)
  Richard 25* (GN-240)
  William 41* (GN-239)
DURCKIM
  Wiley 18* (LW-103)
DUREFIELD
  James H. 2* (LW-58)
DURIFIELD
  Emma 65* (LW-51)
  John 24* (LW-90)
  Thos. 32 (LW-90)
DUTTON
  James 42 (JO-109)
DUVALL
  Martin 53* (GN-201)

Mary A. 22* (GN-223)
DUZAN
  Eli C. 10* (CT-220)
DYER
  Calvin F. 31 (PI-458)
  Cynthiann 30* (LW-105)
  Francis 55 (MG-124)
  Gardner 32 (MG-100)
  Margarett 28 (MG-101)
  Nancy J. 9* (MG-101)
  Nelson 53 (MG-167)
  Preston H. 22 (MG-125)
  Sarah 87* (LW-83)
  William 18* (FO-459)
  William 20* (MG-123)
  William 20 (MG-124)
  Wm. 15* (LW-86)
DYER?
  William 10* (MG-99)
DYKES
  Isom 50 (FO-425)
  James 34 (FO-451)
  Mary 88* (FO-453)
DYLES
  Absolom 40 (PI-485)
  John 35 (PI-475)
DYZARD
  H. S. 19 (m)* (GN-250)
  Isaac G. 47 (GN-252)
  Milton 23* (GN-255)
EADIN
  William 19* (PE-404)
EADS
  Temperance 44* (LW-92)
EARLS
  James 28 (FO-417)
  Jesse 45 (FO-408)
  John 30 (FO-407)
EARTHEM
  Adaline 2* (CT-222)
EASLEY
  Silas 35 (FO-435)
EAST
  John 33 (GN-245)
EASTEP
  Fanny 37* (GN-253)
  William 20* (GN-252)

Index

EASTERLING
  Henry jr. 26 (MG-89)
  Henry sr. 50 (MG-91)
  Lucinda 29* (MG-162)
  Silas 27 (MG-162)
  Walters 32* (MG-157)
  Walters C. 24 (MG-145)
  William 54* (MG-118)
  William M. 25 (MG-163)
EASTERLONG
  Thomas 46 (MG-89)
EASTHAM
  Elba 47 (f) (GN-213)
  James 32 (GN-213)
  John 18* (GN-206)
  John C. 22 (CT-224)
  John H. 34* (CT-224)
EASTLEY
  James J. 24* (MG-145)
EASTRAM
  Elizabeth 15* (LW-69)
EASTRIGE
  Ephragm 34 (PE-399)
  William 38 (PE-399)
EASTWOOD
  Jesse 24* (LW-78)
EDWARDS
  E. 30 (m)* (GN-210)
  Edward 35* (CT-227)
  Humphrey 23 (PI-453)
  Isaac 27 (LW-57)
  Isom 28 (PI-453)
  Jackson 26* (BE-34)
  James 30* (FO-439)
  James 37 (MG-97)
  John 60 (PI-453)
  Meredith 37 (LW-94)
  Susan 64* (LW-93)
  Volatine 18* (CT-228)
  Wm. 25 (LW-56)
EICHER
  Joseph 45* (GN-166)
ELAM
  Daniel 28 (MG-168)
  Elizabeth 21* (MG-157)
  Elizabeth 3* (MG-165)
  Frances 49 (MG-160)
  Gilbert 54 (MG-168)

James S. 25 (MG-87)
James sr. 45 (MG-88)
Jeremiah 38* (MG-90)
Jeremiah sr. 70* (MG-162)
Joshua 25 (MG-168)
Samuel sr. 45 (MG-114)
Walters 70* (MG-119)
Walters W. 52 (MG-139)
Watters 23* (MG-114)
William 22 (MG-139)
William H. 30 (MG-88)
William W. 45 (MG-139)
ELDRIDGE
  Benj. 20 (LE-144)
  Druzy 15 (f)* (MG-116)
  James 3* (MG-122)
  James 38 (MG-122)
  Jesse 44 (MG-122)
  Levi 44 (LE-144)
  Wm. 24 (LE-144)
  sarah 14* (LW-59)
ELDRIGE
  James 32 (CT-282)
  Mary 29 (CT-280)
  William 31 (PE-400)
ELIOT
  Michael 17* (PI-453)
ELISON
  J. B. 79 (m) (GN-229)
ELKINS
  Harvey 21 (PI-452)
  James 20 (PI-452)
  James 47 (PI-487)
  Miles 24 (LW-65)
  William T. 22 (PI-487)
ELLINGTON
  Abram 57* (MG-98)
  Alfred 26* (MG-101)
  Benjamin 33* (MG-102)
  David 86 (MG-104)
  Dorothy 15* (MG-94)
  E. Wells 33 (MG-126)
  Elizabeth 15* (MG-141)
  Isaac 28 (MG-99)
  Isaac sr. 59 (MG-104)
  Jacob 24 (MG-101)
  Jacob sr. 61* (MG-104)
  John 50 (MG-101)

John M. 14* (MG-173)
John W. 30 (MG-103)
Martha 21* (MG-94)
ELLIOTT
  Araminta 7* (JO-102)
  Jackson 34 (MG-138)
  James 48 (MG-115)
  James sr. 79 (MG-138)
  John 30 (FO-413)
  John L. 55 (CT-286)
  John M. 26 (FO-473)
  Perry 21 (MG-173)
  Robert 23 (FO-413)
  Samuel R. 37 (CT-260)
  Samuel sr. 47 (MG-106)
ELLIS
  John 52* (GN-253)
  Mary 18* (PE-430)
  Polly 50* (PE-415)
ELLISON
  John 6* (FO-459)
  Mary 61* (GN-186)
ELSWICK
  Bradly 44* (LW-120)
  William 26* (CT-271)
ELY
  James F. 27 (MG-148)
  Martha 47 (MG-153)
  Michael M. 14* (MG-155)
  Woodson B. 21 (MG-153)
ELZIC
  Jacob 24 (PI-453)
  Johnethan 22 (PI-448)
ELZICK
  Jane 28* (GN-171)
ELZIE
  Bradley 22* (PI-449)
  Bradley 65 (PI-455)
  George W. 13* (PI-454)
  James W. 26 (PI-455)
  William 36 (PI-455)
EMERSON
  Elizabeth 65* (FO-473)
EMILEY
  Alexandre 32 (PI-442)
EMMERT
  John W. 24 (PI-496)

Index

ENDICOTT
  Benjm. 35 (LW-119)
  Saml. Jr. 23 (LW-124)
  Samuel 48 (LW-124)
ENGLAND
  Hannah 66 (CT-246)
  Ruele 21 (m) (PI-449)
  Samuel 37 (GN-261)
  Sarah 69* (GN-262)
  Stephen J. 30* (CT-245)
ENNIGER
  Jefferson 21* (GN-193)
ENOCH
  Alfred 39 (CT-241)
  Amariah 32 (CT-239)
ENSTMIER
  Amon 45 (GN-163)
EPLINE
  Isaac 45 (PI-439)
  Isaah 20* (PI-439)
EPPERHART
  Henry 67* (MG-94)
ERWIN
  John B. 25 (CT-235)
  John L. 59 (CT-235)
ESOM
  Robt. 28* (LW-74)
ESTEP
  Ellen 30 (PI-474)
  Isaac 55 (PI-473)
  Joel 19* (FO-429)
  Sampson 28 (PI-473)
  Samuel 47 (FO-429)
ESTEPP
  Samuel 24* (JO-97)
ESTUS
  Bartley Y. 25 (LE-126)
  Micager 24 (LE-129)
  Richard 21* (LE-129)
ETTER
  Henery 53 (PI-488)
EVANS
  A. J. 17 (m)* (CT-273)
  B. M. 27 (m) (MG-90)
  David 29 (GN-207)
  Drew 50 (MG-130)
  Edwin 39 (MG-90)
  Evan 50 (MG-103)

Farrell 66 (PI-471)
Green B. 62 (GN-207)
Greenbury 32* (GN-211)
Griffith 43 (GN-206)
Henry 24* (LW-122)
Henry 49 (GN-207)
Henry J. 24 (GN-210)
Isaac 48 (CT-240)
JEfferson 45 (GN-157)
Jane 33 (LW-93)
John 27* (PE-433)
John 29 (MG-103)
John 48 (LW-95)
John H. 35 (GN-207)
Jonathan 40 (FO-423)
Lowery 30 (PI-468)
Mary 34* (CT-275)
Rebecca 35* (MG-104)
Rolly M. 27 (m) (MG-103)
Samuel 38 (FO-462)
Susan 43 (LW-122)
Thomas 40 (JO-88)
William 13 (PE-425)
Wilson 35* (MG-132)
Zerelda 10* (CT-285)
EVERAGE
  Benj. 26 (LE-154)
  John 23 (LE-155)
  Joseph 60* (LE-155)
  Nicholas 25* (LE-150)
EVERETT
  J.? W. 29 (m) (LW-75)
EVERIDGE
  Solomon 6_ (PE-425)
EVERMAN
  Elza 33 (CT-231)
  Jacob 24 (CT-244)
  John Jr. 20 (CT-243)
  John Sr. 72 (CT-243)
  Moses Jr. 31* (CT-244)
  Moses Sr. 53* (CT-219)
  Samuel 45* (CT-246)
  William 41* (CT-243)
EVERS
  James 18* (GN-193)
EVERSOLE
  Elijah 23 (PE-409)
  John C. 21* (PE-410)

  Joseph 31* (PE-411)
  Joseph 50 (PE-410)
  William 34 (PE-411)
  Woolery 25 (PE-410)
  Woolery 56 (PE-410)
EVERSON
  Irvin 18 (PE-404)
EVINS
  Henry 47 (BE-20)
  John 58 (BE-20)
  Lewis 23 (BE-20)
EVRUDGE
  Gideon 25 (LE-125)
EWING
  Joseph 56 (GN-199)
  Saml. 55 (LE-146)
FABER
  James 35 (CT-255)
FAGAN
  Henry 21* (GN-219)
FAIN
  Arthur C. 32 (CT-271)
FAIRCHILD
  Aaron 27 (JO-91)
  Aaron 61 (JO-100)
  Asa j. 49 (JO-124)
  Ebenezer 24 (JO-124)
  Ely M. 20 (JO-124)
  Enoch 44 (JO-109)
  Hezekiah 23* (JO-95)
  Isaah 34 (JO-95)
  John 26* (JO-88)
  Joseph 41 (JO-100)
  Moses 29 (JO-98)
  Rachel 34 (JO-105)
  Shadrach 28 (JO-104)
FAIRCHILDS
  Benjn. 53* (LW-99)
  Joseph S. 21 (LE-141)
FAIRTRACE
  William 12* (GN-159)
FAIRY
  Michael 23 (GN-210)
FALKNER
  Thomas 19* (LW-119)
  Thomas 7* (GN-183)
FALLEN
  Gabriel 23 (MG-145)

Index

FALLIERS
  Nelson 21 (BE-37)
FANING
  Hannah 7* (GN-262)
FANNER
  Lewis 27* (GN-165)
FANNIE
  David 50 (CT-233)
FANNIN
  Bryan 48* (CT-217)
  Bryant 59 (MG-157)
  Bryant 6/12* (LW-106)
  David 60* (MG-94)
  George 45* (MG-121)
  Jackson 32* (LW-102)
  James 39 (MG-120)
  John 25 (CT-234)
  John 38* (LW-88)
  John Sr. 71* (LW-106)
  Joseph 48 (LW-106)
  Mary 17* (MG-96)
  Rebecca 36 (LW-90)
  Saphira 40 (LW-107)
  Travis 31 (MG-115)
  William 24 (MG-121)
FANNING
  B. 25 (m)* (GN-252)
FANNON
  Briant 24 (LW-107)
  Henry 22 (JO-97)
  William 53* (JO-120)
FARISH
  William E. 26* (MG-173)
FARISH?
  Stephen M. 63 (MG-173)
FARLEN
  William 34* (BE-22)
FARLER
  Jessee 22 (PI-478)
  Samuel 26 (PI-478)
FARLEY
  Thomas 8 (PE-432)
FARMER
  Henry 18* (GN-166)
  Jeremiah 30 (GN-217)
  John 41 (GN-178)
  Mordecai 28 (GN-217)
  Samuel 25 (PE-412)

FARNEY
  David 36 (CT-269)
FARRELL
  Moses 25 (PI-470)
FARRIS?
  George 26 (PE-406)
FARROW
  Mary 42* (GN-242)
FAULKNER
  William 46 (PI-434)
FEE
  Henderson 30* (BE-24)
FEELING
  John 50* (GN-181)
FEELUS
  Jacob 40 (PE-408)
FELKNER
  Adam 35 (PE-398)
  Henry 73 (PE-404)
  Jacob 21 (PE-409)
  Jacob 38 (PE-424)
  Moses 46 (PE-398)
  William 25 (PE-399)
FERAND
  Jane 15* (MG-104)
  Thomas J. 23 (MG-105)
FERGUSON
  A. W. 45 (m) (GN-184)
  Adeline 21* (LW-74)
  Arthur 15* (GN-197)
  David 38* (GN-161)
  Elizabeth 14* (GN-176)
  Elizabeth 21* (GN-187)
  Elizabeth 32 (MG-125)
  Isaac 36 (MG-86)
  Isaac W. 22* (MG-165)
  James J. 28* (MG-120)
  John 56* (MG-172)
  John P. 31 (LW-93)
  John W. 31 (MG-96)
  John jr. 19* (MG-121)
  Malachi 45* (FO-418)
  William 29* (MG-158)
  William 40 (MG-123)
  William 44 (GN-178)
  William 52* (MG-118)
FERRELL
  Charles 26* (LW-66)

FERRIL
  Andrew 22* (LE-148)
FERRILL
  Richard 19* (PI-469)
FERRIN
  J. C. 40 (m)* (GN-234)
FERSHEE
  James 60 (LW-98)
FETTY
  Charles 30 (GN-263)
FIDLER
  John 24* (FO-471)
FIELD
  Joseph 45* (GN-169)
FIELDS
  Abner 45 (LE-138)
  Abram 25 (BE-6)
  Acey 63 (BE-6)
  Chason 25 (PI-465)
  Elizabeth 26 (BE-26)
  Ephraim 32 (BE-14)
  Henry 23 (PE-413)
  Isaac 41 (LE-126)
  James 33 (LW-95)
  James 38* (PE-408)
  Jason 60* (LW-70)
  Joseph 40 (PI-496)
  Malen 32 (PE-428)
  Martha 67 (LE-138)
  Preston 55 (PI-465)
  Richard L. 35 (PI-444)
  Samuel 35 (PI-445)
  Stephen 55 (PE-428)
  Stephen B. 23 (BE-6)
  Thomas 25 (PI-444)
  Turner 35 (BE-6)
  William 28 (PI-465)
  William 52 (LE-125)
  William 9* (PE-397)
  William J. 30* (CT-279)
FIFE
  Edmond 38 (PI-493)
  John 41* (LW-60)
  Joseph 32 (LW-59)
  Saml. 32 (LW-60)
  Wm. 43 (LW-60)
FIFFE
  John 66 (JO-99)

Index

FINDLAY
  Nancey 56?* (PI-485)
FINKLE
  Harvey 31 (PI-465)
FINN
  Evan 24* (GN-184)
  Martin 51* (GN-184)
  Willis 41* (GN-203)
FIPPS
  James 22* (JO-101)
  James 85* (PI-448)
FISHER
  Francis 48 (GN-261)
  Henry 32* (GN-249)
  Isaac 32 (GN-229)
  Jacob 35 (GN-180)
  Jacob 48 (GN-163)
  John 48* (JO-113)
  Joseph 20* (CT-224)
  Joseph 49 (CT-268)
  William 21 (GN-213)
FITCH
  Champlin 33 (GN-183)
  Daniel 27 (GN-175)
  Elias 29 (GN-175)
  Henderson 2* (BE-8)
  Isaac 45 (GN-182)
  Minerva 32* (GN-205)
FITSPATRICK
  Arthur 26 (LW-120)
  Burgess 38 (LW-95)
  James 28 (LW-100)
  Wm. 26 (LW-100)
  Wm. 67 (LW-100)
FITTY
  Levi 19* (GN-162)
FITZ
  Jerry 12* (MG-163)
FITZPATRICK
  Elizabeth 9* (JO-101)
  Geo. H. 22 (FO-443)
  Isaac 12* (FO-454)
  Jacob 45 (FO-443)
  James 37 (JO-85)
  Jerry 38 (JO-85)
  John 15* (JO-110)
  John 65 (JO-125)
  John 72 (JO-89)

Nathan 40 (GN-173)
Rosey 8* (JO-100)
Tho. S. 41 (FO-419)
Thomas sr. 60* (FO-459)
William 31 (FO-459)
FLANAGAN
  George 30* (GN-224)
FLANEGAN
  Joshua 63* (CT-237)
  Volantine 20* (CT-242)
FLANERY
  Singular 42 (FO-465)
FLANNARY
  Huston 28 (MG-129)
  John 71 (MG-133)
  John jr. 35 (MG-132)
FLANNERY
  Isaac 40 (FO-424)
  James 75 (FO-430)
  John 40 (FO-409)
FLANNIGAR
  Drucilla 18* (JO-122)
FLAWHOR?
  Rebecca 8* (LW-55)
FLEMING
  Fredrick 27 (LE-135)
FLEMMING
  Elizabeth 65 (PI-453)
  Jefferson 25* (PI-453)
  William 27 (PI-453)
FLETCHER
  Alexander 31 (MG-172)
  Alexander 34 (JO-82)
  Elizabeth 64* (FO-457)
  George 53 (FO-449)
  Henley 25 (FO-449)
  Isaac 29 (FO-449)
  James 38 (BE-12)
  John S. 45 (PI-481)
  Reuben 26 (FO-449)
  Simon 23 (FO-449)
FLICK
  Valuntine 45* (GN-247)
FLIN
  John 20* (GN-251)
FLINCHUM
  Danl. 33 (BE-31)
  John 36* (BE-31)

FLINN
  George A. 2* (GN-206)
  Michael 24 (GN-202)
FLINT
  John 40 (FO-454)
FLOWHER
  James 29* (CT-217)
FLOYD
  Hickman 46* (GN-260)
  Peter 45 (GN-264)
  Thomas 40* (CT-257)
FLUTY?
  Aron 24 (LW-124)
  Francis 58 (LW-124)
  Francis Jr. 22 (LW-124)
FOLER
  James 3* (PE-397)
FOLMER
  Charles 21* (GN-158)
FORBS
  Christopher 30 (GN-159)
FORD
  James T. 35* (FO-473)
  John 28 (GN-225)
  John H. 38 (GN-215)
  Mary 58 (PI-462)
  Nancey 40 (PI-495)
  Rebecca 49* (PI-442)
  William 29* (PI-443)
FORGUSON
  James 45 (PI-495)
FORNERS?
  Nancy 15* (PE-404)
FORTNER
  Alexr. 38 (LW-86)
  Jacob 46 (MG-140)
  John 20* (LW-73)
  John 44 (FO-421)
  John 45 (FO-442)
  Joseph 34* (BE-44)
  Wm. 23 (LW-109)
FORTUNE
  Jesse 55 (FO-465)
FOSSET
  Charles 60* (B) (GN-242)
FOSTER
  Alexander 32 (PE-428)
  Charles 20* (LW-84)

Index

FOSTER
 Farris 60 (PE-428)
 Hampton 56 (MG-137)
 Isaac 62 (LW-83)
 Jacob 33 (LW-66)
 James S. 22 (MG-137)
 John 28 (PE-428)
 John 38 (FO-456)
 John B. 54 (GN-236)
 John M. 40 (GN-164)
 Joseph 34 (GN-160)
 Lucinda 35 (LW-118)
 William 32 (GN-234)
 William 38* (GN-217)
 Wm. A. 26* (LW-89)
FOUCHE?
 William 23 (MG-97)
FOUTZ
 Wm. 40* (BE-32)
FOWLER
 William 27* (PI-491)
FOX
 Asa 65 (GN-176)
 Benjamin 23 (GN-238)
 John 28 (BE-39)
 Joseph 25 (GN-176)
 Martha 16* (BE-21)
 Nancy 16* (BE-34)
 Ransom 30* (GN-260)
FRACKER
 Augustus 20* (GN-260)
FRAD
 Charles 27* (CT-222)
FRAIL
 John 25* (GN-176)
FRAILY
 Alexr. 26 (LW-71)
 Isaac 72 (LW-71)
 James 37 (LW-71)
FRALEY
 Andrew 27* (CT-284)
 Benjamin 43 (FO-460)
 Britain 42 (CT-282)
 Daniel 60 (FO-464)
 Frederick 35 (MG-97)
 Honor 31 (f) (MG-101)
 James 45* (GN-186)
 Jesse 50 (CT-285)
 John 48* (FO-468)
 Julia A. 52 (CT-285)
 Phillip 26* (MG-129)
 Samuel 24 (FO-471)
 Susan 8* (MG-94)
 Tempa 18* (JO-119)
 William 23* (CT-285)
 Wilson 25 (MG-96)
 Wm. B. 25 (CT-285)
FRANCE
 Samuel 39* (LE-150)
 Simeon 32 (LE-150)
 Thos. 77 (LE-150)
FRANCES
 Elijah 21 (PI-466)
 James 24 (PI-466)
 William H. 54 (PI-466)
FRANCIS
 Hansperd 17* (PE-401)
 Hiram 25 (PE-417)
 Hiram 50 (BE-16)
 James 70* (PE-417)
 John 28 (PI-484)
 Mary 18* (LW-92)
 Sally 40 (PE-417)
 Temperance 19* (BE-16)
 William 50 (BE-16)
 Wm. 20* (LW-98)
FRANCISCO
 Jacob 60 (PI-478)
FRANK
 C. W. 26 (m)* (GN-246)
FRANKLIN
 Abel 53 (FO-469)
 Bird 18* (JO-118)
 James 30 (LE-152)
 James 45 (JO-84)
 James M. 19* (JO-125)
 John 76 (JO-80)
 Joseph 33* (JO-119)
 Lawson 45 (GN-179)
 Martin 38 (JO-80)
 Thomas 67* (MG-148)
 William 23 (FO-469)
FRASURE
 Geo. 48 (LW-117)
 Irvin 25 (LW-50)
 Saml. 37* (LW-105)
FRAZEL
 George 25* (GN-226)
FRAZER
 John 45 (PI-473)
FRAZIER
 Elizabeth 68 (LE-130)
 George 22 (LE-130)
 John 45 (BE-24)
 Nancy 60* (FO-412)
 Robert 36 (FO-411)
 Solomon 19 (LE-130)
 Solomon 32 (LE-131)
 Squire 49 (LE-130)
 Thomas J. 38* (BE-32)
 Wm. B. 47 (FO-422)
FREDERICK
 Martin 50* (GN-198)
FREDRIC
 John 19* (PI-479)
 John 37 (PI-466)
 Nathan 21 (PI-466)
FREELS
 Frank C. 37* (GN-176)
FRENCH
 John 21 (GN-163)
 Rebecca 21* (LW-64)
FRESE
 Melton 30* (FO-472)
FRIAMOUTH
 Nicholas 36* (GN-249)
FRICK
 Christena 20* (GN-175)
FRIEND
 Charles 65 (FO-472)
 Charles W. 24* (MG-164)
 Isaac B. 40* (FO-473)
 John 59 (FO-472)
 John P. 21* (FO-472)
 Jonas 30* (CT-231)
 Nancy 75* (FO-407)
 Percival 35* (CT-231)
 Samuel K. 49 (JO-80)
FRIER
 A. W. 24 (m) (GN-218)
FRILEY
 Andrew 27 (BE-27)
 Henry 24* (BE-1)
 Sally 55 (BE-3)

Index

FRILEY
  William 45 (GN-167)
FRISBY
  Cornelius 28* (MG-119)
  Jasper N. 6* (MG-106)
  John J. 25* (MG-106)
  Sarah 12* (MG-114)
  William 8* (MG-150)
FRIZZELL
  Alfred H. 42 (CT-265)
FRUMDEN?
  Hiram 26 (B) (PE-404)
FRY
  Andrew J. 24 (PI-451)
  David 49 (LW-124)
  Elizabeth 62* (GN-172)
  Jacob 30* (GN-176)
FUGATE
  Andrew 20 (BE-17)
  Andrew 42 (BE-17)
  Charles D. 63* (BE-29)
  Eli 55 (BE-43)
  Hannah 49* (BE-7)
  Henley 25 (PE-419)
  Henly 49 (BE-30)
  Henly Jr. 23* (BE-30)
  Isaac 22 (BE-17)
  Jesse 28* (BE-7)
  John 20 (BE-7)
  John 24 (BE-15)
  John 25 (BE-17)
  John B. 35* (BE-31)
  Jonathan 96* (BE-7)
  Levi 21 (PE-413)
  Levi 55 (PE-419)
  Martin 20 (BE-17)
  Martin 30 (PE-419)
  Mary 70 (BE-17)
  Samuel 25 (BE-15)
  William 18* (BE-7)
  William 25 (BE-30)
  Wm. 19* (BE-31)
  Zachariah 33 (PE-419)
  Zeckariah 22 (BE-30)
FUGATT
  Moses H. 35 (CT-271)
FUGETT
  Benjm. 59* (LW-80)

  Benjm. H. 21* (LW-117)
  Elizabeth 6* (LW-117)
  Geo. 21* (B) (LW-87)
  James jr. 27 (MG-88)
  James sr. 57 (MG-117)
  Mary 43 (MG-106)
  Rutha 85* (MG-157)
  Solomon B. 33 (LW-75)
  William M. 29* (MG-107)
  William W. 22* (MG-106)
FUGITT
  B. E. 27 (m) (LW-77)
FULKERSON
  James 35 (LW-77)
  Martin 31* (PI-444)
FULLER
  Calvin 32 (PI-434)
  Elijah 60 (PE-420)
  Frances 25* (GN-190)
  George W. 23 (GN-189)
  Hosea 50* (MG-88)
  James 50 (GN-190)
  Jessee 45 (PI-444)
  John 35 (PI-451)
  Obadiah 48 (LW-62)
FULNER
  John 40 (GN-210)
FULTS
  Harrison 22* (GN-211)
  Hezekiah 53 (GN-186)
  Hiram 25* (GN-166)
  William 24 (GN-186)
FULTYS
  John 60 (MG-96)
FULTZ
  A. 54 (m) (GN-250)
  Calvin 22 (MG-150)
  Daniel 30* (CT-236)
  Joseph 31 (CT-233)
  Morgan 32 (MG-172)
  Robert 43 (CT-235)
  Wesley 34* (CT-233)
FULWIDER
  William 28* (GN-210)
FUQUA
  J. C. 37 (m) (GN-226)
FURGASON
  Elijah 40 (CT-220)

  Jeremiah 27 (CT-221)
  Vincent 26* (CT-221)
FURGURSON
  Joseph 39* (PI-496)
  Stephen 26* (PI-491)
FURRELL
  Clay 29* (PI-468)
GABBARD
  Michael 56* (BE-19)
GABLE
  N. 28 (m) (GN-244)
GALASPIE
  Thomas 23* (LW-75)
GALAWAY
  Mary 16* (CT-223)
GALION
  Hiram 23 (CT-274)
  Johnathan 27* (CT-216)
  Thomas 56 (CT-216)
GALLIHER
  John 24* (GN-248)
  John 51* (GN-221)
  Neal 28* (GN-234)
GALLION
  William 24* (GN-175)
GALLOWAY
  James 26 (GN-199)
  John 51 (FO-407)
GAMBELL
  Hargus 28 (JO-98)
GAMBLE
  B. F. 49 (m)* (GN-246)
  Elizabeth 50 (LW-61)
  Henderson 29 (LW-95)
  John 24 (BE-43)
  John 24 (LW-58)
  Martin 34 (LW-58)
  Wm. 31 (LW-58)
  Wm. 51 (BE-27)
GAMBREL
  Nancy 54* (CT-273)
GAMMON
  George 15* (GN-238)
  J. S. 51 (m) (GN-242)
  John 52 (GN-243)
  Martha 52 (GN-240)
GANNON
  Jesse 25* (LW-89)

Index

GANNON?
  Barnabas 27 (PI-483)
  Daniel 56 (PI-483)
  Robert 1* (PI-483)
GANTS
  Joseph 39* (GN-168)
GAPPS
  William 35* (GN-260)
GARD
  John 54 (GN-200)
  William 33 (CT-226)
GARDINER
  Joseph 56 (PI-443)
GARDNER
  Benjamin F. 40* (MG-164)
  James 26* (GN-252)
  James 81* (CT-253)
  Joseph H. 29* (MG-164)
  Perlina S. 32* (MG-145)
  Virginia 13* (GN-258)
GARMER
  Joshua 66 (GN-217)
GARNER
  William 54* (BE-14)
GARRED
  James 57 (LW-78)
  Jane 75* (LW-97)
GARRET
  Thomas J. 73 (GN-227)
GARRETT
  Barton 38 (LW-82)
  Elkana 34* (MG-151)
  Francis 50* (MG-173)
  George 29* (FO-467)
  Henry 53 (MG-173)
  Jane 55 (FO-407)
  Marshall 19 (LW-77)
  Rebecca 39 (FO-408)
  Sarah 83* (FO-408)
GARTHEE
  Catharine 49* (GN-163)
GARUTT?
  Bernard 26* (FO-473)
GARVEY
  John 54* (LW-72)
GARVIN
  James 33 (CT-254)
  John 40* (CT-252)

John S. 37 (LW-109)
Joshnson 63 (CT-241)
William H . 38* (CT-254)
GASTIN
  Robert 44 (GN-161)
GAUSE
  Alex 31* (PI-491)
GAVER
  Charles P. 26 (GN-167)
GAVETT
  Ezekl. 52* (LW-117)
GAVITT
  Elliott 21* (LW-86)
GAW
  Joseph 55 (LW-81)
GAY
  Henry 45* (PE-406)
  Joseph 30 (PE-411)
  Nelson 37 (PE-406)
  Samuel 67 (CT-226)
  Thomas 33* (GN-203)
  William 27* (CT-226)
GEARHART
  Adam 66 (FO-472)
  Adam jr. 26* (FO-419)
  Allen 36* (CT-227)
  Daniel 30 (FO-425)
  Joseph 52* (FO-436)
  Joseph jr. 27 (FO-439)
  Peter 22* (FO-425)
  Valentine 40 (FO-426)
  Woodson 22 (FO-437)
GEARHEART
  Hansford 17* (LW-94)
  John 46 (PE-420)
  Joseph 49 (PE-422)
  Richard 42 (PE-421)
  William 17 (PE-421)
  William 55 (BE-9)
GEE
  Champness M. 45* (CT-214)
  David P. 38 (CT-243)
  Micajah 33 (CT-272)
  Robert 83 (CT-244)
  Robert A. 32 (CT-271)
  William 29* (GN-175)
GEHRON
  Jacob 30* (GN-249)

GEIGER
  D. D. 29 (m)* (GN-210)
  John 23* (GN-194)
  William L. 30* (GN-215)
GELLAR
  Wm. 29* (LW-83)
GENT
  Ellen 11* (MG-86)
  Jane 14* (LW-54)
  Rachel 10* (LW-54)
GEORGE
  Alexander 60 (MG-124)
  Henry 50* (LW-83)
  John 55 (FO-462)
  John M. 32 (MG-145)
  Robert 27 (FO-466)
  Robert M. 50* (FO-464)
  Wilson 29 (FO-461)
GHENT
  William 41 (JO-96)
GHOLSON
  Malinda 54* (GN-169)
  Willis 25 (GN-168)
GIBBONS
  Charles 30* (GN-199)
  Richard 50* (GN-210)
GIBBS
  Ebenezer 34 (MG-114)
  Green B. 21 (BE-4)
  James 36* (MG-116)
  John 63 (BE-4)
  John O. 54 (GN-259)
  Mason 24 (MG-154)
  Milton 34 (MG-107)
  Nancy 5* (JO-104)
  Nathan 56* (MG-144)
  Sarah 60* (GN-228)
GIBSON
  Alexander C. 34 (BE-20)
  Brison 65 (FO-434)
  Burwell 30 (BE-21)
  Cynthia 26* (FO-447)
  Duvenberry 30* (BE-9)
  Hiram 66 (PE-421)
  Joel 15* (FO-431)
  Joel 39 (PE-421)
  Joel 40 (PI-434)
  Leonard 35 (FO-431)

Index

GIBSON
 Sarah 63* (LE-134)
 T. J. 9 (m)* (BE-41)
GILBER
 Samuel 25 (CT-221)
GILBERT
 Ellen 65* (PI-457)
 George 17* (MG-108)
 George 33 (LE-140)
 Isaac 28 (PE-413)
 Jackson 30* (BE-21)
 James 32* (CT-251)
 Jane 20* (CT-220)
 John 22 (CT-220)
 John 31* (CT-252)
 Joseph 40 (BE-9)
 Samuel 23 (PI-457)
 Sarah 52 (CT-255)
 Stephen 23 (CT-269)
 Stephen 45* (MG-108)
 Thomas 27 (CT-269)
 Thomas 30* (GN-164)
 Thos. 65 (LE-153)
 William 32 (CT-262)
 William 34 (CT-255)
GILBRUTH
 Irwin 22* (LW-89)
GILES
 Edmond 23 (GN-251)
 William D. 30 (FO-473)
GILISPIE
 Alexander 21 (JO-114)
GILKERSON
 Francis M. 13* (CT-231)
 Jeff 28 (LW-111)
 John 43* (GN-217)
GILKEY
 Greenville 15* (LW-69)
 John 23* (GN-230)
 Mary 13* (GN-245)
 Robert 14* (GN-259)
 William 42 (GN-254)
GILKISON
 Malinda 62* (CT-245)
GILKY
 Margaret 40* (GN-188)
GILL
 Edward 25* (GN-210)

GILLAM
 Isom 38* (LW-70)
GILLEM
 Chesley 39 (CT-281)
GILLESPIE
 Alexander 45 (MG-140)
 Calvin S. 25* (MG-143)
 Elijah 49 (MG-147)
 Henry 18* (MG-111)
 John G. 31 (MG-145)
 John P. 34 (MG-141)
 William 17* (MG-142)
GILLEY
 Joseph 22* (GN-186)
GILLIS
 George 30* (GN-170)
GILLISPIE
 James J. 24 (PI-492)
 Mathew 58 (PI-492)
 William H. 22 (PI-493)
GILLMAN
 William 29* (MG-145)
GILLMORE
 Daniel 23 (MG-148)
 James 52* (MG-142)
GILLOM
 Chesley 21 (LW-71)
 Isiah 35 (LW-71)
 Martin 73 (LW-71)
GILLS
 Washington* (BE-1)
GILLUM
 Archablad 29 (CT-238)
 Charles 43 (MG-139)
 Isaac 34 (MG-125)
 James A. 23* (CT-238)
 Jesse 22 (MG-124)
 John 30* (PE-429)
 Peter H. 16 (MG-124)
 Richard 50 (CT-234)
GILLY
 Alfred 26 (GN-179)
 Preston 31 (LE-125)
GILMOON
 Perry 6* (JO-83)
GILMORE
 Enoch 49 (MG-140)
 Henry 28 (GN-265)

GIPSON
 Abraham 52 (JO-111)
 Buck 20* (PI-473)
 Elijah 25 (PI-447)
 Henry 20* (LE-146)
 Isom 19* (PI-447)
 John 23 (LE-146)
 John 53 (LE-145)
 Pricey A. 19 (f)* (PI-443)
 Riley 36 (B) (FO-473)
 Samuel W. 23* (FO-471)
 Spencer 35 (JO-81)
 Squire 25* (B) (LE-151)
 William 80* (PI-447)
GLANCY
 Thomas 38* (CT-273)
GLASMER
 William 27 (GN-247)
GLASS
 W. H. 24 (f)* (GN-249)
GLASSFORD
 Sarah 45* (CT-219)
GLIN
 William 40 (GN-261)
GLOVER
 J. R. 11 (m)* (GN-187)
 Sarah 35 (GN-240)
 Thomas J. 45 (CT-221)
GOAD
 Elizabeth 20* (CT-271)
GOBBLE
 David 25 (FO-465)
 Elijah 28* (FO-419)
 Jacob 58 (FO-467)
 William 30 (FO-419)
 William 46 (FO-465)
GOBLE
 Amos 16* (CT-217)
 Ephraim S. 30* (CT-241)
 G. V. 40 (m)* (LW-80)
 Isaac 19* (JO-118)
 Lewis 10* (GN-191)
 Stephen M. 38 (CT-214)
GODSEY
 A. C. 34 (m) (PE-415)
 Augustus C. 23* (LW-80)
 Clinton 25* (PE-433)
 James H. 23* (JO-113)

Index

GODSEY
  John J. 31* (PE-433)
GOFF
  Edward 46 (PI-481)
  George 18 (PI-481)
GOINGS
  Caroline 15* (LW-74)
  Geo. W. 22 (LW-62)
  Harriett A. 10* (LW-58)
  Mary 13* (LW-86)
  Mary 45* (LW-65)
GOLAHU
  Mary J. 4* (CT-277)
GOLAHUE
  John 39 (CT-277)
  Ruth 37 (CT-277)
GOLLIHER
  Charles 23* (GN-178)
GOOCH
  Martha A. 10* (MG-88)
GOOD
  William 47 (CT-277)
GOODAN
  Daniel 69* (CT-250)
  Levi W. 43 (CT-250)
  Philip W. 41* (CT-250)
GOODE
  Andrew M. 13* (PI-442)
  John 9* (PI-441)
GOODMAN
  Alla 54 (f)* (FO-436)
  Andrew 38 (FO-440)
  Calvin 34 (MG-130)
  Enoch 35 (BE-9)
  Pleasant 42 (FO-439)
GOODPASTER
  George W. 39* (MG-107)
GOODWIN
  James 46 (GN-242)
  Jane 37 (LW-92)
GOOSLING
  Hammond 23 (PI-469)
  John 29 (PI-479)
GORDON
  Joel W. 39* (MG-172)
GORE
  Gracy 70* (CT-228)
  James 27* (GN-223)

James C. 22 (GN-175)
  Mary 17* (GN-250)
GORMAN
  David 45* (CT-236)
GOSE
  James 45 (MG-111)
  John 75 (MG-167)
  John jr. 25 (MG-111)
  Mason 34 (MG-98)
  Phillip 25 (MG-166)
GOURD
  Hiram 52* (MG-110)
GRAHAM
  Benjm. 38* (LW-50)
  James 44* (LW-57)
  Jesse 41 (LW-57)
GRANAHAN
  L. D. M. 25 (m)* (LW-80)
GRANT
  Sarah R. 31 (CT-278)
  Warren 40* (LW-83)
GRAVES
  Hardy 55 (LE-140)
GRAY
  David 43 (LW-109)
  Durin C. A. 35 (MG-133)
  Elias 62* (GN-230)
  Gatsey 47 (f)* (MG-133)
  James 40 (CT-271)
  James M. 30 (MG-130)
  Jane 83* (GN-199)
  John L. 54* (GN-219)
  Joseph G. 47 (GN-222)
  Loyd 25 (GN-219)
  Maria 47* (CT-240)
  Marium J. 27* (GN-186)
  Mary 45 (MG-139)
  Mary 90 (GN-222)
  Mellender 39 (m) (PE-423)
  Preston 26 (CT-239)
  Sarah F. 18* (CT-239)
GRAYSON
  John 24* (GN-193)
GREEN
  Adell 39 (GN-160)
  Alexander 45 (GN-237)
  Caney 25* (CT-270)
  Charles J. 45 (JO-110)

David 24 (JO-93)
  Elijah 36* (BE-8)
  Elizabeth 15* (LW-54)
  Enoch 38 (LW-114)
  Evaline 50 (GN-254)
  F. F. 17 (f)* (GN-159)
  Francis 25* (FO-472)
  Giles 50* (JO-94)
  Helma? 62 (CT-245)
  John 35 (GN-209)
  Martha 7* (JO-104)
  Mary 26* (LW-103)
  Nancey 76* (PI-463)
  Sarah 40* (LW-118)
  Thos. 29 (LW-115)
  William 27 (GN-210)
  Wm. 32* (LW-71)
GREENE
  James P. 35 (PI-449)
GREENSLATE
  George 34 (GN-239)
  Mason 33 (GN-218)
  Silas 41 (GN-239)
  Susan 36 (GN-236)
GREENWOOD
  James 27 (MG-117)
GREER
  William C. 30* (GN-259)
GREGORY
  Jamison 30* (MG-104)
  Joseph 54 (GN-222)
  Richard 26 (GN-222)
GREY
  Joseph 22* (FO-465)
GRICE
  Elias 27* (GN-234)
GRIFFET
  John 100 (PI-489)
GRIFFETH
  David 67* (LW-93)
  Elizabeth 57* (LW-68)
  Evan 35 (LW-93)
  Evan 52* (LW-94)
  James 48 (LW-56)
  Jesse 42 (LW-67)
  John 46 (MG-112)
  Reece 36 (LW-93)
  Robt. 36* (LW-93)

Index

GRIFFETH
  Robt. 57* (LW-72)
GRIFFEY
  David 19 (PI-440)
  George 21 (PI-480)
  Houston 23 (GN-236)
  James 64 (PI-440)
  Richard 22 (PI-440)
  Wesley J. 24 (PI-441)
GRIFFIN
  Andrew 60 (GN-222)
GRIFFING
  Louisa 25* (MG-145)
  Wm. L. 35 (BE-32)
GRIFFITH
  Abel 35 (CT-283)
  Abraham 23 (LW-57)
  Danl. 20 (BE-40)
  John 8* (LW-67)
  Nelly 7* (LW-57)
  Susannah 16* (PI-441)
  Thomas 80 (BE-35)
GRIFFITS
  James H. 21* (GN-175)
GRIFFY
  James 22* (FO-435)
  Mary 7* (FO-450)
  Sarah 17* (MG-140)
GRIGSBY
  Benjamine 21 (PE-424)
  Benjamine 28 (PE-423)
  Edward 76 (PE-423)
  James A. 23* (MG-140)
  John 59* (PE-422)
  Samuel 18 (PE-423)
  Thomas 35 (PE-416)
  William 38 (PE-416)
GRIZZEL
  John 38 (CT-267)
GROSS
  Henry 26* (BE-35)
  Peter 21 (PE-413)
  Simon 52 (BE-36)
  Thomas 25* (BE-36)
  William 60 (LE-127)
GRUBB
  Andrew 21 (LW-86)
  Geo. Jr. 32* (LW-72)

  Isaac 50 (LW-105)
  James 36 (LW-66)
  William 33 (GN-159)
GRUBBS
  Absalom 46 (LW-74)
GUARD
  Sarah 70* (GN-190)
GUESS
  John 33 (PI-435)
GUILKEY
  Scott 37* (GN-157)
GULLET
  Christopher 24* (GN-168)
  Christy 26 (m) (GN-211)
  Daniel 28 (GN-177)
  Daniel 45 (GN-177)
  John 55 (CT-217)
  Moses 30* (GN-176)
  Reason 28 (GN-253)
GULLETT
  Andrew 33 (MG-167)
  Christopher 70* (FO-455)
  Daniel 28 (MG-166)
  Ezekiel 49 (MG-91)
  Francis 13* (FO-424)
  Franklin 36 (MG-165)
  Ira 29 (JO-98)
  Jesse 34 (MG-163)
  John 87 (MG-166)
  Martin 21 (FO-455)
  Mason 30 (MG-167)
  Nancy 50* (MG-167)
  Tempa 51 (JO-101)
  Westley 24 (MG-168)
  Wiley 31 (FO-455)
  William 29 (PE-397)
GULLY
  Branson 8* (CT-236)
  John 36 (CT-237)
GUNDRY
  Joseph 40* (GN-181)
GUNELLS
  Austin 47* (FO-410)
GUNNELLS
  Jane 74* (FO-410)
GUSTIN
  Robert 42 (GN-213)

GUSTON
  Ashbel 76 (LW-63)
GUTHERY
  Mary Ann 6* (GN-162)
GUY
  David 54 (CT-219)
GWIN
  William 51 (PE-417)
GWYNN
  Drury F. 24* (BE-31)
  James 17* (BE-31)
  John 28 (BE-43)
  Wm. 55* (BE-31)
GYLEY
  Henry 35 (PE-406)
HABE?
  Lewis 17* (PI-453)
HACKER
  Dudley 24 (BE-39)
  John 82* (PE-415)
  Samuel 45 (PE-413)
HACKETT
  James L. 38 (CT-245)
HACKNEY
  Charles 27 (PI-440)
  John 30 (PI-440)
  Ruell 20 (PI-438)
  Thomas 54 (PI-440)
HACKWITH
  John 41 (GN-191)
  Reuben 62* (GN-196)
  Thomas 34 (GN-229)
HACKWORTH
  Abner 40 (FO-460)
  Benjamin 30 (FO-443)
  Charity 17* (FO-468)
  Esther 60 (FO-443)
  George 40 (FO-459)
  Joseph 20 (MG-150)
  William 13* (JO-103)
HADDIX
  George C. 17* (BE-26)
  Henly 70 (BE-30)
  Jo. E. 23* (BE-31)
  John S. 39 (BE-33)
  Saml. B. 41 (BE-28)
  William 22 (BE-21)
  William sr. 66* (BE-29)

Index

HADDIX
 Zechariah 41 (BE-27)
HADDOX
 Ann 14* (GN-190)
 Samuel 34 (MG-155)
HADEN
 Thomas 65* (FO-410)
HAGAR
 Harmon 29 (FO-463)
 James 50 (FO-463)
HAGER
 Daniel 48 (JO-112)
 Elizabeth 56* (JO-81)
 Henry G. 26 (JO-80)
 John J. 27* (JO-113)
HAGERTY
 Hugh 23* (CT-228)
HAGGERTY
 Eliza 20* (GN-169)
HAGINS
 Danl. 42* (BE-41)
 David 38 (BE-26)
 Thomas 50 (BE-11)
HAGIS
 William 30 (FO-461)
HAIL
 Mary 14* (LW-103)
HALBROOK
 John jr. 30 (BE-12)
HALE
 A. D. 38 (m)* (LE-155)
 Brice 53* (FO-445)
 Caroline 21* (PI-490)
 Franklin 26 (FO-418)
 Harris 19 (LW-81)
 Henderson 21* (FO-466)
 James 11* (B) (FO-407)
 James 45 (FO-432)
 James 45 (FO-444)
 John 17* (PI-487)
 John 21* (CT-258)
 John 25 (FO-421)
 John 34 (LW-76)
 John 48 (FO-446)
 Mary A. C. 6* (CT-263)
 Sarah 61 (FO-422)
 Sarah 79* (FO-436)
 Smith 32* (FO-420)
 Thomas 63 (CT-237)
 Wm. 27 (LE-151)
 Zachariah 58* (LW-55)
HALEY
 Louisa 17* (GN-259)
HALL
 Alexander 25 (LE-148)
 Alexander 63* (LE-128)
 Alexnder 39 (LE-148)
 Alfred 24 (FO-427)
 Alfred 35 (LE-131)
 Allen 21 (LE-135)
 Ausey 27 (f)* (FO-430)
 Clinton 19 (FO-427)
 Cynes 75 (FO-425)
 David 20* (MG-104)
 David 22 (FO-414)
 David 28* (PE-397)
 David 46 (FO-429)
 Elias 41 (PE-432)
 Elijah 42 (FO-412)
 Elisha M. 22* (LW-96)
 Eliza 10* (PI-453)
 Elkana 25 (CT-285)
 Ezekiel 39 (PE-429)
 Fielding 21* (CT-225)
 George 21* (GN-175)
 Henderson 22 (FO-414)
 Henery 30 (PI-460)
 Henry D. 16* (LE-125)
 Hiram 36 (LE-148)
 Isaac 30 (CT-279)
 Isaac 47 (MG-94)
 Jacob 44 (MG-105)
 James 24 (CT-277)
 James 25 (FO-414)
 James 27 (CT-225)
 James 29 (FO-429)
 James 50 (LE-148)
 Jarvy 46* (FO-412)
 Jesse 55 (FO-414)
 John 20* (BE-37)
 John 21 (LW-61)
 John 26* (CT-273)
 John 27 (LE-148)
 John 28 (GN-238)
 John 30 (PE-418)
 John W. 42 (LE-148)
 Johnethan 17* (PI-460)
 Jonathan 51 (LE-149)
 Levi 25 (GN-163)
 Lewis 32 (MG-134)
 Lucinda 37 (LE-149)
 Lydia 40* (FO-430)
 Mary 17* (LW-77)
 Mary 57* (LW-51)
 Morgan 19 (PI-460)
 Nancy 13* (B) (FO-473)
 Nimrod 23 (FO-411)
 Owen 30 (FO-425)
 Phillip W. 27 (PE-423)
 Randolph 39 (LE-149)
 Rebecca 9* (PE-398)
 Reuben 26 (LE-149)
 Reuben 75* (LE-155)
 Rheuben 32 (LE-134)
 Richard 42 (PI-456)
 Richd. 53* (LW-99)
 Riley 21* (PI-455)
 Riley 25 (PI-460)
 Riley 44 (FO-427)
 Robert 24 (FO-413)
 Rodden 66 (FO-414)
 Samuel 35 (FO-431)
 Samuel D.? 14* (LE-134)
 Samuel sr. 53 (PI-456)
 Sarah 10* (LW-89)
 Squire 50* (FO-411)
 Wesley 16* (CT-225)
 William 32? (CT-226)
 William 33 (PI-456)
 William 51 (CT-234)
 William 54 (FO-429)
HALLEY
 Thomas 33 (GN-214)
HALLIOME
 Samuel 20* (CT-256)
HAM
 Alexander 42 (CT-253)
 Bazzel 52* (CT-251)
 Harvey 34 (CT-239)
 Ignasius G. 44 (CT-251)
 James H. 31* (LW-58)
 Jeremiah 29 (CT-239)
 Joseph 58 (CT-239)
 Malinda 39* (CT-251)

Index

HAM
  Peter A. 25 (CT-239)
  Thomas W. 20* (CT-239)
HAMBLETON
  Jessee 19* (PI-460)
HAMILTON
  Anna 79* (JO-98)
  B. 23 (m)* (GN-249)
  Benjamin 44 (MG-122)
  Benjamin S. 24 (JO-99)
  Benjamin jr. 23 (MG-122)
  Cynthia 45* (FO-459)
  David 23 (LW-64)
  David 57 (FO-444)
  David K. 45 (CT-248)
  Elizabeth 11* (MG-121)
  Isaac 18* (CT-273)
  Jabez L. 27 (PE-428)
  James 26 (FO-459)
  James 35 (PE-421)
  James 40* (PI-439)
  Jesse 49 (FO-412)
  John 57 (MG-124)
  Nancy 24 (CT-248)
  Nelson 31 (PI-496)
  Preston 23 (FO-412)
  Samuel 30 (MG-124)
  Samuel 50 (FO-413)
  Sarah 18* (CT-282)
  Stephen 36 (FO-459)
  Susan 55* (PI-446)
  Thomas 29 (JO-92)
  Thomas 33* (GN-248)
  Thomas 50 (FO-412)
  William 38* (FO-412)
HAMLET
  Wade 7* (PE-407)
HAMMON
  Benjamin 50 (MG-92)
  Ephraim 48 (MG-166)
  Jilson P. 42 (MG-90)
  Richard 22 (CT-228)
  Robert 28 (CT-228)
HAMMOND
  John 34 (GN-203)
  Stephen 33 (FO-427)
HAMMONDS
  Elizabeth 8* (PI-455)

HAMMONS
  Andrew J. 31* (MG-90)
  Elizabeth 27* (FO-428)
  Esau 38 (PE-424)
  George W. 24 (MG-166)
  James 44 (MG-107)
  James sr. 62 (MG-151)
  John 30 (LW-124)
  John 66* (MG-90)
  Joseph 35 (FO-428)
  Joseph 80 (MG-92)
  Josiah 22 (MG-166)
  Larkin 26 (LE-136)
  M. J. 13 (f)* (GN-252)
  Martin 24 (LE-132)
  Silas 28 (MG-151)
HAMON
  John 18* (MG-138)
HAMONDS
  John 55* (LW-119)
HAMPTON
  Calep 23 (LE-143)
  Elijah 37 (MG-153)
  Henry 36 (GN-193)
  Jeremiah 37* (LE-143)
  Joseph 35 (LE-134)
  Levi J. 33* (GN-194)
  Levisse 64 (m) (FO-457)
  Preston 31* (CT-246)
  Silvester 30 (LE-134)
  Turner 60* (LE-143)
  William 32 (LE-143)
  William 42 (MG-193)
HANEY
  Absalum 55 (MG-170)
  Ancil T. 37 (CT-226)
  James 31* (MG-156)
  James 48* (MG-164)
  Jariel 18 (m)* (MG-159)
  John 21 (LW-121)
  John 63* (CT-274)
  Martin 32* (GN-260)
  Martin 35* (GN-261)
  Mary 24* (CT-216)
  Paschal 32 (MG-159)
  Philip 65 (LW-121)
  Sarah 61* (GN-259)
  William 57* (MG-118)

William 99 (LW-99)
William jr. 28 (MG-165)
Wm. 25* (LW-121)
HANKS
  Cudmelon 35 (m)* (MG-116)
  George 33* (MG-151)
  Louisa 17* (GN-259)
  William 17* (B) (CT-241)
HANNA
  Ebenezer B. 37* (JO-118)
  John S. 50 (JO-86)
  Samuel 48* (JO-119)
HANNAH
  Alexander 48 (CT-215)
  Ann 62* (GN-177)
  Elizabeth 38 (GN-178)
  James W. 27* (LW-76)
  Joseph H. 56* (LW-59)
HANNAHS
  Ann 60* (GN-175)
  Perry 30 (GN-176)
HANNEARD?
  Fredric 26* (PI-491)
HANNER
  Gabriel 27 (GN-255)
  George 53 (GN-255)
  Judith 83 (GN-255)
  Mary 76 (GN-255)
HANNON
  Daniel 23* (FO-471)
  Lorenzo D. 48* (FO-462)
  Roseannah 70 (FO-461)
HANSHAW
  Andrew 58 (FO-444)
  Harris 30* (FO-438)
  Samuel 22 (FO-464)
HANSHEW
  Henry 22 (FO-443)
HANY?
  John 40 (LE-137)
HARBER
  Abner 37 (MG-103)
HARD
  Moses 43 (GN-159)
HARDESTY
  Geo. 25* (LW-62)
HARDIN
  Amanda 19* (MG-104)

- 365 -

Index

HARDIN
- Frances 26 (GN-172)
- Henry 17* (BE-22)
- Isaac 46 (MG-105)
- Jackson 16* (MG-94)
- James 46* (LW-111)
- John 24* (MG-106)
- John 65 (PI-468)
- Savel 48 (m) (MG-105)

HARDING
- Fielding 30 (GN-177)
- Leander 25* (GN-179)
- Semar? 39 (m)* (GN-178)

HARDIS
- Andrew J. 8* (CT-226)

HARDWICK
- Henry 46* (GN-167)
- Jordan 45* (GN-168)
- Nimrod 41* (GN-168)
- Richd. 47 (LW-119)
- Samuel 52* (GN-168)
- William 33* (GN-168)

HARDY
- Henderson 19* (LW-105)

HARE
- Ferman 38* (GN-237)
- Joshua 30 (GN-237)
- Thomas 28 (GN-237)

HARGAS
- Thomas 41 (PI-493)

HARGET
- Benjamin 26 (CT-240)

HARGIS
- Jacob 23 (LE-149)
- John 48 (BE-18)
- John S. 29 (BE-32)
- Mary 50* (BE-21)
- Samuel V. 59 (LE-133)

HARKINS
- Barney 22* (CT-273)
- Hugh 41* (FO-472)

HARLOW
- William 26 (CT-257)

HARMAN
- Adam 49 (FO-419)
- Daniel 34* (MG-111)
- Rachael 24* (FO-419)

HARMON
- Aquilla 49 (JO-84)
- Joseph 25 (JO-105)
- Mary 25* (MG-143)
- Nancy 10* (MG-118)
- William 52 (FO-462)
- William B. 18* (JO-113)

HARN
- George 48* (GN-172)

HARNWELL
- Elizabeth 52* (GN-225)

HARPER
- Allen 38 (CT-256)
- David M. 46* (CT-217)

HARPEREE
- Elias 51 (GN-221)

HARRELL
- Robert 62 (JO-93)

HARRIS
- Asbury 28* (LW-51)
- Catharine 12* (GN-169)
- David K. 32 (CT-234)
- Edward 30* (FO-470)
- Enoch 37* (LW-85)
- Ephraim 22* (GN-164)
- Jacob 45 (LE-136)
- James 23 (MG-96)
- James 30 (PI-469)
- James 42 (FO-460)
- James P. 38* (FO-473)
- John 23* (MG-172)
- John 27 (JO-93)
- John 33 (FO-439)
- John B. 39* (FO-418)
- John M. 10* (CT-277)
- Joseph S. 36 (FO-459)
- Kelsey N. 41* (JO-80)
- Lawrence 30 (FO-464)
- Littleton Y. 28 (JO-82)
- Luanna 16* (JO-82)
- Nancy 70* (MG-165)
- Saml. 33* (LW-63)
- Sarah 18* (JO-106)
- Susannah 38* (FO-432)
- Thomas 34 (PI-469)
- Thomas H. 25 (PI-469)
- William 34* (BE-29)
- William 55* (JO-108)
- Willis 26* (CT-273)

HARRISON
- George 33 (PI-480)
- George 58 (GN-188)
- Nelly 13* (PI-455)
- Robert J. 49* (GN-199)

HARRISS
- William 33 (PI-460)

HART
- Angaline 28* (GN-225)
- Counsel 44 (GN-224)
- Sarah 53* (GN-185)
- William 26* (GN-211)

HARTLEY
- Abraham 35 (GN-262)
- John 23 (GN-256)
- John 65* (GN-262)

HARTLONG
- Charles 43 (GN-186)

HARTSBROOK
- John 61 (GN-197)

HARVEY
- Andrew 22* (GN-177)
- Calvin L. 66* (CT-220)
- Isaac 48 (GN-169)
- James J. 42 (GN-165)
- John 31* (GN-248)
- William 23 (BE-15)
- William 40* (BE-15)

HASLETT
- Robt. 46 (LW-95)

HASTEY
- James 19* (MG-104)

HASTINGS
- Hiram 35 (GN-170)

HATCHER
- Anthony W. 26* (FO-410)
- Geo. F. 41 (LW-118)
- James G. 45* (FO-410)

HATFIELD
- Andrew 26 (FO-466)
- Ephraim 37 (PI-475)
- Farrell 39 (PI-475)
- George 46 (PI-470)
- Jeremiah 41 (PI-471)
- John 33* (PI-471)
- Joseph 63 (PI-470)
- Madison 22 (PI-471)

Index

HATFIELD
 Nuson 17* (FO-459)
 Raptre? 22 (m) (PI-458)
 Richard 29 (PI-475)
 Richard 29* (PI-476)
 Samuel 57 (FO-471)
 Stephen 15* (GN-176)
 Thomas 24 (PI-470)
 Valentine 28 (PI-471)
 William 41* (PI-475)
 Winney 38 (FO-464)
HATTEN
 Edmd 35 (LW-111)
HATTON
 John 18 (BE-5)
 Melville 23* (LW-63)
 William 60 (BE-5)
HAUBELL
 James 50 (LE-140)
HAVENS
 Joel 29* (MG-140)
 Josiah 37* (MG-90)
 Thomas 35 (MG-118)
HAVINS
 William 60* (MG-106)
HAWES
 Elkijah 54 (JO-93)
HAWKINS
 Isaac T. 36 (GN-190)
 John B. 77 (GN-172)
HAWS
 John W. 30* (LW-118)
HAY
 Henry 33 (LW-116)
 James 49 (LW-60)
 Thomas 36 (LW-60)
 Ursula 46 (BE-31)
 Wm. 16* (LW-72)
HAYES
 Jonathan 75 (LE-137)
HAYNES
 Martha 36 (GN-239)
HAYS
 Alexr. 38 (LW-86)
 Anderson 30* (FO-435)
 Basiel 44* (LW-96)
 Daniel 32 (FO-439)
 David 22 (FO-435)

Harvey 17* (LW-107)
Henry 54* (GN-163)
Isaac 20 (LW-96)
James 37 (LW-87)
John 36* (FO-434)
John 76 (FO-435)
John B. 17 (BE-14)
Montraville 9* (LW-105)
William 22 (LW-96)
William 27* (FO-430)
Wm. 25* (BE-28)
HAYWOOD
 John 54 (FO-443)
 Lewis 56 (FO-421)
HAZELRIGG
 John W. 40* (MG-173)
HEAD
 John 18* (GN-246)
HEDGE
 Eliza 14* (GN-190)
HEDGES
 Catharine 18* (GN-183)
 John 18* (GN-158)
HEDLEY
 George 25* (GN-209)
HEGREITE
 James 20* (GN-177)
HEISLER
 Edward 30 (GN-159)
HELM
 Benjamin 20* (GN-162)
HELMORE
 Daniel O. 4* (CT-232)
HELMS
 James 45* (GN-197)
HELONY
 Thomas 22* (CT-227)
HELTON
 Andrew 32 (FO-452)
 Benjamin 65* (JO-94)
 Elephus P. 30 (JO-94)
 Francis J. 22* (BE-7)
 Nathan P. 34 (JO-111)
HELVEY
 Henery 40 (PI-463)
HENDERICKS
 James 29 (PE-402)

HENDERSON
 Alexnader M. 31* (CT-241)
 Hervey H. 30* (CT-252)
 James 33 (CT-238)
 James 67 (CT-241)
 Mary F. 48* (GN-194)
 Robert 68* (CT-252)
 Robert J. 34 (CT-238)
HENKLE
 William 61 (PI-464)
HENNIFUR
 Matthew 23* (GN-175)
HENROTT?
 E. 30 (m)* (GN-181)
HENRY
 Amey 21* (GN-193)
 Cincinnatus 29 (MG-172)
 Isaac 34* (MG-157)
 Jacob 25* (MG-156)
 John jr. 27 (MG-110)
 John sr. 37 (MG-115)
 Lewis jr. 28* (MG-106)
 Lewis sr. 59* (MG-156)
 Michael 30 (MG-112)
 Samuel W. 28 (GN-165)
 Susan 18* (MG-173)
 William 23* (GN-185)
 William 43* (MG-157)
HENSE
 Joseph 34* (GN-248)
HENSLEY
 Abraham 25 (PI-467)
 Aron 21 (PI-467)
 Cornelius 24* (GN-193)
 Edward A. 26 (MG-174)
 George 62 (GN-213)
 George W. 26 (GN-214)
 Jane 21* (GN-175)
 Joel 26 (GN-213)
 John 22 (BE-17)
 John 23* (BE-29)
 John 28 (LW-89)
 Lewis 19 (BE-17)
 Lewis 20 (BE-29)
 Madison M. 37 (CT-222)
 Milton 23 (GN-214)
 Nelly 50 (PI-452)
 Sarah 24* (LW-57)

Index

HENSLEY
 Stephen 26* (MG-93)
 Stephen M. 21 (PI-470)
 William 26 (BE-21)
 William 30 (PI-467)
 William 32 (GN-213)
HENSLY
 Campbell 23* (MG-144)
 James 26* (LW-68)
 Rebecca 49 (LW-68)
 Sarah 60* (LW-122)
 Wm. 23 (LW-68)
HENSON
 James 60* (MG-135)
 James jr. 22 (MG-100)
 Lewis 36 (MG-136)
HENWOOD
 Benjamin 29 (GN-197)
HERALD
 Reuben? 53 (LE-151)
HEREFORD
 James H. 53* (FO-460)
HERELD
 George W. 18* (GN-186)
HERN
 Harrison 35* (GN-171)
 Harvey 32 (GN-168)
 Mary 30 (GN-215)
 Perry 29 (CT-214)
HERRALD
 Alexander 65 (BE-19)
 Harris 23 (BE-19)
 John 30 (BE-40)
 Thomas 37 (BE-38)
 William 33 (BE-40)
HERRELL
 James 40* (FO-419)
 William 43* (FO-459)
HERRINGTON
 James 25* (GN-181)
HERRON
 James 50* (FO-409)
 Thos. 39 (LW-88)
 William 27* (FO-408)
HERTEL
 Joanna 43 (GN-158)
HERVEY
 Calvin 23* (CT-266)

HESS
 Mary 34 (PI-482)
HEWETT
 Lydia 60 (m?) (MG-144)
HEYNIGHT
 Joseph 24 (PE-406)
HEYTON
 Jacob 28 (PI-491)
 John 35 (PI-492)
HIBBARD
 John W. 28* (PI-463)
HICKMAN
 Francis 42* (LW-101)
 Pleasant 12* (FO-412)
HICKS
 Aulse 70 (FO-442)
 Caleb 25 (PE-421)
 Charles 55* (B) (GN-261)
 Charles 55 (PE-421)
 George W. 34* (FO-434)
 Henry 28 (CT-264)
 Hiram 44 (FO-443)
 Isaac 30* (JO-119)
 James 19* (LW-70)
 James H. 30 (FO-435)
 Jesse 36 (LE-154)
 John 18* (LW-71)
 Rebecca 21 (PE-421)
 Reuben 55 (FO-434)
 Robert 25 (BE-14)
 Smith 25 (FO-435)
 William 24 (FO-435)
 William J. 35 (CT-266)
HIGGENS
 James 54 (LE-140)
HIGGINS
 Gilbert 55 (LE-153)
 James 10* (GN-208)
 John V. 25* (LE-150)
 Sarah 74* (GN-212)
HIGHNIGHT
 Peter 40 (PE-407)
HIGHTON
 John 28* (GN-165)
HIGLEY
 L. M. 24 (m)* (GN-245)
HILDRITH
 Uriah 48 (GN-224)

HILES
 William 21* (GN-215)
HILL
 Burton 28 (FO-442)
 Edward 56 (MG-124)
 Edward P. 30 (FO-472)
 James 20* (LW-59)
 John 22* (FO-472)
 John P. B. 43* (GN-218)
 Lucy 51 (JO-99)
 Sarah E. 20* (MG-120)
 Spencer 31 (MG-123)
 Thomas 33* (CT-251)
 Thomas R. 25* (FO-473)
 Wesley 47 (LW-59)
 Wiley 23 (LW-59)
 William 25 (MG-124)
 William 54 (CT-228)
 William P. 29* (BE-22)
 Wm. R. 27 (LW-60)
HILLIS
 James 15* (CT-246)
HILTON
 Daniel 15* (PI-454)
 Ellen 15* (PI-449)
 George 27 (PE-405)
HINKLE
 Alford 24* (LW-102)
 Geo. 31 (LW-119)
 John 29 (LW-101)
 John 40* (GN-176)
 Lorenzo D. 33 (PI-486)
 Nancy 36* (LW-104)
 Randal 58 (LW-100)
 Wm. 26 (LW-100)
HINKLEY
 Silvester 28* (GN-221)
HINTON
 Richard 45* (PI-459)
HISEY
 Willis 29 (CT-239)
HITCHCOCK
 Alexander 1* (JO-105)
 John 46* (JO-107)
 Nimrod 22 (JO-105)
 Parker 20* (JO-90)
 S. F. 41 (m) (GN-240)
 Sarah 40* (PE-431)

Index

HITCHUM?
  Jeremiah 34 (PE-409)
HITE
  Erastus 21* (GN-193)
  Susan 15* (LW-81)
  William 39 (GN-198)
HIXON
  James 52 (PE-400)
  Wilson 26 (PE-400)
HOBBS
  Hardin 24* (FO-460)
HOCKASAY
  E. J. 39 (m) (GN-163)
HODGE
  Mary A. 64* (LW-118)
  Wilson 31 (LW-79)
HODGES
  Gabl. 28* (LW-79)
HOFF
  John 75 (FO-432)
  William 32 (FO-432)
HOGAN
  David 91* (CT-222)
  Isom 43* (CT-222)
  Samuel 48* (GN-198)
HOGG
  Hiram 49* (LE-130)
  James 24* (LE-126)
  James 45 (BE-25)
  James Jr. 24 (LE-125)
  James Sr. 73* (LE-125)
  Kelly 30 (LE-125)
  Silas 22 (MG-152)
  Stephen 36 (LE-125)
  Stephen sr. 79* (BE-26)
HOGSTON
  John 28 (PI-446)
HOLBERT
  John sr. 60* (FO-423)
  William 28 (FO-423)
HOLBROOK
  Albert 36* (CT-260)
  Ambrose 52* (LW-54)
  Braddock 54 (MG-131)
  Caleb 20 (LW-83)
  Elizabeth 24 (LW-56)
  Jesse 24 (CT-260)
  John 42 (LW-58)
  John 53 (BE-12)
  John 65 (LW-56)
  Menard 32 (LW-58)
  Randol 34 (LW-58)
  Randol 72 (LW-59)
  Robert 22 (CT-283)
  Simeon 32 (CT-256)
  William 25* (MG-90)
  William 61* (CT-260)
  William B. 50 (CT-260)
  Winfry 48* (LW-91)
  Wm. L. 30 (LW-56)
HOLBROOKS
  Kelsey 21* (FO-458)
HOLD
  Jabez 43 (GN-184)
HOLDER
  John 35 (LW-91)
HOLDERBY
  James P. 38* (MG-141)
HOLEBROOK
  Pleasant 47 (JO-99)
  William 39 (JO-99)
HOLEBROOKS
  Benjamin a46 (LE-140)
  Elizabeth 75 (LE-140)
  Randolph 21 (LE-135)
  William A. 27 (LE-131)
  William B. 41 (LE-140)
HOLIDAY
  Wm. H. 40 (LW-109)
HOLIGAN
  John 78* (GN-196)
HOLLAND
  Ambrose 38* (BE-1)
  Drusilla 70* (CT-262)
  Elisha 9* (MG-151)
  George 61* (BE-1)
  Hiram 32 (BE-1)
  James 31 (BE-3)
  John 29 (BE-1)
  John 72 (BE-4)
  Oliver 31 (CT-238)
  Simon 19 (BE-2)
  William 42 (BE-4)
HOLLEDAY
  Eligah 65 (PE-429)
HOLLIDAY
  Abley? 48 (f) (PE-418)
  Martha 35 (MG-170)
  Tolbert 24* (PE-418)
  William 23 (PE-418)
HOLLINGSWORTH
  Beasley 60 (PI-449)
  Edward 33 (GN-159)
  Squire 29* (PI-452)
  Susan 4* (PI-448)
HOLLISTER
  Hudson 32* (GN-179)
  Lyman 37* (GN-159)
HOLMES
  Samuel 38 (BE-23)
HOLT
  James 29 (GN-186)
  Nancy 65 (GN-203)
  Oma 13* (PI-466)
HOLTCOM
  Henderson 46 (PE-431)
HOLTCOMB
  Hardin 52* (PE-430)
  Henderson 28 (PE-431)
HONAKER
  Charles W. 42 (CT-231)
  Hugh 23* (GN-193)
  Louisa 56* (PI-494)
  Thomas D. 33* (PI-490)
HONEYCUTT
  Nancy 45* (PE-422)
HOOBLER
  Samuel 40 (CT-236)
HOOD
  Albert 26 (GN-204)
  Andrew 47 (LW-89)
  Andrew 66* (GN-162)
  Elizabeth 23* (CT-223)
  Hiram 30* (GN-204)
  Jacob 43* (GN-166)
  John 40* (CT-266)
  Lucas 35 (GN-204)
  Thomas 35 (GN-205)
  Thomas J. 30* (CT-266)
  William P. 45 (CT-221)
HOOLBROOK
  Nancy 25* (MG-157)

Index

HOOP
  James 26* (GN-252)
HOOVER
  Emanuel 90* (CT-216)
  John 25* (FO-438)
HOPKINS
  Columbus 20 (PI-435)
  Cornelius 72 (PI-434)
  Elisha 35 (PI-444)
  Joseph 25 (PI-459)
HORD
  John N. 44 (CT-215)
  Philip B. 47 (CT-217)
  Polly 32?* (CT-246)
  Thomas T. 54* (CT-218)
HORN
  Edward 24* (JO-80)
  James 23 (LW-123)
  John 19 (JO-86)
  John 45 (GN-182)
  Jonathan 27 (GN-240)
  Thomas 56* (JO-85)
HORNBUCKLE
  Luke 21* (GN-216)
  Samuel 31* (GN-168)
  William 45 (GN-224)
HORNE
  Michl. 44 (LW-75)
HORNER
  Joshua 15* (CT-226)
HORR
  Elizabeth 33* (CT-265)
  Emly V. 7/12* (CT-265)
HORSELY
  James 55 (GN-232)
HORSLEY
  Gabriel 30 (CT-229)
  James 89* (GN-227)
  Matthew 25 (GN-233)
  William 39 (GN-232)
  William 55 (GN-233)
HORTEN
  Harvey 22* (FO-471)
HORTON
  Daniel 40 (MG-127)
  Elijah 39 (CT-257)
  John 28 (CT-284)
  Louretta 2* (CT-284)

  Rees D. 34 (CT-284)
  Rhoda 34 (MG-128)
  Robert A. 34 (MG-117)
  Travis 32* (CT-284)
HOSKINS
  John 29 (PE-400)
  Moses 54* (FO-452)
  Robert 24* (FO-452)
  Thomas 40 (PE-400)
  William 48 (PE-408)
HOSKINSON
  Mary M. 19* (GN-164)
HOSLEY
  Hiram 41 (CT-219)
HOUGHMAN
  Allen 52 (GN-230)
  Solomon 50 (GN-262)
HOUKS
  Jesse 40 (PI-452)
HOUNSHEL
  Franklin 50 (BE-6)
HOUR
  Joseph 22* (PE-398)
HOURSHEL
  Andrew 35 (BE-23)
  Geo. W. 22* (BE-34)
  Jacob 30* (BE-32)
HOUSE
  James M. 29 (JO-85)
  John 39 (JO-80)
HOUSER
  Philip 26* (GN-249)
  Philip 27* (GN-249)
HOW
  John 24* (GN-231)
  John W. 42* (JO-81)
  Milton 25* (GN-243)
HOWARD
  Andrew 35 (MG-93)
  Ben 34 (BE-11)
  Benjamin 43* (FO-448)
  Boon 48* (MG-108)
  Celia 60* (BE-8)
  Cornelius 46 (MG-126)
  David J. 22 (CT-252)
  Driden 49 (BE-32)
  Dyer 27 (MG-127)
  Elizabeth 19* (FO-446)

  Elizabeth 43 (PE-417)
  George 20 (BE-11)
  George 69 (MG-134)
  Henry sr. 40* (MG-92)
  James 48 (FO-467)
  James 90* (BE-8)
  James jr. 29 (MG-92)
  James sr. 42 (MG-92)
  Jesse K. 23 (MG-127)
  John 21 (FO-446)
  John 40 (PE-403)
  Joseph 33 (MG-128)
  Lewis 23 (FO-445)
  Micajah 26 (BE-13)
  Micajah 27 (BE-32)
  Mongomery 27* (BE-44)
  Moses 27* (JO-101)
  Moses 53 (MG-93)
  Nancy 60* (CT-252)
  Patrick 25 (BE-36)
  Phillip 27 (MG-128)
  Preston 40 (BE-7)
  Reuben 36 (MG-92)
  Samuel 25 (BE-10)
  Samuel 31* (FO-445)
  Suddath 21 (m) (MG-95)
  Thomas 28 (MG-134)
  Thomas 34 (MG-126)
  Thomas 80 (MG-92)
  William 47* (MG-138)
  William 50 (MG-92)
  William 67 (BE-10)
  William jr. 23 (MG-92)
HOWARDS
  Gideon 30 (MG-129)
HOWE
  Daniel 39* (GN-178)
  Edward 29* (GN-205)
  Geo. W. 40 (LW-106)
  Hosey 26 (m) (GN-160)
  Jacob 60* (GN-160)
  James M. 27 (LW-88)
  Martha 66 (GN-263)
  Mary E. 4/12* (CT-223)
HOWELL
  Alexander D. 54 (GN-190)
  David 37* (FO-415)
  Henderson 32* (FO-415)

Index

HOWELL
 James 60 (PI-464)
 James 62* (CT-274)
 Jesse 22 (FO-415)
 John 28* (FO-415)
 John A. 30 (GN-190)
 Mainard 48 (GN-191)
 Samuel 42 (PI-447)
 Thomas 42 (GN-190)
 Thomas 59* (FO-409)
 William 60 (GN-218)
HOWER
 Elexious 61 (JO-108)
 William W. 22 (JO-107)
HOWERTON
 Andrew J. 31 (MG-88)
 James 54 (MG-86)
 John 56 (MG-171)
 Perry 24 (MG-116)
 Preston 32 (MG-171)
HOWLAND
 Benjamin 50 (GN-231)
 Mary L. 3* (GN-228)
 Milley 20* (GN-228)
HOXWORTH
 J. M. 26 (m) (GN-231)
HOYT
 W. B. 27 (m) (GN-244)
HUBBARD
 Sarah 30* (FO-470)
 Solomon 50* (FO-418)
 William 45 (FO-470)
HUCHERSON
 Geo. W. 42 (LW-86)
 John 22 (LW-66)
 Lewis 47 (LW-65)
 Logan E. 37 (LW-109)
 Luther R. 26 (LW-86)
 Nancy 25* (LW-70)
HUDDLESON
 Able 36 (GN-244)
HUEY
 Robert S. 30* (FO-471)
HUFF
 Caleb 28 (CT-232)
 Daniel 26 (PE-405)
 H. J. 32 (m) (LW-64)
 Hiram 25 (MG-124)

James 58 (MG-125)
HUFFMAN
 Albert 21* (PI-496)
 Anderson 25 (PI-495)
 George 22* (GN-202)
 James 29 (PI-462)
 Joseph 35* (GN-209)
 Solomon 50* (PI-496)
HUGG
 Jerman 36 (JO-80)
 John 41* (PE-407)
HUGHES
 Absalom 21* (GN-168)
 Daniel 82* (FO-433)
 Elizabeth 36* (MG-110)
 Emily 4* (MG-149)
 Gabriel 37 (MG-109)
 James 26 (MG-109)
 James 60 (FO-451)
 John 30* (GN-168)
 Martha 16* (MG-110)
 Mary A. 7* (MG-110)
 Susan 8* (MG-110)
 Tolaver 43 (FO-435)
HUGHS
 Gabriel 30 (LE-147)
 Israel 45 (LW-82)
 James 40 (LE-152)
 John 32 (LE-136)
HULCOMB
 Linsy 45* (PE-429)
HULETT
 H. B. 43 (m)* (LW-73)
 J. D. 34 (m) (LW-65)
HULL
 David 30 (GN-251)
 Moses 45 (GN-184)
HUMPHREY
 Rufus 35 (MG-119)
HUMPHREYS
 John 37 (CT-271)
HUMPHRIES
 Charles 25 (GN-246)
HUNDLEY
 James H. 30 (LE-130)
HUNT
 A. D. D. 36 (MG-102)
 A. J. 25 (m)* (GN-238)

Barnet 31 (MG-100)
Carlisle 35 (GN-218)
Charles 16* (MG-137)
George 44 (PI-441)
George M. 27 (MG-95)
Hannah 54 (GN-249)
Harrison 35 (GN-238)
Henery 28* (PI-441)
J. S. 32 (m) (GN-231)
James 26 (FO-421)
John 45 (PI-441)
Joseph 41* (MG-102)
Lewis 53 (MG-102)
Mary 23 (PI-479)
Melvina 15* (GN-219)
Moses 24 (PI-477)
Moses 37* (PI-441)
Thomas 50 (PI-477)
William 20* (GN-211)
William 40 (PE-413)
William 50 (FO-407)
William H. 30 (CT-214)
HUNTER
 David M. 19* (FO-410)
 Francis 58 (MG-137)
 Robert 30 (BE-10)
 Saml. 40 (LW-105)
 Spencer 30 (MG-120)
 Squire 25 (CT-282)
 Sylvester D. 31 (MG-134)
 William 48 (FO-423)
HUNTSMAN
 James E. 27 (CT-257)
 John 25* (CT-220)
HURSLY
 Lewis 30* (GN-210)
HURST
 Campbell 35 (MG-122)
 Hardin 26 (BE-4)
 John 67* (MG-122)
 Samuel H. 50 (MG-116)
HURT
 Absolom 47 (PI-464)
 Garland 30 (m)* (JO-80)
 Robert 27* (PI-458)
 William 80 (PE-423)
HURT?
 Washington 26 (PE-416)

Index

HUSMAN
  E. 20 (m)* (GN-248)
HUTCHESON
  Franklin 29 (MG-120)
  Peter 61 (MG-120)
HUTCHINSON
  Benjamin 47* (GN-165)
HUTCHMAN
  James 55* (GN-164)
HUTTON
  James G. 38* (FO-418)
HUX
  Ishmael H. 33* (CT-263)
  Nathan 65 (CT-263)
HYATT
  _____ 30 (m)* (GN-215)
HYDEN
  John 34 (PE-398)
  William 28 (JO-121)
HYLE
  Julius 42 (FO-466)
HYLTON
  James 23* (PI-441)
  Patton 11* (PI-447)
  Samuel 24 (MG-93)
  William 41 (PI-441)
HYMER
  Asa 21 (MG-103)
HYSE
  John 38* (GN-250)
HYTON
  William 25* (FO-442)
HYTTON
  Rodrick 74* (CT-267)
IDE
  Timothy 39 (LW-86)
IGO
  Daniel 45 (MG-109)
INGLAND
  John 30* (GN-253)
  William 50* (GN-222)
INGLE
  Daniel 35 (LE-126)
  Eliza 41* (LE-152)
  Enoch 18* (LE-145)
  Henry 34 (PE-423)
  Thomas 26 (FO-428)
  William 40 (PE-422)

INGRAM
  Abram 34 (MG-112)
  Alexander 26 (PE-431)
  Isaac 29 (MG-111)
  Jane 13* (GN-235)
  John 52 (PE-431)
  Mary 50* (MG-111)
  Sarah 49* (MG-112)
  Silas 35 (CT-236)
  Sylvanus 24 (CT-236)
  Thomas 29 (CT-236)
  Washington 24 (PE-431)
IRICK
  John 64 (PI-460)
  William 30 (PI-459)
IRONDUFF
  Elisha 20* (LW-108)
IRONS
  Henry 38 (GN-169)
  Solomon 27 (GN-183)
IRVIN
  Isaac 23 (CT-227)
ISAACS
  Fielding 39* (LW-76)
  Samuel 36 (FO-430)
  William 54* (FO-430)
  Wm. 31 (LE-148)
ISABELL
  William 30 (PI-493)
ISHAM
  Gideon 70* (BE-30)
ISOM
  Ann 60 (PE-432)
  Bird 34 (MG-136)
  Charles 48 (CT-234)
  Doctor 33 (MG-136)
  George 40 (LE-130)
  Gideon 47 (PE-431)
  Hetty 46 (CT-278)
  Ira 39 (MG-135)
  Isaac 44* (MG-122)
  Isac 68 (PE-432)
  Isom 21 (CT-279)
  Martin 23 (CT-235)
  Nancy 40* (CT-282)
  Welson 22 (PE-432)
ISOM?
  Lewis 38* (CT-273)

ISON
  Arch 70 (LW-71)
  Argalis 29 (LW-71)
JACKSON
  Anderson 41 (B) (MG-98)
  Charles 61 (GN-241)
  Elizabeth 24 (PE-399)
  Elizabeth 59 (PI-487)
  Hawkins 30* (PI-486)
  Isaac 25* (B) (CT-272)
  Iven 50 (GN-257)
  James 36 (PE-416)
  James 45 (JO-101)
  James M. 27 (PI-486)
  James S. 26 (GN-158)
  John 27 (PE-399)
  Larkin 48 (PE-399)
  Lucy 49 (LE-139)
  Richd. 39 (LW-77)
  Saml. 24* (LW-70)
  Samuel 38 (MG-115)
  Sarah 49 (CT-281)
  Thos. 28 (LW-69)
  William 40 (B) (MG-98)
  Wm. 30* (LW-89)
JACOBS
  Carter H. Jr. 25 (CT-216)
  Carter H. 56* (CT-216)
  J. H. 33 (m) (GN-250)
  John 33 (FO-433)
  Mary 50 (FO-433)
  Roley 32 (CT-228)
  Shelton 39 (GN-227)
  Shelton 39 (GN-251)
  William 28 (PE-421)
  William 42 (CT-221)
  William A. 40* (GN-190)
JAMES
  A. W. 23 (m)* (GN-166)
  Abner 46 (FO-467)
  Andrew J. 26 (CT-242)
  Andrew T. 31* (CT-274)
  Bazel 43* (CT-242)
  Edward 50 (CT-274)
  Ephraim 31 (LW-121)
  Ephraim 49* (CT-272)
  George 22 (CT-258)
  George 53* (CT-242)

Index

JAMES
  John 75 (CT-273)
  John M. 28* (CT-264)
  John W. 41 (CT-257)
  Mary 17* (CT-236)
  Pennina 56* (FO-468)
  Phebe 14* (CT-219)
  Sidney 7/12 (f)* (LW-121)
  Soloman 24* (LW-100)
  T. S. 39 (m) (CT-257)
  William 20 (FO-469)
  William 22 (CT-272)
  William 24* (CT-270)
  William 31 (CT-257)
  William R. 30 (CT-243)
JAMESON
  David 65 (GN-232)
  James 33 (GN-256)
  John 42 (GN-220)
  Wilkshre 25 (GN-232)
JARREL
  Parks 49 (MG-127)
JARRELL
  Aulse? 25 (m)* (FO-422)
  Carrel 64 (FO-420)
  Elizabeth 38 (FO-417)
  Hiram 19* (FO-417)
  Hiram 39 (FO-466)
  Levi 21* (LW-118)
  Lucy 38 (FO-417)
  Ruel 44 (FO-417)
  Thomas 52 (FO-416)
JARVIS
  John 22 (CT-258)
  Joshua 19 (CT-258)
  Mathias 27 (CT-253)
  Solomon 48* (CT-236)
JASPER
  David 1* (CT-283)
JAYNE
  Henry 46 (JO-98)
  William 74 (JO-91)
JENKINS
  Elizabeth 24* (MG-113)
  Hannah 33 (FO-460)
  Isaac 29 (MG-124)
  Isaac 35 (GN-211)
  John 25 (FO-461)

Levi 27 (CT-272)
Robert 35 (JO-100)
Robert 62 (MG-124)
Samuel H. 23 (MG-138)
Solomon 54 (MG-113)
William 23* (MG-126)
Willis 21 (MG-113)
JENNES
  John 50* (GN-192)
JENNINGS
  Abram 30 (JO-85)
  John 30 (MG-95)
  Lacey 40 (m)* (GN-236)
JENT
  Carlos 16* (GN-168)
  Elias 33 (PE-425)
  Henry 27 (PE-426)
  Joshua 74 (PE-424)
JERVIS
  James L. 28 (FO-419)
JESSE
  John 45 (FO-411)
  Joseph 21* (FO-472)
JETT
  Curtus 31 (BE-34)
  Newton 41 (BE-19)
  Stephen jr. 22* (BE-19)
  Stephen sr. 75 (BE-19)
JEWELL
  Nancy 26* (LW-122)
JILES
  Nancy 43* (GN-212)
JIVEDEN?
  John jr. 27 (MG-160)
  John sr. 62 (MG-160)
  Joseph 24 (MG-160)
JOBE
  Wm. 21* (LW-53)
JOHNS
  Danl. W. 34 (LW-86)
  Harrison 31* (LW-91)
  Mary J. 30 (LW-118)
  Thomas P. 33 (FO-421)
JOHNSON
  Abisha 37 (FO-428)
  Abm. 53* (LW-74)
  Agnes 41* (FO-436)
  Ambrose 39 (GN-203)

Amos 23 (GN-170)
Andrew 58 (JO-114)
Andrew J. 27 (PI-496)
Ann 14* (GN-238)
Arch 37 (LW-84)
Bailey 29 (PI-457)
Barnabas 74* (PI-484)
Benjamin 55 (MG-147)
Benjamin 65 (LE-126)
Campbell 39 (PE-412)
David 35 (FO-428)
Elijah 40 (LW-66)
Elijah 55 (MG-146)
Elisha 30 (FO-429)
Elisha 48 (PI-453)
Eliza 30 (GN-172)
Elizabeth 14* (GN-192)
Elizabeth 40 (PE-413)
George 28* (JO-115)
George 59 (GN-214)
George W. 24 (MG-146)
Harvy 33 (FO-428)
Hiram 48* (CT-276)
Isaac 27* (GN-192)
Isaac 28 (PI-449)
Israel 35 (MG-88)
Jacob 65 (FO-407)
Jacob jr. 28 (FO-407)
James 28 (MG-136)
James 30 (PE-412)
James 35 (PI-454)
James 37 (CT-240)
Jefferson H. 31* (MG-145)
Jeremiah 16* (GN-238)
John 23 (PI-459)
John 28* (PI-490)
John 29 (MG-171)
John 40 (MG-156)
John 43 (FO-428)
John 53 (LW-97)
John P. 26 (MG-141)
John T. 25 (GN-185)
John W. 38 (MG-156)
John W. R. 23 (CT-240)
Joseph 24* (LW-50)
Joseph 29* (GN-262)
Joseph 37 (LW-101)
Joseph W. 13* (GN-179)

Index

JOHNSON
  Levi 33* (GN-215)
  Levi 54* (LE-153)
  Lucinda 46? (PI-459)
  Malinda 37* (LW-69)
  Martin 20 (JO-96)
  Martin 26 (PI-449)
  Mary 5* (LE-139)
  Mitchell 26* (PI-455)
  Paine 44 (PI-457)
  Patrick 79* (FO-428)
  Peter 31* (FO-424)
  Pleasant 31 (PI-457)
  Preston 24* (PE-420)
  Robert 40 (PI-457)
  Ruth 47 (FO-411)
  Saml. 23 (LW-118)
  Samuel 25 (GN-180)
  Sylvester 40 (GN-209)
  T. W. 24 (m)* (GN-171)
  Thomas 23* (GN-219)
  Thomas 26 (PI-453)
  Thos. 22* (LW-118)
  Tilmon 35 (MG-142)
  Washington 35 (LE-149)
  William 26* (PI-442)
  William 35 (PI-454)
  William 38 (PI-456)
  William 45 (GN-214)
  William 48 (PI-489)
  William 55* (GN-242)
  William S. 28 (GN-185)
  Wm. 33 (LE-154)
  Wm. H. 31* (LW-75)
  Woodson 18* (MG-152)
  Zachariah 20* (MG-129)
  Zachariah 60* (FO-415)
JOHNSTON
  E. J. 6 (f)* (BE-20)
  Eada 87* (CT-265)
  Elisha 27 (BE-33)
  Elizth. 22* (BE-34)
  Elliott 32 (BE-39)
  Emily 4* (BE-19)
  Ephraim 29* (BE-30)
  Isaac 22 (GN-180)
  Isaac 33 (BE-19)
  James 26 (BE-29)

  James 46 (BE-39)
  Jesse 50* (CT-282)
  Jesse Jr. 22 (BE-33)
  Jesse Sr. 56 (BE-33)
  John 22 (BE-17)
  John 32 (BE-9)
  John 33 (GN-180)
  John 35 (BE-29)
  Madison 16* (BE-34)
  Paschal 26 (BE-39)
  Philip 53 (CT-259)
  Robert sr. 72 (BE-39)
  Saml. 23 (BE-31)
  Thomas 23 (BE-34)
  Thomas Sr. 79 (BE-33)
  William 26* (GN-166)
JONES
  Allin 24 (GN-238)
  Barella 10* (CT-231)
  Benjamin 18* (MG-138)
  Charles 60* (FO-447)
  Charlotte 45 (GN-214)
  Claborn 45 (FO-431)
  Daniel 28 (BE-6)
  David 26* (CT-227)
  David 51* (GN-238)
  Decind? 13 (f)* (PI-484)
  Elijah 6* (CT-270)
  Elijah 72 (CT-237)
  Elizabeth 67* (BE-26)
  Evan 38* (CT-227)
  Eveline 8* (CT-236)
  Franklin 25 (GN-256)
  George 19* (MG-144)
  George 39* (BE-24)
  Griffith 44 (CT-218)
  Henry 27* (LW-124)
  Henry C. 27 (MG-172)
  Isaac 26* (CT-227)
  Isaac 29 (MG-95)
  Isom 21* (FO-464)
  James M. 34 (CT-236)
  James jr. 22 (MG-104)
  James sr. 50 (MG-104)
  Jane 46 (CT-277)
  John 17* (GN-176)
  John 26 (CT-235)
  John 30* (GN-175)

  John 33* (GN-234)
  John 39* (PI-467)
  John 40 (FO-413)
  John 40 (PE-417)
  John 49 (FO-444)
  John 56 (MG-172)
  John 57 (GN-227)
  John 60* (BE-13)
  John 60* (BE-9)
  John C. 2* (CT-250)
  John D. 24* (GN-181)
  John M. 5* (CT-249)
  John P. 25 (GN-182)
  Johnethan 70 (PI-484)
  Joshua 77* (LW-121)
  Josiah 16* (MG-102)
  Luraney 14* (CT-276)
  Mary 45 (GN-221)
  Mary 54* (CT-243)
  Maryan 38 (LW-82)
  Matilda 1* (GN-175)
  N. 27 (m) (GN-240)
  Nathaniel 20* (PI-457)
  Peggy 8* (PE-418)
  Polly 25 (PE-418)
  Polly ann 17* (BE-27)
  R. D. 53 (m)* (GN-235)
  Rachael 9* (MG-102)
  Rebecca 37* (FO-447)
  Richard 49* (GN-196)
  Robert 17* (FO-471)
  Robert 18* (GN-200)
  Robert 47* (GN-250)
  Ryal M. 42 (CT-249)
  Saml. 32 (LW-100)
  Samuel 45 (GN-189)
  Susanna 8* (CT-249)
  Telitha 18* (LW-75)
  Thomas 43* (FO-470)
  Thomas 65 (GN-246)
  William 24 (B?) (MG-98)
  William 25* (GN-237)
  William 26 (CT-225)
  William 27* (FO-470)
  William 40 (MG-149)
  William 57* (CT-217)
  William 7* (MG-95)
  William B. 30* (GN-183)

Index

JONES
William C. 15* (GN-181)
William D. 19* (CT-265)
Wm. 66 (BE-41)
Zachary 63 (CT-251)
JONSON
Malinda 36* (CT-281)
Mason 43 (CT-281)
JONSTON
Lightle 30 (CT-281)
JORDAN
Benjm. 25 (LW-66)
Benjm. 30 (LW-58)
Covey 65 (m)* (LW-51)
Eleanor 35 (LW-93)
George W. 28 (CT-233)
James 17* (CT-219)
James 34 (CT-234)
James 75 (CT-234)
Jesse 50 (LW-84)
John 30 (LW-57)
John 31 (LW-51)
John 39 (CT-242)
John 9* (FO-448)
John J. 29 (LW-65)
Jonas 27* (LW-93)
Jonas 55* (LW-83)
Joseph 39* (CT-233)
Lindsey 34 (CT-234)
Phebe 65 (LW-92)
Richd. 49 (LW-90)
Robt. 20* (LW-54)
Sarah 36 (FO-450)
JORDON
George 34 (CT-233)
Julia 38 (CT-232)
JOSEPHS
John 46* (FO-448)
William 28 (FO-452)
JOURDAN
Ann 48 (CT-276)
James 23 (CT-276)
John 23* (GN-182)
JOURDON
Edward 33 (CT-258)
JUDD
John T. 50* (GN-194)

JUDE
Sarah 15* (PI-467)
JUDSON
William 24* (GN-181)
JUSTACE
Abner 25 (PI-436)
Absher 25 (m) (PI-437)
Andrew 33 (PI-438)
Booker 40 (PI-437)
Claiborne 30 (PI-437)
Edward W. 25* (PI-442)
Geenville 25 (PI-444)
George 45 (PI-434)
Gillmore 18 (PI-436)
Harvey 27 (PI-437)
Hiram 31 (PI-438)
Joab 35 (PI-438)
Nancey 70 (PI-437)
Nathan 12* (PI-434)
Peyton 38 (PI-437)
Peyton 59* (PI-435)
Rhoda 58 (PI-438)
Simeon 27* (PI-490)
Simeon 29 (PI-490)
Simeon 62 (PI-437)
Thomas 25 (PI-435)
William 18 (PI-435)
William 23 (PI-486)
William 29 (PI-437)
William A. 40* (PI-436)
JUSTICE
Abraham 21 (FO-438)
Abyram 41 (JO-94)
Amos 50 (FO-415)
Aulsy 37 (m)* (FO-426)
David 29* (LW-85)
Eli 40 (LW-81)
Eliut? 35 (LW-54)
Elizabeth 45* (LW-91)
Geo. 45 (LW-97)
Hamilton 22 (LW-115)
Harrison 18* (CT-227)
Harrison 22* (GN-212)
Izra 45* (FO-427)
Izra 57 (FO-426)
James 29 (FO-425)
Jonathan 54 (FO-425)
Neal 25 (FO-440)

Pilot 24 (LW-115)
Samuel 30 (JO-95)
Sarah 23* (LW-66)
Sarah 5* (LW-57)
Timothy 21 (LW-120)
Wm. 27* (LW-62)
Wright 47 (FO-473)
KANARD
Samuel 45 (FO-453)
KANES
Jackson A. 35 (PI-489)
KAPLER
William 20* (GN-260)
KARKIN
Thos. 26 (LW-99)
KASH
Andrew 30 (MG-149)
Caleb 22* (MG-153)
Caleb 49* (MG-141)
James 43 (MG-112)
James sr. 77* (MG-140)
Levi 28* (MG-110)
Shelby 23 (m)* (MG-111)
William 41 (BE-27)
KAY
Thomas 36* (CT-250)
KAYSER
J. M. 36 (m)* (GN-165)
KAZED
Nelson 2* (GN-191)
KEAN
John 21 (PI-440)
Lewis 25 (PI-440)
KEATH
William 41 (FO-409)
KEATLEY
William 50* (CT-220)
KEATON
Elizabeth 87* (GN-186)
Jefferson 36* (GN-176)
KEEL
Marshall G. 18* (PI-443)
KEELS
Samuel 23* (PI-461)
KEEN
John 32 (BE-38)
Joseph H. 28 (PI-438)

Index

KEENE
 James 4* (PI-438)
 Margaret 15* (FO-427)
KEESER
 Martin 40* (CT-223)
 Thomas 22 (CT-223)
KEETH
 Louisa E. 10* (PI-488)
 Norman T. 12* (PI-486)
KEETHLEY
 Henery 55* (PI-490)
 William 75* (PI-490)
KEETHLY
 Sympkins 46 (PI-462)
KEETLEY
 Evaline 17* (GN-229)
KEETON
 Edmund 37 (MG-123)
 Elijah 30* (MG-116)
 George W. 41 (MG-91)
 Harvy 22 (MG-167)
 Isaac 20* (MG-91)
 Jane 71* (MG-169)
 John 86 (MG-139)
 Joseph 29 (MG-122)
 Madison 20 (MG-169)
 Mary 15* (CT-252)
 Nelson 68 (MG-122)
 Samuel 38 (MG-100)
 Thomas B. 46* (MG-90)
 Vina 48 (MG-169)
 William 25 (MG-122)
 William 56 (GN-251)
KEITH
 Sarah 30* (JO-103)
KEITLY
 William 30 (GN-192)
KELLAY
 Henry 30 (GN-197)
 Samuel 27 (GN-211)
KELLER
 John W. 29 (JO-81)
KELLEY
 Ephraim 17* (GN-167)
 Frederick 49 (JO-99)
 John 31* (GN-260)
 John 40* (GN-261)
 Pagneman? 46 (m) (GN-226)

Washington 23 (PE-424)
KELLY
 James 35 (FO-431)
 James 55 (LW-60)
 James P. 32 (FO-468)
 John 19 (CT-283)
 John 25 (LE-153)
 John 67* (LE-151)
 Joseph 24 (LW-114)
 Joseph 40 (FO-463)
 Joseph T. 30 (FO-473)
 Nathan B. 50 (LE-153)
 Plesant 44 (LW-88)
 Rebecca 50 (LW-68)
 Saml. 27 (LW-76)
 William 22 (GN-201)
KEMPLETON
 John H. 27 (MG-120)
KEMPLIN
 Henry 39 (MG-121)
KENADAY
 Andrew 48 (PI-471)
 Thomas 48 (PI-465)
KENARD
 Jane 52* (FO-454)
KENBELL
 James 61 (MG-95)
KENDALL
 Allen 45 (MG-156)
 Elizabeth 63* (MG-174)
 James P. 55 (MG-94)
 Jesse 47 (MG-117)
 Jesse jr. 23 (MG-156)
 Lewis 42 (MG-136)
 William H. 52* (MG-137)
 William jr. 32 (MG-95)
KENDLE
 F. 17 (m)* (GN-246)
 Smith 40 (GN-241)
KENDRICK
 Margaret 36* (FO-436)
 William 55 (FO-457)
KENEDA
 John 22* (CT-270)
 Milton 30 (CT-279)
KENEDAY
 Aly 25 (m)* (PI-471)
 Harrison 18 (PI-465)

KENNARD
 David 43 (MG-163)
KENNEDY
 Elijah 40 (FO-423)
 Lewis A. 33* (JO-120)
 Wayne 38 (CT-246)
KERBY
 John 40* (GN-207)
KERNOOT
 William 39 (CT-260)
KERREL
 James 26 (GN-205)
KETCHUM
 George 33 (BE-26)
 Joseph 55 (BE-27)
 Philander 38 (GN-189)
KEYTON
 Lovina 32 (CT-229)
KEZEE
 Benjamin 58* (GN-188)
 C. H. 7 (m)* (GN-182)
 Lewis 36* (GN-181)
KIBBEY
 Jacob 46* (CT-219)
 James H. 23* (CT-244)
 Oliver 28 (CT-221)
 Sarah 67* (CT-244)
KIBBLE
 Marcus L. 35* (GN-193)
KIBBY
 William 31 (CT-265)
KICHEN
 Geo. 25? (LW-67)
 James 34 (LW-57)
 John 66 (LW-68)
 Wm. 28 (LW-73)
KICKER
 Paull 47 (GN-263)
KID
 Edmund 35 (MG-106)
 Harrison 35 (MG-151)
KIDD
 Ellen 45* (JO-111)
 George 36 (FO-410)
 Jesse 46 (LW-88)
 John 25 (BE-2)
 John 72 (JO-112)
 Mary 50* (MG-116)

Index

KIDWELL
  John 21* (MG-102)
KIFFER
  Hiram 26 (GN-166)
KILE
  Peter 26 (GN-262)
KILGORE
  Charles 29 (MG-158)
  John 23* (MG-165)
  John 51 (MG-170)
  Madison 5* (FO-449)
  Nancy 14* (MG-110)
KILKANNON
  Franklin 26 (MG-147)
KILLBURN
  George 35* (BE-41)
KILLEN
  James 27 (GN-193)
  Morgan 18 (MG-160)
KILLGORE
  Jane 19* (MG-156)
KIMBERLING
  John W. 31 (MG-163)
KIMBLER
  Abee 47 (JO-105)
  Solomon 23* (JO-87)
  William 27 (JO-87)
KIMMONEY
  Anthoney 22* (GN-261)
KINARD
  Mary 82* (FO-455)
KINCADE
  James D. 31* (GN-193)
KINDER
  Barnabus 51* (CT-239)
  William G. 26 (CT-239)
KINDRICK
  Adah 50 (FO-439)
  David 29 (FO-419)
KINDRIE
  Harvey 26 (PI-435)
  Milton G. 4 (PI-435)
KING
  B. F. 39 (m) (GN-241)
  Benjamin 43* (GN-260)
  Benjamin 53 (GN-237)
  Elias 45* (CT-284)
  Elkana 34 (CT-268)

Fleming 30 (BE-1)
Franklin 51* (PI-464)
George 35 (BE-3)
George J. 11* (MG-106)
Hiram 34* (BE-41)
Jeremi 39 (BE-2)
John 40* (GN-158)
John 54 (PI-464)
Lewis 23 (BE-1)
Lewis 44 (PI-441)
Lewis 49* (FO-430)
Marcus L. 30 (JO-120)
Mary 25* (B) (GN-157)
Milla 6* (PI-488)
Moses 57 (BE-3)
S. Darrell? 20(m) (BE-22)
Samuel W. 16* (GN-159)
William 26* (GN-250)
William P. 9* (GN-226)
KINGSBURY
  Charles 37 (GN-234)
KINKEAD
  Andrew H. 42* (LW-87)
  Mary 15* (GN-182)
  Wm. C. 19* (LW-82)
KINNEAR
  Alexander 30* (GN-171)
KINNER
  David 29* (LW-112)
  Greenvill 27 (LW-107)
  Hansford 25* (LW-112)
KINNEY
  Charles 24 (GN-244)
  John 35 (PI-460)
  William 34* (PI-454)
KINNIER
  Joseph 60* (GN-169)
KINSER
  David 15* (LE-137)
  Fredrick 20 (LE-136)
  Harvy 24 (PE-426)
KIRK
  Alexander 56 (MG-96)
  George 27 (CT-224)
  Solomon 29* (CT-223)
  Susan 60* (CT-223)
KISE
  Chancy C. 34 (LW-79)

KISEE
  Anderson 64* (MG-131)
  Avery 44 (LW-93)
  Charles 53 (MG-114)
  Elias 52 (LW-72)
  Frances 34 (LW-94)
  Jeremiah 27 (CT-274)
  John 20 (LW-58)
  John 30 (LW-97)
KISER
  Hiram 27 (GN-179)
  Richard 27* (MG-158)
KISOR
  Naman 29 (LE-147)
  Nimrod 26* (LE-149)
KISSEE
  Jessee 46 (CT-276)
KISSICK
  Robert 47* (CT-249)
KISSNER
  William 62 (JO-109)
KISTNER
  Christopher 29* (JO-125)
KITCHEN
  Alexander 36 (CT-233)
  Andrew 58* (CT-276)
  Andrew __ * (CT-280)
  Fleming 29 (CT-276)
  John 36* (GN-201)
  Lewis H. 23 (CT-277)
  Nehemiah 24 (CT-234)
  William 33* (CT-264)
KIZER
  David 33* (GN-208)
  Frany 19* (GN-184)
  Harvey 22* (GN-203)
  Jacob 85* (GN-184)
  John 35 (GN-215)
KNAP
  Joshua 76* (CT-240)
KNIPP
  Alexander 29 (CT-261)
  George 60 (CT-268)
  William 34 (CT-268)
KOUGH
  Mathias 40* (GN-249)
KOUNS
  Christian 36 (m) (GN-217)

Index

KOUNS
 David 34* (GN-185)
 Eleanor 8* (GN-171)
 George W. 46* (CT-224)
 Henry 42 (GN-204)
 Jacob 18* (GN-160)
 Jasper 16* (GN-216)
 John 12* (GN-213)
 John C. 63* (GN-179)
 Martha 22* (GN-195)
 Nelson 22* (CT-271)
 William 48 (GN-255)
 William S. 33 (GN-159)
KOUT?
 John 38 (GN-160)
KRAUSS
 John 37 (LW-106)
KRING
 Elizabeth 33* (GN-217)
 Henry 40 (GN-194)
KUCKER
 Thos. J. 26* (CT-273)
KYLE
 Henry 27* (GN-166)
LACEY?
 Philomen 49 (CT-277)
LACKEY
 Alexander 78 (FO-441)
LACKINS
 John 58 (PI-485)
 John D. 21 (PI-485)
LACY
 Edy 44 (f) (MG-152)
 George 30* (B) (GN-181)
 Harvy 40 (MG-153)
 John B. 58 (MG-89)
 Mark 56 (MG-153)
 Paris 25* (MG-142)
 William 61* (MG-153)
LAD
 Martha 63* (PE-410)
LADD
 Thomas 24* (BE-37)
LAFFERTY
 Daniel 25* (GN-210)
LAINE
 John 21* (PI-473)

LAMASTER
 Elijah 18* (GN-256)
 Lewis 23 (GN-260)
LAMASTERS
 Benjamin 32* (MG-151)
 John 36 (MG-168)
 Lancaster 45 (MG-124)
 Richard 22 (MG-125)
 William 36 (MG-168)
LAMBERT
 Burrel 49 (CT-220)
 Ezekiel 48 (CT-221)
 Fannin 34 (m)* (GN-214)
 James 53 (GN-263)
 James 54 (JO-122)
 James C. 15* (CT-217)
 Jeremiah 27 (LW-87)
 Jobe 24 (LW-108)
 Josiah 45 (LW-106)
 Philip 51 (CT-221)
 Polly 57* (CT-221)
 Saml. 13* (LW-106)
 Sarah 63* (LW-64)
 Wm. 23 (LW-93)
LAMMONS
 William 30 (CT-266)
LAMONDS
 John 26 (LW-118)
LAMPTON
 James 59* (CT-226)
LAMSTERS
 John 35 (MG-169)
LANCE
 Peter 26* (GN-248)
LANCEFORD
 William 21* (GN-175)
LANDRUM
 R. W. 39 (m)* (BE-33)
LANE
 Alexander 53 (PI-441)
 Austin 29 (PI-462)
 Corbin 47 (CT-268)
 Harvey 26 (CT-226)
 John N. 33 (PI-496)
 Lewis 35* (MG-164)
 Lewis P. 25 (CT-268)
 Marideth 39 (PI-482)
 Reubin 22* (GN-167)

 Samuel 23* (CT-268)
 William 23 (PI-463)
 William 56 (PI-473)
LANGDON
 Isaac T. 35* (PE-403)
 Samuel 69 (PE-407)
LANGHSIRE
 Thomas J. 38 (GN-179)
LANGLEY
 Joseph 55 (FO-442)
LANGLY
 John 25 (FO-444)
LANSAN?
 James 38* (MG-118)
LANSDOWN
 A. J. 33 (m)* (CT-265)
 David S. 26 (CT-251)
 Hiram 38* (GN-253)
 James W. 33* (CT-251)
LARGE
 Andrew 30 (LW-73)
 Joseph 23 (LW-73)
 Milly 95* (LW-90)
 Robt. 50 (LW-66)
 Solaman 21* (LW-117)
 Thomas 43 (CT-234)
 William 48 (LW-112)
 Wm. 35 (LW-65)
 Wm. 38* (LW-50)
 Wm. G. 24 (LW-50)
LARKINS
 Presley 91* (JO-104)
LASLEY
 Allen 57* (PI-488)
 James H. 28 (PI-488)
 Martin 42* (PI-488)
 Pharmer 47 (PI-488)
LASLIE
 Andrew 14* (LW-87)
 John B. 21* (LW-89)
 John P. 40 (LW-108)
 Orpha 19* (LW-88)
LAUGHLIN
 Robert 46 (GN-241)
LAVENDER
 Edward P. 21 (JO-86)
 Mary 53* (GN-181)

Index

LAVINDER
 Lewis 41 (GN-264)
LAW
 Marcus 36 (MG-106)
LAWDON
 William 34* (GN-164)
LAWHOM
 Catharine 20* (FO-467)
LAWHORN
 Disa 76* (FO-469)
 Elijah 27* (BE-10)
 George W. 57 (CT-218)
 J. B. 43 (m) (GN-233)
 Melissa 6* (GN-157)
LAWRENCE
 Joel 60 (GN-173)
LAWSON
 Amanda 18* (PI-479)
 B. 21 (m) (GN-242)
 Catharine 61 (GN-219)
 Dailey A. 17 (f)* (PI-495)
 David 16* (MG-112)
 Edmund R. 29 (MG-109)
 Hezekiah 30 (PI-442)
 Jacob 45* (GN-218)
 James B. 31 (MG-111)
 James N. 33 (GN-218)
 Jere 42 (m) (MG-143)
 John 50 (GN-241)
 John 56 (MG-142)
 John Y. 30 (GN-219)
 Joseph 54 (MG-108)
 Joseph jr. 25 (MG-150)
 Mark 53* (PI-490)
 Sarah 24* (PI-468)
 Travis 37 (MG-111)
 William B. 25* (GN-223)
 William H. 24* (MG-110)
 William P. 33 (MG-110)
LAYNE
 David 41 (JO-125)
 Elizabeth L. 41* (FO-408)
 Elizabeth M. 40 (FO-408)
 Isaac 35 (LW-86)
 James 37 (FO-472)
 James L. 43 (LW-63)
 James S. 69* (FO-409)
 Lindsey 38* (FO-409)

Martha A. 16* (FO-417)
 Nancy 55 (FO-407)
LEACH
 Judith 54 (MG-114)
LEAKEN
 John R. 28 (LW-62)
 Joseph 52 (LW-107)
 Thos. 44* (LW-113)
LEARS?
 Elisabeth 47 (LW-69)
LEATH
 David 25 (GN-249)
LEATHERS
 Elizabeth 30* (GN-162)
LEDINGHAM
 Jacob 34 (CT-280)
 Peter 65 (CT-280)
LEE
 David 27* (LW-81)
 Derius 42 (GN-246)
 Elizabeth 7* (PI-490)
 Ellis P. 24* (GN-168)
 Garred 64* (LW-79)
 Green 25 (GN-225)
 Harvey 45* (GN-247)
 James 25* (CT-227)
 James 29 (LW-105)
 Matthew 32 (MG-97)
 Richard 28 (GN-225)
 Sarah A. 13* (PI-488)
 Simeon 4* (JO-86)
 Wilson 51 (GN-231)
LEEDS
 Benjamin 19* (FO-418)
LEEDY
 Randolph 20* (PI-495)
 Randolph 21* (PI-484)
LEEK
 Mary 40 (FO-441)
 Shelton 54* (FO-463)
LEETON
 Elizabeth 38* (MG-153)
LEIZURE
 Marget 22* (GN-197)
LEMASTER
 Daniel 30 (JO-82)
 Eleazar 90* (JO-87)
 Eleazur 36 (m) (JO-96)

Elijah 62 (JO-107)
 Francis 56 (JO-91)
 James 48 (JO-87)
 John 52 (JO-96)
 Joseph 48 (JO-89)
 Lewis 25* (JO-96)
 Lewis 58 (JO-104)
 Richard 43 (JO-96)
 William 14* (JO-103)
 William 28 (JO-87)
 William 34 (JO-90)
LEMASTERS
 Thomas 20 (JO-88)
LEMING
 Saml. 69 (LW-67)
LEMINGS
 Wm. 41* (LW-67)
LETCHER
 John 21* (LW-81)
LEVETMAN?
 Neri? 72 (m) (LW-53)
LEVEY
 John 23 (GN-195)
LEVITMANN
 E. M. 34 (m) (LW-55)
LEWELLING
 William 21* (GN-251)
LEWIS
 Andrew 28 (CT-283)
 Barbara 12* (MG-114)
 Bazel M. 25 (PE-430)
 Charles 25 (GN-209)
 Charles 36* (CT-257)
 Charles 43 (CT-282)
 Daniel 27 (PE-400)
 Daniel P. 23 (MG-101)
 David 27* (GN-166)
 Edmund P. 46* (MG-150)
 Elizabeth 44* (JO-102)
 Enoch 20* (GN-247)
 Enoch 48 (MG-87)
 Eveline 15* (MG-89)
 Francis 64 (MG-126)
 Francis jr. 33 (MG-88)
 Gardner sr. 48 (MG-116)
 Geo. W. 42 (FO-410)
 Gideon 29 (PE-401)
 Gideon 46 (MG-86)

Index

LEWIS
  Hannah 84* (MG-99)
  Harmon 27 (MG-159)
  Henry H. 42* (MG-99)
  Isaac 20* (CT-272)
  Jackson 30 (LW-124)
  James 24 (PE-406)
  James 74* (PE-411)
  James C. 21* (MG-150)
  Jeremiah 22 (CT-282)
  John 68* (MG-136)
  John C. 24 (MG-150)
  John P. 35* (MG-101)
  John P. jr. 29 (MG-119)
  John jr. 36 (MG-136)
  John sr. 61* (MG-162)
  Johnson 34* (PI-458)
  Joseph 39 (MG-120)
  Joseph 55 (PE-403)
  Juder 30 (m) (PE-410)
  Juder 48 (m) (PE-406)
  Kadern 65* (PE-401)
  Milton 42* (CT-257)
  Nathan 62 (CT-282)
  Rebecca 20* (BE-31)
  Samuel 40 (CT-282)
  Samuel 56 (PE-402)
  Solomon 32 (MG-135)
  Squire 44 (FO-407)
  Stephen 38 (GN-202)
  Thomas 32 (MG-162)
  Thomas 39 (FO-407)
  Thomas 9* (MG-91)
  Thomas E. 27 (MG-118)
  Thomas L. 28 (MG-120)
  Thomas sr. 80 (FO-420)
  Timothy 33 (PE-402)
  Washington 12* (MG-160)
  William 23* (CT-271)
  William 35 (PE-428)
  William 48 (MG-135)
  William 62* (MG-101)
  William H. H. 37 (MG-100)
  Wilson 24 (LE-127)
  Winney 13* (CT-283)
  Zera 30 (BE-35)
LIDDINGHAM
  Jesse 26 (MG-132)
LIFORD
  Lazarus 23* (FO-445)
LIGHT
  Anderson 23 (PE-398)
LIKENS
  John M. 29* (LW-105)
LINDNER
  Ernest 31* (LW-106)
LINDON
  David 50* (MG-148)
LINDSEY
  James 29 (LW-64)
  Walter 40* (GN-260)
LINK
  Samuel 66 (PE-427)
LION
  Humbros 20* (PI-490)
  Jesse 61 (LW-55)
LIONS
  David 30 (LW-52)
  Levi 34 (LW-91)
  Lewis 55 (LW-70)
  Martha 2* (LW-83)
  William 51 (LW-95)
LITREL
  Daniel? 39 (MG-95)
LITRELL
  Johnson 27 (LW-67)
LITTERAL
  H. S. 11 (m)* (GN-222)
  John 32* (FO-454)
LITTERALL
  Elizabeth 58 (JO-101)
  George 35* (JO-110)
  Hurston 41 (JO-106)
LITTERELL
  James 30* (GN-167)
  Perry 29 (GN-179)
LITTLE
  Allen 80 (GN-214)
  Charles 44* (MG-149)
  David 21 (PI-460)
  Edmund 31 (BE-23)
  Harrison 22 (MG-155)
  Henry 21 (GN-214)
  Isaac 26 (FO-428)
  James 25 (BE-43)
  James 27 (FO-428)

  Jason 25 (BE-28)
  John 22 (MG-153)
  John 24* (PI-460)
  John 37 (BE-42)
  John F. 38 (MG-149)
  Joseph 35* (BE-41)
  Paulina 19 (BE-22)
  Peter 32 (MG-142)
  Phillip 44* (MG-142)
  William 31 (PI-455)
  William 41 (BE-44)
  William 63 (PI-462)
LITTLEJOHN
  Webb 28 (GN-236)
LITTLETON
  George C. 19 (CT-265)
  John 60 (CT-265)
LITTON
  James 55 (PI-487)
LIVINGSTON
  Henry A. 59 (JO-82)
LOAR?
  Charlotte 19* (LW-53)
  Moses 21* (LW-54)
  Susan 22* (LW-74)
LOASER?
  Peter 35* (FO-472)
LOCEY
  John 28 (GN-251)
LOCK
  James A. 31 (MG-141)
LOCKE
  Lindsey 38 (CT-226)
  Rachael 59* (CT-227)
LOCKERS?
  Andrew 56 (CT-240)
LOCKWOOD
  Elizabeth 43 (LW-108)
  Jacob 74 (LW-109)
  Wm. 45* (LW-109)
LOCY
  Abrel 19 (m)* (GN-215)
  James 21 (GN-204)
  Mary 57* (GN-208)
LOGAN
  Abraham 36* (GN-228)
  Edward 45* (GN-228)
  James 22 (GN-232)

Index

LOGAN
- Stephen 26* (LE-146)
- Tobias 30* (CT-239)

LOGGINS
- Joseph 75* (MG-158)

LOGUE
- Patrick 25* (GN-210)

LONG
- Benjamin 21 (CT-269)
- Benjamin 33 (GN-225)
- Benjamin 57 (MG-156)
- Charles 38 (GN-223)
- Elijah 30 (GN-221)
- Elisha 30 (GN-221)
- George 22 (MG-154)
- George W. 29 (CT-244)
- Henry 68* (GN-160)
- John A. 34 (LW-89)
- Martin 69 (GN-221)
- Solomon 25* (MG-145)
- William 19* (GN-167)

LOONEY
- John 23 (PI-445)

LOOTS
- John 27 (LW-114)
- Nathanl. 55 (LW-114)

LORVINE?
- Henry 68 (LW-77)

LOUKS
- Anthony P. 26 (PI-444)

LOVEJOY
- David 24 (CT-222)
- Elizabeth 16* (LW-108)
- James 21 (LW-108)
- Margaret 14* (GN-231)

LOVELACE
- Jeremi 65 (BE-2)

LOVELESS
- Thomas R. 46 (MG-113)

LOVELEY
- Ruben 20 (BE-10)

LOVELY
- William 45 (BE-10)

LOW
- Alfred 23 (CT-215)
- Aron 75 (PI-478)
- James 27 (PI-478)
- Orrison R. 42 (PI-467)

- Sarah A. 15* (PI-439)
- Stephen 61 (JO-114)

LOWDER
- James 40 (GN-228)
- Lewis 22* (LW-105)
- William 37 (GN-228)

LOWE
- Baley 25* (CT-268)
- Hannah 39 (LW-103)
- Miles 34 (CT-262)
- Nathaniel B. 39 (PI-466)
- William 31 (JO-114)
- William 51 (CT-262)

LOWER
- Katherine 45?* (PI-469)

LOWES
- John 41 (GN-201)

LOWRY
- George 37* (GN-178)
- William 33 (GN-165)

LOWTHER
- Thomas 30* (GN-166)

LUCAS
- Margaret 60* (FO-461)

LUCEY
- Harvey 28 (BE-39)

LUCKY
- John M. 14* (MG-150)

LUCUS
- Aaron 23 (LE-133)
- Emanuel 33 (LE-130)
- Parker 60 (LE-130)
- Willis 26 (LE-130)

LUCY
- Frances 50 (MG-147)

LUMDEL
- Wm. 24* (LW-90)

LUMPKINS
- Frances M. 2* (MG-88)
- George 13* (MG-157)
- Jane 13* (MG-115)
- Joseph 15* (MG-156)
- Manerva 19* (MG-115)
- Mary 45* (MG-90)
- Wiley 6* (MG-156)

LUNDA
- Elisha 25* (MG-143)

LUNFORD
- John 13* (CT-216)

LUNSEE?
- Elizabeth 24* (PI-452)

LUNSFORD
- Alexandre 12* (PI-449)
- Eliza 11* (PI-450)
- James 27 (CT-273)
- Moses 77 (MG-109)
- Thomas 10/12* (PI-452)

LUNTS
- Archibald 20* (MG-145)
- Dicy 50* (MG-132)

LUSK
- James 34 (CT-225)
- Sarah 72 (CT-225)

LUSTER
- Harvey 44 (LW-58)
- Lindsy 37* (LW-57)
- William 5* (LE-139)
- Wm. 37 (LW-55)

LYKINS
- Caleb 27 (MG-117)
- David 59* (MG-115)
- David K. 29 (MG-158)
- David P. 31* (MG-86)
- E. Isaac S. 22* (BE-6)
- Eli 48* (MG-173)
- Isaac 28 (MG-158)
- John 38 (MG-93)
- John 39 (MG-168)
- John C. 34 (MG-156)
- Milton 31 (MG-158)
- Peter 49 (MG-158)
- Peter D. 30 (MG-165)
- Rolly C. 20 (MG-168)
- William 39* (MG-115)
- William 55 (MG-169)
- William S. 53 (MG-168)
- William V. 25 (MG-170)

LYNCH
- William 33* (FO-410)

LYNN
- Christian 45 (LW-89)

LYNTICUM
- Jerishia 65* (FO-463)

LYON
- Francis 58* (MG-155)

Index

LYON
 Jesse 37 (CT-261)
 John 23 (MG-155)
 Nathaniel 32 (CT-263)
 Susannah 55 (CT-263)
LYONS
 Ann E. 15* (GN-259)
 James 30* (JO-96)
 John 21* (MG-149)
 William 38 (JO-99)
LYTTLE
 Edmund 76 (PE-405)
MACE
 Stephen 57 (PI-491)
MACKEN
 Hiram 50 (LW-81)
MACLEESE
 Daniel 41* (GN-233)
 Daniel 69 (GN-233)
MADDEN
 Jonathan 44 (GN-232)
 Matthew 24 (CT-229)
 Nancy 23* (LE-140)
 Nancy 60 (PE-426)
 Reese 27 (PE-426)
 William 24 (PE-426)
MADDEX
 John 31* (CT-268)
MADDIX
 William 32 (CT-266)
MADDOCKS
 John H. N. 40 (LE-141)
MADDOX
 Abraham 52 (CT-263)
 Nathaniel 52* (CT-262)
 Syrus G. 22 (CT-263)
MADDUX
 James 44 (MG-91)
MADEN
 Arch 18 (LE-150)
 Peter 58 (LE-155)
 Wm. 28 (LE-150)
MAGGARD
 David 45 (LE-128)
 Henry 29* (LE-126)
 Isaac 25 (LE-128)
 James 24 (LE-129)
 James 33 (LE-127)

John 53 (PE-402)
John H. 24 (LE-128)
Moses 27 (PE-402)
Moses 31 (LE-128)
Rudolph 50 (LE-128)
Samuel 20 (LE-128)
Samuel 20 (LE-129)
Samuel Jr. 36 (LE-128)
Samuel Sr. 76 (LE-128)
MAGILL
 Ferdinand 22* (GN-168)
MAGINIS
 David 21* (GN-257)
 Harvey 25 (GN-257)
MAGLONE
 John 48 (GN-238)
MAGOVERN
 Daniel 35* (GN-210)
MAHAY?
 John B. 19 (CT-279)
MAINARD
 Alvis 42* (PI-469)
 David 29 (GN-201)
 Henderson 30 (PI-470)
 James 25 (GN-201)
 Moses 34* (PI-469)
 Pleasant 37 (BE-22)
 Thomas J. 3* (GN-184)
 William 45 (GN-201)
MAINER
 Allen 27* (PI-481)
 David 60 (PI-483)
 James 28 (PI-487)
 Thomas 21 (PI-483)
MAINOR
 Benjamine 34* (PI-486)
 Christopher 36 (PI-485)
 Edward 26 (PI-484)
 Edward 52 (PI-468)
 James 77 (PI-485)
 Lewis 30* (PI-485)
 Marcus 58 (PI-484)
 Moses 35 (PI-484)
 Rhoda 36 (PI-468)
 Stephen 33 (PI-485)
 William 26 (PI-468)
MALONE
 William 26 (GN-236)

MALONEY
 John 39 (BE-3)
 McKinley 32 (BE-1)
MANER
 Lewis 25 (LW-124)
MANES
 Thomas 21 (MG-153)
MANIER
 Linsey 24* (PI-496)
MANIN
 Elizabeth 22* (MG-106)
MANION
 Joseph 26* (FO-421)
MANKINS
 John 19* (JO-110)
MANN
 George 21* (FO-467)
 John 27 (BE-11)
 Thomas 28 (BE-11)
 William 41 (BE-10)
MANNEN
 Isaac 25 (CT-249)
 John 50 (CT-249)
 John B. 35 (CT-249)
 Meradith 48 (CT-248)
 Thomas 24 (CT-249)
MANNIN
 Charles 54 (MG-141)
 John 24 (MG-140)
 John D. 30 (MG-141)
 John W. 29* (MG-140)
 Meradith 70* (MG-144)
 Tarlton 39 (CT-238)
 Tube 40 (m)* (MG-112)
MANOR
 Charles 51 (LW-85)
 Isaac 27 (JO-117)
 James 22 (JO-459)
 Jeremiah 19 (JO-116)
 Jesse 27 (LW-119)
 Jonathan 21 (JO-116)
 William 24 (PI-466)
MANUAL
 Elisha 23 (FO-470)
MAPLEWHITE
 Polly 46* (BE-32)
MARANDA
 Isaac 18* (GN-210)

Index

MARCUM
  A. J. 27 (m) (LW-76)
  Alfred 47 (BE-32)
  Fleming 26* (LW-105)
  James 58 (LW-105)
  Lurena 30 (LW-118)
  Thos. 20 (LW-122)
MARILLER
  Cinda 26* (PE-397)
MARITY
  William F. 46 (GN-213)
MARK
  Joseph 32* (GN-209)
MARKHAM
  James 22* (BE-23)
MARKS
  James 19* (GN-209)
  Thos. 29* (LW-110)
MARKWELL
  Sandy 28 (CT-240)
MARLOW
  Joel 27 (CT-262)
MARPLE
  John 32* (MG-173)
MARRS
  John 36 (PI-460)
  Samuel 59 (PI-491)
MARSHAL
  William 45 (BE-12)
MARSHALL
  George 36 (FO-451)
  Hugh 49 (FO-415)
  James 34* (LW-69)
  John 16* (FO-410)
  Johnson 41 (FO-442)
  Mason 27 (FO-451)
  Moses M. 33 (GN-186)
  Reuben 39 (JO-84)
  Reuben 69 (FO-451)
  Ruben 34 (BE-28)
  Washington 20 (FO-442)
  William 13* (FO-410)
MARTIN
  Alexander 35 (FO-431)
  Alexander 63 (GN-205)
  Allen 28 (FO-431)
  Andrew 36 (FO-436)
  Ann 45* (GN-170)

Benj. 26 (LE-154)
Booker J. 26 (LW-124)
David 26 (FO-437)
Ezekiel 45* (GN-190)
Fitney 24 (f)* (BE-44)
George 34 (CT-244)
George 59 (GN-264)
George 66 (GN-213)
Henry 33* (GN-248)
Hester A. 4* (GN-182)
James 24* (BE-25)
James 30 (GN-213)
James 72 (JO-120)
Job 40 (FO-424)
Joel 58* (FO-435)
Joel D. 32 (FO-424)
John 18* (CT-214)
John 19* (GN-261)
John 32 (LE-153)
John 45 (FO-433)
John 50 (GN-232)
John P. 39 (FO-472)
John P. 51 (CT-274)
Joseph 26 (GN-264)
Joseph 28 (GN-262)
Labon 22* (GN-191)
Labon sr. 25 (GN-191)
Morgan 32 (JO-93)
O. W. 44 (m)* (LW-50)
Peter 25* (GN-210)
Phillips 34 (GN-179)
Pleasant 38* (MG-112)
Simpson 30 (FO-424)
Susannah 18* (FO-434)
William 24 (PE-424)
William 26 (GN-243)
William 41 (MG-113)
Wm. 29 (LW-119)
Wyatt 34 (FO-431)
MASON
  James 38 (MG-120)
  Jefferson 40 (MG-135)
  John 43* (MG-144)
  Joseph 40 (GN-181)
  Martin 28* (GN-172)
  Susan 15* (MG-162)
MASSY
  John 23 (LW-111)

MASSY?
  Henderson 40 (PE-422)
MASTERS
  William 9* (B) (MG-137)
MATHES
  Thomas 61* (PI-487)
MATHEWS
  Samuel 25 (FO-434)
MATHUS
  Lucy 42* (JO-116)
MATNEY
  Alex. 25* (PI-445)
  John 30 (LW-115)
MATTHEWS
  A. A. 50 (m) (GN-237)
  Anderson 22* (GN-237)
  James 44* (GN-207)
MATTOCKS
  Emery 38 (BE-12)
MAUK
  Daniel 21* (CT-255)
  Joseph 34 (CT-260)
  Peter 69 (CT-255)
  Peter C. 32 (CT-237)
MAUPIN
  D. G. 28 (m) (GN-189)
  William 37 (MG-111)
MAWHAN
  Henry 57 (JO-105)
  Johial 23 (JO-105)
MAXEY
  Christopher C. 20* (MG-141)
  Clark 12* (MG-173)
  Jacob 19* (MG-174)
  Raney 44 (MG-140)
MAY
  Blair 42 (FO-458)
  Caleb 20 (FO-455)
  Caleb 25 (MG-113)
  Caleb 27 (JO-102)
  Campbell 23 (MG-166)
  Daniel 28 (PI-475)
  Daniel 65 (PI-476)
  David 31 (PI-475)
  David 43 (FO-454)
  David T. 25* (PI-490)
  Elizabeth 34 (PI-476)
  Elizabeth 46* (GN-203)

Index

MAY
  Gideon 44* (PI-447)
  Harvy 25* (FO-467)
  Harvy 28* (MG-162)
  Henery 26* (PI-443)
  James 22 (PI-475)
  James 45 (PI-445)
  James M. 24 (PI-476)
  James jr. 38 (MG-164)
  James sr. 52* (MG-165)
  John 27 (PI-459)
  John 30* (GN-209)
  John 48* (MG-160)
  Johnethan 31 (PI-448)
  Mary 22* (MG-155)
  Mary 50* (FO-458)
  Mary A. 28 (PI-476)
  Rebecca 20* (PI-490)
  Samuel 34* (MG-147)
  Samuel 67* (FO-472)
  Samuel jr. 29 (PI-459)
  Sarah 39 (FO-440)
  Thomas 27 (PE-412)
  Thomas P. 34* (PI-488)
  Thomas sr. 63* (PI-460)
  William 50 (PI-476)
MAYABB
  John 25* (BE-25)
MAYBERRY
  Josiah 23* (GN-185)
  Levi 26 (MG-130)
MAYBERS?
  Charles 32 (GN-181)
MAYHEW
  Elizabeth 13* (GN-181)
  Frances 12* (GN-188)
  James H. 23 (GN-210)
  John 24* (GN-181)
  Melinda 20* (GN-187)
  Rebecca 63* (GN-203)
  William 18* (GN-211)
  William 45* (GN-181)
MAYLONE
  George 23 (GN-160)
  John 25 (GN-159)
MAYO
  Elisha 22* (MG-131)
  George 32 (FO-471)

Jacob 50* (FO-441)
John W. 18* (FO-422)
Lewis 54 (JO-121)
Lewis P. 25* (FO-418)
Mial 55 (FO-441)
Wm. J. 29 (FO-433)
MAYRES
  Thomas 26 (FO-409)
MAYS
  David 7/12* (BE-38)
  Ehud 47 (m) (MG-127)
  Grace 48* (BE-36)
  John 27 (BE-35)
  Lydia 29* (BE-35)
  Moses 33* (BE-37)
  Nathan 33 (MG-127)
  Sarah 42 (MG-89)
  Thomas 43* (BE-36)
  William 26 (BE-36)
  William jr. 37 (MG-133)
  William sr. 73 (MG-133)
  Winston 36 (JO-125)
MCADAMS
  Robert 50* (GN-167)
MCALISTER
  Alexander 36 (CT-232)
  George W. 39 (GN-174)
  Hervey 25* (CT-271)
  James 30* (GN-178)
  John 64 (GN-255)
  John V. 35* (GN-175)
  Joseph 54* (GN-240)
  Robert 28* (GN-174)
MCBRAYER
  Solomon S. 24 (CT-222)
MCBROYER
  James 46 (CT-224)
  Louis P. 23* (CT-224)
  William G. 35* (CT-224)
MCCALASTER
  Mary 45* (FO-460)
MCCALISTER
  Louisa 29 (PI-457)
  Susan 20* (PI-490)
MCCALL
  John 24* (GN-193)
  Robt. 21* (LW-62)

MCCANE
  Mariah 13* (CT-258)
MCCARRAN
  Daniel 23* (GN-176)
MCCARTY
  Eliza 5* (GN-174)
  Henry 35 (GN-183)
  Jeremiah 34 (FO-449)
  John 26 (JO-101)
  John 32 (GN-208)
  John 35 (JO-103)
  John 35 (LW-86)
  Milla 38* (CT-214)
  Sarah 38* (CT-217)
  Thomas 54 (JO-101)
  William 33 (CT-236)
MCCAY
  Reuben 22* (LW-74)
MCCLAIN
  Archibald 30 (MG-159)
  Beverly 42 (m) (MG-100)
  Charles 50 (MG-147)
MCCLANAHAN
  Moses 52 (MG-93)
MCCLAVE
  G. W. 34 (m) (GN-236)
MCCLEESE
  Marshall 27* (CT-229)
  Thomas 51* (CT-229)
MCCLELAND
  John 27 (GN-252)
MCCLURE
  Ezekiel 37 (MG-99)
  Geo. C. 26 (LW-85)
  James H. 33 (MG-99)
  John 46 (LW-74)
  Matthew 29 (MG-116)
  Matthew 70* (MG-99)
  Strother 44 (LW-85)
  Wm. 60 (LW-116)
MCCLURG
  Alexander 19* (GN-212)
MCCOINE
  Joshua 10/12* (PI-448)
MCCOLLEY
  James 44 (PI-447)
MCCOMAC
  Madison 17* (LW-118)

Index

MCCOMAC
  Malisse J. 7* (LW-89)
  Meredith 32* (LW-76)
MCCONAHA
  J. L. 28 (m)* (CT-224)
MCCONNAC
  Wiley 29 (LW-72)
MCCONNELL
  C. L. 24 (m)* (GN-162)
  Matthew 31 (GN-177)
MCCORMAC
  Lorenzo D. 16* (LW-88)
  Wm. 40 (LW-85)
MCCORMICK
  Martha A. 23* (GN-194)
  Samuel 56 (GN-203)
MCCOWAN
  Hugh 65 (PI-461)
  John 28* (PI-460)
  Linsey 24 (m) (PI-492)
  Mitchell 30* (PI-494)
  William 34 (PI-460)
MCCOY
  Acy H. 23 (PI-474)
  Allen 25* (PI-470)
  Barbary 19* (PI-473)
  Benjamine 27* (PI-473)
  Curtus F. 37 (BE-11)
  Eliza J. 2* (PI-473)
  Geo. 46 (LW-90)
  Geo. 67 (LW-91)
  Geo. W. 20* (LW-106)
  John 11* (PI-473)
  John 45 (PI-478)
  Joseph 55 (PI-481)
  Mary 35 (PI-473)
  Nancey 11* (PI-474)
  Pierce 25 (PI-470)
  Randolph 49 (PI-463)
  Richard 50 (PI-472)
  Ryland D. 35 (CT-263)
  Samuel 66* (PI-470)
  Susan 19* (FO-471)
  Thomas 50 (PI-481)
  Uriah 24 (PI-477)
  William 25 (PI-472)
  William 27 (PI-477)
  William 35 (FO-468)

William 39* (PI-478)
MCCRARY
  John 75 (PE-407)
MCCRAY
  Levicy 43* (LE-134)
MCCREAN
  Mariah E. 14* (CT-265)
MCCROSKEY
  William 35 (GN-216)
MCCROSKY
  John 35* (GN-191)
  Margaret 65 (GN-191)
MCCRUM
  Mary 15* (GN-161)
MCCULLOUGH
  Addison 33* (GN-194)
MCDANIEL
  Daniel 18 (BE-23)
  George 35* (MG-95)
  Hezekiah jr. 23 (MG-98)
  Hezekiah sr. 66 (MG-98)
  John 22* (BE-24)
  John 60* (BE-7)
  Joshua 27* (PE-431)
MCDAVID
  George 58 (CT-280)
  James 35* (LW-69)
  John 33 (CT-280)
MCDEER
  John 30 (LW-74)
MCDOLE
  Peter 20 (CT-276)
MCDONALD
  Arthur 30 (BE-11)
  Elizabeth 60 (BE-6)
  Mike 35* (GN-175)
  Thomas 28* (GN-261)
MCDOWELL
  Jahue 47 (LW-74)
  James 23 (JO-97)
  John 51 (LW-103)
  John jr 24* (LW-103)
  Johns 25* (LW-98)
  Joseph 31* (JO-96)
  Mary 23* (LW-110)
  William 26 (JO-97)
  Wm. 61* (LW-114)

MCFADDEN
  William 21* (GN-176)
MCFARLAND
  Geo. 15* (LW-113)
  Virginia L. 7* (CT-256)
  William 23 (FO-452)
  Wm. 50* (LW-117)
MCFARLANE
  Hiram 26* (CT-261)
  John 33 (CT-267)
  William 66 (CT-267)
MCGEE
  Coonrod 46 (GN-212)
  James 25 (PI-459)
  James 60 (PI-443)
  Michael 23* (GN-210)
MCGEORGE
  P. W. 35 (m) (BE-39)
MCGINIS
  Leonidas 19* (PI-469)
MCGINLEY
  Roger 28* (GN-178)
MCGINNIS
  Hiram 41 (JO-117)
  James 38 (CT-224)
  Reuben 28* (CT-219)
  Thomas 35 (CT-224)
  William 5* (GN-214)
  William 66* (GN-256)
MCGLOME
  James 42 (CT-230)
MCGLONE
  Alfred 35 (CT-230)
  Ambros 30 (CT-230)
  Joseph 36 (CT-230)
  Owen 70 (CT-230)
  Robert 44 (CT-231)
  Squire 39 (CT-231)
  William Sr. 47* (CT-232)
MCGLOTHLAN
  Jacob 39 (CT-249)
MCGLOTHLIN
  James 38 (CT-258)
MCGOWEN
  William 25 (CT-228)
MCGOWN
  John 38 (GN-261)

Index

MCGRAW
  John V. 17* (LW-110)
  Lorana 13* (GN-188)
  Martin 23 (MG-163)
MCGREW
  William H. 25* (GN-164)
MCGUIN
  Ambrose C. 40 (MG-93)
  Cyntha 7* (GN-199)
  James 24 (MG-98)
  John 16* (GN-206)
MCGUINE
  Elizabeth 29* (PI-458)
MCGUIRE
  Eada 21* (CT-275)
  Elijah C. 33 (MG-158)
  Elizabeth 48* (FO-408)
  Harrison 23 (MG-108)
  Isaac 38 (FO-420)
  JAmes sr. 70 (MG-172)
  James 22 (CT-244)
  James 56 (MG-108)
  James B. 14* (PI-487)
  James C. 20* (MG-163)
  Jesse J. 25 (MG-89)
  Jilson P. 35* (MG-169)
  John 27* (MG-158)
  John 32* (CT-242)
  John 48 (CT-276)
  Joseph 12* (LW-103)
  N. B. 52 (m)* (LW-117)
  Newton 21* (MG-100)
  Robert 28 (CT-269)
  Samuel 35 (FO-420)
  Samuel 59 (MG-117)
  Samuel W. 28 (MG-91)
  Temperance 52* (CT-269)
  William 24 (PI-489)
  William 48 (FO-469)
MCILHANY
  Elizabeth 15* (MG-97)
MCINTIRE
  Benjamin 66 (PE-425)
MCINTOSH
  Absalom 39 (BE-29)
  Ben. 31 (BE-33)
  Edward 29 (BE-29)
  Henly 30 (BE-35)

James 55 (BE-17)
John 35 (BE-36)
Levi 35 (PE-413)
Nimrod 27 (BE-15)
Peter 30 (PE-413)
Peter 35 (BE-35)
Roderick 67 (PE-398)
Samuel 23 (PE-413)
Sarah 22* (PE-409)
William 24* (PI-491)
William 29 (PE-398)
Wm. 30 (BE-35)
Wm. 60* (BE-35)
Zechariah 30 (BE-15)
MCINTYRE
  Harrison 36 (GN-209)
  James 20* (GN-184)
MCKEE
  Geo. W. 26 (LW-108)
  Jesse 25 (FO-441)
  John 27 (GN-226)
  John 65 (GN-226)
  John 79* (GN-247)
  Roda 5* (LE-155)
  William 55* (FO-435)
MCKENYER
  Harrison 36 (MG-87)
MCKENZIE
  Henly 27 (MG-87)
  Hugh 32 (JO-91)
  John 31 (JO-105)
  Seargant N. 25 (JO-87)
  William 20* (MG-97)
  William 45 (JO-105)
MCKINNEY
  Daniel 59* (CT-265)
  Elijah 36 (FO-414)
  Mary 52 (PI-461)
  Shelton 30 (MG-147)
MCKINNY
  Peter 47 (FO-412)
MCKINSTER
  Allen 19 (LW-73)
  Clemintine 22* (LW-65)
  Elizabeth 45 (LW-115)
  Jackson 15* (LW-116)
  James 26 (LW-115)
  Mack 20* (LW-92)

Thos. 29 (LW-84)
MCKINZIE
  Isaac 86 (MG-100)
  James 47 (JO-98)
  John 56* (JO-98)
MCKOY
  Moses 50 (GN-244)
  Obediah 42* (GN-226)
MCLAIN
  Daniel 40* (GN-178)
  Nancy 28* (MG-146)
  Otho 19* (GN-195)
MCLARKEY
  Samuel 28* (GN-211)
MCLEMORE
  Hiram 70? (PE-403)
MCLONG
  James 50 (CT-252)
  John 4* (CT-251)
MCLOVY?
  William 28 (CT-264)
MCLOWERY
  Jelson 23 (JO-101)
MCMAHAN
  Alexander 48 (CT-235)
  Jesse 30 (GN-209)
  John 25* (GN-210)
  Stephen 56 (GN-162)
MCMAHON
  Isaac W. 25* (CT-242)
MCMARR
  Godfrey 56* (B) (BE-22)
  Letty 84* (B) (BE-25)
MCMEAR
  James P. 40* (MG-118)
MCMULLAN
  James 57* (GN-158)
MCMULLEN
  J. S. 31 (m)* (GN-160)
MCNEALAN
  William 21* (GN-249)
MCNEILEY
  Benjamin 23 (JO-116)
MCNEW
  William 29 (FO-454)
MCPEEK
  George 32 (PI-449)
  James 20* (PI-448)

Index

MCPEEK
  James 63* (PI-449)
MCPHERSON
  Jesse 24* (GN-249)
MCQUILLON
  Thomas 46 (GN-246)
MCQUIN?
  Andrew R. 51* (PI-468)
MCQUINN
  Alexander 62 (MG-156)
  Charles B. 30* (BE-23)
  Charles B. 60 (BE-6)
  James 31 (MG-155)
  Wiley 35 (BE-28)
  Wm. 58 (BE-27)
  Zechariah 22* (BE-24)
MCQUINN?
  Francis 20* (BE-27)
MCREYNOLDS
  Mary 10* (B) (FO-472)
  William 14* (B) (FO-473)
MCROBERTS
  John 10* (CT-249)
MCSORLEY
  Edmd. 23 (LW-112)
MCVAIN
  James 30* (LW-109)
MCWURTER
  Harvey 33 (GN-213)
MEAD
  Abm. 32 (LW-103)
  Abraham 22 (FO-411)
  Albert G. 47* (GN-216)
  Ann 30* (FO-411)
  Armstead 44 (GN-179)
  Benjamin F. 32 (GN-162)
  Benjamine 28 (PI-493)
  Elizabeth 77* (GN-164)
  Gilbert 14* (LW-83)
  Isabel 20* (LW-98)
  Jesse 47 (LW-96)
  Kisiah 35* (LW-103)
  Larkin 14* (CT-219)
  Lorenzo 11* (FO-466)
  Malinda 28 (LW-112)
  Margaret 28* (PI-485)
  Martha 17* (LW-57)
  Mary J. 14* (LW-102)

Moses 63* (FO-409)
Nancy 35* (CT-233)
Noah 16* (LW-101)
Reuben 37 (PI-493)
Rhodes 44 (PI-492)
Robert 31* (JO-102)
Robert 36* (PI-466)
Robert 54 (FO-415)
Samuel 20* (JO-120)
Susan 18* (LW-50)
Susan 70 (LW-103)
Thomas 46 (FO-427)
Thomas jr. 23 (FO-427)
Tolbert 19* (GN-193)
William 21* (PI-442)
William 30 (FO-411)
William 33* (PI-484)
MEADDOWS
  Darcas 30 (LE-140)
MEADOWS
  Elisha 37* (FO-464)
  Isah 50 (FO-442)
  John 22* (FO-442)
  Matthew 36 (MG-161)
MEAK
  Madison W. 15* (LW-50)
MEANS
  Hugh 35* (GN-194)
MEARS
  Susan 53* (GN-160)
MEDDAUGH
  Benjamin 18* (GN-223)
  Charles 47 (GN-223)
  Elijah 38 (GN-240)
  James 39* (GN-223)
MEDLEY
  Johnson 60* (GN-256)
  Julius 22* (FO-457)
MEDLOCK
  James 20* (BE-33)
MEDOWS
  Abraham 42* (GN-257)
MEE
  David 55 (GN-165)
MEEK
  Anna 14* (GN-158)
  Isaac 39 (JO-109)
  James 24 (GN-231)

James 76 (GN-236)
Jesse P. 33* (LW-92)
John 30 (GN-236)
John 60* (LW-53)
Joseph 30* (GN-157)
Joseph 54 (GN-235)
Raburn 21* (LW-118)
Richard 13* (LW-117)
Samuel 37* (GN-231)
Suter 27 (m) (GN-236)
William 39 (JO-102)
MEEKS
  Edwd. 22* (LW-76)
MELLEN
  Patrick 45 (FO-471)
  William P. 36* (FO-471)
MELMAN
  Wm. 37 (LW-82)
MELVIN
  George 36 (JO-103)
MERRIDD
  William 71 (PE-417)
MERRIL
  Albert 22* (GN-223)
MERRILL
  J. P. 24 (m)* (GN-223)
MERRITT
  John 30 (FO-466)
MERRIX
  Charles 37 (FO-451)
  Charles 76* (FO-451)
MERRIX?
  James 40 (FO-450)
  John 43 (FO-450)
MESSE
  Richard 22 (GN-245)
MESSER
  Agness 20* (PE-433)
  Benjamin 25* (GN-264)
  Daniel 24* (GN-248)
  Eligah 9* (PE-416)
  Jacob 65* (LW-123)
  Jinsey 20 (f)* (PE-433)
  Moses 22 (PE-422)
  Reuben 25 (PE-420)
  Sally 40 (PE-423)
  Saml. 36 (LW-89)
  William 32 (GN-264)

Index

MESSER
  William 37* (CT-270)
MEW?
  Thomas 15* (PI-476)
MEYER
  John 50 (GN-261)
MICHELL
  David 35* (LW-98)
MIDDLETON
  James 26 (CT-283)
  Luraney 56* (CT-261)
MIFFORD
  George 25* (GN-220)
  Nathan 18* (GN-220)
MIKLES
  Henry 20* (LW-111)
MILAM
  Elizabeth 35 (FO-461)
  Esther 25* (PI-488)
  Lewis 54 (PE-398)
MILES
  Anderson 35 (LE-150)
  Emily 80 (m?)* (PI-467)
  George 35* (GN-199)
MILLARD
  Elijah 25 (PI-469)
  Malvina 21* (CT-265)
MILLER
  Adison 26 (CT-285)
  Adrian 22* (GN-259)
  Andrew 51 (PE-417)
  Asher 15* (LW-104)
  Benjamin 51 (BE-14)
  Charles 25* (GN-171)
  Charlotta 23* (PI-480)
  Danl. 40* (LW-77)
  Edwd B. 52 (LW-84)
  Elias 50 (BE-16)
  Elijah 24 (BE-14)
  George 46 (BE-5)
  George 6* (BE-6)
  George W. 20* (GN-202)
  Henly 26* (PE-423)
  Henry B. 49 (LW-97)
  Hiram 32* (BE-41)
  Hiram 70* (MG-151)
  James F. 29* (LW-96)
  Jeremi 22* (BE-24)

John 14* (GN-249)
John 27 (BE-14)
John 28 (PI-440)
John 35 (GN-209)
John 36 (BE-16)
John 49 (CT-237)
John 50 (BE-15)
Joseph 31* (GN-166)
Marcus 30 (CT-266)
Martin 45 (BE-28)
Mary 63* (BE-12)
Owens 23 (BE-6)
Philip 45 (JO-118)
Robert 66* (CT-284)
Robt. 39 (LW-103)
Saml. 20 (LW-104)
Samuel 38 (BE-16)
Samuel 46* (BE-8)
Samuel 8 (PE-423)
Sarah 22* (PE-406)
Sarah 45* (PI-449)
Stephen 20* (GN-212)
Timmothy 47 (PI-466)
Uriah 41 (GN-259)
Wiley 31 (BE-31)
William 30 (PE-428)
William 42 (BE-15)
William 58 (CT-241)
William 61 (GN-212)
William H. 30 (CT-268)
Wm. 22* (CT-277)
Wm. 42 (LW-113)
MILLS
  Geo. 40 (LW-123)
  John 21 (FO-462)
  John 49* (LW-123)
  William 45 (PI-487)
MILTON
  Preston 27 (PE-403)
  Terry 59 (f) (PE-402)
  William 22 (PE-403)
MILUM
  Edward 33 (FO-426)
MIMS
  Abigal 45 (PI-495)
  John D. 42* (PI-495)
MINCY
  Elizabeth 49 (PE-400)

MINTON
  Evan 32 (MG-155)
MIRANDY
  William 51 (CT-214)
MIRES
  Wm. R. 38 (LW-76)
MITCHEL
  Jane E. 12* (GN-248)
MITCHELL
  George W. 39 (LE-125)
  Leonard 28 (MG-140)
  Stephen 50 (FO-419)
  Wiley 18* (FO-419)
MITCHUM
  William A. 30 (PI-473)
MOBLEY
  Harris 22 (CT-268)
  Telitha 45 (CT-257)
MOCKABY
  Murte? 70 (m)* (MG-132)
MOCKBEE
  David 39 (CT-250)
  Hamilton 10* (CT-250)
MOLES
  Emanuel 37* (FO-470)
MOLLETT
  David 38* (JO-114)
  Hiram 33 (JO-116)
  James 30 (JO-114)
  John 28 (JO-114)
MOMAN
  G. W. 35 (m)* (GN-197)
MONEYPENNY
  Frederick 21 (MG-141)
MONROE
  Jacob 28* (GN-223)
MONSEY
  Benjamin 27 (BE-25)
MONTGOMERY
  Edington 31 (CT-266)
  Elizabeth 60* (MG-126)
  George 27* (MG-157)
  George 28 (CT-226)
  James 29 (FO-451)
  James 35 (MG-102)
  James 49 (CT-227)
  John 24* (GN-247)
  John 42 (MG-163)

Index

MONTGOMERY
John 50 (GN-226)
John 57 (FO-452)
John Y. 40 (CT-214)
Joseph 20 (MG-90)
Lucretia 18* (MG-109)
Margarett 32 (MG-126)
Nathan 26* (CT-227)
Sarah 25* (GN-178)
Silas 26 (FO-451)
Watson 31 (MG-95)
Wiley 19* (MG-164)
William 28 (MG-124)
William 36* (CT-246)
William 41* (MG-145)
MOODY
George 31* (CT-242)
MOOR
Frances A. 16* (CT-264)
MOORE
Abner 1* (BE-32)
Allen 50 (BE-41)
Ananias 40 (PI-448)
Andrew 24* (FO-418)
Andrew 63 (B) (FO-426)
Archibald 27 (FO-426)
Aron 35* (PI-449)
Charles 42* (GN-249)
David 26 (LW-104)
David 32 (LW-72)
David 56 (LW-53)
Edmond 50 (FO-426)
George 35* (CT-280)
Hiram 30* (CT-241)
Isaac 60 (PI-448)
Isac 30 (PI-449)
James 42 (LW-50)
Jeremiah 39* (GN-256)
John 24 (LW-104)
John 25* (LW-121)
John 39 (CT-229)
John 39 (LW-92)
John 40 (B) (FO-426)
John W. 74* (JO-92)
L. Y.? 21 (m) (LW-75)
Langford 24* (PI-496)
Lucinda 47 (LW-96)
Obadiah 58 (B) (FO-459)

Paul 30* (LW-83)
Rycene 24 (f)* (FO-426)
Saml. 23* (LW-92)
Saml. T. 26 (LW-81)
Sampson 19* (JO-103)
Samuel 36 (FO-467)
Stuffley 22* (B) (LE-146)
Timothey 23* (GN-248)
William 28* (GN-188)
William 37 (JO-116)
William 40* (PI-448)
Wm. 25 (BE-32)
Wm. T. 35 (LW-92)
MOORES
Silas 42* (CT-231)
MORAN
John 26 (GN-264)
William 49 (GN-218)
MOREFIELD
David 23 (BE-13)
MOREHEAD
Katharine 80* (LW-76)
Mary 57* (LW-82)
MORGAN
Able 34 (PE-400)
Adrian 27 (PE-399)
Arta 33* (FO-424)
David 45 (FO-417)
David 50 (PE-399)
Elisha 30 (PE-400)
Enoch 47 (BE-10)
Isom 39 (LE-148)
James 31 (PI-440)
James 35* (LE-149)
James 63* (LE-148)
Jesse 46 (PE-399)
John 35* (PE-398)
John 5* (PE-415)
Johnson 35 (MG-142)
Mary A. 26* (PI-443)
Reuben 25 (FO-446)
Rhoda 29* (B) (FO-472)
Saml. 29* (LW-106)
Washington 12* (PE-413)
Washington 26 (PE-400)
William 7* (PI-490)
Wm. 43 (LE-148)
Zachariah 24 (PE-415)

MORMON
Joseph 30 (GN-205)
MORRIS
Alcey J. 16* (GN-205)
Allin 8* (GN-259)
Ambrose 33 (PI-465)
Benjamin 33* (GN-252)
Benjamin 7i5 (CT-215)
Benjm. 32 (LW-94)
Calvin 10* (GN-231)
Daniel 37 (FO-418)
Elias 44 (BE-43)
Elizabeth 24 (PE-420)
Elizabeth 65 (LW-94)
Ezekiel 60 (PE-420)
Henry 30 (LW-90)
Isaac 55* (GN-171)
J. C. 25 (m) (GN-171)
Jamima 30* (MG-153)
John 33 (CT-270)
John 68* (FO-435)
Joseph 63 (PE-409)
Larkin 22 (PE-409)
Luana 35 (CT-215)
Martin 28 (GN-252)
Mathew 19 (LW-94)
Pendin 39 (LW-94)
Phil 24* (GN-180)
Thomas G. 18* (GN-252)
Wesley 19 (BE-43)
William 21* (GN-173)
William 55 (GN-213)
MORRISON
Emma B. 12* (GN-231)
Mary 50 (PI-486)
N. B. 50 (m)* (GN-250)
Prudence 66* (GN-165)
Raleigh 22* (PI-487)
William H. 35 (GN-204)
MORROW
Danl. 34 (LW-97)
Francis 30* (LW-86)
Francis 38 (LW-112)
Hiram 23 (LW-63)
John 35 (GN-180)
MORTON
George 26 (GN-220)
Hezekiah 53 (GN-219)

Index

MORTON
 James 28 (GN-243)
 John 60 (GN-244)
 John A. 34 (GN-224)
 Richard 27 (GN-241)
 Richard 52* (GN-245)
 William A. 38 (JO-81)
 Willis 30 (GN-244)
MORTRIDGE
 William 16* (PI-440)
MOSELEY
 James 22* (GN-210)
 Peggy 47* (FO-441)
 Prston 34 (GN-204)
MOSELY
 Martha 38 (LW-121)
 Samuel 24 (FO-467)
 William 29 (FO-471)
MOSIER
 Henry 35 (GN-261)
MOSLEY
 D. P. 66 (m) (GN-249)
 James 28 (BE-39)
MOTT
 Almarian 32 (m) (MG-105)
MOULDER
 John 21 (GN-237)
 John 58 (GN-236)
 William 23* (GN-216)
MOUNTS
 Elijah 41 (PI-472)
 Michael 30 (PI-472)
MOUTHEN
 James 24* (CT-271)
MOWRY
 John 22* (CT-264)
MOXLEY
 Henry 34 (LW-58)
MUCKMELON
 John 27 (MG-126)
 William 60 (MG-126)
MULINAX
 Geo. W. 18* (LW-78)
MULLENS
 Aelxandre 40 (PI-452)
 Allen 22 (BE-8)
 Ambrose 47 (BE-9)
 Booker 31 (PI-450)

 Elias 24 (CT-270)
 Elijah 23 (PI-459)
 Elijah 25 (PI-450)
 Elizabeth 56* (PI-453)
 Franklin 18* (BE-43)
 Isaac 34 (BE-9)
 Isom 47 (CT-233)
 James 21* (CT-275)
 James 21* (PI-486)
 James 23 (CT-270)
 Jesse 27 (BE-36)
 John 27 (PI-453)
 John 33 (PI-455)
 John 53* (PI-453)
 Joseph G. 28 (BE-28)
 Joshua 55 (BE-34)
 Larkin 18 (CT-284)
 Pleasant 49 (CT-284)
 Richard 32 (PI-455)
 Solomon 21 (PI-452)
 William 65 (PI-455)
MULLETT
 Elias jr. 35 (JO-112)
 Elias sr. 65 (JO-112)
 Nathan R. 64* (JO-94)
MULLIN
 James 44 (GN-201)
MULLINS
 Benjamine 32 (FO-466)
 Booker 46* (PI-452)
 Booker 55 (FO-423)
 Burgandin 24 (m) (PE-405)
 Daniel 51 (LE-155)
 Elijah 26 (PE-421)
 Elijah 27 (FO-468)
 Hetta 6* (LW-103)
 Isom 55 (FO-468)
 James 64 (PE-421)
 John 18 (LE-139)
 John 22 (LE-150)
 John 52 (CT-285)
 Jonston 23 (CT-280)
 Joseph 21 (LE-155)
 Joshua 33 (LE-153)
 Joshua 40 (LE-139)
 Marshall 28 (FO-468)
 Nancy 14* (LE-139)
 Nancy 15* (LE-137)

 Noah 20* (LW-83)
 Owen 23 (PI-452)
 Owens 27 (FO-429)
 Rachal 48* (LE-150)
 Smith 40 (PI-452)
 Solomon 30 (FO-468)
 Valuntine 27 (LE-150)
 William 28 (FO-424)
 William 46 (FO-429)
 William sr. 84* (FO-429)
MULLIS
 Ambrose 75* (BE-1)
MULTER
 Christopher 15* (JO-117)
MUMBOWER
 Eve 71* (MG-121)
MUNCY
 David W. 20 (LW-79)
 Sally 34 (LW-122)
 Skidmore 50 (LW-78)
MUNDY
 John 22 (PE-399)
MUNSEY
 Levi 45 (PI-467)
 William 45 (PI-468)
MURDOCK
 Elijah 28* (GN-207)
MURPHEY
 Alexandre 23 (PI-478)
 Arch 29 (LW-67)
 David 69* (LW-73)
 Gabriel 25 (PI-482)
 John 27 (LW-57)
 John 30 (PI-445)
 Mary 40 (GN-169)
 Pearce 34 (GN-165)
 Wm. 29* (LW-54)
MURPHY
 David 21* (CT-222)
 Emily 17* (GN-185)
 Jane 57 (GN-198)
 John 30* (CT-227)
 John 39 (MG-149)
 Miles 31* (MG-140)
 Monroe 27 (MG-103)
 William 57 (MG-148)
 William jr. 24 (MG-149)

- 390 -

Index

MURRAY
  Daniel 33* (MG-117)
  Dulcena 36 (MG-100)
  M. 21 (m)* (GN-210)
  Reece 43 (MG-133)
MURRELL
  Larkin 24 (BE-35)
  Thomas 43 (PE-411)
MURRY
  Eleanor 13* (LW-108)
  George W. 23 (JO-115)
  Hiram 45 (LW-110)
  Jane 18* (LW-108)
  Jesse 27 (JO-120)
  Patrick 25* (GN-261)
  Roderick H. 28 (JO-120)
  Saml. 60* (LW-102)
  Samuel 33 (JO-85)
MUSIC
  Charles 21 (GN-252)
  Elevius 22 (PI-475)
  Lucinda 42 (GN-253)
  Martha 11* (GN-253)
MUSICK
  Eligha 41 (LE-152)
  Ephram 54 (JO-118)
  James 38* (MG-148)
  James 44 (JO-122)
  John 24 (FO-469)
  John 63 (JO-121)
MUSSELWHITE
  Joseph 35 (LE-129)
MUTTER
  Franklin 22* (GN-215)
  Isaac 26 (GN-213)
  John 45 (PI-440)
MYER
  Antone 30* (GN-246)
  Henry 25* (GN-260)
MYERS
  Allen 48* (GN-158)
  Henry 59 (GN-161)
  James 35 (GN-161)
  Jameson 30 (CT-253)
  John 38* (GN-158)
  Joseph 55 (MG-94)
  Michael 58 (BE-18)
  Samuel 31 (MG-104)

  Samuel C. 51* (GN-162)
MYNHIER
  Solomon K. 45 (MG-105)
  William 28 (MG-86)
NAPIER
  Edmund 23 (PE-409)
  Elizabeth 50 (PE-416)
  James 29 (PE-417)
  Micager 57 (PE-416)
  Patrick 28 (BE-16)
  Patrick 34 (PE-400)
  Patrick 46 (PE-416)
  Samuel 31 (PE-415)
  Stephen? 31 (PE-423)
NAUGER?
  Frederick 43* (GN-180)
NEACE
  John 63* (GN-222)
  William 21 (GN-228)
NEAL
  Andrew 26 (LW-99)
  John 34 (FO-438)
  Jonathan 21* (GN-217)
  Larkin 40* (GN-176)
  Wm. 59 (BE-39)
NEALY
  Margaret 17* (LW-108)
NEEDHAM
  Christian B 26(m) (MG-140)
NELSON
  Andrew 12* (JO-121)
  David 35 (GN-236)
  Elizabeth 34* (LW-98)
  Emeline 44 (GN-160)
  Emml. 74* (LW-102)
  Isaac 10* (LW-102)
  James 10* (GN-234)
  James 10* (LW-86)
  John 24* (GN-237)
  John 28 (GN-238)
  Kisiah 37* (LW-104)
  Rachel 2* (LW-103)
  Rowland 30* (GN-188)
  Tom 45 (B) (GN-160)
  Wm. 45 (LW-117)
NESBITT
  John 40* (FO-417)

NETHERCUTT
  George 20 (CT-259)
  George 58 (CT-214)
  Jourdan 59 (CT-259)
  Moses 25 (CT-255)
  Stephen 14* (CT-256)
NEW
  David 19* (PI-471)
NEWELL
  Aaron 48 (CT-263)
NEWMAN
  Henry 30 (GN-261)
  Henry 44 (LW-99)
  Lemuel 38 (GN-185)
  Reynolds 45 (LW-111)
  Thomas 28 (GN-191)
NEWSOM
  Davenport 34 (PI-461)
  Fredric 36 (PI-461)
  Harrison 38* (PI-455)
  Hartwell 47* (PI-461)
  Henry 26 (FO-413)
  Henry 43 (PI-454)
  James 21 (FO-468)
NEWTON
  William 46 (BE-6)
NIBERT
  James 30* (JO-120)
NICHELL
  Alexander W. 22 (JO-95)
  George 19 (JO-97)
NICHOLAS
  Thos. 40* (B) (LE-151)
NICHOLL
  Shelby 18 (m)* (JO-108)
NICHOLS
  B. B. 43 (m) (GN-254)
  Elizabeth 2* (PI-464)
  Elizabeth 38 (PI-486)
  Elizabeth 55 (FO-450)
  James 5* (PI-459)
  James E. 59 (GN-165)
  Joseph 28* (FO-457)
  Rachel 65 (GN-157)
  W. T. 41 (m)* (GN-192)
  William 24* (GN-160)
NICKELL
  Andrew 48 (MG-116)

Index

NICKELL
Andrew B. 56 (MG-154)
Andrew P. 25 (MG-154)
Caleb 24 (MG-154)
Caroline 20* (MG-140)
Fowler 32 (MG-97)
George 25 (CT-272)
Georgean 14 (f)* (MG-114)
Greenup 25 (MG-163)
Isaac 23* (MG-149)
Isaac 23 (MG-165)
James 30 (MG-98)
James K. 29* (MG-110)
Jane 13* (MG-152)
John 31 (MG-142)
John 43 (MG-87)
John 67* (CT-248)
John D. 24 (MG-89)
Joseph 40 (CT-248)
Joseph 57* (MG-142)
Joseph D. 19 (MG-164)
Joseph D. 27 (MG-111)
Martha 40 (MG-160)
Martha 8* (MG-162)
Mary 51 (MG-150)
Matilda 52 (MG-89)
Milton 35 (MG-110)
Perry A. 29 (MG-153)
Reuben 36* (MG-130)
Silas 39* (MG-89)
Stewart 32 (MG-154)
Thomas sr. 84 (MG-155)
William 73* (MG-146)
William K. 35 (MG-146)
William P. 35 (MG-146)
NICKOL
Joseph 41 (GN-174)
NICOLS
Rebecca 12* (PI-490)
NIECE
Austin 23 (BE-28)
Austin 65 (BE-31)
Jackson 25 (LE-147)
Jacob 26 (LE-147)
Jacob 63 (BE-30)
Jacob B. 36 (BE-28)
Jacob Jr. 28* (BE-31)
Saml. Jr. 26* (BE-31)

NIPP
Elizabeth 29 (CT-275)
NIX
Leonard 42* (BE-29)
NOBLE
Blair Sen. 70 (JO-123)
Enoch 53 (BE-28)
George 26 (BE-32)
Henry 23 (BE-30)
Ira 35 (BE-16)
Jackson 37* (BE-15)
James 24 (BE-16)
James M. 38* (GN-180)
John 18 (BE-7)
Lawson 39 (BE-30)
Nathan 66 (BE-30)
Sally 22* (BE-7)
Samuel 19* (MG-116)
William 16* (BE-14)
William 41 (BE-31)
NOBLED
James 43 (BE-30)
NOBLES
John 26 (BE-15)
NOE
Jackson 26 (BE-18)
John D. 38 (BE-22)
NOLAND
Jesse 24 (CT-263)
Leonard 23* (CT-277)
NOLCINA
Charles 21* (CT-265)
NOLEN
Jeremiah 22* (GN-177)
Stephen 22 (FO-432)
NOLTE
Wm. 41* (LW-78)
NOLUND
Nathaniel 45 (PE-422)
NORMAN
Stephen 55 (GN-170)
Thomas 27 (MG-163)
NORRIS
Abraham 23 (GN-255)
Edward 55* (B) (CT-244)
George 20* (GN-171)
John 25* (GN-173)
Philip 69* (GN-162)

William 20* (GN-180)
NORTH
John 47 (GN-187)
Loyd 28 (CT-223)
NORTON
Pleasant 48 (CT-225)
NOTT
Arbuth A. 57 (m)* (JO-81)
NUNLEY
Daniel 35 (GN-215)
Elijah 22 (GN-250)
Mary 3* (CT-269)
William 33 (GN-213)
NUNNERY
John 58 (PI-493)
Mitchell 19 (PI-493)
NUSOM
Elizabeth 40 (FO-468)
NUTTER
Levi 22* (GN-212)
William 28 (GN-179)
NUTTY
William 29 (GN-261)
OAKLEY
Anderson 45 (CT-260)
Austin 47 (MG-107)
George Ann 15* (MG-107)
Margarett 58* (MG-114)
Napolean B. 35 (MG-113)
Richard M. 37 (MG-93)
William 25 (MG-100)
OAKS
James 41* (BE-24)
OBRIAN
John 25* (GN-210)
OBRIANT
Herrald 59 (LW-100)
OBRIEN
John 75* (LW-78)
OBRYAN
Henry 26* (GN-210)
James 30 (JO-81)
James 77 (JO-81)
Stephen 34 (JO-86)
OBRYANT
Harrison 28 (JO-93)
OCCOMAN
Samuel 25 (GN-183)

Index

ODANIEL
  Thos. 20 (LW-89)
ODEL
  Henry 35 (MG-152)
ODOR
  William S. 37* (GN-202)
OFFELL
  James 52* (CT-258)
OFFICE
  Elzaphan 45* (CT-253)
  James 31 (CT-255)
OFFICE?
  Alem 46 (CT-254)
  John 56* (CT-250)
OHAIR?
  William 43* (MG-144)
OHORIN?
  Sidney 25 (f)* (MG-140)
OLDFIELD
  George W. 33 (MG-159)
  J. M. 35 (m)* (GN-246)
  Jesse 72* (MG-140)
OLFORD
  Milly 44* (LW-60)
OLIVER
  Betsey 22* (GN-241)
  Betsy 24* (BE-34)
  Cyntha 23* (GN-227)
  James 41 (PE-410)
  Joshua 64 (PE-409)
OLLIVER
  Martha 21* (GN-158)
OLVER
  Daniel 35 (CT-283)
ONEAL
  Patrick 30* (GN-261)
ONEY
  John A. 21 (PI-464)
  Martha 23 (CT-285)
  William P. 26 (MG-116)
ONY
  Allen 36 (FO-440)
  William 43 (FO-437)
ORSBURN
  Alexander 22 (MG-135)
  James 65 (MG-150)
  John 73 (MG-110)
  John P. 35* (MG-110)

Joseph 31 (MG-155)
Samuel 22 (MG-146)
Stephen 37 (MG-150)
Wilkerson 30 (MG-135)
William 38* (MG-155)
OSBORN
  Alford 22 (JO-111)
  Andrew 24 (JO-88)
  Calvin 21 (JO-111)
  Edward 24* (GN-252)
  Edward 37 (JO-100)
  Henry 22 (JO-87)
  James 51 (GN-252)
  James 59 (GN-247)
  Jemima 40* (FO-407)
  Jerremiah 36 (PI-449)
  Jesse 70* (JO-87)
  Lewis 40 (JO-88)
  Silas 23* (GN-223)
  Squire 25* (GN-225)
OSBORNE
  Albert 31 (FO-422)
  Edward L. 45 (FO-423)
  Hannah 84* (PI-460)
  Hiram 51 (PI-461)
  J. W. 25 (m) (PI-448)
  Jesse 25 (PE-405)
  Louisa 52 (PI-461)
  Salsbury 27 (PI-461)
  Shadrac 23* (PI-461)
  Solomon 82* (PI-456)
  Stephen 31 (PI-461)
  Thomas 51 (FO-422)
OSBURN
  John G. 37 (CT-231)
  Paul 35* (GN-186)
  Walter 47* (LW-56)
OSENTON
  Henry K. 29* (CT-244)
  J. T. 21 (m)* (GN-247)
  James 38* (CT-246)
  Samuel 67* (CT-241)
  Samuel 68 (GN-263)
OSETER
  Casper 31* (CT-227)
OSTER
  Andrew 27 (CT-266)
  John 30* (CT-271)

OVERBEE
  Alexander H. 33 (BE-19)
OWAN
  Harvy 24 (PE-404)
OWENS
  Ann E. 4* (PI-462)
  Berry 30 (FO-411)
  Elijah 31 (JO-93)
  Elizabeth 45* (CT-270)
  Hardin 53 (FO-434)
  Hardin 69 (PE-423)
  Hugh 28* (CT-270)
  James 25 (PE-416)
  James 38 (FO-466)
  Jane 9* (PE-420)
  Reese 50 (FO-432)
  Rhodes M. 26 (PI-457)
  Robert S. 26 (PI-457)
  Squire 24 (FO-423)
  Thomas 70* (PI-457)
  Thomas J. 24 (PI-458)
  William 19* (PI-446)
  William 25 (PE-424)
  William 27 (CT-275)
  William 28* (PE-408)
  William F. 30* (PI-494)
OWINGS
  Robert 47* (FO-448)
OWSLEY
  Benjamin 25 (FO-423)
  Fleming 28 (LW-104)
  Josiah 35 (LW-94)
  Shadrick 50 (FO-422)
OXIER
  Rebecca 70* (CT-246)
PACE
  John D. 32 (PE-400)
PACK
  Balley 33 (JO-114)
  Berry 52* (JO-111)
  Cornelus 37 (LW-120)
  Geo. 26 (LW-120)
  George 40 (LW-84)
  Isaac 38 (LW-84)
  John 24 (LW-119)
  Wm. 39 (LW-114)
PACKWOOD
  Stephen 21* (LW-93)

Index

PADGET
  Nicholas 33* (CT-236)
PAGE
  Jacob 29 (B) (GN-165)
  Saml. 30 (LW-76)
PAINE
  James 36* (PI-455)
PALMER
  Amanl. 29* (LW-99)
  John 23 (GN-261)
  Samuel 45* (GN-188)
PAMINGTON
  Levi 40 (PE-401)
PARECUE
  Henry 45* (LW-90)
PARISH
  James 20* (GN-201)
PARK
  John J. 24* (CT-253)
  Thomas J. 38* (CT-251)
  William O. 24 (CT-240)
PARKER
  Andrew J. 27 (CT-265)
  Drury 21* (BE-30)
  Eliza 13* (GN-218)
  H. W. 35 (m)* (LW-65)
  Hannah 44* (GN-225)
  J. 23 (m)* (GN-210)
  James 67 (LW-53)
  Joel 56 (MG-97)
  John 30 (LW-55)
  John 38 (CT-250)
  John 47 (FO-471)
  Lydia 33* (MG-171)
  Mary A. 19* (FO-418)
  Matilda 40 (PE-417)
  Nancy 19* (MG-96)
PARRISH
  Oliver P. 65 (CT-240)
PARSCALL
  John 63* (CT-246)
PARSONS
  David 31 (LE-139)
  Gabriel 25* (CT-217)
  Gabriel 28 (FO-468)
  George 48 (FO-469)
  John 25 (CT-267)
  Robert 21* (CT-225)
  Robert 40* (MG-138)
  Thomas 30 (CT-267)
PARTON
  Cintha 16* (GN-211)
PASSLEY
  Polly 45 (GN-187)
PASSONS
  Richard 40* (PI-434)
PATRICH
  Emanual 25 (GN-226)
PATRICK
  A. B. 31 (m) (BE-18)
  Allen 29 (FO-456)
  Archibald 22 (MG-168)
  Brice 33* (FO-450)
  Charlotte 57 (MG-166)
  Emily 35 (MG-163)
  Greenbury 20* (PI-464)
  Henry 50 (MG-167)
  Hiram 28 (MG-146)
  Hiram 40* (FO-458)
  Hugh 45 (JO-123)
  Hugh 45 (MG-92)
  James 25 (PE-419)
  Jeremiah 35 (FO-447)
  Jeremiah 52 (FO-457)
  Jesse 43 (MG-168)
  Jilson P. 29 (JO-124)
  John 35 (FO-450)
  John 36 (MG-163)
  John 45* (FO-448)
  John 53* (FO-455)
  John S. 14* (FO-454)
  Lewis 34 (MG-166)
  Meethe? M. 23 (m) (FO-456)
  Meredith 46* (FO-456)
  Nancy 50 (CT-238)
  Robert J. 24 (MG-144)
  Thomas C. 26 (FO-457)
  William 31 (MG-147)
  William 56 (FO-456)
  Wilson 26* (FO-454)
PATTEN
  Alexander 34 (GN-258)
  Daniel 19 (PI-473)
  James 45 (CT-232)
  Mary 60* (GN-157)
  Westen F. 40 (LW-81)
PATTERSON
  Erastus J. 32 (PI-458)
  James 23 (GN-252)
  James 55* (GN-211)
  Samuel 30* (GN-193)
  Samuel 31* (GN-210)
  William 33 (GN-202)
PATTINGALE
  Stephen 37 (GN-224)
PATTON
  Charles 29 (FO-436)
  Charles 9* (MG-151)
  Christopher 35* (FO-461)
  Christopher 61* (FO-460)
  David 42 (FO-436)
  David 43 (FO-458)
  Delila 32 (FO-439)
  Elizabeth 39 (FO-450)
  Ellen R. 9* (GN-169)
  Frazier 38 (FO-440)
  George 23* (BE-11)
  Granville 45 (BE-9)
  Henry 35 (FO-439)
  Henry 70 (FO-441)
  J. 26 (m)* (GN-247)
  John S. 44 (GN-169)
  Malinda 39 (FO-439)
  Samuel 62 (FO-440)
  Sarah 35 (BE-9)
  Sarah 40* (FO-436)
  William M. 46* (GN-169)
PAUL
  Doctor 28* (MG-174)
PAWLEY
  Skidmore 53 (JO-115)
PAYNE
  Cornilius 33* (GN-195)
  Lucy A. 24* (GN-164)
  Mary 56* (PI-440)
  Noah 30* (GN-206)
  Richard 67* (GN-195)
PEARCE
  Charles 29 (GN-176)
  Daniel T. 53 (CT-253)
  Gilbreath 25* (GN-162)
  Green B. 25 (MG-103)
  Harris 56 (GN-197)
  Jacob 61 (MG-108)

Index

PEARCE
 Luther 34* (GN-194)
 Mordeica 63* (MG-104)
 William 29* (MG-88)
PEARPOINT
 Lot 40* (GN-248)
PEARY?
 Low B. 39 (FO-467)
PECK
 Geo. C. 38 (LW-116)
 Isaac 38* (MG-144)
 Joseph 66 (LW-116)
PEERY
 Wm. 37 (LW-63)
PELFREY
 James 36 (CT-250)
PELFRY
 Alexander 21 (BE-4)
 Alexander 22* (BE-2)
 Isaac 31 (LW-59)
PELPHREY
 Alixander 54* (JO-104)
 Daniel 22* (JO-107)
 James 35 (JO-105)
 Stephen 32 (JO-90)
 William 28* (JO-90)
 William 56* (JO-104)
PENDLETON
 A. 34 (m) (GN-248)
 H. 19 (m)* (GN-210)
 Hiram 25 (MG-124)
 James 40 (FO-424)
 Joshua 57 (MG-124)
 Milly 40* (MG-88)
 William 33 (MG-124)
PENICKS
 John 31* (GN-175)
 John 31* (GN-177)
PENINGTON
 Abel 60* (LW-69)
 Alford 40 (LW-67)
 Elijah 36 (LW-68)
 Elisha 34* (LW-68)
 Elisha Jr. 24 (LW-69)
 Hardin 30 (LW-99)
 Isaac 27 (CT-259)
 James 20 (JO-100)
 James 22* (CT-280)

James 30 (LW-69)
James W. 51 (LW-69)
John 54 (LW-68)
John W. 23* (LW-68)
Jonathan 32 (CT-259)
Wm. 28 (LW-69)
Wm. 35 (LW-70)
Wm. 43* (LW-69)
Wm. J. 19 (LW-67)
PENIX
 Allen 45 (JO-109)
 Daniel 22* (MG-164)
 Henry 36 (MG-125)
PENLAND
 George 53 (CT-239)
PENNINGTON
 David 29 (JO-88)
 Ephraim 57 (PE-401)
 H. 21 (m)* (GN-210)
PENSE
 Andrew 51 (BE-1)
 John S. 24* (BE-1)
PEONIX
 William 26 (JO-112)
PERATT
 Eli 32 (MG-111)
 John 59* (MG-114)
 Thomas 30 (MG-112)
 Volentine 32 (MG-147)
PERCELL
 Quinton 42 (MG-159)
PEREBOYS?
 Jacob 24* (CT-274)
PEREGOE
 Jacob 25* (LW-118)
PERKINS
 Agnet 23 (f) (LW-68)
 Elean 18 (f)* (MG-116)
 Elizabeth 38 (MG-149)
 George 10* (FO-455)
 Isaac 22 (MG-92)
 James 28 (B) (MG-93)
 Joshua 47 (MG-161)
 Joshua C. 33* (LE-127)
 Lewis 24 (FO-455)
 Lewis 24 (GN-176)
 Lewis 25 (B) (MG-93)
 Lewis 26 (GN-175)

Margarett 9* (MG-164)
Squire E. 25* (MG-145)
Thomas 23 (FO-452)
Thomas 9* (MG-93)
William 23 (GN-257)
PERREY
 Robert H. 40 (CT-235)
PERRY
 Amanda 29 (CT-252)
 Andrew 42* (MG-152)
 Cyrus jr. 29 (MG-172)
 Cyrus sr. 38 (MG-107)
 Daniel 53* (MG-98)
 David 28* (GN-198)
 David 55 (GN-181)
 J. S. 36 (m)* (GN-210)
 John 24 (MG-156)
 Joseph 34* (MG-107)
 Mitton 22 (MG-96)
 Thomas 20* (MG-119)
 Thomas D. 53 (MG-87)
PERSMAY?
 Pelina 14* (FO-450)
PETERMAN
 Lavisa 46* (GN-198)
 Wm. 23* (LW-112)
PETERS
 Amanda 18* (GN-159)
 Jacob H. 38 (LW-73)
 John H. 53 (BE-19)
PETERSON
 John 41 (GN-251)
 William 34 (GN-251)
PETITT
 Benjamin 20* (MG-101)
 Jackson 4* (MG-162)
 Martha 16* (MG-107)
 Samuel 39 (MG-106)
PETRE
 Joel 27 (LW-82)
PEYTON
 Daniel 53* (MG-101)
 Daniel jr. 23 (MG-107)
 John 28 (MG-149)
 John 29* (PI-463)
 Western 35 (MG-148)
PHELPS
 William 35 (CT-239)

Index

PHETTA
  Samuel 24* (GN-253)
PHILBURN
  Thomas 25* (GN-210)
PHILIPS
  Elizabeth 63 (PI-482)
  Thompson 35 (PI-482)
  Zachariah 24 (PI-482)
PHILLIPS
  Abraham 44 (MG-152)
  E. L. 35 (m) (GN-219)
  Gabriel 21* (GN-240)
  George D. 39* (MG-174)
  Henry 26* (MG-116)
  Jessee 39 (PI-482)
  Merrida 20* (PI-442)
  Sarah 93* (JO-119)
  William 29 (GN-258)
  William W. 32* (MG-159)
PHILLUPS
  Iredel 33 (LW-95)
PHIPPS
  Eli 24 (MG-159)
  Isaiah 60 (LE-130)
  John 48 (MG-93)
  Levi 40 (MG-115)
  Preston M. 23 (BE-26)
PHIPS
  Patience 27* (LE-149)
PICKEL
  Frank 26* (GN-181)
PICKENS
  William 44* (GN-225)
PICKEREL
  Bazel 50* (GN-182)
  Henry 28 (GN-182)
  Joseph 37 (LW-75)
PICKET
  Eli 39* (GN-206)
PICKLE
  Sarah 50 (FO-452)
PICKLESIMER
  James 31* (FO-450)
PIERCE
  Dixon 43 (GN-218)
  Hannah 25* (GN-260)
  John 45 (GN-218)
  William 39 (GN-220)

PIERCEFIELD
  V. 44 (m) (GN-249)
PIGG
  James 62 (LW-80)
  John 31 (LW-74)
  John J. 12* (LW-79)
  Mary 24* (LW-50)
PIGMAN
  Campbell 21 (LE-152)
  John 56 (LE-152)
  John A. 26 (LE-151)
  Madison 21 (LE-154)
  Umphry 23 (LE-152)
  Wesley 28 (LE-151)
PILES
  Henry 24* (GN-170)
PILFREY
  John 41 (MG-120)
PINKERTON
  Susan 27* (FO-447)
PINSON
  Allen 65 (PI-464)
  Aron 42 (PI-464)
  George 33 (PI-465)
  Henery 70* (PI-489)
  Hiram 19* (PI-485)
  Jarrett 65* (PI-484)
  John 38 (PI-489)
  Thomas 22* (PI-464)
  William 59 (PI-490)
PITNEY
  Levi 24* (GN-196)
  William J. 26 (GN-196)
PITTS
  Thomas 30 (FO-440)
  Thos. N. 32* (LW-106)
PLAIN
  Alfred 26* (FO-470)
PLUM
  John 23* (CT-226)
PLUMBURG
  J. 29 (m)* (GN-249)
PLUMMER
  Elizth. 42 (BE-20)
  John 55 (CT-231)
  Reuben 52* (CT-243)
  Samuel 25* (BE-20)

PLYMALE?
  Isaac 44 (PI-451)
POAGE
  Cyrus 35 (GN-196)
  Eliza M. 53 (GN-195)
  G. B. 29 (m) (GN-196)
  Nancy 49 (GN-195)
  Pelina 35 (B) (GN-195)
POAGE?
  John 74* (GN-182)
  Samuel 21* (GN-193)
POAGUE
  Elizabeth 16* (LW-77)
  Geo. B. 27* (LW-86)
POE
  Edmd. 36 (LW-92)
  Hugh 26 (FO-448)
  James 34 (LW-66)
  James 60 (FO-443)
  John 22 (FO-443)
  Merida (m) (FO-450)
  Nancy 27* (FO-457)
  Saml. 33 (LW-64)
POGUE
  William L. 56* (GN-182)
POLLARD
  A. C. 24 (m) (GN-188)
  Henry B. 40 (GN-189)
POLLOCK
  John 26* (GN-166)
  Joseph 38* (GN-159)
POLLY
  Anna 35 (PI-444)
  Clabron 22* (LE-149)
  David 40 (LE-132)
  Edward 48 (LE-137)
  Edward Jr. 24 (LE-131)
  Henry 56 (LE-137)
  James 26 (LE-137)
  John 24 (B) (PI-435)
  Randolph 20 (LE-132)
  Spencer 21* (B) (PI-435)
  Stephen 24* (LE-129)
POND
  Samuel 19 (GN-252)
POPE
  Evaline 23* (CT-265)
  Jacob 85* (CT-269)

Index

POPE
  Lewis 43 (CT-265)
PORTER
  Bartlett 21 (CT-281)
  Benjamin 41 (JO-114)
  Benjamin sr. 52 (JO-117)
  Caroline 22* (GN-192)
  Cornelius H. 28 (JO-121)
  Elijah 45 (PI-442)
  Henry 20* (JO-81)
  John 50 (FO-465)
  John P. 52* (MG-131)
  John W. 24 (MG-131)
  Joseph 30 (PI-488)
  Samuel 55* (JO-89)
  William 19* (FO-464)
  William 48 (MG-132)
  William B. 39 (FO-462)
  William G. 23 (FO-470)
  Zepheniah 49* (GN-248)
POSEY
  John 32 (GN-160)
POST
  A. C. 37 (m) (GN-218)
POTEET
  Thomas J. 38 (GN-198)
POTELE?
  Ben F. 31* (BE-23)
POTTER
  Abraham 46 (PI-450)
  Benjamine 54* (PI-448)
  Isaac 49 (LE-135)
  Levi 32 (PI-448)
  Richard 18 (PI-450)
  Richard 50 (PI-446)
POTTS
  James 50 (FO-443)
POWELL
  Abel 45 (GN-200)
  Burr 39* (LW-111)
  Ellis 27* (GN-163)
  George 37?* (PI-435)
  John 15* (GN-222)
  John M. 28 (GN-256)
  John W. 34* (FO-408)
  Joseph 25 (GN-174)
  Lewis 28* (FO-471)
  Luke 28* (GN-163)

Reason 39* (GN-237)
Samuel 45 (GN-180)
Skelton 57* (GN-202)
T. 23 (m)* (GN-249)
William 32* (FO-470)
POWELLS
  Bartholomew 25 (GN-202)
POWER
  Archibald 36 (MG-167)
  Francis 65 (GN-190)
  Francis jr. 31 (GN-190)
  Holloway 38* (FO-456)
  Jeremiah 49* (MG-109)
  John 42 (FO-454)
  Lewis 64 (FO-454)
  Thomas 25 (MG-109)
POWERS
  Lewis 30 (MG-141)
  Noah 28 (GN-198)
  William B. 30* (CT-252)
POYNTER
  Edwin 31* (GN-255)
  J. K. 40 (m) (GN-255)
  Jesse 66 (GN-255)
PRAGMORE
  Mary 40 (PI-467)
PRATER
  ARchibald 40* (MG-160)
  Adam 37 (FO-438)
  Biddy 56* (FO-438)
  Elias 24 (FO-443)
  Elijah 30 (MG-166)
  Elijah W. 15* (MG-90)
  George W. 35 (MG-159)
  Harvey 16* (CT-217)
  Harvy 30 (FO-437)
  Ibba 19* (FO-448)
  Irvin 22 (FO-454)
  James 23 (FO-438)
  James 65 (MG-157)
  James W. 21 (MG-159)
  James W. 27* (MG-164)
  Jilson 24 (FO-455)
  John 25 (FO-438)
  John 65* (FO-456)
  Jonathan 35 (FO-447)
  Jonathan 60 (FO-437)
  Joseph 34 (FO-438)

Letta 24* (PI-473)
Lorenzo D. 30 (FO-437)
Richard M. 14* (FO-456)
Robert 41 (MG-90)
Samuel 28 (FO-440)
Samuel 39 (MG-165)
Thomas 26 (FO-456)
Thomas 57* (MG-91)
Thomas 60 (FO-444)
Thomas L. 24* (FO-454)
Washington 24* (FO-454)
William 26 (FO-438)
William 27 (PI-472)
William 28* (FO-457)
William C. 22 (MG-140)
William D. 32* (MG-91)
William T. 9* (MG-163)
William sr. 63* (FO-454)
PRATT
  Ben F. 13* (GN-165)
  Eliza 47 (GN-239)
  Enoch 22 (JO-100)
  George 27 (GN-205)
  Henry 30 (MG-160)
  Henry 41 (LE-143)
  Hiram 22* (PE-432)
  James 86 (JO-99)
  Nelson 35 (GN-264)
PRESLEY
  James R. 28 (LW-90)
  Rachael 17* (CT-236)
PRESTON
  Arthur 43* (LW-101)
  Burgess M. 33* (JO-118)
  Clarinda 9* (JO-115)
  Eliphus 55 (JO-109)
  Eliphus jr. 26 (JO-89)
  Greenville 27* (JO-110)
  Henry 45 (LW-102)
  Isaac 62 (LW-100)
  James 31 (JO-110)
  James W. 28* (JO-83)
  Jeffrey 58 (JO-109)
  John 36 (LW-100)
  John 48* (LW-98)
  Moses sr. 53 (JO-81)
  Nathan 30 (JO-82)
  Redeford 24 (JO-92)

Index

PRESTON
  Reuben 33 (LW-99)
  Robt. 18 (LW-98)
  Robt. 28 (LW-120)
  Stephen 54 (LW-98)
  Thomas 45 (JO-111)
  William 23 (JO-110)
  William W. 4* (JO-102)
PREWETT
  Henry 25* (GN-177)
  Rachel 59 (LW-121)
PRICE
  Addison 29 (GN-202)
  Andrew J. 30* (JO-102)
  Benjamin D. 61 (GN-183)
  Daniel 18* (FO-471)
  David 23* (JO-102)
  David 27 (CT-249)
  David J. 25* (JO-118)
  George 37* (JO-106)
  Hansford 24* (LW-105)
  Harrison 19 (JO-108)
  Henry S. 35* (LW-76)
  Jacob 22* (GN-165)
  James 28* (LW-100)
  James 45 (LW-111)
  Jane 11* (LW-101)
  Jesse Jr. 24 (JO-125)
  Jesse sr. 60* (JO-102)
  John 33 (LW-100)
  John 35 (GN-197)
  Marinda 24* (LW-114)
  Moses 41* (LW-101)
  Neally 37 (m) (GN-200)
  Rebecca 33* (FO-410)
  Richard W. 55 (CT-244)
  Richd. 52 (LW-99)
  Richd. C. 8/12* (LW-100)
  Robt. 50 (LW-65)
  Thomas 67 (PI-492)
  Thomas J. 30 (JO-120)
  William C. 30 (PI-492)
PRICHARD
  Geo. W. 29* (LW-107)
  James 52 (LW-96)
  John 69* (GN-250)
  Lewis 55 (LW-111)
  Willis 24 (GN-251)

PRIDEMORE
  Daniel 34 (FO-434)
  Emily 20* (LE-145)
  John 23* (GN-177)
PRIEST
  Cornelus 24* (LW-122)
  John 26 (FO-468)
PRILE
  John 45 (LW-99)
PRINCE
  David 35 (CT-245)
  James 31 (LW-68)
  Jane 20* (CT-228)
  John 32* (LW-93)
  Mary 78 (CT-285)
  Nicholas 48 (LW-94)
  Rachel 46* (LW-68)
  Rebecca 22* (LW-68)
  Thomas 40 (CT-255)
  Thos. 26 (LW-68)
  Wilson 25 (LW-61)
  Zachariah 24 (LW-68)
PRITCHET
  Charity 40 (LE-132)
  Harvy 15* (LE-132)
  Zecheriah 29 (GN-200)
PROCTOR
  Jeremiah 43* (CT-248)
PROFIT
  William 31* (GN-249)
PRUETT
  Henry 26* (CT-272)
  Henry 56* (CT-243)
  John W. 20 (MG-115)
  John W. 24 (MG-86)
  Moses 50 (MG-115)
PSIMER
  David 33 (JO-107)
  Nathaniel jr. 22 (JO-107)
  Rachel 35 (JO-107)
PUCK
  Elizabeth 75* (LW-96)
PUCKET
  Gardner 16* (MG-143)
PUCKETT
  Caleb 26 (BE-12)
  Isaac 40 (FO-452)
  Joshua 28 (JO-112)

  Meredith 25* (BE-1)
  Morgan R. 49 (BE-3)
PUGH
  David 36 (GN-261)
  E. W. 21 (m)* (GN-234)
  James G. 40* (GN-231)
  Joseph 37 (MG-172)
  Martin 36* (CT-217)
  Samuel 30 (GN-239)
PULLY
  John 77 (GN-173)
PURVES
  Elizabeth J. 16* (CT-248)
PUTHUFF
  J. B. 37 (m)* (GN-219)
  John 27* (GN-219)
  John 27* (GN-253)
PUTHUFF?
  John 65* (GN-172)
PUTMAN
  Michael 47 (GN-225)
PUTTHUFF
  B. F. 32 (m) (GN-255)
  Henry 62 (GN-255)
  James M. 22 (GN-255)
QUALL
  George 29 (GN-223)
QUEEN
  Absalom 20* (LW-111)
  John 45 (LW-107)
QUICKS
  George 40 (GN-261)
QUICKSELL
  Aaron 32 (MG-157)
  James 38 (MG-158)
QUILLEN
  Henry 27* (LE-134)
  Teague 19* (LE-134)
  Teague 78 (LE-134)
  William 25 (LE-135)
QUILLON
  Anderson 30* (MG-134)
RABORN
  Henry 25 (GN-251)
RABOURN
  Henry 59 (CT-239)
RAINEY
  James W. 19* (LW-62)

Index

RAINEY
John 45 (LW-114)
Joshua 45 (LW-61)
RAINS
John 45 (PI-481)
RAINY
Thadeus 36 (LW-61)
RAISIN
C. L. 28 (m) (GN-158)
RALEIGH
Elizth. 16* (BE-29)
Jacob 22 (BE-28)
James 25 (BE-27)
William 28 (LE-138)
RAMACH?
Elizabeth 12* (CT-230)
RAMEY
Byram 44 (GN-262)
Daniel 40 (PI-446)
Ephraim 37 (FO-461)
John 30 (PI-445)
Moses 40 (PI-446)
Samuel 27 (MG-97)
Tabitha 50* (PI-446)
Thomas 38 (MG-103)
Thomas jr. 21 (GN-159)
William 67 (PI-446)
RAMSEY
Daniel 61 (PI-460)
David J. 27* (FO-471)
James W. 14* (PI-460)
John 23 (PI-442)
John H. 31* (MG-131)
Letitia 67* (PI-442)
Margaret 19* (PI-442)
RAMY
Charles 41 (CT-234)
RANDALL
Peres? 46 (LW-77)
RANDOLPH
Wm. 25* (LW-101)
RANEY
William 35 (BE-23)
RANION
Mitchell 20 (PI-476)
RANKIN
Hugh 27* (JO-120)

RANKINS
Alexander 49* (GN-220)
RATCLIFF
Charles W. 30 (GN-263)
Elijah 44 (LW-67)
James 24 (GN-230)
Jer. 45 (m) (GN-230)
John T. 28 (CT-246)
Samuel 55 (GN-259)
William 19* (CT-219)
William 20* (GN-260)
Wm. 18* (LW-94)
Wm. 20* (LW-67)
RATLIFF
Alexandre 32 (PI-447)
Elizabeth 26* (PI-495)
Elizabeth 45* (MG-119)
Harrison 34* (PI-462)
Henry 21* (JO-104)
Isaac 12* (LW-68)
James 22* (MG-145)
James 23* (MG-144)
James 40 (CT-258)
Jarrett 33* (PI-494)
John 24 (MG-101)
John 26 (PI-445)
John sr. 58* (PI-495)
Joseph 35 (FO-470)
Judy 63 (MG-101)
Lucinda 38* (PI-458)
Mary 45 (PI-496)
Milford 16* (MG-115)
Nathan 22 (PI-463)
Nathan 34 (PI-447)
Reuben 37 (MG-101)
Reuben 83* (MG-115)
Richard 37 (PI-493)
Richard 47 (MG-159)
Richard 51 (PI-451)
Robert 24 (MG-170)
Robert 30 (PI-451)
Samuel 22* (MG-118)
Sarah 40 (MG-170)
Silas 27* (PI-434)
Silas 33* (PI-492)
Silas 36 (PI-448)
Silas 41 (JO-106)

Silas 74 (PI-493)
Solomon 16* (MG-156)
Sparley 23 (m) (PI-445)
Squire 36 (PI-463)
Susan 61* (PI-493)
Thomas 50 (PI-494)
Thursday 22* (PI-494)
William 21* (PI-490)
William 30 (FO-444)
William 34 (MG-116)
William 36 (FO-467)
William 39 (FO-468)
William 43 (PI-493)
William F. 24* (PI-458)
William jr. 56* (PI-462)
William sr. 70* (PI-490)
Zachariah 37* (LW-57)
RATSY
Adam 62 (GN-197)
RAVENSTART
John 22* (GN-174)
RAWLING
Lemuel 23* (GN-198)
RAWLINGS
A. 30 (m)* (GN-230)
Franklin 35* (GN-226)
Joshua 62 (GN-220)
RAY
G. W. 46 (m)* (GN-239)
Samuel 52 (CT-238)
Susan 20* (MG-166)
William 23* (GN-210)
REA
James 22 (FO-453)
Sarah 70 (FO-453)
REED
A. L. 25 (m)* (GN-222)
Asa J. 35 (JO-100)
Daniel 45 (MG-118)
Dowe 24 (PI-465)
Gilbert 33 (PI-466)
Hannah 57* (JO-105)
Hiram 43 (PI-469)
Humphrey 71 (PI-465)
James 30 (GN-224)
James 40* (PI-495)
Lewis 20 (MG-169)

Index

REED
  Martha 86* (MG-119)
  Mason 25 (JO-105)
  Newton P. 30* (MG-173)
  Reuben 21 (PI-469)
  Rodney 26* (GN-224)
  Samuel 20* (CT-271)
  Sandford 46* (MG-164)
  Sarah 16* (MG-102)
  Stephen B. 51* (GN-172)
  William 30 (JO-100)
REEDER
  Joseph 39 (CT-240)
REEVER
  Powles 35* (GN-249)
REEVES
  Bartlett 59 (CT-276)
  Brackston P. 24 (CT-228)
  Holt 18* (LW-64)
  Jasper N. 20* (CT-276)
  John 45* (CT-228)
  Miram 16* (CT-275)
  R. 50 (m) (GN-241)
REFFIT
  John 24 (MG-164)
REID
  Ananias 43* (MG-117)
REMINE?
  John W. 20* (PE-433)
REMY
  Daniel 31 (JO-87)
  James 48 (JO-125)
  John 27 (JO-105)
  Nancy 64 (JO-87)
  Owen 32 (JO-94)
  Thomas 23 (JO-105)
  Thomas L. 8* (JO-104)
  William 30 (JO-92)
RENTFROE
  William 28 (CT-262)
REPHIT
  James 23 (PI-491)
REY
  Daniel 38 (FO-458)
  William 30 (FO-458)
REYNOLDS
  Hamilton 40 (FO-427)
  John 23 (LW-79)

John B. 36 (CT-256)
John H. 41* (PI-494)
Joseph 45 (LE-152)
Michael 31* (FO-407)
Pleasant 27 (CT-256)
Susannah 25* (FO-409)
Thomas 65 (PI-458)
William M. 30 (PI-494)
Wm. 26 (LW-99)
RHEA
  James 33 (PI-484)
  John W. 43* (PI-461)
  Linsey 45 (m) (PI-462)
  Pheeby 19* (PI-462)
RHEED
  John 25 (GN-165)
RHODES
  A. 21 (m)* (GN-210)
RIBBLO
  Henry 41 (GN-157)
RICE
  Andrew J. 20 (JO-104)
  Andrwe J. 27 (JO-124)
  Archibald 55* (CT-274)
  Benjamin 45 (GN-188)
  Danel 29 (CT-258)
  Delina 16* (CT-273)
  Elijah 19* (CT-241)
  Elijah 43* (CT-215)
  Elijah 63 (CT-258)
  Elizabeth 40* (JO-103)
  Elizabeth 71* (CT-277)
  Ellen 14* (LW-93)
  Ezekiel 30* (CT-259)
  Ezekiel 72 (CT-277)
  Ezekiel T. 37 (CT-275)
  Fereler 55 (f) (PE-406)
  Fleming B. 46 (CT-275)
  George 22* (GN-248)
  George 50 (BE-15)
  George W. 32 (MG-166)
  Isaac 27* (JO-124)
  Jacob 22* (PE-406)
  Jacob 44* (CT-277)
  James 62 (GN-202)
  James 65 (LW-89)
  James M. 47* (LW-75)
  Jane 23* (CT-271)

Jehu 56* (GN-163)
Jelina 16* (CT-242)
Jeremiah 49 (PE-406)
John 20* (MG-174)
John 30* (JO-94)
Joseph C. 7* (GN-205)
Joseph W. 50 (GN-190)
Margaret A. 28 (CT-275)
Martha A. 25* (CT-241)
Martin M. 41 (JO-89)
Martin R. 40 (JO-124)
Nancy 39 (CT-221)
Nancy 63 (JO-124)
Nancy 9* (LW-93)
Samuel 38 (FO-457)
Samuel 54* (JO-104)
Samuel K. 24 (JO-105)
Sherod 46 (CT-274)
Susan 37 (LW-94)
Susan 7* (LW-68)
William 25* (FO-409)
William 36* (JO-113)
William P. 27* (CT-258)
Wm. 14* (LW-72)
Wm. 22* (LW-81)
Wm. 27 (LW-79)
Wm. 94 (CT-274)
Wm. C. 27 (LW-56)
Wm. M. 24 (CT-259)
RICHARD
  Jeremiah P. 32* (CT-286)
RICHARDS
  Daniel 34* (CT-227)
  Elijah 28* (CT-254)
  George W. 47 (CT-251)
  James 68 (CT-236)
  John 29* (GN-225)
  M. 23 (m) (GN-218)
  Pheola A. 4* (CT-219)
  Thomas 56* (GN-238)
  Zachariah 45 (GN-220)
RICHARDSON
  Daniel 48* (FO-458)
  John 16* (GN-165)
  John N. 38* (PI-458)
  Lewis H. 42 (MG-101)
  Nelvin 17* (MG-141)
  Thomas 46 (PE-408)

Index

RICHESON
  Mary 64 (GN-243)
RICHIE
  Alexander 21 (PE-424)
  Crockett 60 (PE-419)
  Gabriel 37 (PE-423)
  Hira 35 (PE-421)
  James 40 (PE-419)
  John 35 (PE-424)
  Jurem? 37 (m) (PE-419)
  Nicholas 25 (PE-419)
  Polly 40 (PE-424)
  Thomas 45 (PE-424)
RICHISON
  Lydda 19* (GN-231)
RICKETS
  John 26 (GN-194)
RIDENOUR
  John 12* (GN-224)
RIDER
  Conrad 41* (LW-107)
  Martha J. 20 (PI-496)
RIDGEWAY
  Benjamin 30 (CT-227)
RIDGWAY
  Ann 23* (GN-194)
RIDNER
  Lucy 13* (JO-102)
RIFE
  John 60* (LW-87)
RIFELL
  Crisa 22* (LE-153)
RIFFE
  Coonrod 56 (GN-187)
  Daniel 29 (GN-185)
  Gabriel 33* (GN-187)
  Lexius 31* (GN-184)
RIFFET
  William 34 (MG-153)
RIGG
  Joseph 40 (GN-212)
  Joseph 66* (GN-164)
  Townley 51 (GN-222)
RIGGLE
  Daniel 38* (GN-190)
  Jackson 28 (GN-261)
RIGGS
  Charles B. 67* (CT-225)

George W. 42 (CT-220)
John 30* (GN-195)
RIGHT
  Calvin 24* (CT-280)
  Elizabeth 60* (PI-468)
  Henry 25 (CT-280)
  Malinda 15* (CT-280)
  Samuel 30 (PI-452)
RIGSBY
  Drury 48 (LW-60)
  Lewis 40 (LW-95)
  Thos. 73 (LW-95)
  Travis 47 (MG-123)
RILEY
  G. B. 21 (m)* (GN-157)
  James 24 (PE-412)
  James 40 (PE-412)
  James C. 8* (MG-161)
  James W. 22* (CT-226)
  John 25* (GN-188)
  John 45 (BE-39)
  John 47 (GN-262)
  John 50 (BE-39)
  Miles 25* (LE-155)
  Richd. 20* (BE-33)
  Saml. 22 (BE-39)
  Samuel 45 (PE-411)
  William 45 (GN-252)
  William H. 23 (GN-164)
  Wm. 46 (BE-41)
  Zachriah 30 (BE-39)
RILY
  James 34 (PE-412)
RIMES?
  Isaac 25* (BE-12)
RING
  andrew 43 (LW-75)
RINKES
  Benjamin 30* (GN-205)
RIPATOE
  Sophia 34* (GN-200)
RISNER
  Eli 35 (FO-452)
  Jacob 35 (FO-448)
  James 41 (FO-448)
  John 27 (MG-163)
  John 35 (MG-92)
  Merida 20 (m) (FO-448)

Michael 30 (FO-454)
Michael 60* (MG-164)
William 35 (FO-447)
RISTER
  John 64* (CT-220)
  John J. 47 (CT-228)
ROACH
  Daniel 15* (GN-246)
  Griffin 52 (GN-187)
  Hiram 24* (CT-278)
  Ruth 81* (GN-222)
ROADS
  John 28* (GN-209)
ROANE
  Barbary 69 (PI-451)
ROARK
  John 58 (BE-18)
  John B. 25* (BE-26)
ROBBINET
  John 25* (PI-485)
ROBBINS
  Joshua 40 (BE-11)
  Kiza 18 (f)* (BE-11)
ROBBINSON
  David 48* (PI-434)
  Elizabeth 56* (PI-436)
  James 30 (PI-439)
  James H. 27 (PI-443)
  John 24 (PI-434)
  Samuel 28* (PI-457)
ROBERSON
  James H. 36 (JO-84)
  John sr. 69 (JO-92)
  William 45 (JO-84)
ROBERTS
  A. 30 (m) (GN-235)
  Absalom 67 (GN-235)
  C. L. 40 (m) (LW-75)
  Clabourn 60 (GN-221)
  David 24* (MG-156)
  Elkana 28 (MG-108)
  Geo. 62 (LW-51)
  Geo. W. 36 (LW-54)
  George W. 36* (CT-246)
  Hiram 37 (MG-128)
  Horrace 40 (JO-80)
  Isaac 56 (LW-119)
  Isaac Jr. 24 (LW-119)

Index

ROBERTS
James 35* (FO-430)
James 64 (PE-427)
James 78 (PI-455)
John C. 42 (LW-82)
John jr. 40 (PI-455)
Mark 40 (GN-227)
Martha 12* (LW-80)
Moses 45 (BE-19)
Niel 22* (PI-455)
Owen 25 (FO-428)
Sampson 47 (BE-25)
Samuel 52 (PI-467)
Sinclare 57* (LW-105)
Sympfield 50 (PE-399)
Thomas 25 (PE-399)
Vicey 30* (BE-35)
Wm. A. 23* (LW-106)
Wm. F. 25 (LW-54)
ROBERTSON
Charity 29* (CT-280)
Elizabeth 18* (LW-69)
Frances 20* (CT-270)
Harvey 16* (PI-454)
Isaac 39 (CT-263)
Jacob 38 (CT-280)
James 26 (CT-266)
John 17* (PI-434)
John 22* (MG-119)
John 42 (JO-89)
Martha 14* (CT-282)
Nathaniel 41 (PI-439)
Richard P. 23* (PI-457)
Samuel 28 (PI-481)
Samuel 37 (JO-86)
Sarah 37* (PI-454)
Sarah 40 (CT-280)
Siba 73* (CT-280)
ROBINET
Nathan 27 (PI-474)
Nathan 56 (PI-471)
William 25 (PI-474)
ROBINETT
Wesley 27 (LW-117)
ROBINS
Daniel 42 (CT-278)
Joshua 21 (CT-278)

ROBINSON
Elizabeth 40 (GN-212)
Elizabeth J. 19* (PI-442)
Isaac 45 (PI-458)
John 25 (PI-443)
John 30 (GN-208)
John 32?* (FO-471)
John 38 (BE-26)
John 64 (MG-143)
Joshua 50* (PI-493)
Rebecca 79* (LW-121)
Richard P. 54 (PI-496)
Samuel 15* (GN-178)
Sarah 24 (PI-444)
Susan 40* (FO-418)
William 40 (MG-147)
William 45 (FO-422)
William C. 22* (GN-234)
ROBISON
Elizabeth 11* (CT-244)
George 34 (CT-227)
RODEN
Rebecca 19* (CT-243)
RODGERS
George 18* (GN-217)
John 52 (GN-244)
Roland 19* (GN-211)
ROE
David 39* (MG-131)
Eleanor 54 (CT-259)
George E. 22* (GN-239)
Isom 31 (CT-255)
James 46 (MG-133)
John 26 (CT-259)
Joshua 49* (CT-220)
ROGAN
James 30* (GN-176)
ROGERS
David 40 (CT-278)
Jonathan 44 (CT-278)
M. A. 44 (f) (GN-161)
Nancy 20* (CT-265)
S. M. 37 (m) (GN-163)
Susan 43* (CT-266)
ROGGERS
John 23* (FO-471)
ROMAN
Isaac 23 (LW-88)

Mary 15* (CT-222)
Nathan? M. 33 (LW-88)
ROOK?
George 25* (CT-272)
ROOP
John 26 (FO-468)
ROOS
John 28 (GN-216)
ROSA
Jareal 27 (m) (PI-467)
ROSE
Anderson N. 32 (BE-3)
Bowen 25 (MG-152)
Bowen 56 (BE-2)
David 62* (MG-152)
David jr. 22* (MG-152)
Edward 16* (LW-57)
James 14* (LW-57)
James 21* (MG-165)
James N. 20* (MG-152)
James W. 40 (LW-54)
Jesse 35 (FO-454)
John 59 (MG-152)
John D. 24* (MG-152)
Nancy 24* (LW-104)
Nancy J. 7* (LW-59)
Robert 38* (CT-267)
Sarah 21* (LW-66)
Thomas 35 (JO-99)
William B. 35 (MG-152)
Winney 30* (MG-171)
Wm. 34 (LW-59)
Wm. 65 (LW-59)
Zachariah 80* (LW-73)
ROSS
David 90 (JO-96)
Elizabeth 21* (MG-140)
Henely 20* (PI-438)
James 30 (LW-70)
John N. 31 (CT-236)
John D. 42* (LW-87)
Joseph? 25 (CT-250)
L. D. 39 (m) (GN-253)
Mary 23* (JO-92)
Reuben 26* (CT-236)
Robert 29 (JO-92)
Samuel 58* (CT-236)
Susana 25* (CT-237)

Index

ROSS
 Susannah 23 (CT-264)
ROTEN
 Betsey 47* (CT-230)
 Luvicey 16* (PI-494)
 Mary 33 (PI-462)
ROUS
 James 53 (GN-202)
 Samuel 58 (GN-192)
ROW
 Catharine 22* (GN-196)
 James 73* (PI-444)
 Johnithan 43 (PI-444)
 Wiley 20* (PI-441)
 William 16* (FO-445)
ROWARK
 James 65 (LE-138)
ROWE
 Alexander 7* (FO-445)
 Anna 35* (FO-445)
 Charles 20 (PI-447)
 Charles 45* (PI-438)
 Elizabeth 64* (PI-440)
 Franklin 32 (PI-439)
 Huffman 21 (PI-451)
 Hyram 37 (PI-444)
 Jacob 50 (PI-446)
 James 29* (LW-90)
 John 21* (PI-439)
 John 44* (PI-442)
 Joseph 34 (PI-443)
 Loyd 22 (PI-445)
 Reuben 36 (PI-447)
 Stephen 20 (PI-446)
ROWLAND
 Armstrong 45 (JO-83)
 Daniel R. 39 (JO-119)
 Isabella 66* (FO-442)
 John 48 (JO-103)
 John jr. 21 (JO-109)
 Peggy 20* (JO-84)
 Richard 11* (JO-102)
ROY
 Isaac 40 (FO-470)
ROYAR
 Alford 33* (LW-87)
 John B. 41 (LW-89)

ROYCE
 Benjamin 48 (MG-96)
 John 43 (MG-97)
 John 80* (MG-95)
RUBEL
 Napoleon 27* (LW-74)
RUBY
 John 34* (GN-165)
RUCKER
 Absailom 40 (CT-272)
 Bazzel 40 (CT-278)
 Elizabeth 50 (CT-277)
 Elzaphan 32? (CT-278)
 Elzaphan 70* (CT-278)
 Syria 34 (m) (CT-277)
RUCKLES
 Elizabeth 13* (LW-106)
RUDD
 Riley 59 (LW-57)
 Thos. 27 (LW-72)
RUGGLES
 James 17* (CT-217)
 James 52 (CT-264)
 John 44* (GN-176)
 Michael 65* (CT-269)
RULE
 Andrew 63* (JO-103)
 Andrew W. 35* (JO-81)
 Harrison B. 39 (JO-107)
 James M. 31 (JO-107)
RUNDY
 Christian 40 (m)* (GN-172)
 Lewis 34 (GN-165)
RUNION
 Adam 30? (LW-122)
 Adron 49 (PI-477)
 Henery 29 (PI-486)
 Henery 62 (PI-477)
 Lewis 19* (PI-468)
 Moses 22 (PI-477)
 William 36 (PI-477)
RUNNELLS
 Archibald 32 (GN-188)
 James 37 (GN-189)
RUNNELS
 J. 25 (m) (GN-240)
 Reuben 30 (GN-196)
 Thomas 34 (GN-196)

RUNNER
 Isaac 55 (CT-241)
RUNYAN
 Harvey 39 (CT-223)
RUNYON
 William 39* (GN-197)
RUSSEL
 Charles 49 (GN-255)
 Mahala 38* (CT-222)
RUSSELL
 Henery 25* (PI-467)
 Ira 35* (FO-468)
 John 33 (BE-14)
 Mary 50* (LW-62)
 Sarah 14* (GN-171)
RUST
 Henery M. 23* (PI-457)
RUTHERFORD
 Eliot 29 (PI-471)
 James 58* (PI-479)
 Joseph 54* (PI-479)
 Reuben 52 (PI-477)
 Robert 48 (PI-465)
 Scott 28 (GN-173)
 William 38* (CT-214)
RUTTER
 William 49 (GN-165)
RYE
 Henry 28 (GN-159)
RYOST
 Michael 27* (CT-227)
SADDLER
 William 62 (MG-103)
SADLER
 Saml. 27 (LW-88)
 Valentine 22 (LW-89)
SAGRAVE
 Joseph 38 (JO-96)
 Thomas 28 (JO-91)
 William 34 (JO-97)
SALIERS
 Benjamin 52 (JO-87)
 Bracken 19 (JO-95)
 David J. jr. 22 (JO-87)
 Elizabeth 35 (JO-92)
 Henry 33 (JO-101)
 Jacob 45* (JO-101)
 Jerry 22 (JO-101)

Index

SALIERS
  John 39 (JO-95)
  Joseph 40 (JO-87)
  Martin 41 (JO-95)
  Mary 43* (JO-92)
  Thomas 41 (JO-95)
  William 34* (JO-106)
SALLARS
  Sarah 15* (GN-219)
SALLINS
  Susan 19* (BE-19)
SALMON
  Elizabeth 21* (FO-460)
SALMONS
  Carter 38 (FO-422)
  Jonathan 55 (FO-465)
  Joseph 26 (FO-465)
  Miles 27 (LW-123)
  Thomas 48 (FO-420)
  Thos. 26* (LW-124)
  Weeks 34 (FO-408)
  Wm. C. 23* (LW-123)
SALSBERRY
  Elijah 65 (FO-426)
  Greenville 24 (FO-425)
  Hiram 47* (FO-424)
  Lucky 33 (FO-415)
  Milton 46* (CT-265)
  Morgan 28 (FO-424)
  Sarah 7* (FO-409)
  William 65 (FO-424)
SALYER
  David J. 30 (JO-107)
  Henderson 25 (JO-86)
SALYERS
  Abner 52 (FO-449)
  Benjamin 20 (JO-95)
  David 34 (FO-446)
  Isaiah 36 (FO-446)
  Isiah 50* (LW-101)
  John 23 (FO-450)
  John 48 (FO-447)
  Nancy 63 (LW-98)
  Samuel 34 (FO-450)
  Thomas 26 (FO-449)
  Thos. 26 (LW-98)
  William 24 (FO-449)
  William 26 (FO-446)

  William M. 71 (FO-436)
SAMMONS
  Fleming 41 (CT-269)
  Lewis 49 (CT-284)
SAMONDS
  David 21 (LW-124)
  Rowland 51 (LW-124)
SANDERS
  Jesse M. 50 (LW-68)
SANDFORD
  Augustus 34* (MG-97)
SANDLIN
  John 24 (BE-39)
SANDSAN
  Lorenzo D. 37 (MG-148)
SANDYS
  Hendrick 35 (MG-164)
SANFORD
  Meese 70* (MG-170)
  Thornton W. 41 (MG-97)
SANSOM
  John jr. 38 (PI-470)
  John sr. 90 (PI-470)
SARGANT
  Robert 30* (GN-178)
SARGENT
  Bales 34* (MG-135)
  Elijah 73* (MG-138)
  Joseph 28 (MG-98)
  Lovel 41 (MG-99)
  Martha 1* (MG-101)
SARGENTS
  William 73* (MG-95)
SARO
  Joseph 27* (GN-251)
SARTIN
  Elijah 26 (FO-462)
  Elijah 30* (CT-230)
  Jane 14* (GN-233)
SAULBY
  William H. 25 (MG-111)
SAUNDERS
  Elizabeth 42 (PI-492)
  Greenville 27 (PI-449)
  Ichabod 21 (PI-453)
  John 26 (PI-492)
  Nancy 46* (MG-158)
  Wade H. 29 (PI-453)

SAVAGE
  Ann 10* (GN-176)
  C. P. 26 (m) (CT-269)
  Edward 52 (CT-270)
  Isaac 27 (CT-275)
  James 43* (CT-258)
  James N. 22* (CT-252)
  John 29 (CT-285)
  John 44* (CT-285)
  Nickolas 49* (GN-196)
  Peter 34 (CT-225)
  Tabitha 15* (CT-266)
SAWVILER?
  John 82 (PE-407)
SAWYER
  James 26 (CT-238)
SAXTON
  John 37* (GN-212)
  Preston 20* (MG-114)
SAYER
  Asa 68 (GN-243)
  Charles 31 (GN-243)
  J. 22 (m)* (GN-242)
SAYNE
  Daniel 48 (JO-89)
SCAGG
  John L. B. 24 (LW-115)
SCAGGS
  Christian 42 (LW-56)
  Hervey M. 26* (CT-267)
  James 30 (LW-59)
  Jeremiah 53 (CT-267)
  John 53 (LW-59)
  John Jr. 25 (LW-59)
  Lewis 31* (LW-59)
  Lewis 62* (LW-72)
  Moses 47 (LW-56)
  Peter L. 36 (LW-83)
  Retha 24* (LW-56)
  Solomon 53 (CT-267)
SCAGS
  David 32 (CT-283)
SCALF
  Aggy N. 18* (GN-212)
SCARBURY
  David 52 (PI-475)
  Robert 20 (PI-475)

Index

SCARF
  Jeremiah 27 (FO-421)
SCHER
  Mary A. 20* (GN-164)
SCHLOVOM
  Henry 40 (GN-186)
SCISSON
  Charles 50* (LW-113)
  Joseph 20 (LW-113)
  Miles 23 (LW-113)
SCOTT
  Andrew 41 (PI-489)
  Andrew J. 33 (CT-218)
  Axton 36* (PI-480)
  Barnabas 28 (JO-115)
  Catharine 55* (GN-214)
  Crawford 49 (GN-214)
  Daniel 35 (PI-478)
  Evans 28 (PI-489)
  Gabriel 60 (CT-241)
  Henry 34* (CT-228)
  Henry 42* (CT-218)
  J. R. 23 (m) (GN-203)
  James W. 37 (CT-242)
  John 2* (GN-214)
  John 26* (GN-203)
  John 36 (PI-488)
  Judy 58 (CT-229)
  Richard 56 (GN-200)
  Sarah 35 (LW-110)
  Thomas 25 (PI-478)
  Thomas 69 (CT-218)
  William 28* (FO-457)
  William 64* (PI-489)
SCOWDEN
  Solomon 36 (GN-257)
SCREACH
  John S. 23 (LW-70)
  Saml. 46* (LW-69)
SEATES
  Michael 25 (GN-197)
SEATON
  N. K. 55 (m) (GN-159)
SEBASTIAN
  David 26 (BE-37)
  Henderson 29 (BE-37)
  John 35* (MG-170)

SECREST
  David 47 (LW-91)
  Jacob 25 (LW-91)
SECTON
  Polly 9* (LE-145)
SEEGRAVE
  Stephen 40 (CT-235)
SEELEY
  Samuel 71* (GN-218)
SEGIMOREL?
  John 35 (FO-473)
SEGRAVES
  Saml. 44 (LW-95)
SELLARDS
  Andrew 44 (GN-262)
  Susannah 55 (FO-408)
  Thomas A. 42 (FO-421)
SELLERD
  Elizabeth A. 11* (JO-111)
SELLERS
  ____y 41 (f)* (CT-272)
SELSOR
  George 40 (JO-80)
SELVAGE
  Isaac 30 (MG-137)
  James 56 (CT-245)
SENATE
  Thomas 40* (CT-227)
SERGANT
  Elijah 29* (GN-222)
SERGEANT
  Robert 28* (CT-279)
  William 16* (CT-279)
SERGENT
  David 41 (LE-127)
  Stephen 27 (LW-66)
SETTSER
  Abner 36 (JO-123)
SETZER
  Adam 60 (FO-469)
  Samuel 21* (FO-467)
SEWELL
  Joseph 50 (BE-44)
  Margaret 38 (BE-6)
  Thomas 47 (BE-23)
  William 22* (BE-23)
SEXTON
  Alva 24 (m)* (CT-277)

  Andrew 40 (LE-145)
  Dilly 16* (LE-139)
  Huldy 30 (LE-147)
  Isaac 30 (LE-145)
  Isaah 38 (LE-147)
  James 52 (CT-217)
  John 75* (MG-146)
  Mark 37* (CT-274)
  Moses 45 (LE-131)
  Riley 19 (LE-146)
  Samuel 28* (LE-140)
  Solomon 42 (LE-145)
  Stephen 24 (LE-155)
  Stephen B. 45 (MG-108)
  William 27 (CT-268)
  William 40* (LE-146)
  Wm. 35* (LE-147)
SHACKELFORD
  Abner T. 53 (BE-27)
  Alfred 25 (BE-5)
  Sandford 31 (BE-5)
SHAFER
  David 23* (GN-167)
  George 32* (GN-174)
  Larkin 23 (GN-185)
  Philip 42 (GN-170)
SHAFFNET
  Henry 26* (GN-249)
SHAMBAUGH
  J. H. 48 (m) (GN-231)
SHANNON
  Floyd P. 28* (LW-83)
  Geo. 30 (LW-116)
  James 54* (LW-116)
  Jane 65* (LW-113)
  Joseph 27 (LW-78)
  Thomas 46 (LW-115)
SHARP
  William 35 (GN-176)
SHATTON
  Tandy L. 27 (FO-466)
SHAVER
  Fanny 24* (JO-103)
SHAVERS
  James 42 (JO-104)
  Susan 46 (JO-108)
SHAW
  Abm. 54 (B) (LW-118)

- 405 -

Index

SHAW
  John Aa. 45 (CT-220)
SHEARER
  Walter 36* (CT-275)
SHEARMON
  Henry 42 (JO-109)
SHEELER
  Jacob 50 (GN-182)
  Jeremiah 23 (GN-182)
SHEETS?
  John 43* (FO-418)
SHELL
  George 28 (GN-216)
  Samuel 68* (LE-150)
SHELTON
  Hardin 44 (GN-209)
  John 35* (MG-133)
  Mahalah A. 9* (JO-95)
SHEPHERD
  Benjamin 28* (BE-8)
  Benjamin F. 39 (CT-244)
  Brice 28 (FO-443)
  Brice 33 (FO-446)
  Charlton 59* (GN-164)
  David H. 57 (BE-8)
  George 38* (FO-459)
  Henderson 26 (BE-8)
  Jacob 25* (FO-445)
  Jacob 68* (FO-446)
  John 30 (FO-446)
  John 38 (FO-437)
  John M. 51 (BE-4)
  John T. 26* (CT-219)
  Sylvester 25 (FO-446)
SHEPPARD
  Anderson 23 (PE-402)
  Calvin 26 (PE-400)
  Elias 45 (PE-429)
  Elizabeth 26 (PE-402)
  Hugh 20 (PE-429)
  Huriah? _1 (PE-401)
  Levi 37 (PE-402)
  Louvina 16* (PI-480)
  Sarah 45 (PI-480)
  William 53 (PE-401)
SHERMAN
  James 26 (GN-166)

SHIELDS
  Alexander 26* (CT-240)
  James L. 24 (CT-239)
  W. W. 47 (m) (GN-235)
SHIERER
  Joseph 31 (GN-240)
SHIFLY?
  James Turner 46 (BE-38)
SHINGLETON
  James 22* (GN-163)
  James 23* (GN-206)
SHIPTON
  Barnabas 58 (GN-182)
SHOAF
  John 27 (GN-166)
SHOAT
  Richard 68 (CT-258)
SHOBIT
  Crist 23 (m)* (GN-176)
SHOCKEY
  Geo. 32* (LW-108)
SHOEMAKER
  Amassa 27 (GN-245)
  Isaac 25* (GN-224)
  John 27 (GN-224)
SHORES
  Daniel 32 (GN-261)
SHORT
  Aaroon 35 (CT-276)
  Andrew 45 (LW-53)
  Danl. 43* (LW-62)
  Elizabeth 20* (FO-430)
  Granderson S. 26 (JO-85)
  James 27* (LW-54)
  James 32 (LW-65)
  John 48 (LW-98)
  Rebecca 20* (GN-163)
  Saml. 38* (LW-86)
  Stephen Sr. 39* (CT-227)
  Thomas 55 (JO-103)
  William 25 (GN-172)
  Wm. 38* (LW-64)
  Wm. 54 (BE-33)
SHORTRIDGE
  Andrew 40 (PI-464)
  John 34* (PI-484)
SHOVER
  Andrew 28* (GN-247)

SHROAT
  John 19* (GN-174)
SHUBERT
  Samuel 38 (GN-217)
SHUFF
  Solomon 34 (GN-181)
SHUFFIELD
  James 60 (BE-6)
  Wm. P. 26 (BE-5)
SHUFFLE
  Jane 42 (GN-244)
SHULTS
  Phebe 7i2* (CT-254)
SHUMATE
  Alfred 27 (CT-254)
  George W. 15* (CT-250)
  William 50 (CT-252)
SHUTTS
  Phebe 32* (CT-251)
SHY
  Jeremiah 37 (GN-191)
SIBASTIAN
  John 66 (BE-37)
SICK
  Jacob 39* (PI-495)
  James 27 (PI-485)
  William 35* (PI-495)
SILVERTHORN
  John T. 2* (GN-197)
SIMER
  Andrew P. 24 (JO-86)
  Charlotte P. 17* (FO-450)
  Eilzabeth P. 76* (JO-100)
  Emely P. 51* (JO-87)
  John P. 22 (JO-87)
  John P. 42 (JO-104)
  Nathaniel P. 48 (JO-87)
SIMMONS
  Rolen 40 (CT-229)
  William 28 (MG-165)
SIMPKINS
  George 18* (GN-252)
  George 60 (GN-228)
  Hiram 34 (GN-252)
  James 21* (GN-247)
  John 34 (GN-264)
  Polly 38 (BE-2)
  William 19* (BE-2)

Index

SIMPSON
  Allen 28 (LW-79)
  Fredk. 25* (LW-106)
  Margaret 53 (GN-212)
SIMS
  Lydia 47* (GN-207)
  William 33* (CT-222)
SINK
  Simon 42 (MG-105)
SINNETT
  Jefferson 24 (GN-160)
  John H. 51 (GN-159)
SITH
  George 25 (GN-229)
SITZER
  John 26* (FO-467)
SIZEMORE
  Ephraim 3 (PE-423)
  Felix 22 (BE-23)
  George 22* (FO-436)
  Granville 15* (FO-451)
  Harvey 26 (PE-415)
  Jane 42 (FO-439)
  Lewis 50* (FO-425)
  Russell 25 (BE-36)
  William 35* (FO-435)
  William 53 (BE-24)
SKAGGS
  Amos 39* (MG-131)
  Peter 40 (MG-131)
  Peter 47 (JO-97)
  Squire 32 (MG-132)
SKAGS
  John T. 33 (MG-131)
SKATH?
  Telitha 49 (PI-486)
SKEAN
  Wm. 30 (FO-419)
SKEEN
  Joseph 25 (GN-167)
  Joseph 45 (FO-459)
SKEIN
  Elcanah 52* (CT-242)
SKEINS
  Hiram 53 (LW-51)
  Wm. 49 (LW-62)
SKELTON
  Peter 47* (GN-208)

SKIDMORE
  Joicy 73* (CT-265)
SLACK
  Jeremiah 29* (LW-79)
  Samuel 22 (GN-245)
SLATER
  John 46* (CT-270)
  Mary 28 (PI-469)
  William 38 (PI-468)
SLATTEN?
  Charles 64 (PI-479)
SLIDHAM
  Preston 35 (BE-21)
SLOAN
  Alexander 26 (FO-432)
  Harvy 25 (FO-414)
  Joab 50 (GN-214)
  John 22* (CT-248)
  Lawrence 8* (GN-202)
  Reuben 30 (FO-432)
SLOANE
  James 29* (GN-234)
  James 43* (CT-225)
  Jane 8* (LW-86)
  John 65* (GN-234)
  W. C. 37 (m) (GN-230)
SLOAS
  John 36 (FO-442)
SLOES
  Henry 36 (CT-281)
  Jesse 29 (CT-281)
SLONE
  Amos 30 (PI-436)
  Archibald 25 (PI-436)
  Archibald 33 (PI-435)
  Archibald 45* (PI-439)
  Cudbetts? 25 (FO-447)
  Elijah 30* (PI-436)
  Franklin 21 (PI-473)
  Greenville 26* (FO-433)
  Hiram 53 (FO-427)
  Isom 25* (PI-439)
  Isom 56 (FO-432)
  Isom jr. 27 (FO-433)
  James 35* (PI-434)
  James 35 (PI-436)
  James 36 (FO-432)
  John 40 (PI-440)

  Lucinda 35? (PI-482)
  Martha 19 (FO-427)
  Marvel 28 (FO-427)
  Mary 79* (PI-435)
  Milley 50 (PI-436)
  Mitchell 27 (PI-435)
  Nancy 55* (FO-446)
  Randolph 26* (PI-435)
  Samuel 65* (B) (PI-484)
  Shade 22 (FO-433)
  Shade 62* (FO-432)
  Shadrac jr. 38 (PI-438)
  Shadrack 70 (PI-438)
  Spencer 21* (PI-440)
  Thomas 23* (PI-436)
  William 40 (FO-433)
  William 40 (PI-442)
  William 47 (FO-447)
  Wimea 17 (f)* (PI-442)
SLUPER
  Henry 57* (LW-81)
SLUSHER
  Philip 42 (FO-420)
SLUSSER
  Havey? 24* (LW-118)
SMALL
  Wm. B. 38 (LW-74)
SMALLEY
  John 41 (GN-200)
SMALLWOOD
  Elijah 31 (PI-454)
SMEDLY
  Samuel 52* (MG-104)
SMILEY
  James 39 (GN-170)
  Polly 54* (CT-226)
  Uriah 26* (GN-209)
  William 40* (GN-243)
SMITH
  --- 25 (f)* (CT-214)
  Abraham 31 (CT-285)
  Alexander 22 (PE-426)
  Aly 38 (m)* (PI-469)
  Ambrose 24 (CT-233)
  Andrew 21* (LE-151)
  Andrew 4* (PE-430)
  Ann B. 28* (GN-203)
  Anthoney 41 (GN-243)

Index

SMITH
Aron 28 (PI-436)
Benjamin 46* (GN-157)
Benjamin 72 (BE-7)
Caswell 35 (CT-229)
Charles 23 (PI-485)
Charles 40* (GN-229)
Claiborn 48 (CT-225)
David 26 (LW-123)
David 32 (MG-123)
David 46 (GN-204)
Edmd. 30* (LW-111)
Edmund 54 (B) (BE-6)
Edward G. 23 (CT-215)
Elcana D. 23* (BE-4)
Elijah 28 (MG-152)
Elijah 84 (MG-123)
Elijah jr. 39 (MG-123)
Elisha 30* (MG-123)
Elisha 70* (PE-418)
Elizabeth 16* (LW-76)
Francis 27 (LW-111)
G. W. 30 (m) (GN-232)
George 22 (PI-482)
George 28* (GN-242)
H. C. 22 (m)* (GN-222)
Hardin 37 (BE-2)
Henery 22* (PI-474)
Henery 26 (PI-480)
Henery 33 (PI-480)
Henery 40* (PI-494)
Henry 28 (GN-181)
Henry 46 (MG-125)
Hiram 23 (MG-125)
Isaac 29 (PE-418)
Isaac 30 (PI-482)
Isaac 35* (LW-122)
Isaac 48 (PI-483)
Jacob 28 (PI-479)
James 21* (GN-249)
James 23* (FO-473)
James 24 (PI-480)
James 45 (PE-422)
James 51 (BE-25)
Jeremiah 52 (PE-411)
Jeremiah 70 (PI-463)
Jesse 25 (PI-480)
Jesse 45 (JO-121)
John 18* (JO-89)
John 24* (GN-235)
John 25* (GN-242)
John 28* (GN-176)
John 29 (PE-423)
John 30 (FO-469)
John 34* (GN-221)
John 37 (PI-480)
John 52* (GN-249)
John 59* (GN-249)
John 63 (PI-480)
John B. 25 (LE-151)
John P. 25 (GN-188)
John W. 24 (FO-472)
Johnathan 23 (PE-430)
Johnethan 24 (PI-482)
Joshua 31 (PE-418)
Joshua 32 (BE-39)
Katharine 30 (FO-437)
Lewis 27 (MG-123)
Linsey 24* (LW-74)
Lorenso D. 33 (PE-419)
Margaret 17* (GN-198)
Margaret 65* (PI-451)
Maria L. 6* (CT-217)
Martha A. 30* (CT-261)
Martin 50 (PI-482)
Martin L. 28 (GN-158)
Mary 13* (JO-113)
Mathew S. D. 12* (CT-243)
Melvina 5* (GN-222)
Nancey 58* (GN-229)
Nicholas 44 (LE-154)
Pernina 20* (FO-409)
Peter 37 (GN-257)
Preston 30 (PI-458)
Preston 33 (PE-413)
R. 45 (m)* (GN-241)
Rheuben 58* (PE-432)
Richard 24 (PE-424)
Robert 22* (MG-103)
Sally 100* (CT-229)
Samuel 41 (PE-418)
Sarah 14* (CT-220)
Tempa 45* (PI-489)
Thomas 32 (MG-86)
Thomas 52* (BE-12)
Thomas 69 (LW-105)
Thomas J. 27 (CT-235)
Thomas Sr. 59 (CT-229)
Walter 28* (FO-471)
Whitley 34 (BE-39)
Wiley 45 (MG-146)
William 23 (GN-225)
William 24 (PE-426)
William 25 (BE-12)
William 27* (FO-409)
William 28 (PI-486)
William 29 (CT-226)
William 38 (GN-235)
William 40 (PE-423)
William 50* (CT-229)
William 59 (GN-258)
William B. 45* (MG-138)
William M. 26 (JO-80)
William P. 38 (CT-235)
William R. 45 (GN-232)
Wm. 50 (LE-150)
Wm. B. 52 (LE-151)
SMOOT
Barton 55* (MG-148)
Eliza 25* (MG-86)
SMOUT
John 32* (GN-181)
SNEED
Henery 19* (PI-467)
SNIDER
Daniel 26 (GN-181)
SNODDY
Jacob 40 (GN-200)
John 30 (GN-199)
SNOW
Fielding 40 (PI-446)
Thomas 42 (GN-191)
SNYDER
C. 58 (f)* (GN-221)
SONGER
Nancey 42 (GN-221)
SORD
Sena 21* (PI-490)
SOUTH
Jeremi W. 41 (BE-33)
Richard L. 38* (BE-22)
SOUTHARD
Sarah 50 (FO-414)

Index

SOUTHERLAND
  Cornelius 25* (CT-266)
SOUTHERS
  Abram 42 (BE-15)
  Isaac 42 (BE-14)
SOWARDS
  Lewis 37* (PI-442)
SPALDING
  Alfred 30 (GN-160)
  Francis 76 (LW-116)
  John 55 (LW-104)
  John Jr. 22* (LW-85)
SPANGLER
  Ann H. 11* (GN-217)
  Hannah S. 16* (GN-158)
  Leonora 23* (GN-162)
  Leonora M. 24* (GN-194)
SPARKMAN
  Elizabeth 7* (LE-152)
  John 23 (FO-433)
  Rear? 24 (m) (PE-431)
  William 60 (FO-433)
SPARKS
  Allen 55 (JO-91)
  Calvin 43 (LW-60)
  Colburn 27 (BE-23)
  Danl. 43 (LW-115)
  Dinah 23* (JO-87)
  Elijah 38 (JO-95)
  Elisha 38 (JO-95)
  Ephraim 27* (BE-33)
  Etheldred 34 (PI-463)
  Garred 47 (LW-60)
  Geo. 54* (LW-70)
  Hiram 30 (LW-70)
  Isaac 21* (CT-249)
  James 27 (CT-256)
  James 40 (MG-151)
  Jesse 53 (CT-285)
  John 16* (BE-41)
  John 24 (CT-286)
  John A. 29 (MG-125)
  Levi 72* (LW-60)
  Martha 1* (LW-72)
  Martha 50 (PI-463)
  Mathew 40 (JO-96)
  Nelson 31* (CT-255)
  Nicholas 48 (JO-91)

  Reuben 24* (JO-91)
  Reuben 33 (LW-70)
  Richard 21* (GN-171)
  Richard 24 (PI-489)
  Richard L. 19* (GN-254)
  Solomon 25 (GN-257)
  Solomon 30 (CT-285)
  Thomas 48 (JO-95)
  Wesley 44 (LW-70)
  Wiley 42 (LW-55)
  William J. 22 (GN-203)
  Wm. 38 (LW-71)
  john 26 (CT-262)
SPEAR
  Enoch 41 (JO-119)
SPEARS
  Geo. W. 30 (LW-89)
  George W. 26* (PI-435)
  Paul 41 (GN-189)
  Roseann 40* (JO-118)
  Ruth 60 (JO-121)
  Thomas M. 21 (JO-117)
  Vincent 27* (JO-122)
  Wiley M. 24 (JO-122)
  William 30 (FO-416)
SPELMAN
  Hiram 43 (LW-53)
SPENCE
  Amon 53 (FO-463)
  Archibald 31* (GN-239)
  Henry 7* (GN-242)
  Jobe 37 (JO-97)
  John 37 (GN-257)
  Joseph 55 (MG-170)
  Stephen 26 (PI-463)
SPENCER
  Alfred 24 (BE-42)
  Andrew 20 (BE-4)
  Charles 22 (LW-104)
  Charles 41 (LW-97)
  Elijah 47 (BE-4)
  Franklin 23* (BE-28)
  Henry 21* (CT-259)
  Isac 43 (PE-405)
  James 23* (LW-103)
  James R. 47 (LW-85)
  Jesse 18 (LW-108)
  Jesse 51 (BE-23)

  John 37 (LW-96)
  John 81 (PE-405)
  Jourdon 31 (JO-89)
  Marion 20 (MG-151)
  Thos. 27* (LW-114)
  William 35 (MG-151)
SPERRY
  Alfred 40 (CT-216)
  Benjm. 43 (LW-63)
  James 34 (LW-77)
  Rudelph 46 (LW-63)
  Saml. 74 (LW-108)
  Sarah 23* (LW-76)
SPICER
  Benjn. 55* (BE-35)
  Edward 37 (BE-37)
  Eviline 7* (BE-20)
  Jackson 24* (BE-35)
  James 23* (BE-23)
  Roger S. 30* (BE-22)
  Saml. 22* (BE-35)
  Samuel 66 (BE-40)
  William 35 (BE-26)
SPRADDEN
  Edward 18* (FO-445)
SPRADLEN
  Evan 28 (JO-83)
SPRADLIN
  Abraham 50 (FO-421)
  Benjamin 54* (JO-81)
  Cajor 20* (FO-460)
  Henry 25 (FO-458)
  Henry J. 29* (MG-173)
  James 26 (JO-124)
  James 65* (JO-119)
  Jesse 60 (FO-467)
  John 20 (JO-124)
  Jonathan 27 (FO-442)
  Margaret 46* (FO-442)
  Michael 25 (FO-467)
  Nehemiah 45 (FO-464)
  Richard L. 26* (FO-461)
  Thomas 30 (FO-461)
SPRADLING
  Jerry 28* (GN-171)
  John 26 (GN-173)
  Robert 52* (GN-170)

Index

SPRAGG
  Elen 7* (GN-248)
  N. B. 46 (m) (GN-239)
SPRIGG
  Farris A. 13* (LW-120)
  Polly 30 (LW-120)
SPRIGGS
  Benjamin 38 (GN-248)
  C. 18 (m)* (GN-248)
SPURLOCK
  Jesse 72* (BE-26)
  Margaret 40* (GN-193)
  Martha 54* (FO-424)
  Saml. 33 (BE-26)
  Wm. 20* (LW-110)
  Wm. 39 (BE-26)
  Wm. 51 (LW-94)
  Wm. 62* (BE-40)
SQUIRES
  Betsey 16* (GN-242)
STACEY
  James T. 29 (PI-484)
STACY
  Allen 27 (MG-159)
  Benjn. 30 (BE-33)
  Calvin 80 (PE-397)
  Claboum 38 (MG-143)
  Elizabeth 16* (MG-164)
  Elizabeth 55 (FO-468)
  Felix 3 (PE-397)
  George 49 (MG-161)
  Henderson 28 (MG-165)
  Hugh A. 25 (MG-160)
  James 24* (PE-408)
  James 59 (PE-418)
  John 26 (PE-419)
  John 52 (MG-159)
  John jr. 25 (MG-160)
  Mashack 59* (MG-165)
  Sally 40 (PE-398)
  Shadrick 38 (PE-425)
  William 18* (MG-165)
  William 25* (PE-433)
STAFFORD
  Compton 45 (PI-470)
  Flemming 36 (PI-471)
  James 24 (JO-81)
  James 35 (MG-132)
  James 72* (CT-230)
  John 27* (LW-117)
  John 45* (JO-81)
  John sr. 71* (JO-120)
  Nancey 50?* (PI-478)
  Ralph 22* (JO-81)
  Sally 14* (LW-122)
  Wm. 33 (LW-122)
STAGG
  George 56 (GN-161)
  William 24 (GN-254)
STAGGS
  John M. 37 (CT-255)
STAMBAUGH
  Dicey 50* (JO-111)
  James 24 (JO-93)
  John 63* (JO-82)
  Philip 21 (JO-121)
  Samuel 54 (JO-113)
  Sylvester 25 (JO-108)
STAMFUR
  George W. 32 (MG-89)
STAMPER
  Eli 23 (MG-145)
  Enoch 40* (BE-40)
  George W. 40* (MG-142)
  Isaac D. 34* (LE-145)
  Isam 43 (PE-432)
  Jackson 23* (CT-233)
  Jackson 32 (MG-148)
  James 52 (MG-154)
  James W. 40* (BE-3)
  Joel 45 (BE-37)
  Joel 72* (BE-34)
  John 50 (CT-234)
  Jonathan 68 (BE-40)
  Jonathan Jr. 30 (BE-40)
  Lewis 22 (BE-40)
  Lewis 30 (BE-40)
  Lucinda 38 (LE-151)
  Margarett 60 (MG-148)
  Martha 72* (BE-36)
  Matilda 41* (MG-150)
  Richard 72* (BE-3)
  Richard S. 27 (MG-120)
  William 29 (MG-160)
  William M. 29* (LE-139)
STAMPER?
  James C. 38 (MG-142)
STANDEFORD
  William 40* (PE-408)
STANDERFER
  William 23* (FO-461)
STANFIELD
  Jackson 21 (PE-412)
STANFORD
  William 25* (FO-471)
STANLEY
  Andrew J. 21 (CT-276)
  James 28* (CT-236)
  Jasper 30* (GN-167)
  Moses 50 (PI-479)
STANTON
  Malinda 32* (PI-442)
  Richd. 46* (LW-88)
STAPLETON
  Bazle 49 (JO-82)
  Charles 42 (JO-98)
  Charles 45 (CT-237)
STARE
  Samuel 44 (PI-467)
STARK
  C. F. 28 (m)* (GN-259)
  Caroline L. 24* (PI-458)
  Henry 27* (GN-263)
  Jeremiah 33 (GN-260)
  Nancey 55 (GN-259)
STARKEY
  Sherod 47 (GN-184)
STATEN
  Solomon 30 (GN-201)
STATON
  Amanda 14* (MG-94)
  Solomon 27 (GN-264)
STATTEN
  John B. 17* (LW-122)
STEAGALL
  Drinkard 47 (MG-129)
  Jesse 22* (MG-129)
  Lewis 25 (MG-139)
  Mastin 45 (MG-127)
STEAGULL
  George S. 75 (MG-129)
STEDHAM
  John 25 (PE-409)

Index

STEDHAM
  Samuel 65 (PE-409)
STEEL
  Andrew 22 (PI-450)
  Daniel 59* (FO-407)
  George S. 36 (MG-171)
  Henery 25* (PI-489)
  Jeremiah W. 24 (MG-170)
  John 28 (PI-472)
  Samuel 50 (PI-450)
STEERER
  John 25* (GN-176)
STEERUP
  Nancy 23* (GN-229)
STEPHEN
  George 33* (PE-427)
STEPHENS
  Andrew 21* (MG-130)
  Benjamin 49 (MG-105)
  Daniel 34 (MG-136)
  George 30 (FO-444)
  Gilbert 91 (MG-137)
  James 52 (CT-225)
  James 81 (MG-136)
  James M. 21 (CT-263)
  Jane 24 (PE-427)
  Jesse 30 (MG-136)
  John 44 (CT-263)
  John A. 28 (LW-110)
  Samuel 49 (FO-441)
  Solomon 39 (MG-137)
  Stephen 38 (MG-136)
  William 23* (CT-262)
STEPHENSON
  William 30* (FO-470)
STEPLER?
  John 32* (PI-467)
STEPP
  James 28 (JO-116)
  Joseph 54 (JO-116)
  Moses 19 (JO-116)
  Nancey 57 (PI-467)
  Robert 26 (JO-116)
STEPTER
  James 32 (GN-242)
  John 34 (GN-225)
STERLING
  Abraham 31* (GN-214)

Clarinda 33* (GN-214)
STEVENS
  Andrew 49 (MG-133)
  Jacob 22 (GN-202)
  Jesse 24 (MG-133)
  John 27 (MG-132)
  John M. 37 (GN-192)
  Stephen 52 (GN-202)
  Thomas 18* (GN-195)
STEVENSON
  John 21* (GN-235)
  John 59 (MG-131)
  Matthew 63* (GN-223)
  William 33 (MG-131)
  William 40 (FO-464)
STEWART
  Alex 22* (GN-177)
  Andrew 53 (CT-275)
  Bird 19 (PE-421)
  Charles 40 (CT-275)
  Charles 72* (GN-239)
  Charles A. 27* (GN-222)
  Charlotte 13* (LW-85)
  George 33 (GN-177)
  Hiram 27* (CT-273)
  Jackson 30 (GN-187)
  James 26* (GN-209)
  James 45 (GN-201)
  James 47 (CT-218)
  James 51 (GN-162)
  James 54* (GN-187)
  James J. 26 (PE-421)
  James R. 32* (CT-270)
  John 35* (FO-471)
  John 51* (GN-165)
  John G. 46 (GN-254)
  Jonston 25* (CT-275)
  Lerenzo D. 44 (GN-205)
  Lewis 31 (CT-264)
  Matthew 52 (GN-254)
  Molissa 23 (GN-238)
  P. H. 19 (m)* (GN-248)
  Paull 60* (GN-263)
  Rebecca 7* (LW-116)
  Robert 22* (GN-166)
  Robert 42 (GN-256)
  Sandford 31 (GN-212)
  Sarah 15* (GN-222)

Sarah 46 (GN-207)
Thomas 30* (PI-450)
William 26 (CT-245)
William 27 (GN-234)
William 27 (GN-263)
Wm. 50 (LE-153)
STEWERT
  Absalom 45 (LW-63)
  Absalom Jr. 42 (LW-107)
  Chales? 43 (LW-63)
  Clay 32 (LW-88)
  Geo. S. 27* (LW-64)
  Harvy 37 (LW-65)
  John 27 (LW-63)
  John 45 (LW-106)
  Madison 28 (LW-112)
  Mary J. 30 (LW-92)
  Michel 59 (LW-91)
  Nancy 68* (LW-112)
  Ralph 51 (LW-110)
  Ralph 78 (LW-112)
STIDHAM
  James 38 (BE-44)
STINSON
  Zackariah 30* (FO-463)
STITH
  James 30 (LW-111)
  Nancy 27* (GN-198)
  Wm. 25* (LW-110)
STOCKHAM
  P. 27 (m)* (GN-166)
STOCKUM
  William 49* (GN-240)
STONE
  Charles 30* (FO-466)
  Cudbert 35 (CT-228)
  Elizabeth 12* (LW-64)
  Enoch 24 (CT-228)
  Enoch 70* (FO-445)
  Ira 7* (LW-55)
  Iraby 30 (CT-228)
  James 47 (GN-233)
  Jane 28 (FO-439)
  John 67 (GN-233)
  Levi 21 (LE-154)
  Mary 40 (JO-123)
STONEBRAKER
  Joseph 39 (LW-81)

Index

STOPHER
  Charles 45* (B) (CT-246)
STORMS
  Alfred 15* (GN-159)
STORY
  Elizth 11* (BE-36)
STOTH
  Margaret 63* (GN-200)
STRAILY
  Wm. M. 36 (LW-82)
STRAIN
  Barney 25* (CT-273)
STRAIT
  Henry 22* (GN-198)
  John 26* (GN-209)
STRATTON
  Elizabeth 34* (FO-472)
  Harvey G. 26 (FO-408)
  Henry 76 (FO-408)
  James W. 31 (FO-409)
  John J. 32* (FO-409)
  Solomon 52 (FO-408)
  Tandy 52 (FO-408)
STRICKLAND
  Britten 67 (FO-464)
STRICKLING
  Britian 25 (m) (MG-113)
STROAD
  Mark? 75 (LW-114)
STRONG
  Edward (Col.) 59 (BE-42)
  Edward C. 26 (BE-29)
  Hiram F. 30 (JO-80)
  Robert 26 (BE-32)
  Thomas 40 (LE-140)
  William 52 (BE-42)
STROTHER
  John R. 44* (CT-266)
  Joseph H. 32 (CT-242)
  Philip 71* (CT-242)
STRUMBO
  Frederick 40 (FO-425)
STRUTTEN
  Solomon 35* (PI-487)
STRUTTON
  Harry 43 (PI-489)
  Hiram 38 (PI-489)

STUART
  Abraham 30 (PI-446)
  John W. 21* (PI-450)
STUDD
  Joshua 23 (GN-196)
  Levi 50* (GN-196)
STUFFLEBEAN
  Hiram 46* (BE-5)
STUMP
  George 33 (PI-483)
  Sarah 1* (GN-229)
STURGELL
  Amy 60* (JO-86)
  Jesse 35 (JO-84)
  Joseph 28 (JO-86)
STURGEON
  Alvin 50 (LW-71)
  Blackburn 24* (FO-414)
  Dicy 34* (FO-415)
  Eli 46 (FO-414)
  Elijah 39 (JO-112)
  Fanny 30* (BE-34)
  John 19* (PI-462)
  Lewis 33 (FO-415)
  Lucinda 24* (FO-438)
  Nimrod 35 (FO-460)
  Patsy 40* (FO-411)
  William 36 (BE-23)
  William 45 (FO-453)
STURGETT
  John W. 39 (JO-120)
STURGIL
  Benjamin 23 (CT-279)
  David 25 (CT-285)
  Hervey 30 (CT-279)
  Solomon 45* (CT-279)
STURGILL
  Andrew 19 (LE-129)
  David 50 (LE-129)
  Francis 21 (LE-129)
  Francis 42 (LE-129)
  James 16* (LE-128)
  John 21* (LE-129)
  Jordon 21 (LE-129)
STUTTER
  Francis H. 50* (LW-88)
SUBLETT
  James 25* (MG-99)

Mathew 32 (JO-82)
SUCHER
  Julia 9* (PI-491)
SUDBROOK
  P. 28 (m) (GN-248)
SULIVAN
  Pryor 25 (MG-92)
SULLIVAN
  Patrick 24* (GN-210)
  Voluntine 47 (GN-208)
SUMMERS
  John 24* (GN-173)
  John 49 (GN-182)
SUMNER
  James 50 (LE-143)
  John 34 (LE-143)
SUMPTER
  Caziah 64 (f)* (GN-186)
  Christopher J. 27* (GN-188)
SUMPTOR
  Lewis 19 (LE-127)
  Sarah 53 (LE-127)
SUTERS
  John 81 (GN-236)
SUTHERLAND
  Nelson 38* (GN-171)
  Nelson 40 (GN-184)
SUTHERN
  Henry 29* (PE-416)
SUTHERS
  Andrew 10* (PE-417)
SUTTER
  John 34* (CT-238)
  Uriah T. 30 (CT-238)
SUTTLE
  John 40 (GN-226)
SUTTON
  Lewis 23* (FO-426)
  Seatta 30 (FO-435)
SWANGO
  Abraham 59* (MG-148)
  Harrison 34* (MG-143)
  Stephen 30* (MG-143)
  Washington 38 (MG-152)
SWANN
  Resin 38 (LW-114)
SWANSON
  Levi 95 (MG-132)

Index

SWATNAM
  Wm. P. 27 (BE-32)
SWEARENGEN
  John 27 (CT-223)
SWEARINGEN
  William 21 (GN-227)
SWEARINGER
  Clem 41 (GN-250)
  Samuel 44 (GN-250)
  Van 58 (GN-263)
SWEATMAN
  Zepheniah 41* (JO-110)
SWEATNAM
  Hamilton 32 (MG-174)
  John J. 38* (MG-149)
SWEED
  Thomas 35* (GN-247)
SWEENEY
  Anna 16* (PI-454)
  James 45 (PI-447)
  Joshua 25* (PI-448)
  William 13* (PI-447)
SWEET
  Benjamin 32 (GN-208)
SWERINGIN
  Wm. 26* (LW-89)
SWETNIM?
  C. L. 43 (m) (LW-57)
  Neri 36 (LW-57)
SWIM
  Barbary 15* (CT-258)
  Michael 48 (CT-252)
SWINN
  Sanford 21* (CT-252)
SWORD
  Francis 50 (PI-495)
  John 53 (PI-459)
  Lucas B. 43* (PI-442)
  Richard P. 26 (PI-459)
  William 30 (PI-458)
SYFERS
  Jeritta 4* (MG-141)
SYPHERS
  John 22* (MG-145)
  William 3* (MG-144)
SYRAS
  Levi 26 (LW-109)

SYRUS
  Benjamin 95* (B) (CT-216)
TABER
  Alfred 30* (CT-286)
  Robert 72 (CT-260)
  William 24 (CT-248)
TABOR
  Addison 27 (CT-238)
  Bazel M. 51 (CT-238)
  Laurderdale 23 (CT-237)
TACKER
  Richard 37* (GN-164)
TACKET
  Charles 33* (GN-259)
  Lucy 60* (GN-176)
  Nancy 4* (MG-137)
TACKETT
  Charles 28* (GN-205)
  Dorcus 21* (LW-99)
  Francis 66 (PI-460)
  George 46* (PI-456)
  Hardin G. 25 (CT-277)
  Henry 25* (GN-212)
  Hiram 27 (JO-90)
  Isaac 33 (PI-455)
  James 28 (CT-260)
  John H. 42 (MG-132)
  Joshua 33 (FO-426)
  Levi 30 (JO-90)
  Lewis 31 (GN-177)
  Moses 44 (CT-249)
  Nancy 25* (FO-427)
  Philip 53* (PI-455)
  Rachel 18* (JO-101)
  Robert 35 (CT-260)
  Solomon 20 (PI-456)
  Taply 23 (FO-414)
  Thomas 47 (GN-164)
  Thomas 80* (JO-103)
  William 20 (PI-456)
  William 24* (CT-272)
  William 26 (PI-461)
  William 41 (PI-456)
  William 54* (JO-103)
  William 72 (PI-456)
  Willliam 22* (JO-101)
TAILEN
  Edward 55 (PI-440)

TAILOR
  Allen 38 (PI-466)
  Burgess 49 (PI-446)
  Elizabeth 20* (PI-441)
  Jessee 45 (PI-467)
  John 35 (PI-487)
  Mary 21 (PI-477)
  Mary A. 10* (PI-470)
  Syrus 37* (PI-469)
  William 40 (PI-486)
  William A. 44 (PI-477)
TANAHILL
  Joseph 30* (GN-249)
TANNER
  George 49* (GN-181)
  John 22* (CT-266)
  John P. 49 (GN-160)
  M. 5 (m)* (GN-262)
  Pearce L. 42 (GN-216)
TATE
  Joel 23 (FO-462)
TAULBEE
  Isaac 19 (BE-1)
  Saml. 22 (BE-2)
  William 48 (BE-13)
TAULBY
  John 46 (MG-154)
  John D. 23 (MG-158)
  Lurena 16* (MG-170)
  William 20 (MG-150)
TAYLOR
  Edwd. 56 (LW-88)
  Elizabeth 19* (LE-147)
  Ellis 27 (LW-91)
  George 14* (GN-205)
  Gideon 24 (LE-148)
  Isaac B. 31* (FO-420)
  Isabell 10* (LW-85)
  Joseph 22* (MG-172)
  Joseph 23* (MG-162)
  Mary J. 10* (GN-180)
  Stephen 24 (CT-271)
  William 30* (GN-168)
  Wm. 22 (LW-89)
TEASTER?
  Benjamin 48 (MG-150)
TEGARDEN
  J. M. 40 (m) (GN-246)

- 413 -

Index

TEGARDEN
  John M. 33* (GN-221)
TELEY
  John 41 (GN-245)
TEMPLEMAN
  Enoch G. 27* (MG-96)
TEO?
  William 27* (GN-186)
TERREL
  Hezekiah 46 (MG-155)
  Timothy 21 (MG-155)
TERREY
  Jirel? 38 (m) (PE-421)
TERRIL
  Peter 50* (GN-198)
TERRY
  Elisha 30 (BE-19)
  Isaac 30 (BE-32)
  John 32 (LW-59)
  Joseph P. 42* (PI-490)
  Leonard 56 (FO-432)
  Miles 36 (FO-434)
  Miles 60* (LW-59)
  Rebecca 55 (MG-135)
  Thomas 53 (CT-264)
  William 21* (GN-194)
  William 26 (FO-432)
  William 60 (FO-433)
THACKER
  Abner sr. 70 (PI-437)
  Absolom 24 (PI-435)
  Absolom 26 (PI-436)
  Daniel 30* (CT-250)
  Elisha jr. 33 (PI-436)
  Elisha? sr. 67 (PI-436)
  Greenville 21 (PI-436)
  Jesse 46 (LE-153)
  John 34 (PI-436)
  John 34 (PI-437)
  Nathaniel 47 (PI-443)
  Randolph 38 (PI-437)
  Reuben 45 (PI-437)
  Reuben 70 (FO-443)
  William 30 (PI-437)
THARP
  Robert 43 (CT-261)
THOMAS
  A. 11 (f)* (GN-221)

Abraham 47 (GN-221)
Catharine 60* (MG-144)
David 25* (FO-471)
Evan 23* (CT-227)
Evander 26 (GN-180)
Greenbury 30 (LE-147)
Isaac 51* (BE-29)
James 2* (GN-204)
James 55 (MG-95)
James 59 (PE-403)
James 65* (GN-228)
John 30 (MG-96)
John 35* (CT-227)
John 76* (GN-246)
Jonathan 31 (CT-217)
Madison 32* (GN-179)
Nancy 14* (LE-139)
Peter 25* (BE-20)
Susan 21* (BE-23)
Susannah 13* (CT-262)
Tartia 16* (LW-90)
William 34* (CT-216)
William 38 (GN-201)
William 66 (GN-180)
Wm. 21* (BE-29)
THOMPSON
  Adrom 16 (m)* (MG-135)
  Alfred 31 (GN-228)
  Anderson 25 (GN-246)
  Andrew 30 (LW-104)
  Andw. 72 (LW-104)
  Anthoney 34 (GN-226)
  David 23* (GN-246)
  David 26 (LW-105)
  Eleanor 32* (LW-104)
  Eli 21* (BE-24)
  Elizabeth 65 (PI-496)
  Geo. 24 (LW-104)
  Granvill 28 (LW-105)
  H. 39 (m) (GN-244)
  Hudson C. 60* (GN-199)
  Jackson 34* (GN-235)
  James 25 (GN-228)
  James 26* (LW-67)
  James W. 33* (CT-266)
  Jeremiah 40* (LW-81)
  John 22 (LW-67)
  John 32 (LW-104)

John 44 (FO-469)
John 50* (CT-241)
John 67* (LW-62)
John H. 35 (GN-191)
John H. 35 (LW-76)
Johnson 38 (LW-77)
Johnson 43 (LW-80)
Martin 48* (LW-66)
Matthew 66 (MG-129)
Moses 35* (GN-252)
Patten 30 (LW-122)
Rachel 24* (LW-117)
Reuben 37 (GN-244)
Richd. 45 (LW-104)
Richd. W. 49* (LW-64)
Russell 39 (LW-83)
Saml. 22 (LW-104)
Saml. 26 (LW-81)
Saml. 72* (LW-115)
Samuel 47* (GN-260)
Thomas 19 (GN-243)
W. 41 (m)* (GN-245)
Wesley 41 (LW-115)
William 23 (PI-487)
William 40 (PI-463)
William 68* (GN-228)
William 70 (FO-469)
Wm. 29 (LW-104)
THOMSON
  Charles 28* (CT-254)
  James J. 25 (CT-253)
  John L. 30* (CT-254)
  Thos. T. 43* (CT-285)
THONESBERRY
  Walter 38 (FO-432)
THORN
  N. F. 35 (m) (GN-220)
THORNHILL
  James 24* (LW-91)
THORNSBERRY
  Eleanor 47 (FO-431)
  Geo. 25* (FO-431)
  James 23* (FO-431)
  John 50 (FO-438)
THORNSBURGY
  John 37* (PI-441)
THORNSBURY
  Edward 38* (CT-227)

Index

THORNSBURY
  Levi 29 (PI-462)
  Martha 48 (GN-212)
  Martin 64 (PI-441)
THORNTON
  E. C. 33 (m) (GN-158)
THROOP
  Benjamin B. 36 (CT-246)
  Joseph 30 (CT-265)
TIMBERLAKE
  Thomas 43 (GN-245)
TIMMONS
  Emly 33* (GN-258)
TINCHER
  James 23 (BE-20)
  William 45 (BE-20)
TINGLER
  Solomon 25 (GN-229)
TINSLEY
  William 43 (GN-199)
TIRA?
  Judah 18 (f)* (FO-432)
TODD
  Lewis 35 (JO-80)
TOLBY
  Ira 20* (BE-28)
  Jefferson 25 (BE-14)
TOLER
  Caleb 53* (GN-192)
  Christopher 45* (CT-264)
  Elijah 50 (GN-192)
  Henry 40* (CT-257)
  Stephen 77* (CT-243)
  William 38 (GN-192)
TOLIVER
  Elijah 58 (MG-97)
  Hamton 35* (CT-275)
  Nancy 22* (MG-141)
  William 21* (CT-275)
TOLLEY
  Elkaney 97* (PI-462)
TOLSTON
  Peter 57* (BE-14)
  Thomas 25 (BE-14)
  Wm. 22* (BE-3)
TOMILSON
  Rhoads 17* (GN-240)

TOMLIN
  Alexr. 36 (LW-113)
  Henderson 32 (LW-113)
  Isom 63 (LW-112)
  John 35 (LW-84)
  Solomon 22 (LW-107)
TONG
  William 50 (GN-223)
TORRENCE
  James 22* (GN-248)
TOWNSEND
  Jackson 55 (GN-180)
TRAMER
  Peter 50 (GN-164)
TRAVIS
  Grenville 18* (FO-462)
TRAYLOR
  David 25 (GN-222)
  Jane 17* (GN-235)
  Jesse 22 (GN-226)
  John 67 (GN-258)
  Lewis 32 (GN-248)
  Nancy 13* (GN-227)
  Ransom 21* (GN-226)
  William 12* (GN-251)
TRENT
  Alexr. 25 (BE-4)
  Henry 43* (BE-3)
  Isaiah 22 (BE-26)
  Wm. 24 (BE-4)
TRICK
  Frederick 40 (GN-262)
TRIMBLE
  David 31 (MG-87)
  David S. 28* (MG-146)
  Edwin 42 (FO-474)
  Elizabeth A. 33* (CT-246)
  James 24 (JO-97)
  James G. 26 (MG-144)
  Lewis 37 (MG-150)
  Mark 74 (MG-156)
  William 63* (MG-144)
TRIPLETT
  Bryant 27 (FO-430)
  Daniel 50 (FO-430)
  Elijah 18* (CT-270)
  Jesse 21 (FO-433)
  Joel 28 (FO-431)

  John 22 (CT-279)
  Lee 36 (FO-431)
  Linville 35 (FO-433)
  Wilson 28 (FO-430)
TROUT
  Daniel 43 (CT-273)
TRUEMAN
  Hiram 27* (BE-43)
TRUET
  Mary 52* (GN-228)
TRUMBO
  George 28 (CT-231)
  John J. 30 (MG-102)
  John L. 58 (CT-253)
  Oliver H. 29 (CT-253)
TRUSTY
  Daniel 28* (BE-14)
  David 27 (BE-11)
  John 29 (BE-11)
  William 70 (MG-123)
TUBLETT
  Francis 32 (GN-216)
TUFFTS
  Wealthy A. 50 (f)* (GN-172)
TUFTS
  William 26 (GN-172)
TUPLETT
  Lurana 56 (GN-215)
TURMAN
  James L. 39 (LW-96)
  Permelia 15* (LW-111)
  Renee? 80* (LW-111)
TURNER
  Adam 38 (FO-424)
  Alexander 23* (FO-425)
  Andrew W. 47 (MG-174)
  Burris? 25 (FO-424)
  David 53 (BE-38)
  Edward 50 (BE-40)
  Edward jr. 34 (BE-37)
  Edward sr. 69 (BE-37)
  Edwin S. 23* (JO-104)
  James 50 (BE-4)
  James W. 54 (JO-93)
  Larkin 30 (BE-38)
  Martin 44 (GN-167)
  Rachel 24* (JO-104)
  Roger 55 (BE-40)

Index

TURNER
 Roger jr. 24 (BE-38)
 Saml. 35 (BE-38)
 Samuel R. 43 (MG-172)
 Shadrach 12* (BE-37)
 Stephen 36* (B) (CT-223)
 Thomas 40 (BE-37)
 Thomas sr. 60 (BE-37)
 Wiley 24 (BE-38)
 Wm. 25 (BE-35)
TURNER?
 John 41 (BE-36)
 Thomas 38 (BE-37)
TURNEY
 Rebecca 50* (GN-201)
TURNMIRE
 Jemimah 38 (FO-469)
TURPIN
 Andrew 19* (B) (CT-272)
TURRY
 John 28 (GN-196)
TUSSY
 Craig 25 (FO-444)
 Jacob 36 (FO-446)
 John 34 (FO-444)
 Jonathan 57 (FO-444)
TUTT
 James B. 36 (MG-147)
 John 48* (MG-141)
 William 36 (MG-118)
TUTTLE
 James 17* (GN-196)
TWYFORD
 John B. 23* (GN-260)
TWYMAN
 James 35* (GN-208)
TYLINGER
 Reuben 36* (JO-120)
TYRA
 John 35 (BE-4)
 Sarah 15* (FO-433)
TYRE
 David 22 (LE-139)
TYREE
 Jerome 29 (CT-241)
 Zachariah 44 (CT-241)
ULEN
 Benjamin 60 (GN-171)

 Charles 26* (GN-194)
 Elba 30 (m) (GN-198)
 Elizabeth 12* (GN-216)
UNDERWOOD
 Dolly A. 20* (CT-251)
 George W. 36 (CT-254)
 Gideon 42 (CT-254)
 James 43 (CT-254)
 Matthew 50 (B) (GN-232)
 Nelson 22* (CT-252)
 Samuel A. 55 (GN-232)
 Stephen 34* (CT-250)
 William 22 (GN-228)
UNRUE
 Danl. 36 (LW-116)
URICK
 Elizabeth 14* (GN-165)
UTTERBACK
 Harmon 66* (MG-94)
 Joseph 41 (MG-104)
 Paterson 35 (MG-94)
 William 31 (MG-118)
UTZ
 George 22 (GN-160)
VALANCE
 Carter 30* (GN-220)
 Harvey 35 (GN-227)
 Samuel 28 (GN-227)
 Samuel 70 (GN-227)
VANBIBBER
 Adney 38 (m) (GN-220)
 Cyrus 51* (GN-158)
 Ezekiel 36 (GN-185)
 James 48 (GN-158)
 James 7* (GN-229)
VANCE
 John W. 35 (FO-430)
VANCLEAVE
 Andrew S. 25 (BE-2)
 Ebenezer 73 (BE-1)
VANDEGRIFF
 James L. 40 (GN-240)
VANDERPOOL
 John 27 (FO-452)
VANDERVERT
 James 22* (GN-248)
VANDERVORT
 James 22* (GN-249)

VANDINE
 Ellen 66* (GN-172)
VANDOVER
 Nicholas 14* (GN-188)
VANHOOSE
 Bracken 30 (JO-86)
 James 27 (JO-86)
 James sr. 59 (JO-86)
 Jane 70* (JO-120)
 Jesse 24 (JO-110)
 John 22 (LW-103)
 John 30* (JO-102)
 Joseph 46 (FO-460)
 Levi 54 (JO-123)
 Reuben 43 (LW-85)
 Reuben jr 11* (LW-100)
 Sirena 13* (JO-102)
 Thos. 36* (LW-101)
 Valentine 30 (JO-108)
 Valentine 52 (JO-111)
 William 10* (JO-102)
 William 28* (JO-102)
VANHORN
 Charity N. 9* (GN-199)
VANHORNE
 John 20 (LW-106)
 John 37* (LW-109)
VANKIRK
 John 32 (GN-234)
VANOVER
 Eli 27 (PE-399)
 Nealus 25 (PI-453)
 William 56 (LE-133)
VANSANT
 William H. 30* (MG-132)
VARNEY
 Alexandre 53 (PI-478)
VARNUM
 John 34 (PI-476)
VAUGHAN
 Burwell 26 (FO-472)
 Burwell 56 (FO-470)
 Iris? sr. 60 (m) (FO-469)
 Ivie jr. 27 (FO-471)
 Jacob 20* (FO-473)
 John 48 (JO-80)
 John P. 45 (FO-461)
 Leroy 37 (FO-462)

Index

VAUGHAN
  Patrick 50* (FO-459)
  William 31 (FO-471)
VAUGHN
  Benjamin 9* (CT-223)
  D. B. 31 (m) (LW-77)
  Jane 31 (MG-173)
VEACH
  J. W. 51 (m) (GN-234)
  Nancy 38 (GN-228)
VENTERS
  Geo. M. 21 (LW-114)
  John 27 (LW-112)
VERMILLION
  Douglas J. 33 (LE-140)
VEST
  Edmund 66* (MG-114)
  Hamilton W. 28 (MG-114)
VICARS
  Thomas 23* (JO-89)
VICKERS
  Jacob 22 (GN-185)
  John 25 (LW-85)
VIER
  David 30 (BE-33)
  Fleming 32 (BE-34)
  Moses 37 (BE-22)
  Randal 27 (BE-33)
VIERS
  Anna 35* (BE-13)
  Daniel 49 (CT-245)
  Henry 21* (CT-218)
  William 23* (CT-257)
VINCENT
  Gabriel M. 28 (FO-473)
  John 64 (CT-284)
VINSON
  James 35 (LW-82)
  Lazrus 25 (LW-73)
VIRES
  William 25 (CT-227)
VIRGIN
  Lamack 41* (CT-217)
  Rezin 46* (CT-243)
  Samuel 17* (GN-256)
VIST
  Thomas 17* (MG-99)

VOLDINER
  L. C. 26 (m)* (CT-272)
VOLUNTINE
  John 21* (GN-250)
  Nancy J. 12* (GN-208)
VURNEY
  Andrew 30 (PI-479)
WADDELL
  James 46 (CT-281)
WADDLE
  Alfred 21 (CT-282)
  Jordan 23 (LW-70)
  Mary A. 57* (CT-217)
WADE
  David 42* (GN-176)
  Jackson 21* (CT-228)
  Mary 25* (CT-278)
  Peter 30* (FO-419)
  William 12* (CT-216)
WADKINS
  Andy 21* (BE-5)
  Benedict 95 (FO-443)
  Jackson 26 (BE-5)
  Reese 20* (FO-470)
  Sylvester 23 (FO-446)
  Thomas 31 (FO-459)
  Thomas 33 (FO-445)
  Thomas 98* (FO-445)
  William 30 (BE-8)
  William 43 (FO-449)
WAGES
  Alfus 22 (MG-167)
  Benjamin 24 (MG-167)
  Moses 55 (MG-167)
  William 29* (MG-167)
WAGGONER
  Daniel 32 (MG-132)
  David 27 (CT-282)
  Jacob 23 (CT-282)
WALDECK
  N. C. 38 (m)* (LW-56)
WALDICK
  Alexander S. 36* (MG-174)
WALES
  Caleb P. 46* (JO-81)
WALFORD
  Michael 35 (CT-271)

WALK
  Benjamin 50 (GN-175)
WALKER
  Alexander 21 (PE-422)
  Alexander 32 (PE-419)
  Amanda 19* (LW-80)
  Christopher 56 (FO-434)
  Cristopher 24 (PE-420)
  Deleware 47 (m) (JO-108)
  Elizabeth 38 (GN-225)
  Elizabeth 44* (FO-467)
  George 22* (GN-164)
  Henery W. 19 (PI-488)
  James 24* (FO-434)
  James 42 (GN-225)
  James 51* (PE-420)
  Jeremiah 37 (CT-266)
  Jesse 45* (FO-437)
  John 33 (PE-420)
  John 41 (CT-284)
  John 60 (PE-422)
  Mary 43* (CT-223)
  Mordecai 15* (CT-280)
  Rachel 66 (CT-266)
  Robert 52 (GN-225)
  Thomas 21 (FO-434)
  Wyett 7* (MG-86)
WALKINSHAW
  H. 58 (f)* (GN-242)
WALLACE
  Elizabeth 20* (LW-106)
  George 34 (GN-186)
  George 55 (CT-268)
  James 18* (GN-167)
  James 25* (GN-187)
  Major L. 23 (MG-165)
  Mary 23* (GN-264)
  Otha 28 (m) (GN-264)
  Solomon 30 (PI-469)
  Thos. 38* (LW-76)
WALLEN
  John 45 (FO-434)
  John 55 (FO-436)
  Preston H. 32 (LE-139)
WALLER
  George 24 (FO-465)
  Henry 45 (LW-92)

Index

WALLER
  Jacob 52 (JO-109)
WALLIS
  Mary 51* (GN-264)
WALSH
  David 36 (MG-126)
  John 40* (MG-173)
  Lucy 33* (MG-156)
  Mary 25* (MG-171)
WALTER
  Hiram G. 24* (GN-193)
WALTERS
  Andrew 26 (MG-155)
  B. 41 (f) (BE-21)
  George 48 (GN-197)
  Harrison 32 (GN-175)
  John 12* (JO-113)
  Matilda 16?* (LE-143)
  Matilda 44 (MG-155)
  Nancey 38* (PI-484)
  Robt. 51 (LW-72)
  Shadrach 19* (JO-110)
  Wm. 52* (LW-57)
  Zachariah 47 (PI-491)
WALTON
  Charles 56 (JO-80)
  Jame 23* (CT-214)
  L. D. 32 (m)* (GN-193)
WAMACK
  Ann 34* (CT-226)
  William 41 (CT-218)
WAMOCK
  James 69* (GN-259)
  William 60* (GN-205)
WAMSLEY
  Uriah 62 (GN-207)
WARD
  Bluford 25 (JO-112)
  Charles L. 25 (CT-244)
  Cyrus 65* (MG-112)
  Daniel 51 (GN-262)
  Elizabeth 56 (JO-115)
  George W. 26* (CT-266)
  Hezekiah 47 (JO-84)
  Hiram 41 (JO-114)
  Isaac 22* (GN-164)
  J. B. 33 (m)* (CT-257)
  James 23 (JO-116)

James 26 (MG-145)
James 54* (CT-257)
James 55 (JO-112)
James A. 32 (JO-118)
James M. 32* (JO-92)
Jesse 30 (JO-110)
John 21 (JO-112)
John 22* (GN-164)
John 52* (MG-146)
John H. 26 (JO-92)
John H. 26 (MG-92)
Joseph R. 52 (CT-278)
Malinda 39 (JO-111)
Martha 23* (GN-172)
Mary 70* (CT-257)
Mary A. 60 (MG-110)
Nancy 36* (MG-110)
Nathanl. 25 (LW-121)
Shadrach 37 (JO-112)
Shadrach 64* (JO-113)
Solomon 43 (JO-102)
Solomon S. 22* (JO-102)
Stephen 23 (JO-89)
T. 20 (m)* (GN-210)
Theresa A. 46* (CT-243)
Wells 31* (JO-115)
William 22* (JO-111)
William 23 (GN-181)
William 26 (MG-173)
William 30* (CT-227)
William jr. 31 (JO-89)
William sr. 58 (JO-89)
Wm. 51 (LW-57)
WARE
  A. 35 (m) (GN-241)
WAREN
  Harrison 31* (CT-250)
WARING
  Bazel 49 (GN-258)
  C. H. 69 (m)* (GN-222)
  Humphrey 69 (GN-257)
  J. H. 33 (m) (GN-265)
  J. W. 5 (m)* (GN-229)
  Jane 52 (B) (GN-258)
  R. W. 36 (f) (GN-220)
  Sarah W. 49 (GN-257)
  Tabitha 43 (GN-257)
  Thomas T. G. 70 (GN-256)

Y. G. 35 (m) (GN-218)
WARMAC
  Wm. 18* (LW-99)
WARNER
  H. 50 (f) (GN-241)
  James 23 (BE-20)
  Larkin 39 (GN-197)
  N. S. 60 (m)* (GN-219)
WARNOCK
  J. W. H. 39 (m)* (GN-230)
  Jackson 35 (GN-234)
  Matthew 43 (GN-258)
  Nelson 35 (B) (GN-160)
  William H. 27 (GN-239)
  William H. 37 (GN-230)
WARREN
  Allen 24 (MG-170)
  David L. 32* (MG-171)
  Hugh 26 (MG-171)
  John 45* (LW-69)
WARRICK
  Thomas 26 (PI-459)
WATERS
  Jane 30 (BE-29)
WATKINS
  Daniel B. 21* (GN-193)
WATSON
  Abraham 32 (FO-415)
  Hannah 56* (CT-236)
  John 43 (CT-281)
  Jonathan 45 (FO-416)
  Rolly 38 (m) (MG-135)
  Teryan 45 (m) (MG-161)
WATTERS
  Bradford 41 (BE-30)
  Mathias 54 (CT-253)
  Wallen 30* (FO-471)
WATTS
  Ambrose 27* (BE-44)
  Emilia 22* (BE-44)
  Enoch 42 (PE-426)
  George 75 (BE-43)
  Polly 30 (BE-43)
  Thomas 35 (PE-432)
  Washington 30 (BE-43)
WAUGH
  John 28 (CT-264)
  John 59 (CT-264)

Index

WAUGH
  Thomas P. 30 (GN-168)
  William 33* (CT-258)
WEATHERS
  E. 47 (m) (GN-241)
WEAVER
  Danl. 19* (LW-92)
WEBB
  Alexander 50 (GN-185)
  Benjamin 66 (LE-136)
  Edward 33 (JO-82)
  Elizabeth 58* (LW-68)
  Enoch A. 39 (LE-136)
  George J. 30 (JO-93)
  George W. 38 (JO-91)
  Grandvill 26* (GN-260)
  Hezekiah 26* (FO-438)
  James W. 27 (JO-101)
  Jason L. 30 (LE-136)
  John 25 (JO-122)
  John 62 (JO-88)
  John M. 33 (LW-91)
  Jonathan 331 (JO-88)
  Jonathan 42 (FO-417)
  Marthan 5* (LW-68)
  Miles M. 28 (LE-137)
  Polly 35* (PE-429)
  Rhoda 28 (LW-104)
  Thomas 20 (JO-122)
  William 24* (GN-261)
  William 34 (JO-122)
  William 35 (JO-92)
  Wm. R. 35 (LW-89)
WEBSTER
  William 65 (FO-465)
WEDDINGTON
  Jacob 38 (PI-457)
  Jacob 45 (PI-493)
  Jacob 73* (MG-137)
  James 46* (PI-491)
  William 43 (PI-492)
WEDINGTON
  Wm. 22* (LW-92)
WEEKS
  Cornelus 44* (GN-168)
  J. C. 30 (m)* (GN-243)
WEGNER
  Abram 39 (GN-194)

WELBOURN
  Jackson 35 (CT-265)
  Robert 63* (CT-277)
WELCH
  Andrew 24 (JO-119)
  James 45 (JO-90)
  Napoleon 21* (CT-217)
  Thos. 40* (LW-88)
  Walter 50* (GN-212)
  _____ 1 (m)* (GN-211)
  michael 41* (GN-176)
WELKER
  James 48 (GN-202)
  John 20 (GN-202)
WELLMAN
  John H. 12* (CT-242)
WELLS
  Anderson 19* (BE-33)
  Benjamin F. 48 (MG-156)
  Cristena 15* (LW-55)
  David 50 (MG-171)
  Dennis B. 28 (JO-80)
  Elihu 31 (PE-401)
  Franklin 29* (CT-280)
  George 50 (JO-117)
  James 19 (MG-158)
  John 26 (MG-89)
  John 30 (BE-29)
  John 35 (JO-122)
  Levi 30* (LW-70)
  Lewis 25* (LW-69)
  Lewis 26* (CT-281)
  Margaret 18* (BE-22)
  Moses 46 (JO-122)
  Oliver P. 24 (MG-109)
  Peter 45 (GN-203)
  Richard 27 (MG-106)
  Richard 46 (MG-109)
  Susanna 71* (JO-118)
  Thomas 32* (MG-157)
  William 44 (MG-144)
  William G. 32* (JO-121)
  William Jun. 24 (JO-122)
  William jr. 24 (MG-119)
WELMAN
  Bennett 34 (LW-52)
  Calvin 27 (LW-86)
  Elisha 66 (LW-52)

  Elisha Jr. 27 (LW-52)
  Fleming 26 (LW-80)
  James 32 (LW-52)
  James 57* (LW-91)
  Jarred D. 36 (LW-80)
  Jeremiah 65 (LW-78)
  John 40 (LW-55)
  John R. 33 (LW-96)
  Joseph 68 (LW-85)
  Lewis 40 (LW-77)
  Lot 34* (LW-96)
WELTCH
  Jane 34* (GN-197)
WENER
  Lao 28 (m)* (GN-248)
WERST?
  Alexander 56 (JO-116)
WESLEY
  James 28 (GN-259)
WEST
  Bluford 31 (GN-187)
  Charles 30 (LW-107)
  Greenville 22 (PI-480)
  James 27* (LW-74)
  Joel 23 (GN-187)
  John 41 (PI-480)
  Jordan 53 (GN-261)
  Joseph 32 (JO-102)
  Joseph 66 (GN-187)
  Joshua 32* (GN-187)
  Matthew 38* (GN-181)
  Thomas 23* (GN-167)
  Thomas 38* (GN-163)
WESTFALL
  John W. 10* (GN-158)
WESTPOLE
  Inglebert 40* (GN-205)
WETHEROW
  James W. 22* (LW-72)
WHEELER
  Amos H. 32 (LW-113)
  Daniel 32* (JO-110)
  Edward 46 (GN-173)
  Elizabeth 45* (GN-173)
  George W. 30* (MG-90)
  James 50* (LW-54)
  Jesse 38 (JO-83)
  John 27 (JO-97)

Index

WHEELER
 John 36 (JO-109)
 John 38 (JO-98)
 John B. 19 (JO-83)
 John R. 29 (LW-51)
 John sr. 40 (JO-119)
 Joshua 26* (LW-62)
 Katherine 64 (JO-109)
 William 52 (JO-96)
 William R. 40 (JO-83)
WHISMAN
 David 33* (CT-256)
WHIT
 Henery 36 (PI-482)
WHITAKER
 Edmund 20* (BE-41)
 Edmund 20* (BE-44)
 Esquire 37 (PE-432)
 Francis 56* (FO-449)
 Isac 41 (PE-432)
 Isac 72 (PE-432)
 James O. 46* (FO-448)
 Johnson 58* (FO-445)
 Peter 45 (PE-411)
 Susanna 17* (PE-411)
 W. J. 21 (m)* (BE-23)
 Wiley 24 (FO-445)
 William 22* (CT-271)
 William J. 29 (BE-6)
WHITE
 Alsor 23 (BE-41)
 Andrew 21* (GN-196)
 Bethena 38 (B) (PI-479)
 Danl. 48* (LW-112)
 David 40 (LW-118)
 Edward 25 (CT-246)
 Francis 34 (LW-99)
 George 24* (GN-181)
 George 50 (MG-97)
 Horatio 49 (PI-445)
 J. W. 30 (m) (GN-158)
 James 22 (MG-136)
 James 55* (LW-50)
 James 67 (CT-223)
 Jonas 50 (GN-228)
 Lear 21* (LW-106)
 Manlius 19* (CT-266)
 Martha 25* (PI-495)

 Mary 39* (CT-223)
 Nancey 68 (PI-445)
 Nancy 50* (GN-159)
 Nathan 52* (MG-133)
 Nelson 18* (LW-71)
 Rachel 50 (BE-42)
 Samuel 48 (CT-222)
 Sarah 71* (LW-109)
 Simeon 20 (PE-411)
 William 41* (GN-161)
WHITEBEARD
 Washington 46 (PE-411)
WHITEHEAD
 Wiliam 23 (PE-412)
WHITEKER
 Nelly 37 (LE-125)
 Stephen 19 (LE-125)
WHITELY
 Alexander 65 (MG-169)
 George 46 (MG-169)
 John 24 (MG-169)
 Moses 29 (MG-170)
 Robert 22 (MG-169)
 Thomas 24 (MG-170)
 Timothy 40 (MG-159)
WHITLEY
 Wm. J. 27 (LW-70)
WHITLOCK
 Lewis 34 (CT-271)
WHITON
 William H. 25* (GN-180)
WHITT
 Abijah 37 (CT-267)
 Bunyan 50 (FO-440)
 David 47 (PI-476)
 Emund 24 (CT-256)
 George W. 22* (MG-128)
 Hannah 77 (CT-267)
 Hezekiah 25 (FO-440)
 Jesse 45 (PI-480)
 John L. 32 (FO-439)
 Martin 35 (MG-127)
 Miles 22 (MG-127)
 Moses 34 (MG-128)
 Richard 54* (CT-256)
 Richard P. 43 (CT-267)
 Richard S. 42 (MG-119)
 Richard jr. 28 (MG-127)

 Richard sr. 52 (MG-128)
WIATT
 Jacob 23 (GN-250)
WICKER
 Jesse 22 (FO-434)
WIESS
 Daniel K. 34 (CT-257)
WILBORN
 Burrell 32 (CT-271)
 William 29 (CT-271)
WILBOURN
 Elizabeth 29* (CT-270)
 Lewis 42 (CT-264)
 Mary 22* (MG-102)
 Robert 34 (CT-258)
WILBURN
 Cynthian 16* (CT-241)
 Patterson 30* (CT-220)
 Reuben 22 (CT-242)
 Wm. 24* (LW-88)
WILCOX
 Gains (m)* (GN-165)
 James 41 (FO-463)
 Owen 38 (FO-463)
WILDER
 Deniss W. 30* (GN-177)
 Joseph 80 (PE-405)
 Wilson 35 (PE-405)
WILEY
 Adam 53* (JO-111)
 Andrew J. 19* (JO-101)
 John 19* (JO-108)
 Lucinda 13* (JO-119)
 Richard 24 (JO-110)
 William 48* (JO-100)
 Wm. 20* (LW-99)
WILHITE
 James A. 33 (CT-279)
WILKINS
 Sarah 31* (GN-192)
WILKS
 James F. 41* (GN-188)
WILLCOX
 Samuel 29? (PI-453)
WILLIAMS
 Abraham 28 (FO-411)
 Achilles 24 (PI-483)
 Alexander 22* (FO-467)

Index

WILLIAMS
Alfred 25* (FO-462)
Alfred 39 (CT-273)
Ambrose 23 (MG-117)
Ambrose 31 (MG-119)
Anderson 30 (MG-87)
Andrew 19 (PE-404)
Caleb 20* (BE-13)
Caleb 40 (MG-167)
Catharine 65* (FO-463)
Charles 30* (FO-461)
Charles 31 (GN-237)
Coleman 60 (BE-6)
Daniel 39 (MG-116)
Don 21* (GN-176)
Edward 40 (FO-470)
Eli 24 (MG-166)
Eli 25 (CT-284)
Eli 26* (PI-442)
Eli 69* (CT-279)
Elijah 44 (MG-90)
Elizabeth 34 (MG-91)
George S. 28 (GN-174)
George W. Sr. 50 (CT-237)
Gilbert 36 (BE-28)
Hardin H. 31* (JO-99)
Hardy 54 (PE-404)
Henry 36* (BE-7)
Henry 37 (GN-164)
Hiram 27 (GN-260)
Isaac 27 (LE-132)
Isaac 30 (FO-409)
Isaac 52 (MG-168)
Jackson W. 21 (FO-411)
Jacob 24 (JO-113)
Jacob P. 21 (LW-62)
James 22* (FO-411)
James 25 (GN-172)
James 35 (PE-404)
James 46* (MG-117)
James 63 (CT-257)
James H. 26 (MG-168)
James H. 30 (MG-157)
James Y. 35 (PI-483)
Jane 57 (MG-125)
Jefferson B. 37 (CT-235)
Jeremiah 23 (PE-418)
John 18* (BE-26)

John 22 (PE-419)
John 26 (PE-404)
John 30* (BE-19)
John 51* (FO-410)
John 55 (LE-132)
John 6* (LW-59)
John 68* (MG-118)
John 68 (PE-419)
John J. 26* (BE-25)
John J. 27 (FO-470)
John M. 32 (JO-99)
John T. 26* (MG-173)
John W. 28 (PI-483)
Joseph 40 (JO-90)
Joseph 54 (B) (PE-427)
Joseph 57 (PE-405)
Joseph 65 (FO-461)
Katharine 60* (FO-410)
Laban 39* (CT-263)
Lameck 38 (CT-235)
Lewis 43 (LW-62)
Lucas P. 35 (CT-235)
Lucy 14* (MG-135)
Malan 22* (CT-243)
Malinda 17* (MG-161)
Marcus 37* (GN-195)
Margaret 3* (PE-401)
Mary 70* (CT-225)
Mary A. 4* (FO-452)
Mason 70 (MG-157)
Nancy 33 (BE-26)
Nancy J. 17* (GN-177)
Nicholas 35 (PE-419)
Noah 41 (LW-61)
Owen 28 (JO-116)
Phillip 21 (PE-404)
Pleasant 35 (PE-419)
Richard F. 33* (MG-172)
Risey 17 (f)* (GN-245)
Robert 26 (PE-404)
Robert 62 (JO-99)
Robert R. 39* (JO-88)
Roxe A. 45 (f)* (GN-212)
Samuel 29 (PE-404)
Shedrick 35 (GN-264)
Stephen 27 (BE-13)
Thadeus 9* (MG-146)
Thomas 30 (CT-284)

Thomas 37* (JO-91)
Thomas 45 (CT-251)
Watkin 32* (FO-470)
William 19* (MG-119)
William 22 (PI-441)
William 4* (CT-244)
William 40 (FO-434)
William 44* (GN-215)
William 65 (PI-482)
William F. 38* (MG-88)
Wm. R. 28 (LW-87)
Wyatt 33 (BE-7)
winney 16* (MG-162)
WILLIAMSON
Alden 65 (LW-121)
Anna 36 (PI-483)
Anthony 25* (LW-121)
Benjamin 33 (PI-480)
Benjamin 70* (PI-469)
Benjm. 22 (LW-120)
Elijah 43 (LW-121)
Eliza 24* (GN-194)
Farrell 24 (PI-464)
Franklin 26 (PI-491)
Hibbard 24 (PI-464)
James 27* (PI-480)
James 37 (LW-121)
John 28 (PI-469)
John 35 (PI-483)
John 69 (PI-483)
Jonah 16* (PI-470)
Moses 20 (PI-468)
Peeter 35* (PI-486)
Richard 35 (PI-465)
Shadrach 30* (LW-123)
Soloman 49 (LW-120)
Stephen 21 (LW-121)
William 23* (FO-418)
William 26 (JO-115)
Willis 26* (MG-174)
Wm. 43 (LW-72)
WILLIS
Alfred 22 (GN-179)
Ambrose 37 (GN-258)
Ammill 40* (LW-87)
George 23 (FO-436)
Isiah 47* (LW-80)
Jacob 22 (GN-179)

- 421 -

Index

WILLIS
 John 60 (GN-179)
 Joseph 68 (GN-263)
 Joshua 36 (GN-259)
 William G. 27 (GN-178)
WILLMAN
 Moses 21* (GN-193)
WILLOBY
 Harden 28 (GN-243)
WILLS
 James 71 (GN-229)
 John 46* (GN-245)
 Samuel 35* (GN-158)
 Shelton 25 (m) (MG-109)
 Thomas 59 (MG-141)
WILLSON
 Henery 25 (PI-473)
 Robert 12* (PI-490)
WILSON
 Abijah 24 (MG-103)
 Abraham 30 (PI-475)
 Andrew 23 (GN-175)
 Andrew 50 (PE-430)
 Andrew 52 (MG-154)
 Auskin 22* (BE-29)
 C. M. 47 (m)* (GN-158)
 Charles 70 (GN-198)
 Charles S. 30* (MG-102)
 David 26 (GN-159)
 Elizabeth 70* (GN-183)
 Elzy A. 42 (f)* (GN-168)
 Guy 42* (GN-227)
 Harvy 20 (MG-169)
 Henry 29 (CT-227)
 Isaac D. 24* (CT-226)
 Isaiah 38* (MG-103)
 Jackson 24 (MG-154)
 James 30 (CT-216)
 John 18* (LW-111)
 John 21* (CT-271)
 John 23* (GN-194)
 John 24* (CT-226)
 John 28 (BE-41)
 John 49 (LE-128)
 Joseph 51 (MG-153)
 Joshua 47 (MG-169)
 Preston 26* (MG-156)
 Robert 24 (LE-129)
 Robert 42 (MG-155)
 Samuel 17* (GN-171)
 Sarah 16* (MG-141)
 Seth 37 (GN-174)
 Shelby 37 (m) (MG-154)
 Susan M. 33* (GN-158)
 Wiley 22* (MG-142)
 William 34 (CT-261)
 William 54 (CT-276)
WIMER
 George 36 (GN-245)
WIN
 Robert 28* (FO-471)
WINCHELL
 Henry 21* (LW-91)
WINDFIELD
 John G. 32* (GN-238)
WINEGAR
 John 25* (CT-263)
WINEKER
 Christian 33 (m) (GN-186)
WINER
 Jophnn 24 (CT-261)
WINKLE
 James 50* (MG-145)
 John 35 (JO-87)
 William P. 29* (MG-153)
WINN
 John E. 31 (GN-157)
 Mary 75* (CT-246)
WISE
 Francis 40 (GN-188)
 James 30 (GN-182)
 Wesley 14* (GN-182)
WISEMAN
 Jacob 27 (FO-445)
 Jacob 55 (MG-151)
 John 21 (FO-445)
 John 32 (MG-151)
 John 54* (FO-445)
 Thomas B. 49 (BE-18)
WISHON
 C. 30 (m)* (GN-245)
WITHEROW
 Saml. 20 (LW-93)
 Wm. 48* (LW-67)
WITLEN
 William 58 (JO-125)
WITT
 Mary 15?* (PI-471)
WITTEN
 George H. 26 (JO-93)
 Isaac 24* (JO-103)
 John W. 28 (JO-113)
WIZEMAN
 Abraham 53 (FO-465)
WOLFINGTON
 Jeffery 29 (PI-462)
WOLFORD
 Fredric 24 (PI-474)
 George 33 (PI-474)
 John 63* (PI-474)
WOMAC
 William A. 22* (GN-259)
WOMACK
 A. L. 34 (m) (GN-263)
 Archer 52 (GN-161)
 Charles 45 (GN-174)
 Richard 37 (CT-278)
 Samuel W. 36 (MG-173)
WOMBLES
 Cornelius 40* (BE-40)
WOOD
 Andrew 19* (CT-271)
 Andrew J. 21* (CT-226)
 Hiram 32 (MG-142)
 Jackson 36* (GN-211)
 James F. 26* (CT-226)
 Joshua 35* (CT-257)
 Luke 35* (BE-2)
 Robert 71* (CT-239)
 Shadrack 21 (JO-120)
 Washington 57 (MG-142)
 William 29 (GN-256)
 William 30* (GN-200)
 William 30 (GN-251)
 Zebede 41 (FO-471)
WOODROW
 W. G. 33 (m) (GN-254)
WOODS
 Alexander 40 (FO-416)
 Andrew 41 (LW-52)
 Delila 30* (FO-416)
 Elizabeth 86* (FO-419)
 Fanny 20* (FO-416)
 James 43 (LW-61)

Index

WOODS
  John 55 (LW-64)
  John W. 23 (LW-74)
  Walter 27 (LW-115)
  Woodson 30 (BE-16)
WOODWARD
  Silas 35* (GN-213)
WOODY
  Everett L. 30* (LW-90)
WOOLDRIDGE
  Samuel 45 (GN-178)
WOOLFORD
  Michael 41* (CT-216)
WOOTEN
  Silas G. 46 (LW-82)
  Thomas 24* (CT-231)
WOOTON
  Charles 42 (PE-403)
  Davis 47 (PE-403)
  Hiram 50 (PE-402)
  John 77 (CT-223)
  Polly 53 (PE-398)
  Randal 42 (CT-220)
WORKMAN
  Elizabeth 24* (JO-123)
  Jesse 35* (LW-77)
  Stephen 19 (LW-78)
WORLEY
  Sarah 42* (GN-183)
WORMAN
  Edmund 35 (GN-198)
  F. 29 (m)* (GN-251)
WORSHAM
  Thomas 24* (FO-408)
WORTHINGTON
  Alex 34* (GN-169)
  J. T. 40 (m)* (GN-193)
  James 47* (GN-173)
  John 49* (CT-228)
WRDS
  John 50* (MG-118)
WRENER
  Leo 28* (GN-249)
WRIGHT
  Andrew 23 (LE-135)
  Bailus 31 (JO-99)
  Betsy 57* (BE-6)
  Charles 64 (CT-219)

James 30* (JO-94)
James 39 (LE-135)
Joel 33 (LE-136)
John 37 (LE-134)
Susannah 65 (wid.) (LE-135)
William 36 (CT-219)
WURTS
  George 40* (GN-159)
  Samuel 39* (GN-164)
  William 32* (GN-260)
WYATT
  Nathaniel 20* (BE-28)
  Reuben 54 (JO-103)
WYETT
  Hezekiah 36 (MG-120)
YARBOROUGH
  Randle 43* (MG-108)
  Thomas 66 (MG-108)
YARNALL
  David 30 (CT-272)
YATES
  Eluster 18* (FO-411)
  George 9* (JO-94)
  James 32* (PI-440)
  James 40 (FO-416)
  John 16* (CT-280)
  John 38 (PI-492)
  Joseph 25* (GN-171)
  Levi 27 (CT-230)
  Luke 24 (FO-409)
  Mary 76 (MG-120)
  Richard 19* (PI-440)
  S. J. 34 (m) (LW-79)
  Sarah 57* (GN-167)
  Susannah 50 (FO-411)
  Thompson 23* (LW-69)
  Wiliam 56 (CT-230)
YOCUM
  William 31 (MG-112)
YONTS
  William 42 (LE-134)
YONTS?
  David 21* (LE-134)
  Solomon 44* (LE-134)
YORK
  Francis 23* (GN-157)
  John 34 (LW-117)
  Joshua M. 49 (LW-119)

Nancy E. 14* (B) (CT-242)
YOUNG
  Absolom 95 (PI-466)
  Charles 37 (JO-125)
  Eddy 33* (CT-250)
  Gabriel C. 34 (GN-203)
  Harrison 40* (LW-54)
  Isaac 31 (PE-428)
  James 20 (PE-428)
  James 44* (LW-58)
  Jesse 51 (LW-52)
  John 35 (PI-466)
  John 38 (MG-87)
  John 39 (PE-402)
  John 48 (LW-52)
  John 84 (GN-178)
  John B. 32* (MG-110)
  John Jr. 18 (LW-54)
  Joseph 43 (GN-194)
  Lady? 70* (LW-50)
  Lucy 45 (PE-397)
  Nancey 24* (PI-485)
  Paschal 3* (GN-167)
  Poss? 29 (m)* (GN-174)
  Saml. 32 (LW-53)
  Sarah 60* (FO-464)
  Thomas 28 (PE-428)
  Thomas 69 (PE-428)
  William 16* (GN-236)
  William 68 (LE-137)
  Wm. 52* (LW-103)
YULETT
  William 52* (CT-241)
ZEEK
  William 54 (GN-180)
ZORNS
  Andrew 56* (CT-219)
  Andrew Jr. 32 (CT-232)
  Eli 23* (CT-231)
  Jeremiah 23 (CT-231)
  Martin 28 (CT-232)
  Martin 29* (CT-238)
  Philip 65* (CT-231)
ZORNS?
  Elizabeth 40 (GN-233)
  Philip 33 (GN-232)
  Thomas 30 (GN-232)
  William 29 (GN-235)

www.ingramcontent.com/pod-product-compliance
Lightning Source LLC
Chambersburg PA
CBHW071226290426
44108CB00013B/1308